OXFORD READINGS IN CLASSICAL STUDIES

The series provides students and scholars with a representative selection of the best and most influential articles on a particular author, work, or subject. No single school or style of approach is privileged: the aim is to offer a broad overview of scholarship, to cover a wide variety of topics, and to illustrate a diversity of critical methods. The collections are particularly valuable for their inclusion of many important essays which are normally difficult to obtain and for the first-ever translations of some of the pieces. Many articles are thoroughly revised and updated by their authors or are provided with addenda taking account of recent work. Each volume includes an authoritative and wide-ranging introduction by the editor surveying the scholarly tradition and considering alternative approaches. This pulls the individual articles together, setting all the pieces included in their historical and cultural contexts and exploring significant connections between them from the perspective of contemporary scholarship. All foreign languages (including Greek and Latin) are translated to make the texts easily accessible to those without detailed linguistic knowledge.

D1526971

Oxford Readings in Classical Studies

Greek Religion
Edited by Richard Buxton

Homer's *Iliad*
Edited by Douglas L. Cairns

Virgil's *Aeneid*
Edited by S. J. Harrison

The Roman Novel
Edited by S. J. Harrison

Ancient Literary Criticism
Edited by Andrew Laird

Euripides
Edited by Judith Mossman

Aristophanes
Edited by Erich Segal

Greek Tragedy
Edited by Erich Segal

Menander, Plautus, and Terence
Edited by Erich Segal

The Greek Novel
Edited by Simon Swain

All available in paperback

Oxford Readings in Classical Studies

Aeschylus

Edited by

MICHAEL LLOYD

OXFORD
UNIVERSITY PRESS

OXFORD
UNIVERSITY PRESS

Great Clarendon Street, Oxford OX2 6DP

Oxford University Press is a department of the University of Oxford.
It furthers the University's objective of excellence in research, scholarship,
and education by publishing worldwide in

Oxford New York

Auckland Cape Town Dar es Salaam Hong Kong Karachi
Kuala Lumpur Madrid Melbourne Mexico City Nairobi
New Delhi Shanghai Taipei Toronto

With offices in

Argentina Austria Brazil Chile Czech Republic France Greece
Guatemala Hungary Italy Japan Poland Portugal Singapore
South Korea Switzerland Thailand Turkey Ukraine Vietnam

Oxford is a registered trade mark of Oxford University Press
in the UK and in certain other countries

Published in the United States
by Oxford University Press Inc., New York

© Oxford University Press 2007

The moral rights of the author have been asserted
Database right Oxford University Press (maker)

First published 2007

British Library Cataloguing in Publication Data

Data available

Library of Congress Cataloguing in Publication Data

Oxford readings in Aescylus / edited by Michael Lloyd
p. cm.
ISBN–13: 978–0–19–926524–4 (alk. paper)
ISBN–10: 0–19–926524–0 (alk. paper)
ISBN–13: 978–0–19–926525–1 (alk. paper)
ISBN–10: 0–19–926525–9 (alk. paper)

1. Aeschylus–Criticism and interpretation. I. Lloyd, Michael.
PA3829.O94 2006

882'.01–dc22   2006007425

Typeset by SPI Publisher Services, Pondicherry, India
Printed in Great Britain
on acid-free paper by Biddles Ltd., King's Lynn

ISBN 0–19–926525–9   978–0–19–926525–1
ISBN 0–19–926524–0 (Pbk.)   978–0–19–926524–4 (Pbk.)

1 3 5 7 9 10 8 6 4 2

Preface

The library of University College Dublin has nine copies of Erich Segal's *Oxford Readings in Greek Tragedy* (Oxford, 1983) at the time of writing, most of them rather battered and the newer ones evidently replacements for copies which had disintegrated under the pressure of use. This testifies both to Segal's good judgement in making his selection, and more generally to the potential value to students of collections of this kind. The needs of university students taking courses on Greek tragedy were to the forefront of my mind when compiling the present volume, although I hope that other kinds of reader will also find it useful.

I allotted roughly equal space to the seven surviving plays. The contribution by Timothy Gantz (ch. 1) places them in the context of Aeschylus' work as a whole. I am aware that the book contains little discussion of lost plays, but believed that the available space was more usefully devoted to the plays which survive intact. The inclusion of an article on the *Prometheus Bound* implies no judgement on its authorship, but merely reflects its traditional inclusion in Aeschylus' oeuvre. The book represents a reasonably broad range of critical approaches, but cannot hope to be comprehensive.

I did not consider items reprinted in the Segal collection mentioned above, or in other collections with substantial Aeschylean content (e.g. R. P. Winnington-Ingram's *Studies in Aeschylus* (Cambridge, 1983)). It could be argued that the articles by Dodds and Macleod (chs. 8 and 9) come into this category, having already been reprinted in volumes of collected essays by their respective authors. I decided that their inclusion was justified both by their intrinsic quality and by the advantages of printing them together.

The decision to reprint an article is a slightly different exercise from recommending that it should be consulted in its original location. Some classic pieces seemed rather dated when considered for reprinting, however significant they may have been in the history of Aeschylean scholarship. It is sometimes the fate even of outstandingly good articles to be absorbed into the bloodstream of the subject to such an extent that their original impact fades. Others devote too much space to technicalities or long-forgotten controversies to be reprinted in a volume of this kind. I am convinced that all the items included here retain their value not only for their contributions to particular issues but also for an overall quality and coherence which makes them worth reprinting in (more-or-less) their original form.

Three articles have been translated into English, two from German and one from French. Translations have been added for the Greek quotations, in some cases quite extensive, in several more. Three authors have supplied a foreword or postscript, and others have made fairly minor revisions. No contribution has been substantially revised, although two chapters are excerpts from longer pieces. I hope that the index will add value even to articles which are reprinted in their original form.

The introduction is intended principally to put each chapter in context. Some account is given of the background to each contribution, its main arguments, and subsequent discussion of the issues. I hope that this will give students and other non-specialist readers a better sense of the significance of each piece. I have treated this task fairly broadly, but there are still topics which are omitted because they do not figure prominently in any of the articles included in the book (gender issues in the *Oresteia*, for instance). I see myself more as an impresario than as an embalmer (cf. R. Buxton (ed.), *Oxford Readings in Greek Religion* (Oxford, 2000), 10).

Suzanne Saïd and Wolfgang Rösler kindly took an interest in my translations of their contributions, and made many helpful suggestions. I am especially grateful to Hugh Ridley for looking over my translation of the chapter by Kurt von Fritz and answering a number of queries. None of them should be held in any way responsible for such errors and infelicities as remain. Three exceptionally well-informed and constructive Press readers commented on my selection, and if I have sometimes disagreed with them it was also enlightening to see how much they disagreed with each other.

Dublin

M.A.L.

August 2005

Acknowledgements

Permission to reprint the following items is gratefully acknowledged.

1. T. Gantz, 'The Aischylean tetralogy: attested and conjectured groups', *American Journal of Philology* 101 (1980), 133–64.

2. S. Saïd, 'Tragédie et renversement: l'exemple des *Perses*', *Métis* 3 (1988), 321–41. Translated by Michael Lloyd.

3. M. Griffith, 'The king and eye: the rule of the father in Greek tragedy', *Proceedings of the Cambridge Philological Society* 44 (1998), 20–84. Pp. 44–65 are reprinted in the present volume.

4. K. von Fritz, 'Die Gestalt des Eteokles in Aeschylus' *Sieben gegen Theben*'. In *Antike und moderne Tragödie* (Berlin: Walter de Gruyter & Co., 1962), 193–226. Translated by Michael Lloyd.

5. W. Rösler, 'Der Schluss der *Hiketiden* und die Danaiden-Trilogie des Aischylos', *Rheinisches Museum* 136 (1993), 1–22. Translated by Michael Lloyd.

6. P. Burian, 'Pelasgus and politics in Aeschylus' Danaid trilogy', *Wiener Studien* 8 (1974), 5–14.

7. J. J. Peradotto, 'The omen of the eagles and the *ΗΘΟΣ* of Agamemnon', *Phoenix* 23 (1969), 237–63.

8. E. R. Dodds, 'Morals and politics in the *Oresteia*', *PCPS* 6 (1960), 19–31. Reprinted in *The Ancient Concept of Progress* (Oxford, 1973), 45–63.

9. C. W. Macleod, 'Politics and the *Oresteia*', *Journal of Hellenic Studies* 102 (1982), 124–44. Reprinted in *Collected Essays* (Oxford, 1983), 20–40.

10. B. H. Fowler, 'Aeschylus' imagery', *Classica et Mediaevalia* 28 (1967), 1–74 [published in 1971]. Pp. 53–66 are reprinted in the present volume.

11. A. Lebeck, 'The first stasimon of Aeschylus' *Choephori*: myth and mirror image', *Classical Philology* 62 (1967), 182–5.

12. A. M. Bowie, 'Religion and politics in Aeschylus' *Oresteia*, *Classical Quarterly* 43 (1993), 10–31.

13. M. L. West, 'The Prometheus trilogy', *Journal of Hellenic Studies* 99 (1979), 130–48.

Contents

Notes on Contributors

TIMOTHY GANTZ (1945–2004) taught at the University of Georgia from 1970 until his death. His publications include *Early Greek Myth: A Guide to Literary and Artistic Sources* (Baltimore, 1993), and several articles on Aeschylus.

SUZANNE SAÏD is Professor of Classics at Columbia University, New York. Her publications include *La Faute tragique* (Paris, 1978), *Sophiste et tyran ou le problème du Prométhée enchaîné* (Paris, 1985), and (with Monique Trédé) *A Short History of Greek Literature* (London and New York, 1999).

MARK GRIFFITH is Professor of Classics and Theater Arts at the University of California at Berkeley, where he has taught since 1976. His publications include *The Authenticity of Prometheus Bound* (Cambridge, 1977), and editions of *Prometheus Bound* (Cambridge, 1983) and Sophocles' *Antigone* (Cambridge, 1999).

KURT VON FRITZ (1900–85) was dismissed from his professorship at the University of Rostock in 1935 for refusing to swear the requisite oath of loyalty to Hitler, and emigrated first to England and then to the USA, where he taught at Columbia University in New York from 1938 to 1954. He returned to Germany to take up chairs in Berlin (1954–8) and Munich (1958–68). His books include *The Theory of the Mixed Constitution in Antiquity: A Critical Analysis of Polybius' Political Ideas* (New York, 1954), *Die griechische Geschichtsschreibung* (Berlin, 1967), and *Platon in Sizilien und das Problem der Philosophenherrschaft* (Berlin, 1968). His article in the present volume was first published in his collection *Antike und moderne Tragödie: neun Abhandlungen* (Berlin, 1962).

WOLFGANG RÖSLER (b. 1944) has been Professor of Greek at the Humboldt-Universität Berlin since 1994, before which he taught at the University of Konstanz (1971–94). His publications include *Reflexe vorsokratischen Denkens bei Aischylos* (Meisenheim am Glan, 1970), *Dichter und Gruppe. Eine Untersuchung zu den Bedingungen und zur historischen Funktion früher griechischer Lyrik am Beispiel*

Alkaios (Munich, 1980), and *Polis und Tragödie. Funktionsgeschichtliche Betrachtungen zu einer antiken Literaturgattung* (Konstanz, 1980).

PETER BURIAN (b. 1943) is Professor of Classical and Comparative Literatures at Duke University, where he has taught since 1968. His publications include many articles on fifth-century Greek drama, and translations (solo and in collaboration) of Aeschylus and Euripides. He edited *Directions in Euripidean Criticism: A Collection of Essays* (Durham, NC, 1985), and an edition of Euripides' *Helen* (Warminster) is forthcoming.

JOHN PERADOTTO (b. 1933) taught at the State University of New York at Buffalo from 1966 to 2000. His publications include *Man in the Middle Voice: Name and Narration in the Odyssey* (Princeton, 1990), (as editor, with J. P. Sullivan) *Women in the Ancient World: The Arethusa Papers* (Albany, 1984), and articles and reviews on Greek myth, epic, and tragedy. He was co-founder of the classical journal *Arethusa*, and was its editor-in-chief from 1975 to 1995.

ERIC ROBERTSON DODDS (1893–1979) was Regius Professor of Greek in the University of Oxford (1936–60). His books include editions of Euripides' *Bacchae* (Oxford, 1944) and Plato's *Gorgias* (Oxford, 1959), *The Greeks and the Irrational* (Berkeley, 1951), and *The Ancient Concept of Progress and Other Essays on Greek Literature and Belief* (Oxford, 1973). He also published an autobiography, *Missing Persons* (Oxford, 1977).

COLIN MACLEOD (1943–81) was Student (Fellow and Tutor) of Christ Church, Oxford from 1968 until his death. He edited Book 24 of Homer's *Iliad* (Cambridge, 1982), and his *Collected Papers* was published by Oxford University Press in 1983.

BARBARA HUGHES FOWLER (1926–2000) taught at the University of Wisconsin-Madison from 1963 to 1991. Her publications include *The Hellenistic Aesthetic* (Bristol, 1989), and translations of poetry from several ancient and modern languages.

ANNE LEBECK wrote *The Oresteia: A Study in Language and Structure* (Washington, DC, 1971).

ANGUS BOWIE is Lecturer in Classical Languages in the University of Oxford and Fellow of The Queen's College. His publications include

The Poetic Dialect of Sappho and Alcaeus (New York, 1981) and *Aristophanes: Myth, Ritual and Comedy* (Cambridge, 1993).

MARTIN WEST (b. 1937) was Senior Research Fellow at All Souls College, Oxford (1991–2004), having previously been Fellow of University College, Oxford (1963–74) and Professor of Greek at Bedford College, University of London (1974–91). He edited the Teubner text of Aeschylus and wrote a companion volume, *Studies in Aeschylus* (both Stuttgart, 1990). His other books include editions of Hesiod's *Theogony* (Oxford, 1966) and *Works and Days* (Oxford, 1978), *Greek Metre* (Oxford, 1982), an edition of Euripides' *Orestes* (Warminster, 1987), *Ancient Greek Music* (Oxford, 1992), and *The East Face of Helicon: West Asiatic Elements in Early Poetry and Myth* (Oxford, 1997).

Abbreviations

DK   H. Diels and W. Kranz (eds.), *Die Fragmente der Vorsokratiker* (6th edn.; Berlin, 1951–2)

FGrH   F. Jacoby (ed.), *Die Fragmente der griechischen Historiker* (Berlin and Leiden, 1923–58; Leiden, 1994–)

Fraenkel   E. Fraenkel (ed.), *Aeschylus: Agamemnon* (3 vols.; Oxford, 1950)

IG   *Inscriptiones Graecae*

K–A   See *PCG*

LSJ   H. G. Liddell and R. Scott, *A Greek-English Lexicon* (9th edn., revised by H. Stuart Jones and R. McKenzie; Oxford, 1940; with *Revised Supplement* edited by P. G. W. Glare, 1996)

OCD   *The Oxford Classical Dictionary* (3rd edn.; Oxford, 1996)

PCG   R. Kassel and C. Austin (eds.), *Poetae Comici Graeci* (Berlin and New York, 1983–)

PMG   D. L. Page (ed.), *Poetae Melici Graeci* (Oxford, 1962)

P. Oxy.   Oxyrhynchus Papyri

Radt   See *TrGF*

TrGF   *Tragicorum Graecorum Fragmenta* (5 vols.; Göttingen, 1971–2004). Vol. 3, edited by Stefan Radt, is the standard edition of the fragments of Aeschylus.

Abbreviations for ancient authors and their works, and for modern periodicals, should be readily intelligible with the aid of *OCD* pp. xxix–liv or LSJ pp. xvi–xlv.

The two texts of Aeschylus which are most frequently cited in this book are those edited by D. L. Page (Oxford, 1972) and M. L. West (Stuttgart, 1990; corrected edition, 1998).

Square brackets generally enclose material supplied by the editor, e. g. translations of Greek quotations or references to reprints of works cited.

Titles of Aeschylus' Plays

No attempt has been made to harmonize the differing approaches to the rendering of Greek names adopted by contributors to this volume. Some prefer straight transliteration (e.g. 'Aischylos'), others the more familiar Latinized versions (e.g. 'Aeschylus').

Titles of fragmentary plays are usually transliterated, but titles of the seven extant plays appear either transliterated, Latinized, or translated into English. The most commonly used abbreviations derive from the Latin titles.

Greek Title	English Title	Latin Title	Abbreviation
Persai	*Persians*	*Persae*	*Pe., Pers.*
Hepta Epi Thebas	*Seven Against Thebes*	*Septem Contra Thebas*	*Se., Sept.*
Hiketides	*Suppliants*	*Supplices*	*Su., Supp.*
Agamemnon	*Agamemnon*	*Agamemnon*	*Ag.*
Choephoroi	*Libation Bearers*	*Choephori (-oe)*	*Cho.*
Eumenides	*Eumenides*	*Eumenides*	*Eum.*
Prometheus Desmotes	*Prometheus Bound*	*Prometheus Vinctus*	*P. V.*

Introduction

Michael Lloyd

THE AESCHYLEAN TETRALOGY

The catalogue of Aeschylus' plays lists 73 titles, and at least nine more were known to ancient scholars.[1] The Byzantine encyclopaedia called the *Suda* (*c.* AD 1000), which preserves much valuable information from antiquity, credits him with 90 plays. The article by Timothy Gantz (Ch. 1) addresses the question of how many of these plays belonged to tetralogies. In an earlier article which dealt with some preliminary issues, he defined 'tetralogy' as 'a set of four plays presented together *and* related in plot'.[2] He argued that this was also the meaning of the Greek word τετραλογία. Narrative continuity is thus a requirement for a tetralogy, and Gantz does not include sets of four plays on different subjects such as Aeschylus' plays of 472 BC. He recognizes that the satyr play was somewhat more loosely connected than the three tragedies. He remarks, however, that it 'seems to have been linked to the main story by characters and myth, even if it did not directly continue the plot of the tragedies'.[3] This was evidently the case in the four attested tetralogies, and there are enough plausible titles to supply satyr plays on this basis for several more tetralogies.

---

[1] For this catalogue, transmitted by several medieval manuscripts of the surviving seven plays, see *TrGF* T 78; also p. 335 of D. L. Page's Oxford Classical Text of Aeschylus (Oxford, 1972).

[2] T. Gantz, 'The Aischylean tetralogy: prolegomena', *CJ* 74 (1978–9), 289–304, at 293.

[3] Gantz (n. 2), 293. On Aeschylus' satyr plays, see R. G. Ussher, 'The other Aeschylus', *Phoenix* 31 (1977), 287–99; M. Griffith, 'Slaves of Dionysos: satyrs, audience, and the ends of the *Oresteia*', *ClAnt* 21 (2002), 195–258.

Gantz argues that Aeschylus produced at least ten tetralogies, which would account for nearly half of his 22 or so productions. It is thus reasonable to investigate whether other lost plays also can be assembled into tetralogies.[4] He is well aware that titles can mislead. It would have been natural to place *Prometheus Pyrkaeus* with the other Prometheus plays if we did not happen to know that it was produced with the *Persians* and two other unconnected plays in 472 BC. On the other hand, he observes there are some cases where there are compelling narrative links between two lost plays, and other cases (e.g. Memnon) where it is difficult to see how a particular myth could have yielded two completely separate plays. Furthermore, there are titles like *Choephori* which give no indication of plot, and are thus available to complete tetralogies where there seem to be too few relevant titles.[5]

PERSIANS

Suzanne Saïd's discussion of *Persians* (Ch. 2) starts from the observation that it is the tragedy *par excellence*, in that it focuses more intently than any other on the reversal from prosperity to disaster (cf. Aristotle, *Poetics* 1453^{a}7–12). She substantiates this observation with detailed discussion of the language of the play, showing, for example, how the words which emphasized the vast numbers of the Persian forces in the first half of the play are used in the second half to express the scale of their losses.

Saïd's analysis may be predominantly linguistic, but she also has something to say about the way in which Aeschylus' imagery takes on concrete form in the stage action. She acknowledges here the work of Oliver Taplin, which is undoubtedly one of the most important contributions to the understanding of Aeschylus' skill as a dramatist.[6] Taplin consistently challenges the view that Aeschylus' dramaturgy is primitive or naïve, and stresses that he was already an experienced

---

[4] Gantz (n. 2), 301–3.

[5] On Aeschylus' tetralogies, see further A. H. Sommerstein, *Aeschylean Tragedy* (Bari, 1996), 53–70, 337–5, 451–2.

[6] O. Taplin, *The Stagecraft of Aeschylus* (Oxford, 1977). He discusses *Persians* in ch. 2 (pp. 61–128).

dramatist by the time of *Persians* (472 BC). He thus observes that the play's choral prologue is not merely an archaic feature, but has the dramatic effect of bringing out the impact of the Persian disaster on the whole people. He also analyses Atossa's two entries (155, 598) as a pair of 'mirror scenes', a dramatic device which he defines as the 'repetition or reflection of an incident or scene in such a striking way as to recall the earlier event' (p. 100). Taplin's point is that the stage action is not mere spectacle, but an integral part of the meaning of the play. There is thus is a significant contrast between Atossa's first entry, on a chariot, magnificently dressed, and accompanied by several attendants, and her second entry, on foot, dressed in black, and probably without attendants. This 'visual meaning' is as important as the words. 'The sight embodies and interprets the words, it is indivisible from them, and without the sight the words cannot be fully appreciated' (p. 100). Taplin also insists that every significant stage action is implicit in the words, and that there is never reason to assume stage action which is essential to the play but not indicated in the text ('dumb show'). Atossa's first entry seems in fact to be the strongest counter-example to this principle, as there is no reference to her chariot until she remarks on its absence in the second scene (608–9). Taplin's answer is that Atossa's chariot-entry only becomes significant retrospectively, once she has realized the fragility of the pomp which she had formerly taken for granted (pp. 75–9). Saïd develops Taplin's discussion of the preparation and significance of Xerxes' appearance, and of how Aeschylus uses it to express (e.g. through his clothing) the disaster which has struck the whole of Persia.[7]

Saïd concentrates on the reversal of Persian fortune, but does not go into the reasons for it beyond remarking that the very number of the Persians was a factor in their destruction. Other scholars have focused on this issue. Winnington-Ingram pointed to an interesting contrast in the interpretation of the disaster in the Darius scene and in the rest of the play.[8] He observed that divine power is identified in rather vague terms in the first half of the play: 'a god' (94, 454, 495, 514), 'a *daimon*' (345, 354, 472, 515), 'the gods' (347, 362, 373). This

[7] Taplin (n. 6), 121–7; cf. W. G. Thalmann, 'Xerxes' rags: some problems in Aeschylus' *Persians*', *AJP* 101 (1980), 260–82.

[8] R. P. Winnington-Ingram, 'Zeus in the *Persae*', *JHS* 93 (1973), 210–19 ≈ *Studies in Aeschylus* (Cambridge, 1983), 1–15.

divine power is deceptive (93–100, 495–507), malicious (346, 354, 472, 515), and resentful of human prosperity (362). Fate is merely τὸ μέλλον ('what is going to happen'; 373, 454). These ideas were widespread in popular Greek thought, and especially common in Herodotus. Aeschylus rejects them in the *Agamemnon* (750–62), and Winnington-Ingram argues that he also shows their inadequacy in *Persians*. Darius was outstandingly prosperous and fortunate (554–7, 709–12), yet he lived out his life without attracting the envy of the gods.[9] Darius himself explains why. He is horrified to hear that Xerxes bridged the Hellespont (721–5), not only because it was an impious attempt to control the sea-god Poseidon (744–50) but also because it symbolized Xerxes' misguided desire to extend his rule from Asia to Europe (cf. 762–4). He tried to yoke Asia and Europe together (cf. 50, 72, 181–99).[10] Darius proceeds to elaborate on how Xerxes has brought disaster on himself by acts of impiety and *hubris*. Winnington-Ingram observes that Zeus is only mentioned by name on five occasions in the play: three times by Darius (740, 762, 827), once by the chorus just before the Darius scene (532), and once by Xerxes immediately after it (915). The divine power was anonymous in the first half of the play, but 'Now we can give him a name; now we know on what principles he acts'.[11] Winnington-Ingram concludes by

[9] It has often been observed that the contrast between Darius and Xerxes was in reality much less sharp than it is presented as being by Aeschylus, and that Darius' Scythian campaign in particular would be open to the criticisms which he makes of Xerxes (Herodotus 4.87–9). Herodotus presents Xerxes' expedition against Greece as the logical continuation of a tradition of Persian expansionism of which Darius was very much a part. See (e. g.) S. Saïd, 'Darius et Xerxès dans les *Perses* d'Eschyle', *Ktèma* 6 (1981), 17–38.
[10] Yoking imagery: Taplin (n. 6), 78; B. H. Fowler, 'Aeschylus' imagery', *C & M* 28 (1967), 1–74, at 3–5; D. J. Conacher, *Aeschylus: The Earlier Plays and Related Studies* (Toronto, 1996), 120–1.
[11] Winnington-Ingram, *Studies in Aeschylus* (Cambridge, 1983), 13. M. Gagarin, *Aeschylean Drama* (Berkeley, 1976), 46–52, denies that Darius has any special insight and argues that the 'Herodotean' interpretation of the Persian disaster is essentially correct. A. F. Garvie, 'Aeschylus' simple plots', in R. D. Dawe et al. (eds.), *Dionysiaca: Nine Studies... Presented to Sir Denys Page* (Cambridge, 1978), 63–86, at 67–71, takes similar view to Gagarin, arguing that the 'basic contrast of the play is between former splendour and present ruin' (70). Gagarin and Garvie are criticized by L. Lenz, 'Zu Dramaturgie und Tragik in den *Persern*', *Gymnasium* 93 (1986), 141–63, stressing that tragedy does not merely present the fall from prosperity to adversity but also offers an interpretation it.

pointing out that these lessons are ignored by the chorus, and that both they and Xerxes relapse in the final scene into the superficial level of understanding of the first part of the play.

Saïd's discussion draws attention to aspects of the Persian expedition which were distinctively barbarian, but on the whole treats the play as a tragedy of universal significance. Persia does indeed have features which resemble the mythical settings of other Athenian tragedies.[12] It is a place far removed from Athens, the main characters are royal, and in the absence of the king its court is dominated by a powerful woman (cf. *Agamemnon*). It resembles mythical Troy, an oriental country which laments defeat by the Greeks. On the other hand, this disaster was an historical event, which took place a mere eight years before the production of the play, and in which Athens was centrally involved. Much modern discussion has thus dealt with such questions as the historical reliability of the play and the ways in which Aeschylus has moulded historical events into a dramatic form.[13] *Persians*, written so close to the events with which it deals, has inevitably been sifted for evidence for such matters as the course of the battle and domestic Athenian politics.[14] More generally, the play raises the problem of Athenian spectators' response to the suffering, not merely of mythical figures, but of their own enemies.

Discussion of these topics was placed on a new footing by Edith Hall.[15] She exploited both the structuralist concept of the 'other' and modern discussions of 'Orientalism' to show how Aeschylus'

[12] Cf. S. Goldhill, 'Battle narrative and politics in Aeschylus' *Persae*', *JHS* 108 (1988), 189–93, at 189.

[13] Saïd has herself contributed to this debate elsewhere. See (as well as the article cited in n. 9 above), 'Pourquoi Psyttalie: ou comment transformer un combat naval en défaite terrestre', *CGITA* 7 (1992/3), 53–69. Saïd argues that Aeschylus plays up the Psyttaleia episode in order to turn Salamis into a comprehensive Persian defeat on both land and sea. J. T. Kakridis, 'Licht und Finsternis in dem Botenbericht der Perser des Aischylos', *GB* 4 (1975), 145–54, argues that Aeschylus adapted the historical material in order to bring out the symbolic association of the Greeks with light and the Persians with darkness.

[14] See A. J. Podlecki, *The Political Background of Aeschylean Tragedy*[2] (London, 1999; 1st edn., 1966), ch. 2. For a well-balanced discussion, see C. B. R. Pelling, 'Aeschylus' *Persae* and history', in C. B. R. Pelling (ed.), *Greek Tragedy and the Historian* (Oxford, 1997), 1–19.

[15] E. M. Hall, *Inventing the Barbarian* (Oxford, 1989), ch. 2; cf. her edition of *Persians* (Warminster, 1996). On 'orientalism', see E. Said, *Orientalism* (London, 1978).

presentation of the Persians serves to define the Greeks' sense of themselves. 'Aeschylus' *Persae*... is the earliest testimony to the absolute polarization in Greek thought of Hellene and barbarian, which had emerged at some point in response to the increasing threat posed to the Greek-speaking world by the immense Persian empire' (p. 57). Aeschylus may have known something about Persian culture, but his representation of it is largely controlled by the need to highlight what is distinctively Greek. The Persians are thus presented as hierarchical, luxurious, and emotional precisely in order to develop a contrast with the egalitarian, austere, and self-disciplined Greeks. This approach is illuminating, but can also coarsen into a rigidly binary mode of interpretation which relentlessly emphasizes Greek superiority by taking the worst possible view of every feature of Persian behaviour.[16]

An even more extreme anti-Persian bias has been attributed to the play by Thomas Harrison.[17] He suggests that any sympathy which has been seen in the play for the Persians is 'the product of wishful thinking, a projection of modern values onto the Greeks' (p. 111). His argument that the Persian monarchy is presented as intrinsically flawed has particular difficulty in accounting for the impressive figure of Darius. He writes, for example, 'The idea of Xerxes as the exception to the rule of Persian kings is also undermined by Darius' own words in his recounting of the achievements of his predecessors: he concludes by saying that none had done as much damage as Xerxes (785–6)—hardly a ringing endorsement' (p. 85). But the lines mean that *all the earlier kings put together* (ἅπαντες) would not be found to have done as much damage as Xerxes. The contrast between Xerxes and his predecessors is reinforced, not undermined. Harrison further argues that Darius failed because of 'wishful thinking' to understand oracles predicting the Persian disaster, 'with the result that the tragedy of the Persian defeat is discovered too late'

---

[16] This tendency is more noticeable in Hall's edition than in her earlier book (above, n. 15). See the reviews by A. H. Sommerstein, *JHS* 118 (1998), 211–12, and D. Rosenbloom, *Prudentia* 30 (1998), 35–41. These scholars point to distortions caused by Hall's excessively negative view of the Persians in her discussion of several passages (e.g. 247, 374–83, 495–7, 845–8). For a more balanced view, see Sommerstein (n. 5), 71–96, esp. 76–7, 89, 93–4.
[17] T. Harrison, *The Emptiness of Asia* (London, 2000).

(p. 87). The relevant lines (739–42) do not, however, show that Darius would have understood the oracles better if he had consulted more widely about their meaning, but that even the gods cannot take account of wilfully self-destructive misjudgement by humans (cf. Hom. *Od.* 1.32–43). This is central to the theology of the play, and raises issues which will be explored in greater depth in Aeschylus' later plays. The fullness of Darius' belated understanding is comparable to the *anagnorisis* of such figures as Heracles (Soph. *Trach.* 1145) and Oedipus (Soph. *OT* 1182), adding to his stature as a tragic character.[18]

Mark Griffith's discussion of the play (Ch. 3), by contrast, gives proper weight to Darius' appearance. It is taken from the second of two long articles which develop the perhaps surprising view that Athenian tragedy, while obviously promoting in many respects a democratic view of the *polis* and its institutions, at the same time consistently validates the authority of an aristocratic élite.[19] In the earlier part of the article from which the extract reprinted here is taken, Griffith raised the question why tragedy continued 'to focus so heavily on kings and royal or noble families, despite the ostensible irrelevance of such monarchical structures and hierarchies to the Athenians' democratic practices and institutions' (p. 21). He points out that an aristocratic élite continued to play a leading role in the Athenian democracy, and that a hierarchical social order in which everyone knows their place can be reassuring for both leaders and led. There are several examples in tragedy of idealized kings (e.g. Pelasgus in Aeschylus' *Suppliants*), but even the least satisfactory kings do not cause royal power itself to be overthrown or called into question. Lower-class characters are repeatedly shown to be ineffectual and small-minded, and to depend on their betters for protection. They are sometimes even slightly comic (e.g. the Watchman, Herald, and Nurse in the *Oresteia*, and the Guard in Sophocles' *Antigone*). Griffith relates this theory of the politics of tragedy to a theory of its psychology. The authority and stature of tragic kings is, he thinks, essentially paternal. The sense of an ending in Athenian

[18] For further discussion of Harrison's argument, see P. J. Rhodes, 'Nothing to do with democracy: Athenian drama and the *polis*', *JHS* 123 (2003), 104–19, at 116–17.

[19] The other is 'Brilliant dynasts: power and politics in the *Oresteia*', *ClAnt* 14 (1995), 62–129; cf. his edition of Sophocles' *Antigone* (Cambridge, 1999).

tragedy depends on the reaffirmation of the continued domination of a strong father-figure.

Griffith thus proposes a view of the Athenian audience's response to *Persians* which qualifies the view of Hall and others that the Persians are entirely and essentially 'other'. He argues that both *Persians* and Sophocles' *Antigone* (the other play which he discusses in this article) 'end up strongly reaffirming the need, and the inevitability and even desirability, of élite political rule of a kind that draws much of its power and appeal from the model of the ideal or idealized father of the family' (p. 43). Xerxes may bring disaster on Persia through his foolish and arrogant behaviour, but there is still no danger of his being deposed at the end. The play also presents, in the figure of Darius, a powerful image of kingly and paternal power. Griffith stresses that the appeal of this image is by no means simply a matter of political allegiance, although there will no doubt have been members of the audience who would indeed have preferred Athens to be governed in a less democratic way, but that it would have been possible even for a convinced democrat to admit in the special context of the theatre a 'nostalgic' attraction for social and political behaviour which he would have repudiated outside it.[20]

SEVEN AGAINST THEBES

Von Fritz discusses the character of Eteocles in *Seven Against Thebes* (Ch. 4). This had been the subject of a series of articles, mostly in German, in the 50 years before the appearance of his own contribution in 1962, and he gives a good account of the debate. He begins by discussing the older view that Eteocles is consistently a good king, and that his behaviour serves the interests of the city throughout. This remains the case when he goes off to fight his brother, it was argued, since Thebes will always be in danger while it is ruled by the accursed family of Oedipus. Eteocles' death is thus a sacrifice (the German word *Opfertod* is often used in this connection) which is necessary for

---

[20] See further Griffith (n. 19), 118 n. 171. These nuances are largely ignored in the critique of Griffith by Harrison (n. 17), 105–8.

the salvation of Thebes. Von Fritz follows Wilamowitz in objecting that lines 274–8a (where Eteocles vows offerings to the gods if the city is saved) imply that he expects to survive, and that there is no clear statement that the brothers must die for Thebes to be saved. The latter argument is stronger than the former. If line 278a is interpolated, as seems likely, then there is no clear evidence in this passage that Eteocles necessarily expects to make these offerings himself.[21]

Von Fritz then discusses the view that there is a sharp break in Eteocles' character at line 653, when he responds to the news that Polynices is at the seventh gate. Up until that point, it was argued, he had been a competent and composed military commander, who takes all necessary steps for the defence of Thebes, but after it his behaviour is irrational and self-destructive. Von Fritz discusses two possible explanations for this change. Wilamowitz argued that the discontinuity results from Aeschylus combining two different versions of the myth. Solmsen found a more tragic dimension here, arguing that he is overcome at this point by Oedipus' curse.

Von Fritz also discusses Wolff's view that Eteocles does what he says he is going to do in lines 282–6, and allocates warriors to the seven gates before he reappears for the shield scene or *sieben Redepaare* ('seven pairs of speeches'). He thus has no choice in matching the defenders to the attackers, and the pairings are supernaturally determined by some combination of the curse, the Erinys, and the gods.[22] The matter is complicated by the variation in the tenses which Eteocles uses for his allocation of the seven warriors: 'I will appoint' (408), 'he has been allocated' (448), 'he has been sent' (473), 'he was selected' (505), 'we have a man' (553), 'we will appoint' (621), 'I will go and face him' (672). Wolff argued that the present and past tenses are further evidence that the allocations have already been made, while the futures refer only to the actual execution of the decisions. Von Fritz objects that Eteocles' statement of intent in lines 282–6 would not be so firmly lodged in the minds of the spectators as

---

[21] See G. O. Hutchinson (ed.), *Aeschylus: Septem contra Thebas* (Oxford, 1985), ad loc. For further criticisms of the *Opfertod* theory, in the context of an adverse assessment of the character of Eteocles, see A. J. Podlecki, 'The character of Eteocles in Aeschylus' *Septem*', *TAPA* 95 (1964), 283–99, at 295–9.

[22] Wolff's view was revived by A. P. Burnett, 'Curse and dream in Aeschylus' *Septem*', *GRBS* 14 (1973), 343–68.

to overcome the strong impression that in the shield scene he is actually making a series of choices in response to the Scout's description of each attacking warrior, and not just describing choices already made.[23] The perfects signify the instantaneity of his decisions.[24] More recently, there has been considerable support for Wilamowitz' view that the tenses should be taken at face value, so that Eteocles has already allocated three warriors before the scene begins and makes the remaining four appointments during it.[25] Von Fritz rejects this view, and the obvious symmetry of the scene seems to be a strong objection to it.[26] What would be the dramatic point of treating Eteocles' allocation of the warriors asymmetrically? Lesky offers the most plausible reply. He argues that the variety of tenses creates uncertainty about how much has been decided, simultaneously conveying the impressions both that Eteocles has a choice and that he does not. 'Only in this way could [Aeschylus] reveal both aspects of Eteokles' decision: the fulfillment of the family curse that fate has foreordained, and the moment of decision toward which events develop before our eyes.'[27]

Von Fritz himself offers a modified version of the *Opfertod* view.[28] He does not believe that there is an explicit and supernatural

[23] Taplin (n. 6), 142–6 is sympathetic to von Fritz's view that the whole shield scene should not be distorted to fit lines 282–6, but still wonders about the point of this false preparation and suggests that the lines may be interpolated or displaced.

[24] Von Fritz's defence of line 472 has not impressed recent editors: it is omitted by Page, Hutchinson (n. 21), and West. His interpretation of *Eum.* 894 is also unsatisfactory: καὶ δὴ δέδεγμαι is not instantaneous, but means rather 'suppose that I do accept it'. See A. H. Sommerstein (ed.), *Aeschylus: Eumenides* (Cambridge, 1989), ad loc., Hutchinson (n. 21), on 472.

[25] U. von Wilamowitz-Moellendorff, *Aischylos Interpretationen* (Berlin, 1914), 61–2. Cf. Winnington-Ingram (n. 11), 24; Sommerstein (n. 5), 103–6; Conacher (n. 10), 65–8.

[26] Taplin (n. 6), 154 describes Wilamowitz' solution as 'scholastic and oversubtle, because the entire shape and disposition of the structure make the audience assume that the same thing is happening each time'.

[27] A. Lesky, *Greek Tragic Poetry* (Eng. tr. of German original published in 1972; New Haven and London, 1983), 60; cf. 'Decision and responsibility in the tragedy of Aeschylus', *JHS* 86 (1966), 78–86, at 83–4 = E. Segal (ed.), *Oxford Readings in Greek Tragedy* (Oxford, 1983), 13–23, at 20–1.

[28] Von Fritz is supported by G. M. Kirkwood, 'Eteokles *oiakostrophos*', *Phoenix* 23 (1969), 9–25, who concludes: 'Eteocles the helmsman achieves by his death the preservation of Thebes; the Curse-driven brothers bring by their death an end to the frenzy of the Erinys' (25). The consistency of Eteocles' character is also defended by Conacher (n. 10), 36–74.

requirement that Eteocles must die to save the city (like Menoeceus in Eur. *Pho.*), but that this is in practice how things work out. Polynices' impious and boastful allies, as well as Amphiaraus' condemnation of the expedition, make clear that he would be a bad king and that Eteocles cannot yield the throne to him.[29] Eteocles has turned out to be the most appropriate defender of the seventh gate, and it would be an intolerable dereliction of duty for him not to go there. His decision is thus free in the sense that it expresses his character, but unfree in that he could not in this situation act differently without being a different person. He is doomed even if he kills Polynices, since he could hardly continue to rule Thebes after doing so.[30] Von Fritz regards the chorus's objections merely as evidence of their failure to understand the situation. This view is strongly rejected by Lesky, who points out that Eteocles never contradicts the chorus's condemnation of his deed, which should therefore be accepted as having some validity: 'the king's defense of Thebes, which proves his heroism, becomes at the same time the terrible crime of fratricide.'[31]

Von Fritz is quick to dismiss the possibility raised by Patzer that Eteocles' response to the chorus in the first episode displays a nervous irritability which betrays his inner insecurity.[32] This view restores the consistency of Eteocles' character by making him consistently flawed. The role of women in tragedy has been the subject of much useful work since he wrote, and it has become clearer why Eteocles' attempt to suppress the chorus here cannot be assessed in purely military terms.[33] Some progress was made in an article by

---

[29] Von Fritz does not suppose that the earlier plays of the trilogy would have clarified the moral issues. For discussion of the trilogy, see (e.g.) Winnington-Ingram (n. 11), 40–8; Hutchinson (n. 21), pp. xvii–xxx; Sommerstein (n. 5), 121–30.

[30] Winnington-Ingram (n. 11), 49 n. 86 objects that there is not enough support in the text for von Fritz's assumption here.

[31] Lesky, *Greek Tragic Poetry* (n. 27), 61; cf. id., 'Decision and responsibility' (n. 27), 84 = 21.

[32] Hutchinson (n. 21), on 187–95, similarly argues that 'the harshness of Eteocles' invective is by no means exceptional'. He is criticized in the review by S. Goldhill, *LCM* 12 (1987), 24–8, at 26–7. See Winnington-Ingram (n. 11), 27–9 for discussion of various views of Eteocles' behaviour in this scene.

[33] e.g. F. I. Zeitlin, *Playing the Other: Gender and Society in Classical Greek Literature* (Chicago, 1996); H. P. Foley, *Female Acts in Greek Tragedy* (Princeton, 2001).

Helen Bacon which appeared only two years after von Fritz's.[34] Bacon observes that the imagery of storm and animality which describes the invading army is also applied by Eteocles to the behaviour of the chorus inside the city: 'There is a danger "outside" which must not be let in, and a danger "inside" which must not be let out. The same images of an alien and overwhelming force and noise are used of both. The problem is to know who really *is* the stranger, the outsider, the enemy' (p. 27). Bacon argues that in the house of Laius it is the internal danger, associated with women and incestuous rivalry, which is the more threatening. Eteocles may succeed in suppressing the chorus, but 'the harshness of his language and the intensity of his horror of women' (p. 27) leave an impression that his success is unnatural and unstable. It should be noted that Bacon analyses the situation more in structuralist terms than by trying to psychoanalyse Eteocles.[35]

The paradoxical relationship between women and the *polis* in *Seven Against Thebes* can be examined in more general terms. Roger Just, for example, argues that in Greek (male) thought the emotionalism and irrationality of women were regarded as posing a threat to social order.[36] Eteocles does not only say that women should refrain from spreading panic round the city in wartime, but that he does not even want to share a house with them in peacetime (187–90). On the other hand, the ensuing choral ode (287–368) shows that the women also represent the city's values of kinship and religion, which are being threatened by the masculine strife between the two brothers. 'The Theban women's lack of self-control endangers the state; but if the women represent a disorder that Eteokles as ruler of Thebes must repress, it is nevertheless clear that women are also the

[34] H. H. Bacon, 'The shield of Eteocles', *Arion* 3 (1964), 27–38 = Segal (n. 27), 24–33. Bacon's discussion of the meaning of the shield devices has been taken up by several later scholars, notably F. I. Zeitlin, *Under the Sign of the Shield: Semiotics and Aeschylus'* Seven against Thebes (Rome, 1982), and P. Vidal-Naquet, 'The shields of the heroes', in J.-P. Vernant and P. Vidal-Naquet, *Myth and Tragedy in Ancient Greece* (Eng. tr. of French originals published in 1972 and 1986; New York, 1988), 273–300.

[35] Winnington-Ingram (n. 11), 27 cites the famous observation of Méautis, 'C'est la maternité qu'Étéocle haït, car il ne l'a connue, dans sa famille, que souillée par l'inceste' (*Eschyle et la trilogie* (Paris, 1936), 108–9); cf. R. Caldwell, 'The misogyny of Eteocles', *Arethusa* 6 (1973), 197–231.

[36] R. Just, *Women in Athenian Law and Life* (London and New York, 1989), 198–204.

representatives of an order that Eteokles fails to grasp.'[37] The roles are reversed in the later scene when the chorus tries to restrain Eteocles from going to fight Polynices (677–719). The play thus dramatizes, in an extreme form, the tensions in the role of women in society.

The play also, to look at the matter the other way round, questions ideas which were prominent in Athenian public discourse about the primacy of the *polis* over private relationships. This is stressed by Creon in Sophocles' *Antigone* (175–91; cf. Demosthenes 19.247; Thucydides 2.35–46, 60; Plato, *Crito* 51a), a play in which the limitations of such an attitude are made clear. It was expressed in the Athenian mythology of autochthony, the idea that they were in some sense the children of the city itself.[38] Similar ideas are expressed by Eteocles in his opening speech (10–20), and the effect seems to be to elide the role of women and families in producing children. Martha Nussbaum has given an interesting account of the way in which Eteocles sees himself in purely political terms: 'Eteocles has made it his lifelong practical aim to dissociate himself, in imagination and feeling, from the family that bore him, regarding himself simply as a citizen and the city's helmsman.'[39] It is in keeping with this that he regards Polynices purely as a public enemy, against whom it is appropriate for him to fight. He is in no way restrained by considerations, pressed upon him by the chorus, that Polynices is his brother and therefore someone whom he should be reluctant to fight. He may or may not have any choice about fighting Polynices, but it is highly significant that he feels eagerness rather than reluctance to do so. Von Fritz's conviction of the essential unity of Eteocles' character is thus to some extent substantiated, although the resulting view of it is of course very different.[40]

---

[37] Just (n. 36), 202.

[38] Cf. N. Loraux, *The Children of Athena* (Eng. tr. of French original published in 1984; Princeton, 1993).

[39] M. C. Nussbaum, *The Fragility of Goodness* (Cambridge, 1986), 39.

[40] The whole question of 'character' in drama has been much discussed since von Fritz wrote. See (e.g.) J. Gould, 'Dramatic character and "human intelligibility" in Greek tragedy', *PCPS* 24 (1978), 43–67 = *Myth, Ritual, Memory, and Exchange* (Oxford, 2001), 78–111; M. C. Clark and E. Csapo, 'Deconstruction, ideology, and Goldhill's *Oresteia*', *Phoenix* 45 (1991), 95–125, at 119–25; C. B. R. Pelling (ed.), *Characterization and Individuality in Greek Literature* (Oxford, 1990).

SUPPLIANTS

Wolfgang Rösler's paper on *Suppliants* (Ch. 5) addresses several of
the most difficult problems in the play and the trilogy of which it was
part. The first of these is the reason for the Danaids' rejection of
marriage with the sons of Aegyptus. The debate has traditionally
revolved around the question whether they object to the sons of
Aegyptus in particular, or whether they reject sexuality and marriage
altogether.[41] There can certainly be no doubt that they have a violent
aversion to the sons of Aegyptus, and they repeatedly characterize
their behaviour as *hubris* (30, 81, 104, 426, 528, 817, 845). They
loathe the idea of being forced to marry against their will (39, 227–8,
1031–2), and regard marriage to them as being equivalent to servi-
tude (335, 392–3). The marriage is prohibited by Themis ['Right']
(37; cf. 9), and the suitors are compared to hawks pursuing doves
(223–6; cf. 511, 750–2).[42] Other expressions, however, are more
general. Rösler quotes the Danaids' words at the beginning of
the play: 'We have not been exiled by our people on account of any
blood-guilt, condemned by a vote of the city, but of our own volition
we are in flight from men' (5–8). The last ten words here translate just
two words in Greek (αὐτογενῆ φυξανορίαν), which could more
literally be rendered 'self-generated flight from men'.[43] The expression
seems at least to leave open the possibility of an unnatural objection
to men and marriage more generally, and this is suggested by several
later passages (e.g. 141–53, 332, 392–3, 643–5, 787–91, 804–7).

[41] Aversion to the sons of Aegyptus in particular: H. Friis Johansen and E. W. Whittle
(eds.), *Aeschylus: The Suppliants* (3 vols.; Copenhagen. 1980), i. 29–37. Aversion to
marriage generally: A. F. Garvie, *Aeschylus' Supplices: Play and Trilogy* (Cambridge,
1969), 215–25, Winnington-Ingram (n. 11), 60.

[42] On this imagery, see Fowler (n. 10), 13–15. R. D. Murray, *The Motif of Io in
Aeschylus' Suppliants* (Princeton, 1958) discusses the Danaids' sense of themselves as
reincarnations of Io, arguing that they have a distorted and partial understanding
of her (ignoring the Zeus who *pursued* Io). See further Gagarin (n. 11), 130–2;
Sommerstein (n. 5), 163–8; F. I. Zeitlin, 'The politics of eros in the Danaid trilogy
of Aeschylus', in *Playing the Other* (n. 33), 123–71.

[43] This is the reading of Page, West, and Friis Johansen and Whittle (n. 41).
M. Griffith, 'A new edition of Aeschylus' *Suppliants*', *Phoenix* 40 (1986), 323–40, at
330 and Conacher (n. 10), 81 n. 15 both think that the phrase also has the overtones
of both 'from inborn man-hatred' and 'flight from men of our own race / kin'.

The advice of the secondary chorus at the end confirms this view of the Danaids' motivation (1034–51). Danaus' advice to his daughters (991–1009) has sometimes been thought to imply that they might be tempted by men other than the Aegyptiads, and that they are therefore not opposed to marriage altogether. Mark Griffith rightly responds that the lines 'need only imply that Danaus' daughters always did, and always will, regard their beauty and virginity as delicate possessions ever threatened by male aggression, and ever to be protected at any cost and by any means'.[44]

Richard Seaford has offered an interpretation of the Danaids' motivation in terms of Greek marriage which elegantly combines the two conflicting views outlined in the previous paragraph.[45] He argues that, from the point of view of the bride, there is inevitably a negative and threatening aspect to marriage. The bride regrets the loss of her virginal innocence, is anxious about the transition to a new life, and fears the brutality of the male. The wedding ceremony itself can be represented in terms of abduction and rape, and repeatedly exploits imagery of the yoking and taming of a girl who was previously wild and free. These negative associations will normally be overcome by a more positive view of the natural and social order, but there are a number of examples in tragedy where there is a perverse victory of the negative aspect of marriage. The Danaids thus fear marriage generally, Seaford thinks, precisely because they see it solely in terms of domination by a violent and hubristic master. The problem is exacerbated by the fact that their suitors are also their cousins, so that they will have no independent natal family to turn to in the event of marital conflict.[46] 'The attitude of the Danaids

[44] Griffith (n. 43), 325, rebutting the argument of Friis Johansen and Whittle (n. 41), i. 32–3 that there are passages in which the Danaids express a more positive view of marriage. See also A. H. Sommerstein, 'The beginning and the end of Aeschylus' Danaid trilogy', *Drama* 3 (1995), 111–34, at 114 n. 18.

[45] R. A. S. Seaford, 'The tragic wedding', *JHS* 107 (1987), 106–30, at 110–19.

[46] Cf. G. D. Thomson, *Aeschylus and Athens* (3rd edn., London, 1966; 1st edn., 1941), 298–309, relating the Aegyptiads' claim to an Athenian law awarding marriage rights to next-of-kin in certain circumstances. There is certainly some evidence that this is the basis for the Aegyptiads' claim (387–91; cf. 918, 932–3), but the view that the Danaids reject the marriage because it is endogamous depends on controversial interpretations of two key passages (8, 335–41). For a good discussion of Thomson's view, see J. K. MacKinnon, 'The reason for the Danaids' flight', *CQ* 28 (1978), 74–81, arguing that it is only an enforced marriage that the Danaids

resembles in several respects the attitude associated with the Greek bride or her female companions, but taken to an exotic extreme.'[47]

An entirely different explanation was offered by Martin Sicherl in an article published in 1986.[48] He drew attention to a number of ancient sources for a story that Danaus had received an oracle that he would be killed by a son-in-law. The crucial evidence that this story was associated in antiquity with Aeschylus' Danaid trilogy is a scholion on line 37 of *Suppliants*, explaining why Themis ('Right') prohibits the marriage: διὰ τὸ μὴ θανατωθῆναι τὸν πατέρα, 'so that their father might not be killed'.[49] Danaus was therefore determined to prevent his daughters from marrying, and may even have caused the conflict with his brother by rejecting a proposal from him to join their children in marriage. One objection to Sicherl's theory is that there is no clear evidence in *Suppliants* either for the oracle or for any feud between Danaus and Aegyptus.[50] He argued that spectators are kept in suspense about this background until it is resolved later in the trilogy. Another problem is that the emphasis seems less on the motivation of Danaus himself than on that of his daughters. Sommerstein replies that the Danaids will by now have thoroughly internalized Danaus' hostility to marriage and made his wishes their own.[51]

Rösler offers an answer to the problem of the audience's knowledge of the oracle by addressing another of the great issues of *Suppliants*, its place in the trilogy. He revives a view, which goes

reject, and that the trilogy finally shows the importance in sexual union of mutual attraction and consent. Rösler's theory would of course allow for the basis for the Aegyptiads' claim to have been made clear in *Aigyptioi*.

[47] Seaford (n. 45), 110.

[48] M. Sicherl, 'Die Tragik der Danaiden', *MH* 43 (1986), 81–110.

[49] A. F. Garvie (*EMC* 18 (1999), 129) queries whether this is actually a correct translation of a phrase which in classical Greek would more naturally mean 'because their father had not been killed'. Sicherl (n. 48), 92 recognized that his desired sense would be clearer with βούλεσθαι or θέλειν before θανατωθῆναι ('because they did not *want* their father to be killed'), but also supplies parallels for διά expressing purpose (e.g. Thuc. 4.102.4).

[50] See Friis Johansen and Whittle (n. 41), 33, 47; Garvie (n. 41), 171 (opposing earlier attempts to relate the Danaids' attitude to hostility between Danaus and Aegyptus).

[51] Sommerstein (n. 44), 119–20. Sommerstein also suggests (against Rösler § iii) that Danaus never informed his daughters of the oracle.

back to the nineteenth century, that *Suppliants* was not the first play in the trilogy, but the second. He argues that *Aigyptioi* was the first play in the trilogy, and that it both explained the oracle and dealt with the origin in Egypt of the quarrel between Danaus and Aegyptus. He observes that this makes better sense of the title (which means 'Egyptians', not 'Sons of Aegyptus'), and avoids the problem of how the sons of Aegyptus could have been the chorus of a play in which their murder was plotted. Rösler's theory also explains some otherwise puzzling elements in Danaus' advice to his daughters (991–1009). It is nevertheless still a problem for him that there is no reference in *Suppliants* to the oracle. He suggests that the Danaids rest their case exclusively on the rights of suppliants, but it has been objected that a threat to Danaus' life from the suitors could only strengthen their claim.[52]

One objection to placing *Aigyptioi* first has been that *Suppliants* provides an adequate introduction to the trilogy. Garvie thus writes: 'The situation is made abundantly clear in the Parodos and in the stichomythia between the King and the Danaids'.[53] Rösler aptly retorts that the endless dispute about the Danaids' motivation hardly suggests that the initial situation in *Suppliants* is at all clear. Another objection is that this ordering of the trilogy leaves too much material to be passed over between the second and third plays. By the beginning of *Danaides* the war between Argos and Egypt will be over, Pelasgus (probably) slain, Danaus king of Argos, and all the sons of Aegyptus apart from Lynceus murdered on their wedding-night. Rösler points out that Aeschylus was under no obligation to treat the myth in a continuously linear fashion, and that the events between *Suppliants* and *Danaides* could have been filled in by means of flashback and narrative. Sommerstein reinforces this suggestion by pointing out that other trilogies by Aeschylus probably

[52] Conacher (n. 10), 109–11. Rösler addresses this question in his 'Postscript (2004)', below pp. 195–8. Sommerstein (n. 44), 115–16 observes that Danaus' determination to keep his daughters in permanent spinsterhood may actually have been a motive about which it was wise to keep quiet.

[53] Garvie (n. 41), 185. Griffith (n. 43), 324 observes that there is actually very little in *Suppliants* about events in Egypt, apart from a few enigmatic references (83–5, 741–2, 1008), and that the Danaids have much more to say about the distant past (Io and Epaphus). Cf. arguments about whether *Prometheus Bound* gives too much background for there to have been a play before it (below, p. 36).

passed over important events. In the Theban trilogy, for example, the quarrel between the brothers and Polynices' expulsion from Thebes were probably not represented.[54] Rösler argues that *Danaides*, the final play of the trilogy, featured the trial and acquittal of Hypermestra by a popular Argive court, and that the surviving fragment of a speech by Aphrodite was spoken in her defence (*TrGF* F 44). A number of objections had already been made to earlier versions of this view.[55] It has been objected that it is difficult to see why Danaus would have prosecuted Hypermestra rather than punishing her himself, and also how he could have hoped to gain a conviction on the unlikely charge of failure to kill her husband. Rösler concludes by developing parallels with the trial in *Eumenides*. Sommerstein argues against this that Aeschylus would have been unlikely to repeat himself in this way and suggests that the story of the trial of Hypermestra goes back no further than the fourth-century *Lynceus* by Theodectes (cf. Aristotle, *Poetics* 1452[a]27–9, [b]29–32).[56] These objections are not wholly convincing. The trial of Hypermestra is attested by Pausanias, and if Theodectes could find a plausible dramatic framework for it then so too could Aeschylus. The alternative context for the Aphrodite fragment is a second marriage by the Danaids to Argive bridegrooms.[57] Sommerstein adds that the marriage would have been preceded by the killing of Danaus by Lynceus, surely an inevitable event if the Sicherl–Rösler theory is correct.[58]

Peter Burian's article (Ch. 6) deals with an issue which is briefly touched upon by Rösler, the strikingly democratic character of Argos in *Suppliants*. Pelasgus refuses to make a decision about accepting the suppliants until he has brought the matter before the Argive assembly (365–9, 397–401, 517–18), and considerable emphasis is then placed on the decision of that assembly to accept them (601, 605–24,

---

[54] Sommerstein (n. 44), 118.

[55] Advanced by Murray (n. 42), 86–7; opposed by Garvie (n. 41), 205–11; Friis Johansen and Whittle (n. 41), 53–4.

[56] Sommerstein (n. 44), 123–4 (also criticizing Rösler for saying that Hypermestra was acquitted unanimously).

[57] Winnington-Ingram (n. 11), 58–9, 70; Garvie (n. 41), 225 ff.; Friis Johansen and Whittle (n. 41), 51–2.

[58] Sommerstein (n. 44), 124–30, with a speculative reconstruction of the play; cf. his book (n. 5), 141–52.

739, 942–9, 963–5). Burian rightly dismisses the once-popular attempts to relate this to the constitution of Argos at a particular historical period,[59] and also rejects the view that the role of the Argive *demos* is mainly significant here as a preparation for what will happen later in the trilogy.[60] He focuses rather on the dramatic function of Aeschylus' portrayal of Pelasgus' relationship to his people, stressing that he is not obliged to refer the decision to the *demos* but rather chooses to do so because of its serious consequences for the whole *polis*. Burian shows that Pelasgus' referral of the decision to the demos is itself a tragic choice which has the power to give dramatic focus to the action. He concentrates so intently on *Suppliants* itself that he refuses to make the tragic nature of Pelasgus' predicament in any way dependent on the possibility that it would lead to his death later in the trilogy, although he accepts that this would provide a suitably tragic conclusion. Burian's admiration for Pelasgus goes along with a negative assessment of the Danaids, in whom he sees a 'limited, self-absorbed and barbarian mentality' (p. 206).[61] The Athenians prided themselves on their acceptance of suppliants, and Pelasgus thus resembles the good Athenian king Theseus in Euripides' *Suppliants*.[62]

Burian considers briefly whether Aeschylus' portrayal of the Argive constitution should be regarded as anachronistic. He alludes in passing to a point stressed by Lloyd-Jones, that popular assemblies are a prominent feature of the heroic world described by Homer. The people look to their kings for leadership, but the kings are in turn aware of their responsibilities to the people and of the possibility of being reproached by them if things go wrong.[63] This approach has

[59] H. Lloyd-Jones, 'The *Supplices* of Aeschylus: the new date and old problems', *Ant. Class.* 33 (1964), 356–74, at 357–61 = *Greek Epic, Lyric, and Tragedy* (Oxford, 1990), 262–77, at 263–6 = Segal (n. 27), 42–56, at 43–5, concludes that the 19th-cent. scholars who dated the play to the later 460s on the basis of supposed allusions to contemporary Argos may have been proved right about the date but failed to give convincing reasons for believing it.

[60] Winnington-Ingram (n. 11), 67.

[61] Cf. Hall, *Inventing the Barbarian* (n. 15), 192–3, 199.

[62] Gagarin (n. 11), 126–30 questions the wisdom of the decision to accept the suppliants. Pelasgus is also criticized by A. H. Sommerstein, 'The theatre audience, the *demos*, and the *Suppliants* of Aeschylus', in Pelling (n. 14), 63–79, at 75–8. The Sicherl–Rösler view implies that he was deceived by Danaus.

[63] Lloyd-Jones (n. 59), 358–9 = 264 = 44.

been developed by Easterling, arguing that the dramatists retain a sense of the integrity of the heroic world in which the action is set even when they are introducing into it features which really belong to fifth-century Athens.[64] Voting plays no part in the Homeric assembly, but it has a place in the heroic world in other contexts and is thus not too incongruous when it is employed in the Argive assembly in *Suppliants* (600–10), the earliest surviving reference to voting in a democratic assembly. Aeschylus uses language which evokes the Athenian democracy, and thus raises political issues of contemporary relevance, while being careful to avoid breaking the illusion of a heroic world which is distanced from the world of the audience. Easterling's work here reinforces Burian's stress on the dramatic coherence of Aeschylus' portrayal of Pelasgus' choice. Scholars (e.g. Rösler in the present volume) have recently been more inclined to relate the issue of democracy in *Suppliants* to contemporary Athenian politics, and especially to the reforms of Ephialtes (462/1 BC), than to anything which happened in Argos in any historical period.[65]

ORESTEIA

The discussions of the *Oresteia* by Peradotto (Ch. 7), Dodds (Ch. 8), and Macleod (Ch. 9) are all in different ways rebuttals of D. L. Page's famous statement that 'Aeschylus is first and foremost a great poet and a most powerful dramatist: the faculty of acute or profound thought is not among his gifts'.[66] Peradotto attacks the 'literalism' which had been a damaging feature of Aeschylean interpretation in the 1950s and 1960s,[67] and focuses on the omen of the eagles (*Ag.* 104–59) as an example of the working of poetic logic in

---

[64] P. E. Easterling, 'Anachronism in Greek tragedy', *JHS* 105 (1985), 1–10.

[65] *Suppliants* is, however, dated to the 470s by S. Scullion, 'Tragic dates', *CQ* 52 (2002), 81–101.

[66] J. D. Denniston and D. L. Page (eds.), *Aeschylus:* Agamemnon (Oxford, 1957), p. xv.

[67] Another notable example of such literalism appeared, somewhat paradoxically in a festschrift for Dodds, shortly after Peradotto's article: K. J. Dover, 'Some neglected aspects of Agamemnon's dilemma', *JHS* 93 (1973), 58–69 = *Greek and the Greeks* (Oxford, 1987), 135–50.

Aeschylus. He surveys various answers to the question why Artemis is angered by the behaviour of the eagles, and agrees with Lloyd-Jones that the fate of the hare symbolizes the fate of Troy. 'The eagles stand for the Atreidae; so it is natural to infer that the hare must stand for some other figure or figures belonging to the real world. We can hardly avoid supposing that it stands for the Trojans and their city. So when Calchas says (137) Artemis abhors the eagles' feast, he must mean that Artemis abhors the coming destruction of Troy, which the Atreidae are destined to accomplish.'[68] Peradotto rejects Lloyd-Jones's idiosyncratic argument that Artemis is merely a partisan of the Trojans, and develops a view similar to that of Hammond, that Artemis 'is the goddess of the weak and helpless, and she abominates the brutality of the impending war'.[69] He argues that the omen 'dramatizes' Agamemnon's *ethos* (moral disposition), and goes on to explain that Artemis, as 'patroness of innocent youth and fertility', loathes the indiscriminate slaughter which will be involved in his conquest of Troy.[70] He relates the episode to the cult of Artemis at Brauron and its associated traditions, and explores the imagery by which Aeschylus expresses these issues.[71]

[68] H. Lloyd-Jones, 'The guilt of Agamemnon', *CQ* 12 (1962), 187–99, at 189 = *Greek Epic, Lyric, and Tragedy* (Oxford, 1990), 283–99, at 286 = Segal (n. 27), 57–72, at 60. Page's view ((n. 66), pp. xxiv–xxv) that Artemis is angry with the eagles themselves rather than with what they symbolize has been revived by S. E. Lawrence, 'Artemis in the *Agamemnon*', *AJP* 97 (1976), 97–110, and A. H. Sommerstein, 'Artemis in the *Agamemnon*: a postscript', *AJP* 101 (1980), 165–9 (more briefly in his book (n. 5), pp. 361–2).

[69] N. G. L. Hammond, 'Personal freedom and its limitations in the *Oresteia*', *JHS* 85 (1965), 42–55, at 46 = M. H. McCall (ed.), *Aeschylus: A Collection of Critical Essays* (Englewood Cliffs NJ, 1972), 90–105, at 96 = *Studies in Greek History* (Oxford, 1973), 395–416, at 402; cf. H. D. F. Kitto, *Form and Meaning in Drama* (London, 1956), 4–5; M. L. West, 'The parodos of the *Agamemnon*', *CQ* 29 (1979), 1–6, at 5. West also has some observations on the difference between the black- and the white-rumped eagle, which Peradotto discusses in his Appendix.

[70] D. J. Conacher, *Aeschylus' Oresteia: A Literary Commentary* (Toronto, 1987), 79–80, objects that Calchas makes no specific reference to the destruction of the young in his forecast of the total destruction of Troy (126–30), and that this is only made explicit in the next ode (359). Peradotto has in fact already addressed this point when he observes that Calchas' explanation of the omen in terms of Artemis' love of young wild things is a veiled and euphemistic reference to this very point (this volume, pp. 224–6).

[71] For further discussion of the cult of Artemis at Brauron, see H. Lloyd-Jones, 'Artemis and Iphigeneia', *JHS* 103 (1983), 87–102 = *Greek Comedy, Hellenistic*

Peradotto shares with Dodds a determination to show that Agamemnon had a choice, although he interprets that choice somewhat
differently. He recognizes, as does Dodds, that divine intervention does
not absolve humans of responsibility, but goes beyond Dodds in
stressing very specifically that Agamemnon had a choice and in arguing
that his decision was wrong.[72] He argues that such statements as 'the
mighty Zeus who guards hospitality sends (πέμπει) Atreus' sons
against Paris' (*Ag.* 60–2) are religious interpretations rather than empirical statements, and that Agamemnon was not actually ordered to
punish Paris in the way that Orestes was later ordered to punish
Clytemnestra.[73] Peradotto goes on to criticize Page's argument
that Agamemnon was under any compulsion on the purely human
level to proceed with the war, which is a theme developed only later in
Sophocles' *Electra* and Euripides' *Iphigenia in Aulis*. Peradotto believes
the Trojan War to be disproportionate to its cause. 'The war is thus
a demonic perversion of society's extermination of the offender recognized as a public menace' (p. 235).

Peradotto concludes by showing how Agamemnon came to make
this disastrous choice. Dodds stresses that Agamemnon had a choice,
but does not explain in any detail why he makes his decision, beyond
hinting at a flaw in his nature which may have something to do with
the crime of his father Atreus. Peradotto is more critical, and argues

Literature, Greek Religion, and Miscellanea (Oxford, 1990), 306–30. Lloyd-Jones
retreats somewhat from his earlier view of Artemis' motivation, and focuses now
on her role as the 'mistress of animals' who both cherishes and (as huntress) destroys
them: 'warriors, like hunters, may not kill without appeasing her' (101 = 328).
Peradotto denies that the sacrifice of Iphigenia is an appeasement of Artemis
(this volume, p. 226), but he does not overlook Artemis' more bloodthirsty aspect
(p. 223).

Ag. 239 and Ar. *Lys.* 645, both cited in this connexion by Peradotto, are discussed
by T. C. W. Stinton, 'Iphigeneia and the bears of Brauron', *CQ* 26 (1976), 11–13 =
Collected Papers on Greek Tragedy (Oxford, 1990), 186–9. On Brauron, see also the
discussion by Bowie (this volume, pp. 339–43).

[72] Peradotto similarly goes further in condemning Agamemnon than Albin Lesky,
'Decision and responsibility in the tragedy of Aeschylus', *JHS* 86 (1966), 78–85 =
Segal (n. 27), 13–23. Peradotto's unusually hostile view of Agamemnon is queried by
B. Vickers, *Towards Greek Tragedy* (London, 1973), 427 n. 7.

[73] Cf. Winnington-Ingram (n. 11), 85–6; T. Gantz, 'The chorus of Aischylos'
Agamemnon', *HSCP* 87 (1983), 65–86, at 71–5. The reliability of the chorus's view
that 'Zeus has ordained the expedition' is reaffirmed by A. F. Garvie (ed.), *Aeschylus:
Choephori* (Oxford, 1986), p. xxx.

in detail that Agamemnon has inherited a bloodthirsty *ethos* from his father which manifests itself in his decision to sacrifice Iphigenia in the quest for heroic glory.[74] This act recapitulates Atreus' murder of the children of Thyestes and foreshadows the indiscriminate killing of the innocent in the Trojan War. Peradotto rightly observes that Agamemnon's final exit over the purple cloth is another revelation of his *ethos*.[75] Dodds had argued that $\pi\acute{a}\theta\epsilon\iota\ \mu\acute{a}\theta os$ ('learning by suffering') is manifested in the trilogy in a progression in insight from Agamemnon to Clytemnestra to Orestes. Peradotto, by contrast, sees an absolute distinction between Orestes and both his parents, and concludes with a suggestion about how he has been able to break free of his vicious Atreid (and Tyndarid) ancestry.[76]

Dodds's article (Ch. 8) begins with the question of the political relevance of the *Eumenides*. The *Oresteia* was produced shortly after a revolution in Athens' external and internal affairs in 462/1. The Athenians broke off their alliance with Sparta, which had been championed by the 'conservative' Cimon, and made an alliance instead with Sparta's enemy Argos. Cimon was ostracized (Thuc. 1.102.4; Plut. *Cim.* 16–17). Cimon may have been supported by the ancient council of the Areopagus, which was made up of ex-archons and would thus have consisted of relatively wealthy men from the top two of the four Solonian property classes. Ephialtes, who had opposed Cimon's Spartan policy, reformed the Areopagus. This episode is described in chapters 25 and 26 of the Aristotelian *Athenaion Politeia* (*Athenian Constitution*). Ephialtes 'attacked' the Areopagus by stripping it of the 'added powers' ($\grave{\epsilon}\pi\acute{\iota}\theta\epsilon\tau a$) through which it exercised

---

[74] Dodds thus goes too far when he says that Aeschylus believed (simply) in inherited guilt. 'In Aeschylus it seems that the son who inherits the family-curse is never an innocent sufferer. He inherits not just guilt but a propensity to incur fresh guilt himself, and he is thus always in some degree responsible for his suffering' (Garvie (n. 73), p. xxviii). Cf. Sommerstein (n. 24) on *Eum.* 934–7.

[75] Taplin (n. 6), 312 n. 2 suggests that Peradotto's stress on the revelation of *ethos* may lead him to neglect other significances in the scene.

[76] It would be possible to accept all or most of Peradotto's account of what is wrong with Agamemnon's decision and character while giving more weight to the reasons why it is necessary or right for him to proceed with the war. See B. Williams, *Shame and Necessity* (Berkeley, Los Angeles, and London, 1993), 133 for discussion of 'how someone might have to choose between two courses of action both of which involved a grave wrong, so that whatever he does will be bad'. Cf. Lloyd-Jones (n. 68), 191 = 289 = 62.

'guardianship and supervision of the state', and assigning those powers to the assembly and to the people's courts. He was murdered shortly afterwards. The Areopagus retained some judicial powers, in particular the right to try homicide cases. Four years later, in 458/7, its membership was opened up to the third of the Solonian property classes, the Zeugitae. At the time of the production of the *Oresteia* in 458, Athens was thus in the throes of a revolution which made it considerably more democratic and therefore provoked a degree of hostility which could have threatened the very stability of the state.

Aeschylus' attitude to these events has inevitably been scrutinized, especially as the trilogy culminates in the foundation of the Areopagus and the establishment of an alliance with Argos. Dodds begins by discussing an article by Dover which denies that there is anything in *Eumenides* to show that Aeschylus was a conservative. Dover argues that there can be no doubt about Aeschylus' support for the Argive alliance, since this recent *démarche* is treated in the most positive terms on no fewer than three occasions (289–91, 667–73, 762–74), and is given historical validation by being projected back into the heroic age. Aeschylus seems to approve of the foreign wars in which Athens was now engaged, while warning against the dangers of *stasis* (858–66, 976–87). The aggressive foreign policy and the Argive alliance were in practice associated with Ephialtes' reform of the Areopagus, and Dover argues that Aeschylus would hardly have treated them in such a favourable way if he had opposed the democrats' domestic policies. Dover rebuts three considerations which might have told in favour of Aeschylus being a conservative or at least a moderate. He observes that political terms like 'moderation' (cf. *Eum.* 526–30, 696–9) can be claimed by progressives and conservatives alike, and are not necessarily applied by individuals to themselves in the same way as they would be by others. Secondly, he argues that Athena's warning against interfering with the Areopagus (693–5) does not necessarily support a conservative position, since the democrats could have argued that they were in fact restoring it to its original form by removing the 'added powers' ($\dot{\epsilon}\pi\dot{\iota}\theta\epsilon\tau\alpha$) of *Ath. Pol.* 25.2. Finally, Dover points out that the dignity and power with which Athena invests the Areopagus are in no way incompatible with its reduction to a homicide court, since the judgement of homicide is the cornerstone of civil society. Dover thus concludes that 'the political language of *Eumenides* is neutral, and for that very reason reconcilable with unreserved acceptance of the democratic revolution'.[77]

Dodds criticizes some elements of Dover's argument, arguing that Aeschylus' political position really was moderate, and suggesting both that he accepted some aspects of the conservatives' case and that he warned against further developments in that of the progressives. Aeschylus' language is vague enough with regard to the specifics of the changes which had already been made to command a large measure of agreement from supporters of both sides,[78] but he was strongly opposed to the proposed admission of the Zeugitae to the archonship and thus to the Areopagus.[79] Dodds gives a balanced account of the political message of the *Eumenides*, but his main contribution is to relate this message to the more universal moral concerns of the first two plays of the trilogy and thus to establish the coherence of Aeschylus' overall conception. He follows the two principles παθεῖν τὸν ἔρξαντα ('the doer shall suffer') and πάθει μάθος ('learning by suffering') through the trilogy from morals to politics. The crisis in Athens in 458 needed to be addressed with the full weight of Aeschylus' moral thinking.

Dodds observes that the principle 'the doer shall suffer' is 'as dramatically senseless as it is morally revolting' (p. 258) if Agamemnon had no choice but to kill Iphigenia. Page had argued that the

[77] K. J. Dover, 'The political aspect of Aeschylus' *Eumenides*', *JHS* 77 (1957), 230–7, at 235 = *Greek and the Greeks* (Oxford, 1987), 161–75, at 169–70.

[78] This view is endorsed and expanded by Sommerstein (n. 24) on *Eum.* 693–5; cf. Griffith, 'Brilliant dynasts' (n. 19), 104 n. 132.

[79] In 'Notes on the *Oresteia*', *CQ* 3 (1953), 11–21, at 20, Dodds expressed himself more vigorously than in the article reprinted here: 'Aeschylus is not protesting against anything the democrats have already done . . . But to tamper with the composition of the old Chamber—that was too much. Aeschylus was not by temperament a reactionary, but in his old age he had begun to feel that reform was in danger of moving too fast and too far; that is the common experience of elderly reformers.' Dodds draws the irresistible analogy with proposed reform of the British House of Lords. Dodds's suggestion is endorsed by D. J. Conacher, *Aeschylus*' Oresteia: *A Literary Commentary* (Toronto, 1987), 203 (seeing Aeschylus as fairly conservative on the Areopagus issue), but criticized by Podlecki (n. 14), 172 n. 42 and Macleod, this volume, p. 272 (cf. p. 301: 'he clearly accepts the Areopagus as Ephialtes reconstituted it').

expedition against Troy was necessary both on religious grounds, because it was commanded by Zeus, and for purely practical reasons, because Agamemnon could not disband the army and desert.[80] He has not committed any offence, as in other versions of the myth, but he must still be punished. Dodds points firstly to over-determination, the fact that divine intervention is compatible with human choice. Agamemnon plainly goes through the process of making a choice, which is influenced by human considerations and assessed by the chorus in human terms. Secondly, he points out that Agamemnon *puts on* the harness of necessity. The initial choice is free, as is made clear in Aeschylus' description of it, although it has necessary consequences.

Dodds also criticizes a reductive view of the second principle, πάθει μάθος ('learning by suffering'). Lloyd-Jones had rejected the idea that there was 'an Aeschylean Zeus-religion' which was any more advanced than anything in Hesiod or Solon, and saw no place in Aeschylus for elevated modern views of Zeus 'perfecting men in goodness through the discipline of suffering'.[81] He argued that 'learning' in the Zeus-hymn of the *Agamemnon* is merely a matter of recognizing human feebleness and the uselessness of defying Zeus, and that it amounts to no more than Hesiod's παθὼν δέ τε νήπιος ἔγνω ('a fool learns only by suffering the consequences', *Op.* 218).[82] There is, in his view, no evidence in the *Eumenides* of any progression from primitive vengeance to a more enlightened form of justice: 'nothing in the play justifies the belief that the transition from the blood-feud to the trial by jury is the main theme of the trilogy.' He concludes that 'Aeschylus' conception of Zeus contains nothing that is new, nothing that is sophisticated, and nothing that is profound.'[83] Dodds's discussion of πάθει μάθος ('learning by suffering') is essentially a refutation of this reductive view of Aeschylus' religious thought. He argues that Clytemnestra has more insight than

[80] Page (n. 66), pp. xxii–xxix.
[81] H. Lloyd-Jones, 'Zeus in Aeschylus', *JHS* 76 (1956), 55–67 = *Greek Epic, Lyric, and Tragedy* (Oxford, 1990), 238–61 (quotations from pp. 57 = 243 and 55 = 238). Lloyd-Jones observes at the end of the reprint of this article (p. 261) that his views have developed since it was first published.
[82] Lloyd-Jones (n. 81), 62 = 251–2.
[83] Both quotations from Lloyd-Jones (n. 81), 64 = 255.

Agamemnon,[84] and that Orestes represents a further step towards enlightenment: 'the divine purpose, of which both Agamemnon and Clytemnestra were unconscious and guilty agents, is for Orestes something consciously known and humbly, though not easily, accepted' (263).[85] The culmination of this process is 'a new age of understanding' in the Athens of his own day.[86]

Macleod's contribution (Ch. 9) is essentially a development of Dodds's attempt to show how the *Eumenides* is a fitting conclusion to the trilogy. He sums up Dodds's argument as follows: 'the moral lessons implicit or explicit hitherto are in the *Eumenides* addressed to the city as political lessons, and ... Aeschylus was impelled to unfold his trilogy in this way by the pressing problems of Athens in the present' (p. 280). Macleod believes that this may be enough to show how *Eumenides* develops out of what has gone before, but that it still fails to vindicate the artistic coherence of the trilogy. Dodds's argument concedes that *Eumenides* is not an ideally appropriate conclusion to the trilogy in purely dramatic terms, and that it would have been written differently if Athens' political situation had been less critical. Macleod argues that Dodds has failed to escape from the unduly narrow definition of politics by earlier scholars, in terms merely of commentary on specific current events, and that he effectively treats politics as being subordinate to morals. Macleod takes a

[84] Taplin (n. 6), 327–9 agrees with Dodds that there is a growth in Clytemnestra's understanding in her scene with the chorus at the end of *Agamemnon*. For the view that the growth is in the *audience's* understanding, see G. J. P. O'Daly, 'Clytemnestra and the elders: dramatic technique in Aeschylus, *Agamemnon* 1372–1576', *MH* 42 (1985), 1–19.

[85] Dodds's argument here is criticized by Winnington-Ingram (n. 11), 143–5, who believes that it is the audience who learns rather than Orestes himself. Winnington-Ingram is certainly right to question Dodds's reliance on *Cho.* 930 for evidence that Orestes 'is aware that his act is a crime, even before he has committed it' (p. 263; see further Garvie (n. 73), ad loc.).

[86] This kind of 'progressive' reading of the *Oresteia* has been queried by S. Goldhill in several works, e.g. *Reading Greek Tragedy* (Cambridge, 1986), 33–56. Goldhill's less optimistic view of the conclusion of the trilogy has itself been criticized, e.g. by R. Seaford, 'Historicizing tragic ambivalence: the vote of Athena', in B. Goff (ed.), *History, Tragedy, Theory: Dialogues on Athenian Drama* (Austin, 1995), 202–21; J. L. Moles, *LCM* 11 (1986), 55–64, at 62–4, reviewing Goldhill's *Language, Sexuality, Narrative: the* Oresteia (Cambridge, 1984); D. J. Conacher, 'Aeschylus' *Oresteia* and Euripides' *Bacchae*: a critique of some recent critical approaches', *EMC* 19 (2000), 333–49.

much broader view of politics, as being concerned with the whole question of how human beings live together in a *polis*. Politics, for him, subsumes morals in as much as the highest good is a common good, 'and the common good is the sum of every individual's morality' (p. 280). The *Eumenides* is thus a wholly fitting conclusion to a trilogy whose central concerns are in the broad sense political.

Macleod begins by discussing a series of passages which have been thought, by Dodds and others, to have a primarily topical reference. Macleod's method in each case is to show how the passages make perfect sense without such reference, and how they develop themes which have been prominent earlier in the trilogy. Macleod does not actually deny that these passages can be related to contemporary issues, but he insists that Aeschylus is more concerned with the proper functioning of a *polis* in general than with specific historical events.[87] He contests Dodds's belief that *Eumenides* has a specific (moderate) political message, and rejects his suggestion that there is any kind of warning in *Eum.* 690–5 against the admission of the Zeugitai to the archonship. A narrow programme of this kind would be foreign to Macleod's view of the nature of the political engagement of the play, and he sees the passage rather as stressing more generally the importance of stability in a city's laws. He similarly rejects any hint of the partisanship which some scholars have detected in Athena's reference to the Areopagus as 'guardian of the land' (*Eum.* 706), and sees it rather as an ideal court which guarantees the internal harmony of Athens. Warnings against *stasis* are relevant to any *polis* at any time, and are not prompted by specific dangers to Athens. Macleod concludes this section of his discussion with an eloquent paragraph (pp. 278–9) on the way in which the distancing effect of the mythical subject matter of tragedy serves to detach it from specific contemporary issues so that it can instead address more universal questions.

The second half of Macleod's project is to bring out themes in the *Agamemnon* and *Choephori* which are 'political' in the wider sense of

---

[87] Some later scholars have argued that Macleod goes too far in downplaying contemporary allusions: Sommerstein (n. 24), on 292–6; A. J. Podlecki (ed.), *Aeschylus: Eumenides* (Warminster, 1989), on 398 ff.; Winnington-Ingram (n. 11), 170 n. 54.

the term.[88] He begins by examining the role of δίκη ('justice') in the trilogy, observing how it embraces both legal justice and a much broader conception of the natural order as a whole. It is perverted or overturned in *Agamemnon* and *Choephori* but restored in *Eumenides*. The central point here is that the trial-scene in *Eumenides* is an appropriate culmination of the trilogy's pervasive concern with just-ice in the *polis*. The other term which Macleod investigates is τιμή ('honour'), which includes both the social position of an individual and the respect which is evoked by it. He exploits sociology and anthropology to show how characters in the *Oresteia* are defined as social beings, and focuses in particular on the ways in which the inversion of social values created by the murder of Agamemnon is righted in the trial scene of *Eumenides*.[89]

Barbara Hughes Fowler's discussion of the imagery in *Choephori* (Ch. 10) is taken from a study of the imagery in all seven of Aeschylus' surviving plays.[90] The *Oresteia* proved receptive to the study of imagery as an organizational principle in drama, a method which had long been applied to Shakespeare.[91] An early example was Robert F. Goheen's discussion of the cloth on which Agamem-non walks in the *Agamemnon* (908–74), relating it both to verbal imagery of blood on the ground elsewhere in the trilogy and to the robes worn by the Erinyes at the end of the *Eumenides*.[92] The main influence which Fowler acknowledges, however, is that of Richmond

[88] Dodds, this volume, p. 246 already hinted at this when he observed that there are passages in Agamemnon (e.g. 883–4) which suggest that Aeschylus 'is already thinking in political as well as moral terms'.

[89] A similarly broad view is taken, from a different theoretical standpoint, of the question of politics in the *Oresteia* by S. Goldhill, 'Civic ideology and the problem of difference: the politics of Aeschylean tragedy, once again', *JHS* 120 (2000), 34–56.

[90] The term 'imagery' conveniently includes both symbolism and metaphor: see T. G. Rosenmeyer, *The Art of Aeschylus* (Berkeley, Los Angeles, & London, 1982), 118–19.

[91] e.g. G. Wilson Knight, *The Wheel of Fire* (London, 1930); C. Spurgeon, *Shake-speare's Imagery* (Cambridge, 1935). The influence of the 'New Criticism' is evident in (e.g.) R. F. Goheen, *The Imagery of Sophocles' Antigone* (Princeton, 1951).

[92] R. F. Goheen, 'Aspects of dramatic symbolism: three studies in the *Oresteia*', *AJP* 76 (1955), 113–37, at 115–26 = M. H. McCall (ed.), *Aeschylus: A Collection of Critical Essays* (Englewood Cliffs, NJ, 1972), 106–23, at 107–15. Cf. Bernard Knox's explor-ation of the ramifications of the parable of the lion cub at *Ag.* 717–36: 'The lion in the house', *CP* 47 (1952), 12–25 = *Word and Action* (Baltimore and London, 1979), 27–38.

Lattimore.[93] Lattimore illustrates the interplay of 'idea' and 'symbol' by sketching how the 'persistent and thematic' metaphors of entanglement (curb, yoke, snare, etc.) are embodied in the robe in which Clytemnestra actually entangles Agamemnon. Fowler's analysis of *Agamemnon* develops this insight, treating the robe as a symbol of compulsion, which she regards as the major theme of the play. This idea may in the end be too abstract and unitary to be useful, but she nevertheless gives a thorough and sensitive account of various image-complexes in the play: archery, wrestling, hunting, animals, disease, seafaring, agriculture, and light and dark.[94]

Fowler's discussion of *Choephori* begins with another concept derived from Lattimore, what he called *philos-aphilos* ('hate-in-love'). She applies this in particular to hatred within the family, when someone who is *philos* in the sense of being a relative is not *philos* in the sense of being loving or beloved. In *Choephori*, this is expressed above all by the image of the viper, which kills its mate only to be killed in turn by its offspring. She follows through the images which she had examined in *Agamemnon*, beginning again with the robe. Finally, she shows how *Eumenides* completes the image-complexes of the first two plays: sickness is cured, dark gives way to light, and the murderess's robe becomes the festive garments of the Eumenides.[95]

The imagery of the *Oresteia* was studied at length in an influential book by Anne Lebeck,[96] but her article reprinted here (Ch. 11) has a somewhat different focus. The first stasimon of *Choephori* (585–651) is the only example in Aeschylus of an extended use of myth to illustrate the action (cf. Soph. *Ant.* 944–87; Eur. *Med.* 1282–92; *Hipp.* 545–64; *HF* 1016–24; *Hel.* 375–85). The ode comes at the centre of *Choephori*, itself the central play of the trilogy, between Orestes' departure from the tomb of Agamemnon and his arrival at the palace. The first strophic pair announces the theme of the ode as

---

[93] Introduction to the Chicago translation of the *Oresteia* (Chicago, 1953), 15–18 ≈ McCall (n. 92), 73–89, at 77–9.

[94] Cf. Fowler's earlier article 'The imagery of *Prometheus Bound*', *AJP* 78 (1957), 173–84, focusing on images drawn from medicine and from the idea of yoking.

[95] For a concise account of the imagery of the *Oresteia*, with bibliography, see Garvie (n. 73), pp. xxxvi–xxxviii. More recently, J. Heath, 'Disentangling the beast: humans and other animals in Aeschylus' *Oresteia*', *JHS* 119 (1999), 17–47.

[96] A. Lebeck, *The Oresteia: A Study in Language and Structure* (Washington, DC, 1971).

'the hateful love which overcomes the female' (600). This theme is then illustrated by the stories of Althaea (who killed her son), Scylla (who killed her father), and the Lemnian women (who killed their husbands). The first two stories deal with murderous women, but Lebeck observes that since neither involves illicit passion or the murder of a husband 'the resemblance to Clytemnestra's crime is slight' (p. 319). Less obvious meanings must be sought. She argues that both stories have a significance which goes beyond the chorus's intention to condemn Clytemnestra, and that is to give 'a looking-glass reflection of the parallel crimes committed by Agamemnon and Orestes' (p. 321). The crimes of Althaea (mother killing son) and Scylla (daughter killing father) thus reflect those of Agamemnon (father killing daughter) and of Orestes (son killing mother). Lebeck relates these reflections to the way in which the plot of *Choephori* both recapitulates and reverses that of *Agamemnon*. The effect is to suggest a proliferation of crimes, one reflecting another. The Lemnian atrocities form a climax to these vicious reciprocities, where wives first kill their husbands and then husbands kill their wives.

Lebeck's article illustrates the challenges posed by the paradigmatic use of myth in Greek poetry. The stories are obviously relevant to the action on one level, in that all three deal with the murder of male relatives by 'the devious and consciously destructive sex of women',[97] but this does not seem to exhaust their significance. How far should we go in exploring parallels and contrasts with the situation in the play, especially when the relevant mythical details are not made explicit? The least secure part of Lebeck's argument is her suggestion that 'the Lemnian crime' (631) includes not only the notorious murder of their husbands by the Lemnian women but also the later murder of their wives by the Pelasgians of Lemnos. This is essential to her case that the Lemnian story 'reflects the mysterious way in which crime follows crime and one generation pays for another's wrong' (p. 321). Aeschylus treats the story allusively (631–4), and the chorus's ostensible interest in crimes by women gives no encouragement to see any reference to a crime by men. The Lemnian crime was proverbial for horror, rather

[97] J. Gould, 'Law, custom, and myth: aspects of the social position of women in classical Athens', *JHS* 100 (1980), 38–59, at 55 = *Myth, Ritual, Memory, and Exchange* (Oxford, 2001), 148. Gould 55 n. 125 = 148 n. 125 points to the stress on conscious planning in all three stories (605–6, 620 [reading Porson's προβούλως], 626).

than for reciprocal violence, and the second crime is in any case not retribution for the first.[98] It is however a compelling parallel for the murder of a husband by his wife, and no further significance need be sought for it here. Lebeck's 'mirror-image' theme remains illuminating for the Althaea and Scylla examples, and she has much else of interest to say about the function and structure of the ode.

Lebeck also addresses the question of the order of the stanzas. The stanza which refers to Clytemnestra's deed (623–30), which one might expect to follow the three mythical examples, appears in the transmitted text between the second and the third. It has thus been proposed that it should be switched with the stanza dealing with the Lemnian crime (631–8), so that the actual crime of Clytemnestra comes as a climax after the three stories which illustrate it. Lebeck defends the traditional order, arguing that the chorus is about to apply the stories of Althaea and Scylla to Clytemnestra when it remembers Orestes' injunction to speak 'the right word' (624; cf. 581–2), i.e. not to be too explicit, and turns back to another illustration from myth. The Lemnian story is the climax, the 'crowning example of wrong which engenders wrong' (p. 321). The need for the transposition has been reaffirmed by T. C. W. Stinton, arguing that the overt rhetorical structure of the ode requires Clytemnestra's deed to be the climax, even if Lebeck is right (which Stinton questions) about the secondary significance of the Lemnian story.[99]

Angus Bowie's discussion of the *Oresteia* (Ch. 12) employs a method of analysis similar to that of his book on Aristophanes which appeared in the same year, that of structural anthropology.[100] 'This method assumes that one can analyse a culture by looking for certain patterns of thought which are used to construct, order and

[98] See T. C. W. Stinton, 'The scope and limits of allusion in Greek tragedy', in M. J. Cropp et al. (eds.), *Greek Tragedy and its Legacy* (Calgary, 1986), 67–102, at 70 = *Collected Papers on Greek Tragedy* (Oxford, 1990), 454–492, at 459. Stinton discusses Lebeck's argument in more detail in 'The first stasimon of Aeschylus' *Choephori*', *CQ* 29 (1979), 252–62 = *Collected Papers* 384–96. Cf. D. J. Conacher, *Aeschylus' Oresteia: A Literary Commentary* (Toronto, 1987), 117–18.

[99] Stinton (n. 98), 'First stasimon', 254–7 = 386–90, endorsed by Conacher (n. 98), 116–18. Garvie (n. 73), pp. 202–3 is more doubtful. Stinton's conjecture ἄκαιρ᾽ οὐδ᾽ in 624 ('not untimely either', sc. to mention Clytemnestra) is adopted by West (rejecting, however, the transposition of stanzas).

[100] *Aristophanes: Myth, Ritual and Comedy* (Cambridge, 1993).

talk about the world, and which will appear in a variety of cultural contexts, such as myths, festivals, literature, painting, sculpture and so on' (p. 5). The word 'pattern' is crucial here, since the focus is on underlying rules and structures rather than on individual cultural phenomena studied in isolation. Bowie illustrates his method at the beginning of his book with a brief discussion of how Beethoven's opera *Fidelio* can be related to the story of the death and resurrection of Christ (pp. 1–3). The point is not that the two stories are exactly parallel, but that this Christian 'code' offers a 'filter' (not necessarily the only possible one) through which the opera can be viewed. In his Aristophanes book, Bowie thus examines the plays in terms of myths and rituals which seem particularly relevant to them, for example the festival of the Thesmophoria to *Thesmophoriazusae* or the myth of the Lemnian Women to *Lysistrata*. He recognizes two potential problems with this approach.[101] In the first place, it is often difficult to find evidence for myths and rituals which is contemporary with the plays under discussion. His response to this is that the strong element of conservatism in religious matters mean that evidence for old traditions can be preserved in much later sources. Secondly, there is the question of what counts as a myth in terms of having the power and familiarity—as with the story of Christ for the first audience of *Fidelio*—to impress its relevance on an audience even when the link was not signalled explicitly. This is clearly what Bowie hopes to demonstrate, but he believes that a parallel myth can still be useful for interpreting a play even when it cannot be proved that it was strongly present in the minds of the spectators.

Bowie insists that his Aristophanes book 'is concerned with audience reception rather than authorial intention' (p. 9), and argues that it is futile to attempt to detect Aristophanes' own views in the plays. 'Aristophanic comedy... does not so much lecture or preach at its audience, as offer it ways of looking at itself' (p. 14). He thus begins the article reprinted in the present volume by surveying the remarkably varied political views which have been attributed to Aeschylus over the years, and remarking that the supposed opinions of the playwright regularly seem to reflect the ideological biases of the scholar. The lesson of this is that the political purpose of the *Oresteia*

---

[101] Cf. the review of Bowie's book by A. H. Sommerstein, *JHS* 114 (1994), 188–9.

was not to promote a particular position but rather to offer the
Orestes myth to the audience as a model for thinking about Ephialtes'
reforms. The pattern is of a group being deprived of some of its
previous power (the mythical Erinyes, and the Areopagus in 462/1)
but still retaining a role in the new dispensation.

The Orestes myth can itself be illuminated by a variety of other
myths. The first of these illustrates both the strengths of Bowie's
approach and the kind of objections to which it is open. He plausibly
relates the advance in human civilization which culminates in the
Eumenides to advances on the divine level both of Zeus over his
predecessors and in Zeus's own behaviour. The problem is that there
is no explicit reference to any continuing role for Cronus in the new
order, and Bowie needs to appeal to other evidence for a cult of
Cronus in Athens which is not actually mentioned in the play. The
argument, suggestive as it is, may thus seem somewhat tenuous
in itself, but is reinforced by the similar pattern which Bowie
detects in stories involving Delphi, the Amazons, and Athena. He
thus uncovers something of the deep structure of Aeschylus' thought,
which underlies a number of different myths and is relevant to the
contemporary political situation. The actual political message of all
this is perhaps surprisingly clear-cut, corresponding fairly closely to
that which Bowie quotes from Christian Meier (p. 325).

Bowie's discussion of Athenian rituals relevant to the *Oresteia*
begins with the cult of Artemis at Brauron (founded by Iphigenia)
and the related but distinct cult of Artemis Tauropolos at Halai
Araphenides two miles away (founded by Orestes).[102] He observes
that both cults have plausibly been associated with rites of passage,
and that this pattern is also present in the *Oresteia*. His basic point is
that these rituals represent a less violent form of appeasement of the
goddess than human sacrifice as described in *Agamemnon*, just as
the trial in *Eumenides* is a more civilized method of dealing with
Orestes' crime than the savage punishments initially threatened by
the Erinyes (e.g. *Eum.* 264–8). In both cases, Athens finds a

---

[102] Cf. Peradotto (this volume, pp. 219–23). More recently, M. J. Cropp (ed.),
Euripides: Iphigenia in Tauris (Warminster, 2000), 50–6; A. Tzanetou, 'Almost dying,
dying twice: ritual and audience in Euripides' *Iphigenia in Tauris*', in M. J. Cropp et al.
(eds.), *Euripides and Tragic Theatre in the Late Fifth Century* (*ICS* 24–5; Champaign,
2000), 199–216.

constructive way to reconcile competing claims. Bowie proceeds to discuss the festival of the Anthesteria, a festival which marks the ingenious response of the Athenians to the problem of giving hospitality to the polluted Orestes.[103] The only direct link between the festival and the *Oresteia* is an obscure word in a corrupt passage of *Agamemnon*, but Bowie can nevertheless make use of the Anthesteria as a filter through which to view the trilogy. More firmly based is his development of earlier work on allusions to the mystery cults, and his relation of this to the question of the distinction between ritual and legal absolution.[104] He concludes by examining the ways in which the final procession in *Eumenides* evokes the Panathenaeic procession.[105]

PROMETHEUS

Martin West describes the purpose of his article (Ch. 13) as being 'to reconsider the old but still unresolved problems of the staging of the extant *Prometheus,* to contribute to the reconstruction of the trilogy, and to advance arguments for dating it to the year 440 or shortly after' (p. 360).

West reaffirms the traditional view that *Prometheus Lyomenos* ('Prometheus Unbound') followed the *Desmotes* ('Prometheus Bound') as part of a connected trilogy, and regards it as virtually certain that *Prometheus Pyrphoros* ('Prometheus the Fire-Bringer') was the other play in the trilogy.[106] He is confident that the *Pyrphoros* was the first play of the trilogy not the third, and his main argument for this view is the difficulty of imagining what a third play could have contained.[107]

---

[103] Cf. Bowie (n. 100), 35–9, 146–50 for the relationship of the Anthesteria to Aristophanes' *Acharnians* and *Peace.*

[104] Cf. R. Seaford, 'Dionysiac drama and the Dionysiac mysteries', *CQ* 31 (1981), 252–75; id., 'Sophokles and the mysteries', *Hermes* 122 (1994), 275–88; Bowie (n. 100), 228–53 (on Aristophanes' *Frogs*).

[105] See also B. H. Weaver, 'A further allusion in the *Eumenides* to the Panathenaia', *CQ* 46 (1996), 559–61.

[106] West's second claim is more controversial; see Gantz, this volume, pp. 49–51 for other possibilities. The present discussion follows West and Gantz in referring to the plays by their Greek titles (cf. Winnington-Ingram (n. 11), 175 n. 1, 191 n. 44).

[107] Cf. M. Griffith (ed.), *Aeschylus: Prometheus Bound* (Cambridge, 1983), 283.

A possible objection is that it is impossible to estimate how much mythological material Aeschylus needed to construct a tragedy, or indeed how much potentially relevant mythological material was available to him.[108] Another possibility is that the third play, if there was one, was not about Prometheus at all.[109] West rejects the argument that *Desmotes* contains too much background information (e.g. 199–241) to be anything other than the first play of the trilogy, an argument which was once regarded as conclusive. Winnington-Ingram believes that the real objection is rather that 'the whole technique of exposition . . . is appropriate only to the first play of a trilogy, being spacious, gradual and cumulative, like the expositions of *Supplices* and *Agamemnon*, assuming that the audience knows nothing'.[110]

West accepts Pohlenz' answer to another objection to *Pyrphoros* being the third play, the fact that the scholion on *Desmotes* 94 (= fr. 208a) seems to imply that it deals with a period after or at the end of Prometheus' punishment: 'for in the *Pyrphoros* he says that he was (has been) bound for three myriad (years)'. West rightly observes that the tense of the infinitive ('was bound') is relative to Aeschylus rather than to the dramatic time of the *Pyrphoros*, so that the original could have been in the future tense ('you will be bound for 30,000 years'). He then goes further, and argues that the period of Prometheus' bondage could not have been given after the event as 30,000 years because he was actually released in the thirteenth human generation (*Desmotes* 774). This argument is not so strong, however, because it raises the question why the *Pyrphoros* contained a prophecy or threat which turned out to be incorrect, and ignores the tradition (reflected in *Desmotes* 94) that Prometheus actually was

[108] e.g. Gantz (this volume), p. 50.

[109] e.g. E. R. Dodds, 'The *Prometheus Vinctus* and the progress of scholarship', in *The Ancient Concept of Progress* (Oxford, 1973), 26–44, at 39–40 (Aeschylus died before completing the trilogy); A. L. Brown, 'Prometheus Pyrphoros', *BICS* 37 (1990), 50–6. Winnington-Ingram (n. 11), 194 aptly remarks that 'subsequent to *Desmotes*, there seems too much action to be accommodated in one play, too little for two'.

[110] Winnington-Ingram (n. 11), 188 (but on *Suppliants*, see Rösler (this volume), p. 181). Winnington-Ingram (n. 11), 188 n. 39 refutes West's argument that the naming of Prometheus at 66 is 'not as early as we might expect if he had not been seen before' (p. 363) by observing that Clytemnestra is only named on the third reference (*Ag.* 10–11, 26, 83–4), and commenting that the gradual revelation of the identity of the leading character is appropriate precisely to the beginning of the trilogy. See further Brown (n. 109), 52.

bound for millennia.[111] Griffith ingeniously suggests that the *Desmotes* itself may be imagined to represent the passage of millennia, with lapses of time before (e.g.) 88 or 436,[112] but the contradiction may be due rather to combining a human timescale with a punishment appropriate to the vast scale of this divine conflict.

The *Pyrphoros* is listed in the catalogue of Aeschylus' plays, but the only other evidence for its existence is a single line quoted by Aulus Gellius which is suspiciously similar to *Cho.* 582 and the scholion on *Desmotes* 94 discussed above. One view is that the play is identical with the satyric Prometheus play of 472 BC (the *Pyrkaeus*), and thus nothing to do with *Desmotes* and *Lyomenos*.[113] On the assumptions that the play existed at all, and that it was the first play of the trilogy, West offers a plausible if necessarily speculative reconstruction. He argues that it is reflected in the Prometheus scene in Aristophanes' *Birds* (1494–1552), and that it probably followed Hesiod in various details. He puts some flesh on the bones by suggesting locations in the play for some fragments whose sources do not attribute them to a specific play.

There is considerably more evidence for the reconstruction of the *Lyomenos*. It has usually been thought that Prometheus' mother Ge (Earth) made an appearance, either before or after the Heracles scene. She may have played a part similar to that of Oceanus in the *Desmotes*, advising Prometheus to be less stubborn, or even played an active role as an intermediary in the reconciliation with Zeus (cf. *Desmotes* 210–13). There is however no direct evidence for her participation, and West offers an innovative argument in support of his theory that she did not in fact appear.[114] Heracles certainly did appear, and West argues strongly for the view that he released Prometheus from his bonds as well as shooting the eagle. Prometheus thus did not, as many scholars believe,[115] divulge his secret as a condition of being released. West believes (on the evidence of the scholion on *Desmotes* 167) that Thetis appeared at the end of the play, and that the scene corresponded to the

[111] See D. J. Conacher, *Aeschylus' Prometheus Bound: A Literary Commentary* (Toronto, 1980), 101 n. 3.
[112] Griffith (n. 107), 284.
[113] e.g. Brown (n. 109), 52–5; Sommerstein (n. 5), 320–1.
[114] West's suggestion is entertained by Griffith (n. 107), 286, and described as 'ingenious and quite plausible' by Winnington-Ingram (n. 11), 186 n. 30.
[115] e.g. Conacher (n. 111), 112; Griffith (n. 107), 301.

Io scene in *Desmotes*.[116] West supplements his reconstruction of the *Lyomenos* with an argument that its account of Heracles' travels derived from Pherecydes of Athens.

West's discussion of the *Desmotes* itself focuses on problems of staging, which had been foregrounded two years before the first appearance of his article by Oliver Taplin in *The Stagecraft of Aeschylus* (Oxford, 1977). In particular, he bases his view of the staging of the play on the theory of N. G. L. Hammond that Aeschylus regularly made use of an outcrop of rock, about 5 metres by 5, which would have partly protruded into the *orchēstra* near the *eisodos* on the audience's left.[117] Hammond's main argument is that there are a number of references to rocks and mounds in Aeschylus, including the crag to which Prometheus is bound, and that the rock (*pagos*) would have been useful for representing them. Critics have queried whether the focus of the action could have been so consistently at the periphery of the acting space.[118] The traditional view remains that the outcrop was levelled when the theatre was first established, and that it would never have been allowed to obstruct the *orchēstra*.[119]

The aerial entry of the chorus of Oceanids presents the most perplexing question of staging in extant Greek tragedy. West's entertaining discussion makes abundantly clear just how insoluble the problems are, and how inadequate the solutions which have been offered by scholars. The fact that his own answer is both logical and bizarre offers further support to his low opinion of the playwright's competence. West's arguments have, however, done little to shake the widely accepted view that the Chorus enter in some sort of vehicle(s) on the *skēnē* roof, descend behind the *skēnē* during the Oceanus scene (284–396), and enter the orchestra at 397.[120] The second major problem of staging

---

[116] Winnington-Ingram (n. 11), 187 n. 34 observes that there would then be two scenes in the *Lyomenos* corresponding to the Io scene in *Desmotes*, since that scene has already been 'mirrored' by the Heracles scene.

[117] N. G. L. Hammond, 'The conditions of dramatic production to the death of Aeschylus', *GRBS* 13 (1972), 387–450; id., 'More on conditions of production to the death of Aeschylus', *GRBS* 29 (1988), 5–33.

[118] e.g. Garvie (n. 73), pp. xliii–xliv; J. Davidson, '*Prometheus Vinctus* on the Athenian stage', *G&R* 41 (1994), 33–40, at 33 (arguing that Prometheus' rock was located in the *orchēstra*).

[119] e.g. Griffith (n. 107), 30 n. 93; Conacher (n. 111), 181 n. 12.

[120] e.g. Conacher (n. 111), 183 n. 17; Griffith (n. 107), on 128–92. D. J. Mastronarde, 'Actors on high: the skene roof, the crane, and the gods in Attic drama', *Cl. Ant.* 9

which West discusses is the final cataclysm. Taplin argues that it was all left to the audience's imagination, and that Prometheus and the Chorus then simply walked off (a 'cancelled' exit).[121] West objects to this, and offers some suggestions about how the scene could have been staged.[122] His view that Prometheus was bound to the *pagos* seems to make a realistic staging of his disappearance more difficult than it would be if he had been positioned in front of the *skēnē*, into which he could then have been withdrawn at the end.

West concludes with some observations about the date of the trilogy. He accepts Mark Griffith's arguments that the play is not by Aeschylus, and that it belongs on stylistic grounds to the 440s or 430s. He supports this with a survey of the play's intellectual and stylistic affinities, and a suggestion about the occasion which prompted the composition of the trilogy.[123] Griffith admires the play, for all his doubts that it was written by Aeschylus. West is less impressed, arguing in a later article that, 'Its author writes iambics well, and he has considerable powers of imagination and description. But his construction of scenes and of the play as a whole is inept…He is a gifted but brainless poet working with the literary techniques, stage resources, and sophistic outlook of the 440s or 430s.'[124] West offers arguments in that article in support of the view of D. S. Robertson and E. R. Dodds that the author was Aeschylus' son Euphorion.[125]

(1990), 247–94, at 267 denies that cranes would have been feasible, and makes the interesting suggestion that the Chorus entered on the roof of the skene in 'car-suits', i.e. 'lightweight frames worn around the body of the walking choreuts'. This would answer some of West's objections. Hammond, 'More on conditions' (n. 117), 10–11 reaffirms, against West, that the Chorus entered at ground level.

[121] Taplin (n. 6), 273–5; cf. Griffith (n. 107), on 1080; Conacher (n. 111), 188–9; Sommerstein (n. 5), 312–13. Taplin does not rule out an attempt at realistic staging, but emphatically denies that such a spectacle could have been the work of Aeschylus.

[122] Cf. Hammond, 'More on conditions' (n. 117), 33 n. 90.

[123] Less convincing is West's argument (p. 375) that the *Desmotes* implies a 'transitional' theatre of *c*.445–*c*.435 (see Conacher (n. 111), 183 n. 17).

[124] 'The authorship of the Prometheus trilogy', in *Studies in Aeschylus* (Stuttgart, 1990), 51–72, at 53. For a defence of the play against West's criticisms in that article, see H. Lloyd-Jones, 'Zeus, Prometheus, and Greek ethics', *HSCP* 101 (2003), 49–72. A subtle and challenging argument for a juster and more 'Aeschylean' Zeus in the *Desmotes* is advanced by S. White, 'Io's world: intimations of theodicy in *Prometheus Bound*', *JHS* 121 (2001), 107–40.

[125] Dodds (n. 109), 37–9.

1

The Aischylean Tetralogy:
Attested and Conjectured Groups

Timothy Gantz

For better or worse, it seems generally conceded that the three extant plays presented by Aischylos in 458 BC, the *Agamemnon*, *Choephoroi*, and *Eumenides*, form a narratively connected unit with a continuous plot, called by Apollonios of Rhodes and Aristarchos a trilogy, and termed by the *didaskaliai*, with the satyric *Proteus* added, a tetralogy.[1]

[*Editor's note.* Timothy Gantz, in agreeing to the reprinting of this article, wrote: 'I think it still stands up well', but asked for the correction of a trivial slip on the first page and for the insertion of the fragment numbers from Radt's *TrGF*. Any further changes which he may have contemplated were pre-empted by his sadly premature death on 20 January 2004.]

[1] The present paper is a sequel to one entitled 'The Aischylean tetralogy: prolegomena', in *CJ* 74 (1979), 289–304 (hereafter abbreviated as 'AT:P'). In that previous discussion I attempted to review attitudes on such topics as the number of plays in a *didaskalia*, the ancient definition of the word τετραλογία ['tetralogy'], the *Souda's* note on Sophokles and tetralogy production, the possibility of dilogies, and the interconnection of the satyr play. Here I will say simply that 'tetralogy' is used as antiquity seems to have used it, of four plays connected in plot (though the relationship of the satyr play is less direct). As before, I wish to thank Professor William M. Calder III of the University of Colorado for his kindness in reading an earlier draft of the work and for his very informed comments; if I have not profited by all of them, I must remain responsible. The following frequently cited works are referred to hereafter by author only: F. G. Welcker, *Die Aeschyleische Trilogie Prometheus* (Darmstadt, 1824); N. Wecklein, *Fragmenta Aeschyli* (in vol. 2 of *Aischylou Dramata Sozomena* (Athens, 1896)); H. J. Mette, *Der verlorene Aischylos* (Berlin, 1963); L. Ferrari, *I drammi perduti di Eschilo* (Palermo, 1968). I have made less use of the editions of Droysen (*Des Aischylos Werke*, ii (Berlin, 1832)) and E. A. I. Ahrens (*Aeschyli et Sophoclis Tragoediae et Fragmenta* (Paris, 1842), 177–268) because they largely follow the arrangements and reconstructions set down by Welcker.

Were the evidence for such a form limited to this one instance, it might well be regarded as merely an aberration of the poet's last years. But the matter is of course more involved than that. Hermann's perusal of the scholia to *Thesmophoriazousai* established the existence of a τετραλογία ['tetralogy'] called *Lykourgeia* (so the scholiast), while Franz in 1848 revealed a hypothesis for the *Septem* which assigned to it as coproductions the *Laios, Oidipous, and Sphinx.*[2] More recently the publication of P. Oxy. 2256 fr. 3 [T 70 Radt] has formally linked the *Danaides* and *Amymone*: that *Hiketides* and *Aigyptioi* were part of the same sequence cannot be proved, but the assumption of such a four-play group has raised very little objection.[3] Then there are the Prometheus titles; where authorship itself is still debated it may seem hazardous to apply a conjectural pattern, yet the *Desmotes* and *Lyomenos* surely reflect an attempt to create connection by someone.[4] The result, in any case, is almost certainly four productions in which Aischylos linked the plots of the separate plays to form an overall story. Against this figure we have on the other side evidence for one production in which the plots were surely *not* linked (that of 472 BC).[5]

Given such a ratio in a very limited number of groups (five out of perhaps twenty-two),[6] the question then becomes whether Aischylos might not also have used this method frequently in the productions about which we are less well informed. Welcker, who in 1824 made the first general study of the possibilities, took matters rather to extremes with a list of nineteen such groups involving at times wholly fabricated titles. But the game had been started, and many of the

[2] Cf. below nn. 28 and 16.

[3] Cf. O. Taplin, *The Stagecraft of Aeschylus* (Oxford, 1977) 194–8, where the evidence is subjected to a close and critical scrutiny.

[4] On the whole question of the presumed trilogy and its relationship to a possibly un-Aischylean *Desmotes* cf. most recently M. Griffith, *The Authenticity of Prometheus Bound* (Cambridge, 1977), 13–16, 245–52. Griffith considers a number of possibilities, but he concedes I think that a connected group by someone is likely, or else a deliberate attempt to attach the *Desmotes* to a genuine *Lyomenos*: stronger arguments on the same point are offered by C. J. Herington in his review of Griffith, *AJP* 100 (1979), 424–5.

[5] Against efforts to create some such linkage cf. H. D. Broadhead, *The Persae of Aeschylus* (Cambridge, 1960), pp. iv–ix, and K. Deichgräber, *Die Persertetralogie des Aischylos* (Mainz, 1974), 7–9.

[6] Cf. M. Untersteiner, *Misc. Phil. in mem. A. Beltrami* (Genoa, 1953), 239–45.

suggestions found substantial agreement among scholars to whom, for example, the presence of three plays on the events surrounding Patroklos' death seemed more than coincidence. Further work elim- inated the clearly dubious conjectures and refined some of the more acceptable ones to produce a core of groups considered likely;[7] the latest serious assessment, in fact, that of H. J. Mette, editor of Aischylos' fragments, has pushed the total back up to perhaps eight- een, and offered in many cases detailed reconstructions.[8] Yet the negative scholarly response to some of his conclusions suggests that this is still too sanguine a view.[9] What I hope to do in the following survey is to approach the problem from a more critical bias. I must confess at the beginning that my sense of the matter is much the same as Mette's; on the basis of four connected groups and the common themes of many remaining titles, it seems likely to me that Aischylos did resort to the form in question a good deal of the time. Such a feeling, however, is not tantamount to proof, nor does it justify forcing all the known titles into proper tetralogies. I have tried in what follows to review each attested or conjectured group, to sum- marize what we know for certain of missing plays, and to note at least briefly the more cogent suggestions which have been made; what emerges is hopefully a kind of road map to the possible shapes and probabilities. None of this is likely to convince confirmed skeptics,

[7] Especially important in this process were the efforts of Wecklein (cf. as well as his edition of the fragments the earlier conclusions of the article in *SB München* 1891, 368–85), W. Schmid (*Geschichte der Griechischen Literatur* 1:2, 188–9), and H. W. Smyth (*Aeschylus*, ii (Loeb Library: London, 1926), 377–9).

[8] Mette's actual list (without, however, much in the way of justification) was published as a *Nachwort* to his *Die Fragmente der Tragödien des Aischylos* (Berlin, 1959: 256–60); the sequel volume (above n. 1) then proceeded to describe most of these groups as if they were accepted fact. Nevertheless the results are usually within generally conjectured bounds. The same cannot be said for the still more recent work of Ferrari (also n. 1), who starts from the most dubious of premises, namely that all Aischylos' plays *must* have belonged to groups. As a result we are given twenty-two full 'tetralogies', including among them plays with such hitherto unsuspected titles as *Neleus**, *Bellerophon**, *Mastigosis**, and *Euochias Hetairoi**. Nor is his arrangement of plays much more encouraging: *Bakchai* finds a place with the presumed Perseus group, and *Heliades* with that on Prometheus. On occasion the author has a sugges- tion of real value, but such unrestrained speculation in one's overall approach can only do harm to the study of these matters.

[9] Cf. for example Kamerbeek (*Mnemosyne* 13 (1960), 349); Lloyd-Jones (*CR* 14 (1964), 244–7); Matthiessen (*Gnomon* 38 (1966), 133–4).

but it may put our grasp of the uncertainties on a sounder footing. I have also tried to keep personal hypotheses to a minimum; where these do intrude (as for example in the case of the *Semele* plays), I trust they will be received as nothing more than opinion.[10] As a kind of organizational aid, the groups are presented in three categories: attested, more probable, and less probable. But the reader is reminded again that in the latter two almost everything is guesswork; how much may be justified it is the purpose of this paper to let him decide for himself. In any case the *Persai* production of 472 BC is not included, since there is no reason to suppose anything but the vaguest thematic connection between its plays.[11] Fragments are cited according to Radt's numbering; [s] after a title indicates that it is definitely or very probably satyric.

I. ATTESTED GROUPS

(1) *Agamemnon–Choephoroi–Eumenides–Proteus*[s]. Our only preserved (albeit partially) tetralogy, presented in 458 BC and fully confirmed as a group by the hypothesis and the scholion to Aristophanes' *Batrachoi* [= *Frogs*] 1124. The overall title *Oresteia,* to judge from its appearance in Aristophanes, goes back at least to the second half of the fifth century. Hermann objected that such a title should refer only to the second and third plays, those being the ones

---

[10] Theories on the pattern and arrangement of such groups go all the way back to Hermann, who suggested (G. Hermann, *Opuscula* (8 vols.; Leipzig, 1827–77), ii. 313–18) that a proper trilogy should have a severe play first, then a lyric one, and finally a drama full of novelties. Welcker objected (n. 1), 489–91, but only to replace Hermann's theory with his own, wherein action peaked in the middle play of the series and the last was left to religious and philosophical considerations. In this century the primary contribution to a theory of reconstruction has been that of T. Zieliński, who in his *Tragodoumenon Libri Tres* (Cracow, 1925) developed the concept of rudimentary vestiges in preserved plays which represent elements carried over from lost versions of the same stories (cf. also F. Stoessl, *Die Trilogie des Aischylos* (Baden bei Wien, 1937)). Such an approach would suggest that the playwrights were often barely in control of their material. More promising is C. J. Herington's hypothesis (*Arion* 4 (1965), 387–403) of a thesis–antithesis–resolution pattern, but of course there is no reason to suppose that Aischylos always worked from a set plan.

[11] On efforts to argue the importance of such thematic links cf. 'AT:P' 293.

in which Orestes actually appears, but this is to press a matter of
convenience rather closely.[12] Despite the time lapse between the three
tragedies, the connecting plot line seems clear enough; Wiesmann's
attempt to prove otherwise for the sake of his own theories on the
tetralogy has found no support.[13] As for the lost satyr play, there is no
reason to doubt that it concerned Menelaos' adventures in Egypt as
recounted in *Odyssey* 4.351–75. Early conjectures made the title
figure a king of Egypt who detained Dionysos,[14] but the scholion to
Od. 4.366 (mentioning Proteus' daughter Eidothea as a character in
this very play) should be decisive. The possibilities for burlesque in
Menelaos' efforts to extract information from Proteus are obvious,
but we should also remember that the latter's prophetic powers could
give Aischylos considerable latitude in reassessing the material of the
preceding tragedies.[15]

(2) *Laios–Oidipous–Hepta* (*Septem*)–*Sphinx*[s]. Franz's discovery in
1848 of a hypothesis for this set corrected Welcker's earlier arrangement (which omitted the *Septem*) and created a pattern of crime and
punishment through succeeding generations which still remains
popular in Aischylean interpretations.[16] In fact the tetralogy has
serious problems of reconstruction; given only the final tragedy of
the group, we know the answers to the situations Aischylos was
probing, but not the questions. The matter is further complicated
by scholars' frequent insistence on involving the later productions
of Sophokles and Euripides.[17] The first play, *Laios*, features Laios

[12] *Opusc.* ii. 309. It is to be sure possible that Aristophanes' reference is only to the
Choephoroi (so Schmid, *GGL* 1:2, 222 n. 1); but cf. R. Cantarella, *I nuovi frammenti
Eschilei di Ossirinco* (Naples, 1948), 145.

[13] P. Wiesmann, *Das Problem der tragischen Tetralogie* (Zurich, 1929), 9–25.

[14] Cf. Welcker (n. 1), 507–8.

[15] Cf. L. Levi, *RSA* 1908, 234–7. On the so-called Levi's Law which forms such a
central part of Ferrari's arrangements I have already commented, 'AT:P' 300.

[16] J. Franz, *Die Didaskalie zu Aeschylos Septem contra Thebas* (Berlin, 1848).
Welcker (n. 1), 354–9 desired rather a separate trilogy for each of the three epics
Oidipodeia, *Thebais*, and *Epigonoi*; thus he supported a *Laios-Sphinx-Oidipous*
sequence. Hermann (*Opusc.* ii. 314–15) guessed the truth but then recanted (*Opusc.*
vii. 190–3) in favor of Welcker's view. Oddly enough the correct arrangement was also
perceived (and ably defended) by A. F. Näke, whose paper however was not published
until long after Franz's discovery and his own death (*RhM* 27 (1872), 193–214).

[17] Against this approach cf. the remarks of H. D. Cameron, *Studies on the Seven
Against Thebes of Aeschylus* (The Hague, 1971), 12–13, and his own reconstruction,

himself in the prologue, but beyond that we cannot say certainly whether the action revolved around Laios' disobeyal of Apollo at the conception and birth of Oidipous, or his own death at Oidipous' hands some years later.[18] In the former case the stress would be on the folly of Laios' actions (with perhaps, though I doubt it, some involvement by Pelops and Chrysippos);[19] in the latter (which seems more likely) Laios would relate the oracle and his own response to it, a discussion with Iokasta might follow, he would then set out on his journey (not, however, to Delphi), and a messenger would return with the news of his death (in which case fr. 387a would probably occur here).[20] The *Oidipous* is even less clear.[21] The assumption that the play kept to the lines later followed by Sophokles may seem obvious,[22] but we would then lose the events of his old age, including his neglect by

17–29. The sources are also well screened by H. C. Baldry, 'The dramatization of the Theban legend', *G&R* 25 (1956), 24–37, at 24–9, and W. G. Thalmann, *Dramatic Art in Aeschylus's Seven Against Thebes* (New Haven, 1978), 8–26.

[18] Cf. Mette, 34–5, and A. J. Podlecki, *BICS* 22 (1975), 8–14.

[19] The sources for the story of Laios' abduction of Chrysippos are all late: cf. Apollod. *Bibl.* 3.5.5; Ael. *NA* 6.15; Athen. 13. 602–3; Hyg. *Fab.* 85. Webster (*The Tragedies of Euripides* (London, 1967), 111–13) summarizes what is known of Euripides' *Chrysippos*. The view that this transgression on the part of Laios was included in Aischylos' play has been supported recently by H. Lloyd-Jones, *The Justice of Zeus* (Berkeley, 1971), 120–1; Podlecki (n. 18), 14 reiterates the arguments against it. Lloyd-Jones properly notes that the emphasis in such a reconstruction might well rest on the violation of hospitality in Laios' actions, rather than on the supposedly un-Aischylean sexual aspects. Nevertheless 1 wonder if the play in question really has room for such matters; what the choral odes of the *Septem* stress is rather Laios' disobedience in begetting a child. Cf. also however Thalmann (n. 17), 15–17.

[20] The fragment (which seems to indicate a journey south from Thebes) could of course occur as well in the *Oidipous,* though the plural verb makes it somewhat less likely. Also perhaps from the *Laios* would be fr. 122a, in which a spitting-out of blood for apotropaic purposes is involved: cf. Thalmann (n. 17), 24.

[21] The literature on this play is far too vast for any complete summary here. In what follows I draw heavily on the arguments of E. Bruhn's 1910 edition of the *Tyrannos,* as well as those of C. Robert in his *Oidipus* (Berlin, 1915), 252–83, and O. Klotz, *RhM* 72 (1917–18), 616–25. Robert faces the problems squarely and fully, but like Klotz I see no need for Oidipous to die in the play; the curse is the essential element in this reconstruction. Cf. also the remarks of R. P. Winnington-Ingram in *YCS* 25 (1977), 1–45 [≈ *Studies in Aeschylus* (Cambridge, 1983), 16–54], where despite a generally agnostic position there is some leaning toward the above views.

[22] So Hermann, *Opusc.* vii. 194, Nauck in his edition of the fragments (2nd edn.; Leipzig, 1889) 55, and A. Lesky, *Die tragische Dichtung der Hellenen* (3rd edn.; Göttingen, 1972), 89, to name only a few. Mette, 35, also suggests that fr. 345 could refer to a Sophoklean-type plague at the start of the play.

his sons and presumably his curse upon them.[23] On the other hand, if the play is set at this latter time, the earlier events—Oidipous' discovery of his murder/marriage and his self-blinding—must be relegated to choral odes and speeches of reminiscence. I confess this second arrangement seems to me more Aischylean, and it would also provide background to what remain very puzzling elements in the *Septem*,[24] but that is simply a preference. Such a play (to speculate for a moment) would begin long after the discovery had been made, and concern Oidipous' ill-treatment by his sons, either through the use of Laios' cups, or the serving of a wrong cut of meat, or some other cause.[25] The curse would then follow, and probably at the end some contract between Polyneikes and Eteokles in the hope of avoiding its consequences.[26] With regard to the satyric *Sphinx* the plot is clear,

---

[23] Hermann and others have admittedly argued for an immediate curse by Oidipous against his sons, after blinding himself, simply because they are the products of an incestuous union. I suppose ἐπίκοτος τροφᾶς at *Septem* 786 could mean this, but I do not quite see why Oidipous should curse his children so violently for his own mistake, and only his sons at that. Then too, Eteokles must be old enough to understand the curse. For these reasons it seems to me more natural to refer τροφᾶς, with the scholiast, to the events of Oidipous' old age as recounted in the epic *Thebais* (so Cameron (n. 17), 91–2, who argues from a somewhat different reading). It must, however, be admitted that the text of the *Septem* is very uncertain here, and could be restored in a variety of ways: cf. G. R. Manton, 'The second stasimon of the *Seven against Thebes*', *BICS* 8 (1961), 77–84, for further arguments in support of Hermann. Thalmann (n. 17), 25–6, rather prefers the latter position, and suggests as well that the curse might have surfaced gradually in each of the three plays, demonstrating its strength through repeated *peripeteia*. Such an arrangement would surely weaken the logic of the narrative connection between the plays in order to achieve this thematic unity, but it is attractive nonetheless.

[24] For an ingenious handling of these problems cf. A. P. Burnett, 'Curse and dream in Aeschylus' *Septem*', *GRBS* 14 (1973), 343–68. Mrs. Burnett proposes a cunning division of information between curse and the dream of *Septem* 710–11, so that the one seems to negate the other, and Eteokles fails to grasp their mutual direction until Polyneikes is allotted the seventh gate. The same view might also answer Podlecki (n. 18), 12, who feels that the riddle of the curse is too new to have been a part of the previous play.

[25] For the epic version of both these actions cf. *Thebais* frs. II & III Allen (pp. 113–14). One might also note Ades. fr. 458, a fragment which, though unlikely to be Aischylean, could well draw from an Aischylean original. Apollod. 3.5.9 offers a third possibility, namely that Oidipous' sons failed to help him when he was driven from Thebes.

[26] On the possible form of this contract cf. Hellanikos (*FGrH* 4F98), who tells us that Polyneikes chose to take the chiton and necklace of Harmonia and withdraw permanently from the city. Again, the crucial point of the action would be Eteokles' assumption that through such a bargain the curse of his father had been voided.

though we may find ourselves surprised to see a wretched and deceased figure from the tragic narrative brought back in a leading role.[27] Perhaps the Sphinx's riddles were meant to recall the riddling oracles of Apollo, and Oidipous' ambiguous curse.

(3) *Edonoi–Bassarides–Neaniskoi–Lykourgos*[s]. Here again Welcker made an ingenious try, linking as he did *Edonoi* and *Lykourgos,* but not until Hermann pointed out the notice in the scholia to Ar. *Thesm.* 134 (fr. 61) was the actual arrangement known.[28] The scholiast here not only employs the term τετραλογία ['tetralogy'], but adds the phrase *Lykourgeia,* thereby assuring a general adherence to the story of the Thracian king Lykourgos. We have an early version of this story in *Iliad* 6.130–40, where Lykourgos opposes the coming of Dionysos and is blinded by Zeus, but the scanty fragments of the plays themselves offer no guarantees that that account was strictly followed. For the *Edonoi* it is probably safe to say that the approach of Dionysos and his retinue is described to the king, who orders their capture; subsequently Dionysos is brought in, a confrontation with Lykourgos ensues, and then imprisonment in the palace. From fr. 58 we may further suppose some kind of epiphany of Dionysos, and the palace itself alive with carousal, but nothing more than this. Later accounts[29] include a madness in which Lykourgos kills his son Dryas and perhaps his mother, a cutting-off of his foot, an imprisonment by his own people, and a tearing-apart by horses on Mount Pangaion. How much of this Aischylos used in his plays is an open question; we do not even know if Lykourgos dies in the *Neaniskoi* (where the chorus members are presumably Edonian youths) or becomes reconciled with the god. There is, however, general agreement that the satyr play dealt with a contest between beer and wine, and if as seems likely Lykourgos is converted to the latter, we might

---

[27] For the play cf. Levi (n. 15), 237–9, and the bibliography cited in P. Guggisberg, *Das Satyrspiel* (Zurich, 1947), 97–8. Klotz (n. 21), 623–4, more than adequately refutes the notion of Robert and others that Oidipous himself did not appear.

[28] Welcker (n. 1), 320–7; Hermann, *Opusc.* v. 3–30. More recent attempts at a reconstruction include Wecklein, 593–7; L. Séchan, *Études sur la tragédie grecque* (Paris, 1926), 63–79; K. Deichgräber, *Nachr. Göttingen* 1938–9, 231–309; Mette, 136–41; Ferrari, 367–88.

[29] Primarily Apollod. 3.5.1, but cf. also D.S. 3.65.4–5 and Hyg. *Fab.* 132, 242.

more readily assume a reconciliation in the last tragedy.[30] Thus again the satyr play would offer a lighter view of the tragic material. One final point concerns a passage from Eratosthenes in which we read of Orpheus' destruction by the Bassarides after he climbed Mount Pangaion to honor the sun (Radt, p. 138). Mention of Aischylos in connection with the Bassarides here has led a number of scholars[31] to suppose that the second play revolved around Dionysos and Orpheus, rather than Lykourgos. Yet Eratosthenes does not strictly speaking vouch for more than the name Bassarides as Aischylean, and even should the whole story come from an Aischylean play, it need be no more than an exemplum or warning in a choral ode.[32]

(4) *Hiketides–Aigyptioi–Danaides–Amymone*[s]. The indications of the titles have long made this an obvious possibility, and near-total confirmation has been provided by P. Oxy. 2256 fr. 3 (T 70 Radt), where *Danaides* and *Amymone* are guaranteed as the last two plays. For the reconstruction of the whole A. F. Garvie's thorough survey of evidence and conjectures makes all but the briefest comment super-fluous.[33] Welcker and others did attempt to place the *Aigyptioi* first, but most scholars now agree that the demands of plot and staging are against that view. The majority opinion gives roughly the following: the Danaids arrive at Argos and successfully petition Pelasgos for sanctuary. The Egyptians demand their restitution. After some sort of battle (and possibly the death of Pelasgos) an agreement is reached whereby the Danaids accept the Egyptians, but on the wedding night all save Hypermestra slay their new husbands with daggers provided by Danaos. A crisis ensues, involving either the Danaids (for the murders) or Hypermestra (for disobedience) or both. In any case Aphrodite resolves the conflict with a speech supporting Hypermes-tra's action, and the other sisters are presumably reconciled to

[30] So Deichgräber (n. 28); Levi (n. 15), 239–40 prefers to put the action of the satyr play earlier.

[31] Hermann, *Opusc.* v. 19–20; Deichgräber (n. 28), 281–6; Mette, 138–40; Ferrari, 376–80.

[32] So Séchan (n. 28), 68–9; cf. also Wecklein, 595–6.

[33] A. F. Garvie, *Aeschylus' Supplices: Play and Trilogy* (Cambridge, 1969), 163–233; for a more opinionated (in the best sense) treatment, cf. R. P. Winnington-Ingram, 'The Danaid trilogy', *JHS* 81 (1961), 141–52 [≈ *Studies in Aeschylus* (Cambridge, 1983), 55–72].

marriage.[34] We should note here that the narrative of the tragedies is not only continuous but closely connected. Moreover, the preserved fragments of the satyr play, with their opposition of lust (the satyr) and wooing (Poseidon), offer almost unmistakeably a microcosm of the important themes in the preceding plays.[35]

II. MORE PROBABLE GROUPS

(5) *Prometheus Desmotes–Prometheus Lyomenos–Prometheus Pyrphoros– ——[s]*. For those who still believe that our preserved play is by Aischylos, this category would seem the appropriate place to discuss it; those who do not are welcome to pass over the following remarks.[36] Hermann's objections notwithstanding, the scholion to *Desmotes* 511 has long been accepted as evidence that the *Desmotes* and *Lyomenos* formed a connected group, in that order.[37] Yet Taplin has recently resurrected the argument against this conclusion, taking the words ἐν γὰρ τῷ ἑξῆς δράματι ['in the next play'] to refer to the next item in a book edition (*Lyomenos* could well follow *Desmotes* in an alphabetized order) rather than in a tetralogy sequence.[38] Nevertheless such a line of reasoning, even if correct, would be neutral in weight, and on other grounds the two plays do seem to stand together.[39] As a third play to go with them the *Pyrphoros* would

[34] Pindar, *Pyth.* 9.111–16, recounts a bridal race held by Danaos to marry off forty-eight of his daughters. In discussing this possibility Podlecki (n. 18), 5 suggests that certain allusive lines near the end of the *Hiketides* might anticipate an erotic attraction to the Danaids by some of the Argive men.

[35] Cf. D. F. Sutton, 'Aeschylus' *Amymone*', *GRBS* 15 (1974), 193–202.

[36] Obviously this is not the place to consider the general question of authorship; for arguments against inclusion of a Prometheus group here cf. the work of Griffith cited at n. 4, as well as now M. L. West, 'The Prometheus trilogy', *JHS* 99 (1979), 130–48 [= this volume, Ch. 13]. I confess I remain of the opinion that the thought and dramatic framework of these plays was laid out by Aischylos, whoever may have reshaped the writing (Euphorion, for a group presented in his father's name?).

[37] Hermann, *Opusc.* iv. 253–64.

[38] 'The title of *Prometheus Desmotes*', *JHS* 95 (1975), 184–6; against this reading of the words, West (n. 36), 130 n. 2 [= below, p. 360 n. 2].

[39] Cf. Herington's remarks (above n. 4). I have argued elsewhere (*ZAnt* 26 [1976], 31–42) that Prometheus' often contradictory projections of the future do demand some sort of resolution in a subsequent play, and that the exchange between

seem an obvious choice, since the *Pyrkaeus* is surely satyric, and thus
probably the *Prometheus* presented fourth in the 472 BC production.
Against that several scholars (in this century most especially Focke)[40]
have suggested that the *Pyrphoros is* the *Pyrkaeus* (the latter is not in
the Medicean Catalogue) and thus that there was no third play. But
we should note that (1) the remark on binding in the *Pyrphoros*
(fr. 208a) would then be a problem, (2) there are a number of other
plays also missing from the Catalogue, and (3) Focke's latter statement need not in any case follow from the former.[41] *Pyrphoros* (or
whatever we call it) is of course not without difficulties of its own: if
it was the first play of the group (so Welcker) Prometheus' narration
of his deeds in the *Desmotes* seems rather excessive; if it was the last
(so Westphal) it is hard to imagine what it contained, since Athenaios
(fr. 202) certainly implies a full reconciliation at the end of the
Lyomenos.[42] I would add however that it will not do to underestimate
Aischylos' inventiveness (or those of lost sources); who for example
could have guessed the direction the *Eumenides* would take?[43] Finally,

Prometheus and Cheiron so often cited as the key to the settlement with Zeus is
actually a much more complicated trade between Prometheus and Herakles. For
Taplin's arguments (above n. 38) against such a group on the basis of the three
Prometheus *epicleses*, cf. my remarks at 'AT:P' 303 n. 81, and West (n. 36), 131
[= pp. 361–2 below].

[40] F. Focke, *Hermes* 65 (1930), 263–9. Hermann, *Opusc.* iv. 253–5, summarizes
previous arguments.

[41] Against the identification cf. Wecklein, *Dramata* ii. 29–30, and 'AT:P' 298 n. 52.
Plays certainly missing from the Catalogue include *Alkmene, Glaukos Potnieus,
Hiereiai, Palamedes, Phineus,* and *Oreithyia*; perhaps also *Sisyphos Petrokylistes* (if it
is not the same as the *Drapetes*) and *Thalamopoioi*. On the idea that there might have
been a third play other than *Pyrphoros* cf. for example Lloyd-Jones, *Dionisio* 43
(1969), 211–18, and *The Justice of Zeus*, 97–103, where it is very tentatively suggested
that the *Aitnai* (with the unplaced 'Dike' fragment, 281a) might complete the group.

[42] Cf. Welcker (n. 1), passim, and R. Westphal, *Prolegomena zu Aeschylus Tragödien*
(Leipzig, 1869), 207–24. M. Pohlenz argues against Westphal and surveys more recent
opinion in *Die Griechische Tragödie* (2nd edn.; Göttingen, 1954), i. 77–8, ii. 40–1; so
also now West (n. 36), 131–2 [= below, pp. 362–3]. Space does not permit here even
an attempt to analyse the complexities involved in reconstructing the *Lyomenos*,
where Prometheus was visited by the Titans and perhaps Gaia (perhaps not: cf.
West [n. 36], 141–2 [= below, pp. 381–2]), and released by Herakles with or without
the consent of Zeus. If Athenaios is right the secret was also divulged in this play, but
why is another matter. A. D. Fitton-Brown's treatment ('Prometheia', *JHS* 79 (1959),
52–60) is still I think the most useful account of the problems.

[43] G. Thomson (*Prometheus Bound* (Cambridge 1932), 32–8) offers various suggestions for a final play, including Prometheus' re-entry into Olympos and the

we should remember that *if* the scholion on *Desm.* 511 does mean what
Hermann and Taplin have argued, we would have yet another possibility; thus Podlecki not unreasonably suggests that the missing play
may have been the second one, and recounted Prometheus' adventures
in Hades before he reemerged in the Caucasus.[44] For subject matter we
might draw on encounters with a variety of dead or tormented individuals (Hermes does mention Tartaros), as well as perhaps his fellow
Titans (or Sisyphos, protagonist of at least one Aischylean play). With
regard to the satyr drama we have no evidence whatever. To hazard only
one proposal, Proklos' note on Pandora at Hesiod *Op.* 157 cites an
Aischylean reference to her as τοῦ πηλοπλάστου σπέρματος θνητὴ γυνή
['the mortal woman of clay-moulded seed'] (fr. 369). Such a line could
occur casually in a number of contexts, but the most likely instance is
surely a play about Pandora herself; her creation and bestowal upon an
unwary Epimetheus would certainly provide suitable material for a
satyr drama,[45] and such a topic, involving as it would Zeus' intentions
toward men, might relate very appropriately to the narrative of the
tragedies. For title either *Pandora* or *Epimetheus* would serve (both
would fit into Dieterich's proposed fifth column of the Catalogue),[46] or
perhaps even the attested *Thalamopoioi*, with its chorus of satyrs constructing the bridal chamber.[47]

founding of the lesser mysteries of Demeter. If N. Terzaghi's assignment (*RFIC* 82
(1954), 337–52) of P. Oxy. 2245 (fr. 204) to a tragic *Pyrphoros* was certain, we might at
least have a celebration of the gift of fire in this drama; but his arguments as to satyr
dress are not conclusive, nor must the garlands of fr. 204b20 necessarily be the
expiatory ones described by Athenaios (15.672–3). More likely the fragment is
from the satyric *Pyrkaeus.*

[44] Podlecki (n. 18), 16.

[45] Sophokles uses the same material for his play *Pandora/Sphyrokopoi* (cf.
A. C. Pearson, *The Fragments of Sophocles* vol. ii (Cambridge, 1917), 135–9). Zeus'
gift of Pandora to man, viewed in a beneficent light, might also provide a topic for a
third tragedy in which the god's concern for men is more fully revealed.

[46] Cf. A. Dieterich, *RhM* 48 (1893), 141–6, and my article forthcoming in the same
journal ['Aischylos' lost plays: the fifth column', *RhM* 123 (1980), 210–22].

[47] The title is known only from Pollux. To Welcker's suggestion that the play went
with *Iphigeneia* it has been objected that there never was any marriage intended; to
Hermann's that the title is only an alternate for *Aigyptioi* there is the fact that after the
generous offer of Pelasgos and the city (*Hik.* 1009–11) the Danaids scarcely need new
bridal chambers, nor would they be in process of construction throughout the second
play. Pollux's quotation rather suggests a satyr drama.

(6) *Myrmidones–Nereides–Phryges–* ———[s]. These titles are nowhere actually recognized as a group, but the content of the three separate plays as indicated by the fragments makes such a conclusion virtually inescapable. The plot seems basically that of the *Iliad,* though approach and viewpoint may have been quite different.[48] Various factors complicate the reconstruction: Aischylos' dependence on Homer, Accius' dependence on Aischylos (if any), the authenticity of some of the newer fragments (P. Oxy. 2253, PSI 1211), and the attendability of the younger scholia.[49] New evidence, however, has in part altered the picture,[50] and the following now seems fairly likely. At the start of the first play a chorus of Myrmidons enters, appealing to a silent Achilleus to return to battle. Following their parodos, which elicits no response, two heralds (Talthybios and a silent Eurybates?) enter to make the same appeal, but with no better results. Next comes Phoinix, who may or may not report a threat of stoning by the Achaians if Achilleus does not return. To this (or something Phoinix says) Achilleus finally replies, but it presumably requires a messenger's (Patroklos?) report of the burning ships before he consents to let his friend fight. Patroklos then dons the armor (this may all be offstage) and goes out; the news of his death is brought back by Antilochos (possibly preceded by a messenger) and the play ends in laments (with stress on the sexual aspect of the loss). The second play is

---

[48] For the various reconstructions cf. Welcker (n. 1), 415–30; Hermann, *Opusc.* v. 136–63; Wecklein (n. 7), 327–68; Croiset, *REG* 7 (1894), 151–80; W. Schadewaldt, *Hermes* 71 (1936), 25–69; Mette, 112–21; Ferrari, 91–111.

[49] On the fragments (P. Oxy. 2253 = fr. 451k, PSI 1211 = fr. 132c) cf. Lloyd-Jones' 1957 Appendix to Smyth's Loeb edition of Aischylos (ii. 582–4, 590–3). The Oxyrhynchus lines appear to contain a greeting to the assembled Achaians; *Myrmidones* seems the obvious choice, but *Iphigeneia* or *Telephos* might do as well. The Florentine papyrus presents the famous threat of stoning Achilleus; here the situation is clear, the Aischylean authorship less so (fuller discussion (on the assumption that the lines are by Aischylos) in B. Snell's *Scenes from Greek Drama* (Berkeley, 1967), 1–22, 139–43). With regard to the younger scholion in question (fr. 131: Talthybios and Eurybates before a silent Achilleus), Hermann, Wecklein, and Schadewaldt rejected it, but Bergk (*Hermes* 18 (1883), 481–7), Croiset, and most recently V. Di Benedetto (*Maia* 19 (1967), 374–82) argue more reasonably for its retention. If, however, Herington (*RhM* 115 (1972), 199–203) is right in reading a *plural* verb here, it may be that the passage has nothing to do with Aischylos. Nevertheless the silence of Achilleus at the beginning of the *Myrmidones* seems well established: cf. the excellent discussion by O. Taplin, 'Aeschylean silences and silences in Aeschylus', *HSCPh* 76 (1972), 57–97, at 62–76.

[50] Cf. Di Benedetto (n. 49), 373–4, who argues from a fragment transcribed by Vitelli and subsequently lost [fr. 132b] that Phoinix brings the threat of stoning (Snell supposed Antilochos) and shakes Achilleus from his silence.

less clear, owing to a smaller number of fragments. But certainly the Nereids enter at the start, and after them probably Thetis bearing the new arms. Achilleus would then depart for battle, and a messenger would bring the news of his victory, followed by Achilleus himself with the corpse of Hektor. For the third play we seem to have Achilleus beginning the action in silence again. Hermes comes to tell him he must return the body, and then the chorus of Trojan attendants enters, followed by Priam with the ransom. This last was apparently weighed out against Hektor's body pound for pound, but what passed between Priam and Achilleus we cannot say. A reference to Andromache has been taken by some scholars to indicate her presence, though she may only be mentioned in passing;[51] without her the group nowhere seems to require more than two actors. In any case we apparently have a very close-knit narrative; each play follows directly on the preceding one, with only minor actions occurring between them, much as in the Danaid group (save of course for the murders, which cannot have been shown under any circumstances). For the satyr play there is again no obvious title, but Mette observes that P. Oxy. 2254 [fr. 451l], though very fragmentary, appears to contain the words $Πρίαμε$ ['Priam'] and $θῆρες οἵδε$ ['these beasts'], which if correct would certainly suggest a satyr play about Priam and perhaps Paris.

(7) *Memnon–Psychostasia–Phrygioi* (?)– ——[s]. Given the presence of two separate plays on Memnon's exploits at Troy (for what else could either of these plays contain?) and given the continuous nature of the action (is there much point in the death of Antilochos in the first play without the death of Memnon in the second?) the conclusion of some sort of connection here seems hard to avoid.[52] Nevertheless the lack of an immediately apparent third title has caused doubt in some quarters.[53] Welcker, working from the supposition

---

[51] The question turns on whether $ὦ$ rather than $ἦν$ should be supplied in the first line of fr. 267; Hermann, Smyth, and Ferrari argue affirmatively, but most other scholars favor the indirect reference.

[52] Discussion of these plays in Welcker, *ATP* 430–7; Hermann, *Opusc.* vii. 343–61; Wecklein, 652–6: Mette, 108–12: Ferrari, 131–9.

[53] Typical is Wilamowitz, *Aischylos-Interpretationen* (Berlin, 1914) 59 n. 1, where Hermann's notion of dilogies is resurrected; on this whole question cf. the discussion in 'AT:P' 297–9. Here (as in a number of the following groups) we must remember that our knowledge of the list of Aischylos' titles is not likely to be complete, and

that such a group reproduced the plot of Arktinos' *Aithiopis*, proposed *Toxotides–Psychostasia* (*Memnon*)–*Nereides*, with the epic's three major deaths (Penthesileia, Memnon, Achilleus) arranged in the three plays. Against this Hermann observed that the *Toxotides* is about Aktaion, not Penthesileia, and that Aischylos in any case need not use all of a rather loosely connected source. His own suggestion was to jettison Penthesileia and suppose rather a *Memnon–Psychostasia–Mousai** sequence centered on the deaths of Antilochos, Memnon, and Achilleus. More recently Ferrari has revived Welcker's Penthesileia play under the title *Phrygioi* (with *Memnon–Psychostasia* to follow and no death of Achilleus), while Mette prefers to start the same group with the *Europa* (who like Eos loses a son at Troy). In neither case, however, does the connection seem very satisfactory. Nevertheless Ferrari is surely right in supposing the title *Phrygioi* to have possibilities here; the long-held assumption that it is simply a dittography of *Phryges* in the Catalogue has very little basis in fact.[54] Moreover, we have from Plato (*Rep.* 2.383a7 = fr. 350) an Aischylean fragment in which Thetis bitterly reproaches Apollo for favorable statements made at her marriage and now proved false by Apollo's own share in the slaying of Achilleus. The play to which the fragment belongs is not named, but the lines almost certainly occur in either the third play of this group or the first play of the Aias group. Scholars have taken both positions,[55] but the more likely placing would seem to be here, in a play specifically about Achilleus' death (it is true that Thetis appears in the *Hoplon Krisis*, but Aias is hardly likely to resolve her accusations, nor has he much to do with Apollo). In that case Hermann's reconstruction would be

hence the lack of a title to fill out a group not as significant as it might seem. Then too, there is the fact that no recorded example of such a grouping exists. I have accordingly proceeded on the assumption that where two plays appear closely linked together, we are probably dealing with a full tragic trilogy whose third element is not immediately apparent.

[54] If in fact Aischylos wrote two plays with Phrygian choruses (such as would certainly be likely given the number of dramas located at Troy) there is no reason why he should not have named both of them after those choruses by using the attested Greek variants Φρύγιοι and Φρύγες, nor is there any indication that the author of the Catalogue believed himself to have made a mistake. It is true that there are no citations from a *Phrygioi* play, but that is also the case with a number of other titles mentioned in the Catalogue.

[55] Welcker and Wecklein place it in this group, Hermann, Mette, and Ferrari in the *Hoplon Krisis*. For other guesses cf. Wecklein, 762.

substantially correct. As for plot, the *Memnon* almost certainly presented the arrival of the Aithiopian hero and his victory over Antilochos, while we know that the *Psychostasia* contained Achilleus' triumph over Memnon (represented at least in part by Zeus' weighing of the two souls amid the pleas of the respective mothers).[56] The *Phrygioi* (if title and action are as indicated) would then show the subsequent victory of Paris and Apollo over Achilleus, followed by Thetis' lament and presumably a settlement of her claims. Such a production would of course focus more on Thetis and Achilleus than on Memnon, though there may have been a parallel drawn between Eos' loss of her son in the second play and Thetis' loss of hers in the third. For a related satyr play (marriage of Thetis? escapades of Memnon's foreign retinue?) nothing especially recommends itself.

(8) *Hoplon Krisis–Thressai–Salaminiai–*——[s]. Here again the presence of two plays with a virtually continuous theme (the awarding of the arms in the first play leading to the death of Aias in the second) surely permits some confidence in assuming connection.[57] The preserved fragments establish that in the first play someone summoned Thetis and the Nereids (who seem to have been the chorus) in order to judge the awarding of Achilleus' arms.[58] From the aspersions cast on Odysseus' parentage (fr. 175) it would appear that he and Aias argued the matter out on stage (in which case we would need three actors), but no other conclusions are forthcoming, save for the obvious one that Aias lost. In the *Thressai* we know that Aias killed himself, that the death was described by a messenger, and that the sword bent away several times before a goddess (Athena?) came to show him where he was mortal (the armpit: fr. 83). We do

---

[56] Hermann and subsequent writers have firmly supported Pollux's evidence (Radt, p. 375) for a raised platform for the three deities, in contrast to Welcker. For the *theologeion* in this connection cf. Pickard-Cambridge, *The Theatre of Dionysos at Athens* (Oxford, 1946), 46–7, 128. Welcker also denied that any of the deities spoke, but surely Thetis and Eos were leading characters; if three actors were permitted, Zeus may have made a pronouncement in the fashion of Pylades.

[57] On this group cf. Welcker (n. 1), 438–40; Hermann, *Opusc.* vii. 362–87; Wecklein, 624–9; Mette, 121–7; Ferrari, 141–9. The general lines of the story are known from the *Aithiopis* and *Ilias Mikra,* and also to some extent from the *Nekyia.*

[58] Welcker, however, maintains (*Die griechischen Tragodien*, i (Bonn, 1839), 38) that the summons was not answered, or else that Thetis was called as a witness or on appeal.

not, however, know whether the madness and attack on the cattle were included, nor whether there was any question of Aias' burial, as in Sophokles' play. The third title (*Salaminiai* Herodian; *Salaminioi* Catalogue) is a total blank. Welcker's suggestion that the plot was similar to that of Sophokles' *Teukros* (Teukros returns home to an angry Telamon, who banishes him to Cyprus for failing to save his half-brother) has met with general approval, but the fact is that the few certain fragments indicate nothing of the content or even its location.[59] And though on the analogy of the *Oresteia* and the *Oidipous* plays a jump ahead in time after the death of Aias would not be inappropriate to Aischylos, we have seen that broad expanses of time are not the only principle on which his tetralogies are constructed. Given that both male and female Salaminians would be much in order at Troy, we might do better to assume the missing play to be the middle one (Aias' plotting against the Achaians and his night raid) or even the first (something relating to Achilleus' death and Aias' rescue of the body). The satyr play is completely obscure.

(9)—— –*Phorkides–Polydektes–Diktyoulkoi*[s]. The titles *Phorkides* and *Polydektes,* plus what we know of the content, again seem to suggest a group, since the former play in particular would have a hard time standing by itself as a tragedy. Once again, however, the third title is unknown (and probably lost, though *Thalamopoioi* might do if it is not satyric). Welcker assumed an opening *Danae* on the basis of a dubious reference in Hesychios (fr. 45); the notice today is taken rather to mean the *Danaides.*[60] Hermann for his part conjectured, quite rightly in the event, that Welcker's *Diktyourgoi* (the 'net-makers' of Athamas) was actually a play about Danae's landing on Seriphos, i.e. *Diktyoulkoi* ('net-drawers').[61] But while new papyrus

---

[59] Only Wecklein notes that such a finale is less than certain. Mette suggested locating P. Oxy. 2256 fr. 71 [fr. 451q] here, but though the fragment mentions Aias, it adds little to our knowledge, and Lloyd-Jones (App. Smyth 584–6) seriously questions the attribution. For Sophokles' play cf. Pearson (n. 45), ii. 214–20.

[60] Welcker (n. 1), 378–90.

[61] *Opusc.* vii. 175–7. His own arrangement (*Diktyoulkoi–Phorkides–Polydektes*) subsequently found support from Wecklein, 607–8, Smyth ii. 378, and Séchan (n. 28), 107–13, all of course before the new finds surfaced. More recently cf. Mette, 155–61, and Ferrari, 319–37.

finds vindicated him as to content,[62] they also showed that the play was satyric, and hence not the opening tragedy as he had supposed. In fact there is no very obvious candidate for the missing play among the known titles, nor is it clear where in the sequence it might fall. If it preceded the *Phorkides* it must have concerned either Danae's ill-treatment by Akrisios[63] or the unwelcome attentions of Polydektes and Perseus' rash promise to bring back the head of Medousa. If it came between *Phorkides* and *Polydektes,* it probably described Perseus' taking of the head or his adventures with Kepheus and Andromeda.[64] If it was the closing play, it would recount either the vengeance against Polydektes (shifting the title *Polydektes* over to the first play) or the later death of Akrisios (as in Sophokles' *Larisaioi*). This last supposition would bring in matters scarcely prepared for in the first two plays; to some extent the same is true of an opening Danae-Akrisios play, though the seeming insouciance of Zeus in that tale could pave the way for his later vindication via the punishment of Polydektes. My own preference would be for a fairly tight plot line: Perseus promises to get the head (——or *Polydektes*), Perseus acquires the head (*Phorkides*), Perseus returns to Seriphos with the head (*Polydektes* or——).[65] With regard to the plays themselves, the *Phorkides* seems to have presented Perseus' encounter with the Graiai, sisters and guardians of the Gorgons. From Eratosthenes we learn that he stole their eye and cast it into the Tritonian marsh; beyond that there are mostly questions. Presumably the chorus (minor deities?) was

---

[62] For the main fragments (PSI 1209a and P. Oxy. 2161) cf. Mette's edition, frr. 464 [= fr. 46a Radt] and 474 [= fr. 47a Radt], together with the bibliography there cited. The most exhaustive recent commentary is that of M. Werre-De Haas, *Aeschylus' Dictyulci* (Leiden, 1961), which also contains an excellent account of variations in the myth.

[63] So Cantarella (n. 12), 66–70, and T. P. Howe, 'Illustrations to Aeschylos' tetralogy on the Perseus theme', *AJA* 57 (1953), 269–75. The former resurrects Welcker's *Danae,* pointing out that the Catalogue might have omitted it (haplography after *Danaides*?) along with other missing titles. Against such a play Ferrari argues, perhaps rightly, that one would expect Danae to review much of her fate in the *Diktyoulkoi.*

[64] About Sophokles' *Andromeda* virtually nothing is known; for Euripides' play of the same name cf. Webster (n. 19), 192–9.

[65] Wilamowitz (n. 53), 244 suggests as a title *Seriphioi,* though without precise specification of content; at 154 of the same work he gives the standard *Diktyoulkoi—Phorkides–Polydektes* arrangement.

friendly to Perseus, at least one god (Athena? Hermes?) participated, only one of the two or three Graiai spoke, and the Gorgons may or may not have appeared.[66] As Aristotle suggests, the play may have relied more on spectacle than on conflict.[67] For the *Polydektes* we have only the title in the Catalogue; hence the uncertainty whether it involved the *eranos* before or the vengeance after. The satyr play was as noted above the *Diktyoulkoi*, and concerned Danae's rescue from the sea. The new papyrus fragments leave room for doubt on details, but the general action was apparently an attempt by Seilenos to carry off Danae after Diktys had gone for help.[68] The resemblances to the *Amymone* are obvious, and no doubt here also the satyrs were thwarted. That Seilenos was thus a comic counterpart of Polydektes in the earlier plays seems at least a possibility.

(10) *Psychagogoi–Penelope–Ostologoi–Kirke*[s]. Admittedly this is the weakest of the 'more probable' category, but the interrelation in subject matter between at least *Penelope* and *Ostologoi,* plus two other plays (one designated satyric) unquestionably about Odysseus, still offers grounds to suppose a complete tetralogy. Welcker in fact proposed to form two groups, one (*Neaniskoi–Ostologoi–Penelope*) treating the return to Ithaka, the other (*Palamedes–Psychagogoi–Odysseus Akanthoplex**) relating a broad sequence of events leading up to Odysseus' death.[69] We have seen, however, that Hermann's discovery of the *Thesmophoriazousai* scholion places the *Neaniskoi* in the Lykourgos group, and an Aischylean *Odysseus Akanthoplex* was never more than a figment of Welcker's imagination. Subsequent work has produced general agreement on the arrangement given here, but it must be said

---

[66] The conjectures are endless, especially with regard to the chorus. Nor does it help matters that both the Graiai and the Gorgons are children of Phorkys; we cannot even be sure to whom (both?) the title refers. It is however noteworthy that Aischylos deviates from Pherekydes in eliminating the Nymphs and making the Graiai guardians of the Gorgons. Earlier suppositions (Wecklein, Nauck) that the play was satyric are now almost certainly to be rejected.

[67] *Poet.* 18.1456ª2–3. We should also keep in mind that the arrangement of a connected group will often spread the action out a bit and produce plays that do not necessarily move to a dramatic conclusion; so for example the *Hiketides.*

[68] The only real controversy centers on the identity of the two speakers in PSI 1209a: cf. Lloyd-Jones, App. Smyth 531–4.

[69] Welcker (n. 1), 452–70. His subsequent shift, after the elimination of *Neaniskoi,* to an *Ostologoi–Syndeipnoi**–Penelope* group (*GT* i. 45) was not much help.

that much remains to be explained.[70] The opening play, then, would be
the *Psychagogoi,* in which Odysseus journeys to the edge of the Underworld to consult Teiresias; local residents, perhaps skilled in calling up
the dead, would comprise the chorus. Presumably Odysseus spoke in
turn to a number of shades, and gained from them news of home,
especially as regards the suitors. It is slightly puzzling on this assessment
that our one real fragment (fr. 275) concerns a prophecy of Odysseus'
death from the tail of a sting-ray, but there is after all no reason
to suppose this central to the play.[71] From the second play, the *Penelope,*
we have only one line [fr. 187], the beginning of an Odyssean *Trugrede*
['trick-speech']. Since this suggests a private interview between
Odysseus and Penelope, we might imagine the scene Penelope's bed-
chamber, and the chorus her handmaidens. Various announcements
and speculations might precede Odysseus' arrival, and the actual confrontation of beggar and faithful wife could well lead to the startling
report of the beggar's triumph over the suitors. If this is right the play
would view matters largely from Penelope's vantage point. The *Ostologoi* is usually now taken to have offered a chorus of suitors' relatives
come to gather up the remains and confront Odysseus, and certainly
our two fragments appear to contain a defense by the latter in which
he catalogues the affronts of his antagonists (frr. 179, 180). There
have however been other views: Welcker would make the chorus one
of beggars in the palace, and the play thus precede *Penelope,* while
Hermann argued that the reference to a chamber pot must make the
play satyric.[72] On balance the majority opinion looks correct, but the
links are not as strong, nor the final resolution as obvious, as in previous

[70] For the sequence cf. Wecklein, 689–92, and subsequently Wilamowitz (n. 53),
246–7, Mette, 127–9, Ferrari, 257–67.

[71] Nor has anyone explained why Aischylos, in contrast to Eugammon's *Telegoneia*
and Sophokles' *Odysseus Akanthoplex,* would bring that death by means of a heron
rather than Telegonos. Lloyd-Jones (*CR* 14 (1964), 247) suggests that ἐκ τοῦ in the
third line of fr. 478 Mette [= fr. 275 Radt, which has ἐκ τοῦδ'] might mean simply
'after that' rather than 'from him'.

[72] Against Welcker we might argue that Odysseus relating his troubles to a chorus
of fellow beggars does not offer much in the way of content (especially if they can not
recognize him); moreover ὅδε in the first line of fr. 180 seems to point to the body of
one of the suitors on stage. Hermann's position (*Opusc.* iii. 40) has been supported by
Nauck, F. Kudlien, *RhM* 113 (1970), 297–304, and Sutton, *HSCPh* 78 (1974), 128.
Wecklein, however, long before pointed out the difference between showing such
things on stage and referring to them in a serious context (n. 7, 382). That Odysseus

groups, and quite possibly the whole sequence (aside from the central core of the suitors' death) is wrong. For the satyr play we have the *Kirke* (assuming the *Ostologoi* is tragic), a light-hearted moment from Odysseus' earlier adventures attested as satyric by the Catalogue.[73] Of the specific content, beyond what one could guess from the *Odyssey,* nothing remains.

III. LESS PROBABLE GROUPS

(11) *Perrhaibides–Ixion–* ——— – ——[s]. The presence of two titles indicating fairly closely connected actions (Ixion's murder of his father-in-law, and his dealings with Zeus on Olympos) might seem to group these plays with those discussed previously, but it is troubling that no title suggests itself for *either* of the other two plays, and the actions are not as interdependent as they might be.[74] On the other hand, one might well ask what sort of resolution *Perrhaibides* would have as a monodrama. In any case the title figure is one to whom Pindar's Second Pythian and a variety of later mythographers assign a rather checkered career. He married Dia, daughter of Eioneus, by promising lavish bride-gifts, then lured her father to his death in a fiery pit to avoid paying them. Subsequently no mortal would purify him, but Zeus himself upon supplication performed the ceremony.[75] Divine favor, however, was too much for Ixion; he propositioned Hera, and after lying with a cloud in her form was bound to an eternally-revolving wheel. Whether Aischylos used all of this tale or not is unclear. The *Perrhaibides* (with a chorus of women from Ixion's home Perrhaibia in Thessaly) apparently focused on

might thus describe the arrogant actions of the suitors to their relatives seems to me quite within the bounds of tragedy.

[73] Cf. Levi (n. 15), 241; Guggisberg (n. 27), 90; F. Adrados, *Emerita* 33 (1965), 229–42.

[74] Welcker at first (n. 1, 559) made *Perrhaibides* a play about the Lapiths and Centaurs and thus rejected any grouping. Subsequently, however, he yielded to the obvious implications of fr. 184. For what little is known about the plays, cf. Wecklein, 632–4; Mette, 172–5; Ferrari, 151–63.

[75] Cf. *Eum.* 441, 717–18. Apollo's query as to whether Zeus erred in purifying Ixion seems rather curious in view of the consequences.

Eioneus' claim to the gifts (fr. 184) and presumably concluded with
his death (fr. 186). In that case *Ixion*, of which we know nothing,
might go on to present the purification by Zeus and Ixion's subsequent betrayal of the position accorded him, with the punishment
reserved to a third play. For a satyr drama *Thalamopoioi* (Dia's
wedding chamber) would again be one possibility. The absence of
evidence is especially unfortunate because Zeus was so prominently
involved; one can only imagine the implications of these plays for the
Aischylean view of divine justice.[76]

(12) and 13) *Semele–Pentheus–Bakchai–Xantriai–Trophoi*[s]. The
titles relating to Dionysos' birth and return to Thebes present a rather
different problem from those we have been considering; instead of
too few plays to make up a tetralogy, we have here too many.[77] Since
Welcker it has been customary to begin the group with *Semele*. but
for the following dramas—Dionysos' return and vengeance—some
selection has then to be made from among *Bakchai*, *Pentheus*, *Xantriai*, and *Trophoi*. Of the *Bakchai* we know nothing at all. *Pentheus* is
obviously relevant, and Aristophanes of Byzantium tells us that
Euripides' *Bakchai* draws from it. *Xantriai* means 'wool-carders'; a
scholion to *Eum.* 26 (= fr. 172b) notes that Pentheus' adventures are
located on Kithairon in the play, and thus some scholars have
assumed that the chorus (Agaue and her sisters) figuratively carded
Pentheus in tearing him apart.[78] *Trophoi* is guaranteed by several
sources to concern the nurses of Dionysos, whose story would make a
suitable satyr play. In the face of such abundance several solutions
have been advanced. Welcker supposed *Pentheus* the name of the
whole group, but this goes against practice and attributes a most
unlikely mistake to the Catalogue, where all five plays are listed.
Boeckh, in a view often followed today, removed the *Xantriai* and
referred it rather to the daughters of Minyas who rejected Dionysos'

[76] That Zeus in turn possessed Ixion's wife is recounted by Homer (*Il.* 14.317–18);
for the story that he mated with her in the form of a stallion, cf. Eustathius on the
Iliad, p. 101.

[77] Cf. Welcker (n. 1), 327–35; Wecklein, 591–2; Mette, 141–8; Ferrari, 175–86.

[78] First suggested by Elmsley on the basis of a use of ξαίνειν in this connection by
Philostratos (*Imag.* 1.18) and supported more recently by Ferrari and Pohlenz
(n. 42,i.131). Against such a figurative sense it has been objected that the chorus
would not then become ξάντριαι until the end of the play, but perhaps they carded
wool at the play's opening and then switched to other material.

worship.[79] Admittedly this theory has merit, since a reference to Pentheus in the *Xantriai* need not mean that the play was about him, any more than the *Eumenides* is. Yet it is hard to believe that a scholiast would cite a variant locale in a play *not* about Pentheus, and never mention where Pentheus died in the play Aischylos did write on the subject. It seems more likely therefore that *Xantriai* was indeed the play in which Pentheus was killed. More recently Mette has jettisoned the *Bakchai,* on the grounds that we have no proof the title figures in question were *Theban* Bakchai, and he may well be right.[80] But there is also still another possibility, namely that the basic assumption of an opening *Semele* was wrong to begin with. Welcker patterned his group in large part on the outline of the *Oresteia,* with transgression (by Semele's family) and a return-revenge (Dionysos) in a subsequent generation. Once again, however, it should be emphasized that there is probably nothing typical about such an arrangement, and certainly no pressing reason to retain it here. Omitting the *Semele,* we would then have a group consisting of *Bakchai, Pentheus,* and *Xantriai,* with *Trophoi* possibly the satyr play, and the story of Pentheus spread out over all three tragedies.[81] But as to how the action was distributed, or even of what exactly it consisted, it seems pointless to speculate further, save to say that there must have been parallels with the *Lykourgeia.*[82]

The above hypothesis does of course leave the *Semele* as a single play, and it may indeed have been performed as such. Nevertheless I should like at least to mention a suggestion of Droysen that would

[79] Boeckh (*Graecae tragoediae principium* (Heidelberg 1808), 28–9); so also Wecklein (who thought the play satyric); Séchan (n. 28), 132–8; Mette, 146–7. The last named nevertheless retains the title as a tragedy in his Pentheus group; how he imagines it to relate to the other plays is not stated.

[80] Earlier scholars (Elmsley, Hartung) sought to remove the *Bakchai* by equating it with *Bassarides* and supposing an $\mathring{\eta}$ mistakenly omitted in the Catalogue; so also E. R. Dodds, *Euripides: Bacchae* (Oxford, 1960), p. xxix. It would, however, be a strange mistake on the part of a cataloguer who has no trouble with other duplicate titles, nor are plays with two choral appellations common.

[81] To my knowledge the only previous support for such an arrangement is that of Zieliński (n. 10), 66; no reasons are given.

[82] There are naturally many possibilities: Dodds for example suggests that the Xantriai are originally Theban wool-carders converted to Dionysos. In that case *Pentheus* might come last, and contain the *sparagmos;* much depends on how we interpret the scholiast's τὰ κατὰ Πενθέα at *Eum.* 26. Either way, however, it seems clear that Euripides' *Bakchai* cannot derive *entirely* from the *Pentheus.*

connect this title with the generally ignored *Toxotides*.[83] This latter play, as Hermann pointed out, concerned the death of Aktaion, left to the mercies of his hounds after being turned into a stag. Writers of the Hellenistic and later periods assign as the cause of his demise Artemis' anger because he had seen her bathing.[84] But Stesichoros and Akousilaos both suggest that her motive was rather a desire to prevent Aktaion from marrying Semele, and Akousilaos mentions as well Zeus' annoyance that a mortal would presume to court her.[85] If this earlier version was also the Aischylean one, as seems likely, then Zeus' treatment of Semele would create a strong link between this play and that bearing her name in which she perishes through the machinations of Hera. A further point in support of such a link is the *Semele*'s tantalizing reference to someone killed by Zeus ($Z\epsilon\acute{\upsilon}s$, $\mathring{o}s$ $\kappa\alpha\tau\acute{\epsilon}\kappa\tau\alpha$ $\tauο\mathring{\upsilon}\tauο\nu$, fr. 221); for this 'someone' Aktaion stands as the logical candidate,[86] in which case his death would remain an issue outside the bounds of the *Toxotides*. The whole situation, with Zeus shown in less than the best possible light, has parallels with Io in the *Prometheus Desmotes* and probably also with Europa in the *Kares*.[87] As for the plays, *Toxotides* yields only a few corrupt lines touching on Aktaion's success in the hunt and women who were or were not chaste.[88] From the *Semele*, if the attribution is correct,[89] we do have a

---

[83] Droysen, *Phrynichos, Aischylos und die Trilogie* (Kiel, 1841), 77–8. His complete arrangement (which I do not follow here) would connect *Toxotides, Semele,* and *Pentheus / Xantriai*. with the water carriers of the second play serving to prepare funeral offerings for Aktaion.

[84] Apollod. *Bibl.* 3.4.4; Ovid, *Met.* 3.138–252; Hyg. *Fab.* 180, 181.

[85] Stesichoros 236 *PMG* (from Paus. 9.2.3): $\mathring{\iota}\nu\alpha$ $\delta\mathring{\eta}$ $\mu\mathring{\eta}$ $\gamma\upsilon\nu\alpha\mathring{\iota}\kappa\alpha$ $\Sigma\epsilon\mu\acute{\epsilon}\lambda\eta\nu$ $\lambda\acute{\alpha}\beta\omicron\iota$. For Akousilaos (*FGrH* 2F33) cf. Apollod. cit. above: $\mu\eta\nu\acute{\iota}\sigma\alpha\nu\tauο\varsigma$ $\tauο\mathring{\upsilon}$ $\Delta\iota\grave{\omicron}\varsigma$ $\mathring{o}\tau\iota$ $\mathring{\epsilon}\mu\nu\eta\sigma\tau\epsilon\acute{\upsilon}\sigma\alpha\nu\tauο$ $\Sigma\epsilon\mu\acute{\epsilon}\lambda\eta\nu$. A newly-published papyrus fragment (P. Mich. 1447: T. Renner, *HSCPh* 82 (1978), 282–7) now seems to establish that Aktaion also desired marriage with Semele in the Hesiodic *Ehoiai*. It is not, however, clear from the passage whether he is killed for that reason.

[86] So Droysen; cf. also K. Latte, *Philologus* 97 (1948), 47–56, at 52–3 (where 'Alcmeonis' is surely a misprint for 'Acteonis').

[87] On the latter cf. especially fr. 99, where Europa describes her abduction by Zeus and laments both her abandonment by Minos and Rhadamanthys and the possibility that Sarpedon will shortly be lost to her.

[88] Fr. 243 is anything but clear, yet the speaker seems to be Aktaion, and since the woman who has 'tasted of a man' cannot be Artemis or the chorus, the logical alternative is Semele. Perhaps we see here Aktaion's jealousy of a rival as yet to him unknown.

[89] To my mind, at least, Latte (n. 86) is entirely convincing in his supposition that Asklepiades' referral of these lines to the *Xantriai* is mistaken. The roughly

long papyrus fragment (P. Oxy. 2164 = fr. 168) in which Hera disguised as a beggar speaks with the chorus of water-carriers, but beyond this (and the fact that Aischylos brought Semele on stage pregnant and inspired) we are at a loss. As a third play to join these two we might well consider the *Athamas* as a tentative possibility. In narrative terms, Hera's anger against those (Semele's sister Ino and her husband) who helped to raise the infant Dionysos would certainly further the themes suggested for the first two plays,[90] though how Semele's fate and the apparent chastity-marriage conflict might be resolved is another matter.[91] Neither can we say (on any reconstruction) to what extent Kadmos and Semele's other sisters may have been involved. In closing it must be stressed again that a *Toxotides–Semele–Athamas* group is still simply a guess, but one that I hope bears thinking about. For a satyr play the *Trophoi* would be as appropriate here as in the previous group, with the satyrs as husbands of Dionysos' actual nurses, and both rejuvenated at the end of the drama for their services.[92]

(14) *Argeiai–Eleusinioi–Epigonoi–Nemea*(?). Again there are a number of plays on the same general subject (the expedition of the Seven against Thebes and perhaps also that of their sons) but the content

contemporary treatments of Lasserre (*MH* 6 (1949), 140–56) and Cantarella (n. 12, 108–28) are seriously weakened by their failure to take this possibility into account. It is of course true, as Dodds argues, that Latte cannot *prove* Asklepiades wrong. But we know from later sources (Ovid, Hyginus) that Hera disguised herself to destroy Semele, and Apollodoros (*Bibl.* 3.4.3) also refers to Semele as deceived by Hera; to suppose that Aischylos used the same motif of a disguised Hera in a different play (where she was never thought to belong) surely stretches coincidence. Cf. also Lloyd-Jones, App. Smyth 566–71.

[90] The myths surrounding Athamas are highly involved; presumably Aischylos used the version of Apollodoros (cit. above) rather than the more complex tale with Nephele, Phrixos, and Helle (cf. Hyg. *Fab.* 1–5 and Pearson on the Athamas plays of Sophokles). Athamas was also Sisyphos' brother, and Pindar (fr. 6.5 Snell–Maehler) tells us that the Nereids ordered the latter to found the Isthmian games in Melikertes' honor, but this is hardly sufficient to link the *Athamas* with either of Aischylos' *Sisyphos* plays (assuming there were two).

[91] P. Oxy. 2164 does place a strong emphasis on marriage and childbirth, which may have been an important motif. We should note too Pausanias (2.31.2) and Apollodoros (*Bibl.* 3.5.3) to the effect that Dionysos brought Semele up out of Hades to Olympos; possibly this was the subject of the third play.

[92] On the play cf. E. Maass, *NJKA* 1913, 628–32, and E. Kaibel, *Hermes* 30 (1895), 88–9.

and even degree of connection are most unclear.[93] From Plutarch we learn that the *Eleusinioi* dealt with Theseus' recovery of the bodies of the Seven, and a reference to Kapaneus' death suggests similar material for the *Argeiai*.[94] But whether the latter title would then come before the *Eleusinioi* as a lament for the defeat and the unre-covered bodies, or afterwards as a dramatization of the burial, remains open. Then too, there is no real certainty as to the third tragedy: scholars are divided between those who would begin the group with the *Nemea,* and those who would close it with the *Epigonoi*.[95] Of the *Nemea* we know only that the title figure was the mother of Archemoros, who died in infancy from a snake-bite while the Argives were marching north to Thebes. If Bakchylides and later sources can be trusted,[96] Adrastos founded the Nemean games in his honor and Amphiaraos predicted the death of the Seven in the combat to come.[97] On the other hand, the *Epigonoi* must relate the attack by the sons of the Seven ten years later (whether from the Argive or the Theban standpoint),[98] and this would be a

[93] Welcker originally suggested (n. 1, 372–7) an *Eleusinioi*–*Argeioi*–*Epigonoi* group, but subsequently altered it in order to insert an unattested *Phoinissai**. Hermann (*Opusc.* vii. 190–210) followed a similar approach in the mistaken belief that the *Septem* went with *Argeioi* and *Eleusinioi*. For arrangements subsequent to the discovery of the *Septem's* hypothesis cf. Wilamowitz, *Hermes* 26 (1891), 226–7 and *Aischylos-Interpretationen* (n. 53), 68, 241; Wecklein, 587–9: Robert, *Oidipus* ii. 100, Smyth, ii. 378, Mette, 38–43; Ferrari, 351–65.

[94] The Catalogue and one other source give *Argeioi;* a female chorus is perhaps more likely. M. Schmidt's suggestion (*Philologus* 16 (1860), 161–2) of *Argeia* (daughter of Adrastos and wife of Polyneikes) is also possible (cf. Statius, *Theb.* 12.105 ff., Hyg. *Fab.* 72), though the Kapaneus fragment (fr. 17) argues against it.

[95] Among those favoring the *Nemea* Droysen is followed by Wilamowitz, Robert, Schmid, Mette, and Ferrari. Wecklein, on the other hand, because he agreed with Hermann's linking of *Nemea* to *Hypsipyle* (n. 97), preferred the *Epigonoi*; so also Smyth, though probably not for the same reasons.

[96] Bakch. 9.10–20; Hyp. to Pind. *Nem.*; Apollod. *Bibl.* 3.6.4; Hyg. *Fab.* 273.

[97] Euripides here followed (or invented) a version of the myth which brought Hypsipyle to Nemea to care for the infant Opheltes, son of Lykourgos (cf. Webster (n. 19), 211–15); hence the *Nemea* is sometimes linked with Aischylos' *Hypsipyle* (Hermann, *Opusc.* vii. 205–6; Wecklein, 672–4; Séchan, 341–2). But Euripides' highly melodramatic plot, with Hypsipyle's sons coming to find her, is not likely to have been the subject of Aischylos' play, nor would a drama about the child's *mother* (Eurydike, not Nemea, is her name in Euripides) seem very appropriate to a group of plays otherwise built around the nurse.

[98] The play's one preserved fragment gives no indication of content, but *Epigonoi* is almost never used without reference to the Sons of the Seven against Thebes

considerable gap to bridge (though on the analogy of the Oidipous group not impossible). One other possibility would be to make the *Nemea* the satyr play, with Archemoros' death either ignored (nothing demands that it be the content) or balanced out by the newly-founded games. But all we can really say is that with so many titles there may well be a group hidden here somewhere; Aischylos' purpose in putting it together, if he did so, is far less obvious.

(15) *Argo–Lemnioi–Hypsipyle–Kabeiroi*[s?]. At least three of these plays concern the adventures of Jason, but their actions, though they all revolve around the quest for the Fleece, are not demonstrably related.[99] Of the *Argo* (probably subtitled 'Rowers') we are told that the ship had a speaking beam and that she refused to accept slaves as a crew. The *Lemnioi* exists only in the Catalogue. The *Hypsipyle* recounted how Hypsipyle herself and the other Lemnian women barred the Argonauts from landing until the latter had promised union. And the *Kabeiroi* presented Jason (or at least his men) drunk on stage, presumably as guests of the title figures. Thus the Argo's voyage itself seems the only connecting thread, and even that is not certain in the case of *Lemnioi* (a title which could also indicate the companions of Philoktetes, among other things).[100] Nor can we say for sure which would be the satyr play. E. Maass argued that since the Argo rejected a crew of slaves, the rowers of that play's title must have been free-born Argonauts, not satyrs.[101] But Ferrari's suggestion of satyrs who offer themselves as rowers until the dangers are made

(so Pindar, *Pyth.* 8.41–2; of course the word appears more generically at *Septem* 903, but there it is not the title of a play). The apparent lack of children for Eteokles and Polyneikes in the *Septem* should also be no obstacle to a different view in another drama.

[99] Cf. Welcker (n. 1), 311–18: Mette, 130–2; Ferrari, 165–74.

[100] So Welcker, *RhM* 5 (1837), 466, where *Lemnioi* is proposed as an alternative title for *Philoktetes*. with the Catalogue's inclusion of both explained by the supposition of an otherwise unrecorded *Philoktetes at Troy**. It might be that both attested titles were part of a Philoktetes group, but it is hard to see how the story as we know it could cover much more than one play, and then too we might have expected Dion of Prusa (*Or.* 52) to mention the fact in his survey of the three tragic treatments. It should also be remembered that Lemnians might form a suitable chorus for any play located at Troy (though admittedly one involving Philoktetes would be most appropriate).

[101] Maass (n. 92), 627–8.

clear to them might get around this difficulty. On the other hand, Athenaios' reproach of the inebriation in the *Kabeiroi* is sometimes taken to mean that Aischylos was the first to show excessive drinking in tragedy itself, not just on the tragic stage.[102] Perhaps, however, we overestimate the amount of imbibing that went on in satyr plays. As for the presumed tragedies, Mette and Ferrari both suppose the *Lemnioi* to have related events on Lemnos before Jason's arrival, i.e. the murder of the husbands. Whether we can have a murdered chorus is hard to say; Ahrens's emendation of the Catalogue entry to *Lemniai* would help some, but problems do remain. And while the basic action of the *Hypsipyle* seems clear, its tragic premise and its connection with either *Argo* or *Kabeiroi* are less so.[103] Once again, if there is a tetralogy here, it is well hidden.

(16) *Mysoi–Telephos–* ——– ——[s]. Welcker and Wecklein both refused to consider these two titles part of a single group; though they may of course be right, their assumptions as to the *Mysoi* are questionable, and we do now have evidence of a Sophoklean *Telepheia* with two similar plays.[104] For subject matter there is no lack of material—Auge's pregnancy and imprisonment in a chest, her abandonment of Telephos on Mount Parthenios, his slaying of his uncles the Aleadai, his journey to Mysia and rediscovery of his mother, the defeat of Idas, the combat with the Achaians and wounding by Achilleus, and finally his journey to Argos where Achilleus heals him. For the *Mysoi* we can say with certainty only that it took place in Mysia, and that there was an appeal to the chief priest of the river Kaikos to save someone. The *Telephos* contained an address to

---

[102] Most recently Ferrari, 165–6. In his favor one must add that it is difficult to find a place for the satyrs in a satyric *Kabeiroi*, since the title figures would presumably be the chorus. If there were satyrs, they would probably be the servants who poured the wine, and only one of the Kabeiroi would speak. The arguments in favor of a satyr drama are given by Wecklein, 636–7.

[103] That is to say, we must decide whether the presumed tetralogy is to focus on Jason's adventures (so Welcker) or those of Hypsipyle (Droysen, ii. 237–9). In the latter event the emphasis would be on the Lemnian women's ultimate acceptance of men, as perhaps in the Danaid group; on the other hand, Hypsipyle is not likely to play a part in either *Argo* or *Kabeiroi*, which might seem to favor Jason.

[104] Cf. Welcker (n. 1), 562–3; Wecklein, 670; Mette, 77–99; Ferrari, 79–89. For the Sophoklean group cf. *IG* II² 3091.

Agamemnon; moreover, if the scholion to Ar. *Acharn.* 322 is right, it showed Telephos taking up the infant Orestes at Argos in an effort to secure the healing of his wound. The point has been much debated, since Euripides (whose *Telephos* presented a similar scene) is the expected target of Aristophanes' satire here, but the scholiast may well have cited Aischylos because he was the prior example.[105] Even without this evidence, however, Aischylos' play seems to have had the same theme as the Euripidean *Telephos* and probably Sophokles' *Achaion Syllogos*: Telephos' visit to Argos. The *Mysoi* would then relate an earlier event. Scholars have long conjectured, working from Aristotle's mention of an ἄφωνος ['dumb'] Telephos in a *Mysoi* [*Poet.* 1460ᵃ32], that it concerned Telephos' coming to Mysia for purification after killing his mother's brothers.[106] But Aristotle says nothing about Aischylos in this connection, and his remark likely enough refers rather to Sophokles' *Mysoi,* in which Telephos did seek purification. Aischylos' *Mysoi* could then describe, as Mette holds, Telephos' wounding when the Achaians first landed in Mysia, and a third play might participate in this same close sequence of events, whether before or after the healing (Mette suggests *Iphigeneia,* which is certainly possible if it could be set in Argos). But it must be recognized that with only one play even definitely about Telephos we are on very speculative ground in assuming a tetralogy.

The above survey has attempted to provide a review of the evidence for those groups of Aischylos' plays generally or frequently presumed to constitute legitimate tetralogies. There have of course also been many other arrangements conjectured by individual scholars, and no discussion of the sort intended here will cover all of them. It might, however, be well to at least note several other proposals, such as Welcker's hypothesis of a *Thalamopoioi–Iphigeneia–Hiereiai* set, and Mette's of one including *Philoktetes, Palamedes,* and an unattested *Tenes.*[107] One could also observe (though virtually nothing is known

---

[105] For well-argued support of the scholiast cf. Wecklein, *SB München* 1909, abh. 1, 14–19, and Séchan, 121–7. Wecklein supposes that Telephos threatened to kill the child, Séchan that he merely wished to emphasize his own helplessness.

[106] So Welcker, Wecklein, Séchan, Ferrari. For what it is worth it may be noted that Aristotle's other examples of ἀλογία ['illogicality'] are both Sophoklean.

[107] For Welcker's group cf. *RhM* 5 (1837), 447–66. The *Hiereiai* (who seem to have been priestesses of Artemis) would on this reading attend Iphigeneia in Tauris, but we really know nothing about the play; for doubts on the *Thalamopoioi* in such a

about them) that there are four plays touching on Herakles (*Alkmene, Herakleidai, Kerykes, Leon,* the last two satyric) and two, if they are different, on Sisyphos (*Sisyphos Drapetes, Sisyphos Petrokylistes*).[108] Finally, Aristotle's comments at *Poet.* 18.1456[a]15–19 have been taken by some to mean that Aischylos presented the story of Niobe in several different units, hence a tetralogy; but it may well be too that his criticism is directed at Agathon, and that Aischylos actually handled only a small part of the story in a single play (the attested *Niobe*).[109]

In conclusion I add only one or two brief remarks. It should be clear that the evidence for reconstructing many of the groups in question is painfully thin; nor will arguments from probability always anticipate a playwright who at times certainly wished to surprise his audience. In this respect I have tried to indicate the maximum we can say for certain about each play. Even so there are gaps, and where titles alone remain the dangers are especially high; who would have hesitated to link *Agamemnon* and *Iphigeneia* were there not indications to the contrary? On the other hand, in many of the cases surveyed there is information as to plots, and these often

connection cf. above n. 47. Mette's supposition of a *Tenes** (99–103) stems from P. Oxy. 2256 fr. 53 (fr. 451o53), where Tenes son of Kyknos is purportedly described as leader of the men of Tenedos (island where Philoktetes was bitten); one should note that the references to a 'leader' in the fragment are primarily due to Mette's supplements. *Palamedes* is included because he like Philoktetes was deceived by Odysseus, but this seems more a thematic than a narrative connection.

[108] Welcker, *ATP* 550–9, Wecklein, 716–20, and Mette, 170–2, all suppose separate plays, but say nothing of how they might have been related; Smyth (ii. 457–8) argues for identity, and Lesky (n. 22, 152) notes that the possibility cannot be excluded. In any event all agree that the *Drapetes* was satyric (cf. Guggisberg, above n. 27: 95–7), and that it concerned Sisyphos' return to earth. Our one fragment labeled as from the *Petrokylistes* (fr. 233) also looks satyric, but as Mette points out, the ascription might have been accidentally shifted from the *Drapetes*.

[109] Wilamowitz (n. 53), 57 n. 1 and Schmid (*GGL* 1:2, 189) draw the former conclusion, but the sense of the passage would seem to be that both Euripides and Aischylos (unlike Agathon) knew enough to reduce epic scope to what tragedy could manage. I suppose κατὰ μέρος could mean 'in parts' rather than 'a part', yet it does not entirely follow that Aristotle would find Aischylos less culpable because he told the story of Niobe in three plays rather than one; then again, the *Myrmidones* group does seem to tell the story of the *Iliad* in three parts. For reconstructions of the play cf. Hermann, *Opusc.* iii. 37–58, Séchan, 80–5, and especially Fitton-Brown, *CQ* 4 (1954), 175–80. It may also be useful to append here those remaining titles mentioned by the Catalogue or other sources as Aischylean, but not touched upon in any of the previous discussion: *Atalanta, Glaukos Pontios, Heliades, Theoroi/Isthmiastai, Kallisto, Kerkyon, Kressai, Oreithyia, Propompoi.*

prove to be closely interdependent. A character such as Agamemnon touches on a broad range of time and theme; thus it is not entirely surprising that the *action* of the play bearing his name has nothing directly to do with the death of Iphigeneia. But the same cannot be said of Memnon, or Perseus, or Pentheus, or Aias during the events surrounding his death. In these instances several titles seem to dramatize actions which would normally belong to a single play, sometimes to the point where their reconstruction would be distinctly puzzling without the tetralogy form.[110] The number of and degree of probability for these instances remains a subjective matter, yet it does not seem likely to be less than ten, and if some groups (Jason, Telephos, Semele) are justifiably suspect, others (Herakles?) may have eluded us altogether through lack of evidence. Lest this position be taken too strongly, however, we should also remember that the instance of the unconnected *Persai* production appears supported by the large number of leftover titles offering little or no prospect of linkage. In some of these cases we may overestimate our poet, but surely not in all of them, and thus there is not much point in arguing that Aischylos always used such an approach. On balance I hope to have shown grounds for thinking that the tetralogy is a form typical of Aischylos' dramatic thought, and perhaps peculiarly suited to what he wished to express. Beyond that, and without the poet himself, as another admirer of Aischylos once said, there is only darkness.[111]

---

[110] For example, we should surely have assumed that Aias died in the *Hoplon Krisis*, and Memnon and Pentheus in the dramas bearing their names; yet our evidence shows that each of these plays stopped short of the crucial resolution.

[111] Aristophanes fr. 643 (Edmonds).

2

Tragedy and Reversal:
The Example of the *Persians*

Suzanne Saïd

If tragic action is the story of a reversal, then the earliest surviving tragedy, Aeschylus' *Persians*, is also the tragedy *par excellence*: it deals with a remarkable turnaround of Fate, and consists entirely of a series of reversals. Aeschylus thus gives an exemplary value to an unparalleled disaster by means of a language which is inverted and makes what had seemed to be the very basis of power serve as a demonstration of weakness.

In the *Persians*, as in Herodotus' *Histories*, Persian power rests first and foremost on number.[1] Aeschylus repeatedly emphasizes the significance of an army which does not merely represent the 'élite' ($\overset{\text{\'}}{\alpha}\nu\theta o\varsigma$, cf. 59, 252) of Persia, but moreover 'the power of the whole of Asia' (12), since Xerxes, to form it, has needed 'to empty the vastness of the continent' (718; cf. also 56–7, 61–2, 73, 187).

[*Editor's note.* The author has incorporated some minor corrections. Some of the author's line-references have been transferred from footnotes to the text, with the result that footnote numbers may not correspond to those in the original.]

[1] V. Ghezzo, 'I *Persiani* di Eschilo', *Atti del Istituto Veneto* 98 (1938/9), 427–48, at 433, had already remarked that in the parodos $\pi\hat{\alpha}\varsigma$ ('all'), $\pi o\lambda\acute{u}\varsigma$ ('many'), and $\mu\acute{e}\gamma\alpha\varsigma$ ('great') occur with an extraordinary frequency. The central role of this theme in the *Persians* has been emphasized more recently by H. C. Avery, 'Dramatic devices in Aeschylus' *Persians*', *AJP* 85 (1964), 173–84, at 176–7; E. Petrounias, *Funktion und Thematik der Bilder bei Aischylos* (*Hypomnemata*, 48; Göttingen, 1976), 3–7, 21–2; A. N. Michelini, *Tradition and Dramatic Form in the* Persians *of Aeschylus* (Leiden, 1982), 86–98.

A word like πολύς ('much', 'many') thus recurs like a refrain to describe the multitude of the soldiers who followed Xerxes (25–6, 748, 800, 925) and formerly made up the army of Darius (244, 780), the number of their chariots (46) and their weapons (269), and the immensity of the road which they have travelled (71, 748).

This adjective is itself echoed and amplified by compounds. Thus πολύανδρος ('with many men') describes successively the vast populations of Asia (73), the multitude of the Persians (533), and the peoples of Ionia over whom Darius once reigned (899); πολυθρέμμων ('much-nourishing') expresses the number of people nourished by the Nile (33); πολύχειρ ('with many soldiers') and πολυναύτας ('with many sailors'), which describe Xerxes in line 83, emphasize the number of his troops and his ships.

Πλῆθος ('multitude'), which is attested in Aeschylus almost only in the *Persians*,[2] (it has even been described as a 'theme-word'[3]) serves also to emphasize the number of the Egyptian rowers in the anapaests which open the tragedy (40) and the numerical superiority of Xerxes' fleet in the messenger speech (337, 342, 352, 413).

It remains to cite more concrete words like στῖφος ('mass') and ὄχλος ('crowd') which describe the mass of the foot-soldiers who have left Persia (40) and of the ships which took part at Salamis (366), or the crowd of the Lydians (13) and of the companions of the King (955).

This impression of mass is further accentuated by adjectives like πάμμεικτος and παμμιγής (both words literally mean 'all-mixed', i.e. 'various', 'diverse'), which are perhaps Aeschylean coinages and which set in relief the disparate character of Xerxes' army and the mixture of peoples and arms of which it is made up (53, 269, 903).[4]

The number of the Persians is also made vivid in a more concrete manner by exact figures, by evocative images, and by impressive lists of proper names.

For Aeschylus is not content just to speak of 'innumerable crowds' (40). On one occasion he cites a precise number and gives the complement of the Persian fleet at Salamis, which is 'a thousand

---

[2] Its only other certain occurrence is at *Supp.* 469.

[3] Cf. H. G. Edinger, *Vocabulary and Imagery in Aeschylus'* Persians (diss. Princeton, 1961), 107, 127; Michelini (n. 1), 88.

[4] Cf. the remarks of Michelini (n. 1), 88.

ships, without counting another 207 ships of exceptional speed' (341–3). He makes even more vivid the importance of this figure and the disproportion which exists between the forces of the Great King and those of his adversaries when he mentions that 'for the Greeks, the number of their ships was about 300' and that 'a further ten formed the reserve' (338–40).

But more often he uses numbers in a more subtle and indirect way. He thus mentions in the messenger speech and in the exodos the troops commanded by various officers in Xerxes' army, whether they are 'the 10,000 horsemen of Artembares (302), the 30,000 black horsemen of Atrames (315),[5] the 'five times fifty galleys' of Tharybis (323), or the tens of thousands of soldiers which the King's Eye was charged to count (978–82). He also mentions military ranks which include an indication of number, like χιλίαρχος (304), 'commander of a thousand men' or μυριοταγός (993),[6] 'commander of ten thousand men'. He thus suggests significant numbers of troops without giving precise numbers for them.

Besides number, Aeschylus has not forgotten the prosperity (ὄλβος)[7] of the Persian empire. He frequently mentions the wealth (πλοῦτος)[8]

---

[5] The reference is to Artames if one follows H. Weil and transposes line 315 after line 318, as also do P. Mazon, H. D. Broadhead, J. de Romilly, and D. L. Page. If one wants to keep this line in its place, as do Wilamowitz and, after him, P. Groeneboom (H. J. Rose does not commit himself), it is necessary to accept a lacuna between lines 314 and 315, since it is difficult to see how the same leader can be described successively as 'the leader of 10,000 men' (314) and 'he who leads 30,000 black horsemen' (315).

[6] This correction by Dindorf has been accepted by the majority of editors.

[7] This ὄλβος ('prosperity') which is sometimes described as 'immense' (251–2) and as 'great' (826), is generally attached to Darius who is the creator of it (164, 709, 756).

[8] The importance of this theme in the *Persians* has been recognized by M. Delcourt, 'Orient et Occident chez Eschyle', *Mélanges Bidez* (*Annuaire de l'Inst. de Philol. Orient.*, 1934), 233–54, at 248; Ghezzo (n. 1), 446; O. Hiltbrunner, *Wiederholungs- und Motiv-technik bei Aischylos* (Bern, 1950), 41–2; G. Clifton, 'The mood of the *Persai* of Aeschylus', *G&R* 10 (1963), 111–17, at 112–13; Avery (n. 1), 177–8; W. Kierdorf, *Erlebnis und Darstellung der Perserkriege* (*Hypomnemata* 16; Göttingen, 1966), 51; M. Anderson, 'The imagery of the *Persians*', *G&R* 19 (1972), 166–74, at 170–1 = I. McAuslan & P. Walcot (eds.), *Greek Tragedy* (Greece and Rome Studies 2; Oxford, 1993), 29–37, at 32–3; and W. Thalmann, 'Xerxes' rags: some problems in Aeschylus' *Persians*', *AJP* 101 (1980), 260–82, at 267.

which is the tangible evidence for it and the gold which is its material symbol.[9]

He mentions also the opulent dwellings (τῶν ἀφνεῶν ἑδράνων, 3) of its kings, and the luxury (ἁβρότης) which characterizes the manner of life of the Lydians (ἁβροδιαίτων Λυδῶν, 41) and which manifests itself even in the sumptuous counterpanes which cover the beds of the Persians (λέκτωρ εὐνὰς ἁβροχίτωνας, 543). He emphasizes the prosperity of the cities of Ionia (τὰς εὐκτεάνους, 899) which once formed part of the Persian empire in the reign of Darius.

More concretely, the lustre of Persian gold illuminates the beginning of the tragedy. The adjective πολύχρυσος, 'rich in gold', occurs four times in the parodos to describe the dwelling of Xerxes (3), his army (9), and the cities of his empire like Sardis (45), capital of Lydia (that is to say a country which for the Greeks was synonymous with wealth, as one can see from Herodotus)[10] or Babylon (53).[11] When Atossa appears on the stage for the first time, Aeschylus emphasizes that she comes out of a 'palace adorned with gold' (χρυσεοστόλμους δόμους, 159). This gold glitters even in the ancestry of Xerxes, who is χρυσόγονος (80),[12] 'born of gold', because he is a descendant of Perseus, son of Danaë and of Zeus who had taken the form of a shower of gold. It gleams also in the names of cities in his empire like Chryse,[13] from where comes Matallus, one of the leaders fallen at Salamis (314).

The word πλοῦτος ('wealth') is spoken by Atossa when she mentions in line 163 the 'great wealth of the Persian empire' and acknowledges, in line 169, that this wealth is such that one could find no fault with it. It recurs in the mouth of the messsenger, who greets a Persian land which is a 'haven of immense riches' (250). In the scene in which Darius appears, this πλοῦτος ('wealth'), like the ὄλβος ('prosperity'), is presented as the the fruit of the military exploits of the dead king (751, 755).

[9] See R. P. Winnington-Ingram, 'Zeus in the *Persae*', *JHS* 93 (1973), 210–19, at 214 = *Studies in Aeschylus* (Cambridge, 1983), 8.

[10] The theme of gold runs right through the story of Croesus, with the description of the golden offerings of Gyges and of Croesus (1.14, 50–1, 52, 92) and the mention of the gold dust which comes down from Tmolus (1.93).

[11] In Book 1 of the *Histories*, Herodotus mentions a whole series of gold objects in Babylon (1.181, 183).

[12] This reading is adopted by all editors with the exception of D. L. Page.

[13] This Chryse has been identified with Chrysa, the city in the Troad which Apollo protects in Book 1 of the *Iliad*. But P. Groeneboom (ad loc.), after Wilamowitz, thinks that this name was invented by Aeschylus to symbolize the wealth of the orient. In fact, it is possible that Aeschylus refers here to the Chrysa in Asia Minor, but that he only does so because of the connotations of its name, because this city was itself of little importance and could not in any case supply a contingent of 30,000 horsemen. Cf. R. Lattimore, 'Aeschylus on the defeat of Xerxes', *Classical Studies in Honor of W. A. Oldfather* (Urbana, Ill., 1943), 82–93, at 86.

Persian luxury finally manifests itself on the stage, with the first entrance of Atossa and the apparition of Darius.

After the parodos, Atossa actually arrived on a chariot, surrounded by all the luxury of the Orient.[14] For when she returns to the stage to bring offerings to Darius, after having learned from the messenger of the defeat suffered by the Persians at Salamis, she strongly marks the contrast between this appearance and the one which had preceded it: 'I return here', she says, 'from the palace, without my chariot and without my former pomp' (607–9). The chorus greeted her in lines 150–2, moreover, in terms which indirectly confirm the splendour of her appearance. It did in fact compare the queen to 'the light which shines from the eyes of the gods' ($\theta\epsilon\hat{\omega}\nu$ ἴσον ὀφθαλμοῖς φάος, 150–1). This recherché expression is undoubtedly just an equivalent to the adjective ἰσόθεος ('equal to the gods'). But it is also sufficiently ambiguous for the M-scholiast to have been able to see an allusion to the dazzle caused by the entrance of Atossa. He understands, in fact, that the splendour of the queen is as great in the eyes of the chorus as that of the gods.

Darius would also undoubtedly have appeared in all his glory. This was in any case how the chorus invited him to manifest himself, when it prayed to him saying: 'King of old, king of old, ah! come, appear on the very top of your tomb; raise up the saffron-dyed slipper on your foot, make visible to us the peak of your royal tiara' (658–62). The references to the 'saffron-dyed slipper' (κροκόβαπτον εὔμαριν) and the 'royal tiara' (βασιλείου τιήρας) do indeed combine sumptuousness with local colour. For the εὔμαρις ('slipper') is a form of footwear characteristic of barbarians, as is shown by line 1370 of Euripides' *Orestes* βαρβάροις εὐμάρισιν ('barbarian slippers'). But at the same time saffron, like purple, serves to symbolize royal pomp. One thinks, for example, of Iphigenia's robe died with saffron in the *Agamemnon* (κρόκου βαφάς, Aesch. *Ag.* 239). Similarly, the 'tiara', which in Herodotus is the typical headdress of the Persians,[15] is

---

[14] The importance of Atossa's entrance has recently been demonstrated by Thalmann (n. 8), 268–9. The problems which it poses from the point of view of staging have been well analysed by O. Taplin, *The Stagecraft of Aeschylus* (Oxford, 1977), 75–9.

[15] In Herodotus, the tiara is the typical headdress of the Persians, and he gives this name to the 'cap' (πίλος) which they wear (3.12; 7.61). It is represented on a whole series of Attic vases studied by A. Bovon, 'La représentation des guerriers perses et la

described here as 'royal'. It is undoubtedly difficult, on the basis of these two symbolic details, to imagine exactly what Darius' costume could have been in the *Persians*, even with the help of Herodotus and of representations in art.[16] But it is in any case credible that these two references were confirmed by what the spectator could see in the theatre.

Finally, and perhaps above all, Aeschylus magnifies Persian power by the systematic use of epic language and imagery.[17]

He transports the spectator back to the archaic world of chariot combat with terms like ἱππιοχάρμης ('delighting in horses', 29, 97, 105; cf. Hom. *Il.* 24.257; *Od.* 11.259), ἱππηλάτας (126), and ἵππων ἐλατήρ (32) which is no more than a disaggregation of the Homeric compound ἱππηλάτα (*Il.* 18.331; 19.311; *Od.*3.436, 444, 607). To refer to archers he once uses a periphrasis which improves upon Homer as one can see from comparing the phrase τοξουλκῷ λήματι πιστούς (55), 'confident in their skill in drawing the bow' with the Homeric expression τόξοισι πίσυνος (*Il.* 5.205), 'confident in his bow'.

He also applies to the leader of the Persian army the Homeric title ὄρχαμος[18] στρατοῦ (129, 'chief of the army') and twice uses the Homeric metaphor of the king as 'shepherd of the people' (ποιμὴν λαῶν). This appears first in the parodos, where Xerxes' troops are compared to a 'flock' (ποιμανόριον, 75), then in the mouth of Atossa, who identifies the absolute ruler with a 'shepherd' (ποιμάνωρ, 241). But these two expressions take on a new relief in the *Persians* firstly because of their form: they are both Aeschylean coinages. But also

notion de barbare dans la première moitié du cinquième siècle', *BCH* 87 (1963), 579–602. See also on this point A. S. F. Gow, 'Notes on the *Persae* of Aeschylus', *JHS* 48 (1928), 133–58, at 144 n. 30.

[16] This is what Gow (n. 15), 142–52, tries to do, relying on the texts of Herodotus (7.61) and Xenophon (*An.* 1.5.8; *Cyr.* 7.3.13) as well as on Greek and Persian artistic representations. With the exception of the tiara and the εὔμαρις, about which we have precise information (according to Pollux 7.90 it was a deerskin slipper), nothing in the text allows us to imagine in detail the costume of Darius.

[17] The exceptional importance of epic borrowings and Homerisms in the *Persians* has been emphasized both by W. B. Stanford, *Aeschylus in his Style* (Dublin, 1942), 26 and by A. Sideras, *Aeschylus Homericus: Untersuchungen zu den Homerismen der aischyleischen Sprache* (*Hypomnemata*, 31; Göttingen, 1971), 265.

[18] ὄρχαμος (-ον) ἀνδρῶν: *Il.* 2.837; 6.99; 12.110; *Od.* 3.400, 454, 482; 10.224; 14.22, 121; 15.351, 389; 16.36; 17.184; 20.185, 254. As Sideras (n. 17), 129, remarks, this word is not attested in either Sophocles or Euripides.

from their context: they connect with the image of the yoke[19] which symbolizes Xerxes' wish to constrain men and nature to obey his designs.

Xerxes is even described in line 80 as ἰσόθεος φώς, 'mortal equal to the gods', and the epic coloration of the passage is accentuated by the appearance at the end of the strophe of a formula which in Homer is always placed at the end of a line. But what was no more than a fairly trite epithet in the *Iliad* (it is applied to a whole series of second-rank heroes)[20] takes on more significance here. This adjective does in fact only appear in the *Persians*, where it is applied not only to Xerxes but also to his father Darius (856), and it is further reinforced in the parodos by the adjective θεῖος (75, 'godlike') which characterizes the 'flock' driven by Xerxes.

In the second strophe of the parodos, ('In his eyes flashes the dark-blue glance of the bloody dragon. With many soldiers and many sailors, speeding on his Syrian chariot, he leads an Ares with triumphant bow against heroes famous for the spear', 81–6), the king and his army take on veritably mythical dimensions. This passage has often been compared with the oracle in which the Pythia, if we are to believe Herodotus, had predicted to the Athenians the destruction of their city by 'fire and furious Ares driving his Syrian chariot' (7.140).[21] But the amplification which Aeschylus gives to the oracle's formulation deserves to be emphasized. On the one hand, he identifies the Persian army with the god of war by taking up in ἐπάγει τοξόδαμνον Ἄρη ('he leads an Ares with triumphant bow') the ποιμανόριον θεῖον ἐλαύνει ('he drives his divine flock') of lines 74–5. On the other hand, he suggests a resemblance between the King of Persia and the god who presides over battles by showing a Xerxes 'who speeds on', like the Ares of the oracle, 'his Syrian chariot'.

Described by the adjectives πολύχειρ (83, 'with many soldiers', but literally 'many-handed') and πολυναύτας (83, 'with many sailors'),

---

[19] This central metaphor (well studied by Petrounias (n. 1), 7–15, and Michelini (n. 1), 81–7) occurs three times in the parodos (50, 71–2, 130).

[20] This epithet, which appears 12 times in the *Iliad*, is applied not only to Priam (3.310), Ajax (11.472), Menelaus (23.569), and Patroclus (9. 211; 11.644), but also to Euryalus (2.265; 23.677), Machaon (4.212), Ereuthalion (7.137), Socus (11.428), Melanippus (15.559), and Meriones (16.632).

[21] This comparison has been made by commentators both on Aeschylus (e.g. P. Groeneboom, H. J. Rose) and on Herodotus (e.g. How–Wells).

the King ends by becoming one with his innumerable troops and
vessels, and his 'dark-blue glance' (κυάνεον δέργμα, 80–1) further
contributes to identifying him with his ships with their 'dark-blue
eyes' (κυανώπιδες νᾶες, 559–60).[22]

Xerxes is transformed into a veritable monster. One can indeed
compare this king in whom 'flashes the . . . glance of a bloody dragon'
(81–2) to a creature like Typhoeus, 'with his hundred fearsome
snake-heads' (Hes. *Theog.* 825) which is characterized by Hesiod,
and also by Aeschylus, by the fire which flashes from its eyes.[23] And
πολύχειρ ('many-handed'), evokes by association not only the mass
of the Persian army but also the many hands of Briareus in the *Iliad*
(1.402–4) or of the Hundred-Handers in the *Theogony* (150–1).

In the following strophe: 'Who then will be capable of withstand-
ing this great human flood? As well wish to contain the invincible
surge of the sea with mighty dykes! Irresistible is the army of Persia
and its people valiant of heart' (87–92), the irresistible power of the
Persian army is conveyed by the image of a river which carries away
everything in its path, and then by that of the surge of the sea.

The first image comes directly from Book 5 of the *Iliad*,[24] where
Homer compares Diomedes, who 'goes furiously over the plain' (87)
and throws the ranks of the Trojans into confusion, to an 'over-
flowing river swollen with storm-rains, whose swift waters have
destroyed all the dykes. The dykes do not stop it any more than the
secure   defences   shoring   the   flourishing   orchards'   (87–90).
The ῥεύματι ('flood') of line 88 of the *Persians* does indeed recall
the ῥέων ('flowing') with which Homer described the torrent of a
river in flood (*Il.* 5.88), and one can see in Aeschylus' ἐχυροῖς ἔρκεσιν
εἴργειν ('keep out with secure defences') a reminiscence of Homer's
τὸν δ᾽ οὔτ᾽ ἄρ τε γέφυραι ἐεργμέναι ἰσχανόωσιν οὔτ᾽ ἄρα ἔρκεα ἴσχει
(*Il.* 5. 89–90, 'the sturdy dykes cannot hold it back nor can the banks
restrain it').

---

[22] This variant of the Homeric epithet κυανόπρωρος ('with dark-blue prow', *Il.*
15.693 etc.) can be understood as an exact transposition of the Homeric epithet (with
the prow being compared to a face) or as an allusion to the eye which was painted on
the prow of the ships.

[23] Cf. Hes. *Theog.* 828 and Aesch. *PV* 356.

[24] As has been seen by D. van Nes, *Die maritime Bildersprache des Aischylos* (diss.
Utrecht, 1963), 30, and Sideras (n. 17), 250–2.

But the image of the river is soon replaced in Aeschylus by that of the waves of the sea with the ἄμαχον κῦμα θαλάσσας ('irresistible sea-wave') of line 90 which symbolizes the 'irresistible' (ἀπρόσοιστος) power of the Persian army. One could also cite here a passage in Book 15 of the *Iliad* where the assault of Hector who 'hurls himself into the throng' is compared to a 'violent wave' (*Il.* 15.624–5).

These epic images, which culminate in the comparison of the army to a swarm of bees (σμῆνος ὡς μελισσᾶν, 128–9), do not merely suggest force. They form part of an ensemble which is designed to reveal the essence of an absolutism which concentrates all powers in the hands of a single man.

The parodos in fact suggests the transformation of many into one, with the description of the troops who converge from all parts. The Persians come first: 'Leaving Susa and Ecbatana and the ancient ramparts of Cissia, they departed...' (16–18). A second group comes from Egypt: 'The great and life-giving Nile also sent its people' (40–1). They are followed by the neighbours of Tmolus and the Mysians (49–52). Babylon too 'sends' warriors (52–5). The list culminates with a phrase which expresses the gathering of troops and their union under a single will: 'Flocking from the *whole of Asia*, follow the peoples wielding the short sword, obedient to the dread commands of the King' (56–8). The army is unified to the point of being no more than a single being 'with numerous arms and numerous sailors' (83), which thus appears endowed with a monstrous power. The comparison of the army to an immense flood of humanity (μεγάλῳ ῥεύματι φωτῶν, 88) similarly expresses this fusion into an indistinct mass of a series of elements which have lost all individuality.

A comparison with the Catalogue of Ships in Book 2 of the *Iliad* affords a better understanding of the overall purpose of the parodos. One can indeed contrast this process of fusion in the parodos with a catalogue which starts from an original state of confusion and proceeds to describe the constitution of a series of discrete units. In the *Iliad*, indeed, the initial impression of a confused mass is suggested by two images: 'the vast numbers of the Achaeans' (464) are successively compared to 'the vast numbers of winged birds' (459) and to 'the close-packed swarms of flies' (469). Exact numbers are arrived at by a process of discrimination and classification which is expressed by a third image: the warriors are compared to great flocks of goats which the herdsmen have no difficulty in 'separating' (ῥεῖα διακρίνωσιν, 475) 'when they have mixed together at pasture' (ἐπεί κε νομῷ μιγέωσιν, 475). The Catalogue itself begins at the moment when the Achaeans divide up in order to regroup in contingents, when 'the commanders organized (διεκόσμεον) their men, some here, some there' (476). Homer describes these contingents individually, giving on each occasion the origin of the warriors, the names of their commanders, and the number of their ships. His conclusion: 'Tell me now, Muses, who were the best—of the men and of the horses—of those who followed the sons of Atreus' (761–2), accentuates the impression of an irreducible diversity which alone makes the comparison possible. In this Greek world, the commander cannot be a man who absorbs and incarnates the entire army, as in the barbarian world. He is only its most prominent element, as is shown by the simile which compares Agamemnon to a bull who is pre-eminent among the beasts of the herd, and stands out from the cows which surround him (480–1).

But the parodos only displays Persian power in order better to measure the magnitude of the reversal. After the impressive picture of a multitude of men and a mass of riches united under the command of a single will there follows, after the defeat at Salamis and even as early as the dream of Atossa which prefigures it, the description of a disaster and a disintegration which culminates in the appearance of a king solitary and 'naked' (1036), deprived both of the number which constituted his power and of the wealth which gave him his brilliance.

Thus number, which once described the immensity of the Persian army, now expresses no more than the magnitude of the disaster.

After Salamis, πολύς ('much', 'many') describes the number of the dead (925–7) or of those who grieve for them (287). It emphasizes the multiplicity of the troubles which have crashed down upon the Persians and of the sufferings which they have brought with them (330, 707, 843–4, 845–6). It describes the significance of the troops and the armaments of the expedition only better to contrast with them the tiny number of survivors and the paltry number of arrows brought back by Xerxes (510, 734, 800, 1024).[25] Its compounds like

[25] In Herodotus there is a similar juxtaposition of a great number and a small number in order to dramatize the Persian losses at Plataea (9.70) and Mycale (9.107).

πολυπενθής (547, 'much-mourning'), πολύκλαυτος (674, 'much-lamented'), and πολύδακρυς (940, 'with many tears') express the immensity of the grief and the tears which have followed upon the defeat. And πολύανδρος (533, 899, 'with many men') merely refers to the multitudes destroyed or delivered from the yoke of the Persian empire.

Similarly, the 'crowd' (ὄχλος) of warriors is merely an absence about which the chorus questions Xerxes in line 956. It is replaced, as the chorus feared (121, 124), by the 'crowd' (ὅμιλος) of women in mourning as well as by the 'dense mass' (ταρφύς τις μυριάς, 926–7) of those who have perished.

Πλῆθος ('multitude'), which is a key word for the Persians, no longer describes the menacing crowd of barbarians, but the crowd of troubles and that of the dead (429, 432, 477).

The image of the sea, which in the parodos expressed the irresistible power of the Persian army, is also inverted and serves to describe the 'wave of troubles' which breaks upon the Persians and the 'gulf of misfortunes' which swallows them up.[26]

In order to make more tangible the magnitude of the disaster, Aeschylus also employs figures, descriptions, and catalogues.

Without ever putting a precise figure on the total number of losses suffered by the Persian army, Aeschylus indirectly suggests an impressive number of dead by means of subtle use of number-words. He does indeed accompany the names of certain of the fallen leaders by mentioning the troops which they commanded. The messenger thus mentions the 10,000 horsemen of Artembares (302), the 30,000 horsemen of Artames (315), and the five times fifty galleys of Tharybis (323), while the chorus mentions at the end of the tragedy the tens of thousands counted by the King's eye (986). These officers are also described by a title which sometimes includes an indication of number like χιλίαρχος (304, 'commander of 1,000 men'), μυριόνταρχος and μυριοταγός (315, 993; both words mean 'commander of 10,000 men'). Each death thus turns out to be amplified and to signify symbolically the annihilation of an entire contingent. Number itself serves to

[26] Cf. 433 (κακῶν δὴ πέλαγος, 'sea of troubles'), 599 (κλύδων κακῶν, 'wave of troubles'), 465, 712 (κακῶν βάθος, 'depth of troubles'). On this image, which is particularly appropriate to a disaster which is the consequence of a defeat at sea, see van Nes (n. 24), 35–7.

demonstrate the impossibility of a complete enumeration: the sum of the troubles is such that the messenger could not recount them even if he were to occupy *ten* days with a detailed account (429–430).

The scale of the losses is made apparent also through concrete description of blood and corpses. All the horror of Plataea is expressed by two images: 'the bloody offering' (πελανὸς αἱματοσφαγής, 816) consecrated by the Dorian spear and the 'piles of corpses' (θῖνες νεκρῶν, 818) heaped up on the battlefield. Salamis becomes the tomb of Persian power. For the 'multitude' (πλῆθος) of Persian ships has been replaced by 'a mass of wreckage filling the sea' (ναυαγίων πλήθουσα ... ἀκταὶ δὲ νεκρῶν ... ἐπλήθυον, 419–20) and the countless multitude of their warriors is no more than an army of corpses which 'fills up' the shores, reefs, and approaches of Salamis (272–3, 421), and hides the sea under a torrent of blood (419–20).

The ignominy of a defeat which reduces the vanquished to the status of objects is also expressed by images which show these fearsome warriors buffeted by waves, lacerated by rocks, and devoured by fish (275–7, 568–71, 576, 577–8). It appears above all in a famous comparison which is echoed some fifty years later in the *Wasps* of Aristophanes (1087), that with tunny-fishing. By comparing the Persians to 'tunnies or a catch of fish' which the Greeks 'strike, beating with broken oars and fragments of wreckage' (424–6), Aeschylus transforms what had been a battle into a massacre of defenceless victims by means of an image borrowed from a familiar reality and a form of fishing still in use on the Mediterranean coasts.[27] But he also alludes to an epic model, perhaps Achilles' massacre of the Trojans in a Scamander red with blood, or even more Odysseus' massacre of the Suitors. In Book 21 of the *Iliad*, the Trojans flee and seek a refuge under the overhanging banks 'like fish who flee before an enormous dolphin' (22–3). Odysseus' exploit in Book 22 of the *Odyssey* culminates in the image of the Suitors 'lying in great numbers in dust and blood, like fish which fishermen have pulled from the foaming sea into a hollow on the shore...' (383–6).[28] At the same time, the poet underlines the ironical game of a Fate which

[27] For the reality on which this image is based, see the references assembled by van Nes (n. 24), 161–2 and Petrounias (n. 1), 4–5.

[28] This comparison has been made by Sideras (n. 17), 247–8.

makes use of the wreckage of ships to destroy landsmen who have become sailors in defiance of the will of the gods.

The description of the final catastrophe exceeds in amplitude even that of the original power. To the catalogue in the parodos, which suggested an immense number of warriors by an accumulation of 17 proper names in 30 lines, correspond two lists of victims which are at least as long: the messenger cites 17 names in 26 lines, while the chorus, in the exodos, laments the absence of 26 commanders in about 45 lines. There is thus an ironic counterpoint between the list in the parodos and those which follow it, which is strongly marked by the repetition of names. Tharybis (51, 323, 971), Artembares (29, 302, 972), and Ario-mardos (38, 321, 968) appear in all three catalogues, while Arcteus (44, 312), Arsames (37, 308), Pharandakes (31, 957), and Sousiskanes (34, 960) appear both in the parodos and in one of the two lists of victims. But rather than a strict correspondence, one should speak here of resonant echoes. Various names are lightly changed from one list to another: Amistres (21) is replaced by Amistris (320), Masistres (30) becomes Masistras (971), and Seisames (322) changes to Sesamas (982). Other names recur denoting different persons: Ariomardos, who in the parodos is 'the master of ancient Thebes' (38) causes grief in *Sardis* by his death (321), and Arkteus, described by the chorus as a man from Sardis (44), becomes by contrast an inhabitant of the banks of the *Nile* in the messenger speech (312).

But the continuity of form and even of sound which exists between the parodos, the messenger speech, and the exodos ultimately serves only to emphasize more clearly the reversal and the catastrophe suffered by the Persians.

The parodos presented a parade of all the splendour of the barbarian army in a description modelled on epic, and in particular on the Catalogue of Ships in Book 2 of the *Iliad*. The messenger speech, which is also inspired by an epic form and is a direct descendant of the Homeric ἀνδροκτασίαι ('slaughters of men'),[29] describes the multitude of those who have perished in order to contrast them with a king who appears as the sole survivor. When Atossa asks the messenger 'who are those among the commanders

---

[29] These two epic forms are, moreover, essentially identical, as has been well shown by C. R. Beye, 'Homeric battle narrative and catalogues', *HSCP* 88 (1964), 345–73.

who have not perished?' (296–7), he does in fact confine himself to
one name and one line: 'So far as Xerxes is concerned, he lives and
sees the light' (Ξέρξης μὲν αὐτὸς ζῇ τε καὶ φάος βλέπει, 299). But he
replies to the second part of the question: 'who also are those we
must lament and who, appointed to positions of command, have
died and left their places vacant?' (297–8) by a catalogue of the dead.
The catalogue is impressive first of all for the quality of the victims:
these dead, who stand out from the anonymous mass, are not merely
names; they take on a certain individuality thanks to the details
which characterize them and recall their title, their geographical
origin, or their courage. But above all by its incompleteness: for
these dead represent no more than a tiny fraction of the victims of
rank, and Aeschylus' supreme skill lies in leaving the series open
when he makes the messenger say: 'These are the commanders of
whom I have made mention; but our troubles are countless: I have
only told you a small part of them' (329–30).

Only the king survives. But in the messenger speech, this king, sole
survivor in the midst of a multitude of corpses, still appears in all his
glory and represents for Atossa 'a bright light... brilliant day after
gloomy night' (300–1). The effect of the exodos is to deprive him of
this glory.

When he appears on the stage, the sovereign, who concentrated in
his own hands the power of the whole of Asia and threatened Greece by
the multitude of his troops and of his ships, is no more than a
single defeated man, abandoned by everyone, deprived even of the
company of those few survivors who have succeeded in reaching their
homeland with him (508–12, 734). He commands nothing more than
an army of shades, which is described in a final catalogue. The insistent
questions of the chorus: 'Where is the rest of the multitude of your
soldiers? Where are your lieutenants Pharandakes, Sousas?... And
where is your Pharnouchos? Where is lord Seualkes?...' (955–61,
966–71, 978–85) serve only to emphasize all the more the void left
by these dead.

Xerxes himself emphasizes the isolation which will henceforth be
his lot. He refers to himself with τόδε ('this') in line 1017: ὁρᾷς τὸ
λοιπὸν τόδε τᾶς ἐμᾶς στολᾶς; ('Do you see this remnant of my
expedition?') as all that remains of the forces which he had raised.
He indicates by τόνδε ('this') in line 1020 a quiver which represents

all that remains of the thousands of arrows which armed the Persians. Henceforth, 'stripped of all escort' (γυμνός εἰμι προπομπῶν, 1036), he is reduced to his own powers, that is to say to nothing.

By his presence, alone, the king shows the nothingness of number which was already expressed by the juxtaposition of μάταν ('in vain') and πολλά ('many') in lines 268–71: 'Alas! Greece! it is then *in vain* that the assemblage of *thousands* of arms of every kind have crossed from Asia to an enemy land, the land of Greece'.

Number, which was a factor in the power of Asia, that is to say in a world where people accept absorption into the unity of a régime dominated by a single will, has thus lost all its utility. It has even been transformed into an important factor in the defeat, from the moment when the Persians crossed over into Greece. This would be the logical conclusion of Aeschylus' tragedy, or rather the conclusion which *we* would logically draw. But it is also an idea which is clearly expressed in the text of Aeschylus itself, both in the description of the battle of Salamis and in the account of the retreat of Xerxes.

At Salamis, if the battle, at first evenly balanced, turns into a disaster, it is precisely because of 'the multitude of ships' (πλῆθος ... νεῶν) which 'was crowded together (ἤθροιστ') in a narrow strait' (413–14).[30] Number, in such conditions, far from constituting an advantage and a help (ἀρωγή, 414) is merely an obstacle and a factor in destruction: the Persian ships 'collided and rammed each other with their bronze prows, and shattered all their rowing equipment' (415–16). In the *Persians*, this terminology does not serve only to illustrate, as it would do in Thucydides, the tactical advantages of a 'confined space' (στενοχωρία) for a fleet with inferior numbers but greater skill at manoeuvre.[31] The intelligence which the Greeks demonstrate by encircling the Persian fleet (Ἑλληνικαί τε νῆες οὐκ ἀφρασμόνως κύκλῳ πέριξ ἔθεινον, 417–18) is immediately emphasized. This description expresses in the first place in a very concrete

---

[30] Herodotus also emphasizes on three occasions how large numbers, far from constituting an advantage, become a factor in defeat when they are concentrated in a narrow space: first at Thermopylae (7.177), where it is the result of deliberate tactics by the Greeks, then at Artemisium (8.16), where Herodotus shows, as Aeschylus does at Salamis, how a fleet suffers from self-inflicted damage, and finally at Plataea (9.70).

[31] On this comparison, see J. de Romilly, *Histoire et raison chez Thucydide* (Paris, 1956), 121–2.

way one of the key ideas in tragedy: number, which ought to have assured Xerxes' victory, as the messenger mentions when he says: 'If it had just been a question of number, then you can be quite sure that the barbarian would have triumphed' (πλήθους μὲν ἂν σαφ᾽ ἴσθ᾽ ἕκατι βαρβάρων ναῦς ἂν κρατῆσαι, 337–8), played a decisive part in his defeat.

What applies at sea and for the fleet applies also on land and for the army, for the land 'fights on the side of the Greeks (ξύμμαχος κείνοις πέλει, 792) by destroying by famine *multitudes which are excessively numerous*' (κτείνουσα λιμῷ τοὺς ὑπερπόλλους ἄγαν, 794). That is why sending an expedition even greater in number (στράτευμα πλεῖον, 791) is useless: on Greek land, according to the wise Darius, number is merely a form of excess as is emphasized both by ἄγαν ('excessively') and ὑπερπόλλους ('numerous'), an excess (ὕβρις) which necessarily brings disaster (ἄτη) in its train.

The same applies to wealth as to number.[32] The spectacle of the immense prosperity of the Persian empire, made concrete by gold and by the splendour which surrounds the first entrance of the queen, serves only to make more tangible the ruin which follows.

After Salamis, wealth is merely a notable absence or a past which is mentioned with nostalgia.

When he enters on to the stage, the messenger simultaneously announces in lines 251–2 the destruction of the Persian army and the *annihilation* of great wealth (κατέφθαρται πολύς | ὄλβος). Darius makes Xerxes the epitome of one who has 'poured away great prosperity' (ὄλβον ἐκχέῃ μέγαν, 826) by his desire for something more.

With this prosperity which has been destroyed is contrasted the former splendour of the reign of Darius. These references to the 'happy fortune' of a king who surpassed the felicity of all other mortals, to the 'immense wealth' which he acquired in warfare (709, 755, 897) serve above all to bring home the humiliation of the present. They show what threatens henceforth a wealth which is merely 'plunder offered to the first-comer' (751–2) or emphasize that 'wealth is no longer any use' (842) to a dead man.

The only abundance that remains is of tears. Already in the parodos ἁβροπενθεῖς (135, 'delicately grieving'), looking forward to

[32] See Avery (n. 1), 177–8.

the grief of the Persian women, is a sinister echo of ἀβροδιαίτων (41, 'living delicately'), referring to the luxury and softness of the style of life of the Lydians. Similarly, in the first stasimon, there appear within three lines ἀβρόγοοι (541, 'delicately lamenting'), evoking the long sobs of the widows, and ἀβροχίτωνας (543, 'with delicate coverings'), referring to the luxury which surrounds them and the soft draperies on their beds.

This destruction of wealth is not expressed in merely abstract terms. It is also made present to the imagination and even to the eyes of the spectators by a whole series of images where torn clothing, abandoned finery, the pomp of the dead or the rags of the living symbolize, by contrast with the opulence of past times, the misery of the present.[33]

The parodos already associates defeat with the image of torn clothing. The chorus expresses its fear of one day hearing the cries of women in mourning and seeing their hands fall upon their linen gowns in order to tear them to shreds (βυσσίνοις δ᾽ ἐν πέπλοις πέσῃ λακίς, 124). When it imagines the horror of the naval defeat of which it is about to hear, the first image which comes to mind is that of corpses tossed by the waves 'in their large wandering cloaks' (πλαγκτοῖς ἐν διπλάκεσσιν, 277). The very choice of δίπλαξ ('double cloak') here is significant. This word refers to an actual Persian garment.[34] This could be the sleeveless tunic which is represented on some Attic vases of the first half of the fifth century,[35] the multicoloured tunic with sleeves which is mentioned by Herodotus in his description of Persian troops (7.61),[36] or the large cloak which Xenophon calls κάνδυς.[37] It thus reflects an intention to include in the description of the disaster a reference to the pomp of the Orient, but at the same time it combines this brilliance with the splendour of the world of epic, by means of a term which, in both the *Iliad* and

---

[33] The importance of the theme of clothing in the *Persians* has recently been demonstrated by Petrounias (n. 1), 24–5, and again by Thalmann (n. 8), passim. But neither of them refers to the excellent article by E. Flintoff on this subject, 'ΔΙΠΛΑΚΕΣΣΙΝ at Aeschylus' *Persians* 277', *Mnemosyne* 27 (1974), 231–7.

[34] On Persian costume, see Gow (n. 15), 143–7, and Bovon (n. 15), passim.

[35] See vases 3, 7, 10, and 12 in the numeration of Bovon (n. 15).

[36] This type of χιτών ('tunic') is also mentioned by Xenophon (*An.* 1.5.8; *Cyr.* 8.3.13).

[37] Cf. Xen. *An.* 1.5.8 (τοὺς πορφυροὺς κάνδυς) and *Cyr.* 8.3.13 (κάνδυν ὁλοπόρφυρον).

the *Odyssey*, refers to a cloak which is sumptuous both because of its colour (it is always purple) and because of the woven decoration which adorns it.[38] The association of torn clothes with the grief which follows Salamis recurs finally in the first stasimon with the reference to women who 'tear their veils with their delicate hands' (537–8).

The contrast between Atossa's two entrances is a concrete expression of the passage from wealth to destruction,[39] for it is no longer merely a matter of images which speak only to the imagination of the spectators but of scenes which they can see with their own eyes. When the queen enters on to the stage for the first time, she is the 'all-powerful mistress of the deep-girdled women of Persia' (155), reflecting an aura of epic grandeur with the adjective βαθύζωνος ('deep-girdled').[40] But after the news of Salamis, she returns, as she herself stresses, 'without chariot, without [her] former pomp' (ἄνευ τ' ὀχημάτων χλιδῆς τε τῆς πάροιθεν, 607–8).

There is an even more spectacular contrast between the two kings, the glorious Darius of the second episode and the Xerxes dressed in rags of the exodos. It is also more elaborately prepared by a whole series of images which have their origin in Atossa's dream and develop throughout the entire tragedy.

Atossa's dream begins with an image of opulence, with a barbarian world represented by a woman 'with beautiful clothing' (δύο γυναῖκ' εὐείμονε, 181), 'arrayed in Persian robes' (ἣ μὲν πέπλοισι Περσικοῖς ἠσκημένη, 182). But after Xerxes' unsuccessful attempt to put Greece under the yoke, the contrast between present and past, between the new sovereign and his father, concludes with the description of a king who 'tears the robes which cover his body' (πέπλους ῥήγνυσιν ἀμφὶ σώματι, 199). This destruction of the robes recurs, expressed symbolically, in the omen which the gods then send to the queen. Atossa

---

[38] For δίπλακα πορφυρέην ('purple double cloak'), see *Iliad* 3.126, 22.441, and *Odyssey* 19.241–2. The identification of κάνδυς with the δίπλαξ is maintained by Flintoff (n. 33), 237, on the grounds that the two garments are sumptuous and that they both serve as travelling cloaks.

[39] This contrast was emphasized by Flintoff (n. 33), 234, Taplin (n. 14), 75–9, 98–100, and Thalmann (n. 8), 268–9.

[40] On the epic colour of this word, which like δίπλαξ ('double cloak') contributes to giving Persian clothing a character at once archaic and majestic, see Sideras (n. 17), 52.

sees a hawk which 'with its talons, *plucks* the head (χηλαῖς κάρα τίλλονθ', 208–9) of the eagle which represents Xerxes.

The dream and the omen become reality in the course of the messenger speech, which describes how Xerxes, after the double defeat suffered by his army, by sea at Salamis and on land at Psytta-leia, 'tore his clothes' (ῥήξας δὲ πέπλους, 468). The humiliation of the son is even clearer when it is contrasted with the glory of the father, which is then brought before the eyes of the spectators. Darius would have appeared in all his splendour and power. But it should not be forgotten that this splendour is the splendour of a man who is now dead, and that it does not for a moment cause us to forget the humiliation of the present. Darius himself draws the attention of his listeners to the state of Xerxes' clothing, when he says to Atossa that 'in the grief which he feels at his disaster, his many-coloured clothes are no more than torn shreds about his body' (πάντα γὰρ | κακῶν ὑπ' ἄλγους λακίδες ἀμφὶ σώματι | στημορραγοῦσι ποικίλων ἐσθημάτων, 834–6). And the queen laments in her turn 'the ignominy of the clothing which covers the body of her son' (ἀτιμίαν γε παιδὸς ἀμφὶ σώματι ἐσθημάτων ... | ἥ νιν ἀμπέχει, 847–8).

With the appearance of Xerxes in the exodos, what had been just a metaphor or a distant image becomes a reality which is visible to the spectators.

The parodos showed a king who had departed for the conquest of Greece 'speeding forward his Syrian chariot' (Σύριόν θ' ἅρμα διώκων, 84). Atossa, in her dream, had seen a king who *fell* (πίπτει δ' ἐμὸς παῖς, 197), after having been thrown from his chariot by a horse which rebelled at the yoke (194–6). The spectators in their turn see, in the exodos, a Xerxes whose knees are broken (λέλυται γὰρ ἐμοὶ γυίων ῥώμη, 913), the image of an Asia cast to its knees ('Ασία δὲ χθών ... ἐπὶ γόνυ κέκλιται, 929–30). These words are not merely a metaphorical expression of the exhaustion of the defeated. The staging would no doubt have given the metaphor a concrete value, with a Xerxes who arrives, if not on his knees, then at least on foot, as Taplin has recently argued.[41] This thesis, as Taplin himself recognizes, goes against the generally held view. Most critics have argued that Xerxes made his entrance in a chariot. They rely on a reference by the chorus to Xerxes'

[41] Taplin (n. 14), 123.

covered chariot (ἀμφὶ σκηναῖς | τροχηλάτοισιν..., 1000–1). The reference is incontestable. But it does not necessarily prove the presence of a chariot on the stage. The chorus has in fact been lamenting at length the disappearance of so many commanders who had departed never to return. They have expressed regret for their absence (ποθοῦμεν, 993). When they say ἔταφον ἔταφον οὐκ ἀμφὶ σκηναῖς τροχηλάτοισιν ὄπισθεν ἑπομένους (1000–1, 'I am amazed, amazed, that they do not follow behind your covered chariot'), they could very well be expressing their amazement at a double absence, the absence of the chariot and the absence of the warriors who escorted it.

This king without a chariot is thus the first king dressed in rags to appear on the tragic stage. This apparition is all the more striking because it is at once long-prepared and completely unexpected. It is long prepared by all the accounts of Xerxes rending his clothes. But it is also unexpected because Darius, before disappearing, had told Atossa to go back into the palace 'in order to fetch the most brilliant apparel from there and go to meet her son' (κόσμον ὅστις εὐπρεπὴς λαβοῦσ' ὑπαντίαζε παῖδα, 833–4). And the queen had carried out his instructions and left the stage saying: 'I will go and find new clothing inside the palace' (καὶ λαβοῦσα κόσμον ἐκ δόμων) 'and then I will try to meet my son' (ὑπαντιάζειν παιδί μου πειράσομαι, 849–50). Everything has thus been done to make the spectator expect a Xerxes restored to his former splendour.[42] His entrance in rags would thus be a *coup de théâtre* made possible by Atossa's cautious '*I will try*'.

The misery expressed by Xerxes' rags is further amplified by a piece of stage business involving the chorus. Before the eyes of the spectators, the old men, who are mere reflections of their master, dress in their turn in rags. The former gesture of Xerxes rending his clothes at the sight of his disaster, a gesture which he recalls to the chorus in line 1030: πέπλον δ' ἐπέρρηξ' ἐπὶ συμφορᾷ κακοῦ, is actually reproduced on the stage at the command of the king in line 1060: 'and tear with your hands the robes which cover your breast' (πέπλον δ' ἔρεικε κολπίαν ἀκμᾷ χερῶν). At the command of their sovereign, the chorus goes even as far as ravaging the white hair of their beards and

---

[42] Since Hermann, several scholars (cf. Taplin (n. 14), 122 n. 1) have moreover supposed that the announced meeting took place offstage and that Xerxes appeared with new clothes. But this hypothesis has been very convincingly refuted by Taplin.

plucking out their hair (1056–7, 1062), thus inflicting on themselves a destruction analogous to that which had been suffered by the eagle in the omen from the talons of the hawk (208–9).

The significance of this spectacle is finally made clear by language which suggests, beyond the physical humiliation of the king, the destruction of Persian grandeur.

The equivalence between the clothing of the king and the splendour of Persia is emphasized first of all by the echo of Atossa's laments over the ἀτιμία ('ignominy') of the clothes which cover the body of her son (847–8) in the laments over the disappearance of Persian τιμή ('honour') by the chorus (ὀτοτοῖ ... περσονόμου τιμῆς μεγάλης, 919).

Aeschylus also makes use of the ambivalence of a word like κόσμος, which means successively 'order' and 'clothing'.[43] At the beginning of the tragedy, in the first episode, κόσμος denotes the good order of a disciplined fleet, and is as characteristic of the Persians (οὐκ ἀκόσμως, 374) as of the Greeks (κόσμῳ, 400). It serves also to denounce the *disorder* which accompanies the Persians' flight. But this 'disorder' is already reflected in the disorder of the king's clothing. In lines 468–70, the messenger actually describes a Xerxes who 'rends his clothes' (ῥήξας δὲ πέπλους) before hurling himself into a disorderly flight (ἵησ' ἀκόσμῳ ξὺν φυγῇ). In the second episode, there is a transition from κόσμος-order to κόσμος-clothing. This word, which appears twice, first in the mouth of Darius (833) and then in that of Atossa (849), is indeed used for the 'clothing' which the queen is supposed to fetch from her palace before going to meet her son. In the exodos, when the chorus, in line 920, greets Xerxes and laments over the clothing of the warriors now mown down by Fate (ὀτοτοῖ ... κόσμου τ' ἀνδρῶν οὓς νῦν δαίμων ἐπέκειρεν), the two meanings of the word are reunited: the army becomes Xerxes' clothing, and its destruction is embodied in the destruction of the royal costume.

It is also quite obvious that Aeschylus plays on the ambiguity of στόλος | στολή ('equipment'). For στόλος, in the *Persians*, is first of all a military term: it refers to Xerxes' army (400, 795) or to items of naval gear (408, 416). When στολή appears at line 192 to describe the posture of the woman who represents Persia and who, once placed in

---

[43] See also Thalmann (n. 8), 274–5.

the harness, τῇ δ' ἐπυργοῦτο στολῇ ('towered proudly in her equipment') it takes on a more complex significance. It does indeed refer
to the 'equipment' consisting of the harness and the reins; but, since
it is referring to a woman, the idea of a reference to costume can also
be entertained (Mazon's excellent translation *accoutrement* conveys
the ambiguity of the Greek word). At the same time, its association
with πυργόω ('tower'), which refers to military realities, suggests that
the military connotations of στολή are still perceptible. In line 1017,
when the king asks the chorus: ὁρᾷς τὸ λοιπὸν τόδε τᾶς ἐμᾶς στολᾶς;
('Do you see this remnant of my equipment?') it even becomes
impossible to choose between the two meanings. On the one hand,
τόδε ('this'), by which Xerxes directs the attention of the chorus (and
also that of the spectator) to what remains of his στολή, requires the
meaning 'clothing', more especially as it is followed by τόνδε (connected by τε ['and'] with what precedes), which incontestably serves
to draw attention to another item of Xerxes' costume, that is to say
his quiver (τόνδε τ' ὀϊστοδέγμονα). That is why Groeneboom (on line
1017) glosses τὸ λοιπὸν τόδε τᾶς ἐμᾶς στολᾶς with 'reliquias hasce
meae pallae' ('these remnants of my cloak') and Broadhead asserts
that στολή 'must surely = "robe"'. But, if it is not accepted that στολή
also means 'army', then it is impossible to understand the connexion
between line 1017 and the preceding lines. In lines 1014–15, Xerxes
has in fact exclaimed: 'I have been struck in my army, the numberless
army with which I set out' (στρατὸν μὲν τοσοῦτον τάλας πέπληγμαι),
which prompted the question of the chorus: 'Is anything left of the
Persians, O man of great calamity?' (τί δ' οὐκ ὄλωλεν, μεγαλάτε,
Πέρσαν;). He then replies in line 1017, as it was understood by the
scholiasts and translated by Mazon: 'Tu vois tout ce qui reste des
forces que j'avais levées' ('You see everything that remains of the
forces which I raised').

If the torn clothes of the King can thus symbolize so forcefully the
annihilation of the wealth and power of the Persian empire, the
reason is that in an absolute monarchy the state is identical with
the person of the king. And the same logic, which at the beginning of
the tragedy transformed the sovereign into a creature with a thousand arms and a thousand sailors who contained in himself all the
power of the Persian army, can at the end express the image of total
destruction by the mere spectacle of a king in rags.

3

The King and Eye:
The Rule of the Father in Aischylos' *Persians*

Mark Griffith

1. INTRODUCTION: ÉLITES, MASTERS, AND KINGS IN DEMOCRATIC ATHENS

The relationship between tragedy and democracy in Athens is endlessly debated. Whether *tragōidia* was specifically invented for and by the new democratic system, or merely adapted itself from its Peisistratid origins as the Kleisthenic and Ephialtean reforms began their process of transforming Athenian society,[1] its rich amalgam of elements, archaic and contemporary, distant and familiar, provided a productive medium of experiment and self-examination for the various different components of its (mainly citizen) audience. The combination of linguistic, metrical, mythico-historical, and performative structures, while making this in some respects a panHellenic, and in others a timeless, art-form whose plots and characters have continued to resonate through subsequent centuries, at the same time offered a

[*Editor's note*. This chapter is an abridged version of an article (Griffith 1998) which also contains an extended discussion of Sophocles' *Antigone*. Some theoretical analysis is also omitted, including a section entitled 'Cross-purposes and multiple identifications', discussing the complex nature of an audience's 'identification' with characters in a film or play. The beginning and end of the article have been somewhat abbreviated and recast.]

[1] The first is the suggestion of Connor 1989. The second is the conventional view, based on the traditional date of 534 for the first tragic competition and on the alleged role played by Thespis as a pioneer of this new art-form.

uniquely valuable opportunity for the presentation of competing local interests and ideologies—uniquely valuable, both because of the immense prestige and social significance invested in the annual performances at the Great Dionysia, and because of the special elements of disguise, play, and religious celebration, that made such self-analysis and experimentation less explicit (perhaps also less conscious), and consequently less risky.

Tragedy rarely presents a straightforward 'message' on behalf of any particular political platform or constituency, however, and it should perhaps come as no surprise that we find a rather confusing mixture of democratic and élitist values and relationships represented within the plays. Even as it is true that 'characters of diverse ethnicity, gender, and status all have the same right to express their opinions and the same verbal ability with which to exercise that right',[2] it is also obvious that the plays draw a sharp line between the 'serious' (or 'better kind of') characters (Aristotle's *spoudaioi*), whose decisions, actions, and sufferings form the core (or 'soul') of the plot, and the minor characters (those more 'like us') who form the socio-political context for those decisions and actions, and whose attitudes and desires tend to be affected by, but never to cause or determine, the key crises and reversals of that plot. The 'serious' characters are invariably royal or noble, while the minor characters are of markedly lower status. Thus while it may be correct to describe Athenian tragedy as 'polyphonic' and 'egalitarian' in its form, in so far as it gives generous opportunities for female, servile, foreign, and lower-class voices to be heard, along with—and even in opposition to—the voices of the aristocratic main characters, the trajectory of the plots, along with the costumes and spatial arrangements of the theater itself, tend nonetheless to reassert very strongly the differences between high and low, superior and ordinary.[3]

---

[2] Hall 1997: 118–26; also (p. 125) 'Greek tragedy does its thinking in a form which is vastly more politically advanced than the society which produced Greek tragedy… Tragedy postulates in imagination a world rarely even hoped for in reality until very recently.'

[3] On Aristotle's notion of *spoudaios* ('serious, important') and the moral/social distinction of tragic characters and actions, see *Poet.* 6. 1449^{b}24, 2. 1448^{a}2–18, 13. 1453^{a}9–12 (with D. W. Lucas' nn. *ad locc.*), Halliwell 1986: 153–4; also Plato *Laws* 798d. Of the numerous political and sociological readings of Greek tragedy that have appeared over the last 25 years or so, however, most see the plays as being much less

Greek ideas of what a *polis* was, and how it should be run, were far from homogeneous. Although most Athenians of the mid-fifth century were proud of their democracy and its achievements, they were well aware that the majority of their fellow-Greeks lived under different systems of government, whether hereditary monarchy (e.g. Thessaly and Macedonia), tyranny (e.g. Syracuse, and Athens itself in the time of their own grand-parents), or a more or less narrow oligarchy (e.g. Thebes, Sparta, Corinth); some *poleis* fluctuated between one and another of these systems (e.g. Argos, Syracuse). Such aristocratic or monarchical alternatives to democracy could seem very attractive to a minority (at least) of the Athenian élite.[4] Nor did you have to be an ardent supporter of the *dēmos* to claim credit for Marathon and Salamis, or to promote the ideal of Athenian imperial and cultural superiority. Civic pride came in many forms. So we may be sure that the audience each year in the Theater of Dionysos, drawn as it presumably was from a fairly wide cross-section of the community (though in the 470s the relatively small auditorium, together with the admission-fee, probably resulted in a higher ratio of wealthier spectators than in the later fifth century), contained a broad range of different prejudices and points of views about all kinds of political and social issues, including the desirability (or otherwise) of kingship and aristocratic leadership. But whereas numerous modern studies have focused on the 'tyrannical' excesses of this or that stage hero/ine, and the exotic 'otherness' of tragic foreigners and females, less attention has been paid to the contested status and nature of tragic monarchs in general, or the relations between 'leaders' and 'led'.[5] When we do examine the plays from

concerned with distinctions between rich and poor, well-born and low-born citizens, than between (male) citizens in general, and Others (women, tyrants, foreigners): thus, 'Tragedy... defines the male citizen self, and both produces and reproduces the ideology of the civic community' (Hall 1997: 95); similarly (e.g.) Vernant and Vidal-Naquet 1981; Seaford 1994; Goldhill 1990; Cartledge 1997.

    4 See esp. ps. Xenophon *Ath. Pol.* (The Old Oligarch), and Hdt. 3. 80–3; further Ober 1989: 279–92; Raaflaub 1989, 1996; Donlan 1980; Roberts 1994: 48–70; and below, pp. 97–9. Among 4th-cent. Athenians, warm approbation of kingship (esp. the rule of Kyros 1st of Persia), often in combination with praise of the idealized 'master' operating as a virtual 'king' of his slaves, is found e.g. at Xen. *Cyrop.* 1.1.1–4 (cf. *Oec.* 21.10–12); Plato *Laws* 694a–695e; Isokrates 2 (Nikokles) and 3, 9. (Euagoras).

    5 On monarchs in tragedy, see Easterling 1984, Podlecki 1986; also A. J. Podlecki 'κατ᾽ ἀρχῆς γὰρ φιλαίτιος λεώς: the concept of leadership in Aeschylus', in Sommerstein

this angle, however, they often turn out to convey an attitude towards the dominant 'royal families' that is deeply ambivalent, a super-charged mixture of disgust and admiration, horror and devotion.[6]

We have all been taught from an early age, of course, that one thing that distinguished the Greeks (especially the Athenians) of the Classical period from all other peoples, and that makes them the spiritual and/or biological ancestors of modern Western Man, is their hatred and intolerance of despotism, their love of freedom, equality, and autonomy, and their consequent preference for some kind of republican and/or democratic government in which the citizens were nobody's slave, and no one man could 'lord it' over everyone else. This view, which obviously has plenty of evidence to support it, and which it would be silly to discard completely, is pithily formulated—perhaps for the first time in Western literature—in Aischylos' *Persians*, as the Queen learns just what it is that makes these Athenians so different from her son's Persian troops and allies:

Ba.:   τίς δὲ ποιμάνωρ ἔπεστι κἀπιδεσπόζει στρατῶι;
Χο.:   οὔτινος δοῦλοι κέκληνται φωτὸς οὐδ᾽ ὑπήκοοι.

QUEEN: Who is shepherd over them, who is master of their army?
CHORUS: They are called slaves of no man, and subjects of none.

(*Pers.* 241–2)

Doubtless the Theater of Dionysos in 472 BCE roared with approval at this Churchillian moment, and such expressions became common-place in the decades (and centuries) ahead, as the stereotypes of

1993. On class divisions and attitudes to the élite as reflected in tragedy, Rose 1992; 197–236; Griffith 1995. Elsewhere (Griffith 1995) I have attempted to explore some of the shifting relationships that are staged between the dominant (leading) characters and the more submissive and/or silent minor characters (Guard, Chorus, Messenger, Nurse, Jurymen, etc.), in the *Oresteia* and elsewhere, as well as the analogous relationship that is maintained between those élite leading characters and the theater audience.

6 See Griffith 1995. In the surviving plays, Theseus tends to behave as a more or less ideal king (S. *OC*, E. *Her.*, *Supp.*; cf. Pelasgos in A. *Supp.*); but more often the moral qualities and practical successes of tragic monarchs are mixed and less than ideal [In the unabridged version of this article, the overlap between paternal authority and the rule of a social superior (master, élite elected official, king) is discussed at greater length, with some use also of psychoanalytically oriented theories of the (ancient Greek, and modern Western) family.]

Oriental despotism vs Hellenic freedom and autonomy fixed themselves in the collective consciousness.[7]

But fifth-century Athens provided a complicated and in many respects conflicted environment for its theatrical performances. Even as the ideals of democracy were being extolled by orators and historians, and medical, political and ethical theories concerning the natural superiority of freedom-loving Hellenes to servile Asiatics were proliferating, traditional aristocratic views about inherited worth, excellence of achievement, and entitlement to rule, showed no sign of fading away.[8] Fierce debate, and intermittent bloodshed, attended the struggle for political domination between 'the best' citizens and 'the masses, the laborers', from the time of Kleisthenes right down to the arrival of the Macedonians; and throughout the fifth century (especially in the years before the death of Perikles) the Athenian masses continued to rely heavily on the 'superior' talents of that élite, electing them to office, enjoying the benefits of their wealth, and looking to them (more or less trustingly) for leadership in war and peace.[9]

Outside the strictly 'political' arena (Assembly, ballot-urns, law-courts), there were other social contexts and institutions too in which strict hierarchies persisted and unquestioning obedience was expected and given, even by free males: above all, the family, the army, and the realm of religion. The ideal of a father's rule as $\kappa \acute{\upsilon} \rho \iota o \varsigma$ over his wife and children, and as $\delta \epsilon \sigma \pi \acute{o} \tau \eta \varsigma$ of the whole *oikos*, was never seriously questioned, though the pressures on an ambitious son to assert himself and match or outdo the achievements of his father (especially in aristocratic families) might often cause difficulty (as we shall see).[10] Likewise the need for discipline within the ranks of hoplites or benches

---

[7] See esp. Hall 1989. Of course, in a delicious reversal, the Greeks themselves were in due course to be cast in a quasi-Oriental role by the Romans, as soft, shiftless, parasitical cheats (*Graeculus esuriens*). But that is another story.

[8] See Arnheim 1977; Donlan 1980; Kurke 1991; Roberts 1994; Tatum 1989.

[9] Davies 1984; Ober 1989; Sinclair 1988; 34–43.

[10] $\kappa \alpha \grave{\iota} \ \acute{\eta} \ \mu \grave{\epsilon} \nu \ o \grave{\iota} \kappa o \nu \mu \iota \kappa \grave{\eta} \ \mu o \nu \alpha \rho \chi \acute{\iota} \alpha \cdot \ \mu o \nu \alpha \rho \chi \epsilon \hat{\iota} \tau \alpha \iota \ \gamma \grave{\alpha} \rho \ \pi \hat{\alpha} \varsigma \ o \hat{\iota} \kappa o \varsigma \ldots$ (Arist. *Pol.* 1. 1255^{b}18–19); cf. Foucault 1985: 166–84. Inversions and perversions of domestic patriarchy were of course good material for comedy: e.g. Ar. *Wasps, Lysistrata, Ekklesiazousai*. See further Strauss 1993. It is striking that, whereas the Homeric poems (including the Hymns) frequently present fathers and sons collaborating closely and with affection (e.g., Odysseus and Telemachos, Priam and Hektor, Nestor

of rowers was axiomatic;[11] and it was commonly asserted or assumed in Classical Athens (as in many parts of the world today) that structures of 'good order' and 'economy' that proved appropriate and effective for the family or army must naturally obtain for the political community too. And above all, in the multi-purpose sphere of traditional mythology and religion, the domination of Zeus, 'father of gods and men', remained unchallenged. In the Greek imagination, His eye sees all, His nod directs all; and He judges and punishes all with a sternly parental authority—as Aischylean choruses eloquently remark (*Ag.* 355, 367–9, 1485–7; *Supp.* 101–11, 381–6, etc.). Zeus is no democrat, and in the *Oresteia* in particular his dominant authority as *patrōios* ('patron-of-fathers'), *basileus* ('king'), *teleios* ('completer/perfecter'), and *sōtēr* ('savior') is pervasive and decisive. 'Despotism' of one kind or another, and temporary or permanent 'rule' over others, were thus integral elements of life for every Athenian; and while sophists and philosophers might at times take care to draw sharp distinctions between a master's rule over family and slaves, and a citizen's rule over other citizens, and thus between those whose nature is purely servile (and therefore incapable of ever ruling others) and those who are natural masters (but nonetheless willing to accept the authority of others when appropriate), these distinctions were not always clearly recognized or felt.[12]

The Theater of Dionysos in Athens existed (among its many other functions) as a highly-charged, yet securely-demarcated and ritualized,

and Antilochos or Peisistratos), virtually no friendly scenes between father and son occur in extant tragedy: see further Griffith 1998: 332–4, esp. n. 43, and below, n. 85.

[11] The idea that a *polis* is essentially an army, and that politics is largely the art of security and war, is taken seriously by Aristotle in the *Politics* (7. 1324^{b}1–22), but quickly rejected: this might do for Spartans or Cretans, Scythians or Persians: but it would be 'strange' (ἄτοπον) for a true '*polis*-dweller' or 'statesman' (πολιτικός) always 'to be planning how to dominate and rule over those nearby, whether they like it or not' (θεωρεῖν ὅπως ἄρχηι καὶ δεσπόζηι τῶν πλησίον καὶ βουλομένων καὶ μὴ βουλομένων). Here, as often, ἄτοπον is a pregnant term for Aristotle, signalling a phenomenon that—if true—would be deeply problematic, and that therefore urgently needs to be shown not to be true. On Athenian ideas about the analogy between 'obedience' (*peitharchia*) to one's father and to military command, see further Griffith 1998: 66–9, discussing S. *Ant.* 673–5.

[12] Arist. *Pol.* 1.1254^{a}12–1255^{b}35. One might add that any Athenians who had spent much time with the Greeks of Ionia, or with Lydian or Persian dignitaries (e.g. at symposia or on embassies), would be well aware that a Greek city's 'enslavement' to Persian 'despotism' was largely a metaphor: their subjection was in many respects considerably less oppressive than, e.g. that of Greek Helots to Greek Spartans, or even

arena for the playing out of social/psychological conflicts and contesta-
tions, a 'potential space' in which dangerous and exciting fantasies and
identities could safely be confronted and explored.[13] Through the
medium of tragedy, the audience came to experience a series of shifting
subject positions and multiple levels of engagement that allowed several
different, even competing, impulses to coexist and be satisfied, both
within the citizen body as a whole, and within each audience member.[14]
Imaginations could—were expected to—run riot. And within this
riotous (yet tightly structured) ceremony of play, two of the deepest-
seated and most troublesome sources of fantasy and anxiety involved,
on the one hand, relations between children and parents, and on the
other, power-relations between leaders and led, rulers and subjects,
'them' and 'us'. So I suggest that one of the powerful appeals of
Athenian tragedy was that it presented an occasion for the two to
flow together, in the recurrent and never-ending search to satisfy
deeply-entrenched feelings of need for paternal and despotic authority
and reassurance that still ran strong even within the (by now supposedly democratic and autonomous) male citizen body.

There is not space here to discuss in detail the ways in which plays
(and films) draw audiences into identifying in quick succession, or

that of local Thracian or Siceliot or Egyptian subject populations to their Greek
colonists (to say nothing of the restrictions on the legal and corporal rights of 'free'
Athenian women). As an Ephesian or Halikarnassian or Milesian or Cypriot, you had
to pay taxes to the King, and you bowed if he or his representative showed up in
person; and you weren't allowed to start wars with your neighbors as freely as you
were accustomed to if your city was fully 'autonomous'; but you were free to worship
your own gods, observe your own language, laws and culture, and travel freely to
other parts of the Greek world (as Herodotos, Thales, and Xenophanes did, for
example)—whereas none of these freedoms seems to have existed for the enslaved
population of a Greek *oikos* or *polis*.

[13] The notion of 'potential space' is derived from Winnicott 1971: 'Play is in fact
neither a matter of inner psychic reality nor a matter of external reality... The place
where cultural [= artistic/religious] experience is located is in the potential space
between the individual and the environment...' (Winnicott 1971: 96, quoted by
Green 1979: 1); see too Travis 1996 and p. 118 below).

[14] Elsewhere I have tried to explain this process as generating a kind of 'solidarity
without consensus', i.e. a sense of collective satisfaction and reassurance achieved by
the manipulation of symbols and codes sufficiently ambiguous to allow these different elements each to find the interpretations they desire: Griffith 1995; cf. too Goldhill 1990: 114–29; Pelling 1997*a*: 13–19; Easterling 1997*a*. For the notion (and
implications) of tragedy as a 'talking/watching cure' for the psychological problems
besetting the Athenians, see below, pp. 133–4.

even simultaneously, with more than one character at once, and into feeling strangely mixed emotions while watching a single scene or sequence of scenes. Admiration may be mixed with disapproval, desire with disgust. A character whom we know (at one level) to be debased or far removed from our own conscious aspirations may nonetheless exercise an irresistible fascination for us on stage or on the screen; or we may find ourselves first identifying closely with a lead character, and then a moment later viewing him or her from a quite different subject position, one of implicit inferiority, or superiority, or distance. Such cross-purposes and multiple identifications appear to be characteristic of modern audience response to theater (and film), and they appear likewise to have constituted much of the thrill that the Greeks referred to as *psychagōgia* ('mental-emotional stimulation, affect, psychological identification'). Thus—to cite a well-known example that presents several analogies to Aischylos' *Persians*, as well as provoking the title of the article from which this abridgement is taken—in the Hollywood version of *The King and I*, Yul Brynner, in the role of the Siamese King Mongkut, aroused almost universal feelings of admiration, desire, and sympathy, not only in the English governess Anna (Deborah Kerr) but also in theater audiences around the world, even as his character's cruelty, naiveté, and foreignness also marked him out inescapably (and in a sense justly, in the eyes, e.g., of Anna's son—a virtual 'tragic chorus' for this film— and of the audience too), for rejection, humiliation, and death.[15] In what follows, I shall be attempting to trace some similarly complex processes of multiple identification and mixed audience sympathies in *The Persians*, the earliest of all surviving dramas in which [despotic, abjected] East meets [democratic/civilized] West.

2. THE PERSIAN BOY (THE KING MUSTN'T DIE)

That the young King Xerxes in Aischylos' *Persians* is represented as a hybristic Oriental despot, surrounded by soft, slavish, Asiatic subjects, the very personification of the barbarian Other, is by now well

---

[15] See further Donaldson 1990; Kaplan 1995; and Griffith 1998 n. 61.

documented, and needs no further demonstration.[16] The opulent
costumes and 'luxurious step'[17] of the Persians and their allies, the
elaborate wheeled transportation, the exotic gestures and servile
kow-towing, the Chorus' extravagant language of praise and lamentation, the descriptions of chaotic disorder and flight at Salamis and
Plataia, all mark Xerxes, his family, his entourage, and his people, as
distinctly non-Greek, and in some respects sub-Greek; likewise, the
King's personal cruelty, impiety, and lack of restraint are all highlighted at various points in the play. All these hallmarks of incipient
'Orientalism' are distinctive and unmistakable, as are the various
ways in which Asia in general, and Xerxes in particular, are 'femi-
nized' in the narrative and staging.[18]

In opposition to, or mitigation of, this jingoistic and heavily mor-
alistic reading, however, various critics over the years have pointed
out that the portrait of Xerxes and his fellow-Persians is not nearly as
negative as we might have expected, given the date and circumstances
of the play's production. Indeed, Xerxes has been taken by many to
represent a kind of 'everyman', paradigmatic for Greeks and foreigners alike in his susceptibility to ambition and rashness, his belated
regrets and recognition of mistakes, and his distracted grief at the loss
of friends, dependents, property, and honor. On this reading, Aischylos' partly, or intermittently, sympathetic representation of the
enemy's downfall may be seen as demonstrating his humanistic vision
and broad-mindedness—proof that the Athenians are not cheaply
vindictive, but can rise above petty nationalism to display their good
taste and universal moral concern.[19]

[16] Hall 1989: 69–100, 1993 and 1996 (passim), with further references; also
Georges 1994: 76–114.

[17] ἁβροβάται 1073, cf. ἁβρόγοοι 541, and ἁβροδιαίτων... Λυδῶν 41. For the
associations and significance of ἁβρο- words, see below, p. 103. The suggestion that
habro- represents instead a Hellenizing of Persian *ahura* (D. Korzeniewski, *Helikon* 6
(1966), 548–96, and others) has not convinced many.

[18] For the Persians as the first 'Orientalist' text in Western literature, see Saïd 1978,
Hall 1989. On the 'effeminate' aspects of Xerxes and the Persians, see esp. Hall 1993.

[19] 'Grief is universal...a shattered Persian is not so different from a shattered
Greek', Pelling 1997*a*: 13–14, who suggests further (18–19) that 'the pattern [of
compassionate insight] we have noticed in the *Persae* is not new: indeed it has
close analogies with the *Iliad*'. Commentators have noted that the cult behavior of
the Queen and Chorus is distinctively Greek (esp. 598–622; see Broadhead, Belloni *ad
locc.*), as are the references to 'Zeus', 'Apollo', and the divine apparatus of temptation

It may be a mistake, however, to put the whole issue in such clear-cut, either/or terms. We do not have to choose simply between Xerxes the foolish Oriental despot and Xerxes the allegorical erring every-man, between Other and Us. Rather, we should recognize a more particular set of characteristics that are attached to Xerxes and his family in this play, characteristics recognizable as belonging to a distinct stratum of Greek (as well as Persian) society: for Xerxes is clearly identified by the language of the play as, not just *any* over-reaching, miscalculating youth who needs to be taught a lesson, but more specifically as an aristocratic son and heir of a familiar type and background, one whose relationship to his community, and to his parents, is marked by peculiar dynamics, privileges, and difficulties.

The young king is heir to supreme wealth, manifested especially, we are told, in gold and textiles (as opposed to the democratic silver of the Athenians: 238); he is cosmopolitan, consorting with Lydians, Carians, Ionians, Mysians, and others; he dresses luxuriously and walks in a distinctively delicate manner; he is the owner of horses and chariots; and he spends his time, at home and abroad, surrounded by 'trusty [aristocratic] companions,'[20] as well as by swarms of subor-dinates who treat him as a virtual god. He is the 'light' and 'eye' of his house (168–9 . . . ἀμφὶ δ' ὀφθαλμῶι φόβος. | ὄμμα γὰρ δόμων νομίζω δεσπότου παρουσίαν), terms used elsewhere of the precious sons, father, and husbands of Greek noble families, and also of athletic and military victors;[21] and he faces the supreme challenge of attempting

and punishment: thus the culture and moral sensibilities of these Persians are repre-sented in much more familiar and respectable terms than they might have been. (At 497–8, the worship of Ouranos may be felt to be 'Persian'; more conspicuously, some of the elements in the invocation of Dareios go beyond the norms of hero cult, in treating him as a full-blown divinity; cf. Hall 1989: 89–93; Pelling 1997*a*: 14–15. But there is nothing as 'foreign' and alienating as is presented, e.g. in E. *Orestes* or *Hekabe*, or even A. *Suppliants*). For discussion of the final lamentation-scene (*kommos*), which has struck many as being grotesque or ridiculous (e.g. Hall passim, esp. 1989: 81–4, 131), others as being powerfully emotive and sympathetic (e.g. Broadhead 1960; Taplin 1977; Pelling 1997*a*: 13–15), see below, pp. 108–10.

[20] ἑταῖροι, 989, cf. 441–3, and πιστ- words 443, 681, 979 etc.; also 'age-mates' (ἥλικες, 681, 914; νεολαιά 669), the 'flower' of his nation's youth (ἄωτος 978, ἄνθος 59, 252, 925 (821!), ἥβη 441–4, 512, 544, 681, 733, 923, 978, 987–91); etc. All of these are terms strongly associated with aristocratic *hetaireiai*, and the rhetoric of symposium and praise-poetry.

[21] Cf. *Cho.* 934 ὀφθαλμὸν οἴκων (a son); S. *Tr.* 203 (a husband), *OT* 987 καὶ μὴν μέγας γ' ὀφθαλμὸς οἱ πατρὸς τάφοι; Pindar, *O.* 2.9–10 (the noble family of

to prove himself a fit son and heir to his stupendously successful father, and those other illustriously despotic predecessors.²²

Undemocratic, and even unGreek, though much of this description may sound to us, there were in fact Athenians who would fit this description quite well. Many of the audience in 472 BCE would remember vividly the practitioners of the stylish *habros*-culture, with its Ionic and Lydian dress, gold ornaments, sympotic ethos, dainty parasols, and soft musical styles, that flourished during the later sixth and early fifth centuries in Athens and elsewhere:²³

Ἐν τοῖς πρῶτοι δὲ Ἀθηναῖοι τόν τε σίδηρον κατέθεντο καὶ ἀνειμένηι τῆι διαίτηι ἐς τὸ τρυφερώτερον μετέστησαν. καὶ οἱ πρεσβύτεροι αὐτοῖς τῶν εὐδαιμόνων διὰ τὸ ἁβροδίαιτον οὐ πολὺς Χρόνος ἐπειδὴ Χιτῶνάς τε λινοῦς ἐπαύσαντο φοροῦντες καὶ χρυσῶν τεττίγων ἐνέρσει κρωβύλον ἀναδούμενοι τῶν ἐν τῆι κεφαλῆι τριχῶν· ἀφ' οὗ καὶ Ἰώνων τοὺς πρεσβυτέρους κατὰ τὸ ξυγγενὲς ἐπὶ πολὺ αὕτη ἡ σκευὴ κατέσχεν. μετρίαι δ' αὖ ἐσθῆτι καὶ ἐς τὸν νῦν τρόπον πρῶτοι Λακεδαιμόνιοι ἐχρήσαντο καὶ ἐς τὰ ἄλλα πρὸς τοὺς πολλοὺς οἱ τὰ μείζω κεκτημένοι ἰσοδίαιτοι μάλιστα κατέστησαν ... πολλὰ δ' ἂν καὶ ἄλλα τις ἀποδείξειε τὸ παλαιὸν Ἑλληνικὸν ὁμοιότροπα τῶι νῦν βαρβαρικῶι διαιτώμενον.

The Athenians were the first to give up the habit of carrying weapons, and to adopt a way of living that was more relaxed and more luxurious. In fact the elder men of the rich families who had these luxurious tastes only recently gave up wearing linen under-garments and tying their hair in a knot fastened with a clasp of golden grasshoppers: the same fashions spread to their kinsmen in Ionia, and lasted there among the old men for some time. It was the Spartans who first began to dress simply and in accordance with our modern taste, with the rich leading a life that was as much as possible like the life of the ordinary people.... Indeed, one could point to a number of other instances where the manners of the ancient Hellenic world are very similar to the manners of foreigners today.   (Thucydides 1.6.3–4; tr. R. Warner)

Hieron) ... καμόντες οἳ πολλὰ θυμῶι ... Σικελίας ... ἔσαν ὀφθαλμός, P. 5. 51 ὁ Βάττου παλαιὸς ὄλβος ... πύργος ἄστεος, ὄμμα τε φαεννότατον ξένοισι.... The language of 'radiance' applied to the various members of the royal family in this play (esp. 140, 299–301, may carry distinctively 'Eastern' or 'Persian' associations (Hall 1989: 206); but it (also) finds echoes in other (non-Eastern, non-pejorative) contexts in epinikian and tragedy; indeed, the warrior as 'light of salvation' is a commonplace in Homer (see LSJ *s.v.* φάος IIa) and even in democratic (tyrannicide) contexts.

²² For δεσπότης, cf. 169, 241, 587, 1049 (Xerxes); also Dareios at 666 δεσπότα δεσποτᾶν cf. 675–6, 691 δυνάστης.
²³ See esp. Kurke 1992; Miller 1997; also Zanker 1995: 22–31.

104 *Mark Griffith*

So the difference in appearance and lifestyle between the aristocrats of Greece, and those of Lydia and Persia, had not always been
very marked; and the richer a Greek became, the more likely he was
to start resembling a 'Persian' or 'Lydian'. Herodotos tells us that the
Persians themselves were 'extremely imitative',[24] having, he asserts,
copied the ways of the Medes, and then of the Lydians and Greeks.
A more plausible explanation for the similarities he notes between
these cultures is that their élites were interacting quite frequently
throughout the sixth and fifth centuries BCE (esp. in Ionia), and it
was for *that* reason that they came to share common characteristics
of dress and lifestyle.[25] In short, those Asians were really not so
'Other' after all, even though it might sometimes be desirable to
imagine them that way in the course of promoting a democratic
Athenian self-image. We should bear in mind the careers of such
distinguished Athenians as Hippias, Themistokles, Miltiades, and
Alkibiades (to say nothing of the Spartans, Demaratos and Pausanias,
or subsequently Xenophon, or even Alexander the Great), brilliant
dynasts all, who rubbed shoulders comfortably with Persians and
other nobility, and in some cases went to live among them for a while
as petty kings or courtiers.[26]

Two passages early in our play do indeed emphasize the close
kinship between Greeks and Persians.[27] At 80, the Persians are
χρυσογόνου γενεᾶς ('the race born of gold', i.e. descended from
Perseus, son of Danae and Zeus); again perhaps at 145 Δανάης τε
γόνου... (though the text there is doubtful). And in the Queen's
dream, the two tall, beautiful women whom Xerxes struggles to
keep yoked together as a team to draw his chariot are a 'pair of sisters
of the same family' (185–6 κασιγνήτα γένους ταὐτοῦ—n.b. the dual):
and we might note there that the distinction between their respective
clothing as 'Persian and Dorian' (182–3 ἡ μὲν πέπλοισι Περσικοῖς

[24] ξεινικὰ δὲ νόμαια Πέρσαι προσίενται ἀνδρῶν μάλιστα κτλ. (Hdt. 1.135). See
further Miller 1997, passim.
[25] For example, it appears that the Greek custom of reclining at a banquet or
symposium was borrowed from the East: Miller 1997; W. Burkert, *The Orientalizing
Revolution* (Harvard, 1992), 19.
[26] We may assume too that when a wealthy Athenian such as Kimon or Thucydides went to visit his Thracian estates, he presided there more like a king than an
Athenian citizen.
[27] Cf. Hdt. 7.150; also 6.53–4, 7.61–2.

ἠσκημένη, ἡ δ' αὖτε Δωρικοῖσιν . . .) seems implicitly to recognize the similarity or identity of Persian and *Ionian* women's dress in the early fifth century.[28] For although both Dorian and the more elaborate Ionian-style clothing were quite commonly worn by Athenian women of this period, the requisite contrast between the two women is only possible if 'Dorian' is specified, despite its unAthenian associations.[29]

Confirmation of the notion that the Lydian or Persian lifestyle could be, and often was, viewed by Greeks as impressive, desirable, and not much different from that of their own élite, is easy to find. Margaret Miller has documented in full the cultural borrowings between Persians and Athenians during the fifth century. Equally striking, I think, is the regularity with which (as we noted above) Classical Greek political theorists and moralists of the fifth and fourth century cite, as their prime examples of perfect monarchical government, and of the ideal training, achievements, and behavior of a master and leader of men, not such paradigmatic models of Hellenic achievement as Theseus or Lykourgos, Peisistratos or Polykrates, nor even Solon, Miltiades or Kimon, but the Great King of Persia. And although it was Kyros and Dareios in particular who were most frequently cited as the ideal models of human achievement, we may recall too the anecdote in which Themistokles (in his exile from Athens) compliments King Xerxes as being the human equivalent of Zeus on earth, '. . . for you both are called, and both *are*, Great Kings'.[30]

Over and over again, we find the freedom-loving Greeks—including the democratic Athenians—imagining their ideal of the bold and warlike, but intelligent and wise leader as a *king* (*basileus*), and frequently as *The King* of Persia in particular. Nor should this surprise us. Given that *aretē* ('excellence') was generally considered to involve being *better* than others, and that 'happiness' (*eudaimonia, olbos*) was measured in terms of power, wealth, honor and the regard of others, then no more splendid model of human achievement could be found than the Great King, who had conquered more,

---

[28] Indeed, some modern scholars have argued (unconvincingly) that the quiet, obedient woman in 'Persian' dress represents the Ionian Greeks.

[29] Later in the 5th cent., Athenians get bothered by Spartan styles (hair, clothing, etc.): you need not be 'barbarian' to be 'unAthenian' or élitist.

[30] Plutarch, *Them.* 28.3 μεγάλους γὰρ ἀμφοτέρους εἶναί τε καὶ λέγεσθαι βασιλέας.

ruled over more, and was obeyed and feared by more, than anyone
else on earth.[31]

I should make clear that I am not wanting to claim that *all*
Athenians would have looked on Kyros and Dareios and other
Asian potentates as unequivocally impressive and admirable models
of leadership and achievement—only that *some* might, especially
those who were most familiar with aristocratic lifestyle, military
command, athletic competition, and property-ownership, and
those who were not entirely content with democracy as the fairest
or most efficient system for governing a *polis* and rewarding the
merits of the best citizens. There were always plenty of such people
('oligarchs') at Athens, even if they sometimes had to keep quiet
about it, or disguise their opinions. We may recall that immediately
after the Battle of Marathon, it was believed (perhaps correctly) that
members of the Alkmaionid family had preferred the prospect of
Hippias' return to power in Athens (as tyrant, and vassal of the
Persian King) to that of a continuation of autonomous democracy,
and accordingly had attempted to send secret signals in order to open
up the city to the Persians. Whether or not the accusation was true, a
large number of Athenians believed this to be a likely preference for a
noble family to entertain; and the events of subsequent years (at
Kerkyra and elsewhere, and also within Athens itself in 462–1, 411,
404) would confirm these suspicions.

But what about those two notorious 'Persian' features of the play,
'abasement' (*proskunēsis*), and 'dirge' (*goos*)? Wouldn't the spectacle
of grown men (and upper-class men at that, for the Chorus of
Persian Elders are repeatedly so designated) 'prostrating' themselves

---

[31] In Xenophon's *Cyropaedia*, the idealization of the Persian King goes further.
Indeed, it is hilarious to see through what contortions the Loeb translator will go to
explain that this glowing figure of virtue and manliness is really, in Xenophon's mind,
a cross between a Spartan and an Athenian: 'Cyrus's invincible battle lines are not the
wavering, unwieldy hordes of orientals, easily swept away by the Grecian phalanx like
chaff before the strong south-wind, but the heavy, solid masses of Sparta; and his
tactics on the march and in the fury of battle are not the tactics of a "barbarian" king,
but those of the consummate tactician who led the famous 10,000 Greeks from Asia
back to Hellas' (Walter Miller, ed., Xen. *Cyropaedia* (London 1914), p. ix). More
likely, Xenophon, like other cosmopolitan Greek aristocrats, did not subscribe to
simplistic notions of barbarian inferiority and effeminacy: rather, as an élitist of the
old school, he was firmly convinced that 'kingly qualities', while rare and precious, are
to some degree learnable, and in no way restricted to Greeks.

before their Queen and again before the ghost of their former King, mark this whole scenario as something spectacularly and shamefully unGreek—given that *proskunēsis* was regarded as one of the most notorious features of Persian monarchical behavior, a sticking-point of Hellenism and litmus-test of barbarian servility? And don't the shrill wails of 'Oriental' mourners, the tearing of hair and bloody laceration of cheeks and breast, the rhythmic thumping of ground and/or chests, clash irreconcilably with the more restrained Athenian customs of private funerals and public oration?

The answer is not at all clear-cut. The hated *proskun-* word is not in fact employed in the play: rather, what the Persians are said to do is 'fall down before' their revered mother of the King:

> ἀλλ᾽ ἥδε θεῶν ἴσον ὀφθαλμοῖς
> φάος ὁρμᾶται μήτηρ βασιλέως,
> βασίλεια δ᾽ ἐμή· προσπίτνω.

> Here she comes, equal to the Eyes of the Gods,
> Brilliant Light, Mother of the King,
> my Queen: I fall down before her.

> (*Pers.* 150–2)

προσπίπτειν is a word found quite often elsewhere in tragedy to describe the *supplication*, not just of gods, but also of powerful and respected human figures of authority.[32] That is to say, the Persian Chorus' posture in greeting their Queen and former King, while it would certainly be regarded as excessively submissive and out of place in a contemporary Athenian context (especially in relation to the Queen, since not only is she a woman, but they are not even formally supplicating her), would not necessarily, in the context of high tragedy, be experienced as wholly alienating or unGreek.[33] Later, when Dareios arises from his tomb (i.e., as a genuinely super-human figure of veneration, by any standards), the Chorus' posture is not

---

[32] e.g. S. *Ph.* 485, *OC* 1754, *Aj.* 1181; E. *Her.* 79, *Or.* 1332, *Pho.* 293, 924.

[33] In other (later) descriptions of Persian/Lydian 'prostration', the term προσκυνέω is usually employed: e.g. Hdt. 7. 136, and the 'Gyges-drama' (*TrGF vol. 2 adesp.* F 664.9). For a strong statement of the negative case, however, see Hall 1989: 96–7, 156, 206–7 (and 1996 ad loc. on *Pers.* 152), including good discussion of Klytaimestra's behavior at A. *Ag.* 855–974.

verbally specified, though they indicate that they are too terrified and
overawed to gaze at him face-to-face:

> σέβομαι μὲν προσιδέσθαι,
> σέβομαι δ' ἀντία λέξαι
> σέθεν ἀρχαίωι περὶ τάρβει.
>
> I am in awe to gaze at You,
> I am in awe to address You face-to-face,
> in my old fear of You.
>
> (*Pers.* 694–6)

Much would depend in both scenes, of course, on how the 'abasement' or 'genuflection' was staged. The Elders could be 'grovelling'
full-length in a blatantly exaggerated posture never adopted by real-
life Greeks—or they could be kneeling and showing the unreserved
'awe' and 'reverence' (σέβας) that a god expects from his worshippers,
a protector from a supplicant, and (perhaps?) a Greek tyrant from his
subject citizens, a posture not unknown in tragedy (e.g. S. *OT* 1–150,
esp. 1–3, 15–16, 31–43) and not, it seems, inherently degrading.

As for the scenes of ghost-raising and lamentation, here too critics
may have been too hasty to conclude that behavior normally
excluded from everyday Athenian practice was inherently distasteful
and shameful. On the contrary, the reason for the exclusion could be
precisely that this behavior was felt to be so dangerously appealing
and irresistible. This is certainly the case with ritual lamentation.[34]
From at least the time of Solon, legislators had moved to limit the
extravagance and emotionalism of funerals; and in Athens in particular the state became increasingly involved in the ceremonies of
burial and eulogy during the course of the fifth century.[35] It is clear
from the Homeric epics, and from the literary and visual remains of
the Archaic and early Classical periods (including cities other than
Athens during the fifth century), that elaborate and noisy ritual
lamentation, especially if attended by large numbers of Asian and/

[34] See esp. Alexiou 1974; Foley 1993; Holst-Wahrhaft 1992; also Loraux 1986. For
Greek rituals of lamentation in general, see further Reiner 1938, and the etymological
articles by Frisk and Chantraine *svv.* γόος, θρῆνος.

[35] In the Homeric world (real or imaginary), male tears and demonstrations of
violent grief appear to be more acceptable than in democratic Athens; see Montsacré
1984.

or professional mourners, could serve, not only as an effective emotional release for the family and community of the bereaved, but also as a powerful expression of that family's status, wealth, and interests.

In 472 BCE, the sight and sounds of a full-blast ritual lament, performed by a chorus of exotically-dressed foreigners, must certainly have been disturbingly alien to everyday Athenian experience, and would have elicited barbarian and/or old-style Greek aristocratic associations sharply at variance with their own current customs. A scene like the ending of *Persians* would indeed be utterly shocking and unacceptable in 'real-life' Athens. But tragedy is not real life. Choral lamentation, accompanied by the highly emotive *aulos*, and sometimes including singing solo actors too, was to be *expected* at the most emotional moments of a tragic performance: we need look no further than the *kommoi* of *Seven against Thebes* and *Choephoroi*.[36] The meters and language of such scenes are not markedly different from the *kommos* of *Persians*, apart from a few extra syllables of exclamatory coloring in the latter. The Persian lament differs more in degree than in the particular character of its individual ingredients.[37]

Attempts have been made to distinguish between the (conventional = acceptable) laments performed by *female* choruses or soloists, and the (unacceptable, Orientalized and effeminate) lyrics sung here by the *male* Xerxes and Persian Elders.[38] But any such distinction is undermined, I think, by Orestes' role in the long and passionate invocation over the tomb of Agamemnon in Aischylos' *Choephoroi*: for the young man's lyric alternations with Elektra and the Asian slave-women are powerfully sympathetic and engaging, and in no way effeminate or foreign.[39]

[36] For a full list of tragic *kommoi*, with useful discussion, see Broadhead 1960: 310–17.

[37] Hall 1989: 83–4 'the dirge ... is of inordinate length and emotional abandonment; *excessive* mourning practices were considered barbaric...' (84). On the musical and metrical character of these scenes, see West 1992: 23–4, 349–54; W. Kranz, *Stasimon* (Berlin, 1933), 127–42.

[38] Hall 1989: 84, 1993. She emphasizes too the 'shrillness' of the (male) singing (esp. 332 κωκύματα, 427 κωκύμασιν, 468 ἀνακωκύσας λιγύ), as further evidence of the Persians' effeminacy and degeneracy, and as contributing to the resultant 'effect of near-hysteria' (83). But κωκύω is elsewhere used to describe the (intensely masculine) wails of dismay and grief in S. *Ant.* 1206 ὀρθίων κωκυμάτων, 1227 ἀνακωκύσας (from both Haimon and Kreon; cf. 1079).

[39] That is not to say that no element of danger, of the risqué, may be present there too: Orestes is after all the son of those extravagant and transgressive aristocratic

Numerous texts of the fifth and fourth centuries confirm that melodies (especially 'Asian' melodies) sung and danced to the *aulos* were likely to stimulate an audience to extreme emotional states, and that such a process was felt to be intensely enjoyable.[40] It therefore seems unlikely that the audience's prevailing response to the final scene of *Persians* was ridicule or clear-cut disapproval. An element of disassociation and distaste, perhaps; but also a half-guilty surrender to tears and pity, mixed with the relief of sharing the feelings with others (fellow-spectators, Chorus, even Xerxes?) and the excitement of hearing and seeing such 'forbidden' (unAthenian, undemocratic) sights and sounds.[41] Certainly, two generations later, it is with unmixed delight that Aristophanes' Dionysos recalls the Persian Elders' exotic cries:

ἐχάρην γοῦν, ἡνίκ' ἐκώκυσας περὶ Δαρείου τεθνεῶτος,
ὁ χορὸς δ' εὐθὺς τὼ χεῖρ' ὡδὶ συγκρούσας εἶπεν·"Ιαυοῖ'

I loved it when you wailed around dead Dareios,
and the Chorus right there clapped their hands together
like this, and said 'Iauoi!'

(*Frogs* 1128–9)

The ghost-raising scene (*Pers.* 598–906) shares many exotic and 'forbidden' features with the *kommos*. For necromancy, like other kinds of magic, was never a publicly-approved ritual process; yet it

parents, Agamemnon and Klytaimestra, and his exotic laments may contribute to our ambivalent feelings about him: is he 'savior', or 'lion-cub', to his house and city?

[40] Korybantic ritual was especially well-known for this; and see Alexiou 1974: 10–23; Holst-Wahrhaft 1992 on 'Phrygian', 'Lydian' and 'Ielemistrian' melodies; also W. B. Anderson, *Ethos and Education in Greek Music* (Harvard, 1966).

[41] Similarly mixed responses were presumably elicited in the theater by Euripides' chorus of Bacchant Women, and by Aischylos' terrified but assertive Egyptian maidens (*Suppliants*), or Asian slaves (*Cho.*), and Erinyes (in *Eum.*). In each case, the chorus' exotic and unrestrained character is intermittently but explicitly emphasized, through language, meter, music, choreography, posture, and gesture; and their 'transgressive' character (i.e. their violation of 'normal' Athenian civic codes) is thus highlighted; see Gould 1996. Yet each of these choruses undeniably commands an intensely sympathetic engagement from the audience—sometimes at the very moments when their language and movements are most immodest and self-indulgent, though in each case they are also (intermittently) given spoken and sung passages of great wisdom and sobriety to utter. It is clear in any case that the exotic 'color' of such choruses throws into relief, both positive and negative, the plain and featureless norms of the ordinary citizen (cf. Stallybrass and White 1986).

seems to have been quite widely practised, and is not in any case easily
to be distinguished from conventional hero- and ancestor-cult.[42] In
both cases offerings are made, prayers and/or songs uttered (with or
without the help of music), and the (spirit/body of) the dead person is
invoked. Rarely (we may assume) did the dead actually rise up in
person: but this is of course intrinsically more likely to happen in a
theater, and may at some periods have been almost conventional in
tragic invocations.[43] In any case, both inside and outside the theater,
the seductive—and in certain contexts forbidden—attraction of the
(Greek, or more often non-Greek, male) 'moaner' (γόης) with his
'magic songs' (ἐπωιδαί) is well-attested.[44]

Overall, the spectacle of ritualistic hair-tearing, ground-beating,
and garment-shredding, and the sounds of shrill 'Persian' wailing
and antiphonal chanting, would, I think, repel and attract the various
elements of the Athenian audience in equal measure. Repel, because
such scenes are so far removed from what contemporary Athenians
would ever be allowed to do themselves in 'real life'; but attract too,
because the intrinsic appeal of such glamorous lamentation and soul-
stirring incantations was irresistibly strong.

In general, the racist and ethnic stereotypes of the 'Persian' or 'Asian'
seem to have been much less deeply imprinted on Greek minds (at
least at this early date) than the British or North American racist
fantasies of the nineteenth and twentieth centuries, with their
grotesque misrepresentations of Chinese or African or Native
American characters.[45] (We might think of Marlowe's Tamburlaine,

---

[42] See Broadhead 1960: 302–9; Headlam 1902; S. Eitrem, *SO* 6 (1928), 1–16;
Belloni 1988: 184–7; Hall 1989: 89–91.

[43] See Taplin 1977: 105–6, 114–19, 447–8. In Senecan and Elizabethan drama,
ghosts are quick to appear, and are almost *de rigeur*.

[44] See esp. Dodds 1951; Burkert 1962.

[45] It is difficult, but important, in all of this to recognize both the continuities
and the discontinuities between Classical Athenian attitudes and assumptions about
race, ethnicity, and cultural difference, and those of the modern West. Thus, while it
is true that the insidious and pervasive tradition of 'Orientalism' can be traced
directly and continuously back to 5th-cent. Athens, and to this play in particular,
and true too that we can point to texts (such as, most notoriously, the opening
chapters of Aristotle's *Politics*, and the Hippokratic *Airs Waters Places*) in which
the 'naturally slavish' character of Asians is proposed as a justification for slavery
and for Greek imperialism, and is supported by various empirical and theoretical

or Shakespeare's Othello, as being more closely analogous, with
their ambivalently exotic/admirable heroes.) To some upper-class
Athenians, the Lydians, and even the Persians and Medes, were
probably imagined as being less different from themselves in their
life-style and attitudes than the Spartans—or than their own lower-
class fellow-citizens. A play set in the capital city of Persia, and
presenting the Persian royal family on stage as its leading characters,
was free to develop its own atmosphere and assumptions; for Kyros,
Dareios and Xerxes (like Kroisos, or Priam) were figures who would
resonate very powerfully in the Athenian imagination, as embodi-
ments of élite aspiration, achievement—*and also failure.* And it is
highly significant that the one most conspicuous failing of which the
Great Kings were guilty, according to Plato and other Greek writers,
was the upbringing of their sons.

In Plato's *Laws* (694d), we are told that the one major error
committed by the admirable Kyros was that of entrusting the education of his children to the *women* (because he was too busy leading
armies on campaign: ἔοικεν ἐκ νέου στρατεύεσθαι διὰ βίου, ταῖς
γυναιξὶν παραδοὺς τοὺς παῖδας τρέφειν)—and the natural result was
the despicable Kambyses, just as the great Dareios was succeeded by

arguments, nonetheless there were no systematic theories of inherited racial difference, based on skin-color, brain-size, cranial shape, genetics, etc. (And in any case
the physical features of an Iranian or a Hellene—or for that matter, a Lydian, or
Syrian, or Phoenician—would generally be indistinguishable, once you removed
their slippers and trousers, or χιτών. Only if their περίζωμα was removed as well
would one know that these must be Greeks, since no one else would thus display
themselves in public.) Even the author of *Airs Waters Places*, after an extended
account (12–23) of the natural (i.e., geographical and climatic) causes of Scythian
moistness and flabbiness, and of Asian softness and luxuriance in general, as against
Greek toughness and courage, ends up suddenly adding (23) that of course the reason
lies also in their *nomoi* (customs, laws, political system); and the same ambivalence
between natural and cultural explanations for ethnic difference is constantly detect-
able in Herodotos.

It might be argued, perhaps, that in 472 BCE, just eight years after the Persian forces
had occupied Athens and burnt the temples on the Acropolis, prejudice against the
barbarian must have been running high. But the level of hostility, and the degree of
difference, manifested in the 5th-cent. literary and iconographical representations
seem more akin to, e.g. Saxon resentment of Normans, or 18th-cent. American
opposition to the British, than to post-World War II caricature of fanatical blond
Germans and treacherous slit-eyed Japanese. Yes, the Persians burnt our temples—
but we Ionians had burnt Sardis first....

his inferior son, Xerxes.[46] And, as Plato and other authors make clear, this failure is not to be regarded as a peculiarly Persian weakness: rather, it is seen as being endemic to aristocratic and despotic households in general. Over-protective or ambitious mothers, spoilt and over-aggressive sons, are seldom able to measure up to the achievements of their fathers, who are themselves all too likely to be absent on campaign or preoccupied with the affairs of state. This characteristic 'problem' of dynastic rule seems likewise to be reflected in Athenian society (or at least in the Athenian imagination) in the proverbial inability of the Olympian Perikles to educate his sons to any worthwhile level of achievement, and also in that same regal leader's subservience to the impressive but shameless Aspasia.[47] And, as we shall see, it lies at the heart of Aischylos' representation of his tragic royal family of *Persians.*

The young Xerxes instantiates and embodies the pressures experienced by the aristocratic Greek family at their most unmanageable extreme. His father has built up the largest and most glorious *oikos*-estate in the world:[48] through conquest and wise rule, Dareios came to command the respect and devotion of his innumerable subjects; and he also acquired a wife who herself embodies all the female virtues of glamor, loyalty, piety, fertility, and skill at textile manufacture. How is his son to prove *his* manhood and brilliance, and live up to his father's expectations? Not by sitting around 'indoors'—this is the very taunt that his sympotic buddies keep levelling at him, according to his mother:

ταῦτά τοι κακοῖς ὁμιλῶν ἀνδράσιν διδάσκεται[49]
θούριος Ξέρξης. λέγουσι δ' ὡς σὺ μὲν μέγαν τέκνοις
πλοῦτον ἐκτήσω σὺν αἰχμῆι, τὸν δ' ἀνανδρίας ὕπο
ἔνδον αἰχμάζειν, πατρῶιον δ' ὄλβον οὐδὲν αὐξάνειν.

---

[46] *Laws* 3. 695d–e; cf. Hdt. 1.136 'Before the age of five a boy lives with the women . . .', and 3.3 (the ten-year-old Kambyses' promise to his complaining mother) 'Well, mother, . . . when I'm a man, I'll turn Egypt upside down for you'; we may recall too the account of the education of the young Alkibiades by a Spartan woman (Antisthenes fr. 201, cf. Plato, *Alc.* 121d3–4, with N. Denyer's n.).

[47] On the sons of 'King' Perikles, see Strauss 1993: 132–3. Sokrates was supposed to do better for the young sons of the leading citizens.

[48] For Persia-Asia as private *oikos* of Dareios, cf. Goldhill 1988. (Yet at 682 it is also called a *polis.*)

[49] διδάσκομαι, ὁμιλεῖν, in conjunction with ἀγαθοί vs. κακοί, κτλ., are all thoroughly aristocratic-sympotic terms, esp. in Theognis (e.g. 31–8).

Such were the lessons headstrong Xerxes received
as he passed his leisure among worthless companions.
They kept telling him that you built up huge wealth for your children
with the spear-point, while he for lack of manliness was shafting indoors,
and bringing no increase to his patrimony.

(*Pers.* 753–6)

There are hints that she too has been asking the same question, in her own way (163–4, 211–12 παῖς ἐμὸς | πράξας μὲν εὖ θαυμαστὸς ἂν γένοιτ' ἀνήρ...), even as she has also been smothering him with protective concern and fine garments.

It is important to recognize that, for all the luxurious and delicate language with which Xerxes is surrounded in the text, and for all his own conspicuous failure to prove his manly prowess on the battle-field, he himself is not characterized as effeminate or degenerate: he is no Aigisthos or Paris. Xerxes' errors are due, not to cowardice or laziness, but to the rashness of youth. His standing epithets are νέος ('youthful', e.g. 744, 782; also 13?) and θούριος (73, 718, 754; cf. 136), a word that is often translated 'headstrong' or 'furious', and is derived from the same root as θρώισκω, which means 'leap' or 'mount' (it is the word used notoriously by Apollo to denote the male parent in his paternity argument: *Eum.* 660 τίκτει δ' ὁ θρώισκων): perhaps 'thrust-ing' would best convey the connotations. 'Young thrusting Xerxes' has gone off on his campaign to win himself glory, a campaign that by convention involves imagistically—and often literally—the acqui-sition both of new territory and of a bride (in this case 'Helle/Hellas', with all that concomitant language of 'yoking' and 'taming': 69–73, 131–2, 593–4, 722, 736, 745–8, 799, etc.).[50] But he has been led astray by those seductive feminine divinities *Atē* and *Apatē* (Folly and Delusion), into attempting more than his undisciplined and over-confident strength can manage (93–100, 181–96, 782–3; cf. 826 ἄλλων ἐρασθείς), and instead finds his own 'yoke' and 'strength' broken (190–97, 594 ἐλύθη ζυγὸν ἀλκᾶς, 928–30 αἰαῖ κεδνᾶς ἀλκᾶς... ἐπὶ γόνυ κέκλιται). He himself is the one 'tamed' (279 στρατὸς δαμασθείς, 906 δμαθέντες) and 'stripped naked' (1036 γυμνός εἰμι); and he has left all the Persian bedrooms, which in his father's day were bursting

---

[50] For rape/marriage as a metaphor for conquest and colonization, see Dougherty 1993.

with men and their happy wives, now full of the wails of 'single-yoked' brides (139 μονόζυξ, 579, 734). His own torn and spoilt clothing reminds us of the physical lacerations that his troops have undergone, in a virtual deflowering by the Greek spears, oars, and the rocky coastline itself.[51]

The Persians, and Xerxes among them, are thus represented, not as eternally womanish and weak, but as having *recently lost* their once-proud manhood:[52] the beautiful, precious ἥβη, ἄνθος, and ἄωτος embodied and symbolized by Xerxes and his companions (all terms characteristically used of young aristocratic men in their military-athletic prime) have been dissipated and spoiled, and he has brought back nothing but shame for himself and his family. How will the master, the eye and light of the house, be received? Who will greet him? What are they to say to him, and he to them? How can they—or he—face the eye, or the idea, of his father?

In all this, Xerxes is represented in terms that recall an unsuccessful PanHellenic athlete returning home, an also-ran/fallen wrestler-boxer or pankratiast whose 'loop of *nostos*' now requires him to deal with the prospect of his community's, and his family's shame and scorn. Where Agamemnon in Aischylos' play returns in triumph from Troy to an enkomiastic greeting from his loyal Elders (and the red-tapestry treatment from his faithless wife),[53] Xerxes must face an anti-*enkomion*, as he slinks home alone, shorn of insignia and accoutrements, and thus almost incognito, to his welcoming committee of Elders—and to his *mother*.

That is just how it is for Pindaric failures, too:

τέτρασι δ' ἔμπετες ὑψόθεν
σωμάτεσσι κακὰ φρονέων,
τοῖς οὔτε νόστος ὁμῶς
ἔπαλπνος ἐν Πυθιάδι κρίθη,
οὐδὲ μολόντων πὰρ ματέρ' ἀμφὶ γέλως γλυκὺς

---

[51] On lacerations and rags (and Xerxes), see Hall (passim); Taplin 1977: 92–100; 119–27; Thalmann 1980; also King 1983, esp. 119–21; N. Loraux 'Blessures de virilité', *Le juire humain* 10 (1984), 39–56 (and other pieces).

[52] 'Aeschylus' Darius stresses how different Xerxes is from his predecessors, especially from Darius himself (759–86): Xerxes' aggression is here seen as an *aberration* (Pelling 1997*a*: 15).

[53] See Crane 1993.

ὦρσεν χάριν· κατὰ λαύρας δ' ἐχθρῶν ἀπάοροι
πτώσσοντι, συμφοραῖ δεδαγμένοι.

On four opponents' bodies you hurled yourself fiercely from above,
and they were granted no cheerful return from Pytho:
no sweet laughter provided warm welcome, when they came home
to their mother's side. Down the back-alleys,
out of sight of enemies, they skulk, bitten by failure.

(Pindar, *P.* 8. 82–7)[54]

When a young man returns from the Games as victor, it is his father
and his companions who are routinely mentioned in epinikian
poetry as sharing his joy and honor. As for the *non*-victors—rarely
are we asked to picture their return; but when we are, as here, we find
one of the few mentions of the *mother's* presence.[55] Indeed, it is
specifically to the proximity of her maternal body that the athletes
are imagined as returning (85 παρ ματέρα)—and it remains ambiguous how much is negated by the οὐδέ that precedes—do they 'not
return to the mother' at all, or do they 'return to the mother—but by
back-streets, and without the laughter and χάρις' that the victor
receives? This ambiguity, or quibble, is not trivial, and it presents a
close analogy with *The Persians*. For there is a notorious problem in
our play, concerning the 'false preparation' for a meeting between the
Queen and her son, and for his reception of new clothes from her.

Δαρ.   σὺ δ', ὦ γεραιὰ μῆτερ ἡ Ξέρξου φίλη,
          ἐλθοῦσ' ἐς οἴκους κόσμον ὅστις εὐπρεπὴς
          λαβοῦσ' ὑπαντίαζε παιδί ...
          ἀλλ' αὐτὸν εὐφρόνως σὺ πράυνον λόγοις·
          μόνης γάρ, οἶδα, σοῦ κλύων ἀνέξεται ...

Βα.   ... ἀλλ' εἶμι καὶ λαβοῦσα κόσμον ἐκ δόμων
          ὑπαντιάζειν παιδί μου πειράσομαι·
          οὐ γὰρ τὰ φίλτατ' ἐν κακοῖς προδώσομεν.

---

[54] δεδαιγμένοι might be a preferable reading, ('split, ripped'), though meter tells
against it. I am grateful to Enrica Sciarrino for reminding me of this Pindaric passage.
We may compare too the Spartan mother's proverbial command to her departing son,
'With your shield or on it'—but here Xerxes returns with empty 'quiver' (1020–5).

[55] Another is *P.* 4. 186–7, where the cowardly youth who does not even dare to set
out on the loop of *nostos* is described, 'left behind, he hangs around by his mother's
side all of his unadventurous life, munching' (λειπόμενον τὰν ἀκίνδυνον παρὰ ματρὶ
μένειν αἰῶνα πέσσοντα); cf. *O.* 8. 67–9; Kurke 1991: 28.

DARIUS: But you, old and beloved mother of Xerxes,
             Go to the house, fetch fine and suitable clothing
             and meet your son with it....
             ... Calm him with gentle words;
             For you, I know, are the only one he will bear to listen to.
QUEEN: ... But I shall go and get fine robes from the palace,
             and try to meet my son.
             For I shall not betray my dearest in a time of trouble.

                                               (*Pers.* 832–4, 837–8; 849–52)

In the event, mother and son do not meet on stage, and we are never quite sure *when* Xerxes will actually receive the promised comfort of the maternal embrace. So, even though the earlier scenes of the play were saturated with his mother's references to Xerxes' precious presence within the house, and the scene between Dareios and Atossa has brought this connection even more prominently into our awareness, the final scene significantly follows a different course. Maternal comfort is reserved for later, a private and more intimate sequel to the official 'reception' that Xerxes is actually given on stage—by his father's 'age-mates' and 'trusty companions'.

The emphasis in this play on the Queen's role as mother is obviously crucial in determining our attitude to this royal family, and to Xerxes in particular. As we observed earlier, aristocratic families—and likewise the Persian royal family—were suspected of failing to exercise proper control over their women;[56] and in particular it was claimed that mothers were allowed to play altogether too active a role in the raising of young boys. The Queen's anxious questions and smothering concern for her son, and her complete disregard for the political dimensions of her nation's defeat,[57] thus tend to confirm this stereotype in a manner that is perhaps both disgusting (because shameful in public, Greek, democratic terms) and yet seductively appealing (because every boy or man would secretly wish to be able to count on such a mother).

---

[56] We might add the examples of Herodotos' wife of Kandaules (1. 10–12), and Atossa herself (esp. 3. 133–4, 7. 1–4); see H. Sancisi-Weerdenburg, 'Exit Atossa: images of women in Greek historiography on Persia', in Cameron and Kuhrt 1983: 20–33.
[57] This is well brought out by Goldhill 1988.

The Queen-mother is herself wife of a god, and mother of a god (157), and she 'will not betray her dearest...' (851 τὰ φίλτατ᾽ οὐ προδώσομεν). The promise that she is securely in place (along with the clothing) to greet and comfort the young prince, provides a guarantee (all the more reassuring because it is kept off the public stage) of total acceptance and psychological recuperation for him that on the one hand avoids the embarrassing prospect of Xerxes' public infantilization, and on the other allays the anxiety provoked by his isolation and prospect of parental abandonment.[58] Likewise earlier, in the narrative of the Queen's Dream, Xerxes is described as *seeing his father observe him* crash and fall (197–9 πίπτει δ᾽ ἐμὸς παῖς, καὶ πατὴρ παρίσταται | Δαρεῖος... τὸν δ᾽ ὅπως ὁρᾶι Ξέρξης...), while the dreamer herself (his mother) remains implicitly invisible and non-judgmental. The Queen has no role in the Dream for herself; the images and events are reported just as she 'saw' them, or as they 'came into her view': 200 καὶ ταῦτα μὲν δὴ νυκτὸς εἰσιδεῖν λέγω, 181–3 ἐδοξάτην... εἰς ὄψιν μολεῖν (cf. 176 νυκτέροις ὀνείρασιν ξύνειμι..., 179 ἐναργὲς εἰδόμην..., 188... ὡς ἐγὼ 'δόκουν ὁρᾶν). Xerxes, it seems, does not see *her* in the Dream, and *her* view and experience of the nightmare are virtually fused with *his*, in an identity of perceptions and feelings that links them closely in separation from, and dread of, the stern figure of the by-standing father. And it is to this keenly observant paternal figure that I wish to turn next.

3. DAREIOS: SUPERVISOR AND (GOD-)FATHER

The recuperation and idealization of Dareios, as perfect king-and-father, master-and-god, is staged as an extraordinarily powerful psycho-political event.[59] There is nothing else quite like it in extant tragedy, though it finds significant resonances in the famous

---

[58] Slater 1968; Caldwell 1970; Devereux 1976; Paduano 1978; cf. Adelman 1992.

[59] On psychoanalytic interpretations of son/(absent) father/mother triangles in Greek myth and literature, see Slater 1968; Green 1979; on these issues in *Pers.*, Caldwell 1970: 77–81; Devereux 1976: 1–23; Paduano 1978, 1986. On Aischylos' Dareios in general, Alexanderson 1967; Winnington-Ingram 1983; Gagarin 1976; Saïd 1981.

kommos of *Libation Bearers*, and has parallels too in some of the divine and/or prophetic apparitions of several other tragedies, in which a figure such as Teiresias, or the Dioskouroi, or Herakles, or Athena, appears to the benighted human characters, explains the moral and daimonic dimensions of the situation, and thus directs the action to its proper conclusion. What is unique about Dareios, however, is that he is ritually conjured up from the dead before our very eyes, and that his own personal connection to the other characters is so close and direct, as husband, comrade, father, and king (as Agamemnon would be, were he actually to appear and speak in *Libation Bearers*).

There are critics who think Dareios' appearance must have been experienced as grotesque and distancing: his yellow slippers, tiara, and sumptuous robes, the Chorus' abasement and terrified reaction to seeing him, the effusive iambic and (especially) lyric expressions of praise and awe, including references to his divinity and infallibility— which involve, of course, a curious amnesia about his rise to power, his previous yoking of the Hellespont, his disastrous Scythian expedition, and the Battle of Marathon itself—all of these, it is claimed, mark this scene out as an egregious example of Oriental excess and self-delusion.

But I don't think such a response is plausible. As we have seen, the 'psychagogic wailings' (687 ψυχαγωγοῖς γόοις) that attend—indeed *cause*, through their perlocutionary power—Dareios' ascension from the Underworld, carry a considerable positive, as well as negative, charge. The combination of libation-offerings and incantation is in fact quite closely modelled on real-life nekromantic or hero-worshipping ceremonies, such as might, in some Greek communities and in some contexts of emergency, be directed at a great ancestor or local daimon. And it demonstrably works[60]—the appeal for help *does* reach Dareios in the Underworld, and he responds in all his splendor and good-will.

---

[60] See Taplin 1977: 114–19, Pelling 1997a. We may recall the stories of the bones of Theseus and of Orestes, reclaimed from Skyros and Tegea respectively to be talismans in their native lands; or the predicted hero-cult of Oidipous in S. *OC*. We may think too of Agamemnon's tomb in *Cho.* and of the mysterious heroic ghosts who showed up to assist the Athenians at Marathon.

As Dareios emerges into view, his opening speech interweaves exemplary civic-Greek phrases and images with exotic (but not unfamiliar) details of 'Eastern' ritual and spiritualism:

> ὦ πιστὰ πιστῶν ἥλικές θ' ἥβης ἐμῆς,
> Πέρσαι γεραιοί, τίνα πόλις πονεῖ πόνον;
> στένει, κέκοπται, καὶ χαράσσεται πέδον.
> λεύσσων δ' ἄκοιτιν τὴν ἐμὴν τάφου πέλας
> ταρβῶ, χοὰς δὲ πρευμενὴς ἐδεξάμην.   685
> ὑμεῖς δὲ θρηνεῖτ' ἐγγὺς ἐστῶτες τάφου
> καὶ ψυχαγωγοῖς ὀρθιάζοντες γόοις
> οἰκτρῶς καλεῖσθέ μ'· ἐστὶ δ' οὐκ εὐέξοδον
> ἄλλως τε πάντως, χοὶ κατὰ χθονὸς θεοὶ
> λαβεῖν ἀμείνους εἰσὶν ἢ μεθιέναι.   690
> ὅμως δ' ἐκείνοις ἐνδυναστεύσας ἐγὼ
> ἥκω· τάχυνε δ', ὡς ἄμεμπτος ὦ χρόνου.
> τί ἐστι Πέρσαις νεοχμὸν ἐμβριθὲς κακόν;
>
> (*Pers.* 681–93)

The first two lines immediately establish the reciprocal bonds of aristocratic 'comradeship' (πιστ-, ἥλικες), further underlining their conventional Greek associations by referring to the Persian Empire as a *polis* (681–2). But the next line mentions the 'ripping and furrowing' of the earth, a reference to the extravagant gestures employed in the preceding incantation.[61] Then in 686–8, the reference to the Chorus' 'lamentation' and 'shrill cries' (θρηνεῖτε ... ὀρθιάζοντες) is summed up in the evocative 'mind-bending/ soul-catching wails' (ψυχαγωγοῖς ... γόοις), a phrase that perfectly captures the urgent yet mysterious power of the rhythmic incantation to 'move the spirits' of living and dead alike.[62]

---

[61] On these, see Headlam 1902; Broadhead 1960 ad loc.

[62] ψυχαγωγία is the most commonly used term in the 5th and 4th cent. for the emotional and persuasive effects of music, poetry, and sophistic rhetoric; frequently this process is directly compared to, or equated with, the 'conjuring' effects of 'magicians' and 'incanters' (especially in Plato), cf. J. de Romilly *Magic and rhetoric in ancient Greece* (Harvard, 1975); also Burkert 1962. Aristotle continues to use ψυχαγωγεῖν (casually, in a non-technical sense) in the *Poetics*, for the effects of the best tragedy, perhaps following the example of Gorgias (B 11.60–4 DK): αἱ γὰρ ἔνθεοι διὰ λόγων ἐπῳδαὶ ἐπαγωγοὶ ἡδονῆς, ἀπαγωγοὶ λύπης γίνονται· συγγινομένη γὰρ τῆι δόξηι τῆς ψυχῆς ἡ δύναμις τῆς ἐπῳδῆς ἔθελξε καὶ ἔπεισε καὶ μετέστησεν αὐτὴν γοητείαι. γοητείας δὲ καὶ μαγείας δισσαὶ τέχναι εὕρηνται, αἵ εἰσι ψυχῆς ἀγωγήματα καὶ δόξης ἀπατήματα. (ψυχῆς ἀγωγήματα here is admittedly my own emendation of

We need to be careful, along with our other corrections against chronic Orientalism, not to buy subconsciously into the assumption that all Other (non-Western) gods are necessarily phoney, and that any worship directed towards them must be seen as deluded or blasphemous, even ridiculous. The Athenians would not find it hard to believe that the mightiest King of the mightiest Empire on earth had heroic and demonic powers after death—indeed, many of them might well believe that he had some special divine attributes during his lifetime, as his own subjects believed.[63]

In the imagination of the Elders and of Queen Atossa, and (vicariously) in the imagination of the audience in the Theater, this resplendent figure rising from behind the tomb or altar to the sound of the *aulos* and Phrygian-style wails and chants, dressed (thanks to the special resources and licences of the Theater) more sumptuously than any human being they had ever seen in their lives (though the brilliant robes and crowns of their own gods' statues would presumably provide a comparable display), this figure is the reincarnation, or phantasm, of the grandest grandee the Athenians could imagine. Grander even than Kroisos, or the Egyptian pharaohs, and grander by far than old King Priam or Agamemnon or Minos, this towering figure is conceived of as being virtually perfect, almost super-human—a source of authority, wisdom, power, mastery, and reassurance second to none on earth.[64] And in so far as his sojourn in the Underworld has added an extra dimension of knowledge and uncanniness to his natural wisdom and experience, Dareios is able to speak, and be spoken to, in terms that recall at times the ultimate father and king of all, Ζεύς, ἄναξ ἀνδρῶν τε θεῶν τε.[65] As he narrates the succession-story of Median-Persian kings,

the MSS' pointless ἁμαρτήματα; but even without the emendation, the preceding ἐπαγωγοί . . . ἀπαγωγοί . . . evoke the same dynamic.)

[63] Such terms as *isotheos, isodaimon* would not be intrinsically impious or absurd (given that Homeric and Hesiodic diction gave plenty of parallels; and the language of *makarismos* provided more). In the next century, Alexander the Great, Demetrios Poliorketes, and others, were well aware of all this when they demanded divine honors. And cf. Xenophon's account of the 'divine' (θεῖος) quality of a noble landowner as seen through the eyes of his slaves (*Oikonomikos* 21.11).

[64] On the resources of the Theater of Dionysos (how spectacular could they be?), see Taplin 1977: 434–51 and passim; also Goldhill 1990.

[65] Dareios is described in quasi-divine terms, or in close association with the gods, at 711, 739–41, 762–4, 783, 827–8, 855–6, 914–17, etc.

Dareios emphasizes throughout that these kings were granted their power by Zeus (762–79); and there is nothing in the narrative to suggest that we are supposed to take these claims ironically.

This is the reason, I think, why the Chorus, when they sing their nostalgic praises of their lost king, are led to erase completely any suggestion of failure from Dareios' record, and to reconfigure him as the perfect source of comfort and protection, and the unattainable model of emulation too. One phrase is particularly telling, though it has generally been misunderstood: as they list Dareios' imperial acquisitions within the Ionian Greek world (names that in many cases had recently left the Persian Empire and joined the Delian League—further proof of Xerxes' failure to match up to his immortal father's example), and as they emphasize the many 'glorious expeditions' (857 εὐδοκίμους στρατιὰς) that he led and the 'successful returns' that always kept the households prosperous' (861 νόστοι ἀπαθεῖς . . . εὖ πράσσοντας ἦγον οἴκους), the Chorus remark that he won all these territories 'without even stirring from his fire-side' (866 οὐδ᾽ ἀφ᾽ ἑστίας συθείς). Critics have seized on this as further evidence of misguided Oriental values: barbarians prefer their kings to sit at home and have others do the work and face the dangers for them (precisely Achilleus' complaint to Agamemnon in the *Iliad*). But elsewhere in the play it has been clearly stated that Dareios, like Kyros before him, acquired his wealth by his own 'much labor' (751 πολὺς πλούτου πόνος, the proper term for aristocratic expenditure of effort), and that [he] 'went on campaign many times' (780 ἐπεστράτευσα πολλά), and 'acquired great wealth for [his] children with the spear' (754–5 μέγαν τέκνοις | πλοῦτον ἐκτήσω σὺν αἰχμῆι). So why the apparent contradiction? Because the Chorus in their lyrics are using *sacral* language: and anything a god does should be done 'easily', 'without lifting a finger'.[66] Above all, it is Father Zeus himself who is so described (especially in Aischylos): 'Effortlessly he brings about his will . . . without even moving from his holy seat' (βίαν δ᾽ οὔτιν᾽ ἐξοπλίζει. πᾶν ἄπονον δαιμονίων· ἥμενος ὂν φρόνημά πως αὐτόθεν ἐξέπραξεν ἔμπας ἑδράνων ἀφ᾽ ἁγνῶν, A. *Supp.* 98–103).[67]

---

[66] Hesiod *WD* 1–10 Δί᾽ ἐννέπετε, σφέτερον πατέρ᾽ ὑμνείουσαι, . . . ῥέα μὲν . . . , ῥεῖα δὲ . . . Ζεὺς ὑψιβρεμέτης.

[67] Cf. *Ag.* 182–3 δαιμόνων δέ που χάρις βίαιος σέλμα σεμνὸν ἥμενων. Likewise A. *Th.* 512–13 Ζεὺς πατὴρ ἐπ᾽ ἀσπίδος | σταδαῖος ἧσται διὰ χερὸς βέλος φλέγων (vs

It is only with the arrival of Dareios on stage that the name of 'Zeus' and the theme of 'punishment for over-reaching' become prominent.[68] On the one hand, this can be said to demonstrate Dareios' superior moral stature, and to underline the comparative shortsightedness of the Chorus, and even of the Queen, both of whom have spoken in terms rather of 'the deception of the gods' or 'change of fortune'.[69] But at another level these references to Zeus as the divine 'punisher' and 'overseer' and 'reviewer' (827 Ζεύς τοι κολαστής, 828 εὔθυνος βαρύς), and to 'the present divine fortune' (825 τὸν παρόντα δαίμονα), seem almost to suggest an identification, or at least an analogy, between Father Zeus and Father Dareios himself, now present before us, just as he was imagined previously as 'standing beside' Xerxes in the Dream:

> πίπτει δ' ἐμὸς παῖς, καὶ πατὴρ παρίσταται
> Δαρεῖος οἰκτίρων σφε· τὸν δ' ὅπως ὁρᾶι
> Ξέρξης, πέπλους ῥήγνυσιν ἀμφὶ σώματι.

My son falls; and Father Dareios is standing by,
pitying him. And when Xerxes see Him,
he rips his robes all around his body.

(*Pers.* 197–9)

It was Zeus who gave Dareios his power and authority (739–40, 762–4; cf. 914–17), as previously to 'blessed Kyros' (767–72). Thus the arrival into (our, and the Chorus') view of this embodiment of parental and monarchical authority, previously 'hidden' underground or 'seen' only in dreams, lends to the notion of the royal 'Eye' a renewed element, not merely of the uniquely precious 'light', but of the inescapably observant and judgmental 'gaze'.[70] Earlier (in the Dream) Xerxes was

Typhoeos, emphasizing that Zeus 'just stands [or 'sits'?] there' to throw his thunder-bolt: he doesn't have to run or exert himself). See further Friis Johansen and Whittle on A. *Supp.* 100–3.

[68] Earlier it was the divine *phthonos* theme, and various anonymous *daimones* or θεός τις.

[69] After Dareios' departure, the Chorus do not in fact make a point of lecturing Xerxes about avoiding the gods' displeasure (despite 829–31). Does this mean (as many critics conclude) that neither they nor he has learned anything (dumb barbarians); so e.g. Georges 1994? Or that the closing scene is concerned with something other than moral instruction?

[70] See above, n. 20. Dareios is repeatedly summoned from the 'hidden' depths to 'reveal' himself in the upper light: 630 πέμψατε ... ἐς φῶς, 646 ἐκάλυψεν, 649

overwhelmed when 'he sees <Dareios> standing by' (198 τὸν δ᾽ ὅπως ὁρᾶι, cf. 914 τήνδ᾽ ἡλικίαν ἐσιδόντα); and now Dareios' presence again proves too much for the Chorus, who succumb to 'awe' and 'terror' at the prospect (694–703). Even though (or perhaps because?) Xerxes himself does not witness this demonic apparition nor confront this paternal gaze in person, the demands (cf. 783 τὰς ἐμὰς ἐπιστολάς) that are made on him by the eye and voice of the Father are as irresistible as they are insatiable and unanswerable.

Just as Zeus is the mightiest king and father in the Universe (a figure as masculine and as Greek as could be imagined), so too Dareios, risen from the dead, is figured as a kind of potent deity and supreme Father: all-seeing, infallible, sexually successful, all-replenishing (?), and ever-loving.[71] The fact that this image contradicts certain facts in the historical record (Scythia, Marathon, etc.: cf. *Pers.* 244!) can be taken in one (or more) of three different ways: either (*a*) Aischylos has slipped up and hopes we won't notice (evidence, on the face of it, that his desire to turn Dareios, for dramatic reasons, into a perfect god-father is unreasonably strong); or (*b*) we *are* meant to notice, and to conclude that the Chorus are simply deluding themselves about Dareios' achievements and good qualities—he was almost as foolish as his son—though this seems hard to maintain in the face of the rest of the play, and in any case would confirm the idea that the *imagined* dynastic father is seen to be operating, however erroneously, as a powerful influence on almost all

κέκευθεν, 662 πιφαύσκων, 666 φάνηθι, 694 προσιδέσθαι, 710 ἕως τ᾽ ἔλευσσες αὐγὰς ἡλίου. (Cf. too 603–4 ἐμοὶ γὰρ ἤδη πάντα μὲν φόβου πλέα | ἐν ὄμμασίν τ᾽ ἀνταῖα φαίνεται ᾽κ θεῶν.)

[71] Like Zeus, or a real father, he may be temporarily or partially unaware of recent events (684–93): but (like Zeus, or the ideal/symbolic Father) he will always find out in the end, and duly pass judgment. This discrepancy, or distance, between actual and imagined father is tellingly exploited by Lacan, especially in terms of the phallus, which may be (physical) penis or (symbolic) Word, ultimate Signifier, Law, etc.: '...The phallus is not a phantasy, if by that we mean an imaginary effect. Nor is it as such an object...in the sense that this term tends to accentuate the reality pertaining in a relation. It is even less the organ, penis or clitoris, that it symbolizes...For the phallus is a signifier.... Man cannot aim at being whole...while ever the play of displacement and condensation to which he is doomed in the exercise of his functions marks his relation as a subject to the signifier. The phallus is the privileged signifier of that mark in which the role of the logos is joined with the advent of desire....etc.' (Lacan 1977: 285, 287 [tr. A. Sheridan]; cf. Silverman 1983 passim; Butler 1993).

the other characters; or else, (*c*) we are supposed to be *half-aware*, but no more, of the discrepancy between actual and imagined father, between Dareios' real-life achievements and his divine and paternal image, and we may sense that this discrepancy, or the anxiety to which it points, is an essential component in the dynamics of youthful aristocratic endeavor (as it is for Orestes in A. *Oresteia*, or Aias in S. *Aias*,[72] or Neoptolemos in S. *Phil.*). Achievement under the Eye of the Father: maintaining and increasing the father's house and the Name of the Father in the land—and yet never being able to confront or compete with that real father: this is the unceasing and intolerable demand that every élite Athenian young man faces, within an environment and political system that is now intensely suspicious and restrictive of aristocratic display and individual self-advertisement.

Xerxes and his father do not meet face-to-face on stage—only in the Queen-Mother's Dream; for Dareios' glorious presence and critical eye are mercifully removed before his bedraggled son trudges onstage. It is to be neither the comforting mother nor the stern father, but his less austere and intimidating representatives, the Elders, who will greet Xerxes in the final scene. They were Dareios' 'age-mates' and 'comrades' while he lived (681 ἥλικες ἥβης, 914 ἡλικίαν, 989 ἀγαθῶν ἑτάρων), and they continue now to be his 'trusty advisors and counsellors' (171–5, 441–3, 681), 'overseeing' (7 ἐφορεύειν, cf. 4 φύλακες) the estate that Xerxes has now put in jeopardy. Their interactions with Xerxes in the final scene must play a large part in determining our assessment of him and of his future role as master and king.

Although Xerxes is not subjected to the 'review' (*euthuna*, cf. *Pers.* 213 οὐχ ὑπεύθυνος πόλει, 827 Ζεὺς ... εὔθυνος βαρύς) that an Athenian politician would face upon completing his term of office, he does instead undergo an extended process of 'acceptance' by the representatives of his father's rule,[73] in the form of the lyric exchanges

---

[72] S. *Aj.* 462 is particularly telling as an analogy to the situation in *Persians*: as the humiliated Aias contemplates having to 'face' his mightily successful father back home, he asks himself, ποῖον ὄμμα πατρὶ δηλώσω φανεὶς | Τελαμῶνι; ['What face shall I show to my father Telamon when I appear?'].

[73] It is tempting, but perhaps fanciful, to see this process as a kind of 'eligibility-scrutiny' (*dokimasia*) of the young citizen-soldier, a scrutiny whose outcome remains ambivalent (Xerxes has already failed as a soldier; and no explicit mention is made in the *kommos* of his pedigree and qualifications, as are normally recited in an Athenian

of lamentation and recrimination that take up the last 150 lines of the play. From being alone and 'stripped of escorters' when he first enters the orchestra (1036 γυμνός εἰμι προπόμπων), he ends up in a sympathetic procession of trusty male comrades, who proclaim in the play's final lines, 'We shall escort you with mournful lament' (1077 πέμψω τοί σε δυσθρόοις γόοις), fullfilling Dareios' earlier instructions, 'Then do you escort my son...into the palace...' (529–30 καὶ παῖδα...προπέμπετ' ἐς δόμους). It is significant too that Xerxes passes during this scene from abjectly answering the Elders' questions and complaints (918–1037), to a more assertive issuing of his own commands to them (1038 ff.).

This final scene, with its close alternation of lyrics between leader and escort, King and subjects, accompanied by ritualistic coordination of hair-tearing and garment-shredding in time to the music, provides a powerful and engaging operation of commiseration and reintegration.[74] As Xerxes bids his father's trusty advisors, now his own counsellors, to 'Wet your eyes!' (1065 δίαινε δ' ὄσσε), the sympathetic blurring of their collective vision perhaps serves to

---

dokimasia. But he *is* in the end accepted (back) into his political group.) The Chorus of Elders, as Dareios' ἥλικες, hold some of the political responsibilities of the absent 'Father': they are 'guardians by seniority' (1–7 φύλακες κατὰ πρεσβείαν), chosen by Xerxes himself to 'supervise' in his absence (οὓς αὐτὸς ἄναξ Ξέρξης βασιλεὺς Δαρειογενὴς εἵλετο χώρας ἐφορεύειν. (Cf. 1–7, 140–43, 171–5, 224,–8, 527–31, 681–2, 784, 914, etc.) Their status thus recalls both that of a Homeric Council of Elders (Βουλὴ Γερόντων), and that of the Council of the Areopagos in Athens (which around this period, according to some sources, had been acting as 'Guardian of the Laws' and virtual Emergency Administration). But the Elders are deferential to the Queen (150–8, etc.), and somewhat superseded by her at 700–8, 832–51, though finally it is they who publicly 'receive' Xerxes (529–31, 907 ff.). For analogies between these Elders and those of A. *Ag.*, see Griffith 1995: 76–7, 80–1.

[74] See Belloni 1988: 233 ff. (and pp. xlix–lv) for a detailed account. In Freudian–Lacanian terms, we might say that the young man is shown coming to terms with the Reality Principle, or Symbolic Order, and finding a place for himself as an adult subject: no longer dependent on his mother, nor in direct conflict with his (actual) father, but having (barely, and not without severe trauma) negotiated some kind of reconciliation for himself with the demands of the 'paternal' role that is expected of him. The replacement (displacement) of his (imagined) father's gaze/phallus by (onto) the less intimidating and more mundanely actual Chorus helps to make this possible—though it could be argued that it is the spectators, more than Xerxes himself, who by play's end are the most fully '(re)integrated' into the Symbolic Order, after their disconcerting trip (back) into infantile dependency and Oedipal conflict. See further below, pp. 128–9.

mitigate the sharpness of the imagined glare of the Dream-father. Thus the humiliation of Xerxes, though it is tremendous, is not total. He does not have to face the direct ridicule of his subjects or of his enemies; and his parents and trusty advisors have rallied round to begin the process of restoring him to full authority.

Certainly the contrast is sharply drawn between this reeling and shredded royal household and the victorious Greeks, especially the orderly squads of spearsmen. And yet these victors remain not only anonymous, but also curiously colorless.[75] At one point, admittedly, the possibility is broached by the Chorus that, in the aftermath of this Persian defeat, the lowly subjects of the Empire (whether just Ionian Greeks, or Lydians and Persians too) might rise up in rebellion, their tongues loosened to 'spread rumors freely':

> οὐδ' ἔτι γλῶσσα βροτοῖσιν
> ἐν φυλακαῖς· λέλυται γὰρ
> λαὸς ἐλεύθερα βάζειν,
> ὡς ἐλύθη ζυγὸν ἀλκᾶς.

> No longer are mortals' tongues kept under guard;
> the people have been let loose to mouth off freely,[76]
> now the yoke of power has been removed.

>   (*Pers.* 591–4)

But this prospect is presented only briefly, and in terms hardly more appealing than a slave uprising in a master's household; and it is *not*

---

[75] On the political implications of the description of the battle of Salamis (and the other battles mentioned in the play), see Pelling 1997*a*: 5–13. It is notable that virtually no mention is made of the Athenian sailors, i.e. those poorer members of the population who (in democratic discourse, at least) were entitled to claim the bulk of the credit for Salamis. It may have been 'ships' and the sea (together with the gods) that destroyed Persia's empire; but it was the 'spearsmen' (i.e. hoplites) who in this play are primarily credited with the deed, and even they remain quite nondescript (from the Persian, and hence largely the audience's, point of view).

[76] This is doubtless an overtranslation of ἐλεύθερα βάζειν, but I don't think it is a mistranslation (especially after the mildly pejorative γλῶσσα of 591). βάζω, βάξις, βάσκω can be used of oracular or other benign 'utterance, report'; but increasingly by the 5th cent. the terms seem to carry associations of '(mere) rumor', 'gossip', or outright 'slander, malediction' (as their derivatives βασκαίνω, βάσκανος, βασκανία, κτλ. invariably do). Nor is ἐλεύθερος always a positive term when applied to speech, even in democratic Athens: like παρρησία, it can be used of excessive and inappropriate 'license', as by the shocked Chorus at [A.] *Prom.* 180 ἄγαν δ' ἐλευθεροστομεῖς, or by the domineering Spartan, Hermione, at E. *Andr.* 147–53.

what we see unfolding in Sousa during the rest of the play.[77] The
Persian Empire does not after all seem to be crumbling, the structure
of authority is not in fact challenged. This dynastic family will
recover; its wealth is not all gone; its subjects are still for the most
part loyal. The eye, though wet, can still see.

Or perhaps it would be more accurate to say that this final scene
contrives to *leave open* the precise degree to which élite family-
oriented aspirations are being rejected or reaffirmed. We find ourselves thus simultaneously reminded of the dangerous potential for
mischief posed by overreaching and luxurious élite families within
the context of the Athenian democracy (here equated with Hellenic
freedom at large), and yet also drawn into an intense identification
with the dynamics, needs, and fantasies of a dynastic household in
the throes of an identity- (or authority-) crisis. With the help of the
thick and distancing disguise of Persian garments and gestures, the
Athenian audience is brought to re-experience these anxieties, as they
are played out in ways that offer an appropriately 'mixed' message, to
suit both the élite and their willing 'subordinates'. Along with the

---

[77] A comparable spectre of popular dissatisfaction, criticism, and even insurrec-
tion against the monarchy, is raised repeatedly in A.'s *Agamemnon*, where the
occasion of the King's successful *nostos* prompts a couple of sharp reminders about
the earlier prospect of his defeat or malfeasance (*Ag.* 799–804), and equally powerful
reassurances as to the healing power of victory to repair (or conceal) such cracks in
the political fabric (805–9). In *Persians*, the situation would seem much more
threatening, in as much as the defeat has been so enormous and the humiliation so
conspicuous. But it is striking that 584–97 is, in fact, the only passage in which
the prospect is presented of the end of Persian domination (and cf. 929–30, etc.; also
880–906), as the Chorus imagine the ruin of the King's strength (584–5, 589–90), the
end of respectful bowing and scraping (588–9), the outbreak of popular freedom of
speech (591–3), as imminent perils: the Persian Empire may be coming to an end
(584–5 τοὶ δ᾽ ἀνὰ γᾶν Ἀσίαν δὴν οὐκέτι περσονομοῦνται . . .). The 470s and 460s did
indeed see energetic and largely successful efforts by Athenians and others to recover
Ionian cities and islands from Persian control; and in 472 it would be far from certain
where this campaign would eventually lead, how far back the Empire would be
driven; but in this play overall, the prognosis for military-political developments
that emerges ends up being quite vague (cf. Pelling 1997*a*: 12). Thus, in the Theater in
472 BCE, it would seem that at one level the Athenian audience must read/listen
between the lines and rejoice at the prospect of all those newly liberated Aegean
islands and Ionian cities (880–900), and at the 'freedom-speaking' that the Persian
Elders so fear, while at another level they are inevitably drawn in to sharing the
perspective of these elderly Persian advisers, who are in many ways a sympathetic and
reliable group not unlike (many of) themselves.

(shocking, but not unfamiliar) prospect of aristocratic failure and the triumph of the nameless masses, the spectators are provided with a degree of comfort too (after all, despite their close identification with the chorus and their dejected king, it is not they themselves who have lost their reputation, not they whose clothes are in tatters)—along with a sense of ultimate *control*, in the form of the absent-but-present Father, the supreme king and master, who sees and judges all (from on high or below), and whose symbolic and actual authority is represented and reinforced by (imperfect but) trusty deputies here on earth who can be counted on to continue his rule and maintain his authority in the future. Just as Dareios can rest more comfortably knowing that his kingdom is not indeed to be a 'prey' (ἁρπαγή 752) to all and sundry (i.e., in effect, to the Athenian audience itself, when it reflects on itself as the Persians' enemy), so can we (i.e. that same audience, as it aligns itself with the prime internal audience of the play, the Chorus) rest assured that a supreme paternal overseer is keeping an eye on any young upstarts, monitoring our moral (filial) and political (collective) progress, and guaranteeing our survival and eventual recovery from harm.[78] The enjoyment of simultaneously experiencing the feelings of both the victors and the vanquished, and of participating in the extremes of aristocratic endeavor (and failure) while sitting safely and inertly as (mere) observers and respondents, exploits to the full the spectators' capacity to let themselves be 'led' by the processes of poetic *psychagōgia* to an ending that they know will be harmless, familiar, and secure, however dangerous and exciting the intervening events that they may witness.

4. CONCLUSION

There is no single, correct view of a play, no privileged perspective. What I see and experience (as a member of a theater audience, or as a critic) may not be exactly what others see. I have been suggesting

[78] On the questions, who 'we' are today, who *our* 'paternal overseer' might be, and how 'our' responses might correspond to those of (most of) A.'s audience in 472 BCE, see below, pp. 134–5.

that, among the various subject positions that we come to adopt in the Theater of Dionysos, one to which we give ourselves with particular relish and compulsion is that of 'subjects' of the masterly royal figures that dominate the stage, and especially of such kingly and fatherly figures as Dareios and Zeus. In this article, I purposely chose one of the most unattractive and threatening of the tragic monarchs for this investigation, reckoning that the case is transparently easy to make for such other, more obviously impressive and/or attractive, monarchical/heroic figures as Eteokles, Oidipous, Aias, Herakles, or Theseus (along with their associated divinities and demons).[79]

But where does this get us? And who are 'we'? It is one thing to suggest that the Athenians used tragic drama as a medium through which to explore the tensions and contradictions between democratic institutions and élite leadership, between political egalitarianism and domestic autocracy, and between popular and élite models of the family; but it is perhaps something else to claim (as in places I have appeared to do) that Greek tragedy provides a universal source of pleasure to readers the world over through its insistent re-enactments of Oedipal conflict and reassertions of patriarchal dominance. Let me therefore suggest four main conclusions that have emerged from this study, and outline some of their implications for our reading of Greek tragedy in general:

(i) Even though the dangers of monarchical power and license are frequently problematized in tragedy, a strong current runs through the plays reinforcing élite authority and the precious value of a single, kingly figure (whether actual, or imaginary);

(ii) Much of the authority and stature, and the precious value, enjoyed by this kingly figure derives from his 'paternal' characteristics, as manifested or invoked in relation to his son, and his 'paternalistic' relationship to the internal audiences of the play, especially to the chorus and others in subordinate and dependent relations to him;

[79] In Griffith 1995, I try to make such a case for Agamemnon and Orestes (together with Zeus and Athena) in the *Oresteia*. In Griffith 1998: 65–74 I examine the presentation of Kreon's authority in *Antigone*—in some respects an even less attractive figure than Xerxes, but one whose claims as father and ruler arouse interestingly conflicted responses.

(iii)   The tragedies suggest that élite sons and fathers face especially difficult, yet unavoidable, obstacles to a 'normal' and successful negotiation of inter-generational continuity and succession, in comparison with the rest of the community;[80]

(iv)   The theater audience is regularly brought to accept, and be satisfied by, a particular tragic 'resolution' involving the reaffirmation of continued aristocratic domination, through the play's associated and analogous reinforcement of deeply ingrained habits of filial obedience and dependency on a strong 'father'.

Of these four conclusions (which, I hasten to add, are by no means meant to exhaust the list of functions performed and pleasures provided by Greek tragedy), (i) and (iii) are rooted firmly in the particular historical circumstances of fifth-century Athens, while (ii) floats more indeterminately within the texts themselves and the world of the plays; (iv) by contrast begins to move towards a more general claim on 'us' as universal readers who implicitly share with the Athenians certain basic habits and expectations (natural or acquired) of 'paternal' dependency.

  (i) The notion that strong monarchical/masterly figures on stage might appeal strongly to an audience of Athenian citizens, needs to be tempered by the acknowledgment that this 'appeal' would be to some degree surreptitious and unconscious, and would doubtless work differently, according to the social status and political leanings of each individual audience member.[81] Some (especially those accustomed to presiding over large estates, and to leading armies in the field, and those sympathetic to the stylish 'Ionian' manners of a previous generation) might identify quite closely with the tormented but precious regal heroes: alien though Dareios and Xerxes are, their experiences are not entirely foreign, and they may engage the spectators' fantasies of power, ambition (and humiliation) quite powerfully;[82] thus they are brought to recognize the impossibility (and in some respects, impropriety) of

---

[80] [In the unabridged version of this article (Griffith 1998: 65–74), the quarrel between Kreon and his son Haimon in Soph. *Antigone* is analysed in some detail.]

[81] This first conclusion indeed comprises the main thesis of my earlier article (Griffith 1995). See Griffith 1998: 65–74; 1999: 35–8, 40–3, 155–6.

[82] [The similarities of a leader such as Kreon in Soph. *Antigone* to a real-life 5th-cent. Athenian politician are obviously much greater, and the degree of identification felt by an Athenian audience correspondingly likely to be stronger; see Griffith 1998: 65–74.]

such attitudes in real life. But most Athenians would probably align themselves more consistently with the messengers and Elders in both plays, shocked by their leaders' mistakes, awed but critical, dependent yet supportive, and finally relieved at their community's survival and concerned to cooperate in the process of recuperation. Both sets of reactions (and any mixtures of the two) are permissible (for this is the Theater); indeed both seem to some degree almost inescapable (thanks to the powers of μίμησις and ψυχαγωγία, ὄψις and μέλος, αὐλός and γόος).[83] And I hope I have demonstrated that we need not be too puzzled at the idea that good democratic citizens might find it easy to think themselves (intermittently) into such 'dominant' or 'dependent' mentalities, given the wide range of social roles and performativities which they had to enact and enunciate from day to day.

(ii) In the terms of the kinship/family structures presented by the plays themselves, the final outcomes of each tragic plot tend to reassert a patriarchal norm that is deeply familiar and traditional. A play (like an epic) is not really felt to be over until 'order' of some sort is restored (or at least, disorder removed); and, given that Greek tragedies (to a greater degree than epics, it seems) tend to focus on violence within the family (against φίλοι, as Aristotle puts it), with 'disorder' usually involving some conflict within, and/or inversion of, 'normal' family structures (especially the eruption of dangerous females, or failure/removal of a precious male head of the family), the 'resolution' is frequently brought about by the suppression of the disruptive element(s) and reintegration (implicit or explicit) of the surviving elements into the traditional family pattern of father, wife, and dutiful children (or of marriage and expected future birth of such children). In comedy, this pattern is almost invariable; and even in those tragedies in which the élite family has seemingly been

[83] Similarly, in watching *The King and I* (above, p. 100), most men (surely?) will fantasize themselves intermittently into the King's (Yul Brynner's) role, masterful (yet childishly irresponsible), stylish, and sexually pampered by scores of exotic wives (and potentially by Anna/Deborah Kerr too); and most women will share Anna's/Deborah Kerr's intermittent attraction to him. (Brynner did receive an Oscar for his performance—as did the costume designer, composer and librettist, and choreographer: another triumph of ὄψις and μέλος.) But at the same time, through the dynamics of 'displacement', both male and female members of the audience will tend to align themselves predominantly with the viewpoints of Anna and her (chorus-like) son, whose subject position(s) and surreptitiously colonialist gaze we are encouraged to adopt as being (ultimately) 'proper' and authoritative. See further Kaplan 1995.

smashed beyond recovery (as Oidipous' routinely is), the final scenes usually confirm, or confer, some kind of special power for the presiding/surviving male élite figure(s), whether in cult or in politics. This pattern could be explained as being merely a matter of literary history (traditional myth, inheritance from epic, etc.) and narrato-logical convention (universal story patterns): but it amounts to an irresistible tendency (at least within Classical Greek literature, as in Elizabethan and Victorian) to affirm the Father as the symbol, or representative, or embodiment (Lacan's transcendental Signifier) of social and aesthetic, as well as familial, Order.[84]

(iii) I have suggested at various points in this article that conflict between fathers and sons, and anxieties about the role of the mother within the family, were—or were imagined to be—more intense, and possibly of a different kind, among the aristocracy than they were among the rest of the citizen population at Athens. Thus the curious paucity of scenes in which fathers and sons meet on the tragic stage, and the peculiar violence of their collisions when they do meet, may be a reflection of the particular social and political situation in the early decades of the fully-developed democracy.[85] If so, we may regard these plays as presenting valuable evidence about the shifting power relations and ideologies of the different classes within the citizen body, even as we struggle to disentangle the tightly-woven threads of fantasy and weave them (back) into a recognizable and continuous social and imaginative fabric. At the least, I think we should recognize that, along with the persistent need to confront, problematize, and play/ work through the female and foreign 'Other' in the Theater, as part of the process of defining the male Greek citizen self, the Athenians found it helpful, even necessary, to explore the relations between rich and poor, prestigious and humble,

---

[84] The tendency to equate Law and Order with the rule of the Father is no less strong, of course, in Greek and Judaeo-Christian religion; see above, p. 98 (on Aischylos' Zeus).

[85] See Strauss 1993 and (if used with caution) Slater 1968. There are only seven scenes in extant tragedy that present a father and a son on stage together. Two of these scenes are friendly (Eur. *Herakles*, *Phoinissai*, both involving deceptive moments before calamity). The other five all involve ugly confrontations and/or quarrels: Soph. *Antigone* (Kreon and Haimon), *Trachiniai* (Herakles and Hyllos), *OC* (Oidipous and Polyneikes), Eur. *Alkestis* (Pheres and Admetos), *Hippolytos* (Theseus and Hippolytos). See further Griffith 1998: 30–5.

dominant and dependent, and to map these socio-political opposi-
tions onto a grid of family relations. The prevailing dynamic that
emerges is an even further intensified ambivalence with regard to the
real and imagined father/king: impossibly demanding, judgmental,
and all-seeing, he is both terrifying and reassuring. In some contexts,
it appears that he is best removed from our physical presence, and
replaced with less awesome and troublesome surrogates (the Elders);
yet the deeply-ingrained habits of strong (actual) fatherly supervision
and instruction, and horror of filial disrespect and improper self-
assertion, are constantly mobilized by the plays in the service of élite
authority and control. Thus the 'order' that is (re)imposed at the end
of a tragedy, in the form of the surviving king and/or his representatives (often blessed, or at least confirmed, by Olympian deities as
well), is normalized and naturalized through its assimilation to a
restored family order: the élite father knows best; it is he who can and
should take care of us, and if he errs, he must be rescued or replaced
by (an)other(s) like him.[86]

(iv) This brings me to perhaps the thorniest of my four (tentative)
conclusions, which I will simply rephrase here as a question. Why is
it that 'we' (like those Athenians back then, and those Elizabethans,
and so many others in various times and places...) seem to need
to fall back constantly (instinctively?) on such paternalistic and
monarchical models for a reassuring 'sense of an ending'[87] and

[86] This pattern, for all its specificity to the context of democratic Athens, presents
close analogies with the modern era too: as inequalities of wealth and élite privilege
persist, it appears to be difficult even for zealous and active democrats to avoid falling
back, either into habits of dependency on rich and/or charismatic leaders, 'strong
men' who can take care of business for us and protect us from the dangers of this
world, or into domineering and paternalistic behavior on the part of these 'democrats' themselves, or both. The difficulty of resisting these tendencies is often compounded by the strong conservative agenda of 'family values', religious repression,
and 'mainstream' cultural hegemony—reinforced particularly through the entertainment industry. Like the Theater of Dionysos, Hollywood and the TV networks and
news media play a crucial role in determining, as well as responding to, popular
desires and satisfactions: so perhaps we should be encouraged that The Industry now
occasionally writes women and minorities into leadership roles on screen; maybe
'real-life' America is getting ready for a non-male, non-white, non-Christian Presi-
dent, one day? Even for a non-millionaire Senate? But for now, the occupant of the
White House to whom allegiance must be sworn, still has to be a Dad.

[87] Once again, we may think of the conclusive role of Zeus in the *Oresteia*, or of the
closing lines of S. *Tr.* and *OC*. I will not pursue here the additional dimension of the

restoration of 'order', in our stories and dramas? Or, to put it another way, why does the process of aligning (reintegrating) our various split (or 'displaced') subject positions into a final unified perspective, or psycho-social equilibrium, implicit in our acceptance of a proper 'end' to the tragic story, conform so regularly to this Oedipal pattern? Is this simply a matter of habit and cultural indoctrination? or an even deeper and more original psychological need? Does the 'talking/watching cure' of Dionysiac tragedy necessarily entail conformity to a given (familiar, traditional) norm of parental, sexual, and social authority? Or can other 'symbolic orders' be imagined that would supply an equally reassuring (and aesthetically satisfying) 'sense of an ending'?[88] How much choice do we have as to what kinds of structures we impose on our tragic stories, and what kinds of readings we give to our existing tragic plays?

Any attempt at a responsible answer to these vital questions would launch us immediately into another huge and stormy ocean of controversy, upon which I shall not embark now. But I hope this article has helped, by exposing some of our habits of playing and reading, to suggest ways in which these habits might be resisted and changed (if change is desired). After all, the tendencies of Greek tragedy to reimpose these deeply familiar patterns of aristocratic and paternal domination, while powerful, are not irresistible; we just have to keep our wits about us.[89]

---

playwright's own paternal and dominant role, as (implied, and/or actual) 'author' of 'his' text, though this authorial activity of (re)aligning 'our' subject positions into a final state of equilibrium and acceptance might obviously be said to intersect at several points with that of the transcendental Father and his Word. This in turn may help to explain the fanatical determination of some textual critics to recover and preserve that 'Word' in its most exact and original version—and not to venture a step beyond it in the direction of 'interpretation'.

[88] Or, to put this in Lacanian terms: Is the phallus imaginary, or real? [See further Griffith 1998. 39–43, Griffith 2005.] On these issues in general, see Butler 1993: passim, esp. 203–30.

[89] Indeed, some critics will probably feel that I have argued too narrowly and insistently here for one particular kind of closure to texts that should be allowed to remain more open-ended and indeterminate—and that my anxieties about the origins and effects of this particular kind of closure are therefore misplaced. Certainly, the course of 20th-cent. higher criticism (and stage productions) makes clear just how much leeway the texts give to alternative and resistant readings; and I have no wish to reverse this trend.

REFERENCES

ADELMAN, J. (1992), *Suffocating Mothers: Fantasies of Maternal Origin in Shakespeare's Plays*, New York.

ALEXANDERSON, B. (1967), 'Darius in the *Persians*', *Eranos* 65: 1–11.

ALEXIOU, M. (1974), *The Ritual Lament in Greek Tradition*, Cambridge.

ARNHEIM, M. T. W. (1977), *Aristocracy in Greek Society*, London.

BAKEWELL, G. W. (1998), '*Persae* 374–83: Persians, Greeks, and *ΠΕΙΘΑΡΧΩΙ ΦΡΕΝΙ*', *CP* 93: 232–6.

BAKHTIN, M. M. (1981), *The Dialogic Imagination* (ed. M. Holquist), Austin.

BELLONI, L. (ed.) (1988), *Eschilo: I Persiani*, Milan.

BENNETT, S. (1997), *Theatre Audiences* (2nd edn.), New York.

BOURDIEU, P. (1990), *The Logic of Practice* (Eng. tr.), Stanford.

BROADHEAD, H. D. (ed.) (1960), *The Persae of Aeschylus*, Cambridge.

BURKERT, W. (1962), '*ΓΟΗΣ*: zum griechischen "Shamanismus"', *RhMus* 105: 36–55.

—— (1985), *Greek Religion* (tr. J. Raffan), Oxford.

BUTLER, J. P. (1993), *Bodies That Matter*, New York.

CALAME, C. (1990), *Thesée et l'imaginaire athenien: legende et culte en Grèce antique*, Paris.

CALDWELL, R. S. (1970), 'The pattern of Aeschylean tragedy', *TAPA* 101: 77–94.

—— (1990), 'The psychoanalytic interpretation of Greek myth', in A. L. Edmunds (ed.), *Approaches to Greek Myth* (Baltimore), 342–89.

CAMERON, A., and KUHRT, A. (eds.) (1983), *Images of Women in Antiquity*, London.

CAMPBELL, J. K. (1964), *Honour, Family, and Patronage*, Oxford.

CARTLEDGE, P. (1997), 'Deep plays: theatre as process in Greek civic life', in Easterling 1997, 3–35.

CITTI, V. (1962), *Il linguaggio religioso e liturgico nelle tragedie di Eschilo*, Bologna.

CLOVER, C. J. (1992), *Men, Women, and Chainsaws*, Princeton.

COHEN, D. (1991), *Law, Sexuality, and Society*, Cambridge.

CONNOR, W. R. (1989), 'City Dionysia and Athenian democracy', *C&M* 40: 7–32.

—— (1996), 'Civic society, Dionysiac festival, and the Athenian democracy', in Ober and Hedrick 1996, 217–26.

CRANE, G. (1993), 'The politics of consumption and generosity in the Carpet Scene of *Agamemnon*', *CP* 88: 117–36.

—— (1996), 'The prosperity of tyrants: Bacchylides, Herodotus, and the contest for legitimacy', *Arethusa* 29: 57–85.

CSAPO, E. and SLATER W. J. (1995), *The Context of Ancient Drama*, Ann Arbor.

DAVIES, J. K. (1984), *Wealth and the Power of Wealth in Classical Athens*, Salem, NH.

DE LAURETIS, T. (1987), *Technologies of Gender*, Bloomington.

DE MARINIS, M. (1987), 'Dramaturgy of the spectator', *The Drama Review* 31.2: 100–14.

DEVEREUX, G. (1976), *Dreams in Greek Tragedy*, London.

DODDS, E. R. (1951), *The Greeks and the Irrational*, Berkeley.

DONALDSON, L. (1990), '*The King and I* in *Uncle Tom's Cabin*', *Cinema Journal* 29: 52–65.

DONLAN, W. (1980), *The Aristocratic Ideal in Ancient Greece: Attitudes of Superiority from Homer to the End of the Fifth Century B.C.*, Lawrence.

DOUGHERTY, C. C. (1993), 'It's murder to found a colony', in Dougherty and L. V. Kurke (eds.), *Cultural Poetics in Archaic Greece* (Cambridge), 178–98.

DOVER, K. J. (1974), *Greek Popular Morality in the Time of Plato and Aristotle*, Oxford.

—— (1978), *Greek Homosexuality*, New York.

DU BOIS, P. (1988), *Sowing the Body*, Chicago.

EASTERLING, P. E. (1984), 'Kings in Greek tragedy', in J. Coy and J. de Hoz (eds.), *Estudios sobre los generos literarios*, ii (Salamanca), 33–45.

—— (ed.) (1997), *The Cambridge Companion to Greek Tragedy*, Cambridge.

—— (1997*a*), 'Constructing the heroic', in Pelling 1997, 21–37.

ELAM, K. (1980), *The Semiotics of Theatre and Drama*, London.

FLUGEL, J. C. (1930), *The Psychology of Clothes*, London.

FOLEY, H. (1993), 'The politics of tragic lamentation', in Sommerstein et al. 1993, 101–43.

FOUCAULT, M. (1985), *The Use of Pleasure* (= *The History of Sexuality*, vol. ii), Eng. tr., New York.

FOXHALL, L. (1989), 'Household, gender, and property in Classical Athens', *CQ* 39: 22–44.

GAGARIN, M. (1976), *Aeschylean Drama*, Berkeley.

GEDDES, A. G. (1987), 'Rags and riches: the costume of Athenian men in the 5th C.', *CQ* 37: 307–31.

GEORGES, P. (1994), *Barbarian Asia and the Greek Experience*, Baltimore.

GOLDHILL, S. (1988), 'Battle narrative and politics in Aeschylus' *Persae*', *JHS* 108: 189–93.

—— (1990), 'The Great Dionysia and civic ideology', in Winkler and Zeitlin 1990, 97–129.

GOLDHILL, S. (1997), 'The audience of Athenian tragedy', in Easterling 1997, 54–68.

GOULD, J. (1996), 'Tragedy and collective experience', in Silk 1996, 217–43.

GREEN, A. (1979), *The Tragic Effect* (1969; Eng. tr. A. Sheridan), Cambridge.

GRIFFITH, M. (1995), 'Brilliant dynasts: power and politics in the *Oresteia*', *ClAnt* 14: 62–129.

—— (1998), 'The king and eye: the rule of the father in Greek tragedy', *PCPS* 44 (1998), 20–84.

—— (ed.) (1999), *Sophocles: Antigone*, Cambridge.

—— (2005), 'The subject of desire in Sophocles' *Antigone*', in S. M. Oberhelman and V. Pedrick (eds.), *The Soul of Tragedy*, Chicago.

HALL, E. (1989), *Inventing the Barbarian*, Oxford.

—— (1993), 'Asia unmanned: images of victory in classical Athens,' in J. Rich and G. Shipley (eds.), *War and Society in the Greek World* (London), 107–33.

—— (ed.) (1996), *Aeschylus: Persians*, Warminster.

—— (1997), 'The sociology of Athenian tragedy', in Easterling 1997, 93–126.

HALLIWELL, S. (1986), *Aristotle's Poetics*, London.

HARRISON, A. R. W. (1968–71), *The Law of Athens* (2 vols.), Oxford.

HEADLAM, W. (1902), 'Ghost-raising, magic, and the underworld', *CR* 16: 52–61.

HEATH, M. (1987), *The Poetics of Greek Tragedy*, London.

HERINGTON, C. J. (1985), *Poetry into Tragedy*, Berkeley.

HOLST-WARHAFT, G. (1992), *Dangerous Voices*, New York.

HUMPHREYS, S. (1983), *The Family, Women, and Death*, London.

JAUSS, H. R. (1974), 'Levels of identification of hero and audience', *New Literary History* 5.2: 283–317.

KAPLAN, C. (1995), ' "Getting to know you": travel, gender, and the politics of representation in *Anna and the King of Siam* and *The King and I* ', in R. De La Campa, E. A. Kaplan, and M. Sprinker (eds.), *Late Imperial Culture* (London), 33–52.

KERTZER, D. I. (1988), *Ritual, Politics, and Power*, New Haven.

KING, H. (1983), 'Bound to bleed', in Cameron & Kuhrt 1983, 109–27.

KNOX, B. M. W. (1964), *The Heroic Temper*, Berkeley.

KURKE, L. V. (1991), *The Traffic in Praise*, Ithaca, NY.

—— (1992), 'The politics of *habrosyne*', *ClAnt* 11: 91–120.

—— (1999) *Coins, Bodies, Games, and Gold: the Politics of Meaning in Archaic Greece*, Princeton.

LACAN, J. (1977), *Écrits: A Selection* (Eng. tr.), New York.

LADA, I. (1993), 'Empathic understanding: emotion and cognition in classical dramatic audience-response', *PCPS* 39: 94–140.

Loraux, N. (1986), *The Invention of Athens: The Funeral Oration in the Classical City* (1981; tr. A. Sheridan), Harvard.

—— (1995), *The Experiences of Tiresias: The Feminine and the Greek Man* (Eng. tr.), Princeton.

Lucas, D. W. (ed.) (1968), *Aristotle: The Poetics*, Oxford.

Maitland, J. (1992), 'Dynasty and family in the Athenian city state', *CQ* 42: 26–40.

Miller, M. C. (1997), *Athens and Persia in the Fifth Century B.C.: A Study in Cultural Receptivity*, Cambridge.

Monsacré, H. (1984), *Les larmes d'Achille: le héros, la femme et la souffrance dans la poésie d'Homere*, Paris.

Ober, J. (1989), *Mass and Elite in Democratic Athens*, Princeton.

—— and Hedrick, C. (eds.) (1996), *Demokratia*, Princeton.

—— and Strauss, B. (1990), 'Drama, political rhetoric, and the discourse of Athenian democracy', in Winkler and Zeitlin 1990, 237–70.

Paduano, G. (1978), *Sui Persiani di Eschilo. Problemi di focalizzazione drammatica*, Rome.

—— (1986), 'Drammaturgie della paternita', *SIFC* 3.4: 172–82.

Pelling, C. B. R. (ed.) (1997), *Greek Tragedy and the Historian*, Oxford.

—— (1997a), 'Aeschylus' *Persians* and the historian', in Pelling 1997, 1–17.

Podlecki, A. J. (1966), *The Political Background of Aeschylean Tragedy*, Ann Arbor.

—— (1986), 'Polis and monarch in early Greek tragedy', in J. P. Euben (ed.), *Greek Tragedy and Political Theory* (Berkeley, 1986), 76–100.

—— (1993), 'κατ' ἀρχῆς γὰρ φιλαίτιος λεώς: the concept of leadership in Aeschylus', in Sommerstein et al. 1993, 55–79.

Raaflaub, K. A. (1989), 'Contemporary perceptions of democracy in fifth-century Athens', *C&M* 40, 33–70.

—— (1996), 'Equalities and inequalities in Athenian democracy', in Ober and Hedrick 1996, 139–73.

Reiner, E. (1938), *Die rituelle Totenklage der Griechen*, Stuttgart.

Roberts, J. T. (1994), *Athens on Trial: The Antidemocratic Tradition in Western Thought*, Princeton.

Rose, P. (1992), *Sons of the Gods, Children of Earth: Ideology and Literary Form in Ancient Greece*, Ithaca, NY.

Saïd, E. (1978), *Orientalism*, Cambridge.

Saïd, S. (1981), 'Darius et Xerxès dans les *Perses* d'Eschyle', *Ktema* 6: 17–38.

Seaford, R. (1994), *Reciprocity and Ritual: Homer and Tragedy in the Developing City-State*, Oxford.

Segal, C. P. (1986), *Interpreting Greek Tragedy*, Ithaca, NY.

Silk, M. S. (ed.) (1996), *Tragedy and the Tragic*, Oxford.

SILVERMAN, K. (1983), *The Subject of Semiotics*, Oxford.

—— (1992), *Male Subjectivity at the Margins*, New York.

SINCLAIR, R. K. (1988), *Democracy and Participation in Athens*, Cambridge.

SLATER, P. R. (1968), *The Glory of Hera*, Boston.

SOMMERSTEIN, A. H., et al. (eds.) (1993), *Tragedy, Comedy, and the Polis*, Bari.

STALLYBRASS, P., and WHITE, A. (1986), *The Politics and Poetics of Transgression*, Ithaca, NY.

STRAUSS, B. (1993), *Fathers and Sons in Athens*, Princeton.

—— (1996), 'The Athenian trireme, school of democracy', in Ober and Hedrick 1996, 313–25.

TAPLIN, O. P. (1977), *The Stagecraft of Aeschylus*, Oxford.

TATUM, J. (1989), *Xenophon's Imperial Fiction*, Princeton.

THALMANN, W. G. (1980), 'Xerxes' rags', *AJP* 101, 260–82.

TRAVIS, R. M. (1996), 'Allegorical fantasy and the chorus in Sophocles' *Oedipus Coloneus*' (PhD diss., Berkeley).

VERNANT, J.-P. (1983), *Myth and Thought Among the Greeks* (1965; Eng. tr.), London.

—— and VIDAL-NAQUET, P. (1981), *Tragedy and Myth in Ancient Greece* (1965; Eng. tr. J. Lloyd), Brighton.

WEST, M. L. (1992), *Ancient Greek Music*, Oxford.

WINKLER, J. J. and ZEITLIN, F. I. (eds.) (1990), *Nothing to do with Dionysos?*, Princeton.

WINNICOTT, D. W. (1971), *Playing and Reality*, London.

WINNINGTON-INGRAM, R. P. (1983), *Studies in Aeschylus*, Cambridge.

WOHL, V. J. (1998), *Intimate Commerce: Exchange, Gender, and Subjectivity in Greek Tragedy*, Austin.

ZANKER, P. (1995), *The Mask of Socrates*, Berkeley.

ZEITLIN, F. I. (1996), *Playing the Other*, Chicago.

4

The Character of Eteocles in Aeschylus' *Seven Against Thebes*

Kurt von Fritz

Aeschylus' *Seven Against Thebes* has for some time been the subject of renewed and increasingly lively controversy. This has not so much concerned the problem of the authenticity or inauthenticity of greater or lesser parts of the exodos—although that problem too has been frequently debated—but rather the character of Eteocles. This problem is of particular interest because he is, it seems to me, the most strongly individualized of all Aeschylus' characters. If that is correct, and can be demonstrated in detail, then it would provide evidence that Aeschylus' development as a dramatist was not as linear as literary historians have tended to suppose, as they have with other authors too. The discovery that Aeschylus' Danaid trilogy is to be dated much later than had hitherto almost universally been supposed should really have had a salutary effect—and I readily confess that I was no cleverer than most other people about this—and one should not resist the new discovery, grounded as it is in documentary evidence, but rather take pleasure in the demonstration that artistic development is in reality less predictable and more diverse than the more or less rigid constructions of historians of literature and art.

To return to the subject, it is appropriate to give a brief account of the main lines of the discussion hitherto. The older *communis*

[*Editor's note*. Some of the author's line-references have been transferred from footnotes to the text, with the result that footnote numbers do not all correspond to those in the original.]

opinio, which is still maintained in the latest editions of Pohlenz'
Griechische Tragödie and Schmid's *Griechische Literaturgeschichte*, is
that Eteocles is 'simply the ideal ruler, who in the life-and-death
struggle of his country is dutiful, determined, clear in mind and
strong in hand, and devotes his whole self to the state'.[1] 'He expiates
the guilt of his ancestors, and goes with his eyes open to certain
destruction because a higher duty calls him'.[2] 'The state is saved
by the annihilation of the dynasty, which Eteocles has brought
about by his voluntary self-sacrifice'.[3] This line of interpretation
often supposes that he was determined on self-sacrifice from the
beginning of the play, and that he already knew that there was no
other salvation for the city whose defence he leads, even though the
full horror of mutual fratricide only becomes apparent to him at the
moment when all his other missions are accomplished and nothing
more remains for him than to carry out the unavoidable atrocity as
quickly as possible.

Wilamowitz had already objected to some elements of this interpretation in his *Aischylos-Interpretationen*.[4] That Eteocles has neither
foreseen nor decided upon his death at the beginning is demonstrated by lines 274 ff., in which he makes the vow to sacrifice sheep
and bulls to the gods if the city is saved, to dedicate trophies in the
temples, and to adorn them with the spoils of victory. There is, to say
the least, not the slightest indication here that Eteocles believes that
this vow would have to be fulfilled by anyone other than himself in
the event of the city being saved.

There is neither an explicit statement nor even a clear hint that the
city could only be saved if both brothers fall, and that it is for this
reason that Eteocles must sacrifice himself. Wilamowitz was thus
correct to state: 'It is out of the question that Aeschylus, or anyone
before or after him, had so adapted the material that the death of the
brothers was the condition for the victory over the Seven'.[5]

---

[1] M. Pohlenz, *Die Griechische Tragödie*[2] (Leipzig, 1956), i. 94. [Cf. W. Schmid and
O. Stählin, *Geschichte der griechischen Literatur* (Munich, 1940), I. ii. 211–21.]

[2] Pohlenz (n. 1), 96.

[3] Pohlenz (n. 1), 95.

[4] U. von Wilamowitz-Moellendorff, *Aischylos: Interpretationen* (Berlin, 1914),
56–85.

[5] Wilamowitz (n. 4), 67.

On the other hand, Wilamowitz found a definite contradiction, or at least a lack of consistency, in the fact that the curse of Oedipus seems to be kept in the background in the first half of the play and only comes into the foreground as the decisive factor in the second half. He thought that this discrepancy should be explained in terms of the genesis of the play. Aeschylus thus combined two different versions of the myth: an older one based on the *Thebais*, in which Eteocles, in accordance with his name, was the glorious defender of his fatherland; and another, deriving from later epic, in which Eteocles had become the bearer of the family curse. Wilamowitz thought that an individualized character did in a sense emerge from this, but that the discrepancy permeated the entire play. Aeschylus had doubtless not asked himself how he should represent the character of Eteocles, but had just taken over what was handed down to him by the tradition. He had also not known what a tragic hero was, and would not have understood a theoretician like Aristotle who considered the matter philosophically. In spite of this, his Eteocles would be 'a tragic hero if ever there was one'. It would also fit in with this that he confronts his brother from his own free choice, although what he has chosen to do runs counter to his feelings.

Regenbogen was the first to put forward some qualifications and misgivings about what had been the dominant conception of the freedom of Eteocles' choice.[6] He objects to the excessive influence of German idealistic philosophy: 'It does not make Eteocles free in the sense of idealistic ethics that by his assent... he makes his own the supernatural forces which he feels upon him, but it does initially point to an area in which the question of human freedom can meaningfully be posed. With this qualification, it can be said that Eteocles is the first "tragic" individual in the history of poetry'.

Four years later, an article by F. Solmsen on the Erinys in the *Seven Against Thebes* developed the argument further in the same direction.[7] Solmsen emphasized even more strongly than Wilamowitz the sharp break in the play at line 653. In his view, the working of

---

[6] O. Regenbogen, 'Bemerkungen zu den Sieben des Aischylos', *Hermes* 68 (1933), 51–69 [= *Kleine Schriften* (Munich, 1961), 36–56. The quotation is from p. 69 = *Kl. Schr.* 55–6].

[7] F. Solmsen, 'The Erinys in Aischylos' *Septem*', *TAPA* 68 (1937), 197–211 [= *Kleine Schriften* (Hildesheim, 1968), i. 106–20].

the Erinys, which has hitherto essentially remained hidden, begins
from this point. This finds its expression above all in a fundamental
change in Eteocles' whole frame of mind. While he has demonstrated
hitherto an admirable self-control, which has also given him full
control over his situation, and while in the earlier scenes he has
taken every measure for the defence of the city with the greatest
prudence, and while even in his behaviour towards the chorus there
is no evidence whatsoever of rashness, from this moment on his
mental equilibrium is completely upset. He goes ahead without
paying the slightest attention to the voice of reason, and is also deaf
to the opinions of others. Solmsen thought that the contrast between
Eteocles' frame of mind in the first and second halves of the play is so
complete that it is scarcely possible to combine the Eteocles of the
two halves into the portrayal of a coherent character, as had always
previously been attempted. The tragedy of the play lies precisely in
the fact that Eteocles, who seemed in the first part of the play to be
the ideal ruler, is so overcome by the Erinys, the curse on the family
which was renewed by his father, that he is internally completely
transformed, although he is essentially innocent. The element of free
will in Eteocles' choice, which Regenbogen, albeit with strong reservations, had not disputed, is thereby completely eliminated. 'It is
misleading', wrote Solmsen, 'to speak of his choice or to suggest that
Aischylos when he wrote this play was fascinated by the problem of
free will, the relation of human will and fate or anything of the kind',
and elsewhere: 'there is simply no way of evading what Fate (i.e. the
Erinys) has in store for him'.[8]

E. Wolff tried to substantiate this last conclusion of Solmsen's
through entirely new observations.[9] It had always been supposed
that Eteocles was undoubtedly free in his choice of the captains
whom he posted to the various gates. Wolff now tried to show that
he had already appointed the defenders to the various gates before
the messenger's account of the result of the attackers' division by lot
of the gates of Thebes. He must have assigned them there because he
announced at lines 282 ff. that he intended to do this, and because

    [8] Solmsen (n. 7), 203 [= *Kl. Schr.* 112].
    [9] E. Wolff, 'Die Entscheidung des Eteokles in den *Sieben gegen Theben*', HSCP 63
(1958), 89–95.

there is a long choral ode between this announcement and the messenger's report during which he must have carried out his declaration. The assignments of the attackers and of the defenders were thus entirely independent of each other, and if the result was that Eteocles confronted his brother at the same gate then this would evidently be the result of the curse, whose real meaning, together with its inevitability, becomes apparent at the moment when the results of the assignments are communicated. If this interpretation is correct, then any residue of freedom in Eteocles' decisions would be entirely eradicated.

Finally, H. Patzer fully accepted Wolff's conclusions, but drew entirely new and far-reaching consequences from them.[10] He started from the question how the first part of the play is now to be understood, and by asking whether there is really such an absolute contrast between the first and second halves as Wilamowitz and Solmsen had supposed, for all the difference in their explanations of it. The curse and the Erinys are indeed already mentioned at line 70, although their full influence only comes to the fore in the second half of the play. The two halves cannot therefore be completely opposed to each other. But what, it must now be asked, is the meaning of the whole?

At this point, Patzer brought a further element into consideration for the interpretation of the play. What, he asked, is the significance of Oedipus' curse at the various stages of the play? The answer is that, like an oracle, it has two or more meanings. 'They should divide their inheritance by the sword' [788–90]. That can simply mean that they will not be able to come to a peaceful understanding about it, that it will need to be decided by force of arms, but not necessarily that they must both be killed (in the sense of 'How much land does a man need?' [i. e. only enough to be buried in; cf. 731–3]), let alone that this must happen through mutual fratricide. In the first half of the play, Eteocles believes in the first and milder interpretation. That is shown by the vow which he makes to the gods at lines 271 ff. of what he will do if they grant victory to the Thebans. This vow, which he promises to fulfil himself, would be meaningless or hypocritical if

[10] H. Patzer, 'Die dramatische Handlung der *Sieben gegen Theben*', HSCP 63 (1958), 97–119.

he knew at this moment that he must die in battle with his brother or if he had even decided to sacrifice himself. Furthermore, he does not even know that Polynices will take his stand at one of the gates as the leader of the attackers. He only understands the full terrible meaning of his father's curse when he hears from the report of the scout that Polynices is the attacker at the very gate which he has already decided to defend, and must understand from the situation that there is no further possibility of changing the allocations.

A further question immediately suggested itself to Patzer in connexion with this one.[11] Is the behaviour of Eteocles in the first part of the play really as irreproachable as it had seemed to earlier interpreters, including Wilamowitz and Solmsen? If, as it now appears, he believes in the possibility of the salvation not only of the city but also of his own rule, is he then really so selfless? Further, is his behaviour towards the maidens of the chorus without fault? Does it not show an irritation and excitability which is perhaps the result of an inner insecurity? His behaviour perhaps indicates that, while he may believe in the possibility of salvation, he is still privately oppressed by the curse. In any event, according to this interpretation he seems already in the first part of the play to be by no means the ideal ruler but rather to be the victim of delusion. *Seven Against Thebes* would thus be a kind of forerunner of Sophocles' *Oedipus Tyrannus* as a tragedy of delusion.

Patzer actually poses some considerably more far-reaching questions, which I bring up here because they are not without importance for a correct understanding of the play, although he rightly answers them in the negative. Is Eteocles actually in the right in relation to his brother? Is he even confident that he is in the right? Perhaps he knows, or at least has an uneasy feeling, that he was wrong to banish his brother. Self-seeking determination to keep his throne would then be concealed behind the mask of the ideal prince who is ready to make any sacrifice for his polis. If this is correct, Patzer argues, then the Erinys would be making use of doubly evil behaviour on the part of Eteocles to accomplish its goal: the unjust banishment of his brother and the hypocrisy behind his defence of his fatherland. His exaggerated emphasis on his duty to defend his fatherland could be understood in this sense.

---

[11] Patzer (n. 10), 103 ff.

But Patzer then rejects this interpretation. Aeschylus, at any rate, did not have it in mind. Admittedly the question of the origin of the quarrel, and thus of right and wrong, is not clarified. But if Aeschylus had wanted to put Eteocles in the wrong, then he would have had to make it more explicit. Nor can there be any question of hypocrisy. The way in which Aeschylus portrays the hypocrisy of Clytaemestra in *Agamemnon* leaves no doubt about that. The speeches of Amphiaraus also show, as Patzer explains in detail, that the question of the rights and wrongs of the original quarrel between the brothers remains in the background, as opposed to the contrast between their behaviour in the play, through which Polynices undoubtedly proves himself to be the worse. We will return to this later.

Once the possibility has been rejected of an interpretation, in contrast to earlier views, according to which Eteocles appears as altogether reprehensible, there still remains in Patzer's opinion the undoubted fact of his delusion, not just in line 253 but also far beyond that, even if to a lesser extent. After line 653, he can no longer doubt that single combat with his brother is inevitable. Thus the horror which he expresses in impassioned words. But even then he does not know that he will fall in this duel. There can, if only for this reason, be no question of self-sacrifice. From this moment on, continues Patzer, his fate is separate from that of the city. Eteocles' main goal is still to save the city, but at the same time to maintain his own honour as king. Nevertheless, he must be aware that he can no longer remain as king if he survives the killing of his brother. 'So far as that goes, the family of Laius is fated to destruction . . . This is no longer a tragedy of a moral choice which even in personal destruction remains free; according to the emphases which the poet has made audible enough it is rather the tragedy of one who ostensibly acts freely for the most part, to whom freedom reveals itself as an illusion which can in fact bring about compulsion.'[12]

It is now perhaps not without interest to review once more the history of the interpretation of the play. In the first stage, the character of Eteocles was determined entirely on the basis of his appearance in the first half of the play. Here he appears at first sight to be the ideal leader and defender of the city, in accordance with

---

[12] Patzer (n. 10), 111.

the meaning of his name. This leads on to the idea of his voluntary self-sacrifice at the end of the play. When this interpretation proved unworkable for the second half of the play, the play seemed to fall apart into two conflicting halves. Wilamowitz explained this in terms of its genesis in two contradictory epic versions of the myth which were combined by Aeschylus. Solmsen, on the other hand, thought that he could show that the discrepancy had been intended by the poet: the full horror of the effect of the curse is shown by the very fact that Eteocles is no longer the same person in the second half of the play. Finally, Patzer attempted to re-establish the unity of the play, also with reference to the figure of Eteocles, by explaining it so to speak from back to front. If Eteocles was now wholly at the mercy of the curse in the second half of the play, as seemed necessary in view of Wolff's conclusions, then it was necessary to transform his character in the first half into the complete opposite of what had been supposed by earlier interpreters. If one observes how often in the history of scholarship an extreme antithesis is opposed to an extreme thesis, then Patzer deserves credit for not having given way to this temptation, although he toyed with it, but for trying to bring the interpretation back to a middle ground where the various aspects of the subject can be considered as being of equal importance.

Patzer's interpretation may embody many of his own observations, but it nevertheless depends in one very important point on Wolff's conclusions, and these conclusions need a very careful examination. It is necessary first to say something about the interpretation of dramatic works generally. It goes without saying that a substantial work of art cannot be understood completely at the first seeing or reading. It reveals itself in its true substance only with subsequent reflection. This is also the justification for the repeated search for fresh interpretation by literary scholars. In the case of a *dramatic* work of art, the proposition is nevertheless no less valid that what is necessary for the deeper understanding of its content with regard to purely external events and facts should not be so concealed, or so fleetingly made visible in the stage-action, that it is cannot be grasped by the spectator.

This second proposition admittedly needs a more precise modification or qualification. There are things which cannot readily be apprehended with confidence in the written text, but which the actor can make unmistakably clear to the spectator by means of gesture and intonation. The modern dramatist employs stage-directions for this purpose. The actor and the director must additionally take care to understand the full context of the words, so that the audience's understanding is aided by gesture and expression. The ancient poet was in the best possible position to take care that this happened, since he was himself the director of the play. The second proposition can accordingly be restated to say that nothing in the external events which is necessary for deeper understanding of the play should be so hidden or fleeting that it cannot be made fully intelligible through the art of the director and the actor.

If Wolff's conclusions are examined from this standpoint, then it can easily be demonstrated that they are mistaken and that the interpretation built upon them cannot be sustained. After Eteocles has heard that the leaders of the enemy have begun to draw lots to determine which of them should lead the assault on which gate, and he has then had an altercation with the maidens of the chorus, he explains in lines 282 ff. that he will now go and station himself with six others at the seven gates of the city, before new and urgent messages come and inflame the present emergency. He exits, and then returns after a long choral ode. While one could imagine, after the words which he has spoken, that the captains have in the mean-time been dispatched to the gates, the very fact that he himself reappears on the stage and is thus evidently not standing at a gate makes it clear that he has not completely and literally carried out what he had previously announced. But in view of the shortness of his announcement, which is immediately followed by a long choral ode, and above all in view of the fact just mentioned, it is impossible that the belief was so firmly imprinted upon the spectators' minds that the other defenders have meanwhile taken up their positions at the gates that they hold fast to this belief even when it seems to be contradicted by what follows. So when Eteocles replies to the report of the scout that Tydeus will lead the assault on the first gate 'I *will* oppose the son of Astycus to Tydeus' [408–9], and then goes on to indicate why this man is especially appropriate for the task, the spectators will immediately suppose that the allocation to the gates is being undertaken now for the first time, and if they still remember the precise wording of the announcement at all, they will draw the conclusion that Eteocles has in the meantime accomplished only the first part of the announced action, the choice of the six defenders and the order to them to keep themselves in readiness, but will only now carry out the second part, the actual allocation to the gates. It is furthermore utterly impossible to see how 'I will oppose' could be uttered in such a way by an actor that the spectators could, let alone must, understand it differently.

In the orders by Eteocles which follow with regard to the allocation of the defenders, there are nevertheless two occurrences of the perfect [448, 473] and one of the aorist [505], as well as a second occurrence of the future [621] and one of the present ἔστιν ['there is', 553], which signifies that the appropriate defender is on hand and ready. Some interpreters have taken this literally to mean that three defenders have already been sent by Eteocles to their gates, while the others have come on with him now in order to be sent to the appropriate gates. Yet that is scarcely possible. Mute extras often appear in older tragedy, such as the councillors in Phrynichus' *Phoenissae* and aged representatives of the Theban people in the prologue of *Seven Against Thebes* itself, but it would be ridiculous for the three Theban captains to wait in the background, without Eteocles deigning to address them directly, and then hurry to their posts as soon as he gives the cue with the announcement 'I will send him there'. It is certainly correct that the future, perfect, aorist, and present must all be taken to refer essentially to the same situation. But how then is the change of tenses to be understood?

Instructive in this respect is Eteocles' answer to the boastful appearance of the attacker Eteoclus, on whose shield are written the words 'Ares himself will not drive me from the towers of the city'. Eteocles sends against him Megareus, a descendant of the Spartoi who are closely related to the god whom Eteoclus affronts through his boastful motto, since they sprang from the dragon's teeth which Cadmus sowed at the bidding of Ares (and of Athena); and to make the confrontation even more appropriate, it is said of this Megareus that he does his boasting with his (strong) hands, rather than with his mouth like the braggart Eteoclus. Eteocles' reply to the Scout's report begins now with the words [472–3]:

πέμποιμ' ἂν ἤδη τόνδε· σὺν τύχῃ δέ τῳ
καὶ δὴ πέπεμπται κόμπον ἐν χεροῖν ἔχων.

[I would send him now, but by good fortune
He has already been sent with his boast in his hands.]

Wolff's interpretation is that Eteocles means to say: 'I would send
Megareus to this gate if I had not, by a happy chance, sent him there
already'. But E. Fraenkel, who published his interpretation of the
passage at roughly the same time as Wolff,[13] and was not influenced
by his basic interpretation of the whole play, understood it in an
entirely different way, that is to say that Eteocles first hesitates for a
moment ('I could well send him') but then continues 'but the right
man has already been found'. We will return immediately to the
interpretation of πέπεμπται ['he has been sent'] here.

   Fraenkel would of course prefer to delete the first of these two
lines, on account of the following considerations. Firstly, it does not
suit the character of Eteocles to hesitate about whom he should send
to oppose Eteoclus: 'this man, a picture of absolute decisiveness, has
absolutely no use for a potential optative [i.e. 'I would…']'. Secondly, these perfects, in which it is made clear that a required action
has already been carried out, always in Aeschylus follow immediately
in the next line. Fraenkel gives several examples. But the first reason
for the deletion is not compelling. Absolute decisiveness does not
exclude consideration of how the thing on which someone is determined is to be achieved. Napoleon would have been a bad general if
his decisiveness in battle had prevented him from considering even
for a moment which of his subordinates would be best suited to the
execution of an emergency mission. The second reason is not by itself
sufficient. Even if it were true that in Aeschylus such perfects usually
follow immediately after the demand, that does not show that he
could never have departed from this practice. In the present case, the
divergence is justified not only by the need for variation with regard
to τέτακται ['he has been stationed', 448] in the previous answer, but
the speed of the decision, which arises from Megareus being clearly
the fitting opponent for Eteoclus, is made still more striking by the

[13] E. Fraenkel, 'Die sieben Redepaare im Thebanerdrama des Aeschylus',
SBAW 1957 (3), 30 ff. [= *Kleine Beiträge zur klassischen Philologie* (Rome, 1964),
i. 273–328].

moment of hesitant consideration. Among Fraenkel's parallels for
the immediate connexion of the perfect to the preceding demand
there is at least one in which the perfect cannot refer to the action
which has already preceded the demand, *Eumenides* 892–4:

EUMENIDES: ἄνασσ᾽ Ἀθάνα, τίνα με φῆς ἕξειν ἕδραν;
ATHENA: πάσης ἀπήμον᾽ οἰζύος. δέχου δὲ σύ.
EUMENIDES: καὶ δὴ δέδεγμαι· τίς δέ μοι τιμὴ μένει;

[EUMENIDES: Queen Athena, what dwelling do you say that I shall have?
ATHENA: One free from all distress. Accept it.
EUMENIDES: I have accepted it; what honour awaits me?]

Here the Eumenides could not have accepted the dwelling offered
to them by Athena before she has actually offered it to them. The
perfect thus signifies the instantaneity of their acceptance of the offer.
The perfects in Eteocles' answers could thus in exactly the same way
signify the instantaneity of the decision which arises from the
situation.

It is only a matter of proving that the two perfects could signify a
present decision and that this can be made clear to the spectator by
suitable utterance by the actor, as is indeed clear in the case of
the preceding πέμποιμ᾽ ἂν ἤδη τόνδε ['I would send him now', 472].
Since it is impossible for futures to refer to things which have
long since happened, and since all the answers essentially presuppose
the same situation, the interpretation of the written text must therefore be determined by the future tenses. The aorist ᾑρέθη ['he has
been chosen', 505] presents no difficulty, because the point here is
only that Eteocles has already selected Hyperbolus as a suitable
opponent for Hippomedon, and there is no question that he has
yet been allocated to a gate.

If any doubt should remain about the interpretation which has
been put forward then it must, it seems to me, be removed by the
beginning of the discussion between the chorus and Eteocles after
he has announced his decision to oppose his brother [677–85]. The
chorus begs Eteocles to hold back from carrying out his decision.
If Wolff's interpretation were correct, then there would only be one
possible reply that he could give: 'The defenders already stand at the
gates which have been allocated to them. I have decided upon
the seventh gate for myself. The lots drawn by the enemy, which

have evidently been guided by the gods, have determined that my brother will oppose me at this gate. It is too late to change the allocation, because the attack on the city is imminent. Neither can I leave the seventh gate without a defender. So it is obviously ordained for me to fight against my brother. I cannot escape it'.[14]

But that is not what Eteocles says. He speaks instead of the αἰσχύνη ['shame'] which refusal to go and face his brother would bring on him, which presupposes that he still has a choice if he is prepared to bring shame on himself. Solmsen has indeed described this as a mere secondary theme, and Patzer agrees with him. If, however, as Patzer believes, the whole play is designed to bring Eteocles into a quandary from which he cannot escape, then it is impossible to see why Aeschylus should have introduced a secondary theme which would inevitably obscure his main point, although there was not the slightest necessity to introduce it and he could easily have put words in Eteocles' mouth which would not only have been compatible with his presumed purpose but would actually have elucidated it. Wolff's interpretation therefore seems to me to have been comprehensively refuted. It is a typical scholarly interpretation, that is to say an interpretation which can only be arrived at by reading the text with exclusive attention to the individual lines, without a clear understanding of the conditions governing the effect of the words on the stage. I allow myself to point this out so emphatically because this kind of misguided interpretation is so extraordinarily appealing to scholars because of the nature of their *own* profession.

Patzer's interpretation of the play may have lost one of its fundamental supports with the refutation of Wolff's conclusions, but that certainly does not mean that all his observations are invalidated. The question must still be posed afresh why Eteocles seems to be bent on single combat with his brother from the moment when the scout tells him that Polynices is leading the attack at the seventh gate. The first thing to say is that there is certainly some truth in the idea that Eteocles has been driven by the curse and the Erinys into a corner, in which he must fight to the death with his brother and from which he

---

[14] Wilamowitz (n. 4), 77–8 has already convincingly refuted the objection that Eteocles had no time to dispatch the designated captains to the gates after he had sent for his greaves in order to go armed to oppose his brother.

can no longer escape. But what drives Eteocles into this corner is not of such a mechanical—or mystical—nature as a mere coincidence arising from his allocation of defenders in ignorance of the enemy's lottery for the gates. Eteocles has chosen the defenders of the gates in full knowledge of the enemy's dispositions on the principle that the defender should be appropriate to the attacker. He thus turns out in the end to be the only remaining appropriate opponent for his brother Polynices. His own bitter statement (673 ff.) leaves no further doubt about the matter. There is a much deeper tragic irony here than if the encounter were merely accomplished by the accident of the lot. There is only need for a few more conditions to make his quandary inescapable, and these are brought to light in the dialogue with the chorus, which therefore by no means deals with secondary themes which are of no essential significance for the understanding of the play.

Eteocles' decision, and what he has to say about it in the dialogue with the chorus, are his answer to the scout's report about the posting of Polynices to the seventh gate and his behaviour there. It is here too that the key to the understanding of what follows must be found. The scout reported the curses which Polynices 'wished down' upon the city, and the belief which he thus implied about the outcome of the battle. This is expressed in the following words (634–8):

πύργοις ἐπεμβὰς κἀπικηρυχθεὶς χθονί
ἁλώσιμον παιᾶν' ἐπεξιακχάσας
σοὶ ξυμφέρεσθαι καὶ κτανὼν θανεῖν πέλας
ἢ ζῶντ' ἀτιμαστῆρα τὼς ἀνδρηλάτην
φυγῇ τὸν αὐτὸν τόνδε τείσασθαι τρόπον.

[He prays that standing upon the walls and proclaimed as victor to the land,
Uttering a frenzied song of conquest,
He will meet you in combat, and having killed you die at your side,
Or that if you live, who drove him in dishonour from the land,
Requiting like with like he will exile you.]

Polynices thus does not expect to meet his brother at the gate. But he does hope to capture the city. He will have himself proclaimed as victor, and will himself strike up the victory song. He will *then* meet his brother, and *either* kill him in single combat and fall himself *or* drive him in disgrace from the city, as he had himself been driven out.

This is the basis of Eteocles' behaviour and of his reply to the chorus, and not a situation which in purely military terms allows no other outcome than the meeting of the two brothers at the same gate.

The chorus protests to Eteocles that there is 'no old age' [682] for the pollution of fratricide, that is to say that this stain will neither fade nor disappear. Eteocles' answer is that if one could endure a disaster without shame, so be it; for that (freedom from shame) would be the only profit which still remains for the dead. But good reputation, which must be preserved at all costs, cannot result from unhappiness combined with shame. What decides him in his action, therefore, is that he feels it as an unbearable shame to evade this battle.

In order to see clearly what this means for the overall interpretation of the play, it is necessary to consider the alternatives to Eteocles' decision and to take account of all the presuppositions of the situation. Polynices has not said that he would under any circumstances kill his brother and/or fall at his hand, but has also left open the possibility of driving his brother in disgrace from the city, as he himself was driven: that is, he will do this if his brother does not face up to him in battle of his own accord. It follows from this that the battle could actually be avoided if Eteocles were prepared to go into exile voluntarily and to cede the city to his brother. If this were really the case, then Eteocles would be a power-hungry egoist and—in so far as he talks as if he were a dutiful defender of the city— a hypocrite. Patzer did well to draw attention to the possibility of such an interpretation. Euripides, with his tendency to scrutinize the moral foundations of the old myths and to some extent also of the plays which his predecessors based on those myths, and where he believed that he had discovered a flaw or an inconsistency to make that inconsistency very plainly visible, has drawn in his *Phoe-nissae* the conclusions suggested by Patzer. He has brought out into the open the possibility of Eteocles rescuing the city not by battle but by yielding, and has placed it before the eyes of the spectators in the negotiation between the two brothers which precedes the battle for the city. Eteocles undoubtedly appears here as the one who is in the wrong, or at least more in the wrong. In order to escape their father's curse that they must divide their inheritance by the sword, the brothers have come to an agreement that they will rule the city alternately for a year each. Polynices went into voluntary exile in accordance with this agreement. When he wanted to claim his rights at the beginning of the new year, Eteocles, in breach of the agreement, told him brusquely that, now that he had the kingship in his hands, he was not prepared to give it up even temporarily. Only then did Polynices avail himself of outside help and threaten to claim his rights by force. He is ready to negotiate even now, although he is afraid of his brother's treachery. Eteocles is not prepared to make any concessions whatsoever, so that the battle for the city is only unavoidable because of his lust for power.[15]

This is not the only example of something which appears in Aeschylus only as a possibility on the horizon but which is turned into a reality by Euripides. Aeschylus' Polynices does not expect to find his brother opposing him at the gate. But if, as he hopes, the city is captured, then his brother will have to face him or, if he chooses to evade that, to allow himself to be driven ignominiously from the city, as he himself had been. But there is also another possibility. The attack on the city could be repulsed without the brothers meeting in battle. That is what actually happens in Euripides' *Phoenissae*. Eteocles is not content there with victory and the salvation of the city, but challenges his brother to single combat, after he has already left explicit instructions to his subordinates and followers in the event of his death to forbid the burial of the corpse of his brother if he will have fallen (*Phoenissae* 774–7). There can be no further question here of the dutiful leader who sacrifices himself for the salvation of the city.

If the matter is represented in this way by Euripides, then it suggests a conscious or unconscious question—and personally I do not have the slightest doubt that Euripides was fully aware of what he was doing—to his great predecessor: why does your Eteocles not renounce opposing his brother at the seventh gate, as the chorus recommends, so that at least the possibility remains that the attack will be repulsed without him doing so? A similar question is implied in the negotiations between Eteocles and Polynices in the *Phoenissae*: why does your Eteocles not renounce the sovereignty of the city voluntarily, if he is so concerned for its salvation, since such a

---

[15] Euripides' Eteocles gives an unambiguous statement of this with the famous words (*Pho.* 524–5): εἴπερ γὰρ ἀδικεῖν χρή, τυραννίδος πέρι | κάλλιστον ἀδικεῖν, τἄλλα δ' εὐσεβεῖν χρεών ['If one is going to do wrong, then it is best to do it for the sake of tyranny, and to be pious in everything else'].

renunciation would make the attack on the city superfluous and accordingly prevent it? Or: what does it signify for the character of your Eteocles that in your play he acts in this way and no other?

If one started from the basic assumption occasionally advanced by W. F. Otto, that Euripides had so much reverence for his great predecessor that it could not have entered his head to carry on a controversy with him through his plays in any sense whatsoever, one would be obliged to suppose that it could only have been a false interpretation of a play by Aeschylus that he would want to criticize. His own interpretation of the play, however, agreed exactly with the interpretation considered by Patzer as a possibility, and for that reason Patzer has done a service by throwing open this possibility for discussion.[16] Patzer has, however, rightly rejected the validity of this interpretation for Aeschylus, as will now be demonstrated in detail. This raises the extremely interesting question of the means by which Aeschylus has succeeded in suggesting an entirely different interpretation of Eteocles' behaviour to the spectator, despite the possibility which the critical moralist Euripides has presented in such a clear light; and whether the interpretation which he tries to suggest to the spectator can withstand the critical examination of one who later reflects on the structure of the play, as Euripides had obviously done; and, further, what and how much Euripides had to change in order to force his interpretation of Eteocles' behaviour on his spectator or reader.

It has often been said that Aeschylus leaves the events which preceded his play entirely in the dark. That is entirely correct so far as the purely factual presuppositions of the action are concerned. In contrast to Euripides, nothing whatsoever is said about why Eteocles rules in the city and Polynices is outside as the attacker. Both believe justice to be on their side. The reader or spectator hears nothing of a pact or an arrangement which one of them has observed and the other has violated. It is also very doubtful whether the ancient spectator, who had seen the previous play in the trilogy, would have been any better informed about it than we are. The previous play was called *Oedipus*, and will no doubt have had a similar content to Sophocles' *Oedipus Tyrannus*. Even if Oedipus' curse on his sons

---

[16] Patzer (n. 10), 105 ff.

occurred in it, which is entirely possible, the actual quarrel between
them could hardly have found a place there or even been hinted at. It
would also be inconceivable that there would have been no reference
in the surviving play to an agreement between the brothers if there
had actually been one. But, on the other hand, does the play not
contain in itself everything which is necessary for a full understanding of it? Is it possible that this Polynices could be a good ruler, when
the majority of his six helpers want not so much to conquer the city
for him as to raze it to the ground? Could this sort of man ever have
been a good ruler? And if not, does Eteocles not then have every
reason to prevent him from becoming king, whatever the original
agreement may have been and whatever the original reasons may
have been that Eteocles is now inside and Polynices outside? Is
Eteocles not the true defender of the city precisely because he tries
to prevent Polynices from becoming king? The answer to the first of
Euripides' questions lies precisely in these questions.

If this holds true for the prehistory and for the situation at the
beginning of the play, what then is the situation at the end? Evidently
the same, except that it has come to the most extreme crisis. The
contrast between the brutality and the κόμπος ['boasting'] of the
enemy and the self-restraint of the defence, as well as what the
prophet Amphiaraus says about Polynices, leave no doubt that Eteocles cannot hand the city over to Polynices, and that he cannot give
up his kingship for the sake of peace. The only remaining possibility
is to do everything in his power to avoid a personal confrontation
with his brother, especially as the possibility has not been excluded
that the enemy's assault can be repulsed without Eteocles defending
the seventh gate. But the city would, of course, hardly be saved by
that. The way Aeschylus has portrayed Polynices, he certainly would
not allow himself to be deterred from trying again by one or more
failures of the attack, if necessary with other allies than the ones
whom he has found this time.

For the understanding of the whole, it is very instructive to
examine here once more how Euripides has come to terms with
these possibilities in *Phoenissae*. He has introduced the entirely new
character of Menoeceus into the action, as well as the oracle which
says that the city can be saved only by the sacrifice of a descendant of
the Spartoi. The following scenes result from this: Creon's refusal to

sacrifice his son for the city; his attempt to help his son to escape before the oracle becomes known in the city and the citizens demand the sacrifice; the father's deception by his son, who does not want to evade the sacrifice; and finally the report of his accomplishment of the sacrifice. All this is splendidly realized in detail, and is extremely exciting. But from the point of view of the requirements of the unity of the play, it interrupts the main action and diverts the spectators' attention from it for a considerable period. And yet the Menoeceus episode is from *one* point of view of fundamental significance for the main action: after the oracle has said that the city can only be saved by the sacrifice of the life of Menoeceus, and the assault is then actually repulsed immediately after his death, there can be no further doubt that the city has finally been saved (*Phoenissae* 996 ff.). If Eteocles nevertheless persists in challenging his brother to a duel, then it is clear that he is not sacrificing himself for the city but acting under the influence of the delusion which has affected him because of his father's curse. It is almost as if Euripides had anticipated the explanation by modern scholars of Eteocles' self-sacrifice in Aeschylus. In so far as he has Menoeceus rescue the city by his self-sacrifice, he completely removes the possibility of seeing Eteocles' readiness for single combat with his brother as a self-sacrifice for the city.

The fact that Euripides had to resort to such thoroughgoing changes in the development of the action in order to achieve his purpose shows all the more clearly that the situation in Aeschylus is different. The city is in the most extreme and immediate danger. Eteocles cannot remain detached and wait to see how things turns out. The allocation of the defenders, in which each is matched with an appropriate opponent, has shown with bitter irony that he is the most appropriate man to lead the defence against his brother. The fate of the city is thus not as completely detached from the fate of Eteocles as some recent interpreters have supposed. The city can certainly survive without him, and can indeed do so all the better in that he is burdened by the curse. But he is still king now, and responsible for ensuring that everything possible is done to serve the salvation of the city. He cannot therefore evade his duty without shame, even if it means taking the most extreme measures. But that means stationing himself where he will meet his brother. That is of course the fulfilment of their father's curse, as Eteocles too is well aware at this moment. But the beauty of it is that there is at this point no need for any further supernatural reason for bringing about this fulfilment. Wilamowitz was entirely correct when he insisted that there is absolutely no question of a supernatural reason why the city could only be saved when the curse of Oedipus has been fulfilled by the death of both his sons. Nevertheless it is now apparent that those who have spoken of a self-sacrifice by Eteocles were to some extent correct, if not necessarily in the way in which they supposed. An effective deliverance of the city from the threat is not possible without the death of Polynices. Eteocles cannot evade the task of defending the city at the crucial place. But the situation has developed in such a way that he must face his brother in a combat to the death. It is also clear enough that if he should survive this combat, he could not continue living happily let alone carry on as king. His own death too is thus assured in one way or the other. That is what Eteocles envisages when, after the scout's account of Polynices' behaviour, he goes to face him as the 'appropriate' defender at the seventh gate. It is certainly the case, therefore, that no free choice remains for him in the sense that he can choose or not choose a 'free self-sacrifice' for the city. But he is still 'free' in the sense that the reason why he cannot act otherwise than he does act is that he is who he is, and that means in this case that he is a man who is well aware of his responsibility and cannot endure the shame of shirking it.

   The apparent inconsistency which had seemed to open up between the first and second halves of the play is thus resolved, even though it has in effect been read backwards, rather than forwards as in the older interpretation. The critic is nevertheless not forced to read anything back into the first half on the basis of the interpretation of the second half, which the spectator, who has not yet seen the second half, cannot do. In general, the observations made about various passages by supporters of completely opposing interpretations now fall into place, without any need to be 'eclectic'. The Eteocles of the second half of the play is not a different person from the Eteocles of the first half. And yet there is a tremendous difference. There is even something correct in the theory of the 'tragedy of delusion'. There is no doubt that at the beginning of the play Eteocles still lacks full insight into the hopelessness of his position and into the meaning of his father's curse. He himself still believes in the possibility of a victory, in which he survives and is able to fulfil the vows which he makes now. Nevertheless he is surrounded from the beginning by an atmosphere of complete loneliness, which makes itself felt all the more strongly as he is naturally so closely connected with those around him through his concern about and for the city. Everything rests on his shoulders. Even the chorus itself, which is on his side and addresses him as ὦ φίλον Οἰδίπου τέκος ['dear son of Oedipus', 203] and again later as φίλτατ' ἀνδρῶν ['dearest of men', 677], does not help him, but rather makes his job even harder. That is what finds expression in his vehement harangue of the maidens. Later, in the course of the seven pairs of speeches, he does indeed have the military helpers who will undertake to lead the defence of the city at the gates. But none of them appears on the stage, and there is no hint of any kind of personal relationship between them and Eteocles. Even Prometheus was not so solitary, visited as he was when nailed to his rock by all sorts of fellow-sufferers and sympathizers, and even apart from his visitors through his defiance of his enemy Zeus and his secret weapon against him.

In his final confrontation with the chorus, Eteocles' loneliness and inner isolation become still clearer than in the first half of the play. In addition to the isolation from assistance in the fulfilment of his duty comes the more painful isolation of being completely misunderstood. It is indeed not only Eteocles' 'frame of mind' which is said to have changed in this scene, which would be understandable and in a sense also right and proper in view of what he has learned from the scout's report about Polynices, but the chorus too has allegedly undergone a complete change of character. From the terrified maidens who were no longer capable of rational action and infuriated the king who had to take care of order in the city, they would suddenly have become women who are self-possessed and indeed wise, and oppose the king who has now lost his head. They even address him as τέκνον ['child', 686].[17] We thus have again, as often with modern interpreters, the 'archaic' or even 'strictly classical' poet, who violates in the grossest possible fashion the basic principles of drama which were first formulated not by moderns but by Aristotle himself (who did however, as everyone knows,

---

[17] Cf. Wilamowitz (n. 4), 68–9; Solmsen (n. 7), 200–1 [= *Kl. Schr.* 109–10].

understand nothing of classical Greek poetry). For this violation of the rules, however, Aeschylus must on no account be criticized but must rather be admired instead, since he is after all an archaic or classical poet. But in reality the chorus has not essentially changed its character, even though it may not be so agitated now as it was in the parodos. It is entirely understandable and natural that the maidens should be horrified by Eteocles' willingness to confront his brother in a duel, and that they should refer to the pollution which would arise from it. At the same time this also shows their complete incomprehension. They say, 'No one will call you a coward if it ends well and you save your life' (698 ff.), and 'even a cowardly victory is pleasing to the gods' (716). Wilamowitz has already said everything that needs to be said about this.[18] If the maidens address Eteocles as τέκνον ['child'] and thereby naïvely express their confidence in their own superior wisdom at this moment, then there lies in this an additional irony, which is of course not noticed by the maidens but is located in the human situation. It is by no means the case that Eteocles has become an essentially different person in this scene, whose character has been completely transformed. But his isolation is now complete with regard to those at whom his entire concern is aimed.

The same is true of his relation to the gods. The only difference is that there is a wider span between the first and last scenes. The subject is broached in the very first lines which Eteocles speaks (1–9): 'The man who is at the head of the city must be unceasingly vigilant to do what is right. If things go well, then people thank the gods for it; but if—which god forbid—a disaster should befall the city, then everyone will say that Eteocles is guilty'. This does not yet say a great deal about

[18] Wilamowitz (n. 4), 65: 'The women oppose him with the popular belief: "If it goes well for you (you avoid the duel and repel the assault), no one will call you a coward. The Erinys does not enter a house if the gods accept offerings"... This is the mentality of the seller of indulgences... Aeschylus despises this kind of religion, and so too does Eteocles.' But what Wilamowitz says here somewhat contradicts his assertion that two scenes later the chorus is no longer the chorus of maidens but represents the people of Thebes. It is entirely in character that this new terror completely takes hold of the chorus with Eteocles' announcement of his decision to oppose his brother in battle, and thereby causes it to forget the danger from outside. Wilamowitz' own words, cited above, bear out that their character has not changed in the least. It is indeed correct that the chorus represents the people of Thebes in the negative sense that it is a very effective illustration of Eteocles' isolation with regard to his people.

Eteocles' relation to the gods, and leaves open the question whether ὦν Ζεὺς ἀλεξητήριος γένοιτο ['may Zeus be a protector from these things', 8–9] is anything more than a mere formula. The only thing that is immediately clear is that Eteocles is well aware that he can no more shift any of the responsibility which he has assumed for the city on to the gods than on to his fellow-citizens. He alone bears the full responsibility in this respect too.

A much stronger inner tension is latent in the prayer with which he leaves the stage after the scout's first preliminary report of proceedings in the enemy camp and immediately before the parodos (69–77):

> ὦ Ζεῦ τε καὶ Γῆ καὶ πολισσοῦχοι θεοί
> Ἀρά τ' Ἐρινὺς πατρὸς ἡ μεγασθενής,
> μή μοι πόλιν γε πρυμνόθεν πανώλεθρον
> ἐκθαμνίσητε δῃάλωτον, Ἑλλάδος
> φθόγγον χέουσαν, καὶ δόμους ἐφεστίους·
> ἐλευθέραν δὲ γῆν τε καὶ Κάδμου πόλιν
> ζεύγλῃσι δουλίῃσι μήποτε σχεθεῖν.
> γένεσθε δ' ἀλκή· ξυνὰ δ' ἐλπίζω λέγειν·
> πόλις γὰρ εὖ πράσσουσα δαίμονας τίει.

> [O Zeus and Earth and gods who protect the city,
> Curse, mighty Erinys of my father,
> Do not, I beseech you, utterly destroy
> This city, taken by its enemies, which speaks
> The tongue of Greece, with its hearths and homes,
> And never hold in yoke of slavery
> A free land and the city of Cadmus.
> Defend us! I plead our common cause,
> Since a prospering city honours the gods.]

The words with which he concludes the prayer recall the friendly view of the relation of gods to humans which had developed among the Greeks: that the gods take special pleasure in prayers and sacrifices offered in joyous gratitude and gladness. This corresponds to the fact that human beings, when things go well for them, spontaneously think of the gods and want them to share in their joy. This is a specifically Greek view,[19] which is far removed from the

---

[19]   For a more detailed discussion of this, see K. von Fritz, 'Greek prayers', *Review of Religion* 10 (1945), 5–39, at 8 ff.

rule-observance and fear which are so often to be found in Judaism and Christianity, where people forget God when things are going well for them and need to be brought back to him through suffering.

Eteocles' prayer to save the city and not to allow it to fall under the yoke of slavery does not, however, appeal only to Zeus and to all the gods who protect the city (i. e. enjoy a cult in the city), and for whom such an appeal is highly appropriate, but also to the divine power of the curse and the Erinys of his father, which certainly do not belong to the powers which take a particular pleasure in sacrifices offered with gladness and joy. The best one can hope for from them is that they turn aside their glance and their influence, if only from the city and not from Eteocles, who is the very man on whom they have indeed already directed them. The characteristic ambivalence of Eteocles' attitude both to the city and to the gods is already expressed in this brief prayer—and the way in which it is concentrated into these few lines shows the highest art. He has the closest connexion with the city in the concern which causes him to pray to the gods for it, but is at the same time separated from it in that it can only be saved through separation from the curse which attaches inseparably to him. With regard to the gods, he may still have hope in them for the city, but so long as they include the ἄρα ['curse'] and the Erinys, he cannot really have any hope in them for himself.[20]

There have been many good discussions of how Eteocles' relation to the gods is expressed in the ensuing altercation with the agitated maidens, so that there is not much to be added now. Eteocles is very far from being an atheist. He has experienced the divine powers in his own body and soul too much for him to entertain doubts about their existence. He also has no doubt that they can prove themselves to be helpful, and that one should therefore pray to them as he himself has just done. Yet he is not only convinced that they could not relieve him

---

[20] Wilamowitz (n. 4) seems to me not to have understood this altogether correctly when he says (p. 64) that the Erinys is only loosely introduced into the prayer and that the reminder to the gods of their own profit, while entirely justified for ancient cult, still sounds a discordant note here. The 'profit' of the gods is not only, so to speak, of a material nature. What Eteocles says is no more intended in the sense of a business transaction with the gods than the end of the choral ode (174–81), which Wilamowitz contrasts with Eteocles' prayer. The ambivalence of Eteocles' relation to the gods is brought to the spectators' attention in the most focussed way through the inclusion of the Erinys.

of an iota of his own responsibility, but he also knows too much about how cities and individuals who have also put their trust in the gods and prayed to them have been abandoned, how the gods have literally migrated from a city, and this makes it impossible for him to cling to them (cf. 216 ff.). The contrast between him and the maidens in this respect is very striking. The maidens are full of bewilderment and terror. But even in this bewilderment and terror they have an instinct to cling to something in which they can put their trust. They would still cling to the gods in fearful trust at the very moment when the enemy seized them to cut their throats.

In as much as Eteocles also feels any fear it is an entirely different kind of fear: controlled fear rather than panic. This is another reason why he has no instinct to cling to anything. The gods may exist, but they are distant and one cannot put one's trust in them. This too is part of the atmosphere of loneliness and abandonment which surrounds Eteocles from the start. If we also take into account that the curse and the Erinys of his father are among the divine powers with which he personally has to deal, then it is not such a very big step from the prayer in which this curse is implored along with the other gods to save the city to the insight that he, Eteocles, has been altogether abandoned by the gods. It is therefore also not entirely incorrect to speak of a delusion on the part of Eteocles in the first half of the play which is comparable to the case of Oedipus, in so far as he does not yet recognize the full horror and hopelessness of his situation, but there is nevertheless a complete difference in the presuppositions of the two cases and of the situations which arise from them. Oedipus, entirely innocent so far as the purity of his intentions is concerned, has unintentionally done something which is objectively appalling. He knows nothing of it, and only discovers gradually in the course of the play that he himself is the originator of the whole disaster. Eteocles, on the other hand, is from the beginning well aware of the curse, which rests on his shoulders whether he is guilty or innocent—although he is certainly not entirely without his own guilt—and it is only its consequences which are not yet clear to him in their full horror. Both men are concerned for their city, but Oedipus is entirely at one with it at the beginning, while Eteocles is surrounded by an atmosphere of solitude despite his care for the others. Oedipus, to whom the horror only becomes clear in a process of breathtaking tension in the course of the action represented on the stage, is so overcome by revulsion at what he has now discovered that he tears out his eyes and knows of no other escape either in life or in death, since he dreads meeting his parents again even among the dead. Eteocles, on the other hand, is from the beginning surrounded by horrors, which he alone has to look in the face. After he has, despite everything, tried until the end to do what he regards as his duty, the horrors gather still more closely around him, until at the end he has, so to speak, to go with full awareness through the gate of hell. He is a knight fighting against death and the devil, who not only sits calmly on his horse as in Dürer's engraving,[21] but must go of his own accord to meet the infernal powers.[22]

The situation and the character of Eteocles here are one and the same. The situation can only be what it is because Eteocles is who he is; and, conversely, a character such as Eteocles cannot act without the situation in which he appears. To that extent it was not entirely incorrect for Wilamowitz to try to explain the character of Eteocles, whom he regards as being more individualized than any other character before the *Oresteia*—even, I would say, including the *Oresteia*—in terms of the dramatic situation which Aeschylus created from the combination of the myth of the glorious defender of his fatherland and the version based on the brothers affected by their father's curse.[23] But how far is he correct when he goes on to say, 'The poet has certainly not asked himself how to portray his Eteocles, but took over what was handed down to him'?[24] The first part of this statement is doubtless correct, in so far as it means that Aeschylus did not plan out his characters in detail, but that they formed themselves for

---

[21] [The reference is to Dürer's 'The Knight, Death, and the Devil' (1513), reproduced (e.g.) on p. 265 of M. Brion, *Albrecht Dürer: His Life and Work* (London, 1960), with discussion on pp. 210–11.]

[22] E. Howald, *Die Sieben gegen Theben* (Zürich, 1939), 16, has tried to show that the action of *Seven Against Thebes* is a kind of 'breaking loose of hell', a 'marching forth to battle of the mighty powers of the depths with their retinue', a 'marching forth from the underworld on to earth'. That is certainly a little exaggerated, if only because the play is about living heroes who come from identifiable Greek cities. But it contains an accurate sense that Eteocles' situation really does have something of a battle against infernal powers, in that under the constraint of the curse he cannot without shame escape what are in a sense hellish horrors.

[23] Wilamowitz (n. 4), 64.

[24] Wilamowitz (n. 4), 66–7.

him more or less unconsciously into living shapes. So far as the second part of the statement is concerned, it is possibly correct with regard to all those of Eteocles' individual traits which Wilamowitz adduces: that he does his duty with unshakeable self-confidence (the glorious defender), that he is aware of the curse which drives him with sinister power to a destination at which he shudders (the Eteocles of the later version), and that he would nevertheless regard it as cowardice to disobey the curse (I would say, to evade it), if it were not possible without betraying his duty to the city. But, it seems to me, the individualization of the character goes much further than this, and also beyond the individualization of the characters of the entire *Oresteia*, not just Orestes, who remains relatively unindividualized, but also Agamemnon, Clytemnestra, Aegisthus, and Electra.

Something like the concentrated representation of the combination of the most extreme self-control with the most extreme tension, such as characterizes Eteocles throughout the play, will not simply have been presented to any poet by the material which he inherited. This representation is accomplished, so to speak, in a triple arch, of which each has a wider span than its predecessor. The first arch comprises the prologue. It finds its conclusion in the prayer [69–77], in which the ambiguity of Eteocles' attitude to the gods and to the city finds such a concentrated expression, but at the end of which Eteocles is nevertheless entirely composed and ready for action. The second arch spans the altercation between Eteocles and the chorus after the parodos. His inner tension finds its first outward expression in his outburst here against the maidens. Anyone who accepts the interpretation which Patzer discusses only as a possibility, that a weakness on the part of Eteocles is at least hinted at, that he is in reality not a good leader, would thereby reveal a complete misunderstanding of the play. If Eteocles had remained entirely calm here, this would either have meant that he possessed a tranquillity which is incompatible with a belief in the efficacy of a curse, which would destroy the presupposition of the play, or that he had turned into a lifeless abstraction of an unshakeable leader. The danger of turning him into such an abstraction would have arisen from the influence of traditional versions of the myth, and some modern interpreters have indeed turned him into such an abstraction ('the ideal ruler, responsible, determined, clear in mind and strong in hand' [above, p. 142]).

Aeschylus' greatness as a poet is shown by the fact that he did not give in to this temptation, or possibly that it was not a temptation for him at all. The arch is nevertheless completed at the end of the scene. Eteocles turns, again completely composed, to his next mission, although the maidens have put up resistance to him and he has not entirely finished with their resistance.[25]

The third arch has the widest span. The tension, not only in Eteocles but also in the spectator, slowly mounts until the messenger's report about the seventh gate, which not only leaves no doubt that Polynices will personally take part as leader of the assault and that Eteocles is left as the appropriate defender to oppose him, but also that Polynices' determination to go to the last extremity and do violence to the city has been confirmed. Eteocles' second outburst follows, which expresses itself not just in words like his first but also and especially in the haste with which he reaches the decision to bring the curse, as he now understands its meaning, to fulfilment, and has his weapons brought to him in order to carry it out. But even here he is in the end collected and composed. Now that he sees that there is no other way out, and that the gods assuredly no longer have any care for him, he is ready to take that too on himself. The further objections of the maidens make no impression upon him, unless to make him even more vehement. He is again completely focussed on action, as he had been at the end of the two preceding sections of the play.

The common objection will doubtless now be made against this interpretation that it is 'psychologizing', and thus illegitimately imports into the play something which was far from the mind of an 'archaic' poet. The probability of such an objection can only be a reason for making the attempt to clarify the very vague concepts which have traditionally been employed here, and also to consider the question of the justification of general statements that something could or could not belong to a given period.

Here too a comparison with Euripides is very instructive. A situation was prescribed for him too, when he changed the moral emphasis from *Seven Against Thebes* and tried to show as it were the other side of the coin, from which definite consequences for characterization inevitably followed. In order to incriminate Eteocles, he

---

[25] Cf. 256 ff., and especially the following choral ode, 288 ff.

introduced the negotiations between the brothers and the sacrifice of Menoeceus. But that was not enough by itself, if the character and behaviour of Polynices remained such that the defence of the city against him seemed to be a necessity. In Aeschylus, the very fact that Polynices attempts an assault on his own fatherland with an army of such savage confederates is certainly enough, among other things, to make clear to the spectators that he is not suitable to be the king of this city. It was therefore necessary for Euripides to show him in a different light and to make his campaign understandable. Euripides characteristically uses psychology as a means to achieve this. His Polynices by no means takes the field with savage hatred against his fatherland and his brother. His heart is divided. This is already shown by his very first words which he speaks to his mother when she greets him after he has arrived to negotiate: 'I have come with both good and ill will to those who are my enemies' (*Phoenissae* 357–8). Then he speaks of his love for his homeland, of the sufferings of an exile who must hang around among strangers, and of the friends and relations whom he has left behind in his homeland and of whom he has not had a word of news. His eager enquiries about his father and sisters (376–8) show that there is no hypocrisy in what he says. He is immediately on the defensive in his meeting with his brother, although it is he who has come to exact his rights, and it is only after Eteocles has declared to him that he not only wants to drive him out of the city but also to kill him that he is finally forced to say that his hopes of returning to his homeland are no longer 'sleeping' [634] and that he hopes, after killing his brother, to return to his city as king.

There is an obvious difference between Eteocles' representation of himself in *Seven Against Thebes* and that of Polynices in *Phoenissae*. Euripides' Polynices exposes his heart directly. With Aeschylus' Eteocles, everything is focussed on action and on the matter in hand, and his inner tension is revealed only indirectly. But this difference between direct and indirect expression is not the decisive one. The portrayal of Polynices in *Phoenissae* reveals a far less subtle art of psychological analysis than can be found in several others of Euripides' plays, both early and late: the portrayal of Admetus in *Alcestis*, of Jason and Creon in *Medea*, and of Agamemnon in *Iphigenia in Aulis*. In all these cases, the interior of the characters is revealed not so much by direct expression of their emotions, as in the case of Polynices in

Phoenissae, as through their hesitations, through the half-truths which they utter, and through the contradiction between their words, wishes, and intentions and what they actually do. Aeschylus' portrayal of Polynices and of his leading characters generally is very far removed from this kind of psychological subtlety, a psychology of small revelatory traits and internally fragmented characters. Even when Eteocles' inner tension is revealed in an outburst, he remains entirely focussed on his purpose and there is no ambivalence in him.

It is thus easy to see that it would not have been very difficult to psychologize Eteocles in *Seven Against Thebes* in the Euripidean style. One would only have needed to let some doubt settle into his breast, to have him waver between genuine concern for the city and egoistic lust for power—as has indeed been suggested as a possibility by Patzer—and to let this be expressed in all sorts of small traits, and from the Aeschylean hero a Euripidean one would be created. It would be more difficult to convert Euripides' Polynices into an Aeschylean character, but it would by no means be impossible. His love for his fatherland, instead of being represented directly, could be expressed indirectly through his behaviour with regard to his fellow attackers, and so forth. Here, therefore, there is a genuine difference in the means employed by different poets. This difference is of course to a certain extent a matter of chronology. The question also arises how far it is in each case a matter of inability or disinclination. The character of Oceanus in *Prometheus Bound* perhaps shows that Aeschylus was not altogether incapable of drawing a character in small psychological strokes, but he clearly did not want to do this for his great tragic figures. The theory of the diversity of artistic intention advanced by some historians since the beginning of the century, for which rather too strong claims have been made, is not altogether wide of the mark here, and Aristophanes was also correct when he observed [e.g. *Frogs* 954–67] that Euripides brought things on to the stage which his great predecessors had deliberately shunned.

These plays equally reveal the limits of the explanatory value of historical development. It is a truism that different poets, especially if they belong to different generations, have different intentions and employ different means. But it is often not easy to describe the difference precisely; and modern scholars quite frequently yield to the dangerous temptation of excluding something *a priori* from the interpretation of an earlier poet—as in the case of the psychological here—because it was assumed to make its appearance for the first time in a later poet, and the difference was not made sufficiently clear between what is denoted by the word 'psychological' in the two places.

In the same way, an ancient poet or philosopher could have developed, no less than a modern one; and it is foolish to deny this, as has happened for example with Aristotle, on the grounds that little attention was in general paid in antiquity to artistic development. Here too there is a danger of an unduly linear construction or reconstruction. The greater or lesser prominence of certain forms and means of dramatic presentation is determined not only by the 'inner development' of the poet or the development of his technical means, but to no small extent also by the material which he chooses. This factor is of much greater significance in ancient drama than in modern, because ancient tragedians, with the abundance of their output and their dependence on myth, had far less freedom than modern ones in the selection of their material. To that extent there is a great deal of truth in Wilamowitz' observation that the stronger individualization of Eteocles as compared with Aeschylus' other dramatic characters was determined by the versions of the myth which he inherited, although a lesser dramatist would doubtless not have created such a magnificent character as Eteocles in *Seven Against Thebes* on the basis of the same material.

This effect of the traditional material can perhaps also be illustrated in *Seven Against Thebes* and in Eteocles in another way as well. Nearly all Aeschylus' surviving tetralogies, as well as *Persians* (which was not part of a connected tetralogy), conclude with the restoration of an order, sometimes higher and more complete than that in which the tragic action and suffering came into existence. At the end of *Persians*, the world-order desired by the gods for East and West is thus restored, in which the Greeks of the West have successfully defended their freedom, but the absolute kingship of Xerxes in the eastern half of the world also survives in accordance with divine will, despite all the sufferings which he has brought on his people through his impious attempt to extend it to the West. So also at the end of the Prometheus trilogy, Prometheus was reconciled with Zeus, and an order thereby created in which the defiant enemy of the god of heaven could freely take his place. At the end of the Danaid trilogy, the Danaids were in all probability married to Greek husbands in a Greek wedding,[26] and thus an order was restored which had been violated by the uncouth and violent wooing of the sons of Aegyptus and their ensuing murder by the Danaids on their wedding night. At the end of the *Oresteia*, there is Orestes' acquittal by the Areopagus, the transformation of the goddesses of vengeance into the beneficent protectors of an established order, and the establishment of a court which no longer concentrates exclusively on what has happened but also enquires into people's motives.

Seven Against Thebes is the final play of a tragic trilogy. There should therefore, by analogy, have been something similar at the end here. This is actually to some extent the case. The city has been saved, even if Eteocles has perished. But even in the other single plays or trilogies the conciliatory conclusions cannot undo the tragic suffering, the tragic ruin of individual characters, and the disruption which has affected the human or divine order. There is nevertheless a difference. There also followed in the myth, at least in the versions which are known to us, the story of Antigone and at a still later stage the expedition of the Epigoni and the destruction of the city. There is no hint of this in Aeschylus' play, at least in the parts which he wrote himself. The inauthentic conclusion, in which there are intimations of new tragic developments, shows, however, how strongly it was present to the spectators. The myth of the descendants of Labdacus is one of the most sombre, if not *the* most sombre, of the surviving Greek myths, which least of all offers the prospect of a final restoration or conciliation of the old state of affairs, or even of a higher order. Aeschylus could not altogether eliminate this character of the myth when he made use of it. The city may in the end be saved, and there may be no hint of the later tragic events in the myth, but the death of Eteocles as a result of his father's curse still has something more sombre and disturbing even than the murder of Agamemnon in the *Oresteia*, which was indeed avenged in the later plays of the trilogy and does not stand at the end of the whole.

Sophocles' greatest tragedies were also taken from this very cycle of myths, which to some extent resisted the form of tragedy which

[26] Cf. K. von Fritz, 'Die Danaidentrilogie des Aeschylus', *Philologus* 91 (1936), 121–35, 249–69 = *Antike und moderne Tragödie* (Berlin, 1962), 160–92.

otherwise prevails in Aeschylus' work. This is connected with the fact that Sophocles' form of tragedy is different. It is bleaker than that of Aeschylus. He does not habitually end his plays with the restoration of order or even the establishment of a higher order, or at any rate not in the manner of Aeschylus. It is nevertheless typical of some of his greatest tragedies that the hero not only emerges from terrible sufferings without having been destroyed in his innermost being, but that he has actually been raised far beyond what he had been before them. There are undoubtedly hints of something of this nature in the Eteocles of *Seven Against Thebes*. He does not have the lucidity of the great tragic characters of Sophocles, who stands between Aeschylus and Euripides in that his dramatic figures have well-defined contours while still allowing an insight into their inner lives, whereas Euripides' characters can lose their definition through too much psychology. Eteocles is however the first example of a great tragic character who is entirely individualized; and it is doubtless not without interest to observe that Aeschylus took this step towards a new dramatic form in the process of handling material which by its nature was especially appropriate to Sophocles' style of tragedy.

5

The End of the *Hiketides* and Aischylos' Danaid Trilogy

Wolfgang Rösler

I

The end of Aischylos' *Hiketides* might seem lacking in dramatic tension, or even a little banal. Pelasgos, the king of Argos, has left the stage. The Danaids are alone again with their father, as at the beginning of the play. There are, of course, still slave-women with them, and in particular a detachment of young men armed with spears, who have, as Danaos mentions (985–8), been detailed by the Argives to protect them. The presence of these guards symbolizes the fact that the day has been outstandingly successful for Danaos and his daughters. The city has accepted them; an initial thrust by their pursuers has been repulsed; the citizens have even decided to go to war for them; and, finally, generous living-quarters have been provided. To be sure, the rescue is for the time being only provisional, and a military reckoning with the sons of Aigyptos looms menacingly on the horizon. But in the long final speech, which Aischylos now gives to the father of the maidens (980–1013), this danger figures only at the beginning. What concerns Danaos above all is the immediate present, their removal into the city. He sends his daughters on their way with the following admonition (991–1013):

καὶ ταῦθ' ἅμ᾽ ἐγγράψασθε πρὸς γεγραμμένοις
πολλοῖσιν ἄλλοις σωφρονίσμασιν πατρός·
ἀγνῶθ᾽ ὅμιλον, ὡς ἐλέγχεται χρόνῳ.
πᾶς δ᾽ ἐν μετοίκῳ γλῶσσαν εὔτυκον φέρει
κακήν, τό τ᾽ εἰπεῖν εὐπετὲς μύσαγμά πως.   (995)
ὑμᾶς δ᾽ ἐπαινῶ μὴ καταισχύνειν ἐμέ,
ὥραν ἐχούσας τήνδ᾽ ἐπίστρεπτον βροτοῖς.
τέρειν᾽ ὀπώρα δ᾽ εὐφύλακτος οὐδαμῶς·
θῆρές σφε κηραίνουσι καὶ βροτοί· τί μήν;
καὶ κνώδαλα πτεροῦντα καὶ πεδοστιβῆ   (1000)
†καρπώματα στάζοντα† κηρύσσει Κύπρις
†καλωρα κωλύουσαν θωσμένειν ἐρῶ†,
καὶ παρθένων χλιδαῖσιν εὐμόρφοις ἔπι
πᾶς τις παρελθὼν ὄμματος θελκτήριον
τόξευμ᾽ ἔπεμψεν, ἱμέρου νικώμενος.   (1005)
πρὸς ταῦτα μὴ πάθωμεν ὧν πολὺς πόνος,
πολὺς δὲ πόντος οὕνεκ᾽ ἠρόθη δορί,
μηδ᾽ αἶσχος ἡμῖν, ἡδονὴν δ᾽ ἐχθροῖς ἐμοῖς
πράξωμεν. οἴκησις δὲ καὶ διπλῆ πάρα·
τὴν μὲν Πελασγός, τὴν δὲ καὶ πόλις διδοῖ,   (1010)
οἰκεῖν λάτρων ἄτερθεν. εὐπετῆ τάδε.
μόνον φύλαξαι τάσδ᾽ ἐπιστολὰς πατρός,
τὸ σωφρονεῖν τιμῶσα τοῦ βίου πλέον.

And furthermore inscribe this [in your minds], in addition to the many other lessons from your father which you have inscribed there: that an unknown company is proved by time. In the case of an alien, everyone keeps ready an evil tongue, and a word which causes disgust is easily spoken. I warn you not to shame me, since you are of an age to make men turn their eyes. Tender ripe fruit is difficult to guard; beasts and men destroy it. How could it be otherwise? Kypris summons creatures both winged and earth-treading... [the context is corrupt;[1] it is nevertheless clear that Danaos attributes ultimate responsibility to Aphrodite], and every man that passes, overcome by desire, shoots the seductive arrow of his gaze at the beauty and grace of young maidens. With regard to this, let us not suffer what we

---

[1] The most recent attempt at a restoration is by M. L. West, *Studies in Aeschylus* (Beiträge zur Altertumskunde, 1; Stuttgart, 1990), 165–7. I do not go into textual issues in any detail, either here or in what follows. I have relied throughout on the Aischylos editions of D. L. Page (Oxford, 1972) and M. L. West (Stuttgart, 1990), on the edition with commentary of *Hiketides* by H. F. Johansen and E. W. Whittle (Copenhagen, 1980), and for fragments on the editions of H. J. Mette (Berlin, 1959) and S. Radt (Göttingen, 1985).

endured much toil and ploughed through much sea with our ship to prevent, and let us not give shame to ourselves and joy to my enemies! There are actually two kinds of accommodation available to us. On the one hand it is offered by Pelasgos, and on the other by the city, to live without payment. This presents no problem. Only observe these injunctions of your father, and value virtue more than life!

So ends Danaos' speech. It concerns itself with a hypothetical problem, which in the development of the trilogy will not turn out to cause any serious harm. What, then, is the significance and the dramatic function of this fatherly sermon at this juncture? Lesky observes that 'this remarkably detailed speech should prevent one-sided interpretations of the maidens as being some kind of Amazons'.[2] Kraus thinks that the poet's intention is that the speech should reflect 'a garrulous old man's recollection of his youth', and that 'in the contrast between this recollection and the main thrust of his speech, the notion of Eros suddenly appears for the first time in an alluring light'.[3] Winnington-Ingram similarly supposes that the purpose of these lines is to introduce the theme of Eros which will be important later in the trilogy.[4] Solutions like these seem altogether to confirm the impression of dramatic insufficiency which was mentioned above.

Such a judgement would, however, be over-hasty and misguided, as what follows should demonstrate. The first relevant consideration is that Danaos' speech about living in a strange city is by no means a complete surprise. It has, on the contrary, been very carefully prepared and calculated. A starting-point is the offer made by Pelasgos shortly before, to live either with him in the palace or in the houses of the citizens (957–61).[5] The chorus leaves the decision to their absent father (966–74), but for their own part they already refer to a problem on which Danaos will also focus: the readiness of people to

[2] A. Lesky, *Greek Tragic Poetry*, tr. M. Dillon (New Haven and London, 1983), 66 = *Die tragische Dichtung der Hellenen* (3rd edn.; Göttingen 1972), 103.

[3] W. Kraus, 'Aischylos als Erotiker betrachtet', *WS* NS 17 (1983), 5–22, at 22; id., 'Aischylos' Danaidentetralogie', in *Aus allem Eines: Studien zur antiken Geistesgeschichte* (Heidelberg, 1984), 85–137, at 97.

[4] R. P. Winnington-Ingram, *Studies in Aeschylus* (Cambridge, 1983), 66.

[5] On the nature of these houses, see W. Rösler, 'Typenhäuser bei Aischylos?', in W. Schuller, W. Hoepfner, E. L. Schwandner (eds.), *Demokratie und Architektur: Der hippodamische Städtebau und die Entstehung der Demokratie* (Wohnen in der klassischen Polis, 2; Munich, 1989), 109–12.

speak ill of foreigners. He immediately returns to the stage, and—quite the πρόνοος ('prudent man') and βούλαρχος ('initiator of the plan'), to whose discretion his daughters have previously left things (969–70)—he now delivers the speech which concerns us here. It has, in the context, a remarkable feature. Danaos does not make the decision which is expected of him, the decision between the citizens' houses and the palace. But this omission is, in my opinion, precisely one of the points of the speech. The lesson of the father to his daughters is that where they live is of absolutely no importance. It is much more crucial that they take account of the dangers which accompany their age. The speech takes on an admonitory character from this change of perspective, as can easily be seen. The actual behaviour to which the father's warnings refer may remain implicit, but the unmistakable meaning of what he says is nevertheless that his daughters should avoid appearing in public, and that their place should be in the home.

The recognition that Danaos' admonitory speech is intentionally designed as such, and that it is therefore manifestly not to be explained merely in terms of an indirect dramatic function, nevertheless fails to provide an answer to the question what its positive dramatic function is. For this, a somewhat broader discussion is necessary. We will then return to the problem a little later.

II

In 1986 there appeared in *Museum Helveticum* an article by Martin Sicherl entitled 'Die Tragik der Danaiden'.[6] I am convinced that Sicherl's article has placed the understanding of *Hiketides* on an entirely new basis. Discussion had always revolved around the question why the Danaids refuse to marry the sons of Aigyptos. The play has repeatedly been searched for clues and hidden references, and many hypotheses have been advanced.[7] Sicherl shows, however, that the understanding of the problem requires information which is not

---

[6] M. Sicherl, 'Die Tragik der Danaiden', *MH* 43 (1986), 81–110.

[7] See the list in Sicherl (n. 6), 82–8 who aptly characterizes the various problems.

conveyed by the play itself. This information nonetheless comes down
to us through a series of testimonia, which derive exclusively from
scholia (on Homer's *Iliad*, Aischylos' *Prometheus Bound*, Euripides'
Orestes, and Statius' *Thebais*).[8] In comparison with the sometimes
amazingly subtle interpretations which have been extracted from the
play itself, the explanation derived from the testimonia has a frankly
alarming concreteness and simplicity: Danaos knew from an oracle that
a son-in-law would kill him. The significance of this is (in Sicherl's
words) as follows: 'The reason for the Danaids' refusal to marry the
sons of Aigyptos is that they do not want to be responsible for the death
of their father.'[9] This result is supported by the decisive fact that Sicherl
can demonstrate that the connexion of the oracle with *Hiketides* had in
fact already been made in the ancient interpretation of the play. It is
thus not just a matter of the theory of a modern scholar, but of the
reconstruction of ancient understanding based on a knowledge of the
whole trilogy. The proof is afforded by a scholion on line 37 of *Hiketides*, the significance of which had not been appreciated before Sicherl,
one of the passages in which the chorus stresses the wrongness of
a marriage with the sons of Aigyptos: λέκτρων ὧν θέμις εἴργει ('a
marriage from which Right prohibits us'). The scholion gives the explanation why θέμις ('Right') prohibits the marriage: διὰ τὸ μὴ θανατωθῆναι τὸν πατέρα, 'so that their father will not be killed'—an elliptical
but nonetheless unambiguous reference to the oracle.[10] It fits in with
this that a scholion on *Prometheus Bound* 853, where a brief account of
the myth is given, explicitly confirms that the oracle belonged to the
nucleus of the story (τὸ μὲν ἀληθὲς τῆς ἱστορίας οὕτως ἔχει ('this is the
truth of the story')).[11]

The soundness of the foundation rediscovered by Sicherl is
confirmed at every step of the interpretation. Sicherl himself shows
that in numerous places the terms in which the rejected marriage and
the desire of the sons of Aigyptos are described are typical of kin-
murder.[12] He demonstrates that it is only in terms of the oracle that

[8] For all the details, see Sicherl (n. 6), 88–94.   [9] Sicherl (n. 6), 94.
[10] Cf. Sicherl (n. 6), 92. A connexion of the scholion with the tradition about the
oracle had already been considered by O. L. Smith (ed.), *Scholia in Aeschylum*, i
(Leipzig, 1976), 67 (apparatus).
[11] Cf. Sicherl (n. 6), 91–2.
[12] Sicherl (n. 6), 94–6.

the initiating and controlling role of Danaos can be understood.[13] We can also see now that an apparently significant expression by the Danaids at the beginning of the play, from which above all scholars have attempted to infer a motive for their refusal of marriage, is to be understood without any hidden meaning (5–8):

> ... φεύγομεν
> οὔτιν' ἐφ' αἵματι δημηλασίαν
> ψήφῳ πόλεως γνωσθεῖσαι,
> ἀλλ' αὐτογενῆ φυξανορίαν ...

We have not been exiled by our people on account of any blood-guilt, condemned by a vote of the city, but of our own volition we are in flight from men.

The meaning of αὐτογενής ('of our own volition') is defined by the antithesis to forcibly imposed banishment.[14] The same holds true for the formulation which is explained by the scholion. It suddenly becomes clear why it is precisely θέμις, 'right order',[15] which prohibits marriage, and that is because commitment to the well-being of their parents is the principal duty of children.[16] Moreover the seemingly extravagant threat by the Danaids to hang themselves from the statues of the gods (457–67) now appears in a different light—as the ultimate consequence of the daughters' duty to their father.

If the understanding of the fundamental problem in *Hiketides* of the Danaids' hostility to marriage, and thus the understanding of the whole play, requires knowledge which is not conveyed by the play— knowledge of an oracle given to Danaos—then the question arises urgently of how this knowledge actually was conveyed. In theory there are three possible answers: (1) Aischylos could have worked on the basis that the oracle, if it belonged to the nucleus of the myth, was

---

[13] Sicherl (n. 6), 96. Lines 1006–13, from Danaos' final warning-speech, should certainly be mentioned in this context (see below, § III; the paraphrase of the passage in Sicherl (n. 6), 93 needs to be corrected in the particular point relevant here).

[14] Cf. Sicherl (n. 6), 83, 86. The passage had already been interpreted correctly by K. von Fritz, 'Die Danaidentrilogie des Aischylos', *Philologus* 91 (1936), 122–3 = *Antike und moderne Tragödie* (Berlin, 1962), 161, who then modified his arguments by extracting a motive from it (258–61 (= 182–4)).

[15] Cf. H. Vos, Θέμις (Assen, 1956).

[16] Cf. M. W. Blundell, *Helping Friends and Harming Enemies* (Cambridge, 1989), 39–43.

so well-known to the audience that it did not need to be mentioned explicitly; (2) Aischylos made the situation clear later in the trilogy, i.e. the oracle was introduced subsequently; (3) the oracle had already been introduced previously, in a play which preceded *Hiketides* in the trilogy.

The first of these possibilities can quickly be excluded. The spectators in the Theatre of Dionysus were indeed familiar with the myths which were being dramatized by the tragedians, and the main question was accordingly the particular emphasis of each individual new version. It is, however, everywhere apparent that the result of this basic situation was not an elliptical style of dramatic representation, but that the way in which this emphasis was made was precisely by *how* the myth was dramatically represented in detail. The second possibility is supported by Sicherl. He believes that the oracle was shrouded in silence not only in *Hiketides*, the first play of the trilogy, but also in the second play. 'The spectator was thus kept is suspense, which was probably resolved only in the third play of the trilogy, when after the murder of the Egyptians the motive for the deed must be disclosed. Here for the first time the detailed background to the trilogy was revealed . . .'.[17] But such an order of events seems implausible. Sicherl himself has already given an impressive demonstration that knowledge of the oracle is in fact necessary not only for understanding *Hiketides* as a whole but also many individual passages and many subtle expressions. If one does not possess this knowledge, then the effect is not of a build-up of tension but of misunderstanding and confusion. A compromise position which combined this with the first possibility—the oracle was available to the audience on the basis of its earlier knowledge, and the later mention needed only to confirm it— would moreover be unacceptable to Sicherl, since he attributes the incorporation of the oracle motif into the myth to Aischylos himself.[18] Such a compromise would not, indeed, be especially attractive even for someone who did not agree with this conjecture of Sicherl's.

We must then at this point depart from Sicherl's argument and take another route. The third possibility, however, which would undoubtedly be the most natural, seems to be excluded from the

---

[17] Sicherl (n. 6), 98–9.   [18] Sicherl (n. 6), 107–10.

start. That the oracle was introduced in a play which preceded *Hiketides* in the trilogy is incompatible with the fact that *Hiketides* was the first play of the trilogy. It is precisely because of this that Sicherl never at any stage considers any possibility other than the second.[19] But what is the basis for this fact? In the nineteenth century, opinions about the structure of the Danaid trilogy were still rather divided. Concurrently with the view that *Hiketides* was the first play, there was also an alternative view that it was placed second. This controversy was resolved in favour of the first position by the authority of Hermann, Welcker, and later Wilamowitz, and with such complete success as to give the impression that it was based on certain knowledge.[20] The papyrus fragment of the didascalia (P. Oxy. 2256 fr. 3), which in 1952 effected a revolution in the question of dating, offers no assistance on this point because of a lacuna in the relevant place. The arguments, which since the nineteenth century have been used in favour of *Hiketides* being the first play in the trilogy, thus retained their status. They are vague enough. One refers to the parodos of *Hiketides*, which is said to function as an adequate introduction to the trilogy and to give a full account of the earlier events. It could be objected right away that discussions of *Hiketides* are invariably full of complaints about the unclear motivation of the Danaids' hostility to marriage. Another argument is that so much mythical material remains to be dealt with after the end of *Hiketides*—the future conflict with the sons of Aigyptos, the preparation and accomplishment of the murder of the suitors, the future fate of Danaos and his daughters—that two plays are necessary for its accomplishment. The presupposition of this argument is, however, far from compelling. Aischylos was not forced to treat the myth in a

---

[19] Right at the beginning of his second paragraph he says: 'In the surviving first play, *Hiketides*, ...' (p. 81).

[20] G. Hermann, *Opuscula*, ii (Leipzig, 1827), 314 (see also n. 23 below); F. G. Welcker, *Kleine Schriften*, iv (Bonn, 1861), 100–27 (he had originally advocated the opposite position: see below, nn. 23, 24); U. von Wilamowitz-Moellendorff, *Aischylos: Interpretationen* (Berlin, 1914), 19–21. Cf. A. F. Garvie, *Aeschylus' Supplices* (Cambridge, 1969), 185–6. By way of example, Lesky's account (above, n. 2) gives the impression that it is a matter of established fact (pp. 98, 107 = Eng. tr., pp. 62, 69–70); some reservation may conceivably be implied by the reference to Mette. The *communis opinio* has only very occasionally been questioned since, most recently by A. Brown, 'Why should I mention Io?', *LCM* 8 (1983), 158–60 (but in the context of a quite arbitrary reconstruction of the trilogy).

linear way. He could have covered some parts of the action in the form of flash-back or narration, and omitted others. It cannot even be reconstructed at what point of the myth Aischylos ends the trilogy. We actually have no direct evidence for the content of *Aigyptioi*, whose relationship to *Hiketides* is in question here, and about the content of *Danaides*, which is certainly the final play of the trilogy, we only know a few details. There is thus no impediment to accepting the third possibility. On the contrary, a vital clue for the order of the plays has for the very first time been supplied by Sicherl's discovery.

The trilogy accordingly began with *Aigyptioi*, in which the dispute between the brothers Danaos and Aigyptos was portrayed. We thus return to the less favoured position in the nineteenth-century controversy.[21] But there is now the additional factor of the oracle to reckon with, which plays a decisive part in setting the action in motion. The play can only have been set in Egypt. A chorus of Egyptians, which gave the play its name, fits in most satisfactorily with this.[22] On the other hand, the assumption that *Aigyptioi* was the second play has always raised a twofold problem: 'Aigyptioi' is not a patronymic, and thus cannot mean 'sons of Aigyptos'; but it is precisely the sons of Aigyptos who would have needed to make an appearance in a play with that title which followed *Hiketides*. Even if this were to be conceded, it is in any case difficult to imagine how the planning and preparation for the murder could have been accomplished in the presence of the sons of Aigyptos, who as the chorus could not have left the stage for more than a short time. This difficulty can only be circumvented rather unsatisfactorily by the assumption that the play was named after a secondary chorus which made a brief appearance. The assumption that *Aigyptioi* was the first play, on the other hand, with the oracle as an important element, does not merely render these difficulties immaterial but also explains why the scholion

[21] Cf. K. O. Müller, *Geschichte der griechischen Literatur*, i (4th edn.; Stuttgart, 1882), 543, on *Hiketides* as 'the middle play of the trilogy, which was unquestionably followed by the resolution of the conflict in *Danaides*, just as a preceding play, *Aigyptioi*, must itself have portrayed the motive and beginning of the quarrel in Egypt'. Müller, as is well-known, perceptively anticipated the dating of *Hiketides* to the late 460s (pp. 544–5).

[22] The title *Aigyptos* occurs once as a variant (F 5 Radt [Et. Gud.]; cf. O. Taplin, *The Stagecraft of Aeschylus* (Oxford, 1977), 197–8). A play with this title would easily be conceivable as the first play of the trilogy.

on line 37 of *Hiketides*, the significance of which was recognized by Sicherl, refers to the oracle in such a remarkably elliptical fashion: διὰ τὸ μὴ θανατωθῆναι τὸν πατέρα, 'so that their father will not be killed'. It is merely a matter of a recollection of the previous play in the trilogy.[23] *Hiketides* followed *Aigyptioi*. As between *Choephoroi* and *Eumenides* in Aischylos' *Oresteia*, there is a lapse of time and a change of location between the two plays. Furthermore, the subject in both cases is flight: in the former, the flight of Orestes from the Erinyes, which brings him from Argos to Delphi; in the latter, the flight of Danaos and his daughters from Egypt to Argos. A more detailed exposition is required in *Hiketides* by the lapse of time, by the change of location, and not least by the Danaids themselves, who had obviously not appeared in *Aigyptioi*, as new central characters in the following play, and what is more in the special role as suppliants.[24] The parodos of *Hiketides* accordingly focusses in particular on flight and supplication. It becomes clear that what had seemed to be an introduction to the whole trilogy is in fact just an introduction to *Hiketides*.

In this context, it is also possible to answer the question why the oracle is continually present under the surface in *Hiketides* as the presupposition of the play, but is never mentioned more explicitly. There are two related reasons for this. The first is that the play is

---

[23] An additional argument for *Aigyptioi* as the beginning of the trilogy is provided by the only ancient 'quotation' from the play (F 5 Radt). What is cited as being from *Aigyptioi* (or *Aigyptos* as the case may be: see above, n. 22) is actually a phrase from *Hiketides* (156–7). This form of citation, whether deliberate or mistaken (Radt sees it as the consequence of textual corruption; cf. Mette's version of the text [fr. 121]), is only readily comprehensible in terms of the sequence *Aigyptioi—Hiketides*: the name of the first play would in this case stand for the whole trilogy. This had already been observed by F. G. Welcker, *Die Aeschylische Trilogie Prometheus* (Darmstadt, 1824), 557 n. (with a parallel), but he later changed his mind (above, n. 20, p. 102). G. Hermann reacted to this observation by altering the text (*Opuscula*, viii (Leipzig, 1877), 180–2), the influence of which is visible in Radt.

[24] Welcker (n. 23), before he changed his mind, had already offered very similar arguments (390–1). Hermann 'denied that a play could have preceded *Hiketides* on the grounds that at the beginning of it the Danaids explain who they are and why they are coming to Argos. But the suppliants' explanation was indispensable because they had not appeared in *Aigyptioi* in person, even if the exile recommended to them by their father had itself already been mentioned there; and even if they had done, it was nevertheless necessary to explain to the audience that in the chorus which now enters they see the main characters of the play who do not normally constitute the chorus'.

based on the idea that the only consideration which is relevant to the acceptance of the fugitives into Argos is the divine right to asylum. It is in accordance with this idea that the strategy of the Danaids and their father from the start is to reveal nothing to Pelasgos and his city of the reason for their flight. Already at the beginning of the play, before Pelasgos enters, everything serves to prepare them and to get them in the right frame of mind for the role which they must now play. The king for his part accepts that the newcomers are evidently unwilling to say anything about what has happened beforehand. He and his citizens are motivated solely by the desire not to bring the wrath of Zeus Hikesios down on themselves. This understanding of the omission is obviously related to a second reason, that discussion and assessment of the motives and actions of Danaos and his daughters should be kept back for the third play of the trilogy, where it then takes place with the participation of the gods. This is a question which we will come back to again.

III

We must first, however, return to Danaos' advice-speech. Sicherl did not deal with the end of *Hiketides*, but it is immediately obvious that his discovery is confirmed here too. With the knowledge of the oracle, we understand at a stroke what is worrying the father—the anxiety that his daughters, in the deceptive security of asylum, might forget that the danger by no means comes solely from the sons of Aigyptos. The old controversy, whether the Danaids only reject marriage with their cousins or whether they reject it altogether, is surely resolved by the recovery of the motif of the oracle: they must reject marriage altogether. It is now clear that Danaos himself says this unambiguously (1006–7):

With regard to this [the sexual attractiveness of young maidens], let us not suffer what we endured much toil and ploughed through much sea with our ship to prevent [...].

The subtleties of the text do, indeed, only become apparent with closer investigation. It must be taken into consideration that Danaos can only use veiled language for what he wants to impress upon his daughters. A consistent silence had been maintained in front of Pelasgos and the Argives about the real reason for the Danaids' hostility to marriage, and it is now the presence of the Argive bodyguard which prevents any explicit reference to it. Danaos solves the problem by playing the part of a patriarch who has an exaggerated concern for the good name of his family. The Argives will attribute to his idiosyncratic character that the following speech has a force and elaboration which goes far beyond its ostensible point, to secure the reputation of his family by advance warning to his daughters. It is this disproportion which creates the impression of banality and excess which was mentioned at the beginning of our discussion. But this only describes the surface, behind which, for those who know how to listen—the daughters and together with them the informed spectator—the real concern of the father soon becomes unmistakably clear.

A first signal is the urgency with which Danaos reflects the threatening aspect of the influence of Eros in nature (998–1002). The problem thus takes on a dimension which will inevitably seem incongruous unless it is understood why it actually concerns him. Confirmation follows immediately, with the statement just cited, when those in the know—and only they—understand why the father, who is on the surface motivated only by concern for his daughters, includes himself so explicitly as being also affected (1006–7):

With regard to this, let us not suffer what we endured much toil and ploughed through much sea with our ship to prevent [. . .].

The immediate continuation is also significant (1008–9):

[. . .] and let us not give shame to ourselves and joy to my enemies!

The first striking thing here is the deliberate abandonment of the first-person plural. Danaos says 'my enemies', not 'our enemies'. This exact mode of expression immediately ceases to be puzzling when one brings to bear the knowledge which was communicated earlier in *Aigyptioi*, the knowledge of the quarrel between the brothers and of the oracle.[25] It is generally supposed that kingship was the main issue

---

[25] Cf. Johansen and Whittle (n. 1), on 996–1009.

in the quarrel between Danaos and Aigyptos.[26] The oracle contributes a more specific reason; already in Egypt it prevented a reconciliation of the two families by means of marriage. In this respect,
Danaos was for more than one reason the one who as an individual
attracted the enmity of the other side. He was the rival of his brother
before his flight, and he had forbidden the marriage of his daughters
to the sons of Aigyptos in his dual capacity as father and as the one
affected by the prophecy. His speech here is a logical counter-move
against his personal enemies. The same precision of wording can be
observed immediately before this. The first part of his injunction—
'let us not give shame to ourselves'—seems to recapitulate in an only
slightly modified form the warning which Danaos gave to his daughters just twelve lines earlier (996): μὴ καταισχύνειν ἐμέ ('not to shame
me'). But in the small difference of personal pronouns it is obvious to
the informed spectator that a quite different shame is now the subject
from that feared by a father solicitous for the good name of his
daughters. Instead of this, it has long since been a matter of the
shame which father and daughters would bring jointly on themselves
and which would also affect them jointly, namely the shameful failure
of their flight: first to have 'endured much toil and ploughed through
much sea',[27] to have obtained protection in Argos from pursuit by the
sons of Aigyptos—and then to succumb to the seductive gaze of the
Argive rescuers. And also only the informed spectator understands
specifically how his enemies for their part would derive joy (ἡδονή)
from that: because Danaos must then, according to the oracle, meet
his death.[28]

The father's admonitory speech reaches its climax in its concluding words (1013): '[...] value virtue more than life!'. This exhort-
ation seems exaggerated as an expression of concern for the good
name of his daughters, but, as spectators who have previously seen

---

[26] See Sicherl (n. 6), 88–91.

[27] According to mythical tradition, the first ship was invented for this flight (the
evidence is in L. Preller, *Griechische Mythologie* i. [4th edn., revised by C. Robert],
Berlin, 1894) 217.

[28] The fact that the thought in itself ('No joy for enemies!') is conventional does not
rule out a specific reference here. Cf. Johansen and Whittle (n. 1), on 1008; M. Griffith
(ed.), *Aeschylus: Prometheus Bound* (Cambridge, 1983), on 158–9; M. L. West (ed.),
Hesiod: Works and Days (Oxford, 1978), on 701.

Aigyptioi know, the real message is: 'If you want to save my life, it may happen that you must put your own lives at stake'.[29] The solemnity of Danaos' words is thus fully in accordance with the seriousness of the situation: it is a matter of life and death.

The Danaids' answer (1014–17) shows that they have understood their father. He should be entirely unconcerned:

εἰ γάρ τι μὴ θεοῖς βεβούλευται νέον,
ἴχνος τὸ πρόσθεν οὐ διαστρέψω φρενός.

Unless the gods have resolved on a new plan, we will not deviate from the previous track of our thought.   (1016–17)

But what is interjected as a conventional 'God willing' must have an extremely disturbing effect on Danaos. Although he does not take up the word again in what follows, the daughters' reservation signals the failure of his attempt to find security. The father's worries remain that his rescue-plan with regard to his radiant and marriageable daughters is threatened by failure. They point forward to the development of the trilogy in which, even in an as yet unforseeable configuration, they will prove to be well-founded.

The exodos follows immediately after the Danaids' answer. An entirely new light is now cast on it too. A much-discussed problem arises from the fact that in the concluding choral parts two opposing positions are adopted. One group would like to renounce the goddess Aphrodite, and rejects marriage (this is the position of the Danaids, which they have explicitly affirmed, to remain true to their views). The other group, however, glorifies Aphrodite and sees marriage as a divinely ordained lot for mortals.

Even if clues are lacking in the (notoriously bad) manuscript tradition of *Hiketides*, there are compelling reasons to accept a secondary chorus as a dialogue-partner for the Danaids. Now while at one time the view prevailed that it comprised their serving women, more recently there has been a discernible tendency in favour of the

---

[29] The Danaids have already expressed a readiness to do so earlier in the play, when they threatened to hang themselves from the statues of the gods (457–67). Further-more, the spectator should perhaps be made aware that the words can also be understood as a foreshadowing of the later murder of the sons of Aigyptos: 'Honour virtue more than the life of another!'. There are several ambivalent expressions of this kind in *Hiketides* (cf. Johansen and Whittle [n. 1], on 1033).

Argive bodyguard as the secondary chorus.[30] This view gains substantial, indeed decisive, support from the recently adduced evidence
that the choral parts allude in form and content to the wedding-
song.[31] This was an amoebean song at a wedding, performed alternately by choruses of young men and young women, with a structure
which is attested most clearly in Catullus 62, a poem based on a
Greek model: the male chorus assents to marriage, while the female
chorus expresses reservations. But why has Aischylos formed the
concluding choral parts from the elements of a wedding song? The
subtle point of this reveals itself if one takes account of the external as
well as the psychological situation in which Danaos finds himself at
the end of *Hiketides*. It is then apparent that his anxiety here,
immediately before the end of the play, undergoes an abrupt inten-
sification. For in the quasi-hymeneal the threat, which only recently
had been merely notional, suddenly takes on a concrete form. It does
in fact do so doubly, in both visual and audible ways: Danaos
observes how the young Argives and his daughters make contact
with each other and how a dialogue ensues, and he hears a song
from them which refers to the very realm which endangers his life:
the realm of marriage.[32] The quality of this conclusion now becomes
apparent, a conclusion of high tension and psychological subtlety,
which created impatience for the following third play of the trilogy,
Danaides.

---

[30] There are several reasons for rejecting the older view: see Taplin (n. 22), 230–8;
Johansen and Whittle (n. 1), on 1018–73. In West's edition, too, the Argives are now
understood to be the secondary chorus.

[31] R. Seaford, 'L'ultima canzone corale delle Supplici di Eschilo', *Dioniso* 55
(1984–5), 221–9; cf. id., 'The tragic wedding', *JHS* 107 (1987), 106–30, at 114–15.

[32] Danaos must additionally witness that what he has just represented in his
warning to his daughters as something negative (1000–5) is now transformed by
the Argive chorus into something positive (1035–42). He also has an additional
source of anxiety. Hitherto, for his daughters rejection of marriage and rejection of
those who wanted to marry them (the sons of Aigyptos) coincided; marriage was
something intrinsically hostile for them. Now they discover that marriage is advocated by the young men who are their protectors. Aischylos seems to emphasize this
connexion by the strikingly contrasting descriptions of the sons of Aigyptos as ἑσμὸς
ὑβριστής ('violent swarm', 30) and the young Argives as ἑσμὸς εὔφρων ('friendly
swarm', 1034). In the latter passage, ἑσμὸς is the widely accepted emendation by
Scaliger; the transmitted θεσμός is defended by West (n. 1), 167–8.

IV

We have only *Hiketides*, and, as was said above, only know a few details about *Danaides*. Our main evidence is a seven-line fragment, which comes from a speech by Aphrodite (F 44 Radt). Aphrodite describes the ἱερὸς γάμος ('sacred marriage') of Heaven and Earth, and represents it as the origin of everything which grows on the earth and provides nourishment for human beings and animals. She then adds τῶν δ' ἐγὼ παραίτιος ('For this I am responsible').[33] These statements can be understood—outside their actual context, which will be discussed shortly—as an answer to Danaos' warning-speech at the end of *Hiketides*.[34] There Danaos reflected the danger which threatened his daughters, and consequently himself, from the work-ing of Eros in nature (998–1002)—tender ripe fruit is difficult to guard; beasts and men destroy it—, and he then put the responsibil-ity for it on Aphrodite. She now replies to his attack: that for which I am responsible, the working of Eros, is not destructive but the opposite of that; and what is more, it has something sacred about it, something which has a cosmic dimension.

The location of this speech is controversial. It has seemed obvious to link it to the trial of Hypermestra, one of Danaos' daughters, which is attested by Pausanias, and which was preceded in the myth by a series of events: the acceptance of the sons of Aigyptos into Argos; the trick of the feigned wedding; the murder of the sons of Aigyptos by the Danaids, with the exception of Lynkeus, whom Hypermestra spared through love; and finally Danaos' indictment of Hypermestra on account of this omission. Aphrodite would, it has often been concluded, have appeared in the trial as a witness for

---

[33] The emphatic ἐγώ shows that προ- does not have a limitative force ('co-responsible'). Cf. A. F. Garvie (ed.), *Aeschylus: Choephori* (Oxford, 1986), on 910.

[34] Cf. W. Kraus (ed. and tr.), *Aischylos: Die Schutzflehenden* (Frankfurt am Main, 1948), 165: 'Her [Aphrodite's] words pick up and raise to a sublime level the motif which had been introduced in Danaos' warning speech to his daughters (998 ff.)'. But it is a response rather than a mere reminiscence. Aischylos establishes a linguistic connexion between the two speeches through the repetition of the term ὀπώρα: first by Danaos (998), then in his daughters' answer (1015), and now here in Aphrodite's speech (F 44.6). There is a less striking connexion between ἐρῶ (1002, in the corrupt passage) and ἐρᾷ, ἔρως (F 44.1, 2).

Hypermestra and would have justified her behaviour with the reasoning transmitted in F 44.[35] On the other hand, there have been scholars who question the value of Pausanias' evidence and the reconstruction based on it.[36] It is conceded even by critics that the surviving speech of Aphrodite would fit very well into the context of a trial of Hypermestra,[37] but the decision still depends on the details of Pausanias' evidence. Sicherl's discovery offers an opportunity to give a fresh and more precise analysis of the relevance of this evidence to Aischylos.

In his description of the sights of Argos, Pausanias has three occasions to mention the trial of Hypermestra. In the sanctuary of Apollo Lykios he saw a wooden image of Aphrodite, which Hypermestra was supposed to have dedicated to the goddess after her acquittal (2.19.6); secondly, he was shown a place called Κριτήριον ('Place of Judgement'), the alleged site of the trial (2.20.7); and finally he looked round a sanctuary of Artemis Peitho ('Persuasion'), which was likewise dedicated by Hypermestra after her acquittal in commemoration of her deliverance (2.21.1). In the first of these three passages, Pausanias goes in greater detail into the circumstances of Hypermestra's trial:

ταύτην γὰρ τῶν θυγατέρων μόνην τὸ πρόσταγμα ὑπεριδοῦσαν ὑπήγαγεν ὁ
Δαναὸς ἐς δικαστήριον, τοῦ τε Λυγκέως οὐκ ἀκίνδυνον αὑτῷ τὴν σωτηρίαν
ἡγούμενος καὶ ὅτι τοῦ τολμήματος οὐ μετασχοῦσα ταῖς ἀδελφαῖς καὶ τῷ
βουλεύσαντι τὸ ὄνειδος ηὔξησε. κριθεῖσα δὲ ἐν τοῖς Ἀργείοις ἀποφεύγει τε καὶ
Ἀφροδίτην ἐπὶ τῷδε ἀνέθηκε Νικηφόρον.

She was the only one of Danaos' daughters to disobey his command, and he brought her to trial because he believed that the rescue of Lynkeus was not without its dangers for himself, and considering also that her refusal to share

---

[35] There is some evidence for this interpretation, widely held at one time, in Garvie (n. 20), 205–6. It is to be found, for example, in Preller and Robert (n. 27), II. i (Berlin, 1920), 272. It would fit in well with a trial dealing with the question of guilt that Aphrodite describes herself as παραίτιος ('I am guilty, not Hypermestra'). But the concept is not sufficiently specific that a substantial case could be established from it alone.

[36] von Fritz (n. 14), 249–67 (= 173–89); Garvie (n. 20), 170, 205–11; Kraus, 'Aischylos' Danaidentrilogie' (n. 3), 129–30.

[37] von Fritz (n. 14), 249 (= 173).

in the deed increased the shame both for her sisters and for himself as the initiator of the plan. She was tried before the Argives and acquitted, and to commemorate her deliverance she dedicated an image of Aphrodite Nike-phoros ['Bringer of Victory'].

In the first place, it is clear from the three references in Pausanias that the relevant detail, the trial of Hypermestra, had an important place in the *mémoire collective* of Argos in the second century AD. But what did this tradition go back to? Generally speaking it seems to be most likely that it was nourished by the heritage of classical poetry, as a romantic revival of interest in that heritage is particularly characteristic of this period. More specifically it could be observed that behind Pausanias' summary there is obviously a particular text presenting a distinct version of the myth. This evidently follows in the first place from the fact that as much space is given to Danaos' motives as to the facts, and secondly from the even more remarkable fact that Pausanias fails altogether to explain Aphrodite's interest in the acquittal of Hyper-mestra. It follows from this that Pausanias does not so much want to give a complete account for an uninformed reader as to remind his readers of a text of which he assumed that they were aware, that is to say a text which belonged to the educational curriculum.[38] There is at the same time no reason not to assume that this text is identical with the one on which the relevant Argive tradition was itself based. If one now examines individually the motives of Danaos which Pausanias mentions, there is clearly a perfect correspondence with those which have been established independently for Aischylos' Danaid trilogy. After Sicherl's discovery, it is now clear what is meant by the words '... because he believed that the rescue of Lynkeus was not without its dangers for himself'.[39] We have an elliptical reference to the oracle similar to that in the scholion on *Hiketides*; here too it is evident that Pausanias wants merely to remind the reader. Pausanias' words '... considering also that her refusal to share in the deed increased

---

[38] A sharp contrast is provided by the detailed narrative which Pausanias gave shortly before of how Danaos became king of Argos (2.19.3–4). This story could not be assumed to be generally known, since it dealt with the foundation-legend of the Argive cult of Apollo Lykios (Δαναὸς δὲ ἱδρύσατο Λύκιον Ἀπόλλωνα ἐπ' αἰτίᾳ τοιαύτῃ). Pausanias himself obviously knew it only from oral sources, as he indicates with the parenthetical φασίν ('they say').

[39] The passage could previously only be understood to refer to Danaos' fear of vengeance (cf. von Fritz (n. 14), 133 [= 170]).

Wolfgang Rösler

the shame both for her sisters and for himself as the initiator of the plan' sound like a clear allusion to Danaos' warning-speech at the end of *Hiketides* (1008–9): μηδ' αἶσχος ἡμῖν, ἡδονὴν δ' ἐχθροῖς ἐμοῖς | πράξωμεν, 'and let us not give shame to ourselves and joy to my enemies!'. Finally, the description of Danaos as ὁ βουλεύσας, as the originator of the plan: this too corresponds to his characterization in Aischylos, where he is twice explicitly called βούλαρχος (11, 970), precisely 'initiator of the plan'.[40]

Another piece of evidence in Pausanias deserves attention before these observations are evaluated. Pausanias also saw in Argos statues of the Seven (2.20.5), who did indeed begin their expedition against Thebes from there. Actually, Pausanias adds, the number of the commanders came to more than seven, but the Argives, like others, preferred to follow the poetry of Aischylos on this point (ἐπηκολ-ουθήκασι γὰρ καὶ Ἀργεῖοι τῇ Αἰσχύλου ποιήσει). In view of such a parallel, it seems even less risky to draw the inescapable conclusion from the correspondences of content: that Aischylos' *Danaides* is the text which lies behind Pausanias' summary. This assumption provides the basis for some concluding remarks about the relationship between the Danaid trilogy and the political reality from which it sprang, the Athenian democracy.

V

Hypermestra was thus prosecuted by her father in Aischylos' *Danaides*, but the court acquitted her after Aphrodite had spoken on her behalf. The charge against Hypermestra must have been that through her behaviour, the sparing of Lynkeus, she was guilty of accepting the future killing of her father in exchange. Aphrodite opposed this by referring to the order of nature and to the divine origin of love. The conclusion of this was that Hypermestra could not strictly have been guilty.[41] We do

[40] Cf. § II above, with n. 13.

[41] On the basis of what has now been established, the word παραίτιος turns out to be significant in some degree (cf. n. 35 above). If one disregards the 'guilt' which the goddess has consciously taken on herself in this way, then the plaintiff, Danaos, emerges from the trial as the one who is really guilty. He has involved his daughter in

not know what dramatic form Aischylos gave to the trial.[42] But on one
very important point we yet again have information from Pausanias.
This point is at the same time, as will soon be made clear, a confirmation that Pausanias' summary derives from no other text than Aischylos' Danaid trilogy. The point in question is the statement that
Hypermestra was tried *before the Argives* and acquitted by them
(κριθεῖσα δὲ ἐν τοῖς Ἀργείοις ἀποφεύγει). The significance of this
formulation becomes clear if one takes into consideration how the
constitution of Argos is portrayed in *Hiketides*. It has always been
noted with surprise that it exhibits features of the Athenian democracy.[43] *Hiketides* also has the earliest evidence for the concept of democracy: δήμου κρατοῦσα χείρ, 'the ruling (by means of voting) hand of
the people' (604); τὸ δάμιον, τὸ πτόλιν κρατύνει, 'the body of the
people, which rules the city' (699).[44] Aischylos himself highlights this
anachronism, when he shows the Danaids as being puzzled that Pelasgos fails to behave like a real king, but makes his decision dependent on
the vote of the popular assembly (365–75), precisely on the Ἀργεῖοι
('Argives').[45] Pausanias' ἐν τοῖς Ἀργείοις ('before the Argives') shows
(and it is in any case also dramatically plausible) that the strikingly
democratic constitution of the city of Argos remained significant in the
final play of the trilogy. If in *Hiketides* the popular assembly had given
Danaos and his daughters protection from their pursuers, so now a
citizen court prevents the innocent Hypermestra from being punished.

a plot which brings her into conflict with the natural order, and he has done this in the
misguided hope that a human being can escape an oracle (cf. A. Moreau, 'Déjouer
l'oracle ou la précaution inutile', *Kernos* 3 (1990), 261–79). We do not know in what
way and with what result Aischylos returned in the third play of the trilogy to the
oracle as the central presupposition of the dramatic action. It is plausible that it was
Aphrodite as well who dealt with this aspect of Danaos' guilt.

[42] In view of Aphrodite's speech, the conclusion seems to be inescapable that, as in
the *Oresteia*, the trial took place on the stage (the alternative would be a speech
corresponding to that describing the Argive assembly in *Hiketides*). It is worth noting
that the preceding play, *Hiketides*, required a large number of extras (Pelasgos'
bodyguard, the attendants of the Egyptian herald, the Danaids' serving-women,
Danaos' Argive escort). They could subsequently have taken the parts of jurors.

[43] The analogies extend, as has recently been observed, as far as the external appearance of a particular type of house (cf. n. 5 above).

[44] Cf. D. Lotze, 'Zum Begriff der Demokratie in Aischylos' *Hiketiden*', in
E. G. Schmidt (ed.), *Aischylos und Pindar* (Berlin, 1981), 207–16; P. E. Easterling,
'Anachronism in Greek tragedy', *JHS* 105 (1985), 1–10, at 2–3.

[45] Cf. *Hik.* 605, 625, 739, 980.

New and surprisingly far-reaching parallels with the *Oresteia*
become clear on the basis of this observation. An identical contrast
is displayed in both trilogies. Where the citizens are excluded from
power (in the Egypt of *Aigyptioi*,[46] and in the Argos of *Agamemnon*
and *Choephori*), discord and violence rule; where, on the other hand,
it is the citizens who decide (in the Argos of the Danaid trilogy, and
in the Athens of *Eumenides*), conflict is successfully resolved. In both
trilogies, an individual (Hypermestra and Orestes respectively) conspicuously disregards the unwritten law of the duties of children to
their parents: Hypermestra accepts the killing of her father; Orestes
himself accomplishes the killing of his mother. But neither acts from
base motives, but rather the parents in question have supplied the
reason: Danaos through the design of his plot, which runs counter to
the natural order for which Aphrodite is responsible; Klytaimestra
through the murder of Agamemnon. Regardless of this, the daughter
and the son initially find themselves in the role of fugitives: Hypermestra finds herself exposed to pursuit by Danaos, while Orestes is
hunted by the Erinyes. In both trilogies, matters are finally settled by
a trial before a citizen jury,[47] before which (so one should assume for
the Danaid trilogy as well) both parties can put their cases and which
then gives its judgement by voting. In both trilogies the result is the
acquittal of the accused, after gods (Aphrodite and Apollo respectively) have spoken in their favour.

This series of parallels is nevertheless not intended to give the
impression that the *Oresteia* is some kind of recapitulation of the
Danaid trilogy. The plots and issues of the two trilogies are significantly different, and even where they converge, in the concluding
trial-scenes, the prevailing impression is one of difference. In this
context it can be assumed that Hypermestra was acquitted unanimously, while Orestes by contrast only carried the day by the nar-
rowest of margins. The common element to which the parallels point

[46] We know this, even without knowing the play, from the Danaids in *Hiketides*:
the Argive democracy is completely inconceivable to them from their experience at
home.

[47] In *Eumenides*, Athene chooses 'the best of my citizens' (ἀστῶν τῶν ἐμῶν τὰ
βέλτατα) as jurors (487), but the trial is open to all the citizens (566–73). Cf.
A. H. Sommerstein (ed.), *Aeschylus: Eumenides* (Cambridge, 1989), on 566. Pausanias'
words can thus readily be adapted to apply to Orestes: κριθεὶς ἐν τοῖς Ἀθηναίοις
ἀποφεύγει ('he was tried before the Athenians and acquitted').

may rather lie in the following, which can be considered program-
matic: in both trilogies the conflict-resolution succeeds because it
takes place in an institutional context, on the basis of argument and
voting, and into the bargain in a context of the broadest publicity, ἐν
τοῖς πολίταις ('before the citizens'); in this way, the weaker party also
can obtain justice. The two trilogies are chronologically not far apart:
the Danaid trilogy was not produced before 466 (or perhaps 465),[48]
probably 463,[49] the *Oresteia* in 458. It is highly significant, and certainly no accident, that we encounter this emphasis precisely in the
chronological context of the reforms of Ephialtes, when the Athenian
democracy was by no means stable. It may even have contributed to
the success which Aischylos achieved: on both occasions he won the
first prize.[50]

POSTSCRIPT (2004)

No one who attempts to shake a well-established *communis opinio*
can expect to win general agreement in a short time. The most
that can be attained is to provoke a new debate. The article repub-
lished here has certainly had that effect. It aims to persuade its
readers of two propositions: (1) The presupposition of the action
of *Hiketides* is an oracle which Danaos has received. It states that a
future son-in-law will kill him. This proposition had already been

---

[48] According to C. W. Müller, *Zur Datierung des sophokleischen Ödipus* (Abh.
Mainz, Geistes- u. sozialwiss. Kl., 1984, No. 5; Wiesbaden, 1984), 74.

[49] Thus the *communis opinio* on the basis of P. Oxy. 2256 fr. 3 and Plut., *Cim.* 8.8–9
(= T 57 Radt). Radt himself questions the reliability of this evidence: *The Importance
of the Context* (Koninklijke Nederlandse Akademie van Wetenschappen. Mededelin-
gen van de Afdeling Letterkunde, n.s. 51,9; Amsterdam, 1988), 13–16. A corroborating
argument is supplied by the reference to typical Athenian houses in *Hiketides*
(cf. Rösler (n. 5), 111). At least, the parallels with the *Oresteia* discussed above do
not conflict with the above-mentioned date.

[50] This article derives from a paper which I gave in Blaubeuren in October 1991 at
a symposium organized by the Deutscher Archäologenverband and the Mommsen
Gesellschaft on the subject 'Klassik als exemplarische Bewältigung der Geschichte'.
I am grateful to everyone with whom I have discussed the subject on this or other
occasions. I am especially grateful to Luc Deitz, Martin Hose, Stefan Monhardt, and
Stefan Radt.

advanced in 1986 by Martin Sicherl. In the present article it is
supported by additional arguments. (2) A necessary consequence of
(1) is a reordering of the first two plays in the Danaid trilogy. The
Aigyptioi should be placed first, and the *Hiketides* second. It was in
the *Aigyptioi* that the oracle was introduced into the action.

Three kinds of reaction are possible to this—and can actually be
found: both propositions—(1) and (2)—can be accepted,[51] or both
can be rejected;[52] it is also possible to accept (1) but not (2).[53] In
retrospect, it is clear that doubts have been raised by one difficulty in
particular: the oracle, which is supposedly the presupposition of the
action, is not mentioned in the *Hiketides* at all. Sicherl conjectured
that the oracle was revealed for the first time at the end of the trilogy.
The present article points out the problems which follow from this
hypothesis. They are avoided by the sequence *Aigyptioi—Hiketides*.
This sequence, however, aggravates the difficulty mentioned above.
Anyone who proposes this solution must explain the logic according
to which the oracle is omitted from the *Hiketides* although it had
supposedly been established earlier, in the *Aigyptioi*, as the motivat-
ing factor of the dramatic action.

I would like in what follows to clarify and expand my very brief
observations on this point at the end of §II of the article. The
Hiketides represents in its entirety a dramatization of the ritual
which is fundamental to the Greek institution of supplication. Supplication requires of the suppliant the scrupulous observance of rules
of behaviour.[54] At the same time, however, the status of a suppliant
entails well-defined rights. Since suppliants can appeal to divine law,
which requires on principle that they be assisted, the ritual demands

[51] A. H. Sommerstein, 'The beginning and the end of Aeschylus' Danaid Trilogy',
in B. Zimmermann (ed.), *Griechisch-römische Komödie und Tragödie* (Drama, 3;
Stuttgart, 1995), 111–34; M. J. Lossau, *Aischylos* (Hildesheim, 1998), 66–70.

[52] C. Rohweder, *Macht und Gedeihen: eine politische Interpretation der Hiketiden
des Aischylos* (Frankfurt am Main, 1998), 112–13, 135–6; S. Gödde, *Das Drama der
Hikesie: Ritual und Rhetorik in Aischylos' Hiketiden* (Münster, 2000), 4–5 n.

[53] M. Dreher, 'Hikesie und Asylie in den *Hiketiden* des Aischylos', in M. Dreher
(ed.), *Das antike Asyl: kultische Grundlagen, rechtliche Ausgestaltung und politische
Funktion* (Köln, Weimar, Wien, 2003), 59–84, at 61–5; S. Föllinger, *Genosdependen-
zen: Studien zur Arbeit am Mythos bei Aischylos* (Hypomnemata, 148; Göttingen,
2003), 197–204.

[54] Danaos impresses them on his daughters once again as Pelasgos approaches
(186–203).

no more of them than that they can give a plausible account of the immediate circumstances of their plea, that is to say their actual plight. They are not obliged, on the other hand, to give an account of its wider context. They can even withhold their identity. In accordance with this unstated rule, Arete asks Odysseus in *Odyssey* 7 for an explanation of how he, a shipwrecked sailor, happens to be wearing clothes which she recognizes as coming from her household. When Odysseus answers the question by telling her what is necessary but no more, his reticence is unhesitatingly respected. Only on the next day, when he is no longer a suppliant but has been honoured with lavish gifts and the ship is ready for his homeward journey, does he reveal his name and tell his whole story.[55]

It is this right of suppliants—to be allowed to keep silent about what they cannot or will not say—that makes it not just understandable but absolutely necessary for the suppliants in Aeschylus' play to make no mention of the oracle. They present themselves as refugees, who are being persecuted and have travelled across the sea in a ship; they explain the genealogy on the basis of which they have a particular entitlement to asylum in Argos; above all they put the greatest emphasis on the religious dimension of supplication. But they necessarily leave unstated anything which would cast doubt on the unequivocal nature of their claim. For if the Argives knew that an oracle had predicted Danaos' death, the question would inevitably arise whether a supplication with the aim of avoiding the fulfilment of a divine oracle would not inevitably be regarded as an act of impiety which should be rejected in the interests of the *polis*. The same consequence would also follow from the consideration that the plan is likely to fail (since oracles usually come true) and that pollution for the city would result from the expected killing of Danaos.

The *Hiketides* portrays—in accordance with its title—a complete suppliant action, which extends over the entire play and represents in turn the two components of a supplication, the prayer to the gods

---

[55] Odysseus formally completes his transition to the status of a *xenos* (guest) with this waiving of the suppliant's right to silence (*Od.* 9.16–18): νῦν δ᾽ ὄνομα πρῶτον μυθήσομαι, ὄφρα καὶ ὑμεῖς | εἴδετ᾽, ἐγὼ δ᾽ ἂν ἔπειτα φυγὼν ὕπο νηλεὲς ἦμαρ | ὑμῖν ξεῖνος ἔω καὶ ἀπόπροθι δώματα ναίων ('But first at least you shall have my name—then you will know it henceforth, and if I escape the day of evil I shall remain your guest-friend [*xenos*], although my own home is far from here', tr. W. H. Shewring).

Wolfgang Rösler

(with which the play begins) and the appeal to humans. The inter-vening dialogue between Danaos and his daughters also stands in an immediate and practical relationship to the act of supplication. There is accordingly no place in this play for any mention of the oracle. On the contrary, it might actually have created tension for the spectators in the theatre to observe how the Danaids and their father who leads them satisfy the exigencies of a supplication in which they keep silent about what can on no account be expressed. What scholarly methodology demands as evidence for a reconstruction—the mention of the oracle in the *Hiketides*—is excluded by the dramaturgy of the play and of the trilogy.

6

Pelasgus and Politics in Aeschylus' Danaid Trilogy

Peter Burian

This paper is now more than thirty years old, and in some ways shows its age (as does its author, no doubt). I am glad to see it in print once more, but also grateful to be able to make a brief comment about it from this distance in time.

The most obvious thing to say from this perspective is that no one writing such a piece today would be apologetic about politics as a tragic subject. The intervening years have been marked by persistent and productive scholarly engagement with the relationship between Athenian theatre and civic democratic ideology. At the time of writing, however, those who were interested in specifically political elements of tragedy regularly engaged in special pleading, which usually took the form of claiming that a tragic playwright's political 'message' could be discerned precisely where it led to problems with his dramaturgy—anachronisms, digressions, irrelevancies that betrayed his 'real' interest. It is against such views of the representation of democratic decision-making in Bronze Age Argos that this paper argues, by reclaiming it as an essential part of the dramatic economy of *Suppliants*.

In a general way, I am still satisfied with the argument I made for explaining the shared responsibility of Pelasgus and the Argive demos in accepting the Danaids' supplication 'intrinsically', as a dramatic device carefully crafted to underline the gravity of the decision and intensify our sense of the danger it comports. I am less sure that my treatment of the double decision is entirely correct. (I owe much of that doubt to a recent and fruitful encounter with one of the play's greatest students and advocates, Professor A. F. Garvie.) In the paper I argued that Pelasgus could clearly make the decision himself but chose rather to submit the issue to the assembly. To do this, I took the phrase οὐδέ περ κρατῶν (399) to mean 'even though I have the power', although it might equally well be conditional, 'even if I had the power'. And lines 365–6 ('You are not seated at my own hearth. If the city as a whole is defiled, let the people work out a cure together'), to which I referred only as a picture of 'the threat to the whole state', might suggest that the people, not the king, are responsible for deciding the suppliants' fate. If one accepts these interpretations, it is far less than 'perfectly clear', as I put it, that the king has the power to do so himself. This would alter the dynamic of the situation, but not the thrust of my argument that the deferral of the decision is an effective means of highlighting its significance and needs no external justification.

Finally, looking over the scholarship on *Suppliants* since this article appeared in 1974, one finds the date of the trilogy still being questioned, although within a fairly narrow range of years, roughly the mid-470s to the late 460s, and reconstruction of the trilogy still attracting a great deal of attention, with a number of recent scholars reverting to the old hypothesis that *Suppliants* came second rather than first in order of presentation [e.g. Wolfgang Rösler in this volume]. There has also been important work on the play in relation to issues of gender and ethnicity. What seems to be lacking is serious consideration of the literary and dramatic qualities of the play and a full appreciation of its considerable merits. If the reprinting of this article interests others in exploring *Suppliants* for its own sake, it will have served a useful purpose.

There is general agreement that king Pelasgus is 'the specifically tragic figure' of Aeschylus' *Suppliants.*[1] He must face a heart-rending dilemma: to accept the Danaids' supplication and risk a terrible war, or reject it and incur the wrath of Zeus Hikesios ('Lord of

---

[1] G. F. Else, *The Origin and Early Form of Greek Tragedy* (Cambridge, Mass., 1965), 95.

Suppliants'). It is, as Kitto remarks, 'a tragic situation which will hold its own with any'.[2] But in the end Pelasgus simply refers the whole problem to the Argive assembly for decision. His position as a constitutional monarch appears to create a considerable difficulty for the dramatic action. Scholars have approached this difficulty in two distinct ways. Those who seek contemporary allusions in the *Suppliants* posit here a rupture in the fabric of the play through which they hope to discern Aeschylus' political message. A. J. Podlecki goes even so far as to argue 'that the Argive democracy, proceeding in an orderly fashion to reach a unanimous decision in an Athenian-type assembly, is in some sense the subject of this play',[3] and lets the dramatic chips fall where they may. Those who look for a dramatic explanation of the role played by the Argive *dēmos* invariably fall back on the trilogy: 'the emphasis becomes dramatically important in the following plays'.[4] Both of these approaches are based on the assumption that Pelasgus' recourse to the people is a deliberate anachronism which blunts the effect of the king's dilemma and dispels the sense of a tragic decision. I wish to argue, on the contrary, that it is a coherent part of Aeschylus' dramatic strategy, and that it heightens the impact of Pelasgus' choice.

It has seemed to some scholars an easy step from the assumption of anachronism in Aeschylus' portrayal of the Argive constitution, to the assertion that this portrayal is, in one way or another, motivated by political considerations.[5] But caution is in order here. In the first place, we ought to ask whether the term anachronism is appropriate. If by this were meant merely that Aeschylus is not always careful to distinguish

---

[2] H. D. F. Kitto, *Greek Tragedy*[3] (London, 1961), 8.

[3] A. J. Podlecki, *The Political Background of Aeschylean Tragedy* (Ann Arbor, 1966), 50. The general acceptance of a date in the 460s for the Danaid trilogy has naturally given new impetus to the search for political allusions in the *Suppliants*, since the apparent sympathy for Argos which the play expresses is more easily made sense of at this later date than in the 490s (not to mention the 470s, advocated by M. Pohlenz, *Die Griechische Tragödie*[2] (Göttingen, 1954), 63, and Erläuterungen 24). Indeed, the friendly treatment of Argos, similar in tone to that of the *Eumenides*, has long been a major argument against the early dating of the trilogy. A. F. Garvie, *Aeschylus' Supplices: Play and Trilogy* (Cambridge, 1969), 141–62, offers a judicious survey of scholarly opinion on this and related topics. I make no attempt in these notes to reproduce his ample bibliography.

[4] Garvie (n. 3), 153.

[5] e.g. U. von Wilamowitz-Moellendorff, *Aischylos: Interpretationen* (Berlin, 1914), 11.

the putative world of the myth from his own contemporary world, there could be no objection. Nor should one expect a fifth-century Greek poet to employ the standards of historicity congenial to modern scholarship. But those who speak of anachronism generally seem to expect just this, for they treat elements like the Argive democracy as deliberate deviations from historical verisimilitude.[6] Secondly, we need not assume that the presence of an apparent anachronism is necessarily an indication of some extra-dramatic intention on the poet's part. In the case of the *Suppliants*, it remains to be proved that the references to Argive democracy are designed to mirror the contemporary situation.[7] Even if this could be shown, however, it would not justify the assertion that Aeschylus' motives are to be sought outside the dramatic context. Anachronism cannot be equated with artistic incongruity.[8]

Many scholars, of course, have found it irreducibly incongruous that Pelasgus, the presumed tragic agent, should be incapable of acting for himself. This argument seems, however, to be based on a misunderstanding. Garvie, for example, asserts that 'the king cannot by himself accept or reject the Danaids' plea for asylum. Only the sovereign people can decide'.[9] But to examine the lines he cites in evidence is to reject his conclusion. Confronted by an apparently hopeless dilemma, Pelasgus is unwilling to act alone. At 368–9, after having pictured the threat of pollution to the whole state, Pelasgus declares that he does not wish to make any promise (ἐγὼ δ' ἂν οὐ κραίνοιμ' ὑπόσχεσιν) before he consults those who would be affected by it. Lines 398–9 are perfectly clear on this point:

[6] e.g. J. Vürtheim, *Aischylos' Schutzflehende* (Amsterdam, 1928), ad 259: 'eine historische Fälschung, wie solche dem athenischen Publikum zuliebe gemacht wurden'.

[7] Garvie (n. 3), 153, concisely sums up the main reasons for scepticism on this point: (1) the position of Pelasgus is analogous to that of the Homeric king; (2) the Argives considered their democratic traditions to be very old, and the role of the *dēmos* in the story of the Danaids may well pre-date Aeschylus; (3) Athenian ideals, rather than Argive realities, may lie behind the constitutional monarchy of Pelasgus (cf. the position of Theseus in Euripides' *Suppliants*). See also G. Müller, *De Aeschyli Supplicum tempore atque indole* (Halle, 1908), 10 ff.

[8] Similarly, it will not do to say, with A. Diamantopoulos, 'The Danaid tetralogy of Aeschylus', *JHS* 77 (1957), 220–9, at 224, that the theme of democracy 'in itself has no dramatic interest'. One might fully as well say this, for example, of the theme of genealogy, so much more prominent in the *Suppliants*, and so obviously used for important dramatic ends. Not themes 'in themselves' but their uses must be considered.

[9] Garvie (n. 3), 150.

εἶπον δὲ καὶ πρίν, οὐκ ἄνευ δήμου τάδε
πράξαιμ' ἄν, οὐδέ περ κρατῶν.

I said it before: I will not act without the people, even though I have the power.

Pelasgus does not lack *kratos* ('power', 'rule'), but in this terrifying new situation he is unwilling to exercise it without consent. In the following lines, his fear of popular reproach if he did act alone is further evidence that he could do so.[10]

For their part, the Danaids repeatedly insist on Pelasgus' complete and personal responsibility for their fate. They reply to the king's initial decision to consult the people with a firm reassertion of his *kratos*: 'You are the state, you are the people' (370). No popular vote is needed, for Pelasgus 'rules by the sole vote of his will' (κρατύνεις... μονοψήφοισι νεύμασιν, 372–3). Like a Zeus on earth, he decides every issue 'on the throne of sole sovereignty' (μονοσκήπτροισι δ' ἐν θρόνοις, 374). From this position the suppliants never really weaken. They are satisfied to win the king to their side as πρόξενος ('sponsor', 'protector'; 419, cf. 491), for they still consider his rule absolute (ὦ πᾶν κράτος ἔχων χθονός ('O you who hold all power in this land'), 425), and therefore regard his sponsorship as sufficient.

Once it is understood that Pelasgus' refusal to act by himself is precisely that, and not the result of some constitutional limitation on his power, it becomes possible to search for its dramatic motivation, for its role in the play's artistic economy. There is, in the course of the king's encounter with his suppliants, a clear progression from initial assertions of almost unlimited power to a recognition of the limitations on its exercise that new circumstances make advisable. Pelasgus introduces himself to his suppliants as the eponymous king of a domain including almost the whole of mainland Greece (260–9).

[10] None of the other passages listed by Garvie alter this picture. In 617–18 Pelasgus merely says that he will try to make the people well-disposed. 601 (δήμου δέδοκται παντελῆ ψηφίσματα, 'the votes of the people have decided with finality'), 605 ff. (description of the vote), 739 (τελεία ψῆφος, 'the vote of the Argives was final'), 942 ff. (announcement of the people's action to the herald), 963 ff. (reassurance to the Danaids of protection both by Pelasgus and by the people), are all comments after the fact, naturally enough emphasizing the importance of the popular decision but in no way implying that Pelasgus could not have offered the suppliants asylum on his own initiative. Aeschylus in fact never clarifies the relations of power between king and *dēmos*; he is not describing a constitution, but constructing a drama.

He represents himself quite unabashedly as Argos' ruler (τῆσδε γῆς ἀρχηγέτης ('ruler of this land'), 251; ἐμοῦ δ' ἄνακτος ('[the Pelasgoi, named] after me, their king'), 252; κρατῶ ('I rule') emphatically ending lines 266 and 269). But as he becomes aware of the terrible burden the suppliants would place on his shoulders, these self-confident expressions yield to new and discordant notes of impotence and fear:

> ἀμηχανῶ δὲ καὶ φόβος μ' ἔχει φρένας
> δρᾶσαί τε μὴ δρᾶσαί τε καὶ τύχην ἑλεῖν (379–80).

I am at a loss, and fear seizes my heart, whether to act or not to act and take whatever comes.

The Danaids, although they stress their helplessness (e.g. 360–3, 428–32), are the real wielders of power here. They are fully aware of the strength of their position, and willing to push it to the limit. They threaten Pelasgus with the wrath of Zeus Hikesios,[11] and warn of pollution; the more agonized his hesitation, the more insistent their demands. Finally when the king's search for a 'saving thought' (407, 417) still uncovers no other solution than sacrilege or war, they threaten to hang themselves upon the very statues of the gods (465). It is the fear of this 'miasma that cannot be outshot' (473) that finally compels Pelasgus' limited offer of aid.

The unrelenting, indeed unscrupulous, pressure that the Danaids bring to bear on Pelasgus turns the proud autocrat into a constitutional monarch. What appears at first sight to be a contradiction is in fact a reflection of Pelasgus' understanding of the situation and of his role in it. As he becomes aware of the dangerous consequences of any action he might take, he assesses his *kratos* anew and realizes that it is inadequate to such a responsibility as now lies before him. The whole state is threatened; let the whole state work out a cure (366–7). This first expression of the play's 'democratic' motif is as close as Pelasgus can come to the 'saving thought' he so desperately seeks. Pelasgus'

---

[11] Ζηνὸς ἱκεσίου κότος ('the wrath of Zeus, Lord of Suppliants') is a kind of *Leitmotiv* of this exchange (347, 385, 478–9, 616; in each case κότος ('wrath') comes emphatically at the end of the line). A. Lesky, *Die tragische Dichtung der Hellenen* (Göttingen, 1956), 91, points out the 'besondere, sinnhafte Form der Wiederholung' (= *Greek Tragic Poetry*, tr. M. Dillon (New Haven and London, 1983), 108–9: 'Individual words appear in a special and thematic way scattered throughout widely separated passages in the manner of a leitmotif').

self-imposed limitation of power serves a clear dramatic purpose. The king's initial claim of absolute rule heightens the impact of his increasingly impotent hesitation. His later insistence that the people decide the case underlines effectively the magnitude of his dilemma.

This way of underlining the king's dilemma accords fully with the characterization of Pelasgus, or more precisely, with the consistent contrast of Pelasgus and his suppliants developed throughout the play. Pelasgus is not a highly individuated character, because his dilemma, not his person, is the center of dramatic interest. But, as W. Kraus observed, a good deal of the tension in the supplication scene stems from the contrast of his nature with that of the Danaids.[12] They remain, despite their Argive ancestry, profoundly barbarian.[13] Their use of the rite of supplication, the one Greek element in their otherwise exotic appearance (243), is merely the means to an end, and they do not scruple to pervert it by repeated threats of suicide at the altar.[14] These violent and sacrilegious outbursts betoken an obsessive, hysterical fear of marriage with the sons of Aegyptus. It is such a threat, as we have seen, by which the suppliants extort Pelasgus' aid. Their triumph is not won by the humility and modest demeanor that Danaus recommended (191–203), but by their 'fine device' ($\mu\eta\chi\alpha\nu\grave{\eta}$ $\kappa\alpha\lambda\acute{\eta}$, 459), the bold stratagem that reveals the full extent of their ruthless self-absorption. Pelasgus, by contrast, embodies the Greek virtues of genuine piety and concern for the safety of the state. His anguished hesitation is not the result of indecisiveness, but rather of swift and lucid comprehension of the need to decide between dreadful evils: $\mathring{\alpha}\nu\epsilon\upsilon$ $\delta\grave{\epsilon}$ $\lambda\acute{\upsilon}\pi\eta\varsigma$ $o\mathring{\upsilon}\delta\alpha\mu o\hat{\upsilon}$ $\kappa\alpha\tau\alpha\sigma\tau\rho o\phi\acute{\eta}$ ('nowhere an ending without pain', 442). His most salient characteristics—his awe of the Danaids' supplication, his tortured weighing of the consequences of action, and (later in the play) his manly resistance to the herald's threats—keep the contrast of his nature with that of the Danaids' well in the foreground.

---

[12] W. Kraus, *Die Schutzsuchenden* (Frankfurt, 1948), 141.

[13] W. Nestle, *Menschliche Existenz und politische Erziehung in der Tragödie des Aischylos* (Tübinger Beiträge 23; Stuttgart, 1924), esp. 13 ff. The suppliants' foreignness is emphasized by references to their language (e.g. 118–19 = 129–30), their dress (e.g. 234–7), their physical appearance (e.g. 496–8). These and similar elements are examined by H. H. Bacon, *Barbarians in Greek Tragedy* (New Haven, 1961), 15–63.

[14] Cf. Nestle (n. 13), 17–18, who sees in these threats an offense against Hellenic religious feeling which turns the maidens into hysterical *theomachoi*.

In this light, Pelasgus' insistence that the people decide an issue involving their very survival takes on an almost emblematic quality. Pelasgus' dilemma is the dilemma of a statesman. He must fear the consequences of his action not only for himself, but for his people; and he seeks the 'saving thought' for both together, but first for the state (410–11). Even if he wished to escape his public responsibility, however, he could not, for his people would hold him accountable (399–401, cf. 484–5). The Danaids, on the other hand, have no thought at this point for the safety of their ancestral home, and seem to take no notice of Pelasgus' concern for it. Not only are they obsessed by their own struggle; they appear to have no clear idea of political responsibility. They conceive of power as essentially coercive, and so they use the power of their perverted ritual. For them, Pelasgus' power is limited only by the still greater power of Zeus, certainly not by concern for (or even fear of) those he rules. Whereas Pelasgus imagines the whole state stained by pollution (τὸ κοινὸν δ᾽ εἰ μιαίνεται πόλις ('if the city as a whole is defiled'), 366), the Danaids can portray only personal danger (including that to the king's children and house, 433–6) should he refuse them aid. In short, Pelasgus' recourse to the assembly serves as one more indication of his clear-sighted, public-spirited and thoroughly Greek approach to the tragic dilemma, in sharp contrast to the limited, self-absorbed and barbarian mentality of the suppliants who have thrust it upon him.

The dramatic function of the Argive assembly's decision is surely primary, and whatever praise it implies of democracy, Argive or Athenian, only subsidiary. Dramatically, the king's decision to help the suppliants is the crucial one.[15] In terms of what is actually accomplished for the Danaids' protection, of course, the vote of the people is far more important, for there the whole city guarantees its support. The dramatic weight, however, does not fall on the achievement of protection, but rather on the confrontation that leads up to it, the way in which the tragic choice is made. The exchange between king and suppliants, the longest scene of the play, has as its practical

---

[15] This is demonstrated very clearly by B. Snell, *Aischylos und das Handeln im Drama* (Philol. Suppl. 20; 1928), 59–63; and by M. Class, *Gewissensregungen in der griechischen Tragödie* (Spudasmata 3; Hildesheim, 1964), 30–3.

outcome nothing more than Pelasgus' promise of support in the assembly, but it lays bare the bones of the tragedy. And this dramatic emphasis on Pelasgus' choice robs the theme of a final decision by the people of much of its force.[16] The popular vote, indeed, is treated in an almost perfunctory manner. Danaus' report of the meeting is the shortest episode in extant tragedy,[17] and is largely devoted to Pelasgus' eloquence in presenting the suppliants' case.

In the stasimon that follows Danaus' announcement of the vote, the Danaids at last take cognizance of the Argive state as a whole. The ode is an extended prayer for blessings upon the suppliants' new protectors, and as such wholly appropriate at this point in the drama. Despite a tendency to seek political allusions here, there is no reason to regard it as anything but a conventional prayer, well-adapted to its dramatic context.[18] There is no particular emphasis on democratic themes. The grateful suppliants naturally refer to the vote by which they won asylum in Argos, but only as the token of Argos' reverence for suppliants and of her decision to support the cause of women against that of men (640–5). The only other mention of popular rule (698–700) is a prayer for good government that comes as part of a long series of wishes and admonitions. The dramatic use of the popular assembly is sufficient explanation for such references; if it leads, not unnaturally, to the employment of a certain amount of contemporary political terminology, this need hardly be accounted for by some political program or persuasion. The problems and

---

[16] Albin Lesky, 'Decision and responsibility in the tragedy of Aeschylus', *JHS* 86 (1966), 78–85, at 79 = E. Segal (ed.), *Oxford Readings in Greek Tragedy* (Oxford, 1983), 13–23, at 14–15.

[17] A. Lesky, 'Zur Entwicklung des Sprechverses in der Tragödie', *WS* 47 (1929), 12–13 (= *Gesammelte Schriften* (Bern 1966), 91), following Wilamowitz, points out that 600–24 constitute not so much a true episode as a prologue to the stasimon 625–709.

[18] Garvie (n. 3), 149–50, citing the relevant literature. He points out that the emphasis (in order and relative importance) on the avoidance of war, over against the brief mention given to the avoidance of civil strife, appears to be dictated by the dramatic context. To this we might add the obvious appropriateness of the repeated reference to the claims of suppliants and *xenoi* (627, 640–1, 652–3, 672–3, 701 ff.), and of the related theme of averted pollution (646 ff.). There is a valuable treatment of this ode, emphasizing possible ironic overtones in several of its themes, in R. D. Murray, *The Motif of Io in Aeschylus' Suppliants* (Princeton, 1958), 79–82.

inconsistencies, such as they are, reveal much more about Aeschylus' dramatic technique than about his politics.

Much the same may be said about the view that the popular vote in the *Suppliants* must be understood as preparing a role for the Argive assembly later in the trilogy. Winnington-Ingram argues this case on the basis of an unimpeachable methodology: 'If any feature in the extant play seems to lack relevance or to receive emphasis disproportionate to its dramatic value there, it may look forward to the missing sequel.'[19] In this instance, however, I have tried to show that there is no reason to speak either of irrelevance or of disproportionate emphasis. This need not, of course, imply that the Argive assembly did not play a part in the lost plays, but such an assumption is not necessary to make sense of the *Suppliants*. Certainly, Winnington-Ingram is right to stress the fact that the dramatic action links the fate of Argos to that of the Danaids. But the way in which the trilogy as a whole developed this at least potential 'Tragödie der Polis'[20] remains highly uncertain, and the use of the Argive assembly in the *Suppliants*, linked as it is to the dramatic situation there, does not seem to offer a very firm foundation for reconstruction.

Winnington-Ingram's methodology, indeed, seems better suited to deal with a quite different problem concerning Pelasgus' role. The emphasis in the *Suppliants* upon his dilemma, upon his tragic choice between evils, seems to require an adequate sequel if it is not to be disproportionate to the king's apparently marginal role in the remainder of the trilogy.[21]

---

[19] R. P. Winnington-Ingram, 'The Danaid trilogy of Aeschylus', *JHS* 81 (1961), 141–52, at 141 = *Studies in Aeschylus* (Cambridge, 1983), 56. The principle derives from F. Stoessl, *Die Trilogie des Aischylos* (Baden bei Wien, 1937), 84. In Winnington-Ingram's intriguing reconstruction, Danaus asks the Argive assembly to condemn Hypermestra for sparing Lynceus, but the people decide instead to condemn him and the remaining daughters for killing their husbands.

[20] Pohlenz (n. 3), 51.

[21] Our sources agree that Danaus became king of Argos at some point, although just when and how is unclear. The traditions concerning Danaus' kingship are conveniently summarized by M. L. Cunningham, 'A fragment of Aeschylus' *Aigyptioi?*', *Rh. M.* 96 (1953), 223–31, at 228. In any case, the killing of the sons of Aegyptus, Hypermestra's sparing of Lynceus, and the presumable resolution of the conflicts engendered by these actions appear to leave little room for Pelasgus to emerge again as bearer of the tragic idea.

Many scholars, therefore, have embraced the reasonable view that Pelasgus' tragic choice bore its fruit in the second play of the trilogy, with his defeat and death at the hands of the sons of Aegyptus.[22] This fits what little we know or can infer about the action of the remaining plays, and provides a suitable culmination to the theme of Pelasgus' tragic dilemma. Still, it remains a matter for speculation, not certainty. And the portrayal of the stark, almost stylized anguish of Pelasgus' hesitation between religious duty and political responsibility does not strictly require the king's death in order to be complete and satisfying.

Pelasgus' role is unique in extant Greek tragedy.[23] He is only technically the protagonist of the play; dramatically the protagonist is the chorus.[24] The Danaids, obsessed by their desire to escape the sons of Aegyptus, force a terrible choice upon the king. The power of their ritual and of their threats, the ever-increasing pressure they bring to bear, elevate this secondary figure in the story as a whole into the carrier, if only briefly, of the tragic impulse.[25] This is how Aeschylus gives dramatic shape to the apparently undramatic subject—the arrival of the Danaids in Argos—that he has chosen for the

---

[22] The case is persuasively argued by Lesky (n. 16), 80 (= *Oxford Readings in Greek Tragedy*, 15). If Cunningham (n. 21), 223 ff., is right, and P. Oxy. 2251 is a fragment of the *Aigyptioi*, the reconstruction is almost unavoidable; but cf. the reservations of Garvie (n. 3), 200 ff.

[23] Theseus in Eur. *Supp.* and Soph. *Oed. Col.*, and Demophon in Eur. *Heracl.* share Pelasgus' formal position as host and protector of suppliants; and in Eur. *Supp.* there is a partially analogous division of the central role between chorus and king. But none of these plays present the kings' choice with anything like the emotional intensity and structural concentration of Aeschylus. Although it cannot be proved, there is at least some negative evidence to indicate that Pelasgus' part in the story is Aeschylus' own invention. Cunningham (n. 21), 228, points out that 'no authority other than Aeschylus speaks of an appeal by Danaus to the Argive king, and most accounts make no mention of the former king' (i.e. Pelasgus). Other than Aeschylus, only Σ Eur. *Orest.* 857 and 932, and Ovid *Her.* 14, 23 mention him, and both could depend on the Aeschylean version.

[24] Cf. Garvie (n. 3), 130.

[25] Else (n. 1), 95–6, points out that the technique of achieving dramatic conflict by pitting protagonist against chorus could only be applied in special cases; in fact it appears again only in *Eum.* and Eur. *Supp.* For Else, Aeschylus here is experimenting, and the experiment is only partially successful; for 'if the protagonist happens to be a secondary person for the theme of the trilogy, as Pelasgus is, a certain obliquity and loss of momentum is bound to result'.

first play of his trilogy.[26] The Danaids' supplication, fully as much as their cousins' pursuit, creates this dramatic shape. And Pelasgus is the necessary foil both for the suppliants and for their enemies. Although we cannot be sure what use Aeschylus made of this figure later in the trilogy, there is nothing obscure or problematic about his function in the *Suppliants*. Pelasgus turns the story of the Danaids' flight into a dramatic action.

[26] Kraus (n. 12), 139.

7

The Omen of the Eagles and the *Ethos* of Agamemnon

John J. Peradotto

I

There is a kind of drama which lays claim to some degree of universality. It is, in a sense, the syllogism of literary art. An undistracted rigour governs its movement from premises to conclusions, from cause to effect. It can little afford the exuberance of comedy or the expansive digressions and unhurried pace of epic. A preoccupation with the chain of cause and effect, with responsibility, dominates this kind of tragic composition and forces it to strip away chance, the fortuitous, the coincidental, leaving only a perception of naked law.[1]

The *Oresteia* is just such a dramatic syllogism, and the first premise of its poetic logic is the omen of the eagles feasting on the pregnant hare, together with two closely allied events—the anger of Artemis and the sacrifice of Iphigeneia—in the parodos of the *Agamemnon*

A portion of the present study was presented at the ninety-ninth annual meeting of the American Philological Association in Boston, Massachusetts, December 30, 1967. [*Editor's note*. This article is reprinted here in its original form, although with the addition of translations of Greek quotations. Translations from the *Oresteia* are taken, sometimes slightly adapted, from the version by C. Collard (Oxford, 2002). Other translations are by the editor unless otherwise stated. References have also been added where appropriate to reprints of articles cited.]

[1] Cf. A. C. Schlesinger, *Boundaries of Dionysus* (Cambridge, Mass. 1963) esp. 12–26.

(109–247). The whole trilogy is structured on this incident; images and verbal motifs from this scene recur again and again throughout the work. It sets the 'problem'; the remainder of the trilogy develops a solution. Since this problem is a profoundly moral one, involving the concrete issue of Agamemnon's guilt as well as ultimate questions about the nature of the gods, man, and the world, a misunderstanding of the oblique, oracular terms in which this scene is written will seriously compromise even the most careful reading of the rest of the trilogy, and vitiate its poetic logic. Just how important this passage is can be assessed in some measure by the fact that in most cases a critic's interpretation of this portent turns out to be a capsule-version of his total view of Aeschylean moral and religious thought.[2] And in recent years the most literal and, for that reason, misleading interpretations of this scene have been proposed by critics whose attitude toward the intellectual merit of poetic drama is, to say the least, disconcerting.

That poetry possesses a respectable logic of its own and merits our serious consideration as a means of exploring reality and discovering values is a truth which some Aeschylean critics seem hesitant to entertain without Platonic misgivings or even outright disdain. They create the impression that Aeschylus was singularly unenlightened, distinguished to be sure by a gift for graceful language, but often incoherent, confused, or at best conventional in his thinking.[3] They imply that serious literature may woo us by power and grace of

---

[2] A survey of significant scholarly viewpoints on this passage may be found in E. Fraenkel, *Aeschylus: Agamemnon* (Oxford, 1950), 2.96–9, to which the following must now be added: John Finley, *Pindar and Aeschylus* (Cambridge, Mass., 1955), 252–3 (to whose brief but profoundly thought-provoking reading of this passage I owe a great deal), and *Four Stages of Greek Thought* (Stanford, 1966), 38; H. D. F. Kitto, *Form and Meaning in Drama* (London, 1956), 2–5, 70–9; J. D. Denniston and Denys Page, *Aeschylus: Agamemnon* (Oxford, 1957), pp. xxiii–xxviii [the introduction is by Page]; C. J. Reeves, 'The parodos of the *Agamemnon*', *CJ* 55 (1960), 165–71; William Whallon, 'Why is Artemis angry?', *AJPh* 82 (1961), 78–88; H. Lloyd-Jones, 'The guilt of Agamemnon', *CQ* 12 (1962), 187–99 [= *Greek Epic, Lyric, and Tragedy* (Oxford, 1990), 283–99; and E. Segal (ed.), *Oxford Readings in Greek Tragedy* (Oxford, 1983), 57–72, 411].

[3] See, for example, Lloyd-Jones' essay on tragedy in the collection of essays edited by him, *The Greek World* (Baltimore, 1965), esp. 99; also his 'Zeus in Aeschylus', *JHS* 76 (1956), 55–67 [= *Greek Epic, Lyric, and Tragedy* (Oxford, 1990), 238–61]. For a critique of this literalism, cf. H. D. F. Kitto, *Poiesis: Structure and Thought* (Berkeley and Los Angeles, 1966), 1–115.

language, but still requires the suspension or even suppression of those critical faculties whose meat is consistency, profundity, and discovery. So, for example, Page tells us that 'Aeschylus is first and foremost *a great poet and a most powerful dramatist:* the faculty of acute or profound thought is not among his gifts'.[4] Fraenkel, though he finds the anger of Artemis an unmotivated and embarrassingly arbitrary starting-point for the logic of cause and effect in the trilogy, still ends with the implication that such lapses of coherence are easily overlooked in the heat of impassioned utterance and may even be concealed by poetic legerdemain: 'Aeschylus might be confident that the *power of his song* would keep the hearers firmly in its grip and leave no room for idle speculation or curiosity about details.'[5]

The attitude toward poetry and criticism underlying these statements is one which prevailed in the late nineteenth and well into the twentieth century, and still persists obstinately in classical studies long after the revolution in critical methodology that has occurred in other literary fields. Its major characteristic is the dissociation of intellect and emotion, and the association of poetry only with the latter. It is symptomatic that it was a classicist, A. E. Housman, who should make what was probably the last significant defence of this view of poetry in the Leslie Stephens Lecture for 1933,[6] a decade after *The Wasteland* and a year after F. R. Leavis began his vigorous protest against the Victorian dissociation of emotion and intellect and the conventional exclusion of ideas from poetry.[7] Many of Housman's statements in that lecture read like the first principles upon which Page's conclusions about Aeschylean poetry might have been founded:

I cannot satisfy myself that there are any such things as poetical ideas... Poetry is not the thing said but the way of saying it....Meaning is of the intellect, poetry is not....The intellect is not the fount of poetry....; it may actually hinder its production...and...it cannot even be trusted to recog-

---

[4] Page (n. 2), p. xv; italics added.   [5] Fraenkel (n. 2), 2.99; italics added.

[6] 'The Name and Nature of Poetry', delivered at Cambridge in May, 1933, and published in A. E. Housman, *Selected Prose* (ed. John Carter) (Cambridge, 1961), 168–95. For a sensitive scrutiny of Housman's attitude toward poetry and the state of literary criticism in contemporary classical studies, see Brooks Otis, 'Housman and Horace', *Pacific Coast Philology* 2 (April 1967), 5–24.

[7] In *New Bearings in English Poetry* (London, 1932).

John J. Peradotto

nize poetry when produced.... Poetry indeed seems to me more physical
than intellectual.... I think that the production of poetry, in its first stage, is
less an active than a passive and involuntary process; and if I were obliged,
not to define poetry, but to name the class of things to which it belongs, I
should call it a secretion.[8]

If the critic is convinced that poetry may so easily dispense with ideas
and consistency and still lay claim to our serious attention, and that
the most it can do is lend prose statements 'an enhancement which
glorifies and almost transfigures them',[9] then he will surely make no
great attempt to discover in it any logic other than that of prose, nor
feel any scandal at its absence.[10] This is not the place for a detailed
critique of this view of poetry. It has been mentioned only because, as
we shall see time and again in our analysis, it has profoundly affected
Aeschylean scholarship by its depreciation or intolerance of literary
criticism, and by a literalism in the reading of poetic texts which calls
itself objectivity, but which proves especially impotent before a passage whose fabric is as multilayered and symbolic as the one under
discussion.

Because the omen of the eagles and the hare belongs to a broader
network of symbolic events and images, whose parts illuminate one
another only gradually, it is understandable that they should not
yield their meaning easily or immediately. The difficulty is further
compounded by calculated verbal obscurity in Calchas' interpretation and the chorus' narration, both motivated by the fear that a too
explicit reference to untoward events or their causes will bring them
about. But the effect of this heavy overlay of obliqueness is not to
divert our attention from bad logic, but to make us all the more
aware that there is a problem to be solved.

'The problem', as Whallon[11] summarizes it, 'is why Artemis should
require atonement. She cannot seek retribution for the predation

---

[8] Housman (n. 6), 186–8, 194.   [9] Housman (n. 6), 186.

[10] Interesting, if not wholly convincing, are the arguments of R. D. Dawe in
this connection. In 'Inconsistency of plot and character in Aeschylus', *PCPhS* 189
(1963), 21–62, he finds that the ultimate aim of Aeschylean dramaturgy was
ἔκπληξις—emotional impact (cf. the manuscript life of Aeschylus, 7)—in each
scene, to be achieved at any price, even of consistency of plot and character. Tycho
von Wilamowitz had made a similar claim concerning Sophocles in *Die dramatische
Technik des Sophokles* (Berlin, 1917).

[11] Whallon (n. 2), 81.

against Troy paid in advance, Fraenkel argues (2.97 n. 3), unless the formula δράσαντι παθεῖν ['the doer shall suffer'; *Cho.* 314; cf. *Ag.* 1564 etc.] is changed to δράσοντι παθεῖν ['the one who *will* do shall suffer']. But if she bears a grudge against the Atreidae for a reason unconnected with the sack of the city, the omen is dramatically misleading. The devouring of the hare is most understandably seen as the sacrifice of Iphigeneia or the children of Thyestes told in other terms'. Whallon's summary presents three possible motives for Artemis' anger: the killing of the hare and her young represent (a) the harm that will be done innocent non-combatants at Troy, (b) the sacrificial slaughter of Iphigeneia, and (c) the murder of Thyestes' children by Atreus. We shall return in due course to these three explanations after examining two further interpretations which merit our attention, and reviewing the poetic tradition concerning the events at Aulis.

  The first of these alternate interpretations is that Artemis hates the Atreidae simply *because the eagles typify them,* not because Agamemnon is guilty in the eyes of the goddess.[12] The matter is, of course, the other way round; Artemis hates the eagles because they typify the Atreidae. Or better, perhaps: she hates both eagles and Atreidae for the same reason. If the eagles typify the Atreidae, then it must certainly be for something associated with the dramatic content of the omen—something, that is, which is considered guilty *in Artemis' eyes.* That is a critical point, and Page misses it when he argues that it is the killing of the hare, meant as an encouraging omen, that angers Artemis, not anything that Agamemnon has done or will do, *since his actions congrue with the will of Zeus.*[13] But Zeus is not Artemis, and

[12] J. Conington and C. Robert; see Fraenkel, ii.97. T. Plüss, in 'Die Tragödie Agamemnon und das Tragische', *Wissensch. Beilage zum Bericht über das Gymnasium* (Basel, 1896), 12, goes a fatal step further and claims that Artemis is angry *only* with the eagles, not with the Atreidae at all.

[13] Page (n. 2), pp. xxiii–xxv. Concerning this insistence that Agamemnon is guiltless because he is doing Zeus' will, some further considerations are in order. Must we assume with Page that in willing the punishment of Paris, Zeus also wills the destruction of Troy? And if he does (the text is doubtful), must we assume that he also wills the harm which comes to Troy's innocent non-combatants, protégés of Artemis? And if he does (the text is silent), must we expect that such a state of affairs be 'justified by any reasoning acceptable to man'? On this last point it is hard not to share Winnington-Ingram's suspicion (in his review of Denniston-Page, *CR* n.s. 9 (1959), 25) 'that his [Page's] real quarrel may be not so much with Aeschylus' theology as with the world in which we live'.

Agamemnon's actions may very well congrue with the will of Zeus and yet earn the displeasure of Artemis.

Another interpretation is Lloyd-Jones'—that Artemis' anger against Agamemnon is sufficiently motivated by the fact that 'in the *Iliad* and in the whole poetic tradition Artemis together with her brother Apollo appears as a loyal partisan of Troy against the invaders'.[14] This is inadequate on several counts. As for her presence in the *Iliad*, it is predominantly as a bringer of death to women that she would have been remembered, rather than as a 'loyal partisan of Troy'. Furthermore, it is a dangerous practice to assume anything in Greek tragedy from so variegated a tradition of poetry and cult as lies back of it, unless substantial support in the text warrants our doing so. How easily Aeschylus may dispense with the Homeric tradition and emphasis can be seen in the fact that Apollo, speaking of Agamemnon (*Eum.* 631 ff.), assumes a commendatory tone hardly appropriate for a 'loyal partisan of Troy' regarding the leader of the invaders. Where Artemis is concerned, what is heavily emphasized in the *Agamemnon*, to the exclusion of nearly all her other prerogatives and attributes, is her *protective concern for the young and innocent* (an aspect of her personality which would probably have been uppermost in the mind of a fifth-century Athenian, for reasons we shall shortly note). Indeed, the Artemis who enters battle in *Iliad* 20 is utterly alien to the Aeschylean vision, in which it is precisely the destructiveness of war itself that rouses her anger. As we shall shortly argue in greater detail, Artemis is not angry because the victims of Agamemnon's attack are Trojans, but because they are young and innocent victims. Although Lloyd-Jones is quite right in reading the murdered hare as a symbol for the doom of Troy and its inhabitants, he is wrong in seeing Artemis' anger as motivated by nothing more profound than political partisanship. This might satisfy a romancer or mythographer, but it is the purpose of the present analysis to show that Aeschylus cannot and does not settle for such shoddy aetiology in probing so important a question of responsibility and punishment.

Fraenkel has rightly emphasized the differences between Aeschylus' account and the poetic tradition, though he has, I think, drawn

---

[14] Lloyd-Jones (n. 2), 190 [= *Greek Epic, Lyric, and Tragedy*, 287 = *Oxford Readings in Greek Tragedy*, 61].

incorrect conclusions from those differences. He reasons that, in order to secure Agamemnon's relative innocence and to make his downfall the result of a deliberate choice in a difficult dilemma rather than the disproportionate upshot of a minor offence, Aeschylus 'followed the traditional story in maintaining the wrath of Artemis and her appeasement through the sacrifice of Iphigeneia but eliminated the act of Agamemnon which had incensed the goddess'.[15] He then goes on to suggest, as we noted above, that Aeschylus ventures to distract his audience from the missing link by 'the power of his song'. While for Page and Lloyd-Jones the scene represents nothing more profound than the mythic tradition, Fraenkel at least sees it as an exercise in serious, if slightly flawed, thought.

It is flawed, Fraenkel would conclude, because there is still a disproportion (though smaller than in the *Cypria*) between the cause of Agamemnon's punishment and its severity. In effect, Fraenkel sees Aeschylus reducing the responsibility of Agamemnon by increasing the arbitrariness of the goddess. But there is only a difference in degree, not in kind, between a divinity who punishes a man so severely for a venial offence (as in the *Cypria*), and a divinity who punishes him for no offence at all. This expedient turns out to be no solution at all: the relatively arbitrary wrath of Artemis is still the starting point and primary cause of Agamemnon's fate, not the deliberate moral decision which, as Fraenkel rightly observes, Aeschylus wished to be the primary cause of that fate. My difference with Fraenkel, as I shall argue in greater detail below, is that Aeschylus has not only 'eliminated the act of Agamemnon which had incensed the goddess' (in the *Cypria*), but has substituted in its place an Agamemnon whose moral disposition (*ethos*) is such as to issue in acts at Troy which alienate Artemis. The omen of the eagles dramatizes this moral disposition. If we can demonstrate that the poet has endowed Agamemnon not with less responsibility than he had in the *Cypria,* but with *more,* and that in so doing he has made the king's character and conduct quite proportionate to the punishing anger of Artemis, we shall have the kind of starting point Fraenkel observes here, without feeling constrained to look upon Aeschylean poetry as an incantation to charm away logical difficulties.

---

[15] Fraenkel (n. 2), ii.99.

Towards this end, our first task must be to examine the poetic tradition behind the wrath of Artemis. It is best reproduced in the epitome of the *Cypria* by Proclus. There we learn that during the second gathering at Aulis Agamemnon, after shooting a deer, had angered Artemis by his boast of skill superior to hers.[16] Other accounts either add details or offer minor variations on this version. In Sophocles' *Electra* (558–76), two details are worthy of note: first the goddess is offended not only by the boast but by the fact that the killing takes place in her sacred grove;[17] second, the subsequent storm keeps the ships from sailing either to Troy *or home.* Apollodorus (*Epitome* 3.21) indicates two causes for Artemis' anger: (a) the boast that not even Artemis could have done it better, and (b) the fact that Atreus, Agamemnon's father, had neglected to sacrifice the golden lamb to her.[18] Euripides (*IT* 20 ff. and 209 ff.) introduces a motif common in the folktale tradition,[19] that the sacrifice of Iphigeneia was the constrained fulfillment of Agamemnon's earlier vow to give Artemis the loveliest thing each year should produce.[20]

Two things are noteworthy about these versions in their treatment of Artemis' anger. First, the various inciting causes are altogether prior to and wholly unrelated to the war; second, there is not the remotest resemblance between them and the Aeschylean omen of the eagles and the hare (unless it be in the killing of an animal). These two observations are not unrelated. As I hope to demonstrate, Aeschylus' seemingly deliberate rejection of the tradition is motivated in part by a desire to relate the goddess' wrath causally to the war.

The omen of the eagles and the hare bears no significant correspondence to anything in the poetic tradition about the *second*

[16] The following sources give the same version: Schol. *Il.* 1.108, Schol. Eur. *Or.* 658, Callimachus *Dian.* 263, Dictys Cret. *Bell. Troi.* 1.19–22, Tzetzes *ad Lyc.* 183.

[17] Compare Hygin. *Fab.* 98: *Cervam eius violavit superbiusque in Dianam est locutus* ['he profaned Diana's deer and boasted over her'].

[18] So reads the Vatican manuscript. But the Sabbaitic scribe, misinterpreting the phrase οὐδὲ ἡ Ἄρτεμις ['not even Artemis'], introduces a slight variant: Agamemnon boasted that the deer could not have escaped him *even if Artemis had wished it* (οὐδ' Ἀρτέμιδος θελούσης).

[19] Compare Jephtha's vow in *Judges* 11.30–40, and cf. Wilamowitz, 'Die beiden Elektren', *Hermes* 18 (1883), 214–63, at 253.

[20] Cicero uses this version as an example of a promise better left unfulfilled (*Off.* 3.25.95): *Promissum potius non faciendum quam tam taetrum facinus admittendum fuit* ['it were better not to fulfil the promise than to perpetrate so vile a crime'].

gathering at Aulis. But it does closely resemble the omen observed at
the *first* gathering (*Il.* 2.301–30 and Proclus' summary of the *Cypria*)
forecasting an Argive victory in the tenth year: a snake devouring a
sparrow and her eight nestlings. Aeschylus has seen fit to conflate the
two gatherings at Aulis into one in such a way that the omen of the
eagles and the hare does double service as prediction of an Argive
victory and as emblem of Artemis' wrath. Still, it remains to ask why
the poet should not be satisfied merely to reproduce the omen of the
snake and sparrows so well-known from the *Iliad*. If Lloyd-Jones were
right in positing as the cause of Artemis' anger her loyal partisanship
of Troy (the victims in the Aeschylean omen obviously symbolize the
Trojans), then no change would have been necessary, inasmuch as the
sparrows of the traditional version also symbolize the Trojans.[21] What
poetic purposes were better served by the portent of the eagles
and hare than by that of the snake and sparrows, and—a related
question—what was the experiential or historical raw material out
of which Aeschylus fashioned the portent as it appears in the text?

An answer to the second question, even a merely probable one, will
facilitate our investigation of the first, for it goes without saying that
a literary artist at nearly every stage of his task quite naturally
assumes in his audience a response to associations of the experiential
raw materials of his work which may be lost on the foreign reader
with nothing but the text to rely on. We must, of course, always
exercise care in reconstructing the manner in which a poet has
converted his raw materials into artistic products, keeping in mind
that such reconstructions have at best only probable validity.

An introductory clue to our question is the statement of a scholiast
on Aristophanes' *Lysist.* 645, κᾆτ' ἔχουσα τὸν κροκωτὸν ἄρκτος ἦ
Βραυρωνίοις ['and then, wearing my saffron gown, I was a bear at
the Brauronia']: οἱ δὲ τὰ περὶ Ἰφιγένειαν ἐν Βραυρῶνι φασίν, οὐκ ἐν
Αὐλίδι. Εὐφορίων· Ἀγχίαλον Βραυρῶνα, κενήριον Ἰφιγενείας. δοκεῖ
δὲ Ἀγαμέμνων σφαγιάσαι τὴν Ἰφιγένειαν ἐν Βραυρῶνι, οὐκ ἐν Αὐλίδι
['some say that the events concerning Iphigeneia took place at Brauron,
not at Aulis. Euphorion: "Brauron by the sea, the cenotaph of Iphigeneia"

---

[21] It is true that the sparrows in the omen seem to refer *primarily* to years of war,
but unless they also symbolize Troy, Calchas could not predict an Argive, rather than
a Trojan, victory.

220 *John J. Peradotto*

(fr. 91 Powell). Agamemnon is thought to have sacrificed Iphigeneia at Brauron, not at Aulis']. Brauron (modern Vraona), situated some twenty miles from Athens, was an important centre of the cult of Artemis. Close ties had always existed between the two communities: Brauron was one of the twelve cities in the Attic *synoikismos,* and was the home of the Pisistratids. In the fourth century there was a temple of Brauronian Artemis on the Acropolis, and a century earlier, during Aeschylus' day, young Athenian girls, aged five through ten, customarily participated in the festival of Brauronian Artemis, and were called ἄρκτοι ['bears'] because they imitated bears in the ritual (see the same scholion on *Lysist.* 645).[22] During excavations at Brauron begun in 1948, under the direction of John Papadimitriou,[23] votive statuettes were unearthed representing a young girl (very likely one of the ἄρκτοι) holding a hare.[24] In addition, votive offerings left at the temple indicate that it was a shrine frequented by women in their pregnancy. Euripides, certainly relying on local legend, makes Iphigeneia (after her sojourn among the Taurians) become 'keeper of the keys' and, after her death, recipient of special honours at this shrine (*IT* 1462–6).[25] Papadimitriou sums up the history of the site as follows:

Artemis Brauronia . . . was associated with Iphigeneia and adored as Protectress of birth and fertility—especially animal fertility. But we are able to say now that the name of Iphigeneia is one of the *hypostases* of the great chthonian goddess—the Earth-mother—and the cult remained continually associated with the same site even after the abandonment of the prehistoric town. It was much later that the goddess became confused with Artemis and the name became an epithet of Artemis . . . We must affirm that a faith even

[22] For all the literary sources of our knowledge of Brauronian Artemis, cf. Farnell, *Cults of the Greek States* (Oxford, 1896), 2.435–42, 564–6; see also Ludwig Deubner, *Attische Feste* (Berlin, 1932), 207–8, and M. P. Nilsson, *Gesch. d. Griech. Rel.*[2] (Munich, 1955), 1.484–6.

[23] The death of Papadimitriou has long delayed the correlation and final appraisal of the Brauron materials. For a description of the excavation at various stages, see *Praktika* from 1949 on, and *Ergon,* 1954–61. An up-to-date popular account, relying heavily on conversations with Papadimitriou, may be found in Leonard Cottrell, *Realms of Gold* (Greenwich, Conn., 1963), 186–200.

[24] See reproductions in *Ergon* (1959), 36, fig. 38; Cottrell (n. 23), plate 96; C. Kerenyi, *The Religion of the Greeks and Romans* (New York, 1962), plate 75.

[25] Papadimitriou has actually identified one of the structures at Brauron as the tomb of Iphigeneia mentioned in *IT* 1464: *Praktika* (1955), 118–20.

older than that of Artemis became in time the cult of Iphigeneia who by classical times had become confused with the daughter of Agamemnon and Clytemnestra.[26]

All the basic elements of the Aeschylean version are present here in embryo; Artemis as patron of pregnancy, innocent youth, and wild life; the hare as particularly appropriate to her cult because it is fecund, timid and innocent in appearance, and wild;[27] the association between Iphigeneia and Artemis.

Other intriguing points of correspondence between Brauron and the Aeschylean account appear. Describing Iphigeneia at the moment of her sacrificial death, Aeschylus uses the much discussed expression κρόκου βαφὰς δ᾽ ἐς πέδον χέουσα ['Her yellow-dyed dress streaming to the ground'] (*Ag.* 239). At one level, it takes its place within the important image-patterns of entangling fabric (garments and nets) and of flowing blood that run through the trilogy.[28] But the detail adds a further dimension of pathos and irony as yet unnoticed: Iphigeneia is dressed like an ἄρκτος ['bear'] at the festival of Braur-onian Artemis. The passage in the *Lysistrata* already cited and its scholion emphasize the κροκωτόν ['saffron gown'] as a significant feature of the rite.[29] In a context involving Artemis and Iphigeneia, especially as Aeschylus compels us to envision the latter—young, innocent, unwed (παρθενοσφάγοισιν ῥείθροις, 210 ['slaughter stream-ing from a maiden']; παρθενίου θ᾽ αἵματος, 215 ['a maiden's blood']; αἰῶνα παρθένειον, 229 ['her maiden's years']; ἀταύρωτος, 245 ['an

---

[26] Unpublished address of John Papadimitriou to the *Direction des Musées de France,* cited in Cottrell (n. 23), 193.

[27] Herodotus (3.108), in discussing τοῦ θείου ἡ προνοίη ['divine providence'] which makes animals more prolific in proportion as they are timid and edible, singles out the hare as a prime example. Cf. also Aelian *NA* 2.12 and Pollux 5.73.

[28] On this point, see the excellent analysis by Anne Lebeck, 'The robe of Iphigen-eia', *GRBS* 5 (1964), 35–41.

[29] *Lysist.* 645: κᾆτ᾽ ἔχουσα τὸν κροκωτὸν ἄρκτος ἦ Βραυρωνίοις ['and then, wearing my saffron gown, I was a bear at the Brauronia']. The scholion: Ἄρκτον μιμούμεναι τὸ μυστήριον ἐξετέλουν. αἱ ἀρκτευόμεναι δὲ τῇ θεῷ κροκωτὸν ἠμφιέννυντο, καὶ συνετέλουν τὴν θυσίαν τῇ Βραυρωνίᾳ Ἀρτέμιδι... Ἄρτεμις...ἐκέλευσε παρθένον πᾶσαν μιμήσασθαι τὴν ἄρκτον πρὸ τοῦ γάμου καὶ περιέπειν τὸ ἱερὸν κροκωτὸν ἱμάτιον φοροῦσαν ['They carried out the rite imitating a bear. The girls serving as bears for Artemis wore saffron gowns, and they made the sacrifice to Brauronian Artemis... Artemis... ordered every maiden to imitate the bear before her marriage, and to conduct the rite wearing a saffron gown'].

222   *John J. Peradotto*

unwed girl'])—the detail would have conveyed the ritual significance quite naturally to an Athenian audience most (if not all) of whose young daughters would don the κροκωτόν ['saffron gown'] and dance the bear-mime of Artemis before their marriages.³⁰

Another way in which Brauron may have provided grist for the poet's mill is suggested a few lines earlier, where Iphigeneia is lifted, as the chorus describes it, δίκαν χιμαίρας ὕπερθε βωμοῦ (232 ['like a goat-kid over the altar']). Here, as many scholars have pointed out, an Athenian may well have thought of the 500 χίμαιραι ['goat-kids'] offered yearly to Artemis Agrotera for the victory at Marathon (Xen. *Anab.* 3.2.12, Ael. *NH* 2.25), or of the Spartan custom of sacrificing one before battle (Xen. *Hell.* 4.2.20, Plut. *Lycurg.* 22.2). But a goat was also sacrificed at the Brauronia (Hesych. s.v. Βραυρώνια ἑορτή), according to one tradition, as a substitute for the young girl originally required.³¹ An Athenian, with the rites at Brauron in mind, would be struck by the inversion, at once ironic and gruesome, involved in the Aeschylean substitution.³²

The cult of Artemis at Brauron, then, and the traditions associated with it seem to provide most of the basic materials from which the Aeschylean account could have been created. It also sheds light on the more important question of what poetic purposes are better served

³⁰ A precise parallel can be found at *Eum.* 1028, where the incorporation of the Erinyes into the life of Athens is symbolized by their investiture with the φοινικοβάπτοις ἐνδυτοῖς ἐσθήμασι ['red-dyed clothing'] traditionally worn by the *metoikoi* in the Panathenaeic procession. Cf. Walter Headlam, 'The last scene in the *Eumenides*', *JHS* 26 (1906), 268–77, and George Thomson, *The Oresteia of Aeschylus*² (Amsterdam and Prague, 1966), ii.231–3.
³¹ Eustath. *Il.* 331.26, Bekker *Anec.* 444–5. The scene of the incident in these sources is the Piraeus, where there was a temple of Artemis Munychia, but on the confusion of Brauronian traditions with those of Artemis Munychia, see Deubner (n. 22), 205–7.
³² This assimilation of man to beast in the *Oresteia* is one of the trilogy's more striking image-patterns. In a drama about the progress of δίκη ['justice'] Aeschylus' use of animal imagery is in the tradition of Hesiod who says that the animal kingdom is (or should be) distinguished from mankind by the fact that there is no justice in it: birds and beasts prey upon one another because there is no δίκη ['justice'] among them (*Op.* 276–80). So in the *Oresteia*, as δίκη ['justice'] itself becomes more humane, the poetic identifications between man and beast gradually diminish, both in number and repulsiveness. See Heinrich Weinstock, *Die Tragödie des Humanismus*⁵ (Heidelberg, 1967), 15, and J. Peradotto, 'Time and the Pattern of Change in Aeschylus' *Oresteia*' (diss. Northwestern University, 1963), 149–69.

by the eagle–hare image than by the Homeric snake and sparrows. The Artemis at Brauron is a goddess whose main concerns are fertility, pregnancy, youth, innocence, but around whose cult there are whispers of human sacrifice.[33] The Artemis of the *Agamemnon* is no other; the devouring of a pregnant hare and her brood dramatizes one aspect of her Brauronian character, while the sacrifice of Iphigeneia dramatizes the other. Such a goddess would indeed resent the murder of Thyestes' children, the murder of Iphigeneia, and the murder of innocent youth at Troy. These three analogous events stand to the omen of the slaughtered hare as species to a kind of symbolic genus; the omen subsumes all three events, relating them one to another as cases of the slaughter of innocent youth in the pursuit and exercise of power.

The text supports this triple reference. Treating the hare's death as a *sacrifice*[34] (θυομένοισιν, 136) and a *meal* (βοσκομένω, 119; λαγοδαίτας, 124; δεῖπνον, 138) underscores its relationship with the sacrificial feast of Thyestes' children (σφαγάς, 1096; βεβρωμένας, 1097; δαῖτα, 1242; θοινατῆρος, 1502; ἐπιθύσας, 1504; δαῖτα, 1593; σφαγήν, 1599; δείπνου, 1601), and to the sacrificial death of Iphigeneia (θυσίαν, 150; παρθενοσφάγοισιν, 209; θυσίας, 214; θυτήρ, 225; θυτήρων, 240; ἔθυσεν, 1417; τυθείσης, *Cho.* 242), which, though it is not a meal, does not get by without some allusion to eating (θυσίαν ... ἄδαιτον, 150; εὐτραπέζους, 244).[35] But treated as a *hunt* (λοισθίων δρόμων, 120; πτανοῖσιν κυσί, 135), the omen clearly refers to Troy and its inhabitants[36] (ἀγρεῖ Πριάμου πόλιν, 126; ἐπὶ Τροίας

---

[33] Consult Farnell (n. 22), 2.566 n. 35, for sources which associate human sacrifice with Artemis in other contexts than Brauron.

[34] Cf. Froma Zeitlin, 'The motif of the corrupted sacrifice in Aeschylus' *Oresteia*', *TAPhA* (1965), 463–508, where the sacrificial aspect of the eagle–hare omen is developed.

[35] Iphigeneia's sacrifice might be spoken of as satisfying hunger indirectly by bringing to an end the adverse winds, one of the effects of which was starvation (ἀπλοία κεναγγεῖ ['store-jars empty from not sailing'], 188, πνοιαὶ ... νήστιδες ['winds bringing starvation'], 192–3). Aeschylus may have derived this detail from the Brauronian tradition, according to which the need for sacrifice is precipitated by a λιμός ('famine') which Artemis has caused (Schol. *Lysist.* 645; Suda, s.v. ἄρκτος); in reporting the same tradition, Eustath. *Il.* 331.26 and the author of the note in Bekker *Anec.* 444 speak of a λοιμός ['plague']. None of the other versions of what happened at Aulis mention starvation.

[36] The motif of biting or eating also enters into the description of Troy's destruction: Ἀργεῖον δάκος ['the beast of Argos'] (824), ὠμηστὴς λέων ['the ravening lion'] (827).

πύργοις ... δίκτυον ... γάγγαμον, 357–61; κυναγοὶ κατ' ἴχνος, 695).
This, I would argue, is the *primary* reference of the omen; here we are
in agreement with Lloyd-Jones' conclusion, if not with his reasons. It
is not as an arbitrary partisan of Troy, but as patroness of innocent
youth and fertility that Artemis recoils from the indiscriminate
predation which she knows a war under the Atreidae will be. Fraenkel[37] (and Whallon appears to follow him[38]) denies this on the
grounds that no reference is made to the harm done the young at
Troy in the interpretation of Calchas. But it is certainly implied in
what Calchas says, and Fraenkel seems to recognize this: 'From the
fact that the eagles mercilessly devour the hare with her unborn
young the seer seems to infer that Troy and *all that is in the city
will be completely and violently destroyed.* The violence is strongly
emphasized in λαπάξει πρὸς τὸ βίαιον ['will sack in violence', 130],
and that it is to be wholesale destruction is illustrated by a suggestive
detail: not even the flocks outside will be spared, much less anything
within the walls of the conquered city.'[39] It is quite natural that
Calchas, conscious of the consequences that δυσφημία ['words of
ill-omen'] may have, should avoid being as explicit about the unpro-
pitious half of the omen—the cause of Artemis' anger—as he has
been about the forecast of victory.[40]

But as if this indirect reference to young Trojan victims of
the war were not enough, the poet vividly recalls the detail in the
next choral ode. The motif of the hunt, begun in the parodos
(120, 126, 135), is resumed: the capture of Troy is described as the

---

[37] Fraenkel (n. 2), ii.96–7.   [38] Whallon (n. 2), 81.
[39] Fraenkel (n. 2), ii.96; italics added.
[40] H. Lloyd-Jones, 'Three notes on Aeschylus' *Agamemnon*', *RhM* 103 (1960),
76–80, at 76–8 [= *Greek Epic, Lyric, and Tragedy* (Oxford, 1990), 305–9, at 305–6],
argues that Calchas, in the expression κτήνη ... δημιοπλήθεα, with the tendency
Greek prophets show of referring to people by animal names, is referring to the
Trojans, not to their cattle: 'the herds which are the people'. If this is the case, it should
be further noted that an interpretation as cryptic as the omen itself would be odd,
unless, as I have suggested, the interpreter had good reason to avoid straightforward
speech—the fear of naming undesirable possibilities. No reader will have missed the
sharp contrast between the clarity of lines 122–5 (explaining the propitious side of
the omen, and identifying the eagles as the Atreidae and the hare as Troy) and lines
126–55, where, besides the calculated indirection of the language, one may note that
the expected explanation of the unborn young is never explicitly made.

casting of a hunting-net from which neither old *nor young* can extricate themselves (357–61):

... ἐπὶ Τροίας πύργοις ἔβαλες
στεγανὸν δίκτυον ὡς μήτε μέγαν
μήτ' οὖν νεαρῶν τιν' ὑπερτελέσαι
μέγα δουλείας
γάγγαμον ἄτης παναλώτου.

... you threw your mesh to cover Troy's battlements
so that no one full-grown, nor any of the very young, might rise above
the great dredge-net of slavery which captures all.

Note how οὖν adds emphasis to νεαρῶν ['of the very young'], a word which, as Fraenkel himself points out (ad loc.), is properly, though by no means exclusively, used of young wild animals, and which certainly carries this connotation in the context of the hunting-net. The choice of this word itself and of the whole hunting image at once describes the event and recalls the omen which forecast it.[41] If, as is unlikely, the terms of the omen itself were not sufficient to have reminded a fifth-century audience of the Homeric Agamemnon's desire, memorable in its ferocity, that every Trojan perish utterly, *including the unborn child in the womb* (*Il.* 6.57–60[42]) then this passage would surely have done so, concentrating as it does upon the fate of the young and emphasizing the barbaric completeness[43] of

---

[41] If we accept Weil's φυτάλμιοι παιδῶν γέροντες ['old men, their fathers, (fallen about the bodies) of their children'] or Denniston-Page's φυταλμίων παιδῶν γέροντες ['old men (fallen about the bodies) of children whom they had begotten'] for the clumsy φυταλμίων παῖδες γερόντων ['children (fallen about the bodies) of old men their procreators'] of the manuscripts at 327–8, we have another, though less emphatic, reference to the fate of the young at Troy [translations from Denniston-Page]. Furthermore, in line 528, καὶ σπέρμα πάσης ἐξαπόλλυται χθονός ['the seed was utterly destroyed from the land'], though the metaphor is different, the referent is the same: killing—complete and indiscriminate.

[42] τῶν [sc. Τρώων] μή τις ὑπεκφύγοι αἰπὺν ὄλεθρον | χεῖρας θ' ἡμετέρας, μηδ' ὅν τινα γαστέρι μήτηρ | κοῦρον ἐόντα φέροι, μηδ' ὃς φύγοι, ἀλλ' ἅμα πάντες | Ἰλίου ἐξαπολοίατ' ἀκήδεστοι καὶ ἄφαντοι ['Not one of them (sc. the Trojans) must escape stark destruction at our hands, even the boys still carried in their mothers' wombs—not even they must escape, but all be extinguished together, wiped from Ilios without sight or ceremony' (tr. M. Hammond)].

[43] To a fifth-century Athenian, not to spare the young would be un-Greek. Compare Thucydides' account of the massacre perpetrated by Thracian mercenaries at Mycalessus (7.29.4), where, as in the Aeschylean account, the historian concentrates upon the fate of the children and the indiscriminate slaughter of every living

the havoc (ἄτης παναλώτου [lit. 'all-catching doom', 361]). We are left
with the overwhelming impression that the Argives, especially their
commander, are not mere hunters, but vicious, pitiless, indiscriminate hunters, who must naturally incur the hatred of her in whose
honour young hares, as Xenophon tells us, were traditionally spared
by huntsmen.[44]

II

In the logic of the drama, then, Artemis, particularly under her
Brauronian aspect of fertility goddess and guardian of the young
and innocent, is angry principally over the innocent victims of the
impending war. Yet, we must not, with Daube, regard the sacrifice of
Iphigeneia as an *atonement* or *appeasement* demanded by Artemis of
Agamemnon in advance for what he will do at Troy.[45] The sacrifice of

---

thing in sight: ἐσπεσόντες δὲ οἱ Θρᾷκες ἐς τὴν Μυκαλησσὸν τάς τε οἰκίας καὶ τὰ ἱερὰ
ἐπόρθουν (cf. *Ag.* 527) καὶ τοὺς ἀνθρώπους ἐφόνευον φειδόμενοι οὔτε πρεσβυτέρας οὔτε
νεωτέρας ἡλικίας (cf. *Ag.* 358–9), ἀλλὰ πάντας ἑξῆς ὅτῳ ἐντύχοιεν καὶ παῖδας καὶ
γυναῖκας κτείνοντες, καὶ προσέτι καὶ ὑποζύγια καὶ ὅσα ἄλλα ἔμψυχα ἴδοιεν (cf. *Ag.*
528) ['The Thracians burst into Mycalessus, sacked the houses and temples
(cf. *Ag.* 527) and butchered the inhabitants, sparing neither the young nor the old
(cf. *Ag.* 358–9), but methodically killing everyone they met, women and children
alike, and even the farm animals and every living thing they saw (cf. *Ag.* 528)'
(tr. R. Warner)].

[44] *Cyn.* 5.14: τὰ μὲν οὖν λίαν νεογνὰ [sc. τῶν λαγίων] οἱ φιλοκυνηγέται ἀφιᾶσι τῇ
θεῷ ['Sportsmen leave the very young ones (sc. of the leverets) to the goddess'].
Fraenkel (n. 2), ii.84 n. 1, argues that this passage sheds no light on the omen:
'Neither god nor man can expect of eagles the behaviour of φιλοκυνηγέται ['sportsmen']'—as if the eagles stood for nothing beyond themselves!

[45] B. Daube, *Zu den Rechtsproblemen in Aischylos' Agamemnon* (Zurich, 1938),
147 ff. Fraenkel (n. 2), ii.97 and Whallon with him (n. 2) 81 imply that the only
conceivable relationship between the omen (with the ensuing sacrifice of Iphigeneia)
and the events at Troy can be one of *atonement*. They therefore reject such a
relationship on the grounds that 'the fundamental maxim δράσαντι παθεῖν ['the
doer shall suffer'] cannot be supplanted by a δράσοντι παθεῖν ['the one who *will* do
shall suffer']' (Fraenkel), implying that the death of Iphigeneia is a πάθος ['suffering']
of Agamemnon. How relevant the principle δράσαντι παθεῖν ['the doer shall suffer']
is to Agamemnon as sacrificer of Iphigeneia is at best doubtful; actually, where
the principle is explicitly applied to him, his πάθος ['suffering'] is *his own* (not
Iphigeneia's) death, and what he has *done* to deserve it is the sacrifice of Iphigeneia;

Iphigeneia is itself a partial cause of Artemis' anger. We may not say, with Whallon, that Artemis was 'a deity whose punitive actions became predacious,'[46] unless it can be shown that she desires and causes the death of Iphigeneia. The precise nature of Artemis' demand is a critical adjunct of our interpretation of the omen and must occupy us at this point for the light it throws on Agamemnon's guilt. For in the dramatic economy of the trilogy it is, as Fraenkel insists, the death of Iphigeneia which is, at the level of human agency, the first sufficient cause (πρωτοπήμων, 223) of the ensuing chain of troubles. Aeschylus, again departing significantly from the Homeric tradition, makes it quite clear in the feeble character of Aegisthus, effeminate foil to the masculine Clytemnestra, that the crime of Atreus, though a contributing factor, is not a sufficient cause of what follows.[47] Who then is responsible for the inciting incident—the death of Iphigeneia? The goddess who requires the sacrifice or the man who performs it?

Is it correct to say that Artemis *demands* the sacrifice of Iphigeneia? All the text tells us (in the words of Calchas) is that she caused adverse winds, precipitating (σπευδομένα) the sacrifice (148–50), and that the sacrifice was a μῆχαρ (199), an *expedient* or *remedy* for the bad weather, proposed by Calchas, and uncontested by Agamemnon (μάντιν οὔτινα ψέγων ['blaming no seer'], 186). Artemis compels Agamemnon to nothing. She merely creates a situation in which he may either cancel the war, or else pursue it by inflicting on his own

---

Ag. 1526–7: Ἰφιγένειαν ἀνάξια δράσας ἄξια πάσχων ['suffering what he deserved having done to Iphigeneia what she did not deserve'] (compare 1564: παθεῖν τὸν ἔρξαντα ['the doer shall suffer']). In any case, it will not be for Fraenkel's reason that we reject the notion of Iphigeneia's death as an atonement in the ensuing argument.

[46] Whallon (n. 2), 87.

[47] Cf. Henri Weil, *Études sur la drame antique* (Paris, 1897), 39, and N. G. L. Hammond, 'Personal freedom and its limitations in the *Oresteia*', *JHS* 85 (1965), 42–55, at 42 [= M. H. McCall (ed.), *Aeschylus: A Collection of Critical Essays* (Englewood Cliffs NJ, 1972), 90–105, at 90–1 = *Studies in Greek History* (Oxford, 1973), 395–416, at 395–6]. Here we are in disagreement with Lloyd-Jones and Page who believe that the *fons et origo* of the action of the trilogy is the curse upon Atreus, and that Agamemnon, acting under its compulsion, is punished for the crime of his father. In what follows we will argue not against the notion of son punished for father's wrongs (it is a function of the reconciled Erinyes, *Eum.* 934 ff.), but against the idea that this is the exclusive or sufficient cause of Agamemnon's fate (as it is in Homer), and that Agamemnon is the victim of external compulsion.

household the kind of slaughter he will perpetrate at Troy. αἰτία ἑλομένου· θεὸς ἀναίτιος ['responsibility lies with the person who makes the choice; god is not responsible', Pl. *Resp.* 617e4–5] (or at most μεταίτιος ['jointly responsible']). The result depends less upon the goddess than upon the kind of man Agamemnon is. And it is because Calchas knows what kind of man he is that he can speak of Artemis 'precipitating' Iphigeneia's sacrifice by creating contrary winds. Some critics will, no doubt, find that this condition imposed by Artemis rather vitiates the picture I have drawn of her overmastering concern with the suffering young. But this (as any) estimate of the goddess depends upon whether or not Agamemnon has a reasonable alternative to the sacrifice of Iphigeneia. If such an alternative is wanting, then indeed Artemis at this point is not only inconsistent, but vicious. But is the alternative wanting?

We have suggested that Agamemnon is *free* to sacrifice or not to sacrifice Iphigeneia, to pursue the war against Troy or not to do so. Is this in fact true? Page,[48] Lloyd-Jones,[49] Fraenkel,[50] and Whallon[51] all insist that Agamemnon acts if not under compulsion, at least without a harmless alternative, that the war is a holy command of Zeus Xenios and not to pursue it is to incur punishment at his hands. The text seems to lend strong support to such a position. At 60–2, we are told by the chorus, Ἀτρέως παῖδας ὁ κρείσσων ἐπ' Ἀλεξάνδρῳ πέμπει ξένιος Ζεύς ['the mighty Zeus who guards hospitality sends Atreus' sons against Paris']. They speak even more strongly at 362–3 of Troy's destruction as the work of Zeus (Δία τοι ξένιον ... τὸν τάδε πράξαντα ['Zeus of Hospitality who has carried this through']), and at 367 as his stroke (Διὸς πλαγάν ['Zeus' blow']). Similarly, at 748,

[48] Page (n. 2), pp. xxiii–xxiv.

[49] Lloyd-Jones (n. 2), 193 [= *Greek Epic, Lyric, and Tragedy* 291–2 = *Oxford Readings in Greek Tragedy*, 65].

[50] Fraenkel (n. 2), iii.726: 'The common man may content himself with the wish μὴ εἴην πτολιπόρθης ['may I not be a city-sacker', *Ag.* 472] and hope thus to escape irrevocable conflicts, but the man on whom God has laid the burden of a great undertaking, seeing in front of him two ways open, may feel that whichever way he chooses there is no way out of evil'. See also ii.122–3.

[51] Whallon (n. 2), 83–4: 'Sent by Zeus as an Erinys against Troy, Agamemnon has no attractive choice. He faces the conflict between the punitive forces, Artemis and the Erinyes, and is scourged by the one for satisfying the other.... It is difficult to attach blame to Agamemnon. He sacrifices his daughter with free will, it is true, but an inimical cosmos has confronted him with a dilemma.'

they tell us that Helen, with the Argive army close behind her, brought doom to the Priamids, πομπᾷ Διὸς ξενίου ('escorted by Zeus god of hosts'), and Agamemnon at 853 greets the gods who sent him on the expedition and brought him back again (οἵπερ πρόσω πέμψαντες ἤγαγον πάλιν ['who sent me out and brought me back again']). But what seems 'final and decisive' (in Page's words) is the description at 218 of Agamemnon's sacrifice of his daughter as *inevitable* (ἀνάγκας ἔδυ λέπαδνον ['he put on the yoke-strap of necessity']).

Here again we must be on our guard against the pitfalls of literalism. In particular, we must avoid confusing two quite distinct elements: on the one hand, the descriptive narrative of what happened in purely human causal terms, and on the other, the religious generalization or interpretation of those same events. The first states an individual and contingent fact; the second, usually made after the event, sees it as an instance of universal and necessary law. We must not confuse the statements of the chorus with a dramatic *intervention* of the gods, either offstage or on, as in the *Eumenides* (though these too, I would insist, must be interpreted in other than literal terms). Neither text nor tradition will warrant our assuming that Aeschylus or the chorus mean here an actual epiphany of Zeus to Agamemnon with a mandate to attack Troy, nor do I think any of the critics would defend such an absurd interpretation. How then are we to understand the statement 'Zeus *sent* Agamemnon'? Is there a standing mandate of Zeus which obliges men *under threat of their own punishment* to avenge all violations of hospitality personally and regardless of cost? None at all. In fact, *Eum.* 269–75 (compare *Frogs* 145–6) records the belief that those who go unrequited for harming a guest-friend are punished hereafter. It must be remembered that we are not dealing here with the same kind of situation as vengeance for murder—Orestes' situation—where the kinsman-avenger is himself treated as a murderer if he neglects his duty. To my knowledge, there are no examples from antiquity of punishment meted out to those who do not avenge a crime against hospitality.[52] Indeed, were the

<hr/>

[52] Cf. George M. Calhoun in Wace and Stubbings, *A Companion to Homer* (New York 1963), 450: 'It is worth noting that the offences which invite divine reprobation [in Homer] are precisely those for which human justice in a simple society will be least likely to offer adequate remedies—neglect of the dead, *injuries to suppliants or*

imperative to vengeance as coercive as Page suggests, one wonders why Agamemnon should not employ so compelling an argument in favour of sacrificing Iphigeneia, or why the poet should not use a stronger verb than πέμπειν ['send'] to mean 'command' or 'demand'.

The statement 'Zeus sent the Atreidae...' is a religious interpretation of the chorus, not an empirical description. It does no more than indicate their belief in the right or legal claim under which the war might be justified. Zeus Xenios *permits, justifies, supports* the war, but nothing in the text suggests that he *obliges*. After the event, the chorus sees the destruction of Troy as retribution fulfilled for a crime hateful to Zeus Xenios, and can, therefore, speak of the war as the stroke (367) or the work (362) of Zeus, and of the Atreidae as his avenging instruments.[53] The poet's *Persians* is full of similar statements about the agency of the gods in a historical event that had occurred in his own lifetime.[54] It is not likely that a veteran of Salamis would take Aeschylus literally when his messenger in the play claims that a *daimon* destroyed the Persian fleet, and that the gods saved Athens (345–7, compare 724–5), or when the chorus calls Zeus the destroyer of the Persian force (532–4, compare 739–40). These were not observable phenomena in the literal sense, but interpretations raising the events of the war beyond the realm of contingency and accident, endowing them with some degree of normativeness, and seeing in them the manifestation and verification of laws whose definition was the product of faith and hope more than of experience. Clearly such statements about divine activity and necessity do not devaluate human accomplishment, eliminate human responsibility, or purge decision of its perils. The Greeks who in the *Persians* are heard to shout νῦν ὑπὲρ πάντων ἀγών ['in the struggle now everything is at stake', 405] are less assured of their divine mission than the messenger who later reports the outcome. After the event, what appears is such an interpenetration of divine and human

guests, the perversion of justice' (italics added). Compare Hesiod, whose assurances about the chastisement meted out by Zeus to the unjust man are statements of religious hope rather than empirical observations, as is clear in *Op.* 267–73.

[53] If, on the other hand, a crime against hospitality goes unrequited, Zeus Xenios himself is subject to criticism: cf. Aesch. frag. 496 Mette = *TrGF* 451h.

[54] *Pers.* 94–9, 107–15, 337–47, 353–4, 362, 454–5, 515–16, 532–6, 604, 724–5, 740–2, 772, 918–21.

agency that the line dividing them is blurred: Xerxes, for example, is duped both by the guile of a Greek *and* the φθόνος ['envy'] of the gods (361–2). The ghost of Darius enunciates this double aspect of an action in a general principle (742):[55] ὅταν σπεύδῃ τις αὐτός, χὠ θεὸς συνάπτεται ['when someone strives eagerly himself, the god too lends a hand'].

The other half of the argument against Agamemnon's freedom lies in the poet's use of the word ἀνάγκη ['necessity'] at 218: ἀνάγκας ἔδυ λέπαδνον ['he put on the yoke-strap of necessity']. Page is quite right to insist that it not be toned down to mean 'bodily pain,' or 'anguish', but that it retain the full meaning of *inevitability* its usage elsewhere demands. But there are grounds for disagreement over what precisely ἀνάγκη ['necessity'] refers to. Is it Iphigeneia's sacrifice itself, or the *inevitable consequences* of that action? Page categorically denies the latter, without offering any argument. Yet, what is the overriding preoccupation of the chorus in this ode as throughout the play if not the *inevitable consequences* of unjust acts, both Paris'[56] and Agamemnon's? This automatic chain of cause and effect which springs from a single free act and issues in the ruin of a man or a whole house constitutes the burden of the chorus' inmost thoughts, despite Agamemnon's safe return, right up to the moment of his murder, and long afterwards. What more felicitous metaphor could the poet have found for this idea than to say that Agamemnon himself *'put on*

---

[55] Compare: φιλεῖ δὲ τῷ κάμνοντι συσπεύδειν θεός ['god eagerly assists the one who toils', frag. 673 Mette = *TrGF* 395], and the statement of Themistocles, reported by Herodotus (8.60): μὴ δὲ οἰκότα βουλευομένοισι οὐκ ἐθέλει οὐδὲ ὁ θεὸς προσχωρέειν πρὸς τὰς ἀνθρωπηίας γνώμας ['the purposes of those who do not make sensible plans are not supported by the gods either']. Incidentally, this remark of Themistocles is surely a better index of the state of mind in Athens *during the events themselves* than the later tales of divine intervention collected by Herodotus. In any case, it is not easy to ascertain how popular such tales were or how widely believed.

How much the sophistic separation of the divine and human aspects of an action can lead to a denial of human responsibility and an excuse for misconduct may be seen in Euripides' *Cyclops*. When Polyphemus reproaches the Greeks for having fought a war over one shameless woman, the corrupt and sophistical Odysseus disclaims responsibility (285): θεοῦ τὸ πρᾶγμα· μηδέν' αἰτιῶ βροτῶν ['it was the doing of a god: blame no mortal for it'].

[56] Consistent, if mistaken, Page (n. 2), 104 sees in Paris the same innocence and the same divine compulsion due to a family curse as he sees in Agamemnon.

the harness of necessity'? The verb ἔδυ ['he put on'], with an accoutrement like λέπαδνον ['yoke-strap'], can hardly support a toned-down meaning like 'fell into', 'bowed down beneath', or passive meaning like 'was put on him'.[57] In terms of freedom and compulsion, this passage is analogous to the choice of lives by the souls in Plato's myth of Er (*Rep.* 614b–621b): the choice is free; what follows is necessity. The gods are responsible for the necessary chain of cause and effect; man is responsible for its inception or application.[58]

In a further attempt to exculpate Agamemnon, Page argues that the king is externally compelled not only by the gods but even at the *human* level: Agamemnon (Page tells us) guesses that were he not to

[57] By contrast, all the parallel yoke-metaphors cited by Fraenkel and Headlam–Thomson have *passive* forms (usually of ζεύγνυμι ['yoke']) or neutral meanings, e.g., Eurip. *IA* 443, ἐς οἷ' ἀνάγκης ζεύγματ' ἐμπεπτώκαμεν ['under what a yoke of necessity I have fallen'] and *Or.* 1330, ἀνάγκης δ' ἐς ζυγὸν καθέσταμεν ['we are under the yoke of necessity']. *PV* 108, ἀνάγκαις ταῖσδ' ἐνέζευγμαι τάλας ['I have, in my misery, put on the yoke of these constraints'], is probably an exception. Its meaning is identical with ἀνάγκας ἔδυ λέπαδνον ['he put on the yoke-strap of necessity'] if ἐνέζευγμαι is read as a middle ['I have put on']. Such a reading would seem to be required by Prometheus' insistence, a few lines earlier (101–5), that he had foreknown with utter certainty the *necessary consequences* of his action. Thus, he says, by performing it, he has in effect *put himself* in the yoke of necessity—an idea to which he returns at 266: ἑκὼν ἑκὼν ἥμαρτον ['Deliberately I did wrong, deliberately'].

D. J. Conacher, in a recent study (*Euripidean Drama* (Toronto, 1967), 241 n. 17), points out that Menoeceus in the *Phoenissae* (999–1005) seems to use the expression in a manner hardly different from Aeschylus at *Ag.* 218; 'yet,' Conacher insists, 'it is quite clear that Menoeceus considers himself as having a choice here, for he declares how base and cowardly it would be to choose the alternative of fleeing from this necessity'.

[58] The result of this dual aspect of human action is often the juxtaposition of remarkably strong expressions for compulsion with expressions of human spontaneity and freedom, equally strong, without incompatibility. For example, in the Homeric description of Clytemnestra's seduction by Aegisthus (*Od.* 3.269–72) we read: ἀλλ' ὅτε δή μιν μοῖρα θεῶν ἐπέδησε δαμῆναι... | τὴν δ' ἐθέλων ἐθέλουσαν ἀνήγαγεν ὅνδε δόμονδε ['But when the gods' purpose ordained that she should yield...he took (her) to his own home, and he and she were of one mind', tr. W. H. Shewring]. In the same vein, Plato can say of the Athenians (*Laws* 642c): μόνοι γὰρ ἄνευ ἀνάγκης, αὐτοφυῶς, θείᾳ μοίρᾳ, ἀληθῶς καὶ οὔτι πλαστῶς εἰσὶν ἀγαθοί ['they alone are good without compulsion, naturally, by divine fate, truly and unfeignedly']. In the *Agamemnon* itself, the chorus can, without apparent contradiction, speak of Zeus as παναίτιος πανεργάτης ['the all-causing, the all-doing'] (1486) and fifteen lines later deny that Clytemnestra is ἀναίτιος ['without responsibility'] (1505). So also Aegisthus admits responsibility (1604) for what he has called not too many lines previously the handiwork of the Erinyes (1580). Compare *Eum.* 199: the Erinyes claim that Apollo is παναίτιος ['wholly responsible'] yet they pursue Orestes.

sacrifice Iphigeneia, the other Achaean leaders would do so.[59] He
urges that the only alternative mentioned is to become a λιπόναυς
['deserter of the fleet', 212], which Agamemnon rejects 'immediately'
on the ground that it would not thus save his daughter. This curious
embellishment, it need hardly be stated, has little, if any, substanti-
ation in the text.[60] Fraenkel, without going so far, still sees in
λιπόναυς γενέσθαι ['become a deserter of the fleet'] an unthinkable
and unrealistic alternative: 'such an action would be criminal for any
member of the expedition, how much more for the commander'.[61]
But how can it be criminal for the Atreidae, leaders of the expedition
and 'plaintiffs' (41) in the legal claim justifying (but not *obliging*)
them in the war, to call it off at Aulis? Does Agamemnon face danger
as a 'deserter'?[62] Again, nothing in the text suggests this. In a context
where, if Fraenkel and Page were correct, we would reasonably expect
such a consideration to be prominent, neither Agamemnon nor the
chorus make anything of it.[63] For Agamemnon to call the sacrificial
murder θέμις ['Right'] (217, if indeed that is what he is doing in this
much vexed portion of the text), does not make it so, and must be
considered at best hyperbole, at worst rationalization.[64]

In evaluating Agamemnon's responsibility there has not been sufficient attention paid to the sharply drawn contrast between the pretext
of the war (Helen) and its cost (Iphigeneia and the large number of
Argive and Trojan casualties). Aeschylus' emphasis upon Iphigeneia's
virginity (210, 215, 229, 245) sets her off from Helen, the πολυάνωρ
γυνή ['woman with many husbands', 62], the 'heart-tearing
flower of desire' (δηξίθυμον ἔρωτος ἄνθος, 743). The light, delicate,

[59] Page (n. 2), p. xxvii.
[60] Thomson (n. 30), ii.22 adds a further consideration: even granting the possibility of Iphigeneia's sacrifice by the other commanders, why does Agamemnon
choose to do it himself when he might, if others did the deed, escape blood guilt
μιαίνων ... πατρῴους χέρας ['polluting a father's hands'] (209–10)?
[61] Fraenkel (n. 2), ii.122–3.
[62] Like Achilles in Aeschylus' *Myrmidons* (?) (frag. 225 Mette = *TrGF* 132c).
[63] Aeschylus leaves nothing implied in dealing with a moral dilemma. Note how
fully detailed the consideration of alternatives is in the case of Orestes (*Cho.* 269–305)
and Pelasgus (*Supp.* 468–89).
[64] One is reminded of a remark attributed to Democritus (192 DK): ἔστι ῥάδιον
μὲν ἐπαινεῖν ἃ μὴ χρὴ καὶ ψέγειν, ἑκάτερον δὲ πονηροῦ τινος ἦθος ['it is easy both to
praise and to condemn what one should not; both are signs of a bad character
(*ethos*)'].

234   John J. Peradotto

untrammelled movement of Helen (407, 425, 690–2, 737–40) contrasts with the brutal constraints pressed upon Iphigeneia (235–7). Helen's seductive μαλθακὸν ὀμμάτων βέλος ['eyes throwing melting glances'] (742) recalls its foil, Iphigeneia's piteous but unpersuasive glance at her murderers ἀπ' ὀμμάτων βέλει φιλοίκτῳ ['a bolt from her eyes to move compassion'] (240),[65] just as the sensual hangings of the older woman's bed-chamber ἁβροπήνων προκαλυμμάτων ['filmy chamber-curtains'] (690) ironically sharpen in retrospect the pathos in the image of the young girl's κροκωτόν ['saffron gown'] spilling in saffron folds to the ground at the sacrificial altar (239). As for the disproportionate extent of the Atreid retaliation, the chorus returns to it relentlessly. In their opening anapaests the magnitude of the expedition is emphasized χιλιοναύτην ['a thousand ships'] (45); μέγαν... Ἄρη ['mighty war'] (48), and in a startling jeu de mots the extent of the suffering is ironically compared with its object—πολυάνορος ἀμφὶ γυναικὸς πολλὰ παλαίσματα καὶ γυιοβαρῆ ['because of a woman with many husbands to make many bouts of wrestling heavy of the limbs'] (62–3), an idea repeated at 694 (πολύανδροι ['with many men']). Menelaus' dreamy, erotic grief over the loss of Helen is set sharply against the brooding anguish of the community for the Argive dead (408–36); their ashes, measured against the woman they fought to win back, rouse public indignation (445–51). The Argive elders actually accuse Agamemnon to his face of madness in recovering a 'willing wanton' (θράσος ἑκούσιον) at the cost of dying men (799–804),[66] while only for the king himself is the disproportion in his vengeance a point of pride (823–8). The king's own death in the eyes of the chorus is the crowning achievement of Helen's mass-destructiveness (1455–60):

ἰώ· παράνους Ἑλένα,
μία τὰς πολλάς, τὰς πάνυ πολλὰς
ψυχὰς ὀλέσασ' ὑπὸ Τροίᾳ
νῦν τελέαν πολύμναστον ἐπηνθίσω
δι' αἷμ' ἄνιπτον.

O you demented Helen,
singly destroying those many,

[65] For another version of the young girl's innocent glance and its seductive counterpart, see fragments 420 and 421 Mette = TrGF 242 and 243 from the Toxotides.

[66] For a defence of the manuscript reading, θράσος ἑκούσιον, against Fraenkel's suspicion and Page's absolute rejection, see Headlam–Thomson (n. 30), ii.66.

all too many lives under Troy!
Now you have crowned yourself with the unforgettable flowers of fulfilment,
because of blood not to be washed away.

A young girl's innocent blood is shed to launch a war for an adulterous woman (225–7), involving a holocaust of victims and regicide.
The war is thus a demonic perversion of society's extermination of
the offender recognized as a public menace. The moral condemnation implied in all these contrasts far outweighs the cold comfort that
its legal sanction is the law of hospitality.[67]

In his decision to sacrifice Iphigeneia and pursue the war for Helen
Agamemnon suffers no external coercion.[68] As we have tried to demonstrate, his choice depends less upon Zeus or Artemis than upon
the kind of man he is, his *ethos*. A man's *ethos* is the abiding disposition
or habitual texture of his mind and behaviour. In Greek tragedy it is
usually a relatively uncomplicated matter: one or two basic and easily
definable attitudes which motivate every significant decision a given
character makes. In Aristotelian terms (useful here insofar as they
originate in large measure from both a descriptive analysis of tragedy
[the *Poetics*] and a discursive mode of examining the moral act closer
to our own [the *Nicomachean Ethics*]), *ethos* is the 'ground' of moral
choice (προαίρεσις); in tragedy, Aristotle says, it reveals what course of
action a man will take where this would not otherwise be clear in the
situation itself.[69] Put in slightly different terms, decision or choice

---

[67] The moral implications of the Trojan War in such terms as these are not a major
concern of the *Iliad*, where its *raison d'être* is to provide an arena for heroic achievement
rather than to attain a more specific pragmatic purpose like the return of Helen or the
punishment of Paris. Still, something like the Aeschylean contrast between the alleged
justification for the war and its toll in human lives and suffering is present in Hector's
rebuke of Paris in Book 6, and in Achilles' complaint (9.321–41) that he suffers the
bloody business of battle for other people's women (ὁάρων ἕνεκα σφετεράων).

The most explicit condemnation of the Greek expedition against Troy appears, of
course, in the Persian account of the origins of the antipathy between East and West
reported by Herodotus (1.3–4).

[68] See Albin Lesky, 'Decision and responsibility in the tragedy of Aeschylus', *JHS* 86
(1966), 78–85 [= Segal (n. 2), 13–23]. Lesky's conclusions and those of the present
study are in the main similar, though the line of argument and the interpretation of
Agamemnon's dilemma are different.

[69] *Poet.* 1450[b]8: ἔστιν δὲ ἦθος μὲν τὸ τοιοῦτον ὃ δηλοῖ προαίρεσιν, ὁποῖά τις ἐν οἷς
οὐκ ἔστι δῆλον ἢ προαιρεῖται ἢ φεύγει. Compare *Poet.* 1454[a]17, *Rhet.* 1395[b]13,
1417[a]16, and *NE* 1139[a]23.

discloses the moral motivation of an action and the *ethos* of the agent. Though in the *Ethics* Aristotle lays chief stress upon the *formation* of *ethos,* he is at one with his predecessors in treating it as fairly fixed; once known, the decisions and acts emanating from it are, if not automatic and predictable, at least expected. The constitutive elements of *ethos* are varied, but the early aristocratic emphasis upon heredity as an important (if not its prime) factor never quite disappears. In the *Oresteia* the idea of inherited *ethos* is a motif of major significance.

The chorus presents the idea most explicitly in the second stasimon of the *Agamemnon.* The lion-cub (717–36), despite a τροφή ['nurture'][70] calculated to alter its natural character, ultimately displays its inherited disposition of savagery (χρονίσθεις ἀπέδειξεν ἦθος τὸ πρὸς τοκέων ['Brought on by time however it displayed the nature which came from its parents'], 727–8).[71] Not much later, the chorus transfers the idea of inherited *ethos* from agents to actions (758–65): the unholy act proliferates (πλείονα τίκτει) others exactly like itself (σφετέρᾳ δ᾽ εἰκότα γέννᾳ); old hybris tends to breed (τίκτειν) youthful (νεάζουσαν) hybris, when the day of delivery (φάος τόκου) arrives; black ἄτη ('ruin') comes into being, resembling its parents (εἰσομένας τοκεῦσιν).

Like the lion in the parable, Agamemnon has inherited his father's predatory and teknophonous *ethos,* an *ethos* incidentally which is quite consistent with the portrayal of Agamemnon in the literary tradition.[72] It is this *ethos* that Artemis chiefly hates; it is this *ethos*

---

[70] The emphasis upon τροφή ['nurture'] in opposition to *ethos* is unmistakable: ἔθρεψε ['nurtured'] (717), νεοτρόφου ['nursling'] (724), τροφεῦσιν ['rearers'] (729), προσεθρέφθη ['it was reared'] (736).

[71] Compare especially Pindar (all translations by W. H. Race), *Ol.* 9.100: τὸ δὲ φυᾷ κράτιστον ἅπαν ['What comes by nature is altogether best']; *Ol.* 11.19–20: τὸ γὰρ ἐμφυὲς οὔτ᾽ αἴθων ἀλώπηξ οὔτ᾽ ἐρίβρομοι λέοντες διαλλάξαντο ἦθος ['neither ruddy fox nor roaring lions could change their inborn character (*ethos*)']; *Ol.* 13.13: ἄμαχον δὲ κρύψαι τὸ συγγενὲς ἦθος ['one cannot conceal the character (*ethos*) that is inborn']; *Pyth.* 8.44–5: φυᾷ τὸ γενναῖον ἐπιπρέπει ἐκ πατέρων παισὶ λῆμα ['By nature the noble resolve from fathers shines forth in their sons']; *Pyth.* 10.12: τὸ δὲ συγγενὲς ἐμβέβηκεν ἴχνευσιν πατρός ['by inherited ability he has trod in the footsteps of his father'].

[72] In the *Iliad,* Agamemnon's *aristeia* (11.15–283) is unmatched in its savagery and brutality: his shield bears the dreadful face of the Gorgon (36); in killing his opponents he is compared to a lion crunching in his teeth the νήπια τέκνα ['infant young'] of a deer (101–19); again compared to a lion, he slaughters the suppliant sons of Antimachus (122–42, recalling by contrast the mercy of Menelaus in 6.51 ff., which

that is the source of all three acts symbolized by the portent of the eagles.[73] The situation at Aulis is contrived by the goddess for the disclosure of that *ethos* which will issue in indiscriminate killing at Troy, and which has already led to the murder of Thyestes' children. In so disclosing the *ethos* of Agamemnon, the scene serves a dramatic function similar to his walking over the purple tapestries (944 ff.), which in its relative freedom from external coercion confirms our suspicions about a different but closely related side of Agamemnon's *ethos*, his overweening thirst for ζῆλος—the heroic prestige that makes one the object of emulation and jealousy.[74] At Aulis Agamemnon experiences the existential limitations not only of the particular principle of justice involved in vengeance for violations of hospitality, but of the outmoded quest for heroic ζῆλος ['glory']. His free decision to sacrifice Iphigeneia is a dramatic refusal to honour those limitations, and by it he incurs a punishment more ineluctable than that which he himself inflicts upon Paris. And while a later romantic view of tragic heroism may exalt a self-destructive disdain for the contingencies of human existence, Aeschylean drama is, to use William Lynch's description of true tragedy, 'a sober

occasioned the expression of Agamemnon's blood-thirstiness); a third time he is compared to a lion, now as it slaughters a cow and laps the blood and guts (172–6; cf. *Ag.* 827–8, ὠμηστὴς λέων ᾅδην ἔλειξεν αἵματος ['the ravening lion licked its fill of blood']).

In the tradition, child-killing seems to be an abiding characteristic of the house of Atreus. In Eurip. *IA* (1151–2) we are told that Agamemnon murdered Clytemnestra's infant child by her former husband, Tantalus.

[73] It is not unreasonable to suppose that Plato may have had the *Agamemnon* in mind when, in Er's account near the end of the *Republic,* among the examples of souls whose choice of a life-pattern is largely determined by the character (συνήθεια) of their former existence, Agamemnon is represented choosing the life of an eagle (620b).

[74] Lloyd-Jones (n. 2) 196–7 [= *Greek Epic, Lyric, and Tragedy* 294–5 = Segal 67], accepts Hermann Gundert's thesis (in Θεωρία: Festschrift für W. H. Schuchhardt (Baden-Baden 1960), 69–70) that Agamemnon, against his better judgment, walks the purple because Zeus has taken away his wits (just as at Aulis). But why must Zeus drive Agamemnon mad to make him walk the purple? If, as Lloyd-Jones maintains, Zeus has already determined to ruin Agamemnon for the crime of Atreus, if he is to perish whether he walks the purple or not, what does the action add to the economy of the drama? Nothing, of course, unless it is, like the crisis at Aulis, a means of disclosing *ethos*—the springs of his προαίρεσις ['choice']. It does not bring him any closer to his death; it rather serves to elucidate more fully the relation between his guilt and his punishment.

calculation of the relation of human energy to existence'.[75] Agamemnon's decision cannot be viewed as anything other than what the chorus calls it—παρακοπά, a madness which cannot adjust personal desire and legal claim to the demands of a larger reality, and dares all in the face of doom (τὸ παντοτόλμον φρονεῖν ['to be utterly unscrupulous', *Ag.* 221]). If Agamemnon is victimized, it is by his own *ethos*; the scene at Aulis is Heraclitus' ἦθος ἀνθρώπῳ δαίμων ['Man's *ethos* is his destiny', fr. 119] dramatized.

The various arguments used to exonerate Agamemnon of guilt seem, at least in part, attempts to salvage the tragic integrity of the *Agamemnon*. A morally irresponsible hero, it is assumed, does not engage our sympathy. But we must be on our guard not to confuse dramatic sympathy with moral approval.[76] Even Aristotle, whose tragic pity (ἔλεος) implies a moral judgment, uses the expression τὸ φιλάνθρωπον [lit. 'human-loving'] in situations where it seems to mean a sympathy for human suffering which undercuts moral considerations.[77] There is no question but that Aeschylus elicits profound sympathy for the death of Agamemnon. But we may still insist on his guilt without implying that he arouses our loathing. More important, however, is the fact that Agamemnon is not strictly speaking the hero of the trilogy, nor is the *Agamemnon* itself a complete answer to the questions which are raised in it about crime and punishment. Although in many ways the last two plays of the trilogy lack the artistic polish and dramatic power of the *Agamemnon,* it is clear both from the title of the trilogy[78] and from the dramatic concerns of the final play that Orestes is its central figure.

In the *Choephoroi*, Aeschylus presents Orestes as a moral agent in such a way that a comparison between his *ethos* and that of his parents emerges, and with it the conviction of his innocence and their guilt in other than purely juridical terms. The question at issue in such a comparison is not the relative guilt attached to child-killing, husband-killing, and parent-killing—as the Erinyes and Apollo seem

[75] William F. Lynch, S. J., *Christ and Apollo* (New York, 1960), 75.

[76] Cf. Schlesinger (n. 1), 27.

[77] *Poet.* 1453ᵃ2, 1456ᵃ21. Cf. φιλανθρωπία, *Rhet.* 1390ᵃ20.

[78] That the trilogy was commonly called the *Oresteia* seems fairly certain from the scholion to Aristoph. *Frogs* 1124 and the *didaskaliae* preserved by Aristotle (frag. 575, 1572ᵇ21). Cf. A. E. Haigh, *Tragic Drama of the Greeks* (Oxford, 1896), 114 n. 4.

to imply. This is the discursive content of the final play, and its resolution strikes many readers as somewhat arbitrary. The deeper question, *raised by the intervention of Zeus in Orestes' case,* concerns purity of intent or, if you will, moral sensitivity in the face of the existential limitations of purely legal claims and duties. The purity of intent and moral sensitivity with which Orestes executes his legal claim is a *new* and creative event in the trilogy, for it breaks through the apparently invariable cycle of inherited *ethos*. Aegisthus had appeared as his father in miniature: an adulterer in pursuit of power. Clytemnestra was her sister's double: destructive, adulterous allurement. Agamemnon, like his father Atreus, did not hesitate to take young lives to achieve other ends. The chorus in the first play, aware of this seemingly unvarying sequence of criminal tendencies, derived a *law* from it: the fable of the lion cub and its moral—'sinful deeds proliferate (like plants and animals) after their own kind'. But Orestes as it turns out breaks the pattern and earns, where his father had not, the protective intervention of Zeus.

This is not the place for a detailed study of the *ethos* of Orestes. But a brief examination of the dramatic comparison between him and his parents will be helpful for the light it throws on Agamemnon's guilt as well as on the concept of inherited *ethos* in the trilogy. Orestes has, to be sure, inherited the *ethos* of each of his parents to some degree: he is at once the nestling of the eagle, Agamemnon (*Cho.* 247), and the offspring of the viper, Clytemnestra (*Cho.* 540). He is a lion (*Cho.* 938) like his parents and his aunt Helen. He is, like his father, an Atreid (*Cho.* 407) and a man in the grips of a moral dilemma; he is also like his mother, an avenger, a contriver of guile, a murderer. But there the comparisons end. Orestes' reaction to the unlovely command of the god contrasts sharply with Agamemnon's decision, though superficially they appear alike.[79] His meticulous and agonizing struggle to justify his act and his final hesitancy show a moral

---

[79] Both choose the good of the *polis* (or, in Agamemnon's case, the alliance) as against the good of the family, though it should be hastily added that Agamemnon's action tragically depletes the community; both recognize that their deed is a μίασμα ['pollution'] (*Ag.* 209, *Cho.* 1017); both articulate their sense of mental ἀμηχανία ['helplessness'] (*Ag.* 211: τί τῶνδ' ἄνευ κακῶν ['what is there without evil here?']; *Cho.* 407–9: ἴδεσθ' Ἀτρειδᾶν τὰ λοίπ' ἀμηχάνως ἔχοντα...πᾶ τις τράποιτ' ἄν, ὦ Ζεῦ; ['See here the helpless remnants of the Atreidae...O Zeus, which way to turn?']).

delicacy not evident in Agamemnon's abrupt decision and brutal execution. In contrast to Agamemnon's tenuous rationalization (θέμις κτλ. ['Right', etc.], 214–17), Orestes insists that his strongest incentive was the god's assurance that he would be free of guilt (ἐκτὸς αἰτίας κακῆς εἶναι, 1030–1). While Agamemnon did not stop to question Calchas' interpretation (μάντιν οὔτινα ψέγων ['blaming no seer'], *Ag.* 186), Orestes indicates that, were it not for legitimate personal motives (the recovery of his patrimony, the rescue of Argos from tyranny), the χρησμοί ['oracles'] even of Apollo himself might be repudiated (297–304), even though the alternative to compliance with the oracle is more horrible than any which suggests itself in Agamemnon's case: disease, madness, exile, utter isolation. In this context, even the imagery supports the contrast: Agamemnon puts on (ἔδυ) the constricting harness of compulsion, while Orestes is the young colt yoked (the passive voice is used) to pain's chariot (πώλου εὖνιν ζυγέντ' ἐν ἅρμασιν πημάτων, *Cho.* 794–6). Furthermore, Orestes' act is no heroic quest for ζῆλος ['glory'], the strong motive behind Agamemnon's behaviour, especially in the scene where Clytemnestra induces him to walk the purple; ὁ δ' ἀφθόνητός γ' οὐκ ἐπίζηλος πέλει ['the man free of jealousy never draws envy'] (939), she tells him, and he yields immediately. By contrast, Orestes sees a singular absence of ζῆλος ['glory'] in his victory (*Cho.* 1016–17):

ἀλγῶ μὲν ἔργα καὶ πάθος γένος τε πᾶν,
ἄζηλα νίκης τῆσδ' ἔχων μιάσματα.

I grieve for the deeds and the suffering and the whole family;
and there can be no envy for the pollution my victory here brings to me.

Orestes exhibits even less kinship with his Tyndarid ancestry. Clytemnestra's thirst for power[80] is absent in her son. There is in Orestes' case no adultery[81] complicating the murder-plot and its motivation, and no gloating over his dead victim. There is that

---

[80] On the importance of *kratos* to an understanding of Clytemnestra's character, see R. P. Winnington-Ingram, 'Clytemnestra and the vote of Athena', *JHS* 68 (1948), 130–47 [= *Studies in Aeschylus* (Cambridge, 1983), ch. 6].

[81] Electra, in this as in other respects, shares Orestes' divergence from his parents; cf. *Cho.* 140–1. She is like him an outcast (132 ff.). Her hesitancy before the prospect of vengeance is like his (122). Their respective prayers to Hermes are strikingly similar (compare 1 ff. with 124 ff.), and their hair and footprints identical.

moment of hesitancy to underline the deed's repugnance in his eyes and its discrepancy with his *ethos*, compared to Clytemnestra's triple stroke and the demonic pleasure she admits to have taken in being spattered by her husband's blood. There is unqualified justice in his murder of the other victim, Aegisthus, as usurper and adulterer (*Cho.* 990),[82] while the murder of Cassandra by Clytemnestra (as that of Iphigeneia and Troy's young non-combatants by Agamemnon, and of Thyestes' children by Atreus) was the unjustified slaughter of the innocent. Finally, though he employs guile to enter the house, he does not kill from ambush, as Clytemnestra and Aegisthus had done.[83]

How, in dramatic terms, does the poet account for such divergence from the Atreid *ethos* and the Tyndarid *ethos*? It would seem that the Aeschylean emphasis upon Orestes' (and to some extent Electra's) *alien* τροφή ['nurture'] and fatherless exile serves precisely this purpose. Strophius played the part of father (τρέφει, *Ag.* 880) for him during the ten-year war at Troy, and before that Cilissa nursed him in Clytemnestra's stead. Cilissa's long speech in the *Choephoroi*, with its stress on the τροφή ['nurture']-idea (ἐξέθρεψα, 750; τρέφειν . . . τροφοῦ,[84] 754; τροφεύς, 760; cf. also τροφόν, 731), and its profound expression of grief over the supposed death of her young charge, dramatically explains the weakening of the Tyndarid strain in Orestes,[85] and discloses the

---

[82] Cf. Dem. *In Arist.* 53.

[83] This is no inconsiderable distinction, as we learn later from the trial (*Eum.* 460–1, 627–9). Cf. P. B. R. Forbes, 'Law and politics in the *Oresteia*', *CR* 62 (1948), 99–104, at 100: 'In homicide . . . the kinsman's primitive undiscriminating discretion to kill even the least culpable killer is restricted. The first distinction, e.g. in Israel and in England, is against killing from ambush, "forestealing": and so it seems to have been in Attica, if we may judge by the legal thought inherited by Aeschylus, whose Clytemnestra stands condemned not only on the old criminal count of treason, but also, in the progress of law represented by Apollo, for a killing not open but by deceit.'

[84] Thomson's correction of τρόπῳ.

[85] The attitude toward *ethos*-τροφή ['nurture'] here seems to parallel the implication in Soph. *Ajax* that inherited *ethos* must be fostered and strengthened by a similar τροφή ['nurture']. Ajax claims that his infant son's fearlessness proves fresh slaughter proves his paternity, but that he must still be raised in his father's ways if he is to achieve the same φύσις ['nature'] (545–9): ταρβήσει γὰρ οὔ | νεοσφαγῆ που τόνδε προσλεύσσων φόνον, | εἴπερ δικαίως ἔστ᾽ ἐμὸς τὰ πατρόθεν. | ἀλλ᾽ αὐτίκ᾽ ὠμοῖς αὐτὸν ἐν νόμοις πατρὸς | δεῖ πωλοδαμνεῖν κἀξομοιοῦσθαι φύσιν ['he will have no dread, when he looks on this newly-slaughtered blood, if indeed his inheritance makes him rightly mine. He must immediately be broken in like a young horse in his father's savage ways, and be made like him in his nature', tr. A. F. Garvie].

hollowness of Clytemnestra's ἐγώ σ᾽ ἔθρεψα ['I nurtured you'] (*Cho.* 908) as a plea for mercy from her son.

In the final analysis, the unexpected newness represented by Orestes' moral sensitivity in spite of his Atreid and Tyndarid heredity happily disproved the apparent inevitability of the lion-cub parable and its law of the endless proliferation of evil. An *alien* τροφή ['nurture'] does in fact weaken Orestes' ἦθος τὸ πρὸς τοκέων ['*ethos* inherited from his parents'; cf. *Ag.* 727–8]; his actions do not turn out to be 'like theirs in kind' [cf. *Ag.* 760]. A father whose *ethos* recalls the Aeschylean Xerxes[86] produces a son with the moral sensitivity of king Pelasgus in the *Suppliants*.

The πρώταρχος ἄτη ['primal madness', *Ag.* 1192] of the trilogy is not an external force, but Atreid *ethos,* predacious, teknophonous, aquiline, hateful to the Brauronian goddess whose special concern is its young and innocent victims. The son, Agamemnon, who is punished for his father's crime is himself guilty. The curse on the house of Atreus does not strike Agamemnon from without; it operates in and through *ethos,*[87] inherited by son from father, giving events a predictable afterlife, and issuing in identical decisions. ἦθος ἀνθρώπῳ δαίμων ['Man's *ethos* is his destiny', Heraclitus fr. 119]. The Erinyes that plague the house are truly σύγγονοι (*Ag.* 1190), 'inbred', and the dividing line between them and the human agents is indistinguishable. But the curse is cancelled when the Atreid *ethos* disappears, as it

---

[86] Aeschylus' treatment of Agamemnon suggests the oriental. The walking of the purple tapestries comes immediately to mind, especially Agamemnon's weak protest at 919. In addition, the king's extravagant beacon-relay must by its length have reminded an Athenian of Mardonius' trans-Aegean beacon-relay, which was to have signalled the capture of Athens to Xerxes in Sardis (Herodotus 9.3); note the presence of a Persian word, ἀγγάρου ['courier'] (282), early in the beacon-speech.

[87] Lloyd-Jones (n. 2), 199 [= *Greek Epic, Lyric, and Tragedy,* 298–9 = *Oxford Readings in Greek Tragedy,* 71–2] believes that Agamemnon was externally compelled to do what he did at Aulis, and that his punishment is nothing but the working out of the curse on Atreus by Zeus. This makes illusory puppetry of all the complexity of human action in the play, and turns Zeus' intervention in Orestes' case into something purely arbitrary. He sees the curse here as an external, determining force which apparently overrides the personal decisions of the human agents, and claims that the same pre-determination obtains in Aeschylus' Theban trilogy. For a less literal reading of the *Septem,* see Anthony J. Podlecki, 'The character of Eteocles in Aeschylus' *Septem*', *TAPhA* 95 (1964), 283–99, where the author sensibly sees the curse as operating in and through, rather than external to, the character of Eteocles.

does in Orestes, who turns out to be not so much the nestling of the eagle as the hunted hare of *Eum.* 326, earning the protection of Zeus, who, as the now more benign successor of two violent and arbitrary warlords of Olympus (*Ag.* 168–72), is himself an example of altered *ethos.*

Appendix: Menelaus and the *Proteus*

How concerned Aeschylus was to maintain the thematic continuity of a trilogy in its accompanying satyr-play is not, in the present state of our knowledge, the kind of question that will lead to any but the most tenuous conclusions.[88] But there are certain considerations which at least make us suspect that Aeschylus, in composing the passage on the eagles and the hare in the *Agamemnon,* was anticipating the *Proteus,* in which Menelaus—the other eagle of the omen—survives. The survival of Menelaus, an unalterable *datum* of the poetic tradition, would have presented a touchy artistic problem, if the dramatist were concerned to make the *Proteus* a burlesque projection of the same issues raised in the foregoing tragedies. For if Menelaus is the other eagle of the omen, and if he displays the predatory Atreid *ethos* hateful to Artemis, how is he made to escape punishment? Without the *Proteus,* it would be presumptuous to say. But it is noteworthy that Aeschylus goes out of his way in the *Agamemnon* to emphasize the temperamental difference between the two Atreidae, and thus to prepare his audience for Menelaus in the satyr-play as the comic analogue of the tragic Orestes in his divergence from Atreid *ethos.* The eagle which symbolizes Menelaus in the portent is ἐξόπιν ἀργᾶς ['white behind'] (115), commonly called πύγαργος

---

[88] It will be obvious to readers of the Proteus episode in *Odyssey* 4 what ample opportunities for humour were present to Aeschylus: a chorus of malodorous seals or of Menelaus' men disguised as seals, the ambush of Proteus, the chance for an unrestrained discussion (if not representation) of the πολυάνωρ γυνή ['woman with many husbands'; cf. *Ag.* 62] and of her renewed relationship with the uxorious Menelaus. One is further tempted to wonder whether and how far Aeschylus may have exploited the broad parallels that exist between his own conception of Agamemnon's situation at Aulis and the situation of Menelaus at Pharos as narrated in the *Odyssey*: (a) adverse winds preventing a sea voyage and forcing men to wander about in hunger; (b) the intervention of a goddess (the one hostile, the other friendly); (c) an oracular disclosure of δέξια ['auspicious things'; cf. *Ag.* 145] and κατάμομφα ['inauspicious things'; cf. *Ag.* 145] (in Menelaus' case, the assurance of his safe return and ultimate transfer to Elysium, and the news of Agamemnon's murder); (d) sacrifice to gain favourable winds.

244		*John J. Peradotto*

['white-rumped'] and characterized as, if not cowardly, at least less ferocious in comparison with the μελανάετος ['black eagle'] or λαγωφόνος ['hare-killer'] (κελαινός ['black'], *Ag.* 115).[89] Calchas understands the difference in the birds as the difference in the temperaments of the two Atreidae (λήμασι δισσούς, 122). I would submit that this emphasis upon the difference between the vain, vicious Agamemnon and the gentler, less warlike, more humane Menelaus, so well documented in the literary tradition,[90] is intended in some measure to justify Menelaus' exemption from the punishment meted out to his brother.

---

[89] *EM* s.v. πύγαργος (= Soph., *TrGF* frag. 1085): εἶδος ἀετοῦ· Σοφοκλῆς· ἐπὶ τοῦ δειλοῦ, ἀπὸ τῆς λευκῆς πυγῆς, ὥσπερ ἐναντίως μελάμπυγος ἐπὶ τοῦ ἰσχυροῦ ['a kind of eagle. Sophocles: for cowardice, from its white rump, just as conversely the black-rumped for strength']. Cf. also [Aristotle] *HA* 9.32.1, and Fraenkel's excellent note (n. 2), ii.67–70.

[90] See Headlam–Thomson (n. 30) *ad* 115 for sources. Late in the tradition the character of Menelaus, like that of Odysseus, suffers denigration to such an extreme that Aristotle is prompted to cite his representation in Euripides' *Orestes* as a παράδειγμα πονηρίας ἤθους μὴ ἀναγκαῖον ['an example of unnecessary baseness of character'] (*Poet.* 1454ᵃ28). In Homer, he is a peace-loving man (*Il.* 13.636–9, *Od.* 4 passim), concerned over the sufferings of both Argives and Trojans (*Il.* 3.95–102), fighting for the pragmatic purpose of the war, the return of Helen and his property. The contrast between the brutal *aristeia* of Agamemnon (see n. 72, above) and Menelaus' *aristeia* (*Il.* 17) reveals the corresponding contrast in their characters. Menelaus guards the body of Patroclus 'as over her first-born calf a mother cow stands lowing, who has known no young before this' (17.4–6, contrast Agamemnon's remark at 6.57–60). To be sure, his attack, like his brother's, is compared to that of a lion crunching the back of a cow and licking its blood and entrails (17.63–4 = 11.175–6), but it is significant that in Menelaus' case the killing in question only comes after the victim (Euphorbus) has refused to heed Menelaus when he warns his young challenger not to meet him in battle; in Agamemnon's case the simile refers to the wholesale slaughter of fleeing men. Twice again in Book 17 Menelaus is compared to a lion (109–12, 657–64), but one that grudgingly retreats, harried by overwhelming odds. Here, as in other similes used of him—the persistent mosquito (570–2) and the sharp-eyed eagle (attacking and killing a hare! 674–8)—the point of departure is his sorrow over the fate of Patroclus and his plodding determination to rescue the body against overwhelming odds.

8

Morals and Politics in the *Oresteia*[1]

E. R. Dodds

When Aeschylus wrote, no distinction between morals and politics
had yet been drawn.[2] But in our day the moral and the political
element in the *Oresteia* have usually been examined separately. Thus,
for example, Professor Dover, in his thoughtful paper on 'The political aspect of the *Eumenides*',[3] makes no attempt to connect this
aspect with the moral issues raised in the earlier part of the trilogy.
And Sir Richard Livingstone, in his paper on 'The problem of the
Eumenides', denied, if I understand him correctly, that any real link
exists: 'The last 350 lines of the *Eumenides*', he says bluntly, 'are not an
integral part of the trilogy. They are a loosely connected episode,
stitched on its outside.'[4] If he is right, we may properly ask what
motive was so strong, what need so urgent, as to induce the poet
thus to botch the conclusion of his masterpiece. And if he is wrong,
we should try to prove him wrong by making clear the nature of
the link. To explore these alternatives is the chief purpose of the
present paper.

---

[1] A paper read to the Cambridge Philological Society, 14 January 1960, and
published in its *Proceedings,* No. 186 (1960), after revision in the light of subsequent
discussion at an Oxford class on 'Politics in Greek Tragedy', to whose members I am
indebted for much helpful criticism. [*Editor's note.* Translations have been added for
Greek quotations, and some Greek words have been transliterated or translated.]

[2] Cf. W. Jaeger, *Paideia,* tr. G. Highet, 3 vols. (New York, 1939), i. 323.

[3] *JHS* 77 (1957), 230–7 [= *Greek and the Greeks* (Oxford, 1987), 161–75].

[4] *JHS* 45 (1925), 120–31, at 123–4.

I

The political implications of the *Oresteia* begin to force themselves on the reader's attention only in the scenes at Athens, a fact which is sometimes explained (if one can call it an explanation) by saying that Aeschylus wrote the first two parts of his trilogy for mankind, but the third part for the Athenians of 458 BC.[5] Yet the language of contemporary politics is not wholly absent from the earlier parts.[6] Its most striking intrusion occurs at *Agamemnon* 883, where Clytemnestra describes her fear lest in the King's absence δημόθρους ἀναρχία βουλὴν καταρρίψειεν. Here the first two words surely mean (*pace* Fraenkel) 'the anarchy of popular clamour', and it is most natural to take βουλήν as meaning 'the Council'—a unique appearance of this political term in tragedy, but one which need not too greatly surprise us, since Aeschylus elsewhere admits semi-technical terms with a good deal of freedom.[7] It would be unwise to imagine here any conscious allusion to the contemporary conflict between *demos* and Areopagus, and certainly wrong to draw any conclusion as to the poet's attitude towards it. But this passage and others in the *Agamemnon* do suggest that the author is already thinking in political as well as moral terms. References to the *demos* are more frequent than we expect in a Mycenaean monarchy. What the citizens say about the Trojan war amounts to 'a curse decreed by the *demos*' (456–7); the loss of the fleet is 'a blow to the *demos*' (640); Agamemnon fears what the *demos* may say about him (938); and later the Chorus threaten both Clytemnestra (1409) and Aegisthus (1616) with 'the curses of the *demos*'. Argos is not yet a democracy, as it will be in 458, but the

[5] So, e.g., W. Schmid, *Griechische Literaturgeschichte* (1929), I. ii, p. 253.

[6] This is well brought out by B. Daube, *Zu den Rechtsproblemen in Aischylos' Agamemnon* (Zürich, 1938); see especially pp. 45 ff., 135–6.

[7] Cf. E. Fraenkel (ed.), *Aeschylus: Agamemnon*, 3 vols. (Oxford, 1950), on 534–7; H. Lloyd-Jones, 'The end of the *Seven against Thebes*', *CQ* 9 (1959), 80–114, at 94 (on *Sept.* 1006); and H. G. Robertson's long list of technical phrases in the *Supplices*, 'Δίκη and Ὕβρις in Aeschylus' *Suppliants*', *CR* 50 (1936), 104–9, at 104 n. 3. The alternative rendering, 'deliberation', suits ill with the vividly pictorial word καταρρίψειεν, 'fling to the ground'. If Aeschylus had meant 'reject deliberation', I suspect he would have used ἀπορρίψειεν ['throw aside'], as at *Eum.* 215.

opinions of the *demos* are already important. We may notice also that the rule of Aegisthus is described in the language of politics: it is repeatedly called a 'tyranny' (*Ag.* 1355, 1365; *Choephoroe* 973), from which Orestes 'liberates' Argos (*Choephoroe* 1046, cf. 809, 863). These things are no more than straws in the wind; yet I think they have some importance as suggesting that the political developments of the last play are not something 'stitched on the outside' of the trilogy, but were in the poet's mind from the first, and influenced his choice of words.

Argos is not yet a democracy. But Athens is, or so it would appear. The curious circumstance that in the *Eumenides,* alone among Greek tragedies, Athens lacks a king has hardly received the attention it deserves. True, 'the sons of Theseus' are casually mentioned at line 402; but even if this means Akamas and Demophon rather than the Athenians generally (a point which is open to doubt), they are plainly not sovereign. The only sovereign is Athena, 'queen of the land' (288). She it is who, exercising the same royal function as Pelasgus in the *Supplices,* weighs the grounds for accepting or rejecting the suppliant's claim; she it is who in the trial scene takes the place of the *archon basileus.* In mythical time, as her first words show (397–402), we are still within a few years of the Trojan war, but in historical time we have leapt forward to a new age and a new social order. This telescoping of the centuries is characteristic of the *Eumenides,* and as I believe essential to its purpose. The Athenian audience must have begun to be aware of it when at line 289 Orestes provides a mythological *aition* for the recent alliance with Argos; and when in the next breath he speculates on the possible presence of Athena in Libya, 'helping her friends' (295), I imagine they asked themselves 'What friends?' and quickly guessed the answer: 'Of course, our other ally, those Libyans whose king we are just now helping to break the yoke of Persia'. (That the actual campaigns of 459 and 458 were fought not in Libya but in the Delta is true, so far as our limited knowledge goes, but surely unimportant. The ancients had no war correspondents and no maps of the front. Probably neither the poet nor the majority of his audience would be in a position to know just where the battles were taking place; what they would know is that many of their kinsfolk were overseas, fighting for the Libyans. The phrase χώρας ἐν τόποις Λιβυστικῆς ['in regions of the Libyan land'] (292) is in fact studiously vague,[8] while the reference to Lake Triton is added only for the sake of the necessary mythological link.)

Whether there were any contemporary goings-on in Chalcidice, where also Athena might have been (295–6), or in the Troad, where she actually was (398), I do not know; the supposition can be neither proved nor ruled out.[9] But when we come to the foundation of the Areopagus, no audience in 458 could fail to be reminded of contemporary goings-on. Nearly everyone agrees (the chief exception is Groeneboom) that there is a political point here; but after a century of controversy there is still no agreement on what the point is. I believe myself that this is exactly what the poet would have wished: he was writing a political play, yes; but a propagandist play, no. It is very difficult to suppose with K. O. Müller and Blass that he was fighting a conservative rearguard action. That view is virtually excluded by his three emphatic references to the Argive alliance; on this subject I have nothing to add to Dover's careful discussion. But in the light of Athena's foundation-speech I find it almost equally difficult to see Aeschylus as a consistent and committed supporter of radical reform. Stale though the controversy is, we must consider again the two vital sentences, 690–5 and 704–6.

The first of these says that on Ares' hill awe and terror will restrain the people from wrong-doing, whether open or secret, so long as the citizens themselves do not (do something bad to) the laws. The corrupt participle cannot be restored with certainty, but the next two lines make it plain that its sense was pejorative. To what action did it refer? To Ephialtes' action in cutting down the powers of the Areopagus? That used to be the common view, and if it is right, the poet here emerges, to our confusion, as an out-and-out reactionary. To avoid

---

[8] Despite Dover (n. 3), 237 [= *Greek and the Greeks* 174], it should be remembered that 'Libya' was a general name for the African continent, and that its frontiers were uncertain (Pind. *Pyth.* 9.9 and schol., Herodotus 2.16).

[9] Cf. B. Meritt, H. T. Wade-Gery, and H. McGregor, *The Athenian Tribute Lists*, 4 vols. (Cambridge, Mass., 1939–53), iii. 321 n. 88: 'Very possibly lines 295–6 will refer to some sort of trouble in Pallene, and this would surely mean Poteidaia. It is not impossible that Poteidaia remained recalcitrant till Kimon made his Five Years' Truce in 451'. As for the Troad, Sigeum seems to have been threatened by Persian encroachments in 451/0 (*IG*² i. 32, and B. D. Meritt, 'Greek inscriptions', *Hesperia* 5 [1936], 355–430, at 360–1), and it is *possible* that the trouble began earlier.

this, Dover suggests equating the ἐπιρροαί ['influxes'] of line 694 with the ἐπίθετα ['acquired powers'] of *Ath. Pol.* 25. 2: the bad action will then be, as Verrall thought, the supposed action of the Areopagus in assuming unconstitutional powers; Aeschylus will be echoing the propaganda of the radicals. But will this really do? 'The citizens themselves' [693] cannot mean merely the members of the Areopagus (who are ἀστῶν . . . τὰ βέλτατα, 487 ['the best of the citizens']); we expect it to mean the whole body of citizens sitting in the Assembly. But there is no evidence that the Areopagus either acquired or was thought to have acquired its ἐπίθετα ['acquired powers'] by legislation in the Assembly; most historians believe that the powers in question were in fact pre-Solonian. And in the absence of such evidence I fear that this interpretation will not stand. I still incline personally to a third view, that the action the poet has in mind is something as yet in the future, though already a topic of discussion at the time the play was produced, namely the admission of the Zeugitae to the archonship, and thereby to membership of the Areopagus—a measure which was carried through in the year 458/7. I have argued for this view in print,[10] and I will not repeat my arguments here. If I am right, Aeschylus is neither justifying the recent reforms nor grumbling about them; he is offering something more practical and less overtly partisan, a quiet word of warning for the future.

The other crucial passage is lines 704–6. These are the final words in which Athena declares the Areopagus established and defines its purpose; they are as it were the trust-deed or charter of the new institution. And it is not easy to read them in a restrictive sense, as limiting its functions to those of a murder court. The only way to make this plausible is to accept the scholiast's view that εὐδόντων ['sleepers'] means 'the dead'. Wilamowitz at one time did so, but repented later,

---

[10] 'Notes on the *Oresteia*', *CQ* 3 (1953), 11–21, at 19–20. Jacoby has objected (*FGrH* III b Suppl. ii, p. 528) that Aeschylus could not imply, even indirectly, that the Zeugitae were, even relatively to the λαμπροί ['illustrious'], 'mud'. I am not sure on what this judgement is based. If it means that Aeschylus could not *entertain* an undemocratic sentiment, it begs the question under discussion. If it means that in 458 he could not risk *expressing* an unpopular opinion, I should reply that in the *Persae* he had taken at least as grave a risk: in 472, when Themistocles, if not already ostracized, had certainly fallen from popular favour, it was surely an act of moral courage to recall so frankly his services to Greece.

with good reason.[11] I know no real parallel in Attic Greek for such a use; and if there were one, the metaphor would be quite inappropriate here. With those dead who sleep quiet in their graves a murder court has no concern; its only clients among the ghosts are precisely the *un*quiet dead, the βιαιοθάνατοι ['those who died violently'], and to call *these* 'the sleepers' would be strangely misleading, even if we could reconcile that sense with the wider function implied in φρούρημα γῆς ['guardian of the land', 706]. It is possible that εὐδόντων ['sleepers'] is intended literally, if Lucian's repeated statement[12] that the Areopagus sat by night is anything more than a mistaken inference from the present passage. But it seems more likely that we are to think of the citizens as inactive 'sleeping partners' who entrust their security to the vigilance of the Areopagus: this metaphorical use of εὕδειν and καθεύδειν ['sleep'] is common enough; we find it at *Ag.* 1357 and *Cho.* 881. On either of these views the functions of the Areopagus would seem to be conceived in wider terms than those of a murder court, which does indeed protect the security of the individual, but scarcely that of the country as a whole. The poet's language is vague (I think intentionally so); but the powers of the historical Areopagus are described in equally vague phrases. The *Ath. Pol.* calls it φύλαξ τῶν νόμων ['guardian of the laws'] (4. 4) and ἐπίσκοπος τῆς πολιτείας ['overseer of the constitution'] (8. 4); and similarly Plutarch terms it ἐπίσκοπον πάντων καὶ φύλακα τῶν νόμων ['overseer and guardian of all the laws'] (*Sol.* 19). Aeschylus' phrase, ἐγρηγορὸς φρούρημα γῆς ['watchful guardian of the land'], is most naturally taken as referring to the same powers. And if that is right, the play is no more propaganda for Pericles than it is propaganda for Cimon. It looks to me as if the famous saying about the superiority of τὸ μέσον ['the middle']—which Aeschylus put so oddly into the mouth of the Erinyes (530)—might in fact be taken, not as a political catchword of Right or Left, or even as 'recommending a reflective attitude to politics',[13]

---

[11] Wilamowitz's other suggestion (*Aristoteles und Athen*, 2 vols. (Berlin, 1893), ii. 334), that in founding the Areopagus Athena was 'really' thinking of the Heliaea, must be still more firmly rejected; it has no support in the text (cf. H. Bengl, *Staatstheoretische Probleme in der attischen Tragödie*, 54), and in 458 such a confusion was surely impossible.

[12] Lucian, *Herm.* 64, *dom.* 18. Did the Areopagus provide the model for Plato's Nocturnal Council (which meets in fact at dawn, *Laws* 961b)?

[13] Dover (n. 3), 233 [= *Greek and the Greeks* 167].

but as an honest and correct description of the author's own position. It has often been noticed that in the passage of which it forms
part the goddesses appear to speak less for themselves than as the
poet's persona; they echo the choruses of the *Agamemnon*, exhort
mankind in the second person singular, and anticipate the wisdom of
Athena.[14]

I add a word about the theory of Miss Smertenko, tentatively revived
by Dover,[15] that the curse of the Pelopidae should be seen as a mythological prototype of the curse of Cylon, and Apollo's purification of
Orestes as a prototype of his purification of the Alcmaeonids. My
difficulty about this is not so much the absence of direct evidence
that the Alcmaeonids were ever purified as the feeling that if Aeschylus
had meant to be so understood he would have made the purification of
Orestes at Delphi much more important than it is in our play. As it is,
its importance seems to be deliberately *minimized*. When Orestes
arrives at Athens after long wanderings by sea and land (*Eum.* 75–7,
240), he has experienced not one purification but 'many' (277), a
phrase which allows for the local traditions of his purification at
Trozen, Megalopolis, and various other places.[16] Now he is no longer
προστρόπαιος ['a suppliant seeking purification'] (237), but this is not
due to the unaided efforts of the καθαρταί ['purifiers']. Time has also
done his part (286): Orestes has 'rubbed off' his pollution on the cities
and roads of the world (238–9), so that now 'the blood is getting sleepy
and fading from his hand' (280). (It is futile to delete line 286, for its
content is already implicit in lines 238–9 and 280.) Orestes is in fact
noticeably vague about the efficacy of pig's blood. The Erinyes are not.
For them it has no efficacy. In their view Orestes is still a polluted
creature, food for vampires (302), unfit for any contact with gods or
men (653–6). And finally, even when they are reconciled and settled at

[14] Compare 520–1 with *Ag.* 180–1, 532–7 with *Ag.* 758–62, 538–42 with *Ag.* 381–4,
552–65 with *Ag.* 1005–13; also 517–19 and 526–8 with *Eum.* 696–8. Cf. W. Kranz,
Stasimon (Berlin, 1933), 172–3, and on the 'paraenetic' second person singular Dover
(n. 3), 232 [= *Greek and the Greeks* 165].

[15] Clara M. Smertenko, 'The political sympathies of Aeschylus', *JHS* 52 (1932),
233–5; Dover (n. 3), 236 [= *Greek and the Greeks* 171–2]. Cf. also A. Plassart, *REA* 42
(1940), 298–9.

[16] Cf. L. Radermacher, *Das Jenseits im Mythos der Hellenen* (Bonn, 1903), 138–9;
A. Lesky in P.–W. s.v. 'Orestes', cols. 988 ff.; P. Amandry, 'Eschyle et Éleusis', *Mélanges
Henri Grégoire*, 4 vols. (Brussels, 1949–53), i. 27–41, at 37.

Athens, the doctrine of inherited guilt is *not* abolished; it is reaffirmed at lines 934–5. If Aeschylus was really thinking about the curse of Cylon, the encouragement he offers the Alcmaeonids is singularly limited.

I turn now to the closing scene between Athena and the Erinyes, where for brevity's sake I shall confine my discussion to two passages, both of which have troubled conscientious editors. The first is lines 858–66, where the goddess begs the Erinyes not to start a civil war in Attica. Dindorf excised the entire passage; Weil transposed it to follow line 912. The transposition is impossible; for at 912 the Erinyes are already reconciled, and concerned only with blessings. For the excision a better prima-facie case can be made than for much of the surgery to which the text of Aeschylus has been subjected. It can be argued on the ground of sense, since the Erinyes have never in fact threatened to start a civil war; on that of logical sequence, since τοιαῦτα ['such things'] in 867[17] clearly refers back to the promises made in lines 854–7; and on that of symmetry (such as we expect in an 'epirrhematic' passage), since the omission of these lines will make Athena's four persuasive speeches roughly equal in length—they will contain respectively 14, 13, 13, and 11 lines. On the other hand, who but Aeschylus would introduce those typically Aeschylean mixed metaphors, that wild notion about the cock's heart, and those Aeschylean turns of phrase, οὐ μόλις ['not too little'] (cf. *Ag.* 1082) and οὐ λέγω ['I make no account of'] (cf. *Cho.* 989)? My own guess is that the lines were interpolated by the poet himself, who at some moment when the threat of civil war had grown acute inserted them into an already completed draft, at the cost of dislocating the context and damaging the symmetry. Their author certainly has his own day in mind, as appears from the allusion to foreign war, οὐ μόλις παρών ['not too little present'].[18] And that Aeschylus did at this time fear civil war is plain enough from lines 976–87, lines which would naturally be

[17] Dindorf made the mistake of deleting 867–9 as well as 858–66, thus depriving himself of his best argument.

[18] We possess a casualty-list of the tribe Erechtheis for one of the years 460–458, giving the names of those 'killed in action in Cyprus, Egypt, Phoenicia, Halieis, Aegina and Megara in the same twelvemonth' (*IG*² i. 929, Tod 26). And it is no mere coincidence that the feelings of parents and wives who saw their men 'changed for a handful of dust' are unforgettably painted in the second ode of the *Agamemnon* [438–55].

taken by his first audience as a reminder of the fairly recent murder of Ephialtes and an appeal to the radicals not to pursue a vindictive policy. Such fears were not groundless, as we know from Thucydides' words (1.107.4) about the treachery planned by certain pro-Spartan oligarchs—a kind of treachery which the old poet had experienced once before in his life, in the year 508. This time the danger was averted, but there may well have been moments of real anxiety.

Should we go further than this, and say with Livingstone that since Athena's advice to the Erinyes is in effect the poet's advice to the Athenian oligarchs, we have here a sort of 'allegory'? I have some-times been tempted to do so, especially in view of lines 851–2, where Athena's words, 'If you go to a foreign country, you will long for Attica', seem to fit oligarchs contemplating voluntary exile better than they do the Erinyes. But, as Dover points out,[19] the Erinyes cannot be thus suddenly reduced to allegorical figures when the audience has come to accept them as real beings and active partici-pants in the drama. What we *can* perhaps say is that their case is paradigmatic: their eventual choice is an *exemplum,* showing that even the bitterest feud can and should end in reconciliation. As Zuntz has expressed it, 'In the mirror of the myth, tragedy puts before the city of Pallas the image of what she ought to be and to do.'[20]

The remaining passage to which I would call attention is lines 996–1002, where the Erinyes invoke a blessing upon Athens *in nomine patris et filiae* ['in the name of the father and of the daughter']. It begins with a reference to αἰσιμίαι πλούτου. The word αἰσιμία is otherwise unknown, but presumably means 'just apportionment [sc. of wealth]' rather than simply 'fated apportionment' (which would have little point in the context). The phrase recalls a number of passages about wealth in the choruses of the *Agamemnon,* particu-larly lines 773–80 where Justice is said to honour the ἐναίσιμος ['just'], whereas she has no respect for 'the power of wealth mis-stamped with praise'.[21] Solmsen has observed, quite correctly, that 'in

[19] Dover (n. 3), 236–7 [= *Greek and the Greeks* 173].

[20] G. Zuntz, *The Political Plays of Euripides* (Manchester, 1955), 11.

[21] Cf. also *Ag.* 381 ff., 471, 1008 ff.

the statements of Aeschylus' choruses the κέρδος ['profit'] motive
looms larger than in his plots'; money questions have no real place in
the tragedy of the House of Atreus. He is inclined to attribute this
irrelevant emphasis to the influence of Hesiod and Solon, in whose
scheme of justice wealth does, for good reasons, play an important
role.[22] That may indeed be the true explanation, or part of it; but the
present passage suggests that the poet had in mind not only the
economic conflicts of Solon's day but others more recent, which he
prays may now be ended. For in this last scene, as Weil already saw,
'fabulae pars fiunt ipsi spectatores' ['the spectators themselves
become part of the play'].[23]

More important than this, however, are the implications of line
1000, σωφρονοῦντες ἐν χρόνῳ ['gaining wisdom in time']. Blass and
Groeneboom tell us that ἐν χρόνῳ ['in time'] is 'meaningless' here,
and print instead Weil's conjecture ἔμφρονος ['of the sensible, sc.
Athena']. In this they are certainly mistaken. I cannot find that
ἔμφρων ['sensible'] is used anywhere in Greek literature as an epithet
for a god, nor should we expect it to be. It commends the human
being who is 'in his right mind', sane or rational; but it would be a
poor compliment to the goddess of wisdom to call her ἔμφρων
['sensible']. ἐν χρόνῳ ['in time'], on the other hand, though less
common than the simple dative, is a perfectly good Aeschylean
phrase: it is used at line 498 of this play and at Cho. 1040 with the
meaning 'in course of (future) time'. Here the reference must be to
the present—the actual present, not the mythological one—and the
implication must be that the Athenians have acquired 'over the years'
a σωφροσύνη ['wisdom'] which they have not always possessed. I shall
try to show that this idea of the slow and painful acquisition of
wisdom provides the necessary connection between the moral questions of the first two plays and the political answers of the Eumenides,
To eliminate ἐν χρόνῳ ['in time'] is, in my view, to destroy an essential
clue to the meaning of the trilogy.

[22] F. Solmsen, Hesiod and Aeschylus (Ithaca, 1949), 220 n. 160. Cf. also D. Kaufmann-Bühler, Begriff und Funktion der Dike in den Tragödien des Aischylos (Heidelberg, 1951), 64.

[23] H. Weil, De tragoediarum graecarum cum rebus publicis coniunctione (Paris,
1844), 11.

II

The moral issues raised by the *Agamemnon* are notoriously complex. For simplicity's sake, I shall limit myself to the two principles which the Chorus of Elders enunciate with such solemnity—παθεῖν τὸν ἔρξαντα ['the doer shall suffer'] and πάθει μάθος ['learning by suffering']. Both are associated with the name of the supreme god. It is said of the first that while the rule of Zeus endures it too will endure as a law (1563–4); and of the second, that it was laid down by Zeus, who thereby set mankind on the road to wisdom (176–8). Neither principle, of course, was invented by Aeschylus.[24] But he appears to have designed them as clues which the audience is expected to follow, for we are repeatedly reminded of them in the course of the trilogy. That the doer shall suffer is applied by the Herald to the case of Troy (532–3) and by Clytemnestra to the case of Agamemnon (1527); in the *Choephoroe* it is restated at the beginning of the great *kommos* where the Chorus call it a τριγέρων μῦθος ['a thrice-ancient saying'] (313–14); later they apply it to the case of Orestes (1009). The connection of suffering with wisdom is reaffirmed at *Ag.* 250 and implied at *Eum.* 520. All this has long been recognized. But, strangely enough, it is only in recent years that scholars have seriously asked themselves in what sense these principles operate in the drama of the House of Atreus as the poet has presented it.[25] To this question I now address myself.

First, then, 'the doer shall suffer'. Before the trilogy opens this maxim has already been verified in the cases of Thyestes and Paris; the audience will see it verified for Agamemnon, for Clytemnestra

---

[24] The antecedents of πάθει μάθος ['learning by suffering'] have been scrupulously examined by H. Dörrie, 'Leid und Erfahrung', *Abh. Mainz* (1956), Nr. 5. The rule παθεῖν τὸν ἔρξαντα ['the doer shall suffer'] is formulated in a line ascribed to Hesiod [frag. 286 M.-W.], εἴ κε πάθοι τά τ᾽ ἔρεξε, δίκη κ᾽ ἰθεῖα γένοιτο ['if one suffered what one did, then straight justice would be done'].

[25] Cf. Daube (n. 6), 148–50; Kaufmann-Bühler (n. 22), 59–107; A. Lesky, *Die tragische Dichtung der Hellenen* (Göttingen, 1956), 93–8 [= *Greek Tragic Poetry*, tr. M. Dillon (New Haven and London, 1983), 110–14]; H. D. F. Kitto, *Form and Meaning in Drama* (1956), chaps. i–iii; H. Lloyd-Jones, 'Zeus in Aeschylus', *JHS* 76 (1956), 55–67, at 61–5 [= *Greek Epic, Lyric, and Tragedy* (Oxford, 1990), 238–61, at 250–7]; D. L. Page, Introduction to J. D. Denniston and D. L. Page (eds.), *Aeschylus: Agamemnon* (Oxford, 1957), pp. xx–xxix; F. Solmsen, *Gnomon*, 31 (1959), 472–3.

256 E. R. Dodds

and Aegisthus, even for Cassandra;[26] and for Orestes also, provided we do not arbitrarily limit the meaning of πάθος ['suffering']. But are we to think of it as universally valid? What, for example, of Atreus? We hear much of his crime, but nothing of his πάθος ['suffering']. And what of those many Greeks and Trojans who suffered for what they did not do, ἀλλοτρίας διαὶ γυναικός ['because of another man's wife', *Ag.* 448]? And a further, more disturbing question: does the maxim apply without distinction of circumstance? Is the crime of Agamemnon, who was the unconscious agent of Zeus, or that of Orestes, who was the conscious agent of Apollo, to be equated with the crime of Clytemnestra?

If we are to bring this confused picture into any sort of focus, we must recognize that the moral and logical presuppositions behind it are not those which we take for granted today. I will list a few of them.

(1) Guilt is inherited, and because the son's life is a prolongation of his father's (*Cho.* 503–4), the guilty man may suffer in his son's person, as Atreus suffers in the person of Agamemnon (*Ag.* 1577–82). We must not say that Aeschylus somehow 'transcended' this assumption, for it is implicit in passages like *Ag.* 1338–42, and at the end of the *Eumenides* it is explicitly affirmed by Athena herself (932–7).

(2) Guilt is infectious, not only in the formal sense of contagious impurity but in the sense that the punishment of a guilty individual may require the destruction of an entire community: πολλάκι καὶ ξύμπασα πόλις κακοῦ ἀνδρὸς ἐπαυρεῖ ['often a whole city suffers together because of a bad man', Hes. *Op.* 240]. The fate of Troy is a case in point. When this happens, however, a fresh guilt is created: τῶν πολυκτόνων γὰρ οὐκ ἄσκοποι θεοί ['the gods are not unwatchful of those who kill many'] (*Ag.* 461). The offence of an individual can thus give rise to a situation in which crime is *inevitable*. Of that situation Orestes' dilemma is the classic example. If he refuses his office as avenger of blood, the Erinyes of his father will get him (*Cho.* 283 ff.); if he accepts it, the Erinyes of his mother. Either way, he is doomed and damned.

(3) This sinister capacity of guilt for producing fresh guilt is 'projected' as an evil spirit, or a company of evil spirits, for whom

[26] Cassandra sees her destruction as Apollo's act of vengeance for her offence against him (*Ag.* 1269–76). Yet in the next moment she predicts that she shall be avenged on Apollo's unconscious agents (1279–80).

the terms *daemon, alastor,* and *erinys* are used more or less inter-changeably. It is idle to ask whether Aeschylus believed in the object-ive existence of such beings: this is the sort of question which no dramatist can be made to answer, for it is the function of every dramatist to think in images. But their reality and causative activity is a presupposition of the story as Aeschylus unfolds it. They are not everywhere at work (*Ag.* 761–2); we are to think of them as generated by a specific deed of blood (*Cho.* 327–8, correctly explained by Wilamowitz, cf. 402), or by the curses of its victim (*Eum.* 417, cf. *Sept.* 70, *OC* 1375–6). But once generated they are henceforth active in the human heart, 'constraining' it to fresh crime with the voice of Temptation, Peitho (who is herself a daemon).[27] Such temptation is described as ἄφερτος,[28] 'more than our nature will bear' (*Ag.* 386); and yet it does not relieve us of responsibility. That is surely made plain once and for all in the passage where the Queen claims that not she was the killer but the alastor, using her body as its instrument, and the Chorus reject her claim: the fiend may have been a συλλήπτωρ ['accomplice'], but the guilt is hers (*Ag.* 1497–1508). It is the same judgement which Darius pronounces concerning the daemon who tempted Xerxes (*Pers.* 353–4, 724–5): ἀλλ' ὅταν σπεύδῃ τις αὐτός, χὠ θεὸς συνάπτεται ['when someone strives eagerly himself, the god too lends a hand'] (*Pers.* 742)—without some flaw in our nature the daemon could not gain entrance. As Arthur Adkins puts it, 'though some may be predisposed towards evil by supernat-ural agency, none are so predestined'.[29]

(4) But finally, behind all this intricate interplay of human and daemonic purposes there is still something else, the purpose of Zeus, παναιτίου πανεργέτα· τί γὰρ βροτοῖς ἄνευ Διὸς τελεῖται; ['the cause of all, the doer of all; for what is accomplished for mortals without Zeus?'] (*Ag.* 1485–8). How seriously are we to take that? Very seriously, I think: that whatever happens is the will of God has been said, and

---

[27] Cf. the well-known scyphos by Macron which shows her tempting Helen [*LIMC* s. v. 'Helene', no. 166; cf. R. G. A. Buxton, *Persuasion in Greek Tragedy* (Cambridge, 1982), 45–6, with Plate 2 (a)].

[28] This word is found no less than nine times in the *Oresteia,* and nowhere else in the whole of Greek literature. It would seem that Aeschylus coined it (Fraenkel [n. 7] on *Ag.* 386) as a unique descriptive term for the unique situation created by the curse.

[29] Arthur W. H. Adkins, *Merit and Responsibility* (Oxford, 1960), 124.

seriously meant, many times since; it is a recurrent datum of the
religious consciousness. But the people who say it have never meant
it as a denial of human causation or of human responsibility.[30] Nor did
Aeschylus. We have to recognize here the same willingness to accept
'over-determination' which we already recognize in Homer.[31] Where
Plato said αἰτία ἑλομένου· θεὸς ἀναίτιος ['responsibility lies with the
person who makes the choice; god is not responsible', *Republic* 617e4–
5], Aeschylus is prepared to say αἰτία ἑλομένου· θεὸς παναίτιος ['responsibility lies with the person who makes the choice; god is entirely
responsible']. We may call this a pre-logical or a post-logical way of
thinking; but if we do not accept it for the *Oresteia* we risk being gravely
misled.

For example, logic may assure us that Agamemnon at Aulis can
neither have made a choice nor have incurred any intelligible guilt; for
it was the will of Zeus that Troy should fall (*Ag.* 60–8), and what Zeus
wills must come to pass and must be right.[32] If we follow the prompt-
ings of logic, we shall conclude that δράσαντι παθεῖν ['the doer shall
suffer', *Cho.* 313] stands for something as dramatically senseless[33]
as it is morally revolting—the suffering wantonly inflicted by an
all-powerful deity upon a human marionette. But may it not be better
to follow the text instead? There we see the King go through all the
motions of a man in the act of choice. Like Pelasgus in the *Supplices*
(472 ff.), or like any other man caught in a dilemma, he weighs the
alternatives, and dislikes them both: βαρεῖα μὲν..., he says, βαρεῖα

---

[30] Most of them would, I think, say with Paul Tillich that 'God's directing
creativity always acts through the freedom of Man'.

[31] On 'over-determination' in general see E. R. Dodds, *The Greeks and the Irrational*
(Berkeley and Los Angeles, 1951), 30–1, 51–2. Its modalities in Homer have been
worked out by Prof. Lesky in the paper which he read to the Third International
Congress of Classical Studies at London [cf. 'Divine and human causation in Homeric
epic', in D. L. Cairns (ed.), *Oxford Readings in Homer's* Iliad (Oxford, 2001), 170–202].
That something of the kind must also be admitted for the *Oresteia* is now recognized
by the more perceptive critics: cf. Daube (n. 6), 172–8; Lesky, 'Der Kommos der
Choephoren', *SAWW* 221.3 (1943), 122–3; Kitto (n. 25), 71–2.

[32] Cf. Page (n. 25), Introd. to *Ag.*, pp. xxiii ff.

[33] The *OT* should not be cited as an example to the contrary. The dramatic value of
that play depends not on the acts which Oedipus once committed as the puppet of
destiny, but on the choices which we see him make as a free agent. See E. R. Dodds,
'On misunderstanding the Oedipus Rex', *G&R* 13 (1966), 37–49, at 42–3 [= *The
Ancient Concept of Progress* (Oxford, 1973), 64–77, at 70–1; and E. Segal (ed.), *Oxford
Readings in Greek Tragedy* (Oxford, 1983), 177–88, at 181–3].

δὲ...τί τῶνδ᾽ ἄνευ κακῶν; ['It is grievous to do one thing,...and grievous to do the other... Which of these is without evil?'] (206–11). The considerations which influence him are purely human, and surely he *believes* himself to be making a choice between them; for he does not know that he is the agent of Zeus. And the Chorus too believes it; for it describes his act in terms which have no meaning save in relation to an act of choice. He hesitated, they say ('a veering wind blew through his heart', 219), and changed his mind (μετέγνω, 221); but a man who has no choice can do neither of these things. But what then of the 'harness of necessity' (ἀνάγκας ἔδυ λέπαδνον, 218)? I reply, with Bruno Snell,[34] that the man who wears such harness has indeed lost his freedom, but the man who *puts it on* might have refused to do so. The next sentence shows what is meant: by making the wrong choice Agamemnon placed himself in the power of the alastor, here called παρακοπὰ πρωτοπήμων ['madness, the beginning of disaster'] (223). Henceforth he will listen, not to his own good sense, but to the voice of the tempter: he has *given away* his freedom.

I have dwelt on this passage because in my view the existence of a moment of choice is something which the poet wished not merely to admit but to emphasize. As Fraenkel says,[35] that is why he suppressed the reasons commonly given for the anger of Artemis: had the sacrifice of Iphigeneia been a punishment for boasting, as in the *Cypria*, or for killing a sacred deer, as in Sophocles' *Electra*, or had it been, as in other versions, the fulfilment of a rash vow, then Agamemnon would really have had no choice. But Aeschylus wanted him to have a choice, and though he could not show it on the stage, he has described it for us rather fully and carefully. Certain other moments of choice we are made to witness. The first is in what we must no longer call the carpet-scene. There we see Agamemnon first refuse and then agree to provoke the *phthonos* of gods and men by 'treading on purple'. Why does he agree ? Out of a trivial vanity, or from sheer weakness of will? Neither, I think. He agrees because ever

---

[34] *Aischylos und das Handeln im Drama* (Philol. Supp. 20.1; Leipzig, 1928), 143. A different way of meeting Page's objections is offered by Kitto, *Gnomon*, 30 (1958), 168, who thinks that Agamemnon at Aulis is 'helpless but not innocent' because his fatal choice has already been made, at the moment when he decided to attack Troy. But if so, why the parade of weighing alternatives?

[35] Fraenkel (n. 7), ii. 98–9.

since Aulis τὸ παντότολμον φρονεῖν μετέγνω ['he changed his mind so as to be utterly unscrupulous'] (221). He has given away his power of judgement; now he must follow where the tempter leads, on the path of *hybris* whose end is the palace door—the gateway to death (Ἅιδου πύλας, 1291). Like all that happens at Argos, his choice is the outcome of that older choice. And then comes a parallel[36] scene in which we see Cassandra first refuse and then agree to enter that same gateway. But what the King chose blindly, at his wife's prompting or at the alastor's, Cassandra chooses with full knowledge, yet by a free act of will—ἰοῦσα πράξω τλήσομαι τὸ κατθανεῖν ['I will go and act; I will endure to die'] (1289). Helpless slave though she is, in that act she asserts her status as a human being. But the most dramatic moment of choice is that in the *Choephoroe*, when Orestes hesitates to kill his mother, and Pylades speaks for the first and last time, uttering the will of Apollo (899–903). It was, of course, to kill his mother that Orestes came to Argos; yet it is a real moment of choice, the resolution of an internal conflict of which, if we are at all sensitive, we have been conscious throughout the earlier part of the play. (Schadewaldt succeeded for a time in persuading most scholars that no such conflict exists, but I think his view has been convincingly refuted by Lesky[37]).

Is there a moment of choice in the *Eumenides?* Not for Orestes: his time for choosing is over; he is now, as Wilamowitz said,[38] *corpus delicti* and nothing more. As for the jury, they fail to choose; and in the light of Aeschylus' presuppositions that is inevitable. Orestes' act can neither be simply condemned as a crime nor simply justified as a duty, for it is both; the logic of the vendetta, brought to the test of this limiting case, breaks down in flat contradiction. It is Athena who decides Orestes' case, but on an arbitrary personal ground which seems to deprive the decision of moral significance. The crucial choice in this play is surely that made by the Erinyes when they first refuse and then accept Athena's offer. This is the final liberating moment;

---

[36] The parallelism is brilliantly brought out by K. Reinhardt, *Aischylos als Regisseur und Theologe* (Bern, 1949), 90–105.

[37] W. Schadewaldt, 'Der Kommos in Aischylos' Choephoren', *Hermes* 67 (1932), 312–54 [= *Hellas und Hesperien* (Zürich and Stuttgart, 1960), 106–41]; Lesky (n. 31), 221.

[38] In the Einleitung to his translation of the *Eumenides*, 42.

not, like the others, a choice between evils, but a choice of Good, and one made by deathless beings, not by transient mortality. Moreover, as we have seen, it is so presented as to suggest its paradigmatic value for the poet's own day. The moral issues of the myth are living issues which have still to be faced in the Athens of 458.

What of Aeschylus' other law, πάθει μάθος ['learning by suffering']? The older commentators were strangely incurious about its working out in the *Oresteia*, and often strangely vague about the meaning of μάθος ['learning]. It was left to Mr. Lloyd-Jones and Professor Page to observe that if μάθος ['learning'] involves moral improvement it does not work out at all. As Lloyd-Jones says, Agamemnon, Clytemnestra, Aegisthus, 'are not purified or ennobled; they are simply killed';[39] and Orestes (one may add) is not perceptibly nobler after his sufferings than he was before. We must conclude that μάθος ['learning'] does not signify what is vulgarly meant by 'moral improvement'. But it seems equally clear that to Aeschylus the saying does not mean merely what it doubtless meant originally, 'A burnt child dreads the fire': that sense would be equally irrelevant to the tale of the House of Atreus. The poet's language suggests that μάθος ['learning'] has an intellectual content: he paraphrases it by φρονεῖν ['good sense'] or σωφρονεῖν ['wisdom'] (*Ag.* 176, 181; *Eum.* 521).[40] Let us consider then what it is that the characters of the drama can be said to learn.

Of Agamemnon we can say only that up to (and during) his brief appearance on the stage he learns *nothing*; and ὤμοι, πέπληγμαι ['Oh! I have been struck', *Ag.* 1343] conveys no final flash of insight. But the poet has told us why Agamemnon learns nothing: he is a man already blinded by the alastor, incapable of φρόνησις ['wisdom'] since the fatal hour at Aulis when τὸ παντότολμον φρονεῖν μετέγνω ['he changed his mind so as to be utterly unscrupulous', *Ag.* 221]. Hence the painful impression of mingled arrogance and stupidity which he makes on most readers.[41] He is a παράδειγμα ['example'], not of

---

[39] H. Lloyd-Jones (n. 25), 62 [= *Greek Epic, Lyric, and Tragedy*, 252]; cf. Denniston and Page (n. 25) on *Ag.* 184 ff.

[40] As Headlam rightly said in his note on *Eum.* 520, 'σωφρονεῖν ['good sense'] is synonymous with γνῶναι σεαυτόν, *to know your place* in relation to the gods and to your fellow-men'.

[41] Fraenkel's picture of Agamemnon as 'a great gentleman, possessed of moderation and self-control' [(n. 7), ii. 441] is very hard to reconcile with the indications of the text. Cf. Denniston and Page (n. 25) on *Ag.* 810 f. and 931 ff.

πάθει μάθος ['learning by suffering'], but of that δολόμητις ἀπάτα θεοῦ ['cunning deception of a god'; cf. *Pers.* 93] which slowly strangles all sense in the man who incurs it.

It is otherwise with Clytemnestra; her education—her πάθος ['suffering'] which is also her μάθος ['learning']—is played out before us, if we have eyes to perceive it. It is not an education in morals. At no point does she exhibit the slightest repentance for her deed or pity for her victims. It is an education in insight—insight into the rules of the nightmare world that she inhabits. In her first speeches after the killing she claims sole responsibility for her act, and glories in it as an act of simple justice. Then slowly she comes to see it, first as a sacrifice to the evil spirits whom she still refuses to fear (1432–4), then as a deed done at the prompting of the daemon (1475–80), finally as the daemon's own act, of which she was but the instrument (1496–1504). That this last *is* insight and not 'cold irony' seems to me certain, not only from the parallel with *Cho.* 910, where she makes a comparable[42] claim in no ironic mood, but also from the parallel with Cassandra's insight; for Cassandra too perceives her own action as the action of a supernatural being possessing her and working through her (1269), and Cassandra should know the rules of the nightmare world if any mortal does. In the end, what breaks Clytemnestra down is the Chorus's word, παθεῖν τὸν ἔρξαντα ['the doer shall suffer', 1564]. At that point she offers blood-money to the being in whose power she has placed herself; but in vain, for now she too has 'put on the harness of necessity' and must walk to the end the road she chose. In the *Choephoroe* we see her as a broken woman, haunted by evil dreams, vainly seeking to appease the dead man's ghost, and perceiving everywhere the action of the daemon.[43] She has gained her insight, unwillingly; but it is an insight only into the daemonic level of causation, and it serves only to torture her.[44]

---

[42] It is uncertain whether παραιτία at *Cho.* 910 means 'contributory cause' (like μεταίτιος and συναίτιος), or 'parallel cause', or simply 'cause' (as in later usage). The use of the word at frag. 44.7 [*TrGF*] seems to favour the second or the third view, which would make Clytemnestra maintain the position she took up at *Ag.* 1497 ff.

[43] *Cho.* 691–9 is certainly spoken by Clytemnestra; and comparison with *Ag.* 1497 ff. and 1660 suggests that it is seriously meant. Cf. Lesky, *Hermes* 66 (1931), 207.

[44] Cf. *Cho.* 68–9: Ate keeps the guilty one alive 'until he is filled to the brim with sickness'.

Orestes' case[45] is again different. We see him stand where his mother once stood, in the palace doorway; once again a man and a woman lie dead at the Avenger's feet; but where Clytemnestra carried a bloody sword Orestes carries an olive-branch and a wreath (*Cho.* 1035). The parallelism is intentional and significant; so is the difference. Outwardly, his situation resembles hers; inwardly, there is a deep gulf between them. It is not merely that Orestes is humble where she was arrogant, or that his motives are 'purer' than hers; like her, he has simple human motives, which he does not conceal (299–304). The deeper difference is that the divine purpose, of which both Agamemnon and Clytemnestra were unconscious and guilty agents, is for Orestes something consciously known and humbly, though not easily, accepted. He is aware that his act is a crime, even before he has committed it (930, τὸ μὴ χρεών ['wrong'], cf. 1016–17 and 1029); but receiving it as a duty, he stands as a type of all those who take upon themselves 'the necessary guilt of human action'. Orestes has not merely suffered his situation, he has understood and in a sense mastered it; it is his μάθος ['learning'] which makes him worthy of salvation.

Thus far we seem to have a fairly logical progression, from Agamemnon, the blind instrument of justice, who never learns, through Clytemnestra, the half-blind instrument, who learns too late and incompletely, to Orestes, the conscious instrument, whose insight comes before the deed and achieves contact with the divine will. Is there a fourth term in the progression? My thoughts return to the great central ode of the *Eumenides*, with its renewed insistence that it is good for men σωφρονεῖν ὑπὸ στένει, 'to learn wisdom under pressure', and to those Athenians at the end of the play, σωφρονοῦντες ἐν χρόνῳ ['learning wisdom in time']. May not this be the fourth and final term—πάθει μάθος ['learning by suffering'] no longer illustrated in the life-history of individuals, but writ large in the destiny of a whole people and ushering in a new age of understanding? Such a hope can only be an act of faith; and the poet has set it in a devotional context. It is a hope for the people of the Virgin, 'whose seat is near to Zeus',[46] and should we not here remember what we were told at the outset, that he who has faith in Zeus shall attain to perfect under-standing (*Ag.* 175 τεύξεται φρενῶν τὸ πᾶν)?[47] I will risk the guess that it was this hope for Athens—the hope of achieving a truer insight into the laws that govern our condition—this, rather than the particular squabble about the powers of the Areopagus, that shaped the com-position of the *Oresteia*.

To say, as Jacoby said,[48] that 'Aeschylus wrote his trilogy because of the Areopagus' is to distort the pattern by divorcing the 'political' application from the underlying religious and moral ideas that give it lasting significance.[49] But may we not say that he wrote it in the way he did 'because of Athens'? When he sat down to compose it, his country had just passed through the greatest internal revolution since Cleisthenes, and had just embarked on the greatest foreign adventure she had ever undertaken. It was a moment of high hope, but also of grave danger—both from enemies abroad and from extremists at home. All turned on what Athena prays for (*Eum.* 1012), the ἀγαθὴ διάνοια ['good intent'] of the people. Given that, Athens might achieve a position such as no Greek state had ever held since Agamemnon's day; without it, the whole adventure might collapse in *stasis* and defeat. Is it surprising if behind the lineaments of prehistoric Argos the pressing problems of another and a dearer city thrust themselves upon the imagination of the old poet, faintly and fitfully at first, then with growing insistence, until finally his vision of the past was completely interfused with his hopes and fears for the present, and in the closing scene of the trilogy the two images became one?

ἡμένας [i.e. with Athena rather than the Athenians sitting near Zeus] would express the thought more perspicuously, at the cost of turning poetry into prose.

[47] Solmsen has lately put the same question in a more general form, asking 'Have not these weighty utterances of the Chorus [in the *Agamemnon*] their significance also for the entire trilogy, and especially for the last piece?' (*Gnomon* 31 (1959), 472–3). The answer is surely 'Yes'.

[48] *FGrH* III b 1, p. 25.

[49] The present paper is concerned with those aspects of the *Oresteia* which tie it down to a particular locus in time and place. But it should be unnecessary to add that underneath its time-bound purpose and its archaic presuppositions the *Oresteia* is also an enduring symbol of certain moral tests and torments which will always be part of the human condition. Great works of art can be understood on more than one level of significance.

9

Politics and the *Oresteia*

Colin Macleod

In memory of Eduard Fraenkel
'Nil me paeniteat sanum patris huius'

As a drama and a poem the *Eumenides* is often regarded with unease.[1] It brings the *Oresteia* to a conclusion; but its account of Athens and the Areopagus seems to many readers inspired more by patriotism (of whatever partisan tinge) than a sense of dramatic unity. Hence much attention has been devoted to Aeschylus' supposed political message in the play; as a result, the question of its fitness to crown the trilogy recedes into the background or even vanishes. On the other hand, those whose concern is with Aeschylus' poetry tend to ignore his 'politics'. The purpose of this paper is twofold. First, it seeks to vindicate Aeschylus the artist: to show, that is, how the founding of the homicide court and the cult of the Semnai on the Areopagus in Athens properly marks the end of the troubles of the Argive Atridae, and how the sufferings and guilt of individual men and women are resolved in a city's institutions. In pursuing this aim, it also has to consider, and try to define, the relation of the tragedian to his audience and to contemporary society. My concern, then, is with the individual and the community, both within the play and behind it.

[1] This paper is a revised and slightly enlarged version of one published in Italian in *Maia* 25 (1973), 267–92. I should like to thank Richard Gordon for acute and helpful criticisms, and to thank again David Lewis, Hugh Lloyd-Jones, and Oliver Taplin for their valuable comments on an earlier draft. The *Maia* article appeared about the same time as Brian Vickers' *Towards Greek Tragedy* (London, 1973), whose chapter on the *Oresteia* has said very effectively much that I was trying to say, and more. I hope this paper may be considered complementary to his work.

I

In 1960 E. R. Dodds published an article called 'Morals and Politics in the *Oresteia*.² Some of the valuable insights this piece of work gives into Aeschylus will find a place later in this paper; here I wish to make two criticisms of it, which concern particularly the implications of its title and which bear on two fundamental questions posed by my theme.

First, the word 'politics'. When it is said of the *Eumenides* that the play has a political element, that usually means that it is commenting on the events of the writer's time; and it is clearly in that sense that Dodds uses the term. The 'political' character of the *Eumenides* should, I believe, be understood rather differently; it will, then, be necessary to consider how far the play is in the usual sense 'political'. This in its turn requires the close examination of a number of individual passages.

1. Athenian Campaigns

(*a*) 292–7 (Orestes praying to Athena):

> ἀλλ' εἴτε χώρας ἐν τόποις Λιβυστικῆς
> Τρίτωνος ἀμφὶ χεῦμα γενεθλίου πόρου
> τίθησιν ὀρθὸν ἢ κατηρεφῆ πόδα
> φίλοις ἀρήγουσ', εἴτε Φλεγραίαν πλάκα
> θρασὺς ταγοῦχος ὡς ἀνὴρ ἐπισκοπεῖ,
> ἔλθοι . . .

Whether she be moving or sitting, whether she be in Libya around the waters of Triton where she was born, helping those she loves, or whether like a bold war-lord she be surveying the Phlegraean plain, let her come . . .

Dodds suggests (47 [= 247–8]) that there is an allusion to the Athenians who were then fighting in the Nile Delta on behalf of the Libyans. But even if we allow that the poet and his audience might

² Reprinted, with corrections, from *PCPS* 186, (1960), 19–31, in his *The Ancient Concept of Progress* (Oxford, 1973), 45–63. In what follows I refer to the page numbers of the reprint [= Ch. 8. Page numbers of this volume are added in square brackets].

not distinguish Libya from Egypt, the main reason why that part of
the world is mentioned emerges clearly from the text: Athena might
be near Lake Tritonis because that is where she was born; and if she is
said to be 'helping those she loves', that is because Orestes is calling
on her to help him now. So too she might be in the Phlegraean fields
(Chalcidice), because they were the theatre of the gods' mythical
battle with the Giants in which she played an important part.[3] This
the poet recalls in the phrase 'like a bold war-lord'. So any contemporary reference is at least secondary. The point of mentioning these
two, rather than any other regions, is presumably that they mark a
northern and southern extremity of Athena's sphere of operation.
Since the area in between is large, there is implicit—as always in such
invocations—a praise of the goddess.[4]

(*b*) 397–402

> πρόσωθεν ἐξήκουσα κληδόνος βοὴν
> ἀπὸ Σκαμάνδρου γῆν καταφθατουμένη,
> ἣν δῆτ᾽ Ἀχαιῶν ἄκτορές τε καὶ πρόμοι,
> τῶν αἰχμαλώτων χρημάτων λάχος μέγα,
> ἔνειμαν αὐτόπρεμνον ἐς τὸ πᾶν ἐμοί,
> ἐξαίρετον δώρημα Θησέως τόκοις.

I heard your cry from far off, from the Scamander where I was taking
possession of the land which the Achaean leaders and chieftains assigned
to me, a large share of the spoils, to be entirely and for ever a choice gift for
the sons of Theseus.

In fact, then, Athena has been in the Troad taking up the Athenians'
portion of the spoils. The post-Homeric *Sack of Ilium* includes
Demophon and Akamas among the warriors at Troy;[5] for the mythical kings Aeschylus substitutes the goddess representing her people.[6]

---

[3] Cf. K.J. Dover, 'The political aspect of the *Eumenides*', *JHS* 77 (1957), 230–7, at
237 [= *Greek and the Greeks* (Oxford, 1987), 161–75, at 173–5].

[4] Comparable are the Augustan poets' references to Roman power as stretching
from Britain to Arabia, or the like: see, e.g., Hor. *Carm.* 1.35.29–32; 3.5.3–4; 4.14.41–52;
Virg. *Aen.* 6.798–800. See further, Woodman on Velleius Paterculus 2.126.3. In tragedy,
cf. Eur. *Hipp.* 3–4.

[5] Cf. Schol. Eur. *Tro.* 31; *RE* 1.1143–4.

[6] Θησέως τόκοις is like Θησεῖδαν in Soph. *OC* 1066, Ἐρεχθεῖδαι in Eur. *Med.* 824,
Πριαμίδαι in *Ag.* 537 or παῖδες Κρανάου in *Eum.* 1011. The phrase can hardly refer to
Theseus' sons in the literal sense since the play gives no indication that Athens is a
monarchy.

Likewise, if Akamas and Demophon's booty in the epic was a purely private one, here the booty is a piece of land for the whole state. Now there were struggles between Mitylene and Athens over Sigeum in the sixth century; possibly this piece of mythology was invented to support Athens' claims then. But these lines do not refer, so far as we know, to any specific disputes or battles at the time of the play.[7] Their purpose is rather to point back from a distance to the sack of Troy which bulked so large in the *Agamemnon*. There the destruction of the town made the Atridae guilty, even as they triumphed, and it led to a divine punishment for the Achaeans as a whole, the storm which shattered their fleet; so when the messenger tells of that storm he compares his news to the news of a city conquered (636–45): it is a 'victory-hymn of the Erinyes' (παιᾶνα τόνδ᾽ Ἐρινύων) for the Greeks. But here the sack of Troy is the cause of an honourable reward: the Athenians have conquered, but conquest for them is not ruined by their leaders' guilt. Thus there is here a myth corresponding to the formation of the alliance with Argos later in the play: both show a united people getting a just recompense for their labours. Further, both stories validate something about contemporary Athens, one of her territorial claims or one of her alliances; and that applies too to the account of how the Areopagus and the cult of the Semnai were set up, which is the mythical charter for two of her institutions. So if this passage is relevant to its time it is so in a larger than a merely topical way; and it is also part of a coherent artistic design.

2. The Argive Alliance

762–74 (cf. 287–91, 667–73)—Orestes addressing Athena:

> ἐγὼ δὲ χώρα τῆδε καὶ τῷ σῷ στρατῷ
> τὸ λοιπὸν εἰς ἅπαντα πλειστήρη χρόνον
> ὁρκωμοτήσας νῦν ἄπειμι πρὸς δόμους,
> μή τοί τιν᾽ ἄνδρα δεῦρο πρυμνήτην χθονὸς
> ἐλθόντ᾽ ἐποίσειν εὖ κεκασμένον δόρυ.
> αὐτοὶ γὰρ ἡμεῖς ὄντες ἐν τάφοις τότε

---

[7] Cf. Dover (n. 3), 237 [= *Greek and the Greeks*, 173–5]. L. H. Jeffery, *BSA* 60 (1965), 45 n. 21, is more inclined to find a topical reference, but grants that caution must prevail.

τοῖς τἀμὰ παραβαίνουσι νῦν ὀρκώματα
ἀμηχάνοισι †πράξομεν† δυσπραξίαις,⁸
ὁδοὺς ἀθύμους καὶ παρόρνιθας πόρους
τιθέντες ὡς αὐτοῖσι μεταμέλῃ πόνος.
ὀρθουμένων δὲ καὶ πόλιν τῆς Παλλάδος
τιμῶσιν ἀεὶ τήνδε συμμάχῳ δορὶ
αὐτοῖς ἂν ἡμεῖς εἶμεν εὐμενέστεροι.

I am now going off home; and I swear an oath valid for all the future to this land and your people that no leader of my country shall bring against them a well-equipped army. For I in my grave will punish (?) those who offend against this oath of mine with insurmountable failure: I will make their marches despondent and their paths ill-omened, so that they will repent of their labours. But if my oath is respected and they pay honour to Pallas' city with their alliance, I shall be more favourable to them.

It is generally agreed that these passages imply approval of the Argive alliance of 462 BC which reversed the pro-Spartan policies of Cimon, the leading 'conservative' at Athens at the time, and ushered in a 'radical' democracy.⁹ Nor do I wish to contest that assertion. But the Argive alliance is also a motif which forms a significant part of Aeschylus' play. Paris' guilt, his offence against ξενία ['hospitality'], brought war between Argos and his own city: Athens, which has freed Orestes from guilt, is now bound by an eternal alliance to his city. (συμμαχία ['alliance'] is here, as often, a relationship of ξενία ['hospitality'] in its military aspect).¹⁰ Moreover, the phrase 'I will make their marches despondent and their paths ill-omened, so that they will repent of their labours' recalls the situation at Aulis described in the parodos of the *Agamemnon*: the bad omen of the eagle and the hare, the gloom of the Achaean troops and their leader's hopeless decision; and so too, if in Agamemnon's case respect for his allies (*Ag.* 212–13) led to a crime, the sacrifice of his daughter, the Argives' respect for their alliance with Athens will bring them good fortune. Further, Orestes' position should be compared to that of the Erinyes: they remain, he goes home; they become μετοίκοι ['metics'],

⁸ Probably the corruption in this line is confined to the word πράξομεν, but it may be that, as Page suggests, something has dropped out after the preceding line.
⁹ See J. H. Quincey, 'Orestes and the Argive alliance', *CQ* 14 (1964), 190–206; G. E. M. de Ste Croix, *The Origins of the PeloponnesianWar* (London, 1972), 183–4.
¹⁰ Cf. LSJ, s. v. ξενία, 2. For ξενία abused, see *Ag.* 1590–3; *Cho.* 700–6, 914–15, and below on *Ag.* 699–706 (cf. 60–2, 362–7, 399–402).

he becomes a σύμμαχος ['ally']. This alliance, like their co-residence, is a continuing relationship which expresses both parties' gratitude. Both also are to protect the city for the future and bring it 'victory' (*Eum.* 777, 903): the alliance will save it in war, the Erinyes will guarantee its internal harmony and prosperity. As we shall see, the alliance is also closely linked to the Areopagus. In short, what is significant about the Argive alliance is not what it implies about Aeschylus' political views, but what it represents within his dramatic creation. It is a good and guiltless relationship between states; it is the expression of Orestes' gratitude; and it is one guarantee of Athens' safety. Above all, it reflects, but reverses, the horrors and sufferings of the past.

It is sometimes held that Aeschylus chose to set the centre of Agamemnon's kingdom in Argos rather than in Mycenae, like Homer, or in Lacedaemon, like Stesichorus, Simonides (Schol. Eur. *Or.* 46), and Pindar (*Pyth.* 11), in order to prepare for an allusion to the Argive alliance of 462 BC in the *Eumenides*. That is no doubt true as far as it goes, even if the term 'allusion' in such a context needs careful definition (see below, pp. 278–9). But there are also artistic reasons for this choice. Aeschylus represents Agamemnon and Menelaus as reigning together in Argos, a notion he derived from some passages in the *Odyssey*.[11] Argos is a suitable place for this joint rule, because the city carries the same name as the whole region the two Atridae govern,[12] and because it is not the traditional seat of either of them; so to set their kingdom there avoids subordinating one to the other. And as an Athenian, Aeschylus would hardly have adopted Stesichorus' version with its pro-Spartan *tendance*. The notion of the double kingship is important in the *Oresteia* because it means that Agamemnon is involved no less than Menelaus in punishing the rape of Helen; and so the Trojan war is in large measure the cause of his guilt and his death. It also means that the murder of Agamemnon by Clytaemnestra is more directly linked to Helen's misdeeds and their

[11] For the evidence, see B. Daube, *Zu den Rechtsproblemen in Aischylos' Agamemnon* (Zurich, 1938), 11–25; note also *Od.* 4.561–2 where it is implied that the Argolid is Menelaus' homeland. The *Oresteia*'s use of Odyssean motifs deserves a systematic treatment.

[12] See Jebb on Soph. *El.* 4; and in Euripides' *Heraclidae* Μυκηναῖοι and Ἀργεῖοι are interchangeable terms.

consequences: the two daughters of Tyndareus exercise a common 'dominion' (*Ag.* 1470) grotesquely parallel to the joint rule of the Atridae.[13] So if the *Agamemnon* and *Choephori* are set in Argos, that is a small, but deliberate, part of a poetic design.

3. The Areopagus

(*a*) 681–4 (Athena establishing the Areopagus):

> κλύοιτ᾽ ἂν ἤδη θεσμόν, Ἀττικὸς λεώς,
> πρώτας δίκας κρίνοντες αἵματος χυτοῦ.
> ἔσται δὲ καὶ τὸ λοιπὸν Αἰγέως στρατῷ
> αἰεὶ δικαστῶν τοῦτο βουλευτήριον.

Hear now what I lay down, you citizens of Attica, who are judging the first trial for spilt blood. In the future too the people of Aegeus shall have this council of judges for ever.

In 462 BC the Areopagus, a body composed of all former archons which had in the previous period gained some larger powers, had its functions confined to the trial of murder. This was the work of the 'radical', Ephialtes. So it has often been asked whether in describing the Areopagus' foundation Aeschylus takes up any partisan position over this matter. The passages quoted show that any notion of the Areopagus as other than a judicial power is quite foreign to the dramatist, for two reasons. First, because the Areopagites are identified with the Athenian people. For it is the people (Ἀττικὸς λεώς) who are said to be judging the case; and these judges we also know to be the Areopagites. So the two are one; and indeed the court is addressed or referred to as the people throughout the play (566, 638, 775, 997, 1010).[14] So if the Areopagus is 'the best of the citizens' (487 ἀστῶν . . . τὰ βέλτατα), that is to emphasize not that they are superior, but that they perfectly represent the city, being the flower of its manhood. A 'conservative' too might have spoken of the council in this way, to stress that its membership was drawn from the two highest property-classes in the state; but if Aeschylus echoes such language, it is to give it a larger, and no longer partisan, sense.

[13] Cf. Daube (n. 11), 24–5.
[14] Cf. O. Taplin, *The Stagecraft of Aeschylus* (Oxford, 1977), 392–5.

Second, because the Areopagus is a body of 'judges'. This is to impress on the audience that it is conceived here to be what it was when the *Oresteia* was produced, a court of law. Further, Aeschylus has excluded from his trial scene all the specific features of procedure on the Areopagus;[15] the court thus becomes in our play the representative of law as a whole, and all the more because it is judging the first murder-case of all time.

(*b*) 690–5

> ἐν δὲ τῷ σέβας
> ἀστῶν φόβος τε ξυγγενὴς τὸ μὴ ἀδικεῖν
> σχήσει τό τ' ἦμαρ καὶ κατ' εὐφρόνην ὁμῶς,
> αὐτῶν πολιτῶν μὴ †πικαινόντων† νόμους
> κακαῖς ἐπιρροαῖσι· βορβόρῳ δ' ὕδωρ
> λαμπρὸν μιαίνων οὔποθ' εὑρήσεις ποτόν.

... there will sit Reverence, with its kinsman Fear, that belongs to my people: and it will prevent wrong-doing night and day, if only the citizens themselves do not pollute(?) the laws with evil additions—if you foul clear water with mud you will never find it fit to drink.

Dodds (48 [= 248–9]) argues against Dover that these lines cannot refer to the powers which had accrued to the Areopagus before Ephialtes, because it is very unlikely that these came by legislation in the assembly (which is the natural implication of 'the citizens themselves'): he suggests in his turn that the lines concern the admission of the *Zeugitai*, a lower property-class, to the archonship, which in fact took place a year later. We might object to his objection that πολιτῶν could be used here, as words meaning 'the citizens' are used elsewhere, to refer to the Areopagus itself.[16] But what Athena says is in danger of pollution is neither the powers nor the membership of the court, but the 'laws'.[17] So these lines recall an important Athenian

[15] Cf. U. von Wilamowitz-Moellendorff, *Aristoteles und Athen* (Berlin, 1893), 2.333; Jacoby, *FGrH* iii b Suppl. pp. 24–5. Jacoby makes it plain that it was Aeschylus who made Orestes' the first trial for murder.
[16] Nor would Aeschylus speak of his own class in such insulting terms: cf. Jacoby, *FGrH* iii b Suppl. Notes p. 528. Dodds' answer (49 n. 1 [= 249 n. 10]) scarcely meets Jacoby's point.
[17] For the metaphor of ἐπιρροαί applied to laws, cf. Plato, *Legg.* 793d5; it need not therefore be used of persons, as Dodds, 'Notes on the *Oresteia*', CQ 3 (1953), 11–21, at 20, suggests.

principle, the stability of homicide laws, which is guaranteed in their formulation (Dem. 23.62) and which Antiphon (5.14 = 6.2; 1.3) dwells on with pride.[18] And so it is that Athens will surpass two models of law and order (εὐνομία), the Scythians and the Spartans (700–3). The foundation of such laws is implicit in what Athena here lays down, since this is the first trial for murder, and one of these is later made explicit, namely the principle that equal votes lead to acquittal.[19] If, then, any contemporary event is relevant it is the introduction of the γραφὴ παρανόμων (a restraint on legislation contrary to existing statutes) which may well belong to this period;[20] and that the laws are better unchanged is a commonplace of democratic oratory.[21] The Areopagus' functions risk being impaired by such a change because it is a court for the trial of murder; it is therefore dependent on the laws which guide its conduct.

(*c*) 700–6

> τοιόνδε τοι ταρβοῦντες ἐνδίκως σέβας
> ἔρυμά τε χώρας καὶ πόλεως σωτήριον
> ἔχοιτ' ἄν οἷον οὔτις ἀνθρώπων ἔχει,
> οὔτ' ἐν Σκύθῃσιν οὔτε Πέλοπος ἐν τόποις.
> κερδῶν ἄθικτον τοῦτο βουλευτήριον,
> αἰδοῖον, ὀξύθυμον, εὐδόντων ὕπερ
> ἐγρηγορὸς φρούρημα γῆς καθίσταμαι.

If you stand in just awe of such a reverend body you will have a bulwark to safeguard the country and the city such as no one, whether in Scythia or the Peloponnese, possesses. I establish this tribunal, untouchable by gain, worthy of respect, keen in its wrath, a wakeful guard in the land for those who sleep.

---

[18] Cf. Thomson, ad loc., whose view I share; also H. Lloyd-Jones' translation (1970), 54–5, 75–6.

[19] The formulation of homicide law in Athens is normally ascribed to a historical figure, Draco. But the myth of the *Eumenides*, like the other myths about the foundation of the Areopagus, presupposes a forerunner of Draco's code; and Demosthenes can speak of the Attic law of murder as due to 'heroes or gods' (23.70); see further K. J. Dover, *Greek Popular Morality* (Oxford, 1974), 255.

[20] Cf. C. Hignett, *A History of the Athenian Constitution to the End of the Fifth Century* (Oxford, 1952), 210–13; *contra*, see Andrewes on Thuc. 8.67.2. The same principle is behind the formation of an apparently more short-lived institution, the board of νομοφύλακες mentioned by Philochorus: cf. A. J. Podlecki, *The Political Background of Aeschylean Tragedy* (Ann Arbor, 1966), 96–7.

[21] Cf. Dover (n. 3), 234 [= *Greek and the Greeks*, 168–9]; add Dem. 24.24, 139–43; [Dem.] 26. 25; Aeschin. 1.6.

The functions ascribed to the Areopagus here are often compared to later writers' characterizations of it as it was before Ephialtes: φύλαξ τῶν νόμων ['guardian of the laws'] (*Ath. Pol.* 4.4), ἐπίσκοπος τῆς πολιτείας ['overseer of the constitution'] (ibid. 8.4); ἐπίσκοπον πάντων καὶ φύλακα τῶν νόμων ['overseer and guardian of all the laws'] (Plut. *Sol.* 19). But these parallels prove nothing; there are many ways in which the Areopagus might be 'guardian' of the city, and which is meant here depends first and foremost on the context.[22] We have already had occasion to stress that the Areopagus is in Aeschylus a court for the trial of murder; and Dover (*JHS* 67 (1957), 234–5 [= *Greek and the Greeks*, 169]) has argued powerfully that precisely in virtue of that function it can be conceived to be the guardian of the community as a whole; for homicide law is the basis of all law and order. So even if Aeschylus echoes the language used of the Areopagus' powers before Ephialtes, he gives it a new sense. The court is also closely parallel to the Argive alliance. Both the alliance and the court are to stand 'for all time' (572, 683, 708 and 670, 672, 763); and both are to be 'saviours' (701 and 777 σωτήριον). The alliance is to save Athens in war; the court is to save her from bloodshed and its consequences for the community. In short, they guarantee what every city needs: internal harmony and security against others.

The epithets which Athena goes on to use are also suited to a court of law as such. 'Untouchable by gain', because a jury must be incorruptible (ἀδέκαστος); 'worthy of respect', because Demosthenes (23.65) calls the Areopagus itself in the same breath δικαστήριον ('a court') and σεμνότατον ('most reverend'); 'keen in its wrath', because there is an anger proper to a judge,[23] most memorably embodied in antiquity in the chorus of Aristophanes' *Wasps*, or, in the words of a great modern sociologist,[23a] legal punishment is in essence 'une reaction passionnelle'. Likewise, the Areopagus incorporates, but for the good of society, the anger or lust for vengeance we hear so much of in the trilogy (e.g. *Ag.* 214–17; *Cho.* 40–1, 454; *Eum.* 981). The metaphor of sleep and waking is used to say, again,

[22] For similar language used of the fourth-century Areopagus, see Thomson on *Eum.* 704.

[23] See further R. Hirzel, *Themis Dike und Verwandtes* (Leipzig, 1907), 416–18.

[23a] E. Durkheim, *De la division du travail social* (Paris, 1893), ch. ii, 2.

something about justice; compare the Hindu *Laws of Manu* 7.18 (tr. Derrett): 'Punishment rules all the people. Punishment alone protects them, Punishment is awake while they sleep.' And that metaphor too points back to the past. At the beginning of the play the Furies are asleep: there they are both bloodthirsty and ineffectual, unlike the Areopagus which is to be just and effective. So too when both Agamemnon and Clytaemnestra meet their deaths, help is 'asleep' (*Ag.* 1356–7, *Cho.* 881); the Areopagus on the other hand is to be a 'wakeful guard'. A different, but also significant, contrast is with the sleepless watchman of the *Agamemnon* (see esp. 12 ff.) whose loyal performance of his task serves only to alert the king's murderers: the Areopagus' 'sleeplessness' will prevent wrongdoing.

To summarize: Aeschylus' account of the homicide court's foundation is clearly the mythical charter for the post-Ephialtean Areopagus. That need not mean he is a 'radical'; it could equally imply a hope that the warring factions might be calmed by accepting things as they had become. But again, what counts in the play is the significance ascribed to the Areopagus; and it is significant, to Athens no less than to us, as part of the basis on which any just and happy community must rest.

4. Contemporary references are also sometimes detected at the end of the play. Thus Dodds (51–2 [= 252–3]) finds in lines 858–66 an allusion to a danger of civil war after the assassination of Ephialtes,[24] just as Wilamowitz[25] did in 976–83:

> τὰν δ᾽ ἄπληστον κακῶν
> μή ποτ᾽ ἐν πόλει Στάσιν
> τᾷδ᾽ ἐπεύχομαι βρέμειν,
> μηδὲ πιοῦσα κόνις μέλαν αἷμα πολιτῶν
> δι᾽ ὀργὰν ποινὰς
> ἀντιφόνους ἄτας
> ἁρπαλίσαι πόλεως.

I pray that faction insatiable for evil may never roar in this city, and that the dust may not drink the dark blood of the citizens and in anger gulp down vengeance, murder answering murder, the city's ruin.

---

[24] Cf. Wilamowitz, *Aischylos-Interpretationen* (Berlin, 1914), 226–7.
[25] Wilamowitz (n. 15), 2.342.

Now the genuineness of 858–66 is open to grave suspicion;[26] but to pray for a city that it should be free of faction is natural and normal at any time as indeed the Eumenides' song as a whole asks for the blessings which a city's prayers normally seek, and freedom from the evils they try to avert.[27] Thus an Attic drinking-song (*PMG* 884 Page):

> Πάλλας Τριτογένει᾽, ἄνασσ᾽ Ἀθάνα,
> ὄρθου τήνδε πόλιν τε καὶ πολίτας
> ἄτερ ἀλγέων καὶ στάσεων
> καὶ θανάτων ἀώρων, σύ τε καὶ πατήρ.

Tritonis-born Pallas, queen Athena, keep this city and its citizens upright without sufferings or faction or untimely deaths, you and your father.

And to prefer war to faction is another conventional and natural wish. So Herodotus (8.3) writes: 'Internal discord is as much worse than war waged in concord as war is than peace'[28] (στάσις γὰρ ἔμφυλος πολέμου ὁμοφρονέοντος τοσούτῳ κάκιόν ἐστι ὅσῳ πόλεμος εἰρήνης); and Horace expresses the same idea (*Carm.* 1.2.21–2; 1.35.33–40). So there need be no topical reference in the passages from the *Eumenides*. What is more, 976–83 are designed to recall the *Agamemnon* and *Choephori*; for they bring to mind the series of vengeances unfolded there. The imagery of those lines with its vivid personification of the dust is particularly reminiscent of *Cho.* 66–7:[29] 'Because of blood drunk by earth the nourisher, avenging blood clots and will not dissolve' (δι᾽ αἷματ᾽ ἐκποθένθ᾽ ὑπὸ χθονὸς τροφοῦ | τίτας φόνος πέπηγεν οὐ διαρρύδαν) and both passages recall the Furies' threat to drink Orestes' blood (*Eum.* 264–6). Now with murder goes civil discord (*stasis*): the killing of Agamemnon and of Clytaemnestra and Aegisthus are both acts of *stasis*, the one because it sets up

[26] See Dodds 51 [= 252]. The reasons he gives for deleting these lines are far more cogent than his reasons for preserving them.
[27] Cf. Aesch. *Suppl.* 661–2; Pind. *Pae.* 9.13–20. In general on cult-poetry like the Eumenides' hymn, see E. Norden, *Aus altrömischen Priesterbüchern* (Lund, 1939), 160–1, 268–74.
[28] Quoted by Thomson on lines 977–9; he also adduces the Attic skolion on 957–8.
[29] Cf. further *Ag.* 1017–24; *Cho.* 48, 400–4, 520–1; *Eum.* 647–8. The language also brings to mind the symposium: for distorted sympotic imagery, cf. *Ag.* 1188–93, 1385–7; *Cho.* 577–8; V. Di Benedetto, *L'ideologia del potere e la tragedia greca* (Turin, 1978), 232–3.

tyranny in place of kingship, the other because it liberates Argos from
the tyrants (*Ag.* 1355. 1365; *Cho.* 973, 1046). In Cassandra's mouth
stasis is even personified (*Ag.* 1117–18): 'Let insatiable Discord raise
for the race a jubilant shout over this sacrifice worthy of stoning'
(στάσις δ' ἀκόρετος γένει | κατολολυξάτω θύματος λευσίμου). The
murder of the king generates *stasis*; it also provokes the threat of
stoning, which in ancient Greece is the community's way of removing the miasma induced by murder.[30] The chorus of elders in the
Agamemnon in fact utter that threat against Aegisthus; and this is one
of a number of ways in which popular discontent makes itself felt
there. Clytaemnestra has been afraid of 'anarchy with popular clamour' (883 δημόθρους ἀναρχία); the people have murmured against
their king for involving them in a war for Helen's sake (449–51), and
they have even put their curse upon him (456–7); the chorus threaten
his murderers, as with stoning, so also with the people's curse and
with its sentence of exile (1407–11, 1615–16).[31] Indeed, the chorus of
elders throughout the *Agamemnon,* and even sometimes the chorus
of slaves in the *Choephori* (esp. 55–9, 973–82),[32] stand for the city
harmed or worried by the deeds of their rulers. So the reference to
stasis in the *Eumenides* is amply prepared for.[33]

In 996–1002 Dodds finds a reference to recent 'economic conflicts'
(52–3 [=253–4]). But as he himself observes, questions about the
proper use and the dangerous consequences of wealth arise in the
choruses of the *Agamemnon* (esp. 750–81, 1001–16); and we have
heard the Furies say (*Eum.* 535–7): 'From soundness of mind comes
wealth that all love and greatly pray for' (ἐκ δ' ὑγιείας | φρενῶν ὁ
πᾶσιν | φίλος καὶ πολύευκτος ὄλβος). Nor is 'economics' foreign to the
plots. In the *Agamemnon* it is powerfully suggested that the Greeks'
victory and spoils at Troy are ill-gotten (341–8, 636–80); and the king

[30] Cf. Fraenkel on line 1117. On that passage in connection with *Eum.* 976–87, cf.
Di Benedetto (n. 29), 207–10.

[31] Cf. Dodds 45–6 [= 246–7]; but these things are surely more than 'straws in the
wind'. The presence of a discontented people (δῆμος) when kingship is violated is
another Odyssean motif: cf. above all the assembly in Book 2.

[32] In these lines Orestes is addressing the chorus. There is no reason to suppose
that he enters with some citizen-extras: cf. Taplin (n. 14), 357–8.

[33] Cf. on the plane of imagery, *Ag.* 650–2: fire and water 'conspired' (ξυνώμοσαν)
to destroy the fleet. Disorder in nature is, as all over the *Oresteia*, bound up with
social disorder. For literal 'conspiracy', see *Cho.* 978.

ruins the substance of his house by treading on its precious robes,[34] as
Clytaemnestra boasts outrageously that its supplies are inexhaustible
(*Ag.* 958–62). The robe in which she then ensnares him represents an
'evil wealth' (*Ag.* 1382 πλοῦτον εἵματος κακόν). In the *Choephori* the
poverty of Orestes, his rightful inheritance expropriated while his
mother and Aegisthus enjoy the regal luxury, is one of the motives
that impel him to do the deed (249–50, 301, 973–4; cf. 135–7); and
when he is acquitted he rejoices that he will now again be called an
Argive and come into his father's heritage (*Eum.* 757–8; cf. *Cho.* 865).
In short, the Furies' concern with wealth grows out of the plot as
Aeschylus shapes it. And at the end of the *Eumenides,* in this as in so
much else, there is realized in Athens the just counterpart to the
wrongs and horrors of the past.

What, then, emerges from the discussion of these passages about
the 'political' character of the *Eumenides?* First a few words must be
said in general about the tragedian and his city. To present a tragedy to
the Athenians as an audience at the Dionysia is not the same as
speaking to them in the Assembly or even as producing before them
a comedy; for in tragedy there is no direct address to the spectators[35]
and no reference to contemporaries from the Greek world. It is
therefore fair to assume that the audience, who had an intimate and
instinctive knowledge of the nature and limits of the genre, would
respond accordingly. Indeed, the function of tragedy in its social and
historical context is not to comment directly on the times, but to raise
to universality and touch with emotion the experience of the dramatist and his fellow-citizens, to interpret in myth and drama their
deepest concerns as human beings.[36] Sometimes that includes the
use of myths which explain and legitimate something historical, as we
have already seen in the *Eumenides,* or the treatment of overtly
political subjects, like the value of democracy (Euripides, *Supplices*),
and the authority of the state as against that of the gods (Sophocles,
Antigone); but such themes are completely bound up with the actions
and sufferings of figures who belong in a drama. So it is not surprising
that Attic tragedy is set almost invariably in the world of myth; and

[34] Cf. J. Jones, *On Aristotle and Greek Tragedy* (London, 1962), 86–9.
[35] See D. Bain, 'Audience address in Greek tragedy', *CQ* 25 (1975), 13–25; Taplin
(n. 14), 129–34.
[36] See further Vickers (n. 1), 100–56.

the one surviving play which deals with contemporary events only confirms what has been said here.[37] For Aeschylus' Persians represent human delusion, fear and suffering; and if there is praise of Athens in that play, it is designed to intensify the bewilderment and gloom of the characters on the stage.[38] So it is with the *Oresteia*. Even when Aeschylus draws closer to his own time, he is rather giving a certain significance to something contemporary than commenting on it for its own sake: the Areopagus and the Argive alliance, as we have begun to see, have in the trilogy a meaning and a value which are not confined to any historical situation; and if the audience recalls those institutions in their contemporary form, it is meant to see that, since they were indeed, as the play says, set up 'for all time', their value is confirmed by history. We have begun to see too that in those places in the *Eumenides* where topical allusions have been detected, there are rather—or at least also—links with the rest of the trilogy. So if we speak of 'politics' in the *Oresteia* it may be helpful to give the word a different sense, 'a concern with human beings as part of a community'. This will also in itself do much to bridge the apparent gap between the *Eumenides* and the other two plays. For if in the *Eumenides* Athens is above all an ideal representation of human society which pointedly reverses the social disorder of the *Agamemnon* and *Choephori*, then the unity of the trilogy is in essence vindicated.

[37] H. D. F. Kitto, *Poiesis* (Berkeley and London, 1966), 74–115 demolishes the notion that the *Persians* is a merely patriotic play. On Eur. *Suppl.*, cf. C. Collard's commentary (1975), i.29.

[38] Miletus, like Athens an Ionian city and originally one of her colonies, was sacked by the Persians in 494 BC. When the tragedian Phrynichus produced a tragedy about the event, the Athenians fined him 1,000 drachmas for 'having reminded them of their own troubles' (ὡς ἀναμνήσαντα οἰκήϊα κακά) and forbade the play to be read or staged again (Hdt. 6.21.2). Now what it *did*, we are told, was move them to tears; we have no warrant for thinking it was inspired by a political *arrière pensée*. And the reason for the Athenians' outrage was simply that, unlike any other known tragedy, it dealt with a disaster for Athens. Phrynichus offended against the *nomoi* both of the city and its drama. The proper material of Attic tragedy was suffering which could move the audience to pity and fear, but which was not their own; and thus its proper effect required, as all art requires, detachment as well as involvement in its public. For the tragic emotions of pity and fear are evoked by the plight of men *like* ourselves (Arist. *Poet.* 1453^{a}4–5) and by suffering we can *envisage* ourselves or those closest to us undergoing (*Rhet.* 1385^{b}3–5); Herodotus himself makes the distinction between pity for another's suffering and feeling it as one's own in his story of Psammenitus (3.14; cf. Arist. *Rhet.* 1386^{a}17–24); see also Gorgias, *Hel.* 9. For a helpful discussion of the Herodotus passage, see F. Marx. *RhM* 77 (1928), 343–8.

The second criticism of Dodds' article can be dealt with more briefly; for the nub of it is in his own opening sentence: 'When Aeschylus wrote, no distinction between morals and politics had yet been drawn.' Now the thesis of his whole paper is, very broadly, that the moral lessons implicit or explicit hitherto are in the *Eumenides* addressed to the city as political lessons, and that Aeschylus was impelled to unfold his trilogy in this way by the pressing problems of Athens in the present. But the *Eumenides*, I suggested, is a political play in the sense that it is concerned with human beings in a *polis*: it dramatizes, like the *Agamemnon* and *Choephori*, social problems. And if we take seriously Dodds' opening remark, it follows that it is in the very nature of morality as Aeschylus conceived it to include the political sphere. The distinction between ethics and politics goes hack to Aristotle; but for him the one was in fact contained in the other (*EN* 1094^{a}18–^{b}11; cf. 1099^{b}29–32, 1142^{a}9–10). And the purpose of the city is 'living well' (*Pol.* 1252^{b}30). This is because the *summum bonum* is thought of as a common good and the common good is the sum of every individual's morality. So the laws' task—and the task of the Areopagus in the *Eumenides*—quite simply, is to make people good;[39] and the word εὐνομία (literally, 'having good laws') commends not only, not even principally, a city's institutions, but the behaviour of its inhabitants.[40] What is true of good is also true of evil. As we see throughout the *Oresteia*, the consequences of wrong-doing cannot be limited; just as it extends from one generation to another, so also it affects the whole community and its institutions (cf. Hes. *Op.* 240–1). Thus the murderer or wrong-doer can be said not only to endanger the laws[41] or pollute the city,[42] but even, quite directly, to 'kill' them.[43] So by fashioning in mythical Athens the image of an

[39] See also Arist. *Pol.* 1280^{b}6–12, 1333^{a}11–16; Pl. *Protag.* 326c–d; *Apol.* 24d; Isoc. 2.3; Dem. 20.154; [Dem.] 25.16–17. Note also Isoc. 7.41–2 on the Areopagus in olden times: its function, as in Aeschylus, was to make people good and prevent, not merely punish, wrongdoing.

[40] Cf. A. Andrewes, 'Eunomia', *CQ* 32 (1938), 89–102, at 89–91.

[41] Cf., e.g., the conventional phrase 'come to the laws' aid' (βοηθήσατε τοῖς νόμοις) and the like in forensic speeches: e.g. Dem. 22.1; 26.27; 43.84; 45.87; 46.28; Lys. 30.35.

[42] Cf. L. Moulinier, *Le pur et l'impur dans la pensée des Grecs d'Homère à Aristote* (Paris, 1952), 212–25.

[43] See Soph. *OC* 842 (where ἐναίρεται is not to be emended): cf. W. Schulze, *Kleine Schriften*^{2} (Göttingen, 1966), 181 n. 3, and Solon 4a West (if καινομένην is right); Cic. *Pro Mil.* 14; *II Verr.* 4. 26.

ideal city, Aeschylus is presenting goodness achieved, he is also portraying the reversal of the state of things in the *Agamemnon* and *Choephori*. If, then, the *Eumenides* concentrates on society, that need not be explained by his concern about contemporary Athens. The *Oresteia* is unmistakably the work of an Athenian citizen and addressed to Athenian citizens; but its author's patriotism does not have to be invoked to explain his artistry.

It is now time to look closer at Aeschylus' poetic design; and if there is any truth in these reflections, they indicate a path to take. We need to see in more detail how moral and social considerations are one throughout the trilogy, and in particular how the *Agamemnon* and *Choephori* prepare for that emphasis on the community which is often thought peculiar to the *Eumenides*; at the same time we shall have to define more closely the 'political' character of the last play. To this end I shall group my remarks under two headings which are also words Aeschylus continually uses, δίκη and τιμή.

II

It is plain to the most casual reader that δίκη ('justice') is a central notion in the trilogy. The plots and choruses of the *Agamemnon* and *Choephori* describe a self-perpetuating series of crimes and punishments, which begins with the rape of Helen and goes on through the sacrifice of Iphigenia, the sack of Troy and the murder of Agamemnon to the murders of Clytaemnestra and Aegisthus. A converging line of wrongs is revealed in the Cassandra scene. There we learn of the Thyestean banquet and the guilt which hangs about the house; and these too lead to the revenge Aegisthus takes with his consort. Δίκη is constantly invoked as a goddess when these punishments are recalled or enacted (e.g. *Ag.* 383, 911, 1432; *Cho.* 646). So at the very beginning of the parodos of the *Agamemnon,* the imagery sets us in the context of not only justice, but even law. Agamemnon and Menelaus are the ἀντίδικος, the 'plaintiff',[44] against Paris and they set out with an ἀρωγά, 'aid', another term with legal associations. This line of thought

---

[44] Cf. 451 προδίκοις Ἀτρείδαις and Fraenkel ad loc.

is extended in the simile which follows: the two kings are compared to vultures who raise the βοή, the cry which both calls for help and testifies to the injury they have suffered; and a god answers them—for the birds are the gods' μέτοικοι ('co-residents', yet again a word with social and legal overtones)—by sending the Erinys. But the image fits its context less than perfectly; and these imperfections are meant to trouble the spectator. Agamemnon and Menelaus, unlike the vultures of the simile, are themselves the avengers. The gods defend their μέτοικοι not by acting as their προστάται ('spokesmen at law'), but by direct punishment. The loss of children and the mourning of their parents is scarcely like the flight of the 'woman of many husbands' (62 πολυάνορος . . . γυναικός) who was to bring all the toils of war to both Greeks and Trojans; if anything, it squares rather with the death of Iphigenia and reminds us that Agamemnon too is guilty.[45]

The use of legal language is disturbing here, as it is elsewhere in the *Agamemnon*. So at 813–17:[46]

> δίκας γὰρ οὐκ ἀπὸ γλώσσης θεοὶ
> κλύοντες ἀνδροθνῆτας Ἰλιοφθόρους
> ἐς αἱματηρὸν τεῦχος οὐ διχορρόπως
> ψήφους ἔθεντο, τῷ δ' ἐναντίῳ κύτει
> ἐλπὶς προσῄει χειρὸς οὐ πληρουμένῳ.

The gods, without having heard in speech the parties' claims, cast unambiguously into the urn of blood the verdict of death to the men and destruction to the city, and only hope came to the other urn, that was never filled.

When the gods judge a case they do not hear it; they proceed at once to execution. Or *Ag.* 532–7:

> Πάρις γὰρ οὔτε συντελὴς πόλις
> ἐξεύχεται τὸ δρᾶμα τοῦ πάθους πλέον·
> τοῦ ῥυσίου[47] θ' ἥμαρτε καὶ πανώλεθρον
> αὐτόχθονον πατρῷον ἔθρισεν δόμον·
> διπλᾶ δ' ἔτεισαν Πριαμίδαι θἀμάρτια.

---

[45] Cf. Daube (n. 11), 125–78; D. Kaufmann-Bühler, *Begriff und Funktion der Dike in den Tragödien des Aischylos* (Diss. Heidelberg, 1951), 59–60; F. I. Zeitlin, 'The motif of the corrupted sacrifice in Aeschylus' *Oresteia*', *TAPA* 96 (1965), 463–508, at 481–2; A. Lebeck, *The Oresteia* (Washington, 1971), 8–10.

[46] Cf. Lebeck (n. 45), 204–5.

[47] This word can keep its normal sense 'something taken in reprisal', if we take it as the *Greeks'* ῥύσιον.

Neither Paris nor the city that pays jointly with him can boast that they did more than they underwent. Convicted of rape and theft, he has lost what the Greeks seized in reprisal and has stripped his father's house, left it utterly destroyed with all the land. The sons of Priam have paid twofold for their offence.

Payment twice over is a known form of legal retribution; but here such payment means the total destruction of the city. Similarly the word πράσσεσθαι and its cognate πράκτωρ, which are normally connected with the exaction of debts or fines, are applied to Agamemnon's punishment of Paris' rape and robbery (*Ag.* 111, 705, 812, 823); only here the 'fine' is again ruin for the whole of Troy.[48]

What then is this δίκη and why is it so disturbing? It is a retribution which strikes not only the offender but his whole city; it is also a summary justice in which punishment follows directly on crime and whose agents, even though the gods will the punishment, are themselves guilty. It thus stands in contrast to the legal justice of the *Eumenides*. This contrast becomes particularly clear in the scene where Athena questions the Furies and Orestes before the trial (397–489). Only the doer is to be punished, if anyone is; and she refuses a justice which consists simply in both parties' swearing an oath: the case must be heard on either side (428). Further, the plea that the murder was a just one may cause the murderer to be spared (*Eum.* 612–13—contrast *Ag.* 1563–4, *Cho.* 313–14), a principle Demosthenes (20.157, 23.74) finds enshrined in Attic homicide law and in the story of Orestes' acquittal on the Areopagus. Nor can she, for all that she is a goddess, decide it on her own (470–2). There must be a collaboration between gods and man—men are no longer to be simply the instruments, conscious or otherwise, of divine wrath; and this results in a judgement after trial, not immediate destruction. This collaboration is dramatically represented when Athena votes together with the other jurors.[49] Similarly, Apollo is no more what

---

[48] Cf. Daube (n. 11), 108. For violent punishment treated as the exaction of a fine or debt in the *Oresteia*, see also *Ag.* 458, 1503; *Cho.* 275 (where Tucker's interpretation is right), 311, 805; *Eum.* 319, 624. Ultimately, cf. Hom. *Od.* 12.382. Note also the grim analogue of legal justice practised by Hades that the Furies appeal to (*Eum.* 316–20).

[49] Wilamowitz (n. 24), 183–5, is an unassailable statement of this view of the *calculus Minervae* ['vote of Athena']: hers is not a casting vote, it creates an equality of votes.

he was in the *Choephori,* the author of a terrifying and oracular command to kill: he is present in a supporting and subordinate role to share with Orestes the charge of murder and to be his witness and advocate (576–80). Hence the apparently curious unobtrusiveness of his entry and exit in the trial scene:[50] he stands, as it were, beside or behind Orestes, he no longer looms over him.

The two notions of justice are already briefly contrasted at *Cho.* 120 when Electra interjects, as the chorus instruct her how to pray: 'Do you mean a judge (δικαστήν) or an executioner (δικηφόρον)?' And the first time the word δικαστής appears in the *Eumenides* it has the same implication (81):

κἀκεῖ δικαστὰς τῶνδε καὶ θελκτηρίους
μύθους ἔχοντες μηχανὰς εὑρήσομεν
ὥστ᾽ ἐς τὸ πᾶν σε τῶνδ᾽ ἀπαλλάξαι πόνων.

There with judges and with persuasive speeches we will find a way to release you completely from these troubles.

In the court persuasion has a place; and Athena again uses the word θελκτηρίους of her placating the Erinyes (886). Persuasion (πειθώ), which she invokes there and later (970), is no longer as earlier in the trilogy a force that leads to crime or death (*Ag.* 385, *Cho.* 726)—it has been dramatized most vividly in the scene where Agamemnon yields to Clytaemnestra's arguments and walks on the precious robes:[51] it is now the agent of the continuing peace and happiness of the city. And whereas the chorus in the *Agamemnon* (1406–25) could only make a vain attempt to 'sentence' (δικάζειν) Clytaemnestra, now there is a court to pass judgements with authority and power.

In the *Eumenides,* then, legal justice, a pacific and effective solution of quarrels and wrongs, ends and supersedes the *lex talionis.* And in this Aeschylus is again giving expression to something implicit in Attic homicide law, which prevents an infinite series of reprisals by prohibiting revenge against the murderer (Demosthenes 23.39), or indeed in the notion of law itself, which, as Plato puts it, 'civilized' or 'pacified' (ἡμέρωκε) all human life (*Leg.* 937e1). This is not to say

[50] Noted by Taplin (n. 14), 395–407. His suggestion that the text of the trial-scene is gravely disrupted is stimulating, but mistaken; see further ibid. 398 n. 1, 399 n. 1.

[51] Cf. Lebeck (n. 45), 40–1; R. F. Goheen, 'Aspects of dramatic symbolism: three studies in the *Oresteia*', *AJPh* 76 (1955), 113–37, at 126–32.

that divine justice, which still punishes violently and still visits the sins of the father on the children, is overthrown; the Erinyes remain in the city to enforce it,[52] though it is now not they, but Athena, who asserts that function (930–7, 950–5). But here they are not the blood-sucking avengers, concerned only with the rights of kin; they represent universal justice. We have seen them or heard of them in both these roles in the *Eumenides,* and before (e.g. *Ag.* 1190, *Eum.* 210–12 and *Ag.* 59, *Eum.* 269–75). What they lose here by giving up their angry threats is their partisan character, which is the basis of the *lex talionis* and the evils it brings with it. And their sphere of competence is now not merely the family but the human community as a whole.

But to see more clearly how δίκη is achieved at the end of the *Eumenides* we need to consider the two concluding events of the play: the foundation of the Areopagus and the incorporation of the Erinyes.

Athena's speech (681–709) which sets up the court for all time is what above all expounds its meaning. It is to embody τὸ δεινόν ('what instils fear'), in it will reside reverence and fear to prevent wrong-doing; as long as this remains so, then there will be neither 'anarchy' nor 'despotism'. All this echoes the words of the Furies in the previous chorus (517–37). Now their prime concern in the whole ode seems to be with individuals; so that they too should speak of 'anarchy' and 'despotism' is striking. But the sense of these terms is not a narrowly political one.[53] The chorus and Electra in the *Choephori* (58, 102) speak of a bad fear, contrasted with reverence for the true king, in the face of their unjust rulers; and Clytaemnestra in the *Agamemnon* (883) mentions the risk of 'anarchy' when the king is away. In other words, 'anarchy' or 'despotism' can be set against monarchy no less than against democracy. So these words do not refer to forms of constitution; they are what comes about

---

[52] For one specific way in which their functions reinforce the state's justice, see Thomson on 935–8: participants in trials on the Areopagus had to swear on oath sanctioned by a curse on themselves and their descendants, and a prosecutor can refer to the nether gods in pressing for a conviction (Antiphon 1.31). In general, to punish a wrongdoer's descendants is characteristic of divine, as opposed to human, justice: cf. Hdt. 7.137.1–2; Lysias 6.20.

[53] Cf., broadly, Dover (n. 3), 233 [= *Greek and the Greeks*, 166–8]. Note also M. Lefkowitz, 'Autobiographical fiction in Pindar', *HSCP* 84 (1980), 29–49, at 38–9 [= *First-Person Fictions: Pindar's Poetic 'I'* (Oxford, 1991), 136–7], on a similar passage in Pindar, *P.* 11.51–4.

when fear is absent from the state. And fear is at once and indistin-guishably both an individual and a collective thing: it is the right measure and manner of control whether in the person or in the city.

What then exactly is this fear? It is powerfully contrasted with the foreboding or horror in the face of violence and guilt which we have witnessed continually in the trilogy.[54] It is identified with 'soundness of mind' (534 ὑγιείας φρενῶν); it is also the basis of spontaneously just behaviour (550). We have already met this emphasis on free will in *Eum.* 217–18. There Apollo says marriage is guarded not just by an oath, but by δίκη. In this context δίκη clearly implies spontaneous recognition of a bond which has an intrinsic value and is not an arbitrarily imposed duty. Much the same contrast occurs in Sopho-cles' *Philoctetes* (811–12) where Philoctetes refuses to constrain Neoptolemus by an oath to take him away and the younger man replies: 'Indeed it is not *right* for me to go without you (ὡς οὐ θέμις γ' ἐμοί 'στι σοῦ μολεῖν ἄτερ).[55] Naturally there is also punishment for those who scorn δίκη. The Chorus make this quite clear: behind their morality is the recognition of the gods' superior power (*Eum.* 517–25). But this recognition, what Aeschylus calls σωφρονεῖν, corres-ponds to the 'learning through suffering' (πάθει μάθος) of the hymn to Zeus in the *Agamemnon*; what was there only a dimly hopeful speculation, is now achieved.[56] To know the gods' power induces justice inspired by a conscious fear, not blindness—and then terror of punishment for the misdeeds that blindness prompted.

We might then even call the Areopagus the 'conscience' of the city;[57] it embodies an enlightened, not an unseeing fear. It is also within the community what τὸ δεινόν should be within each of its members: the parallelism of city and individual is part of Aeschylus' thinking as much as it is of Plato's.[58] So too the philosopher used an

[54] For the word, see esp. *Ag.* 14, 976; *Cho.* 46, 58, 102, though naturally fear is also widespread in the action. Cf. J. de Romilly, *La Crainte et l'angoisse dans la tragédie d'Eschyle* (Paris, 1958), 107–14.

[55] Cf. *OC* 650–1.

[56] Cf. Dodds 59–62 [= 261–4].

[57] Cf. Durkheim (n. 23a), ch. ii 1: penal law is a manifestation of 'la conscience collective ou commune', which in its turn is 'le type psychique de la société'. Note also Isoc. 17.14: the 'soul' of the state is its constitution (which determines its laws).

[58] For an explicit expression of it, see *Eum.* 522–5; also, e.g., Thuc. 2.64.6; 6.85.1; Eur. *Hec.* 903–4; *Suppl.* 493.

ideal city to express a permanent and universal image of justice; and the dramatist does the same through the Areopagus, an institution set up for all time in a community. Thus the foundation of the court substitutes for the horrors of 'an eye for an eye and a tooth for a tooth' not only legal justice, but justice in a far wider sense; and in that notion of justice is naturally implicit a vision of society.

Let us now turn to the conciliation of the Furies. As we have seen, they remain in the city as agents of universal justice. Just as the Areopagus is its human guarantor, so are the Furies on the divine plane. For human justice needs to be supplemented by divine supervision (992–5):

τάσδε γὰρ εὔφρονας εὔφρονες ἀεὶ
μέγα τιμῶντες καὶ γῆν καὶ πόλιν
ὀρθοδίκαιον
πρέψετε πάντως διάγοντες

If you honour them and show them kindness, as they themselves are kindly, you will surely be pre-eminent, guiding your land and city in the straight path of righteousness.

The picture of what the Eumenides are to bring to the city is long and complex. The benefits are of two kinds, social and material. Let us consider these in turn so as to see what light they throw on the notion of δίκη and the unity of the trilogy. We have already seen that if the Eumenides pray against faction and for a just prosperity, their prayers reverse what has come about in the *Agamemnon* and *Choephori*: we should now try to pursue this relation between the last scene of the trilogy and the rest a little further.

(1) The Eumenides are to be goddesses of marriage and child-bearing (834–6) and they pray to their gods as a whole and to their sisters, the Moirai, for fertility in matrimony (956–67). They thus come in their own way to agree with Apollo about the sanctity of marriage (213–18). We have heard before of the unholy wedding of Helen, the adulteress; we have seen Agamemnon enter with his concubine[59] or Clytaemnestra monstrously posing as the faithful wife and then slaughtering her own husband. These breaches of

[59] An Athenian could at least sympathize with the wife whose husband slept with other women: witness Sophocles' *Trachiniae*. See also K. J. Dover, *Aristophanic Comedy* (London, 1972), 160 n. 16.

marriage are reflected in the imagery. The word προτέλεια, which means particularly a sacrifice before marriage, occurs in a sinister way twice in the parodos (65–6, 227), associated with war and death and in contexts where the evil marriage of Helen and the frustrated marriage of Iphigenia are in our minds. It recurs (720) in the sinister analogy of the lion-cub who grows up to bring destruction to the house with Helen or her fateful wedding;[60] the mildness of the lion-cub in the 'prelude of life' (ἐν βιότου προτελείοις) contrasts with the 'bitter consummation of the marriage' (γάμου πικρὰς τελευτάς). I shall have more to say of this theme in dealing with the trial-scene; further documentation will follow then.

(2) The Eumenides are to have a cult and receive sacrifices (834–6, 854–7; cf. 1006, 1037). We recall the sacrifice Agamemnon performed on his daughter, Iphigenia—'a sacrifice without music and without feasting' (Ag. 151 θυσίαν... ἄνομόν τιν' ἄδαιτον)—or the deceptive sacrifice of thanksgiving performed by Clytaemnestra (Ag. 587–97). The language of sacrifice is also used in a distorted way of the death of Agamemnon (Ag. 1092, 1118, 1277, 1409, etc.): so, for example, for Clytaemnestra Agamemnon is the victim she has offered up to the goddesses Dike, Ate and Erinys (1432–4). Again, when the Eume-nides find Orestes clinging to Athena's statue they see him as their sacrificial victim, who has been 'fattened and consecrated' to them (ἐμοὶ τραφείς τε καὶ καθιερωμένος), and whom they will not kill, but devour alive (Eum. 304–5).[61]

Clytaemnestra's sacrifices were accompanied by an ὀλολυγή, a jubilant cry (Ag. 587, 595) particularly associated with sacrifice or victory. Here again there are recurrent sinister uses of the same word. The chorus in the Choephori pray that they may raise an ὀλολυγμός for the death of the tyrants (386–8); and they do so when it happens (942). In the Agamemnon we have already seen the hideous ὀλολυγή of Discord in Cassandra's prophecy (1118–19). Most fearful and most concrete of all is the one Clytaemnestra makes over the doomed

[60] Cf. Lebeck (n. 45), 48–9, 68–73; Vickers (n. 1), 421. Note also H. Lloyd-Jones, 'Agamemnonea', HSCP 73 (1969), 97–104 [= Greek Epic, Lyric, and Tragedy (Oxford, 1990), 310–17].

[61] Cf. Zeitlin (n. 45); Lebeck (n. 45), 60–3; P. Vidal-Naquet, Mythe et tragédie en Grèce ancienne (Paris, 1972), 135–58 [Eng. tr. in J.-P. Vernant and P. Vidal-Naquet, Myth and Tragedy in Ancient Greece (New York, 1988), 141–59].

Agamemnon (*Ag.* 1236). This disturbance of ritual is also set right at the end of the trilogy, where the chorus of escorts utter a joyful ὀλολυγή as they take the Eumenides to their home (1043, 1047).

(3) The Furies sing a song and a prayer, a ὕμνος for 'a not evil victory' (*Eum.* 903 νίκης μὴ κακῆς). There have been terrible victories before: Agamemnon's over Troy, Clytaemnestra's over Agamemnon (see esp. *Ag.* 940–3, 956, 1237), Orestes' over Clytaemnestra (see esp. *Cho.* 148, 244, 490, 868, 874, 890, 1017). But now the desperate hope of the chorus in the *Agamemnon*, 'May the good prevail' (121 = 139 τὸ δ᾽ εὖ νικάτω) comes true: the victory imagined here is an unambiguously good one. So is the song which hymns it. But hitherto song itself has been perverted. The most striking example is the 'binding-song' of the Furies which both echoes the magical process of κατάδεσις ('casting a spell') and hideously caricatures a sacrificial hymn (*Eum.* 304–6, 328–33 = 341–6), the victim eaten being the living Orestes himself. Likewise the central chorus in the *Choephori* (306–478), besides being the lament owed to the dead man, is the instrument of his retribution; the dirge, which is right and proper, is bound up with the spirit of revenge.[62] The singers not only bewail Agamemnon (θρῆνος), but call on his shade (ψυχαγωγία) to help in the coming murder, and incite his son to perform it. (So too among the proper prayers which accompany the libation to the murdered king Electra includes an 'evil prayer', for the death of the murderers [*Cho.* 145—8].) In the *Agamemnon* the chorus likens its utterance to a song which, unlike the normal singer, 'prophesies uninvited and unrewarded' (979 μαντιπολεῖ δ᾽ ἀκέλευστος ἄμισθος ἀοιδά); or the ode which is to be a thanksgiving for the victory (353–4) becomes a gloomy record not only of Paris' crime justly punished, but of Menelaus' loneliness, of the anger and bereavement of the Argive citizens, of premonitions of doom for the victor. So song itself has to have its value renewed at the end of the trilogy.[63]

(4) The Eumenides also pray for benefits in the natural world. Here again the last play reverses the horror of what went before. In a wealth of images connected with vegetation, with begetting, with weather and with light, Aeschylus had reflected the evil-doing of

---

[62] Cf. M. Alexiou, *The Ritual Lament in the Greek Tradition* (Cambridge, 1974), 178–9.

[63] Cf. J. A. Haldane, 'Musical themes and imagery in Aeschylus', *JHS* 85 (1965), 33–41, at 37–40; Zeitlin (n. 45), 496–7.

men. So Clytaemnestra rejoices when Agamemnon's blood spurts over her 'no less than the sown earth at the bright showers from heaven at the birth time of the bud' (*Ag.* 1391–2 οὐδὲν ἧσσον ἢ διοσδότῳ | γάνει σπορητὸς κάλυκος ἐν λοχεύμασιν). Or the chorus describe Agamemnon when he decides to sacrifice Iphigenia as 'breathing a reverse wind, impious, impure, unholy' (*Ag.* 219–20 φρενὸς πνέων δυσσεβῆ τροπαίαν | ἄναγνον, ἀνίερον). They speak too of the gestation and deliverance of Hybris (763–71); or, in relation to Paris' crime, of the 'baneful brightness' of evil (*Ag.* 389 πρέπει δέ, φῶς αἰνολαμπές, σίνος). These natural images have been recently studied in some detail;[64] here it is enough to recall how they echo the plot: the storm which shattered the Greek fleet, the ill winds that blew at Aulis (both signs of divine anger); the relay of beacons which announces the capture of Troy, whose fire is apparently a light of salvation (φῶς σωτήριον), but in reality the precursor of the conqueror's death and the symbol of the destruction coming to his house; the dream in which Clytaemnestra gives birth to a serpent, her matricidal son.[65] In short, in the *Agamemnon* and *Choephori* there is, both in the imagery and in the events the plays describe, a disturbance and a distortion of nature, which mirrors or even results from human crimes. Such a notion is familiar to English readers from *Julius Caesar* or *Macbeth* or *King Lear*; it is all the more natural in a language where δίκη can mean the world-order as a whole.[66] At the end of the whole trilogy these disturbances are calmed and the distortions straightened. The torch-light procession heralds an epoch of prosperity; and the Eumenides pray for crops and trees to be safe from blasting winds and the young of animals and women from mortal disease. We have already observed how social and religious institutions are also renewed at the end of the *Eumenides*; and the beneficence of nature and the prosperity of the people go naturally with this establishment of δίκη.[67] For δίκη is conceived

[64] See J. J. Peradotto, 'Some patterns of nature imagery in the *Oresteia*', *AJPh* 85 (1964), 378–93; T. Gantz, 'The fires of the *Oresteia*', *JHS* 97 (1977), 28–38.

[65] Note that the motif of *giving birth* is Aeschylus' own touch to the tradition about Clytaemnestra's dream: contrast Stesichorus, *PMG* 219 Page.

[66] Cf. H. Lloyd-Jones, *The Justice of Zeus* (Berkeley and London, 1971), Index s.v. 'Dikē'; Dover on Ar. *Nub.* 1292; H. Fränkel, *Wege und Formen frühgriechischen Denkens*² (Munich, 1960), 162–73.

[67] For δίκαιος and similar words applied to Athens, see 805, 912, 994.

to bring wealth and fertility both in Hesiod (*Op.* 225–37) and the *Odyssey* (19.109–14).[68] There is a significant difference in that in those contexts it is the just judgements of a ruler which bring prosperity; in Aeschylus it is respect for an institution and a cult. In this he writes indeed as the citizen of a democracy.[69] But in either case δίκη affects a whole community and nature itself, just as the individual's crime has been seen to do in the *Agamemnon* and *Choephori.* For δίκη is manifested or upturned in a city and in a world; it is not the lonely righteousness of an individual.[70]

III

That the framework of the action in the *Agamemnon* is a state goes with the fact that Aeschylus never completely separates even his great individuals from the collective ties which encircle them. The clan and the state have a far greater importance for the action in his work than in Sophocles'...
(Daube (n. 11) 50[71])

This quotation will pave the way for the consideration of our second word, τιμή. It may be complemented by a further quotation, from a modern introduction to anthropology:

Social relationships...are...the ways in which people behave when other people are the objects of that behaviour. The social relationship between husband and wife, for example, in a particular society means the ways in which husbands ordinarily behave to their wives, and wives to their husbands, in that society. At this preliminary level, there are always two things to be ascertained about any social relationship; whom it is between (e.g. husband and wife, father and son, ruler and subject) and what it is about

[68] Cf. Vickers (n. 1), 420.

[69] Cf. F. Solmsen, *Hesiod and Aeschylus* (Ithaca, NY, 1949), 215. Pericles praises Athenian democracy for its fear of written and unwritten laws (Thuc. 2.37.3); so too Aeschylus requires fear of the Areopagus and the Erinyes.

[70] For a suggestive statement of this point, see Aristotle, *EN* 1159^{a}25–1160^{a}30; cf. Cic. *Fin.* 5.65–6.

[71] A qualification: Sophoclean drama is certainly concentrated on the lonely individual, but by the same token it concerns his estrangement from his fellow-men or his precarious place among them.

(e.g. the disposition of property, the exercise of authority, the need to show respect). The dual quality of social relationships is often expressed in the distinction between statuses, what people are; and roles, what as occupants of certain statuses they do. The two aspects have sometimes been combined... in the portmanteau concept 'status-role'.   (J. Beattie, *Other Cultures* (London, 1964), 35–6)

Now τιμή is both a 'position' and a 'function' in a society; it is also the 'honour' which a person receives in virtue of them. So the word refers both to a 'status-role' and its acknowledgement, the feeling or behaviour which guarantees it and is evoked by it. And society is no more nor less than a 'system of relationships' (ibid. 221). Therefore when τιμή is at stake, so is society itself.

In order to see how an ancient mind might picture such a 'system of relationships', we could do worse than turn to an ancient anthropologist, St Augustine, who in the passage which follows is reporting, after Varro, the ethical tenets of the later Academy (*De civ. Dei* 19.3):[72]

hanc vitam beatam etiam socialem perhibent esse, quae amicorum bona propter se ipsa diligat sicut sua eisque propter ipsos hoc velit quod sibi; sive in domo sint, sicut coniunx et liberi et quicumque domestici, sive in loco ubi domus est eius, sicuti est urbs, ut sunt hi qui cives vocantur, sive in orbe toto, ut sunt gentes quas ei societas humana coniungit, sive in ipso mundo qui censetur nomine caeli et terrae, sicut esse dicunt deos quos volunt amicos esse homini sapienti.

They say that happiness is sociable, in that the happy man delights in the blessings of those he loves for their own sake as if they were his, and desires for those persons, for *their* own sake, what he desires for himself—whether they are in his home (like his wife and children and any other members of his household) or in the place where his home is, a city for example (like those who are called his fellow-citizens) or in the whole world (like the nations of men, with whom he is joined in the common bond of humanity) or in the universe itself which goes by the name of "heaven and earth" (like the gods, in their view, who they claim are friends to the wise man).

Two ideas underlie this doctrine. First, the individual cannot be fully good or happy unless his society (in the large sense of the term that

---

[72] For similar passages and a discussion of their sources, see S. G. Pembroke in *Problems in Stoicism*, ed. A. A. Long (London, 1971), 121–6. Also relevant to Aeschylus and his period, and foreshadowed in them, is the Stoic idea of the world as a city in which gods and men live together under a natural law: see, e.g., A. J. Festugière, *La Révélation d' Hermès Trismégiste*, ii (Paris, 1949), 272–8.

the passage suggests) is good and happy. Second, all relationships are continuous with one another; and a man cannot exist as a human or moral being outside that growing series of attachments. These notions were formulated at least two centuries after Aeschylus' death, but they are implicitly—and powerfully—present in the *Oresteia*; and they help to understand its artistic unity. For if family relationships and relationships with the rest of 'society' are continuous, it is clear that a concern with the city, the human community, is the natural counterpart of what is more often emphasized in Aeschylus, a concern with the family and with the gods. And as we consider τιμή, we shall have to consider it in all these contexts equally.

In the *Eumenides* τιμή (the word and its cognates recur again and again) is particularly associated with the Erinyes. Their functions or privileges as divine avengers of wrongdoing are, as they see it, in question; and these are confirmed at the end by their receiving a cult and a home in Athens. Thereby a mutual relationship of honour is set up between them and the Athenians (e.g. 917 and 993, 1029, 1038).[73] In the earlier part of the play the goddesses' τιμή is bound up with Clytaemnestra's—indeed, they *are* the curses of the aggrieved parent (417): the ghost of the murdered mother sees herself 'dishonoured' among the dead (95 ἀπητιμασμένη), and the only remedy is vengeance. (So also in *Cho.* 483–5 and 255–61 Orestes had warned both Agamemnon and Zeus that they would be dishonoured if Clytaemnestra was not punished, because they would receive no offerings from the royal house.) Against the claims of Clytaemnestra and the Furies are set the claims of Orestes as a suppliant: the two are most directly contrasted at *Eum.* 230–4,

> Χο. ἐγὼ δ', ἄγει γὰρ αἷμα μητρῷον, δίκας
> μέτειμι τόνδε φῶτα κἀκκυνηγέσω.
> Απ. ἐγὼ δ' ἀρήξω τὸν ἱκέτην τε ῥύσομαι.
> δεινὴ γὰρ ἐν βροτοῖσι κἀν θεοῖς πέλει
> τοῦ προστροπαίου μῆνις, εἰ προδῷ σφ' ἑκών.

---

[73] This is visually represented by the procession in the last scene and by the scarlet over-garments put on them there, which are now used, as the red robes should have been in the *Agamemnon* (921–2; 946–7), to honour the gods: see further C. W. Macleod, 'Clothing in the *Oresteia*', *Maia* 27 (1975), 201–3 [= *Collected Papers* (Oxford, 1983), 41–3]. Red robes are also proper to the cult of the nether gods: cf. Headlam on *Eum.* 1028–30 (pp. 316–17); Plut. *Aristid.* 21.

Chorus: I will pursue my vengeance, led by his mother's blood, and hunt the man down.

Apollo: And *I* will help and rescue the suppliant. The wrath of a suppliant is terrible among men and gods, when he is gratuitously abandoned.

The contrast is stressed by the ambiguity of the word προστρόπαιος, which may denote either, as here, the suppliant for purification or the spirit of a murdered man (e.g. *Cho.* 287) that demands revenge.[74] It could be said, in fact, of Orestes in this play that his role is simply to be a suppliant. It is this which gives him, through the purification it seeks and finds, a foothold among men, a claim to trial and so, after his acquittal, restoration to his kingdom. It is also his suppliant condition which distinguishes him from the other murderers of the trilogy (Dodds 61 [= 263]). He, when the deed is done, looks for purification; 'where Clytaemnestra carried a bloody sword, Orestes carries an olive-branch and a wreath' (ibid.)—though he too carries a sword (for he too is a murderer), as is clear from the priestess' description of him (*Eum.* 42–3). He behaves σωφρόνως (*Eum.* 44), in that spirit of enlightened fear which the Furies praise, the Areopagus embodies and the Athenians are to live by (*Eum.* 1000).

The characters in the *Eumenides*, then, are what they are in virtue of their definition as social beings. Orestes is so unobtrusive, even colourless, because he is a suppliant, and as such must efface himself in seeking help;[75] and the moment he is restored to his own identity and his own community is the end of his tragedy. The Erinyes are so ferocious because they are defending their status in the world, which is to embody and enforce the law of blood for blood among kindred; and their tragedy likewise ends when they are incorporated in a city with the honours that are their due. In the *Agamemnon* and *Choephori* too the characters can only arouse the intense emotions they do because they are set in a society which their deeds or sufferings affect. This should have emerged to a considerable degree already in this paper; so in order not to overburden the reader I limit the discussion

---

[74] See further Moulinier (n. 42), 267–70.

[75] Cf. J. Gould, 'Hiketeia', *JHS* 93 (1973), 74–103, at 94–5 [= *Myth, Ritual, Memory, and Exchange* (Oxford, 2001), 22–74, at 58–60]. His whole paper is an already classic treatment of supplication; also admirable is the chapter of Vickers (n. 1), 438–94, on the subject as material for tragedy.

to, first, the main appearances of the word τιμή and its cognates, and then the central misdeed of the trilogy, the murder of Agamemnon. First, *Ag.* 699–706:

> Ἰλίῳ δὲ κῆδος ὀρ-
> θώνυμον τελεσσίφρων
> Μῆνις ἤλασεν τραπέζας ἀτί-
> μωσιν ὑστέρῳ χρόνῳ
> καὶ ξυνεστίου Διὸς
> πρασσομένα τὸ νυμφότι-
> μου μέλος ἐκφάτως τίοντας.

Wrath that fulfils its purpose brought to Troy a marriage rightly named "woe" [pun on κῆδος] exacting in the passage of time requital for a dishonour done to hospitality and Zeus, guardian of those who share the hearth, from the people who loudly sang in honour of the bride...

Paris offends against a social institution, ξενία (as he does against another one, marriage), and the god who guarantees it. He is thus attacking society as a whole, not merely Menelaus or even Menelaus' city. Compare *Cho.* 429–45:

> Ηλ. ἰὼ ἰὼ δαῖα
>   πάντολμε μᾶτερ, δαΐαις ἐν ἐκφοραῖς
>   ἄνευ πολιτᾶν ἄνακτ',
>   ἄνευ δὲ πενθημάτων
>   ἔτλας ἀνοίμωκτον ἄνδρα θάψαι.
> Ορ. τὸ πᾶν ἀτίμως ἔλεξας, οἴμοι,
>   πατρὸς δ' ἀτίμωσιν ἆρα τείσει...
> Χο. ἐμασχαλίσθη δέ γ', ὡς τόδ' εἰδῇς·
>   ἔπρασσε δ' ἅπερ νιν ὧδε θάπτει,
>   μόρον κτίσαι μωμένα
>   ἄφερτον αἰῶνι σῷ.
>   κλύεις πατρῴους δύας ἀτίμους.
> Ηλ. λέγεις πατρῷον μόρον. ἐγὼ δ' ἀπεστάτουν
>   ἄτιμος, οὐδὲν ἀξία[76]...

Electra: Ah, mother of hatred, you stopped at nothing, you dared, in a funeral of hatred, to bury the king without his citizens, your husband without a lament, unbewailed.

---

[76] On the force of this phrase, note A. W. H. Adkins, 'Aristotle and the best kind of tragedy', *CQ* 16 (1966), 78–101, at 91: Electra is 'unworthy' both as innocent and as a noblewoman. Cf. Isoc. 16.48.

Orestes: In utter dishonour! She will pay, then, for the dishonouring of my
father…

Chorus: And he was mutilated too… She did it, she who buried him thus,
eager to give him a death unbearable to you and your life. I tell you
of the sufferings, the dishonour of your father.

Electra: That was how my father died. And I stood apart, dishonoured
unworthily…

There is here a dishonouring of Electra thrust aside by the usurpers,
as there is of the city and the house,[77] but still more a dishonouring
of the dead man. Agamemnon is buried, but he receives no lament
and is even mutilated. Here, as when Clytaemnestra's ghost appears,
it is the τιμή of the dead that is at stake, for they too are part of
society by virtue of their honours and influence among the living.[78]
This same theme, the lack of a lament over Agamemnon, plays a large
part at the end of the *Agamemnon* (1480–96 = 1513–20; 1541–50)
and the beginning of the *Choephori*: it culminates and ends in the
lament at last achieved by Electra, Orestes and the chorus. So again in
Ag. 1443–6 Clytaemnestra boasts:[79]

> ἄτιμα δ' οὐκ ἐπραξάτην·
> ὁ μὲν γὰρ οὕτως, ἡ δέ τοι κύκνου δίκην
> τὸν ὕστατον μέλψασα θανάσιμον γόον
> κεῖται φιλήτωρ τοῦδε…

They have not lacked their privileges. There he lies, and she, having sung like
a dying swan their lament, lies there too, his lover…

This is another of the queen's blasphemous sarcasms. The τιμή the
two have received is not a proper lament at all, it is only Cassandra's
prophetic wailing (cf. 1313–14).

To consider now the murder of Agamemnon. Here the most
valuable starting-point is the arguments of Apollo and Athena in
the trial scene of the *Eumenides*. Of these Solmsen remarks (n. 69)
193, that they 'are merely an attempt to appraise in rational, or even

---

[77] The word ἄτιμος is applied to the house in *Cho.* 408; and the notion that it and
the city are enslaved and degraded by the usurpers pervades the whole play: see, e.g.,
302–4, 942–5, 961–4, 973–4. In the last passage Aegisthus and Clytaemnestra are evil
μέτοικοι (in contrast to the Erinyes at the end of *Eum.*).

[78] Cf. Dover (n. 19), 243–6.

[79] Denniston-Page rightly interpret ἄτιμα here as 'without honour, without privileges'; but I differ over what honour or privilege is concerned.

doctrinal, terms those features of the situation which long before the trial scene have influenced our responses to the plot'. In other words, though the arguments which secure Orestes' acquittal are one-sided,[80] they are, to the spectator who has seen the whole trilogy, not arbitrary sophistries. The essence of the matter is this: Agamemnon is the man, the husband, the lord of the house, the victorious general, the king; he is treacherously killed by a woman, his wife, the false guardian of the house in his absence (οἰκουρός), who then becomes, with her consort, a tyrant. The king's death is pitiful and fearful because it represents the inversion or destruction of so many social values. The same applies, though on a smaller scale, to the death of Clytaemnestra. She is, though her husband's murderer and a usurper, still the mother killed by her son; this is what the Erinyes are asserting and has been thrust upon us above all in the scene where she bares her breast to Orestes (*Cho.* 896–934), or in the account of her dream where the serpent she bore sucks her blood, even as her son is to kill her (*Cho.* 526–50). And it should by now be clear how all the events and all the people involved in them have such a social significance. The exception which proves the rule is Cassandra. The essence of her tragedy is that she is caught up as a gratuitous and innocent victim first in the destruction of Troy and then in the death of Agamemnon and the doom of his house; she falls a prey not so much to the justice of the gods as, like Io in the *Prometheus Vinctus*, to the arrogance of her divine lover. At the same time, isolated and misunderstood, she knows and reveals, as no other does, what is to come. And it is only from this isolation that she can cry (*Ag.* 1327–30):

> ἰὼ βρότεια πράγματ'· εὐτυχοῦντα μὲν
> σκιᾷ τις ἂν πρέψειεν, εἰ δὲ δυστυχῇ,
> βολαῖς ὑγρώσσων σπόγγος ὤλεσεν γραφήν.
> καὶ ταῦτ' ἐκείνων μᾶλλον οἰκτίρω πολύ.

Oh the life of man! When there is prosperity, it can be likened to a shadow; but when there is misfortune, the dash of a wet sponge wipes out the picture. And this I pity far more than that.

---

[80] Athena's words in 734–40 correspond to the will of Zeus (797–9), but they are not meant to be a solution: what Orestes did remains a fearful crime, and not for nothing are there as many votes for condemnation as for acquittal (cf. 795–6). Aeschylus expects from his audience enough political wisdom to see that law and judgement are no less necessary because some legal decisions are open to dispute.

She alone tastes unmixed sorrow, without pride or guilt.[81]

But let us consider one by one the elements of Agamemnon's tragedy as it is recalled in the trial scene.

(i) Agamemnon as man and husband killed by the woman and his wife (the two pairs of notions are hard to keep apart because of the ambiguity ἀνήρ and γυνή).[82] This theme figures in Apollo's speech (627; 657–66); and the predilection for the male is the main feature of Athena's (734–40). We have already seen the importance of marriage in the trilogy; and that Agamemnon and Clytaemnestra are man and wife is naturally part of the horror of his death. So *Ag.* 1116: 'The net is his wife, who is responsible for the murder' (ἀλλ' ἄρκυς ἡ ξύνευνος, ἡ ξυναιτία | φόνου;) *Ag.* 1543: 'Will you dare to lament your husband when you killed him?' (ἦ σὺ τόδ' ἔρξαι τλήσῃ, κτείνασ' | ἄνδρα τὸν αὑτῆς ἀποκωκῦσαι;). So also the theme of man and woman in *Ag.* 1231: 'The female is murderer of the male' (θῆλυς ἄρσενος φονεύς), with the subsequent comparisons to female monsters. And the notion of the woman's unnatural and criminal supremacy dominates a whole ode in the *Choephori* (585–651).[83] The pervasiveness of this theme is what above all makes Clytaemnestra seem an almost super-human— or better, anti-human—character; and it is represented on the stage when she dominates her husband on his return. So when Apollo and Athena say that the man is the only begetter of the child, that is the statement, in physical terms, of a principle thought necessary for moral and social order (the fusion of the categories 'is' and 'ought' is of the essence in the notion of δίκη); and Aeschylus' poetry has made it immediate to the spectator through his portrayal of Clytaemnestra and the reactions of chorus and characters to her deed. Apollo has not told the whole story, for Agamemnon himself sins against

[81] On the contrast between Cassandra and the other characters (especially Agamemnon), see K. Reinhardt, *Aischylos als Regisseur und Theologe* (Bern, 1949), 90–105; Macleod (n. 73), 202–3 [= *Collected Papers*, 42–3]; id., 'Aeschylus, *Agamemnon* 1285–1289', *CQ* 32 (1982), 231–2 [= *Collected Papers*, 44–5].

[82] On this theme, see R. P. Winnington-Ingram, 'Clytemnestra and the vote of Athena', *JHS* 68 (1948), 130–47 [= *Studies in Aeschylus* (Cambridge, 1983), 101–31], a pioneering article; also Vickers (n. 1) 381, 400–2, 414–16, who corrects an aberration of Winnington-Ingram's on p. 432, n. 33.

[83] On this ode, see the valuable analysis by T. C. W. Stinton, 'The first stasimon of Aeschylus' *Choephori*', *CQ* 29 (1979), 252–62 [= *Collected Papers on Greek Tragedy* (Oxford, 1990), 384–96].

marriage by bringing a concubine into the house and by killing the
daughter he shares with his wife; but neither is the god's argument a
mere sophistry.

(ii) Agamemnon as lord of the house, and Clytaemnestra and
Aegisthus as its false guardians.[84] This theme figures in Athena's
speech (740). So in *Ag.* 1224–5 Aegisthus is the 'cowardly lion, enjoying the freedom of his bed, keeping the house—alas!—for its lord'
(λέοντ' ἄναλκιν ἐν λέχει στρωφώμενον | οἰκουρόν, οἴμοι, τῷ μολόντι
δεσπότῃ); or in *Cho.* 52—3: 'Darkness covers the house at the death of
its lord' (δνόφοι καλύπτουσι δόμους | δεσποτᾶν θανάτοισι). More
broadly, this theme is present in Clytaemnestra's welcome when
Agamemnon returns, seemingly to take his place in the house as its
master, but in reality to die (esp. *Ag.* 966 ff.); it is most vividly
represented when her sudden appearance blocks his entry into his
own palace,[85] or when she boasts of her 'good housekeeping' (606–16).
And in the *Choephori* the death of Aegisthus and Clytaemnestra is
the liberation of the house from its wrongful occupiers (e.g. 942–5,
962–4).

(iii) Agamemnon as victorious general. This theme appears in
Apollo's speech (631–2, 637). 'He fared well for the most part'
(ἠμπολημότα | τὰ πλεῖστ' ἄμεινον) is a bold rhetorical obfuscation
designed to blot out memories of the sacrifice of Iphigenia or the guilty
triumph at Troy; none the less, we have already been responding
to Agamemnon's death as that of the great general. So *Ag.* 1227–8:
'The ruler of the ships, the sacker of Troy, does not know' (νεῶν δ'
ἄπαρχος Ἰλίου τ' ἀναστάτης | οὐκ οἶδεν . . .); *Cho.* 1071–2: 'The war-
lord of the Greeks was struck down in his bath' (λουτροδάικτος δ' ὤλετ'
Ἀχαιῶν | πολέμαρχος ἀνήρ). On a larger scale this theme has been
present in the confrontation of Agamemnon and Clytaemnestra. For
Clytaemnestra fulsomely urges Agamemnon not to place 'the foot
that sacked Troy' (907 τὸν σὸν πόδ', ὦναξ, Ἰλίου πορθήτορα) on the

[84] In general on the wife's role as οἰκουρός see T. E. V. Pearce, *Eranos* 72 (1974),
16–33. In *Ag.* 1225 οἰκουρόν (cf. 809) must have—with the bitter irony revealed by
οἴμοι—its full sense of 'guardian of the house', since it goes with τῷ μολόντι δεσπότῃ.
(The following line is rightly deleted by Fraenkel.) So also at 1626, where a large part
of the horror is that he who watches over the house in its lord's absence also defiles his
bed. The sense 'stay-at-home' is also felt in so far as Aegisthus is contrasted with the
fighter and general Agamemnon.
[85] Cf. Taplin (n. 14), 306–8.

bare ground, but in reality—as is underscored by the language (940–3, 956)—she wins a 'victory' over Agamemnon by persuading him to walk on the precious robes; and so we have the ironic spectacle of the conqueror conquered, which also foreshadows his coming death.

(iv) Agamemnon as king. In Apollo's words he is 'honoured by a Zeus-given sceptre' (626 διοσδότοις σκήπτροισι τιμαλφούμενον). So also in *Ag.* 1451–2: 'Our most kindly lord and guardian has been killed' (δαμέντος | φύλακος εὐμενεστάτου); *Cho.* 431–3: 'You buried the king without his citizens' (ἄνευ πολιτᾶν ἄνακτα... ἔτλας... θάψαι); *Cho.* 479: 'Father, you who died in a way unfit for a king' (πάτερ, τρόποισιν οὐ τυραννικοῖς θανών). Agamemnon's kingship is his most obvious relationship with the community; and the chorus in the *Agamemnon* are naturally conscious of him above all—at times angrily—as their ruler, and their feelings guide and stimulate the audience's. The theme is further stressed by typically Aeschylean inversions. We already saw how Helen and Clytaemnestra are conceived to wield a common rule, by a hideous analogy with the joint kingship of the Atridae (*Ag.* 1470); and how when the queen and her lover come to power, they are usurpers from whom Orestes liberates the city.

I have separated these themes for convenience's sake, when in their contexts they combine, and in so doing, gain intensity; and they have only been selectively illustrated. But they are so pervasive in the trilogy, its words and its action, that no further quotation should be necessary. All that needs repeating is that any response to Aeschylus' characters and their destinies is a response to a society, a society upturned, as in the body of the trilogy, or renewed, as at the end of the *Eumenides.*

IV

I have adopted in dealing with the *Oresteia* a position which might well be attacked as unhistorical. But it was not my intention to deny what a historian might wish to insist on, that Aeschylus was part of his own, a historical, society and that he must have been affected by it and had some views about it. As I hope was clear, I believe it is possible by an examination of the text to suggest something about Aeschylus' political views; for he clearly accepts the Areopagus as Ephialtes reconstituted it and the Argive alliance. More generally, there are important touches in the *Oresteia* which are the work of the citizen of a democracy. For example, for Aeschylus, unlike Hesiod or Homer, δίκη is guaranteed not by a just ruler but by a court and a cult; nor is there any sign of a monarch in his mythical Athens. And Aeschylus' concept of the Areopagus corresponds quite closely to things that the orators say about law and its function in society. But the same Aeschylus who idealizes a democratic Athens also vividly presents through his choruses and characters the sentiments of loyal subjects of a monarchy; and the *Agamemnon* and *Choephori* would be meaningless if we did not accept in imagination the social framework they presuppose.[86] The *Oresteia*, because it spans and penetrates so many conditions of man, tends towards universality; and its conclusion is the picture of much more than a good democracy. The poet's own city here approaches the condition of an ideal city; but the ideal embraces society—and that means also nature and the gods—as a whole. Likewise, the message of the play to its audience is not a narrowly topical one. The tragedian is influenced by his time and circumstances; but they are an influence on the work, not the meaning of it. And it is only through an examination of that meaning that both the lasting greatness of the poet and his position in his own time and city can be illumined.

[86] For some places where the *Oresteia* presupposes non-Attic (Homeric) customs, see Fraenkel on *Ag.* 245, 1109, 1382, 1595.

10

The Imagery of *Choephoroe*

Barbara Hughes Fowler

The *Choephoroe* is in its plot of recognition and revenge more complex than the *Agamemnon*. In its lyric structure it is, however, simpler than that play. Still, it is a part of the story of the doom upon the house of Atreus, and because it is a continuation of that narrative, it is in its drama created out of the same basic contradiction: men and women.

Orestes and Electra slay their mother partly to avenge their father's death, partly to punish her for her affair with Aegisthus; they act partly out of loyalty to Agamemnon, partly out of jealousy for Aegisthus, who claimed from Clytemnestra the affection her children deserved. The *philos-aphilos* ['hate-in-love'] motif has become a conflict now between generations: between mother and son; between mother and daughter; between both the children and their mother's lover, who was also their father's cousin and their own uncle, Aegisthus.

Members of a house, naturally committed to one another, are in the *Choephoroe* forced to turn against one another—and so against themselves—by the compelling force of revenge. Motivation seems simpler now, and this is in keeping with the more archaic, more strictly heroic character of the play. But the revenge theme is far more than a personal one. It is also strongly dynastic. Orestes is an exile and, quite literally, an impoverished one. He is driven by the loss

[*Editor's note.* This chapter is an extract from a long article discussing the imagery in all of Aeschylus' surviving plays apart from *Prometheus Bound.*]

of his rightful inheritance to recover the kingdom Aegisthus usurped. Finally, the revenge motif becomes religious, for it was Apollo, spokesman for Zeus, who commanded Orestes to commit this murder, to appease the Furies' wrath.

The *Choephoroe* is composed of very nearly the same image complexes as was the *Agamemnon*. It develops the themes of the earlier play and uses to do so—with addition, with variation—the same symbols, the same combinations of symbols.

The robe, the murder device, is still in the *Choephoroe* a symbol, provided now not out of action but out of the memory of action, the memory of murder that is to be cause for more murder. Orestes and Electra in their incantation to their father's spirit bid him remember the novel casting net (ἀμφίβληστρον) devised for him (492). He was trapped in fetters (πέδαις) no bronze-smith made (493). In shrouds (καλύμμασιν) contrived in shame (494). Electra in her variation of the figure of the fishing net (δίκτυον) includes the idea for which it habitually stands: the murder of Agamemnon. She and Orestes are like corks that buoy it up; they are voices of salvation to a man even though he is dead (505–6).[1] Though Agamemnon is dead, murdered in a fishing net, his children, the corks that save the net from sinking, will preserve his name and his house.

When Orestes comes to the actual plans for the murder, he demands that Electra keep secret their agreement so that those who killed an honored man with treachery may with treachery be taken in the selfsame snare (βρόχῳ) and die (555–8). The snare now is more than the murder device, more than the robe in which Agamemnon was entangled and slain. It has become a device for revenge. The murderers, Apollo has promised, are to be taken by their own device: by treachery.

When the murder is done, when Clytemnestra and Aegisthus are dead, Orestes to justify his deed holds up the robe, the means for the first, the cause for the second set of murders. Look, he says, at this device, the thing that bound his wretched father, shackles (πέδας) for his hands, fetters (ξυνωρίδα) for his feet (980–2). What shall he call it? A snare (ἄγρευμα) for a wild beast? A shroud (κατασκήνωμα) for a

---

[1] These lines are bracketed by Murray.

corpse (or a curtain for a bath[2]) wrapped round his feet (ποδένδυτον)? Or a net (δίκτυον) perhaps, and robes to entangle the feet (ποδιστῆρας, 998–1000). Spread it out, he says, that Apollo may see the impious deeds of his mother and defend him ἐν δίκῃ (983–6): in the 'vengeance' which he has taken, in the 'trial' which he must face, in what Orestes now mistakenly thinks is 'justice'. His act of unfolding the robe is symbolic of that process of Revenge which will in the *Eumenides* become Right.

Now, however, Orestes and Electra use the robe, the memory of that method of murder, to evoke for their purposes of vengeance the spirit of their father Agamemnon. They are, they say as they stand at his tomb, the orphaned children of the eagle father who died in the meshes (πλεκταῖσι) and coils (σπειράμασιν) of the deadly viper. They are pressed by hunger, for they are not grown enough to bring their father's quarry to the nest (247–51). This is the symbolism of the *Agamemnon*. Agamemnon is again the eagle; Clytemnestra, the viper; the viper's coils, the folds of her robe. But now the orphaned nestlings add to the completed plot of the *Agamemnon* the motivation for the plot of the *Choephoroe*, and that motivation is dynastic as well as purely personal. Agamemnon's children feel the pinch of poverty because they have been deprived by Aegisthus of their rightful inheritance. 'Prey' refers to the provision their father made for them while he was alive and by implication to the provision that ought now to be made for them even though he is dead. Besides this, the word anticipates the vengeance that Orestes and Electra are planning to take. The figure of the hunt because it recalls the manhunt for Helen and Troy, because it anticipates the hounds that will track Orestes down, because it is throughout the trilogy associated with death and revenge, means here the prey that the nestlings will bring to the nest for their father's sake, the vengeance that they will take for him when they are 'grown'; the implication is that their father's support will make them that.

The viper that entangled the eagle in its coils becomes a primary symbol of the *Choephoroe*. It comes to stand for the *philos-aphilos* ['hate-in-love'] motif in all its strongest statements. Clytemnestra, herself the viper before, dreams that she gave birth to a serpent which

---

[2] The lines translate both ways: the ambiguity is deliberate.

she wrapped in swaddling clothes as though it were a child; she offered it her breast and it drew clotted blood with the milk (527–33).[3]

Orestes interprets the dream to mean a man and that man himself. For if it left the same place he did and was wrapped in his swaddling clothes, if it took the breast that nourished him and mixed the sweet milk with clotted blood, and if she then shrieked with terror at this portent, then surely it means that she must die by violence. For he, Orestes, turned serpent, will kill her as this dream declares (549–50). Clytemnestra, when she realizes that Orestes intends to kill her, recognizes him for the snake she bore and suckled (928). When she is dead, Orestes says that had she been born a sea-snake or a viper, her very touch without her bite would have caused a man to rot; so bold and wicked was her spirit (994–6). Orestes, the chorus tells him, set free the whole city of Argives when he cut off the heads of the two serpents, when he murdered Clytemnestra, the viper, and her lover, Aegisthus (1046–7).

This entire complex of image, of the viper and her mate, of the viper and her young, is the most explicit statement in all the *Oresteia* of the *philos-aphilos* ['hate-in-love'] motif. The Herodotus passage (3.109) that sets forth the popular notion of the viper that turns against its own—the female against the male and in retribution for this the young against the mother—is clear exposition of the plot, first of the *Agamemnon* and then of the *Choephoroe*.

Besides the symbol of the viper and its coils, which stands for compulsion as murder and as revenge for murder, other symbols of animals, violent or constrained, stand for compulsion in its several aspects or forms.

Before the murder is actually accomplished the chorus appeals to Zeus to see the orphaned colt harnessed to the chariot of suffering. May he set a measure to the race he is running and grant that they may see him keeping a steady rhythm through the field and a strain

---

[3] Clytemnestra's dream and its symbol of the viper was part of the tradition as Aeschylus inherited it. Cf. Stesichorus 219: 'She dreamed that there came a serpent with bloodied crest, and from it there appeared a king of the line of Pleisthenes.' The use of that symbol as part of the dramatic pattern was undoubtedly Aeschylus' own. On the symbol of the viper see further W. Whallon, 'The serpent at the breast', *TAPhA* 89 (1958), 271–5; B. M. W. Knox, 'The lion in the house', *CPh* 47 (1952), 17–24 [= *Word and Action* (Baltimore and London, 1979), 27–38].

in his finishing stride (794–800). Orestes is constrained by the past sufferings or disasters of his house to suffer another disaster, to commit another murder. May he keep his head, the chorus asks; may caution see him through the deed.

When the deed is done, then Orestes loses control. He no longer is that harnessed colt of steady pace. He is instead, he says, a charioteer who drives his horses outside the course. His wits, hard to control, carry him, defeated, away (1022–4). Compulsion is no longer the disasters of the past; it is remorse now for the present disaster, for the murder that Orestes has himself committed. In both cases, however, the idea behind the image is that of the doom upon the house of Atreus, the curse that made Orestes murder his mother, that will make him pursued now by her avenging spirits.

Just after Orestes takes Clytemnestra into the house to murder her, the chorus says that justice came at last, a heavy retribution to Priam's house, but a twofold lion came into the house of Agamemnon, a twofold slaughter, and the Pythian-advised exile, urged by the gods' counsel, got all that was allotted him (935–41). The twofold lion is Orestes and Pylades or perhaps Orestes and his sister Electra who have come to take vengeance by a double murder for the double murder that another twofold lion, Clytemnestra and Aegisthus, had committed: the murder of Agamemnon, another lion, and his captive mistress, Cassandra.

Other animal images stand not for the act of revenge but for the forces that provoked that revenge. Orestes deprived of his father's wealth is angered like a bull (275). Electra, when her father was murdered, was kennelled in her room like a vicious dog (445–6). Her mother may fawn, Electra says, but their pain is not to be soothed; for the temper they have from their mother is, like a savage wolf, implacable (420–2). Electra's figure here recalls Clytemnestra, the faithless watchdog of the *Agamemnon*; it anticipates too the *Eumenides'* hound-like avengers, for later Clytemnestra herself tells Orestes to guard against a mother's wrathful hounds (924). Orestes was driven by his poverty, Electra by her mother's mistreatment, and both of them by their inherited dispositions to commit this second set of murders. These animal figures too, then, give form to the drama's general theme of compulsion, which has in the *Choephoroe* become revenge.

Animal figures suggest in the *Choephoroe* as they had in the
Agamemnon the image of the hunt. Now, however, that image stands
not for the expedition for Helen's sake and not for the ultimate will of
Zeus but for present revenge. The lament for fathers, the chorus says,
when its cause is just 'acts the hunter' ($\mu\alpha\tau\epsilon\acute{\upsilon}\epsilon\iota$, 329–31). Orestes'
revenge is the hunter now. Soon, however, his revenge will arouse his
mother's avenging huntressess, the Erinyes.[4]

Figures of animals, controlled and uncontrolled, are associated in
the *Choephoroe*, as they were in the *Agamemnon*, with figures of
objects that constrain or fail to constrain. The chorus, while Orestes
and Electra are invoking Agamemnon's spirit, refers to the bloody
stroke ($\pi\lambda\alpha\gamma\acute{\alpha}$) of Ruin that afflicts the race (466–8). They refer here
to the events of the past, but earlier they referred to the incantation
itself as a double scourge ($\mu\alpha\rho\acute{\alpha}\gamma\nu\eta\varsigma$, 375–6). Again, compulsion is
becoming revenge.

The balance, including the *Choephoroe*, as it had in the *Agamemnon*,
the idea of weight, is identified with Dike; for the sinking ($\dot{\rho}o\pi\acute{\eta}$)
(of the scale) of justice swiftly casts a shadow on those in the light
(61–2). The chorus here seems to refer to Dike as Justice but it includes
in its expression the Revenge that is to precede Justice: 'those who stand
in the light' refers to the fortunate in general, but it refers also
to Clytemnestra and Aegisthus who, like the chorus, do not know
the fate that awaits them. Electra anticipates that fate when she asks
when Zeus will bring his hand upon them (394–6). The 'hand of Zeus',
which Electra thinks of as revengeful, includes too the concept of
weight.

The chorus, before the murders are accomplished, says that Dike,
though trampled underfoot ($\lambda\acute{\alpha}\xi\ \pi\acute{\epsilon}\delta o\iota\ \pi\alpha\tau o\upsilon\mu\acute{\epsilon}\nu\alpha\varsigma$), will strike at him
who has transgressed the majesty of Zeus (639–45). Here, it is
implied, the will of Zeus, which is not immediate Revenge but eventual Justice, is the force that, temporarily subdued, will prevail. For,
the chorus has just said, the sword strikes at Dike's command (639–
41). Her anvil is planted firm; destiny is making arms ($\pi\rho o\chi\alpha\lambda\kappa\epsilon\acute{\upsilon}\epsilon\iota$)
and forging her sword ($\phi\alpha\sigma\gamma\alpha\nu o\upsilon\rho\gamma\acute{o}\varsigma$, 646–7). Orestes is, in the eyes
of the chorus, the agent of Dike and Destiny. Just before he murders

[4] G. D. Thomson, *The Oresteia of Aeschylus* (Cambridge, 1938), ii. 189 (on *Cho.*
329–30).

Aegisthus, it speaks of the bloodstained edges of blades (πειροί κοπάνων) that will either destroy entirely the house of Agamemnon—or win Orestes his father's wealth (859–62). Their figure here anticipates the actual weapon with which Orestes will murder Aegisthus and Clytemnestra, but it includes too the sword of Dike and of Destiny. The murders, because they are done at Apollo's will, are the first step in the establishment of Justice;[5] they are a beginning of the setting right of the affairs of the house of Atreus.

When the murders are done, the chorus refers to the curse upon that house as a curb (ψάλιον). They think, at least, that they are freed from the compelling forces of the past (961–2). Orestes, however, realizes that the revenge he has taken is not the end; he declares that he must go, an exile, to Apollo's shrine. The chorus, still not possessed of complete knowledge, asks him not to yoke (ἐπιζεύχθῃς) his mouth to ill-omened speech, for he has by lopping off the serpents' heads freed the whole land of Argos (1044–7). They want him, they imply, to be free as he had freed Argos from the compelling forces of evil that have plagued the house of Atreus and so its subject people in the past.

The figure of the archer or the arrow appears in the *Choephoroe*, as it did in the *Agamemnon*, sometimes in connection with the sword, to represent compulsion. That compulsion is, in this play, specifically Revenge. In its recall, however, of the imagery of the *Agamemnon* and its anticipation of the imagery of the *Eumenides*, it is also the will of Zeus, which is Justice.

The chorus, early in the play, longs for a man strong in the spear (δορυσθενής), brandishing the bow (Σκύθην...Ἄρη [παλίντον'... βέλη]), wielding the sword (αὐτόκωπα...βέλη), to deliver the house (160–3). Orestes, recounting Apollo's orders to him, describes the assault of a father's avenging spirits as the dark arrow (βέλος) of the nether powers (286). Βέλος need not mean specifically 'arrow', though the word is perhaps most frequently so used; it may be a dart, a bolt, anything thrown; in this context, almost certainly a weapon.

---

[5] Thomson comments that πειροί 'edges' is explained by the scholiast as being from πείρειν 'to pierce', a verb regularly used in Homer of setting meat on spits in preparation for sacrifice, and that the word here may be based on the idea of a sacrificial knife. If so, the figure emphasizes the religious nature of Apollo's command to murder (n. 4, ii. 232, on *Cho.* 858–9).

The incantation of Orestes and Electra has pierced Agamemnon's ear like an arrow (βέλος, 380–1). He is to help them take their revenge. When Orestes lyingly tells Clytemnestra that her son (Orestes) is dead, she laments that the Curse has with well-aimed bow (τόξοις) brought down what she had thought was safe (692–4). She pretends that the Curse has deprived her of what she had thought was an agent of revenge; actually, the bow of revenge stands before her.

When Orestes has taken his revenge, he explains that he acted on Apollo's orders. The god of the bow had assured him that if he did not avenge his father, no bow (τόξῳ) could reach such woes as would befall him (1033).

The figure of the wrestler occurs in the *Choephoroe*, as it had in the *Agamemnon*, and includes again the concepts of involvement and weight, aspects of the play's theme of compulsion. Electra asks is it not impossible to throw doom a third time (ἀτρίακτος, 339)? The figure is, the scholiast remarks, taken from wrestling.[6] Orestes, invoking Agamemnon's spirit, asks that he and Electra get grip (λαβὰς λαβεῖν) of Clytemnestra and Aegisthus as those two had of him (497–9). Orestes speaks of immediate revenge, but Clytemnestra, hearing of Orestes' 'death', speaks of the whole series of compelling forces, set in motion by the will of Zeus, when she addresses the curse upon the house as hard to wrestle with (δυσπάλαιστε, 692). When Clytemnestra has sent Orestes and Pylades into the house as her guests, that chorus says that it is time for Persuasion to enter the lists (ξυνκαταβῆναι) with Orestes (726–7). Persuasion, which in the *Agamemnon* had been sex, flattery, wealth, is now allied with Revenge. She begins to be, but is not really yet, a force for good.

When Orestes has gone inside to commit the murders, the chorus says that he, in such a match (πάλην), with none to second him (ἔφεδρος), is about to grapple (ἄψειν) with two (866–8). Their thought now is of present revenge. Ἔφεδρος was a third competitor in a wrestling or a boxing match; he 'sat by' during the round between the first two competitors and then engaged the winner. The implication here is that the first round in the contest was the murder of Agamemnon.[7]

---

[6] Thomson (n. 4), ii. 24 (on *Agamemnon* 179–82).
[7] Thomson (n. 4), ii. 233 (on *Cho.* 865–6).

Medical imagery continues in the *Choephoroe* to define the doom
upon the house of Atreus. It continues to stand for that particular
power that drives its victims to murder and to revenge for murder.

Orestes, in his opening speech, asks, when he sees the black-garbed
women, whether some new anguish (πῆμα) has come upon the house
(13). Πῆμα here, as in the *Prometheus Bound*, has physical as well as
mental connotation. Later, the chorus uses πόνος 'pain' (466) and
ἄλγος 'pain' (470) with the double significance of πῆμα. Their expression is partly medical, as the following antistrophe makes clear. The
house has a cure (ἄκος) to heal these (pains), not from others without,
but from itself, a savage strife of blood (471–4). The cure they see for
all this affliction is blood revenge. What they do not see is that there
must be an antidote for this cure too. Medical imagery in the *Choephoroe*, as in the *Prometheus Bound*, by evoking the ancient concept of
health as a balance of opposites, suggests that the cure to come can
actually be wrought only by a reconciliation of Apollo's directions for
revenge with the avenging forces of Clytemnestra's Erinyes. The cure
of the house will not really occur until the end of the *Eumenides*.

Meanwhile, the sinner is sick of guilt for the murders done in his
house, for the blood, more than earth could drink, that lies clotted
now and cannot drain away. He swells with consuming disease (νόσου,
66–9). For the adulterer there is no cure (ἄκος, 71–4). Nothing can be
done to remove the guilt of Thyestes; nothing can remove the blood
from his hand—or the doom that he brought upon this house.

The sickness that afflicts the house of Atreus, that began with the sin
of Thyestes, continues until the third generation. That is why Clytemnestra, appalled by her dream, sends libations to the dead and
hopes that they will prove a ready cure (ἄκος) for suffering (538–9).
She hopes to avert the coming disaster, to turn aside the wounds that
are yet to be dealt.

When she hears that Orestes is dead, Clytemnestra asks that the
hope that was once in the house, a healer (ἰατρός) for its fair revelry,
be recorded as present (696–9). Clytemnestra's hope was that Orestes,
while he was alive and away from home, while he kept his foot out of
the mud of destruction, would prevent there being another in this
series of murders of kin. Electra's hope, which Clytemnestra unwit-
tingly includes in the expression of her own, is that Orestes by
returning alive will rid the house of its curse, of its many murders of

kin. For Βακχίας 'Bacchic' must refer to the Erinyes, the 'revel band' made bold by human blood that dwells in Atreus' house (*Agam.* 1189).

Aegisthus, when he has been told that Orestes is dead, declares that to lay this too upon the house, wounded (ἐλκαίνουσι) and bitten (δεδηγμένοις) as it is with a former murder, would be a burden dripping with blood (αἱματοσταγές, 841–3). Here again is the figure of the malignant wound, the wound that was murder, that was caused by the viper's fang and her poison. Orestes' death is just one more wound 'dripping' with blood inflicted upon this already wounded house; it is just one more fulfillment of Thyestes' curse upon his brother's house.

The 'house' of Atreus, afflicted with sickness and wounds, with murder and guilt, is again identified with its material symbol, the actual palace at Argos. The chorus of servants sent by Clytemnestra with libations for Agamemnon's tomb bewail the fate of the house. It has been razed to the ground. Sunless gloom, loathed by mortals, shrouds the house now that its master is dead (50–3). When the nurse has gone to fetch Aegisthus, the chorus prays that murder may no longer beget offspring in the house (806). Here is the idea of the 'house' elaborated; it includes now the idea of the 'line', a line of murders to destroy the line of Atreus.

When Orestes has taken his mother into the house to murder her, the chorus predicts that all-accomplishing time will soon cross the threshold of the house, whenever all pollution is driven from the hearth by the cleansings that drive ruin away (965–8). Let the house rise up, they say; for too long a time has it lain fallen to the ground (963–4).

The chorus' joy is false joy. Their hopes for the house of Atreus are deceived when they see Orestes maddened by the 'hounds' of his mother. A third storm (χειμών) of this race, they say, has broken upon the royal halls and run its course (1065–7). And they specify: first came the children slain for food; next, the king murdered in his bath; now a third was come—but whether a savior or a doom, they cannot say. And when, they ask, will it fulfill itself? When will the fury of disaster be lulled to sleep and cease (1073–6)?

Once the chorus identifies the house with the ship. Again, as in the *Agamemnon*, that identification comes through the association of

each with wealth. They will, they say, if Maia's son sends help, sing a
song of deliverance for the house, the song that women sing when the
wind stands fair—'The ship sails well, and this brings gain to me.
Ruin stands off from those I love' (819–26).

Earlier the chorus had used images of ship and storm to define the
play's themes. Against its heart's prow (πρῷρας) wrath has blown
(ἄηται) in hate (390–2). The stormy blast is Agamemnon's still
unavenged spirit, a compelling force, as the chorus and Electra and
Orestes see it, as Apollo has explained it, for revenge. Electra had
herself used the image of the sailor in a storm at sea to describe her
plight, which resulted, of course, from all the compelling forces at
work in the house of Atreus. She calls upon the gods who know by
what things they are tossed like sailors in a storm (χειμῶσι, 201–3).
When Orestes has returned home, the chorus, hoping for Justice at
last, asks that Hermes aid the Avenger. May Maia's son in justice
(ἐνδίκως) help, for he is best at providing a favoring wind (οὐρίσαι)
when he wishes (812–14). Hermes, the patron of guile, or eloquence,
is here enlisted as Persuasion on the side of Revenge. He is to provide
an effective wind for the 'ship' of vengeance.

When Orestes has forced Clytemnestra into the house to kill her,
the chorus, in premature rejoicing, declares that Dike, daughter of
Zeus, breathing (πνέουσ') destructive wrath upon her foes, has
guided the avenger's hand (948–52). Πνέουσ' here suggests strongly
the wind of storm. The verb was used frequently of wind and air (*Od.*
4.361; 5.469; Hdt. 2.20; cf. *Agam.* 191). Again, the chorus mistakes
Vengeance for Justice.

Images of the root, the seed, and the stock, closely associated in the
Agamemnon with imagery of the house, occur too in the *Choephoroe*,
sometimes alone, sometimes with but inevitably for the 'house' of
Atreus. Electra, when she has Orestes' lock, remarks that if they win
safety, mighty stock (πυθμήν) may spring from a small seed
(σπέρματος, 204). When she recognizes and greets Orestes, she calls
him the house's hope of saving seed (σπέρματος, 235–6). Orestes,
appealing to Zeus on behalf of himself and Electra, the impoverished
orphans, reminds him that if he allows the ruling stock (πυθμήν) to
wither, it will not supply his altars with sacrificial oxen (260–1).

Once the chorus uses an image of flowering as it had been used in
the *Agamemnon* (255–6) to stand for the product of sin, which here is

suffering. For the survivor, it says, suffering blossoms (ἀνθεῖ, 1009). Orestes, they imply, will cull the result of his deed. Still, more suffering (πάθος: again mental 'anguish' which is practically physical: a real madness) awaits him.

In the *Choephoroe*, as in the *Agamemnon*, light and dark are both theme and image. Again, they create mood and atmosphere; again they help to define the dramatic issues. As before, images of light and dark, derived in this play primarily from the concept of the under-world and the world of the living, are involved in other images, particularly—again as in *Agamemnon*—that of the house.

Sunless gloom (ἀνήλιοι δνόφοι), the chorus laments, shrouds the house now that its master is dead (51–3). When Orestes has returned, they pray for the house's deliverance. May it see freedom's shining light (φῶς λαμπρόν) from out its gloomy veil (δνοφερᾶς καλύπτρας, 808–11). Just before Orestes takes his revenge they say that the time has come when either the house of Agamemnon will be destroyed entirely or Orestes will kindle a light (φῶς) for freedom and gain his father's kingdom and wealth (863–5). When the murders are done, the chorus says that the light (φῶς) has come—they are freed from the curb upon the house (961–2).

Imagery of light and dark is in this play, as it was in the *Agamemnon*, associated with the trilogy's pervading theme of good and evil. The sinking of the scale of justice swiftly casts a shadow upon those in the light (φάει); lingering sorrows abide at the border of darkness (σκότου) and ineffectual night (νύξ) keeps them in its hold (61–5). The chorus speaks specifically of revenge, but generally too of true Justice, which sooner or later visits all men.

The imagery of darkness is included in that of the archer and here specifically defines the avenging force of the dead father's spirit, as Apollo had described it: the arrow of the nether powers is dark (285–6). Orestes, addressing his dead father, asks him what light (φάος) (revenge) he can give to match his darkness (σκότῳ), which is not only his actual place in the underworld but the murder that put him there (315–19). The chorus assures Orestes that the dead man is conscious, that he lights (φαίνει) afterward what angers him; the dead man is lamented; the guilty man, revealed (ἀναφαίνεται, 324–8).

Finally, the chorus of the *Choephoroe*, like that of the *Agamemnon*, uses imagery of light and dark to speak of its own hopes and dread. Listening to Orestes's and Electra's incantation, they say that their heart is shaken as they hear this lamentation. They are for the moment bereft of hope. Their heart is darkened (κελαινοῦται) as they hear this word (410–14).

The house is veiled in gloom because Agamemnon is dead. Dark is the arrow of the nether powers that want him avenged. Should Orestes send down to him the light of revenge, he will bring light to his house and to the chorus' darkened spirits as well.

The *Choephoroe* is another drama of compulsion. Its characters are driven too by forces and motives beyond their control. This motivation, which includes memory of the murder and much of what that involved, is simpler now; it has become almost solely revenge. The eagle's nestlings stand at his tomb and bid him remember how he was killed in the viper's coils. They themselves become a double lion to avenge one set of slaughters by committing another. For as the viper killed her mate, so her young to avenge their sire kill their mother in turn. The bull angered at the loss of his inheritance, the dog kennelled while her father was murdered, spurn the fawning bitch whose wolf-like temper they have inherited, whose hounds they provoke in their vengeance. They send a double scourge, an arrow, a hunting lamentation to invoke their father's support. Dike casts a shadow with the beam of her balance, points her sword, forges her weapons. The curse upon the house is armed with a bow, is hard to wrestle down; but Persuasion will enter the lists with Orestes, who will enter the bout as a third contestant. The revenge that he is to take is guided by the doom upon the house of Atreus, by the bloody stroke that beats it, by the bit that constrains it, the darkness that shrouds it, the festering wound, the incurable sickness that afflict it. Orestes to avert the disease that Apollo threatens (279 ff.) brings added disease to his house. A third storm breaks upon his race, the result of the stormy wrath of Agamemnon's unavenged spirit. Orestes, the saving seed of the house, will live to see suffering blossom for him. As before there is a constant overlapping and interlocking of symbol and idea: the lions come into the house; the viper's very touch would corrupt; the bit is lifted from the house which was shrouded in darkness, bitten (by the viper) and wounded; the arrow of a father's avenging spirit is dark; Dike is trampled underfoot but points her sword and casts a shadow with the beam of her balance.

The cycle is not yet complete. Orestes, turned serpent, has lopped off the serpents' heads. Now his mother's Furies appear to him—with snakes upon their heads (1049 ff.). He accomplished the deed with measured caution, with the colt's steady pace, but now his wits, like wild horses, drag him off the course. The awful hounds, the avenging spirits of his hound-like mother, pursue him. The story of the hunt is yet to come.

11

The First Stasimon of Aeschylus' *Choephori*: Myth and Mirror Image

Anne Lebeck

Within the structure of the *Oresteia* the first stasimon of the *Choephori* is emphatic by position: it falls at the center of the central drama.[1] That a choral ode so placed should have a significance beyond the immediate context—should touch the farthest reaches of the whole—is not incredible nor even surprising, but almost to be expected. The lyric does not cheat this expectation. Indirectly it directs attention to the central problems of the trilogy.

There are striking parallels between the *Choephori* and the *Agamemnon*. As the action of the second play unfolds one can discern the pattern of the first.[2] Returning home Agamemnon falls victim to a plan for vengeance; Orestes returns home as avenger of the crime. In a climactic scene each comes face to face with Clytemnestra. Guile and deceit, irony and double meaning are prominent in both encounters. As Clytemnestra, exulting over Agamemnon's corpse, justifies her deed to the chorus, so Orestes stands over the corpse of Clytemnestra defending his.

---

[1] W. Kranz, *Stasimon* (Berlin, 1933), 169, calls it a 'Verbindungsstück' which unites the play's two halves.

[2] See A. Lesky, *Die tragische Dichtung der Hellenen* (Göttingen, 1956), 74 [= *Greek Tragic Poetry*, tr. M. Dillon (New Haven and London, 1983), 82], and 'Die Orestie des Aischylos', *Hermes* 66 (1931), 204 ff. These parallels are studied in detail by F. Stoessl, *Die Trilogie bei Aischylos* (Baden bei Wien, 1937), 28–42.

Viewed in a different manner, the situation of the second play reverses that of the first. A victim is received by his murderer, a murderer by his victim. The woman who welcomes him tricks the man who returns; a man who returns tricks the woman who welcomes him. Another aspect of this reversal is brought out by means of imagery. In the parodos of the *Agamemnon* (48–59) the Atreidae are compared to birds mourning loss of their young and all the care they lavished on the nest. With piercing cry they call upon the gods, Apollo, Pan, or Zeus, for vengeance. In *Choephori* 246–51 Orestes uses an image which evokes the long and elaborate simile of the *Agamemnon*. He cries to Zeus for aid: the eagle's orphaned young, their father dead, are left untended, go hungry since they cannot hunt their food. The situation described in the image is the reverse of the earlier simile. Instead of parent birds crying for their young, Zeus hears the cry of young birds bereft of parent.[3]

The reversal of circumstance between child and parent takes another form as well. Agamemnon, the father who slays his daughter, is followed in the next generation by Orestes, the son who slays his mother.[4] The first stasimon explores this inverse parallel, this symmetrical reversal, by means of three mythic paradigms. Each myth plays upon the relation between slayer and slain, that tangle of kin murder which forms the myth of Atreus and his descendants, the myth of the *Oresteia*.

---

[3] The ostensible similarity between the Atreidae and the vultures mourning their children is, of course, the theft of Helen. However, the comparison also suggests Clytemnestra's grief at losing Iphigenia. (This point is noted by B. M. W. Knox in 'The lion in the house', *CPh* 47 [1952], 17–25, at 18 [= *Word and Action* (Baltimore and London, 1979), 27–38, at 28]. Cf. E. T. Owen, *Harmony of Aeschylus* [Toronto, 1952], 66]. Hence choice of the word παίδων (50), used here for the first time of animal rather than human young, and γόον (57), properly a lament for the dead. See E. Fraenkel (ed.), *Aeschylus: Agamemnon* (Oxford, 1950), ii.32 and 30. The latter word is another link between the opening simile and the second play. The birds mourn their loss with a funeral lament which brings vengeance upon the transgressor; the first half of the *Choephori* revolves round a funeral lament and incantation designed to secure vengeance. Metaphorical use of γόος ['lament'] in the vulture simile of the *Agamemnon* prefigures what is acted out in the great kommos of the *Choephori*.

[4] Lesky (n. 2), 75 [= Eng. tr. 82], emphasizes that structural parallels between the first and second play reflect a major theme of the trilogy: the curse passed from one generation to the next and the concept of Dike embodied in the gnomic δράσαντι παθεῖν ['the doer shall suffer', *Cho.* 313]. This statement applies not only to parallelism but also to the reversals discussed here.

The opening thoughts and images of the stasimon grow out of an event narrated in the preceding epeisodion. Clytemnestra dreamed she bore a serpent, a loathsome thing (533), and nursed the fearful monster at her breast (548). The lyric begins, 'Many dread hurts and fears are nursed by Earth; the embrace of ocean swells with creatures cruel to man. And midway in mid-air bloom fiery lights...' (585–90).[5] The monster nursed by Clytemnestra gives the chorus subject for their song.[6] The metaphors they choose reflect the dream's contrast between tender act and cruel recipient. Earth's nurslings inflict hurt, inspire fear; monsters nestle in the sea's embracing arms; ominous comets bloom like flowers. Thus the opening strophe is a stream of associations evoked by Clytemnestra's dream.[7] The lyric closes with a restatement of the dream's meaning: the Erinys brings a child into the house to be the avenger of past wrongs (648–51). As the dream foretold, that serpent brought to birth by Clytemnestra is the son brought home for vengeance of her crime.[8]

[5] The Greek text for this passage is that of P. Groeneboom, *Choephori* (Groningen, 1949), which comes closest to the manuscript reading. Elsewhere the text translated is that of G. Murray, *Aeschyli Tragoediae*[2] (Oxford, 1955).

[6] τρέφω ['nurture'] appears in 548 in reference to that prodigy (τέρας) which Clytemnestra bore and, in 585, to those prodigies which earth produces.

[7] If the opening lines of this lyric are reconsidered with reference to the final member of the trilogy, new connections and further implications come to light. The earth bears hostile angry things which cause man fear and suffering. Of these dread things none is more dread than the Erinyes, 'born for harm since they inhabit harmful dark and Tartarus beneath the earth' (*Eum.* 71–2). 'What earth can boast their rearing without pain?' (*Eum.* 58–9). They are the serpent of Clytemnestra's dream (*Eum.* 129); they are the lion of the parable (*Eum.* 193). When, at the close, crime ceases to engender crime and Justice is no longer blind demand for vengeance, earth ceases to bear ill and brings forth fruit. The Erinyes, once chthonic forces of malevolence, become dispensers of earth's gifts: Eumenides.

[8] T. G. Tucker, *Choephori* (Cambridge, 1901), 150, suggests that the epithets here applied to the Erinyes, κλυτή ['glorious'] and βυσσόφρων ['deep-thinking'] are chosen as a play on Clytem(n)estra's name. P. Mazon, *Eschyle* (Paris, 1925), 2.104 n. 5, adds '...comme cette Erinys est incarnée en Clytemnestre...le poète lui donne des épithètes qui rappellent ce nom, κλυτή, mot rare chez les tragiques, dont le choix ici est certainement voulu, et βυσσόφρων, qui évoque l'idée de μῆτις contenue dans la seconde partie du nom' ['...since this Erinys is incarnated in Clytemnestra...the poet gives it epithets which recall her name, κλυτή ('glorious'), a rare word in tragedy which has certainly been deliberately chosen here, and βυσσόφρων ('deep-thinking'), which evokes the idea of μῆτις ('craft', 'plan') in the second half of her name']. And thus the adjectives would confirm that notion conveyed by the dream: Clytemnestra is the source of her own destruction, her crime producing its own punishment.

The first strophe ends, 'Both the winged and that which walks the ground could tell of tempest's windblown wrath' (591–2). From animals frightened by rage of storm, the antistrophe glides to human passion, a thing more frightful still: 'But how describe man's over-daring mind, of woman's reckless heart all-daring love that herds with human ruin?' (594–8). The last lines join man and beast together: that hateful love which overcomes the female conquers both beasts and men, destroying ties of conjugality (599–601).

In the next strophes these general statements are illustrated by the stories of Althaea (603–11), Scylla (612–22), and the women of Lemnos (631–4). The first two are dealt with in detail. Contrary to what one might expect from the preceding antistrophe, neither exemplifies the overpowering effects of erotic love.[9] And since neither is a case of illicit passion or a husband's murder, the resemblance to Clytemnestra's crime is slight. The last of the three, suitable on both counts, is an allusion only; no narrative underlines the parallel.

Why then are the first myths chosen? What is the relevance of those features which fail to tally with the case in question? Their discrepancies might be dismissed as characteristic of archaic style: the poet chooses examples which he then rejects in favor of one more suitable.[10] Such an explanation, correct as far as it goes, does not go far enough. What passes for discrepancy in the immediate context is meaningful in relation to the whole.

Shortly before the ode begins, Orestes warned the chorus, 'And to you this is my advice: say nothing unlucky, keep silent when you should, and at the right moment speak the right word' (581–2). Here as elsewhere, the need for concealment and careful speech is

[9] In the more common version of Scylla's story, passion is her motive. See Paus. 1.19.4; Apollod. 3.15.13; Nonn. *Dion.* 25.161 ff.; Prop. 4.19.21; Ov. *Met.* 8. 90 ff.; *Ciris* 130. Aeschylus makes no mention of love. His Scylla has a weakness for gold bracelets (617–19).

[10] Kranz (n. 1), 160. E. G. Holtsmark, 'On *Choephori* 585–651', *CW* 59 (1966), 215–17, sees the entire ode as a definition of τὸ δεινόν ['marvel'] proceeding along the lines of a 'priamel' or *praeambulum*, a term defined by Fraenkel (n. 3), ii.407 n. 3: '...a series of detached statements which through contrast or comparison lead up to the idea with which the speaker is primarily concerned...'. In the present instance the marvels of nature are rejected in favor of a greater marvel, human passion; this passion is then illustrated by concrete examples, the last of which represents τὸ δεινόν ['marvel'] best.

stressed.[11] This parting injunction to the chorus affects the tone and
content of their lyric. Instead of open attack on Clytemnestra, they
turn to myths which exemplify the crime of woman, yet are not
parallel with Clytemnestra's crime. On the verge of reference more
direct they break off with the words ἀκαίρως δέ ['unfittingly', 624], as
if remembering Orestes' order in 582: λέγειν τὰ καίρια ['speak the
right word'].[12] They substitute instead another myth, this time one
entirely apposite but barely sketched.

[11] Cf. 265–8 and the scene between the chorus and the nurse.

[12] Orestes' words provide a point of departure for interpreting 622–3, a strophe
that Murray calls 'locus paene desperatus' ['an almost hopeless passage'], on which
remark Groeneboom remarks that the description would be more accurate if 'paene'
['almost'] were omitted. This strophe follows the first two paradigms and introduces
the third which forms the subject of the antistrophe: ἐπεὶ δ' ἐπεμνησάμην ἀμειλίχων
πόνων —† ἀκαίρως | δὲ δυσφιλὲς γαμήλευμ' ἀπεύχετον δόμοις | γυναικοβούλους τε
μήτιδας φρενῶν... H. W. Smyth, *Aeschylus*[2] (London, 1958), II, reverses the meaning
entirely by emending ἀκαίρως ['unfittingly'] to ὁ καιρός ['the fitting time']: 'But since
I have called to mind tales of pitiless afflictions, 'tis the fitting time to tell of a
marriage void of love, an abomination to the house...'. Mazon (n. 8) preserves the
MS reading and translates the line as a question expecting a negative answer: 'Et
puisque j'ai ici rappelé ces tristes forfaits, n'est-ce pas l'heure pour ce palais de honnir
aussi l'épouse abominable...?' A. W. Verrall, *Choephori* (London, 1893), punctuates
after ἀκαίρως δὲ: 'But since the ungentle feats here cited fit not the present theme—it
is from a fell wedlock that this house prays to be delivered...'.

Only F. H. Paley's interpretation, *Tragedies of Aeschylus*[4] (London, 1879), reveals
the connection between use of paradigm and reluctance to speak openly of Clytemnestra, between ἀκαίρως ['unfittingly'] in the lyric and Orestes' parting reminder to
speak τὰ καίρια ['the right word'] and leave the rest in silence. (Paley himself does not
mention this connection. He understands ἀκαίρως ['unfittingly'] to mean, 'It is
inconsistent with the position of a slave and captive'.) An aposiopesis follows πόνων
['afflictions'] in 622; a verb of saying, understood from ἐπεμνησάμην ['I have mentioned'], is to be supplied with ἀκαίρως δὲ ['but unfittingly']. (If desired, one might
follow Paley in smoothing the syntactical irregularity of ἀκαίρως ['unfittingly'] to
ἄκαιρόν [ἐστι] ['it is unfitting']. The scholiast's note, λείπει, μνήσομαι
Κλυταιμνήστρας ['"I will mention Clytemnestra" is omitted'], suggests that he
understood the line in a similar way.)

This then is the train of thought: after the exempla of Althaea and Scylla, the
chorus are on the verge of turning from exemplum to thing exemplified. But they
break off, and by means of *praeteritio*, bring out what should be passed over: 'And
since I speak of cruel acts—but this is not the time for that unlovely marriage and the
wiles of woman's will.' Instead they turn again to myth, that of the Lemnian women,
closest parallel of all.

Several scholars, following the suggestion of Preuss, reverse the order of strophe
and antistrophe. In his *Commentary on the Surviving Plays of Aeschylus* (*Verhand.
Kon. Ned. Ak. Weten.* 44 (1958)), 2.180, H. J. Rose maintains that the manuscript
order is not 'a rhetorically intelligible structure' because the 'case in question,

Each paradigm is operative on two levels. One is determined by the dramatic role of the chorus as participants in the action of the moment. This is the meaning of which they are aware, which they intend. The other corresponds to their lyric role as interpreters of that action. In this capacity their utterance is timeless, universal, endowed with import which they themselves may fail to comprehend. The stories of Althaea, Scylla, and the Lemnians are intended as condemnation of Clytemnestra; in each a woman is author of the crime. This is their relevance to the immediate situation. Also theirs, however, is significance more penetrating, more complex. The first two exempla give back a looking-glass reflection of the parallel crimes committed by Agamemnon and Orestes, reversed in such a way that woman's treachery comes to the fore each time. Thus there is a triplicate reference which calls up the murder of Iphigenia, of Agamemnon, of Clytemnestra. The last exemplum reflects the mysterious way in which crime follows crime and one generation pays for another's wrong.

In the strophe Althaea destroys her son; in the antistrophe Scylla her father. The crime of Althaea is the inverse of that act which Orestes left the stage to commit: instead of son slaying mother, mother slays son. At the same time, since parent slays child, the myth is relevant to the murder of Iphigenia by her father. The crime of Scylla exactly reverses the relationship of the previous paradigm. It inverts the wrong committed by Agamemnon: instead of father slaying daughter, daughter slays father. And, in that it is murder of parent by child, this myth parallels the murder of Clytemnestra by her son.

The Lemnian story forms a climax, a crowning example of wrong which engenders wrong. Each of the first exempla dealt with a single crime, committed by magic and not by violence. The Lemnian atrocities, as told by Herodotus,[13] involve two separate crimes, one

---

Klytaimestra's, is suddenly thrust into the middle of examples illustrating it'. In support of the manuscript order, Holtsmark (n. 10) points out a structural parallel between the gnomic introduction (585–601) and its paradeigmatic corroboration (602–38). When the third strophic pair are considered in connection with Orestes' command to speak τὰ καίρια ['the right word'], one finds added reason for retaining the traditional order.

[13] Hdt. 6. 138.

the reverse of the other. In the time of Thoas the Lemnian women murdered their husbands.[14] At a later period the Pelasgians of Lemnos murdered the Athenian women whom they had carried off along with the children borne them by these women. The Lemnian disaster became a byword because of both crimes, not that of the Lemnian women alone. 'Thereupon the Pelasgians judged it best to slay the sons of the Attic women; and this they did, and slew the boys' mothers likewise. From this and the former deed which was done by the women, when they slew their own husbands, who were Thoas' companions, a "Lemnian crime" has been a proverb for any deed of cruelty.'[15] The murderous act of the Lemnian women, followed in course of time by that of the Pelasgian men of Lemnos, is another case of the impious act which late or soon begets its like.

Thus the three paradigms are relevant not only in so far as each deals with a woman's crime; taken together they play upon the various combinations of kin murder which beset the seed of Atreus. In the first, child is slain by parent, as in the generation of Agamemnon. The second reverses this: parent is slain by child, as in the generation of Orestes. The last alludes to one wrong followed by another, its mirror image. Wives slay their husbands, husbands their wives. And so the myths chosen by the poet at this central point reflect the three crimes of the trilogy, show how a whole house may perish: 'Loathed by the gods, among men dishonored, the polluted line is lost from sight' (635–6).

[14] The fullest account of the first crime is given by Apoll. Rhod. 1. 609 ff. Cf. Pind. *Pyth.* 4. 252.

[15] A. D. Godley, *Herodotus* (London, 1928), 3.295. Commentaries on *Choephori* call attention only to the earlier deed and not to the sequence of crime following crime nor the reversal, both of which are relevant.

12

Religion and Politics in Aeschylus' *Oresteia*

A. M. Bowie

In the light of the remarkable changes of political colour which Aeschylus has undergone in the hands of scholars, there is a certain amusing irony about the fact that the satyr-play which followed the *Oresteia* was the *Proteus*. Sadly, we know too little of the *Proteus* to say whether it would have resolved this debate about the *Oresteia*'s political stance, though one may have one's doubts.[1]

For some, Aeschylus has been a conservative: K. O. Müller and Blass saw him fighting a conservative rear-guard action, and Peter Rhodes has recently found 'it easier to believe that Aeschylus is not expressing enthusiasm for the reform but after the event felt regret at what had happened or at any rate fear that in the future the democrats might go too far'.[2] On the other hand, despite Lloyd-Jones's warnings against the 'incautious liberalism'[3] of writers like Kitto, through the twentieth century Aeschylus has generally become more liberal, though there have been notable reservations, not least

The text of this paper is largely that of the original publication, but I have attempted to bring the bibliography up to date.

[1] For the scanty remains of the *Proteus*, cf. *TrGF* iii. 331–3, and for suggestions concerning the relationship between satyr-play and trilogy, J. J. Peradotto, 'The omen of the eagles and the ἦθος of Agamemnon', *Phoenix* 23 (1969), 237–63, at 261–3 (this vol., pp. 243–4). For the relationship between tragedy and historical events, cf. C. B. R. Pelling (ed.), *Greek Tragedy and the Historian* (Oxford, 1997).

[2] P. J. Rhodes, *A Commentary on the Aristotelian* Athenaion Politeia (Oxford, 1981), 312.

[3] P. H. J. Lloyd-Jones, *The Justice of Zeus* (Berkeley and Los Angeles, 1971), 93.

from feminist writers. Livingstone saw the ending of the trilogy as an allegory, in which the *Eumenides* represents and so prompts the reconciliation of conservatives to the democratic reforms.[4] Dover was more forthright: 'if [Aeschylus] was positively conservative in sentiment, it is difficult to believe that he would have written the *Oresteia* in anything like the form which it actually has. If he was in principle democratic, but mistrustful of the continuation of democratic reform, he has concealed his mistrust impenetrably.'[5] Griffith too saw an essentially aristocratic agenda.[6]

Others have been less certain: 'a moderate democrat—a member of the old nobility who...had espoused the cause of the people, but was opposed to the extreme democracy', was Headlam and Thomson's analysis.[7] Similarly, for Dodds, Athena's foundation-speech contained 'a quiet word of warning for the future';[8] the references to the Argive alliance showed Aeschylus could not be a conservative, but it was 'difficult to see Aeschylus as a consistent and committed supporter of radical reform'.[9] Dodds gave the trilogy a wider significance as expressing a hope 'of achieving a truer insight into the laws that govern our condition rather than concerned solely with the particular squabble about the powers of the Areopagus'.[10] Macleod too argued for a broadened view of the plays' scope, opposing the application of the term 'political' solely to the poet's own time: 'the Areopagus and the Argive alliance...have...a meaning and a value which are not confined to any historical situation...By fashioning in mythical Athens the image of an ideal city, Aeschylus is presenting

---

[4] R. W. Livingstone, 'The problem of the *Eumenides* of Aeschylus', *JHS* 45 (1925), 120–31.

[5] K. J. Dover, 'The political aspect of the *Eumenides*', in *Greek and the Greeks: Collected Papers volume I: Language, Poetry, Drama* (Oxford, 1987), 161–75, at 171 (= *JHS* 77 (1957), 230–7, at 236).

[6] M. Griffith, 'Brilliant dynasts: power and politics in the *Oresteia*', *ClAnt* 14 (1995), 62–129.

[7] G. Thomson and W. G. Headlam, *The Oresteia of Aeschylus* (Cambridge, 1938), 357.

[8] E. R. Dodds, 'Morals and politics in the *Oresteia*', in *The Ancient Concept of Progress and Other Essays on Greek Literature and Belief* (Oxford, 1973), 45–63, at 49 (this vol., p. 249).

[9] Dodds (n. 8), 48 (this vol., p. 248). Cf. for a similar view A. J. Podlecki, *The Political Background of Aeschylean Tragedy* (Ann Arbor, 1965), 63–100.

[10] Dodds (n. 8), 62 (this vol., p. 264).

goodness achieved.'[11] Rose also offered an optimistic reading: 'Thus on the political level the substantial historical progress achieved by Athens may sustain Aeschylus' relatively optimistic vision as at least an attainable goal within its actual institutions.'[12]

Meier gave a complex discussion of how the myth of Orestes was a means of articulating a vision of recent political events: 'what Aeschylus attempted to do was to evolve new concepts by means of which the whole of this new [political] experience could be articulated and brought into equilibrium.'[13] Meier wanted to play down the idea that the tragedy is being used for making party-political points, but ultimately ascribed to Aeschylus a firm view: 'there was no mistaking what the poet was saying: the defeated should accept defeat, and the victors should accord them functions in the new order that partly corresponded to those they had performed in the old.'[14] Sommerstein entered a note of caution, playing down the importance of the views of Aeschylus the private citizen: 'nowhere in *Eu.* is there an avowedly partisan utterance relating to domestic Athenian politics. Athena's advice about the Areopagus is wrapped in ambiguities'. Only one message is clear: ' "unity and victory" '.[15]

There have been other views: for instance, Lebeck saw a humour and parody in the ending of the trilogy which undercuts the apparently triumphant resolution of the problems,[16] and feminists like Millett and Zeitlin have worried about what they see as the blatantly patriarchal nature of the end of the trilogy.[17] Cohen argued that the trilogy institutes 'a cosmic and political order which is neither moral not just, but rather tyrannical, in the sense that its ultimate

[11] C. Macleod, 'Politics and the *Oresteia*', in *Collected Essays* (Oxford, 1983), 20–40, at 28 (= *JHS* 102 (1982), 124–44, at 132; this vol., pp. 279–81).

[12] P. W. Rose, *Sons of the Gods, Children of the Earth: Ideology and Literary Form in Ancient Society* (Ithaca, NY, and London, 1992), 185–265, at 264. Cf. also J. P. Euben, *The Tragedy of Political Theory: the Road not Taken* (Princeton, 1990), 67–95

[13] C. Meier, *The Greek Discovery of Politics* (tr. D. McLintock, Cambridge, Mass., and London, 1990), 89.

[14] Meier (n. 13), 114.

[15] A. H. Sommerstein, *Aeschylus: Eumenides* (Cambridge, 1989), 31–2.

[16] A. Lebeck, *The Oresteia* (Washington, 1971), 134 ff.

[17] Cf. K. Millett, *Sexual Politics* (New York, 1971), 114 ff.; F. I. Zeitlin 'The dynamics of misogyny: myth and mythmaking in the *Oresteia*', *Arethusa* 11 (1978), 149–84 = *Playing the Other* (Chicago and London, 1996), 87–119. Cf. also Rose (n. 12), 221–32, 242–6, 256–60.

foundations are force and fear',[18] and Rosenbloom traced the 'earnest dialectical conflict between freedom and domination.... Aeschylus' tragedy dramatizes the limits of domination in the necessity of freedom, displaying how forms of power are liable to subversion'.[19]

In the face of such ambiguity,[20] then, though each of these readings illuminates something of Aeschylus's text, Goldhill did well to warn not only against confident attempts to get at the author behind the text (there is less such confidence now), but also of the danger that the reader's own ideological biases will be imported into the reading of the text or the constitution of the author.[21] Most recently, Sourvinou-Inwood has stressed the need to avoid privileging the political aspect of the play to the religious in that word's broadest sense.[22]

We may surely welcome the recent growing tendency to shift from consideration of the author to the attempt to reconstruct something of the discourses made available by the plays to the audience, the shift from individual intention to multifarious receptions which do greater justice to the many ambiguities that are apparent in the text, as they explore the kinds of responses which the trilogy may have evoked in the audience generally. We can view the Orestes myth not as bearing a message, so much as offering a matrix, that is, as providing a model for thinking about what has recently happened. Providing a way of thinking about the world is, after all, one of the most important functions of myths in society. They can be used to inculcate a particular ideology, but are also available, via Lévi-Strauss's process of 'bricolage', for thinking about the world and its

[18] D. Cohen, 'The theodicy of Aeschylus: justice and tyranny in the *Oresteia*', *G&R* 33 (1986), 129–41, at 129 = I. McAuslan and P. Walcot (eds.), *Greek Tragedy* (Greece and Rome Studies 2; Oxford, 1993), 45–57, at 45.

[19] D. Rosenbloom, 'Myth, history, and hegemony in Aeschylus', in B. Goff (ed.), *History, Theory, Tragedy: Dialogues on Athenian Drama* (Austin, 1995), 91–130, at 94.

[20] Voices have been raised in different ways against the too easy embrace of 'tragic ambiguity' and 'open-endedness', e.g. R. A. S. Seaford, 'Historicizing tragic ambivalence: the vote of Athena', in Goff (n. 19), 202–21, and the second work of Goldhill in n. 21.

[21] S. D. Goldhill, *Reading Greek Tragedy* (Cambridge, 1986), 32–56, and 'Civic ideology and the problem of difference: the politics of Aeschylean tragedy, once again', *JHS* 120 (2000), 34–56. For other bibliography on politics in the *Oresteia*, cf. A. Wartelle, *Bibliographie historique et critique d'Eschyle et de la tragédie grecque 1518–1974* (Paris, 1978), 672.

[22] C. Sourvinou-Inwood, *Tragedy and Athenian Religion* (Lanham, Boulder, New York, and Oxford, 2003), 231–51.

problems. By displacing consideration of the Ephialtic reforms onto a mythical story, the *Oresteia* is able to articulate thought and discussion of recent events through mythical events which, though historically connected to the more recent ones, are not identical with them; as a result of this difference, the discussion can then take place in a less heated and partisan atmosphere.

The Orestes myth in the *Oresteia* suggests a pattern, in which one group is deprived of some of its previous power but yet retains a role, and this pattern provides a filter through which the Athenians can look at the recent changes to the political scene and make sense of them. The pattern has the possible message that even radical changes can be seen to be leaving behind them something of the situation which they have destroyed. What has happened to the Areopagus is a repetition of its own foundation: this foundation led to the substitution of a new, more rational type of justice which subordinated the old, vendetta system which had operated in the play and the world so far, but did not obliterate it. This change was to the benefit of mankind: might not the recent changes in Athenian justice be similarly beneficial, the next step in an ever-improving judicial system? When there is change, there are winners and losers, but the losses of the latter may be compounded for by the greater good of the wider community: justice after Athena's settlement with the Furies involved a small section of mankind; after Ephialtes's reforms it takes in an even wider group. Indeed, the mythical changes made to justice, which were such as to affect justice in the cosmos as a whole, by the deposition of the Furies and the elevation of mortals to a position of importance, might be said to put into some sort of perspective the recent changes, which in the case of judicial matters affect Athens and mortals alone.[23] The dangers of the abuse of power by the new rulers are also intimated.

This main myth is not, however, the only one to provide a filter through which the action can be viewed, though it has received most attention. There are several other myths and, perhaps more strikingly, rituals which Aeschylus offers for his audience to use to

---

[23] The analysis is very similar to the Marxist notion of 'struggle', in which the worse aspects of an earlier stage of social development are removed and the better retained. For Marx and Aeschylus, cf. S. S. Prawer, *Karl Marx and World Literature* (Oxford, 1976).

explicate the political codes of the *Oresteia*. I shall consider first myths, which also contain a ritual element, and then the rituals, which also involve mythology.

1. MYTHS

(a) Zeus and Cronus

The great myth concerning change of authority was that of Zeus's defeat of Cronus in a competition for the rulership of the cosmos.[24] There are two references to this myth in the trilogy. First, in the more pitiless world of the *Agamemnon* (168–75; tr. Fraenkel):

> οὐδ᾽ ὅστις πάροιθεν ἦν μέγας,
> παμμάχωι θράσει βρύων,
> οὐδὲ λέξεται πρὶν ὤν·
> ὃς δ᾽ ἔπειτ᾽ ἔφυ, τρια-
>   κτῆρος οἴχεται τυχών·
> Ζῆνα δέ τις προφρόνως ἐπινίκια κλάζων
> τεύξεται φρενῶν τὸ πᾶν.

And he who aforetime was mighty, swelling with the boldness of a victor in every contest, shall not even be reckoned, since he is of the past; and he who afterward came into being met his thrower and is gone.

Here, Cronus and his helpers are, unusually, completely destroyed and their names are not even mentioned.[25] On the other hand, in *Eumenides*, when Apollo appeals to Zeus for the justification of his case in favour of Orestes (614–21), the Chorus gleefully pick him up with the second reference to this myth (640–2):

---

[24] Cf. Hsd. *Theog.* 617 ff. For this type of story, cf. J. Fontenrose, *Python: a Study of the Delphic Myth and its Origins* (Berkeley, 1959); F. Vian, *La Guerre des Géants: le mythe avant l'époque hellénistique* (Paris, 1952), 94–113, who offers a critique of Fontenrose's methodology; J. Trumpf, 'Stadtgründung und Drachenkampf', *Hermes* 86 (1958), 129–57, on near-eastern mythology and Pi. *Py.* 1, a poem where this myth has a similarly paradeigmatic function to that proposed here.

[25] Sommerstein (n. 15), 81.

πατρὸς προτιμᾶι Ζεὺς μόρον τῶι σῶι λογῶι,
αὐτὸς δ' ἔδησε πατέρα πρεσβύτην Κρόνον·
πῶς ταῦτα τούτοις οὐκ ἐναντίως λέγεις;

According to your argument, Zeus has a special regard for the death of a father, but he himself bound his old father, Cronus: how does this not contradict what you said before?

Apollo, who is not having an easy time defeating the Furies' arguments, is reduced to a splenetic reply, which nonetheless makes our point once again (644–8):

ὦ παντομισῆ κνώδαλα, στύγη θεῶν,
πέδας μὲν ἂν λύσειεν, ἔστι τοῦδ' ἄκος
καὶ κάρτα πολλὴ μηχανὴ λυτήριος·
ἀνδρὸς δ' ἐπειδὰν αἷμ' ἀνασπάσηι κόνις
ἅπαξ θανόντος, οὔτις ἔστ' ἀνάστασις.

O most hateful beasts, objects of loathing to the gods, he could unlock the fetters, there is a remedy for this and there is many a device to undo the wrong; but when once a man has died and the dust has drunk his blood, there is no resurrection.

In *Eumenides*, then, Cronus is merely bound and the possibility of release remains, in a version of the story closer to the standard one of Cronus's being bound in Hades. There are a number of significances that could be given to this difference in the versions. It may be a case of divine rhetoric, with Apollo choosing a version that better supports his case. Alternatively, it may be that, as the new dispensation comes closer, the picture of Zeus is improved. Furthermore, as Burian has argued, 'the history of the house of Atreus is made not only to replicate the history of the house of Ouranos. The chorus of the *Agamemnon* depicted Zeus's succession in terms of sheer force... Now, Zeus triumphs through persuasion: ἐκράτησε Ζεὺς ἀγοραῖος (*Eum.* 973), the Zeus of the polis, of law, of debate'.[26] Whatever the reason for the shift, in this succession myth we have a change in which a better state of affairs is achieved by the

---

[26] P. Burian, 'Zeus Σωτὴρ τρίτος and some triads in Aeschylus' *Oresteia*', *AJP* 107 (1986), 332–42, at 342; he also notes the parallels between Orestes and Zeus as τριακτήρ and τρίτος σωτήρ (p. 341).

defeat of earlier rulers: the victory of Zeus moves us from a world
in which children are devoured to one where order, peace and
prosperity reign.[27]

In the main story of the trilogy, continued cult is one of the
consolations offered to the defeated: as Athena repeatedly stresses,[28]
the Furies will receive worship from the Athenians. No such cult for
Cronus is mentioned in the play, but Athenians would have remembered that, despite his deposition by his son, he continued to be
honoured in Athens, especially at the Cronia, celebrated in the
autumn.[29] This festival, seen as the equivalent of the Roman
Saturnalia,[30] honoured both Cronus and Rhea, mother of the gods,
that is, the representatives of the divinities who were overthrown
by the Olympians. Furthermore, masters would dine with slaves,[31]
which thus gave a position to this class which, at the human level,
had like Cronus been marginalised.[32] Furthermore, Cronus had a
sanctuary in the enclosure of the temple of Zeus[33] and there was a
tradition that the month Hekatombaion had originally borne his
name.[34] The greatest succession myth of them all, with its cosmic
change that brought Zeus to power and created the world order as we
now know it, thus has lessons for those contemplating recent up-
heavals in Athens.

[27] For a discussion of the play in terms of a Gigantomachy, with Orestes opposing
Clytaemestra and the Furies as dragon-like figures, cf. N. S. Rabinowitz, 'From force
to persuasion: Aeschylus' *Oresteia* as cosmogonic myth', *Ramus* 10 (1981), 159–91.

[28] 804–7, 832–6, 854–7, 890–1; cf. C. Carey, 'Aischylos *Eumenides* 858–66', *ICS*
15 (1990), 239–50.

[29] L. Deubner, *Attische Feste* (Berlin, 1932), 152–5; H. W. Parke, *Festivals of the
Athenians* (London, 1977), 29–30.

[30] So Accius, fr. 3 Morel (p. 34): 'maxima pars Graium Saturno et maxime Athe-
nae | conficiunt sacra, quae Cronia esse iterantur ab illis, | ... nosterque itidem est mos
traditus illinc | iste, ut cum dominis famuli epulentur ibidem'; cf. Philochorus, *FGrH*
328 F 97. Cf. also Farnell, *Cults* i. 32–4 for Cronus's cults; also Deubner (n. 29), 152–5 for
Athens.

[31] Plut. *Mor.* 1098bc.

[32] Cf. C. Sourvinou-Inwood, 'The *Votum* of 477/6 B.C. and the Foundation
Legend of Locri Epizephyrii', *CQ* 24 (1974), 186–98, at 194–5 for the ideology of
festivals of this kind.

[33] Paus. 1.18.7.

[34] Plut. *Thes.* 12.1; *EM* 321.4.

(b) Delphi

Eumenides begins with a succession myth (1–8), which has links with Zeus's own succession myth in that it is Zeus who sets the seal on Apollo's authority at Delphi (17–19).[35] That it prefigures the outcome of the trilogy has been sufficiently noticed.[36]

πρῶτον μὲν εὐχῆι τῆιδε πρεσβεύω θεῶν
τὴν πρωτόμαντιν Γαῖαν· ἐκ δὲ τῆς Θέμιν,
ἣ δὴ τὸ μητρὸς δευτέρα τόδ' ἕζετο
μαντεῖον, ὡς λόγος τις· ἐν δὲ τῶι τρίτωι
λάχει, θελούσης, οὐδὲ πρὸς βίαν τινός,
Τιτανὶς ἄλλη παῖς Χθονὸς καθέζετο
Φοίβη, δίδωσιν δ' ἣ γενέθλιον δόσιν
Φοίβωι· τὸ Φοίβης δ' ὄνομ' ἔχει παρώνυμον.

First in this prayer I honour among the gods Earth, the primeval prophetess, and after her Themis, who was second to sit in this oracle of her mother, as the story goes. In the third dispensation, Phoebe, a Titaness and another child of Earth, sat here, with Themis's agreement and without violence and against no-one's will. She gave it as a birthday-present to Phoebus, who bears Phoebe's name along with his own.

This encompasses a number of movements important to the play. First, that from the representatives of the earlier, chthonic world and the opponents of the Olympians—Earth, Themis her Titan daughter, and Phoebe 'another Titan' (6)—to the Olympian Apollo; and second, that from 'old' deities like Gaia to the 'new'. These two movements prefigure that from the vengeful Furies, the old daughters of Night, to the Olympian justice of the younger Athena and Apollo. Finally, it depicts a movement from the female to the male, which again prepares for the dominance of that sex in the decision

---

[35] For this use of Zeus in such myths, and on the Delphic succession myths generally, cf. C. Sourvinou-Inwood, 'Myth as history: the previous owners of the Delphic Oracle', in J. Bremmer (ed.), *Interpretations of Greek Mythology* (London and Sydney, 1987), 214–41, esp. 225–33, and *Reading Greek Culture: Images, Rituals and Myths* (Oxford, 1991), 217–43; H. Bowden, *Classical Athens and the Delphic Oracle: Divination and Democracy* (Cambridge 2005), 46–75.

[36] See also on this passage and its possible antecedents D. S. Robertson, 'The Delphian succession in the opening of the *Eumenides*', *CR* 55 (1941), 69–70.

over Orestes. The changes in the trilogy thus receive some authenti-
cation from this paradigmatic myth.

Aeschylus's version of the Delphic myth may well be his own,[37] but
it stands in that class of myths which transfer power from more or
less disordered figures, like Gaia, Themis or a dragon, to Apollo, in a
manner that is not violent but peaceful: Themis seems simply to
inherit the throne from her mother; Phoebe is explicitly said to
receive it 'with Themis's agreement, and without violence and against
no-one's will' (5); and Apollo has it as a birthday present, taking
Phoebe's name as his own.

This last element is important. Phoebe appears in no other version
of this myth, and her role is explained by Sourvinou-Inwood as 'a
representation . . . of a positive relationship between Apollo and the
maternal side of his family—perhaps a symbolic counterweight to
Orestes' matricide and Apollo's role in it and in its aftermath'.[38]
Phoebe's gift symbolises also the important aspect of the fate of the
defeated parties mentioned above: though defeated, they are not
entirely obliterated but, in this case quite literally, leave their name
behind them. As in the case of the Furies, names are again important:
they too will continue to play a part in Athenian justice with the new
name of 'Semnai' beside their old one;[39] we may compare too how
Cronus's name continues in the appellation 'son of Cronus' for Zeus,
and the names Pytho, Pythius and Pythia recall the snake which
Apollo defeated at Delphi.[40]

Again, under the new dispensation in Athens, violence will ultimately be subordinated to logos and peitho: the Furies are persuaded
'without violence' but through the words of Athena to abandon their
violent pursuit of Orestes. On the other hand, were it not for another
aspect of this myth which again appears to be Aeschylus's own,
one might be tempted to contrast the smooth manner in which
grandson succeeds grandmother at Delphi with the more troubled

[37] Sourvinou-Inwood (n. 35), 231.   [38] Ibid.

[39] On the *Semnai* and the Furies, cf. A. Lardinois, 'Greek myths for Athenian
rituals: religion and politics in Aeschylus' *Eumenides* and Sophocles' *Oedipus
Coloneus*', GRBS 33 (1992), 313–27.

[40] *H.Ap.* 372–4. On naming in the trilogy as an attempt at controlling language
and so (the narrative of) events, in what is ultimately a political act, cf. S. D. Goldhill,
Language, Sexuality, Narrative: the Oresteia (Cambridge, 1984), 54–63 and Index
s.v. 'naming'.

and threatening transfer in Athens: after all, Athena refers in a scarcely oblique manner to her knowledge of where Zeus keeps his thunderbolt (*Eum.* 827).

The Pythia's account of Apollo's career continues as follows however (9–14):

> λιπὼν δὲ λίμνην Δηλίαν τε χοιράδα,
> κέλσας ἐπ᾽ ἀκτὰς ναυπόρους τὰς Παλλάδος,
> ἐς τήνδε γαῖαν ἦλθε Παρνησοῦ θ᾽ ἕδρας.
> πέμπουσι δ᾽ αὐτὸν καὶ σεβίζουσιν μέγα
> κελευθοποιοὶ παῖδες Ἡφαίστου, χθόνα
> ἀνήμερον τιθέντες ἡμερωμένην.

Leaving the Pool and rocky island of Delos, he landed at Pallas Athena's shores, the haunt of ships, and came to this land and his abode on Parnassus. He was escorted and greatly honoured by the road-building sons of Hephaestus, who made the wild land civilised.

The scholiast (on 11) says of this version that it was created to give special honour to Athens: in the *Homeric Hymn to Apollo*, the god went via Mt. Olympus, Thessaly, Euboea, the Euripus and Boeotia.[41] Furthermore, the scholia identify the 'builders of roads' as the Athenians, who created a road to Delphi for their processions,[42] and most commentators have followed them in seeing the Athenians in the 'sons of Hephaestus', because of Erichthonius's birth from his seed.[43] The scholia on 14 point out that when the sacred embassy went from Athens to Delphi, there preceded it a troop of men carrying axes 'as if to civilise the land'. We have therefore also a move from the chaotic to the civilised, from Gaia to the sons of Hephaestus (a god of craft, *techne*), who are described in 14 as 'making the wild earth civilised'. The Athenians thus play a crucial role in this Delphic succession myth, by civilising the very ground over which the god went to his oracle: it is almost as if their part is more important than that of the Delphians, in that all they have to do is to welcome the god, whose arrival has been made possible by the Athenians. Athens has,

---

[41] 186, 214 ff.; cf. A. J. Podlecki, *Aeschylus: Eumenides* (Warminster, 1989), 130.

[42] Cf. Ephorus, *FGrH* 70 F 31b.

[43] 'Probably only a periphrasis for "craftsmen"' (Podlecki (n. 41), 130), but the point of such a reference is hard to discern, and the scholiasts' comment on the Athenian procession in 14 (which Podlecki quotes) surely suggests the meaning 'Athenians'.

therefore, some time before the arrival of Orestes, established its claim to an association with the civilised transfer of power in a manner both peaceable and ultimately satisfactory to all sides, and demonstrated a superiority over Delphi which has obvious relevance to the ending of the play.[44]

(c) Amazons

These ideas are repeated and reinforced by reference to the Amazons. Athena, at *Eum.* 685–90, speaks of

πάγον δ' †Ἄρειον† τόνδ', Ἀμαζόνων ἕδραν
σκηνάς θ', ὅτ' ἦλθον Θησέως κατὰ φθόνον
στρατηλατοῦσαι, καὶ πόλιν νεόπτολιν
τήνδ' ὑψίπυργον ἀντεπύργωσαν τότε,
Ἄρει δ' ἔθυον, ἔνθεν ἔστ' ἐπώνυμος
πέτρα πάγος τ' Ἄρειος.

this hill of Ares [?], where the Amazons encamped and dwelt, when once they marched against us because of their jealousy of Theseus and built this new, high-walled city against our own, and sacrificed to Ares whence the rock and hill have the name of Ares.

Theseus defeated the Amazons, in an exploit that Herodotus has the Athenians recount as one of their military glories.[45] The Amazons' errant life-style stands as the opposite of normal human life in the polis, and their abnormal sexuality and man-killing ways are the opposite of the normally fertile family life; they thus resemble the Furies, who also lack a fixed abode, have no sexuality and spend their time rending mortals, as Apollo so charmingly points out (*Eum.* 179–97). In Isocrates's version of the Amazons' story they are obliterated,[46] but if Plutarch's information about the shrines to them near the Peiraeus gates, their graves below the Acropolis hill and an 'ancient

[44] For the idea in tragedy of Athens as a locus of civilisation and fertility, cf. F. I. Zeitlin, 'Thebes: theater of self and society in Athenian drama', in J. J. Winkler and F. I. Zeitlin (edd.), *Nothing to do with Dionysos?* (Princeton, 1989), 130–67.

[45] 9.27.4.

[46] 4.70. See most recently, W. B. Tyrrell, *Amazons: a Study of Athenian Mythmaking* (Baltimore, 1984).

sacrifice' that used to be made to them the day before the Theseia can be
referred to the fifth century, then they too, like Cronus, can be said to
continue to receive recognition despite their defeat.[47] In the fourth
century at least there was a shrine to them, the Amazoneium.[48] Even if
these rites did not exist in the fifth century, the play itself provides for
continued recognition of the Amazons, in terms familiar from the
other two myths discussed above. As Athena says, the Areopagus will
have a name which commemorates the Amazons defeated on it: they
made a sacrifice to Ares, who was their father according to Lysias and
Isocrates,[49] and whose name is preserved in 'Areopagus'. Here then, as
with Phoebus and Phoebe and the Erinyes/Semnai, we have a case of a
name acting as an acknowledgement of the significance of a defeated
party, and, as with Cronus, the persistence of cult. The site of Athens'
first law-court is thus emblematic of the way that defeated forces can be
reintegrated into ordered existence.

We may contrast this story about the Amazons with what is said in
Choephori about the Lemnians, another female group which created
a disordered society. The chorus of women put this myth at the end
of their list of female destructiveness (631–6):

> κακῶν δὲ πρεσβεύεται τὸ Λήμνιον
> λόγωι, γοᾶται δὲ δημόθεν κατά-
> πτυστον, ἤικασεν δέ τις
> τὸ δεινὸν αὖ Λημνίοισι πήμασιν.
> θεοστυγήτωι δ᾽ ἄγει
> βροτοῖς ἀτιμωθὲν οἴχεται γένος.

The horrors of Lemnos have pride of place in story, and they are lamented as
abhorrent by the people; one still compares dreadful deeds to the Lemnian
troubles; but the race has perished unhonoured by men because of the
pollution the gods hate.

Here is a myth where women succeeded in taking power by slaughtering their husbands, but their race has disappeared and has no

---

[47] Plut. *Thes.* 27. The possibility should not be ruled out that some or all of these
cults were created in response to myths like those of the *Oresteia*: cf. N. J. Richardson,
'Innovazione poetica e mutamenti religiosi nell' antica Grecia', *SCO* 33 (1983), 13–27;
Sourvinou-Inwood (n. 35), 221 on the cult of Gaia and Themis at Delphi.
[48] Cleidemus, *FGrH* 323 F 18 (ap. Plut. (n. 47)); it was on the Areopagus.
[49] Lys. 2.4; Isoc. 4.68. Aeschylus appears to have invented this sacrifice, which is
not mentioned elsewhere (Sommerstein (n. 15), 214).

celebration. Aeschylus's version is unusual, in that the Lemnians are normally regenerated by the arrival of the Argonauts,[50] but we may, taking up the hint in the text, contrast this tale with what happens in Argos in the play and, equally importantly, in Athens in the case of the Amazons. The crime of the Lemnians and its aftermath is thus a 'limit-case', illustrating the worst that can happen. In comparison with it, the state of affairs in Athens is obviously preferable.

This example of the Amazons is, of course, of a different nature from the first two discussed, in that we do not here have a change of authority but rather the preservation, from attack by forces representing its antithesis, of a better ordering of society. In this case, therefore, one might argue that the myth is open to a double interpretation in terms of Athenian politics, depending on whether one reads the proponents or opponents of the recent changes as the Amazons. On the other hand, it is equally true that the myth, though a standard representation of the victory of civilisation over chaos, is a particular version of this myth-type, in that it does not, like that of Zeus and Cronus, represent an 'original' victory so much as a successful attempt to prevent a return to an earlier, more chaotic state of things which has been transcended. It avoids the kind of regression which the Furies threaten after their defeat (*Eum.* 778 ff.), where wholesale destruction of the fertility of Athens would reduce the city to a chaotic and uncivilised condition. Sommerstein on κατὰ φθόνον (*Cho.* 686) remarks that 'this vague expression tends to suggest that the Amazons' motive for invading Attica was not an honourable desire for revenge, or for the rescue of a captive compatriot . . . , but base jealousy of the glory of Theseus'.[51] There are echoes, therefore, of the Furies' feelings on their defeat, and anger and jealousy in the face of defeat are put forward as negative qualities that contrast with the relative magnanimity of the victors.[52]

---

[50] G. Dumézil, *Le Crime des Lemniennes: rites et légendes du monde égéen* (Paris, 1924); W. Burkert, 'Jason, Hypsipyle, and the new fire at Lemnos: a study in myth and ritual', *CQ* 20 (1970), 1–16.

[51] (n. 15), 214–15.

[52] The fact that the Persians had similarly used the Areopagus as a base for their attacks, which resulted in the murder of suppliants at altars and the destruction of the whole Acropolis, also characterises the Amazons in a negative fashion: cf. Hdt. 8.52–3; n. 136 below on other Persian references in the trilogy.

(d) Athena

Finally, the presence of Athena herself on stage is a reminder to the audience that, in the foundation legend of their city, she defeated the elder Poseidon to become its patron.[53] Her victory led to a turbulent reaction from Poseidon, involving either flooding of Attica or an invasion of the territory by Poseidon's son, Eumolpus. Athena's 'son', Erechtheus, defeated Eumolpus in battle, but was rammed into the ground by the god. Nonetheless, despite his ultimate defeat, Poseidon, like the other defeated parties discussed above, was still worshipped alongside Athena on the Acropolis, and was known as Poseidon-Erechtheus. Mankind benefited because the goddess of craft, intelligence and cultivation triumphed over the elemental Poseidon, despite the fact that he was one of the three most august gods of the earlier generation. Once again, therefore, a change of name and continuity of cult accompanies a major but beneficial change, and this divine reconciliation is made available as another way of thinking about contemporary events. Here too, as in the trial of Orestes, the choice between two possible patrons with powerful cases was, in some versions at least,[54] left to the kings of Athens, Cecrops, Cranaus and Erysichthon; and the choice, though initially involving violence from the loser, was ultimately to the benefit of the city. Their own foundation myth thus also provides a model for the curbing of the existing authority by newcomers.

[53] On this story, cf. Preller–Robert i. 202–4; W. Burkert, *Homo Necans: the Anthropology of Ancient Greek Sacrificial Ritual and Myth* (tr. P. Bing, Berkeley, 1983), 136–61, and on Athena's relation to Poseidon, M. Detienne and J.-P. Vernant, *Cunning Intelligence in Greek Culture and Society* (tr. J. Lloyd; Hassocks and New Jersey, 1978), 187–203; R. Parker, 'Myths of early Athens', in Bremmer (n. 35), 198–200, 203.

[54] The traditions are varied: Apollod. 3.14.1 says 'Zeus appointed arbiters (*kritai*), not, as some have affirmed, Cecrops and Cranaus, nor yet Erysichthon, but the twelve gods'; in Callimachus, there are two versions, fr. 194.66–8 and fr. 260.24. Hesychius associated Cratinus, *PCG* 7 (*Archilochoi*) ἔνθα Διὸς μεγάλου θᾶκοι πεσσοί τε καλοῦνται with the story of how Athena traded a first sacrifice for Zeus's vote, but Kassel-Austin doubt whether the interpretation is correct. For mortals judging such competitions, cf. Paus. 2.15.5 (Cephisus and Asterion assist the river Inachus to judge a competition between Hera and Poseidon for Mycenae) and Simon. fr. 552 (= schol. Theoc. 1.65/6a). In Varro (ap. Aug. *Civ. Dei* 18.9) the whole city voted on the matter.

2. RITUALS

Reference to rituals and especially, as in the case of the myths, peculiarly Athenian rituals is another important device whereby Aeschylus provides perspectives and filters for recent events.[55]

Zeitlin has already shown that the trilogy is structured in the same way as a myth of rite of passage.[56] The pattern of such myths and rituals can be analysed in the same terms as were discussed above: the male is privileged over the female as the son is moved from the sphere of the mother to that of the father, but at the same time the fact that the end of such myths is the achieving of adult male status, including marriage to a woman, means that this privileging is deconstructed and the importance of the female acknowledged. The female is abandoned by the ephebe, who leaves his mother, passive sexual roles etc., but she nonetheless has a part to play in fertility, as even those who accepted Apollo's chauvinistic words at *Eum.* 658 ff. must have allowed. Athena, tender of the city's hearth, is always there in *Eumenides* to remind us of the centrality that the female holds in the *oikos*.

Zeitlin has also traced the way in which, especially in *Agamemnon* and *Eumenides*, the language and conventions of sacrifice are put to perverted use, so that Clytaemestra's murder of Agamemnon is described in terms of libation, the Furies' desire to punish Orestes as an attempt to make him a victim of a perverted human sacrifice, and so on; this perversion of sacrifice is corrected by the end of the trilogy.[57]

There are also references to a variety of different cultic and religious practices which have already been noted by scholars,[58] such as the confusion by Clytaemestra of rituals for dressing for a feast and

---

[55] For other bibliography on ritual and the *Oresteia*, cf. Wartelle (n. 21), 676.

[56] Zeitlin (n. 17). Cf. also A. F. H. Bierl, 'Apollo in Greek tragedy: Orestes and the god of initiation', in J. Solomon, *Apollo: Origins and Influences* (Tucson and London, 1994), 81–96.

[57] F. I. Zeitlin, 'The motif of the corrupted sacrifice in Aeschylus' *Oresteia*', *TAPA* 96 (1965), 463–508. For the perversion of funeral-rites in the trilogy, cf. K. J. Hame, 'All in the family: funeral rites and the health of the *Oikos* in Aischylos' *Oresteia*', *AJP* 125 (2004), 513–38; for corrupted *xenia*, P. Roth, 'The motif of corrupted *xenia* in Aeschylus' *Oresteia*', *Mnemosyne* 46 (1993), 1–17.

[58] A general argument in G. F. Else, 'Ritual and drama in Aischyleian tragedy', *ICS* 2 (1977), 70–87.

dressing a corpse,[59] libations for the dead and lamentations at the tomb of ancestors in *Choephori*,[60] the use of curse-tablets to damage an opponent before a trial in the 'binding-song' of the Furies,[61] refrains[62] and so on. Here, however, I shall be concerned with reference to specific Athenian cults and rituals through which commentary on the political events can be generated.

(a) Arcteia

Peradotto first looked in depth at the importance of the rites of Brauron for the representation of Artemis and the sacrifice of Iphigeneia.[63] Lloyd-Jones discussed the passage more fully in terms of Athenian and other cults of Artemis, especially those at Brauron, Mounychia and Halai Araphenides. These cults are a specific instance of rites of passage: 'there is ground for suspecting that, at least in the earlier stages of its history, the cult of the Tauropolos [at Halai] was concerned with the initiation of males, and was closely related to that of the Brauronia, which was concerned with that of females.'[64] Christiane Sourvinou-Inwood has discussed the dropping of the saffron-coloured robes in 239 (κρόκου βαφὰς δ' ἐς πέδον χέουσα) as a feature of the rites at Brauron: 'the shedding of the krokotos by the bears at the Brauronia was a symbolically charged act marking the end of the arkteia and the beginning of the transition into a new status, and as such it functioned as a very potent and apt *pars pro toto synecdoche* expressing the notion "successful completion of the

---

[59] R. A. S. Seaford, 'The last bath of Agamemnon', *CQ* 34 (1984), 247–54.

[60] W. Schadewaldt, 'Der Kommos in Aiskhylos' Choephoren', *Hermes* 67 (1932), 312–54.

[61] C. A. Faraone, 'Aeschylus' ὕμνος δέσμιος (*Eum.* 306) and Attic judicial curse Tablets', *JHS* 105 (1985), 150–4.

[62] H. E. Moritz, 'Refrain in Aeschylus: literary adaptations of traditional form', *CPh* 74 (1979), 187–213 (esp. 195 ff.).

[63] (n. 1), 244–8 (this vol., pp. 219–23).

[64] P. H. J. Lloyd-Jones, 'Artemis and Iphigeneia', *JHS* 103 (1983), 87–102, at 97 = *Greek Comedy, Hellenistic Literature, Greek Religion, and Miscellanea* (Oxford, 1990), 306–30, at 322. Cf. also K. Clinton, 'Artemis and the sacrifice of Iphigeneia in Aeschylus' *Agamemnon*', in *Language and the Tragic Hero: Essays on Greek Tragedy in Honor of Gordon M. Kirkwood* (Atlanta, 1988), 1–24, who criticises aspects of Lloyd-Jones' interpretation; the criticisms do not affect the current argument.

arkteia, achievement of acculturation, and the status of proper marriageable parthenos".[65]

This shedding of the robes and the sacrifice because of the wrath of
Artemis[66] are perhaps the most striking parallels between play and
ritual, but Aeschylus's picture of Iphigeneia's sacrifice also contains
other references to aspects of these cults. First, Iphigeneia is referred
to as ἀταύρωτος (Ag. 244), an adjective indicating her virginity.[67]
Athenian myth continued the story of the sacrifice of Iphigeneia,
telling of Orestes's subsequent foundation of the rites of Artemis
Tauropolos at Halae Araphenides two miles to the north of Brauron,
and of Iphigeneia's foundation of those at Brauron.[68] As Graf has
shown, Artemis Tauropolos was a goddess connected with rites of
passage of young men,[69] and she was also connected with madness:[70]
both aspects suit Orestes. The bull is a regular feature of maturation
rites for young men, as is shown by Theseus's killing of the Minotaur,
bull-lifting by ephebes at sacrifices, the gift of the bull to the boy
involved in the Cretan rite of passage, the Harpage,[71] and many other
examples. Secondly, Iphigeneia is sacrificed δίκαν χιμαίρας ('like a
goat', 232). This was the sacrificial animal at Brauron,[72] and the rite at
Mounychia, closely related to that at Brauron, was instituted after the

---

[65] C. Sourvinou-Inwood, *Studies in Girls' Transitions: Aspects of the Arkteia and Age
Representation in Attic Iconography* (Athens, 1988), 134. The book should be consulted
on these festivals generally, with ead. 'Lire l'arkteia—lire les images, les textes, l'ani-
malité', *Dialogues d'histoire ancienne* 16 (1990) 45–60. See also on the myths A. Brelich,
Paides e parthenoi (Rome, 1969), 248–9 n. 44; W. Sale, 'The temple legends of the
Arkteia', *RhM* 118 (1975), 265–84. On Iphigeneia in Athens, cf. E. Kearns, *The Heroes
of Attica*, BICS Suppl. 57 (1989), 27–33, 57–8, 174. R. A. S. Seaford, 'The tragic
wedding', *JHS* 107 (1987), 106–30, at 108–9 has discussed the sacrifice of Iphigeneia
in terms of Greek marriage.

[66] The later correlative of this scene is that with Orestes in *Eumenides*, where the
Furies wish to have him killed because they are angered at the death of Clytaemestra;
they refer to him as a 'hare' (26) which recalls the hare in the portent given to the
Atreidae (*Ag.* 119–20).

[67] On the whole phrase ἀγνᾷ δ' ἀταύρωτος αὐδᾷ, cf. D. Armstrong and A. E. Hanson,
'The virgin's voice and neck: Aeschylus, *Agamemnon* 245 and other texts', *BICS* 33
(1987), 97–100.

[68] Eur. *I.T.* 1446–61.

[69] 'Das Götterbild aus dem Taurerland', *AW* 4 (1979), 33 ff.

[70] Lloyd-Jones (n. 64), 96–7 = 321–2.

[71] Ephorus, *FGrH* 70 F 149; cf. J. Bremmer, 'An enigmatic Indo-European rite:
paederasty', *Arethusa* 13 (1980), 279–98.

[72] Hesych. s.v. Βραυρώνια.

death of a bear at the hands of Attic youths: the goddess demanded a maiden as requital and a goat was substituted for the maiden.[73] Embarus offered to sacrifice his own daughter to the goddess but substituted a goat disguised as the girl, who was thus saved.[74] Finally, Iphigeneia's sacrifice is described as the *proteleia* of the ships (*Ag.* 227), the word for the sacrifice made by Athenian girls to Artemis before their marriage.[75] For an Athenian, therefore, the evocation of these rites that moved their children to marriageable status, in the context of the ending of Iphigeneia's young life, would have had an especial poignancy, through the contrast between their daughters' dropping of the saffron robes and Iphigeneia's.

We can distinguish therefore three levels of narrative in this context: (1) the human sacrifice at Aulis, (2) the Athenian rites at Halae and Brauron evoked by the description of (1), and (3) the experiences of Orestes in the *Eumenides.*[76] (2) is an improvement on (1), demonstrating a better solution to the problem of human sacrifice demanded by angered deities. This brings to an end a sequence of killings, but yet makes some reparations to the slighted divinity: young girls in Athens still serve the goddess before going off to be married.[77] The divinity concerned with the rites of passage of young girls is placated so that she is not forced to take her revenge by killing those under her tutelage, and the paradoxes inherent in the need for Agamemnon to sacrifice his daughter because of the death of a hare and her young are avoided. The deity continues to receive cult, without having to resort to continued demands for revenge, and thereby Athenian society is able to continue without being constantly under the threat of divine anger and the compulsion to sacrifice children. The goddess is thus respected, not simply feared.

[73] Schol. Ar. *Lys.* 645; Zenob. *Ath.* 1.8.

[74] Paus. Att. 35 Erbse; Suda s.v. Ἔμβαρος Lloyd-Jones (n. 64), 93–4 = 316–17. The *Cypria* (Proclus 104.12 f. Allen) said that a hind was substituted for Iphigeneia, but Phanodemus, an Athenian, says it was a bear (*FGrH* 325 F 14).

[75] Evidence in Burkert (n. 53), 20.

[76] The question of how these relate together in any realistic chronology is not of importance here.

[77] For the placatory aspect of the Arcteia, cf. Suda s.v. Ἄρκτεια ἤ Βραυρώνια: ἀπομελισσόμεναι τὴν θεάν; also schol. Theoc. 2.66 (on an uncertain festival of Artemis) ἀφοσιώσει τῆς παρθενίας, μὴ νεμεσηθῶσιν ὑπ' αὐτῆς (the reference to the 'basket-bearer' in Theocritus could point to the Brauronia: see Gow ad loc.).

(3), which deals with the brother of Iphigeneia also pursued by divine anger over a murder, is another improvement over (1), again engineered by Athens. At Aulis, 'the judges [βραβῆς][78] in their eagerness for battle cared nought for her prayers, her cries of "father" and her virginal youth' (Ag. 228–30) before she is gagged to prevent unfortunate utterance and sacrificed like a goat; in the play's lawcourt at Athens, these things are again considered by judges but the defendant may speak and is protected by the goat-skin aegis of Athena. The Brauronian and Halai cults thus act as mediators between the stories of brother and sister, and as further signs of the rightness of the justification of Orestes in the play. As the girls go off to be prospective mothers and the boys hoplites, Orestes makes a military treaty with Athens and will re-establish his oikos, taking his father's place at the head of it and re-instituting its fertility destroyed by Clytaemestra, through her marriage to an effete man and the chopping down of the tree that shaded the house (Ag. 966–74). Like Artemis, the Furies are to be respected, not simply feared; they continue to be concerned with justice, but within the context of a civilised society which will honour them in a way that Delphi, for instance, did not.[79] The Furies thus avoid the more catastrophic fate of the Amazons and the Lemnians, which Athena's reference to the thunderbolt held out to them.

Sacrifice is thus restored to its proper role in peaceful communion between god and man, symbolised by the normal animal victims which are substituted for Orestes by Athena (Eum. 1006 f.). This then contrasts with the impossibility of softening the anger of the divinity stated at the start of the play, in Ag. 69–71:[80]

οὔθ᾽ ὑποκαίων οὔτ᾽ ἀπολείβων
ἀπύρων ἱερῶν
ὀργὰς ἀτενεῖς παραθέλξει.

neither by burning sacrifices nor by libations <nor by the spell of(?)> fireless offerings shall he soothe aside the relentless wrath.

---

[78] On the meaning of this word, see Fraenkel ii. 132.

[79] Cf. Apollo's words at Eum. 179 ff.

[80] (παρα)θέλγειν and its cognate noun reappear in the final persuasion of the Furies (Eum. 886, 900).

It contrasts too with the failure of Priam's sacrifices to protect Troy (*Ag.* 1167–72).[81] Athens has found a way. The justification of Orestes in the law-court thus marks a step away from violent types of appeasement,[82] as did the substitutions of the Brauron cult. Law-courts are not without their measure of rhetorical trickery, which would match the cunning of an Embarus, but they offer a rather more open and public demonstration of the solution to the problems of exigent anger. The ultimate justification for the changes is that they created a situation where a civilised existence is possible for all, where competing claims have been and will continue to be balanced. The question of the proper response in Athens, whether to what was done to the Areopagus or to the murder of Ephialtes, needs to be viewed in the light of all of this.

(b) Anthesteria

The solution to the problem of Orestes also features in the second Athenian rite to which *Agamemnon* makes significant reference. In Aegisthus's account of Atreus's serving of his children to Thyestes (1577–1611), there would appear to be a hidden reference 'en fili-grane' to one of the myths of the Anthesteria, in which we have another aspect of the story of Orestes in Athens, his purification: several words and phrases point as easily (if not, in some cases, more so) to Orestes as to his assonant counterpart Thyestes.

The first passage to consider is unfortunately corrupt and the translation thus uncertain (1594–7):

> τὰ μὲν ποδήρη καὶ χερῶν ἄκρους κτένας
> †ἔθρυπτ᾽ ἄνωθεν ἀνδρακὰς καθήμενος
> ἄσημα δ᾽† αὐτῶν αὐτίκ᾽ ἀγνοίαι λαβὼν
> ἔσθει . . .

---

[81] For parallels between this scene and *Eumenides*, cf. A. L. Brown, 'The Erinyes in the *Oresteia*: real life, the supernatural, and the stage', *JHS* 103 (1983), 13–34, at 14.

[82] One might be tempted to say that the Areopagus court is something of an improvement over the court described by Agamemnon in *Ag.* 813–17, where the gods vote οὐ διχορρόπως ('in a decision leaving no room for doubt', Fraenkel), δίκας . . . οὐκ ἀπὸ γλώσσης . . . κλύοντες 'after they had heard by no spoken word the parties' claims'. Against the idea that Zeus changes, cf. Sourvinou-Inwood (n. 22), 242–6.

The feet and the branching tips of the hands †he cut up small on top, sitting apart, and the indistinguishable parts† taking in ignorance, he ate...

The most important feature for the argument is the use of the adverb ἀνδρακάς, *viritim*, 'each separately' (1595), to describe the seating arrangements. Despite the corruption, the rare ἀνδρακάς is unlikely to be a scribal correction or error:[83] one may agree with Fraenkel when he says 'is it too much to hope that future editors will leave ἀνδρακάς alone and no longer play with a charcoal fire as Abresch did in the eighteenth century and Housman in the nineteenth?'.[84] A number of pragmatic explanations have been given for the use of ἀνδρακάς, such as that of Denniston–Page: 'the point of "each man sitting by himself" is of course that there may be no danger of the fatal dish being taken by, or shared with, somebody else'.[85] From the point of view of the practical arrangements of the feast this is eminently sound, but we are dealing with an author characterised more by a densely economical treatment of his material than an obsessive concern with *placements*.[86] Fraenkel argues that 'the statement that Atreus, the host, is sitting at a separate table would be pointless: what really matters is that Thyestes is served with his ghastly meal apart from the rest of the company';[87] this is true, but Greek ritual practice, especially that of Athens, may suggest that the idea of each at a separate table is more likely. The use of this rare adjective remains an unusual and unparalleled detail for this story, but it does have an analogue at the Anthesteria.

---

[83] H. Neitzel, 'Das Thyestes-Mahl im "Agamemnon" des Aischylos', *Hermes* 113 (1985), 406–9 ingeniously suggests that ἀνδρακάς is in fact a noun = 'Mannsportion' (cf. Nic. *Ther.* 643); however, it is perhaps more likely that Aeschylus would have used a Homeric word in the Homeric sense and that a Hellenistic writer should then have created a noun from it, than that Aeschylus should have made the change.

[84] iii. 750. The word appears only in *Od.* 13.13–14. The meaning κατ' ἄνδρα (a *varia lectio* in the *Od.* passage), *viritim* is found in Hesychius and *E.M.* s.v. and *Anec. Bachm.* p. 86.27; the lexicographers tell us that Cratinus used the word to mean κατ' ἄνδρα, χωρίς (fr. 21).

[85] J. D. Denniston and D. L. Page, *Aeschylus: Agamemnon* (Oxford, 1957), pp. 215–16.

[86] Fraenkel's suggestion that Aeschylus is making 'deliberate use of the discrepancy between the customs of Homeric society and those of his own time' (iii. 754 f.) does not give any significance to this (rather recherché) Homeric echo.

[87] iii. 751. Cf. Denniston and Page (n. 85), 215: 'grammar demands that the subject should be Atreus, the context insists that it must be Thyestes'.

This was the one time of the year when the Athenians drank sitting separately, at the drinking competition on 12th Anthesterion, the 'Choes'.[88] This practice commemorated king Demophon's solution to the problem of the arrival of Orestes, still polluted by the murder of his mother, at the time of the festival: not wishing to turn away a suppliant nor to pollute the festival, he sat Orestes at a separate table with his own *crater* and wine-jug, and, to avoid any hint of insult, ordered everyone else to so the same. The story has obvious relevance for the *Oresteia*, in that yet again it records an Athenian resolution of a potentially disastrous problem, and the use of ἀνδρακάς ought to have put the Athenians in the audience in mind of their own sitting separately, in imitation of this mythical event.

This parallel between Atreus's feast and the Anthesteria now allows us to see other parallels between the festival and this passage. Thyestes is described as returning home as a προστρόπαιος ('suppliant', 1587), which is more applicable to Orestes than to Thyestes: we are given no clear reason why the latter went into exile and returned as a suppliant, whereas Orestes came to Athens as a suppliant for purification.[89] In 1590 Thyestes is given hospitality (ξένια), which is what Orestes also sought, on a κρεουργὸν ἦμαρ (1592), a phrase which combines notions of the grisly meal,[90] and also 'festival day' on which sacrificial meat was eaten, as at the Choes.[91] συνεξελαύνει τυτθὸν ὄντ' ἐν σπαργάνοις ('drove me out young and in my swaddling-clothes', 1606) and τραφέντα δ' αὖθις ἡ Δίκη κατήγαγεν ('when I grew up, Justice brought me home again', 1607), said by Aegisthus of himself, are also both appropriate to Orestes. Finally, and perhaps more controversially, could the reason for Aegisthus's use in reference to himself of τρίτον ... ἐπὶ δέκα ('in addition to ten, the third',

[88] On this festival, cf. Parke (n. 29), 107–20; Deubner (n. 29), 93–123; Burkert (n. 53), 213–47; *Greek Religion* (Oxford, 1985), 237–42; A. W. Pickard-Cambridge, *The Dramatic Festivals of Athens* (rev. J. Gould and D. M. Lewis; Oxford, 1988), 1–25. The earliest reference is in Eur. *I.T.* 947–60, and the other main source is Ar. *Ach.*, esp. 960–1, 1000–2, 1076–7, 1224–5 with their scholia.

[89] The word is used of Orestes in *Eum.* 41; cf. also 176, 205, 234, 237, 445; *Cho.* 287 etc. Cf. R. C. T. Parker, *Miasma: Pollution and Purification in Early Greek Religion* (Oxford, 1983), 108; Fraenkel iii. 745.

[90] Cf. Hdt. 3.13.2, 7.181.2 quoted by Fraenkel iii. 747, who notes the words κρεουργεῖν and κρεουργία become in later literature *voces propriae* for the cutting up of Pelops, father of Thyestes and Atreus.

[91] *IG* 2/3² 1672.204 (329/8).

1605), with its archaic ordinal and, to many, strange and apparently unnecessary precision about the number of Aegisthus's sons,[92] result from a desire to emphasise the idea of 'the third': Orestes is Agamemnon's third child, the 'third storm' (*Cho.* 1066), the 'third saviour' (1073), and third murderer in the trilogy after Agamemnon and Clytaemestra? It may be pure chance that this archaic form of expression was used in the Athenian calendar, and that the thirteenth of Anthesterion was the last day of the Anthesteria,[93] the day after Orestes arrived.[94]

In its context, this evocation of the Anthesteria both throws a negative light on Aegisthus's involvement in killing Agamemnon on his arrival, through the contrast with Demophon's treatment of Orestes, and provides an ironic commentary on Aegisthus's crime of revenge, by presaging the appearance of the avenger Orestes who will kill Aegisthus in turn and for similar reasons. At the same time, it associates Orestes with Aegisthus as murderer and raises the question of what will happen to Orestes as a result.

More specifically, in terms of the present enquiry, the connotations of the Anthesteria come into play again in the *Eumenides*, when we see Orestes once more coming to Athens for purification. Delphi has proved ultimately unable to solve the problem, and as before Athens is the place where the solution is found. There is no king in this play; rather, an ancient democracy is created, bringing mythical Athens closer to the audience of Aeschylus's time.[95] The legal solution in the trilogy and so the changes piloted by Ephialtes are thus of a similar

[92] The reading is defended against attacks on it as absurd by Fraenkel iii. 758; Denniston and Page (n. 85), 216 justify their *obeli* by reference to 'a ludicrous multitude' of sons; H. Neitzel (cf. n. 83), 366–70 also opposes thirteen sons, but not convincingly.

[93] Cf. Philochoros *FGrH* 328 F 84 ἤγετο ἡ ἑορτὴ Ἀνθεστηριῶνος τρίτηι ἐπὶ δέκα. As in the case of ἀνδρακάς, the archaic nature of the expression makes it 'hard to believe that the occurrence here is due to corruption' (Fraenkel iii. 760).

[94] A similar custom of solitary dining connected with Orestes is found in Troezen. The people did not take the polluted Orestes into their house until the pollution had been removed, but fed him in the 'booth of Orestes' in the sanctuary of Apollo; the descendants of the men who purified him still dine there on set days (Paus. 2.31.8, with Frazer). Cf. Plut. *Q.G.* 44 (*Mor.* 301 ef, with W. Halliday, *The Greek Questions of Plutarch* (Oxford, 1928), 183–5) for a similar Aeginetan custom deriving from the Trojan War.

[95] Sommerstein (n. 15), 132–3.

kind to the mythical–ritual solution, and offer a greater participation to members of the community in such matters, rather as Demophon involved the whole community in the case of Orestes.[96]

(c) The Mysteries

Building on work initially done by Headlam, Thomson argued for a consistent thread of allusion to mystery cults, and especially to Eleusis.[97] Not all of the claimed allusions are soundly based, but there is enough for us to allow that this is a significant code in the trilogy. The Watchman in the opening lines prays for ἀπαλλαγὴ πόνων ('freedom from toil'),[98] which recalls the function of the Mysteries of guaranteeing happiness in the Underworld after death.[99] This allusion can be justified by the fact that, as if in answer to his prayer, the beacon almost immediately blazes out in the darkness, just as the light blazed from the Anactoron at the climax of the Eleusinian Mysteries.[100] The Watchman's prayer and its fulfilment set up the imagery of darkness

[96] The Anthesteria also permitted for one day the circulation in the city of the 'Cares'. It is debated whether these were spirits or Carian foreigners (cf. Burkert (n. 53), 226–30, but whichever was meant (perhaps both) one has again the idea of full participation in the city by outsiders, like the Furies, Orestes, etc.

[97] W. Headlam, 'The last scene of the Eumenides', *JHS* 26 (1906), 268–77; G. Thomson, 'Mystical allusions in the *Oresteia*', *JHS* 55 (1935), 20–34; Thomson–Headlam (n. 7), Index s.v. 'Eleusinian mysteries'. M. Tierney, 'The mysteries and the Oresteia', *JHS* 57 (1937), 11–21 accepted Thomson's main theory but preferred to refer to matters which were 'simply mystic in general', but his distinctions between Eleusinian and Orphic elements were challenged by Thomson in the commentary (362–6), and need to be reviewed now in the light of F. Graf, *Eleusis und die orphische Dichtung Athens in vorhellenistischer Zeit* (Berlin, 1974). Cf. also Sourvinou-Inwood (n. 22), 246–50; R. A. S. Seaford, *Reciprocity and Ritual: Homer and Tragedy in the Developing City-State* (Oxford, 1994), 373–4. On the Mysteries, see most recently Burkert (n. 53), 248–97, and *Ancient Mystery Cults* (Cambridge, Mass., and London, 1987).

[98] As do the Chorus of *Choephori* (941–2) and Apollo (*Eum.* 82–3); the word σωτηρία appears repeatedly towards the end of *Eumenides*.

[99] Thomson quoted Firmicus, *err. prof. rel.* 22 for the words of the priest at Eleusis promising ἐκ πόνων σωτηρία but, as Tierney (n. 97), 11–12 pointed out, Firmicus does not relate these words to Eleusis. The importance of 'salvation' in Eleusinian cult is, however, enough for Thomson's argument to stand: cf. e.g. Plato, *Phdr.* 70a and Thomson (n. 97), 21–3 for further examples, and Burkert (n. 53), 'Index' s.v. 'salvation'.

[100] Plut. *Mor.* 81e; Posidonius, *FGH* 87 F 36.51, etc.

and light which is to be central to the play and lies at the heart of
the Mysteries.[101]

Initiation was regularly seen as a toilsome journey, made in darkness
and ending in light.[102] Thomson saw an allusion to this at the end of
Choephori.[103] However, one may wonder whether Orestes' use before
the murder of the characteristically Eleusinian verb ἐποπτεύειν,[104]
along with his command for silence from the Chorus, another mystic
idea, is really enough to support the inference that 'a parallel is being
drawn, or is about to be drawn, between the murder of Clytaemnestra
and mystic ritual'.[105] Again, Thomson's claim that, in *Choephori*, in a
reminiscence of the climactic moment of the Eleusinian Mysteries, the
darkness 'is scattered by a sudden burst of light (πάρα τὸ φῶς ἰδεῖν
(961)) from torches seen within the palace as the doors are thrown
open', is open to question in terms of staging.[106] A more persuasive
specific reference to mystic affairs is the suggestion of Tierney that the
Eleusinian image of the journey accounts for the unusual description of
Orestes's wanderings from Delphi to Athens as being over sea and land
(*Eum.* 75–7, 240, 249–51).[107] He noted too that Orestes achieves safety
like the initiate and 'comes to his trial a living dead man;[108] he leaves it
reborn (l. 757), declaring himself "an Argive again" and thanking

---

[101] The Watchman's reference to the silence caused by 'an ox on the tongue' (37)
has Pythagorean and so mystical resonances (Philostratus, *Vit. Apoll.* 6.11). The
opposition light/darkness is also related to the code of rites of passage: cf. e.g.
P. Vidal-Naquet, 'The Black Hunter and the origin of the Athenian *Ephebeia*', in
R. L. Gordon (ed.), *Myth, Religion & Society* (Cambridge, 1981), 147–62.

[102] See esp. Plut., fr. 178.

[103] Thomson (n. 97), 24–7.

[104] *Cho.* 579–84. *Epoptes* was the name given the *mustes* on his second journey to
the Mysteries. For the verb, cf. Harpocr. s.v. ἐποπτευκότων, Theo Sm. *Math.* p. 14
Hiller; C.A. Lobeck, *Aglaophamus: sive de theologiae mysticae Graecorum causis*
(Königsberg, 1829), i. 127–31. It is frequent (*Cho.* 1, 489, 583, 985, 1063, and *Ag.*
1270, 1579, *Eum.* 220, 224), but its normal use is 'in the context of divine, or
semi-divine, superintendence of human affairs' (A. F. Garvie, *Aeschylus: Choephori*
(Oxford, 1986), 201).

[105] Cf. Thomson (n. 97), 24; Thomson–Headlam (n. 7), 203–6 (on *Cho.* 581–2).

[106] O. P. Taplin, *The Stagecraft of Aeschylus: the Dramatic Use of Exits and Entrances
in Greek Tragedy* (Oxford, 1977), 357 has him enter at 973 and Thomson's staging is
also rejected by Garvie (n.104), 313.

[107] Tierney (n. 97), 18.

[108] Both he (n. 97), 13–17 and Thomson (n. 97), 34 point to the similarity between
what Orestes is threatened with and the tribulations of the uninitiated in Eleusinian–
Orphic belief (cf. e.g. Plato, *Rep.* 365a).

Athena, Loxias and Zeus in a speech which three times in eight lines has
a reference to σωτηρία. The notion that initiation ... was equivalent to
rebirth was a widespread one.'[109] These references and the use of
'Eleusinian' vocabulary[110] help to maintain the Eleusinian colouring,
and the general idea of light and safety coming after long tribulation is
one which, it is not over-bold to assume, Athenians would have
associated with their experiences at Eleusis or other mystery cults.[111]

The Eleusinian Mysteries therefore can be said to offer a metaphor
for the experiences undergone by Orestes. They also provide a
slightly different perspective from those we have discussed so far.
Like the Anthesteria, though in a more all-embracing manner, they
offer a model for the acceptance into the city of problematic figures,
like the polluted Orestes or the apparently vile Furies. However,
Orestes's polluted state is, in the context of the Mysteries, a problem:
pollution was one of only two things which precluded one from
participation.[112] It is interesting therefore that in *Eumenides* the
question of Orestes's pollution is complicated. He claims three
times to have been purified, his most explicit statement coming at
Eum. 445–52:[113]

> οὐκ εἰμὶ προστρόπαιος, οὐδ' ἔχων μύσος
> πρὸς χειρὶ τῆμῆι τὸ σὸν ἐφεζόμην βρέτας.
> τεκμήριον δὲ τῶνδέ σοι λέξω μέγα·
> ἄφθογγον εἶναι τὸν παλαμναῖον νόμος,

---

[109] Tierney (n. 97), 20–1. There is nothing about rebirth in 757, but Orestes' move
from the clutches of the chthonic Furies is perhaps enough to let Tierney's point to
stand.

[110] One might add the frequent repetition of words from the root *tel- with its
connotations of 'initiate' etc.; cf. S. D. Goldhill, 'Two notes on *telos* and related words
in the *Oresteia*', *JHS* 104 (1984), 169–76.

[111] Garvie (n. 104), 304 is, therefore, being too reductive when, in discussing
Thomson's claims about the chorus in *Cho.* 935–71, he writes: 'though the parallels
[with the Mysteries] are undeniable it seems unnecessary to interpret the ode in
mystic terms. The language is fully explicable in the dramatic context of the play
itself'. 'Full' explanations of imagery etc. will not necessarily involve merely the
internal relations of the play; broader cultural reference also needs to be taken into
account.

[112] The other was an inability to speak Greek; the prohibitions were proclaimed in
the *prorrhesis*, cf. Isoc. *Paneg.* 157.

[113] Cf. 235–43, 276–98. On the question of Orestes's condition, cf. Taplin (n. 106),
381–4; Parker (n. 89), 386–8; Seaford (n. 97), 92–105; K. Sidwell, 'Purification and
pollution in Aeschylus' *Eumenides*', *CQ* 46 (1996), 44–57.

ἔστ᾽ ἂν πρὸς ἀνδρὸς αἵματος καθαρσίου
σφαγαὶ καθαιμάξωσι νεοθηλοῦς βοτοῦ.
πάλαι πρὸς ἄλλοις ταῦτ᾽ ἀφιερώμεθα
οἴκοισι καὶ βοτοῖσι καὶ ῥυτοῖς πόροις.

I am no suppliant, and I did not sit by your statue with pollution on my hands.
I will give you clear proof of this. It is the custom that the polluted man should
stay silent until, at the hands of one who can free him of his blood-stain, the
blood of a young sacrificial animal washes away the pollution. Long since have
I been thus purified in other houses with victims and running waters.

The Furies, however, are not impressed, claiming the blood is still on his
hands, as indeed the Pythia has also said when she described seeing
Orestes as 'a polluted suppliant sitting at the Omphalos with blood
dripping from his hands' (40–2). There are further difficulties as to
whether the pollution has 'worn off' during the wanderings (238–9,
280) or was cleansed by ritual purification, and, if the latter, whether
this happened once (282–3) or repeatedly (451–2). This problem has
been addressed by reference to formal aspects of the composition of the
play,[114] but it may also be that these confusions have a more central
purpose, as do similar uncertainties in Sophocles. In particular, we have
here to ask how the possibly polluted nature of Orestes tallies with his
triumphant justification proclaimed in Eleusinian terms at the end of
the trilogy. The answer would appear to be that, when a man claims to
have undergone all that ritual prescribes to free himself from pollution
and suggests that he has done this on divine guidance,[115] but other
divinities counterclaim that the pollution is still present, a further
process is necessary to prevent a repetition of the kind of circumstances
in which Agamemnon found himself at Aulis, hopelessly trapped
between two deities and their demands. Athena herself says the matter
is too great for mortals or even for her to decide alone, and that the
Furies have a claim (470–9). The resolution of the problem is to be
found in the debate and voting of the law-court: 'legal absolution' is
thus a necessary complement to the religious, and the old, traditional

[114] e.g. by Taplin (n. 106), 383: Aeschylus 'wants the supplication at Delphi, but he
also wants the salutary suffering of Orestes' wanderings', and both are necessary for
his purification; 'perhaps there is a simple explanation which reconciles these features; but it seems more likely that they are meant to co-exist without this kind of
close scrutiny' (this is accepted by Sommerstein (n. 15), 124–5).

[115] Athena too describes him as καθαρὸς ἀβλαβής (474).

forms of purification are seen to require the new judicial process in order to resolve complex, disputed cases, in which the status of the defendant is not, in religious terms, clear-cut. The decision in the play devolves onto the mortal citizens of Athens, the city that has to decide whether to accept Orestes, and, with the help of Athena's casting vote, a solution is found.[116] There is a parallel in contemporary Athenian politics too, in that in future there will be a greater involvement in the legal processes of those who are affected by the decisions: weighty matters of state are, like the trial of Orestes, a πρᾶγμα μεῖζον, resolution of which is not to be left to a powerful elite alone, be it a goddess or the Areopagus.

(d) Panathenaea

The final example of an Athenian festival evoked in the trilogy is the Panathenaea, to which a number of references are made at the very end of the trilogy.[117] Headlam was the first to explain the red cloaks of the Eumenides as those worn by the Metics in the Panathenaic procession: the Furies are explicitly called *metoikoi* in *Eum.* 1011,[118] and so, as they put on their new raiment, take up a new position in the community of Athens.[119] That the new clothes are put on over the

---

[116] Cf. Seaford (n. 20).

[117] For another play in which the Panathenaea and associated festivals play an important role, see my *Aristophanes: Myth, Ritual and Comedy* (Cambridge, 1993), 45–77 on Aristophanes's *Knights*.

[118] Cf. μετοικίαν 1018, and for the idea also 803–7, 833, 869, 890–1, 916; Headlam (n. 97) and Thomson–Headlam (n. 7), 315–19. The language of 1011 echoes the juxtaposition of μετοίκων and Ἐρινύν in *Ag.* 57–9; for μέτοικος elsewhere, cf. *Cho.* 684, 971 with Garvie (n. 104), ad locc. See also R. F. Goheen, 'Aspects of dramatic symbolism: three studies in the *Oresteia*', *AJP* 76 (1955), 113–37 = M. H. McCall (ed.), *Aeschylus: A Collection of Critical Essays* (Englewood Cliffs, NJ, 1972), 106–23, and on the procession, Taplin (n. 106), 410–15, esp. 411 and Sommerstein (n. 15), 34, 275–82. A. Kavoulaki, 'Processional performance and the democratic polis', in S. Goldhill and R..G. Osborne, *Performance Culture and Athenian Democracy* (Cambridge, 1999), 306–8, and Pompai: *Processions in Athenian Tragedy* (Oxford, forthcoming), warns against taking the connection of red robes as a reference exclusively to the Panathenaea.

[119] For this theme in the play, cf. D. Sider, 'Stagecraft in the *Oresteia*', *AJP* 99 (1978), 12–27; T. A. Tarkow, 'Thematic implications of costuming in the *Oresteia*', *Maia* 32 (1980), 153–65; Macleod, *Collected Essays* (n. 11), 41–3 (= *Maia* 27 (1975), 201–3); R. Drew Griffith, 'Disrobing in the *Oresteia*', *CQ* 38 (1988), 552–4.

old symbolises the blend of old and new justice in which they will share.[120] Headlam also noted Athena's words in 1030–1:

$$ὅπως ἂν εὔφρων ἥδ᾽ ὁμιλία χθονὸς$$
$$τὸ λοιπὸν εὐάνδροισι συμφοραῖς πρέπῃ.$$

... so that this kindly association with the land may be glorified in future by the good fortune of manly excellence.

These he related, first to Hesychius's statement that the Metics carried bowls in the procession ἵνα ὡς εὖνοι ἀριθμῶνται ('so that they should be counted as kindly disposed to the city'),[121] and second to the contest in *euandria* which determined the leaders of the procession:[122] perhaps too the Jurors, specially selected by Athena as 'best of my citizens' (487), recalled the way that older men were specially chosen for their striking good looks, to take part as representatives of their group. Headlam revived a suggestion of August Mommsen that the torches, and the *ololugmos* and singing (1043, 1047) attested for the Panathenaea by Euripides,[123] will have recalled the *pannychis* which took place immediately before the procession, which set off at daybreak.[124] The Areopagus met at night (*Eum.* 704–6), so that the Panathenaic *pompe* in the play will have set off at the same time.[125] One may note too that the goal of the procession was the temple of Athena Polias, where the first scene in Athens is set. Headlam concluded that 'the whole of this procession was designed by Aeschylus as a reflection of the great Panathenaic'.[126]

---

[120] For ἐνδύτοις (1028) = 'additional', cf. G. Hermann's edition (Leipzig, 1852), p. 645.

[121] s.v. Σκαφηφόροι; cf. also similar language in *Eum.* 990–5, 1014–20, 1033–4 (Headlam (n. 97), 273; cf. 276–7 for the significance of 990–5 to Athens' relations with the Metics).

[122] [Andoc.] *Alcib.* 42 (Headlam (n. 97), 274).

[123] *Heracleid.* 777 ff.

[124] Headlam (n. 97), 275; A. Mommsen, *Heortologie: antiquarische Untersuchungen über die städtischen Feste der Athener* (Leipzig, 1864), p. 171; *IG* 2² 334.30. Mommsen also noted the existence, at least in the fourth century, of *hieropoioi* for the Semnai appointed by the Areopagus (Dem. 21.115); the *hieropoioi* were generally in charge of the festival.

[125] Cf. Lucian, *Hermot.* 64. Sommerstein (n. 15), 279 notes that references to light begin at 906 and replace frequent reference to darkness; the Chorus calls on the sun at 926.

[126] (n. 97), 274–5. B. H. Weaver, 'A further allusion in the *Eumenides* to the Panathenaea', *CQ* 46 (1996), 559–61, argues for a coincidence in date between Areopagus trials and the Panathenaic procession.

How many other features of the procession appeared on stage is unknowable.[127] Even if some of these features were not actually brought on stage, the evocation of this schema of the festival means that the trilogy can be considered in terms of the schema. One can only speculate on whether branches were carried, as by the *thallophoroi,* freed slaves and barbarians in the actual procession; these would pick up the suppliants' branch with which *Choephori* ended.[128] Would not the Panathenaic robe, present or otherwise, with its depiction of the defeat of chaos, pick up the imagery of weaving and, with the red robes of the Eumenides, bring that symbolism, which has stood so long for entrapment and death, to an auspicious close? The word *peplos* is actually used of the garment in which Agamemnon was murdered at *Eum.* 635,[129] where it has the epithet δαίδαλος:[130] the *peplos* was highly decorated, as we learn from Euripides:[131]

> ἢ Παλλάδος ἐν πόλει
> τὰς καλλιδίφρους Ἀθα-
>   ναίας ἐν κροκέωι πέπλωι
> ζεύξομαι ἆρα πώ-
>   λους ἐν δαιδαλέαισι ποι-
>   κίλλουσ᾽ ἀνθοκρόκοισι πή-
>   ναις ἢ Τιτάνων γενεάν,
> τὰν Ζεὺς ἀμφιπύρωι κοιμί-
>   ζει φλογμῶι Κρονίδας;

Or in the city of Pallas shall I yoke the horses with their fine chariots on the saffron *peplos* of Athena, decorating it with saffron threads, or the Titans' race, which Zeus son of Cronus lays low with a blazing bolt?

The robe given to Athena at the festival was decorated with a Gigantomachy, and in the play too Athena overcomes chthonic

---

[127] Taplin (n. 106), 411 is sceptical of anything too elaborate. Sommerstein (n.15), 276–8 estimates a total of about 35 people on stage at the end.

[128] Cf. *Cho.* 1035; for branches at the Panathenaea, cf. for the *thallophoroi* schol. Ar. *Vesp.* 544, X. *Symp.* 4.17, and for slaves etc. Bekker, *Anecd.* 1.242–3 (Deubner (n. 29), p. 29).

[129] Cf. Iphigeneia's *peplos* at *Ag.* 233 and *Ag.* 1126–8, 1580–1, *Cho.* 999–1000.

[130] E. Flintoff, 'The treading of the cloth', *QUCC* 54 (1987), 122–3 argues that there is an earlier near parody of the gift of the *peplos* to Athena in Agamemnon's walking on the robes, which are described as ποικίλοις κάλλεσιν (923; cf. for the adjective 926, 936), a phrase suitable to garments in a religious context (Headlam–Thomson (n. 7), p. 96, Fraenkel ii. 925).

[131] *Hec.* 466–74; cf. schol. Ar. *Vesp.* 544.

powers, though in a much less violent manner than in this earlier exploit, which predated Zeus's establishment of the present cosmos. This time, the chthonic beings are not, like the Titans, imprisoned under the earth, but are to be honoured there (*Eum.* 1036).[132]

If we accept Burkert's account of the relationship of the Panathenaea to the festivals at the end of the old year,[133] this evocation of the Panathenaea will be not only a symbol and celebration of the unity brought by Athena, but also another way of viewing the events of the play and of recent months. The festivals at the end of the Athenian year marked dissolution, the break-down of normality and the reversal of roles. At the Scira, the priestess of Athena and the priest of Poseidon left the Acropolis (the gods thus symbolically abandoned the city), men and women were separated so that family life was interrupted, and women unusually gathered together. During this time, the Dipolieia was celebrated, when the Eleusinian Ceryces family 'occupied' the Acropolis of Athena, and carried out the anomalous Buphonia sacrifice to Zeus: the slaughter of an ox which had eaten the sacred cakes resulted in a trial of those involved; the blame was passed from one to another until it fell on the instruments of sacrifice, which were thrown into the sea. At the Cronia, discussed above, the roles of master and slave were reversed.

The trilogy echoes a number of aspects from these festivals. At the Scira, the normal occupants of the Acropolis are absent, just as the murder of Agamemnon and the marginalisation of his son remove the expected rulers from the house. The disruption of the household dramatised by the festival is repeated in the actions of Clytaemestra and Aegisthus: their swapping of the roles of master and mistress is of the same order as the rites at the Cronia.[134] Clytaemestra furthermore sins against two aspects of Greek ideology about women and

[132] N. S. Rabinowitz, 'From force to persuasion: Aischylus' *Oresteia* as cosmogonic myth', *Ramus* 10 (1981), 186.

[133] Burkert (n. 53), 135–61. There is no intention to imply that Athens had any 'new-year' festival of the kind found in Babylon: there was no such neat division. The Scira and Dipolieia took place in the middle of Scirophorion, the last month, the Cronia and Panathenaea in the middle of the first, Hecatombaion. The justification for taking the last as the 'first' festival of the new year is the nature of the festival. Some new officials took up their office after it (cf. Meiggs & Lewis, no. 58A.27–9).

[134] Aegisthus's effeminacy was traditional: Hom. *Od.* 3.262–4, 310; cf. *Ag.* 1224–5, 1625–7, *Cho.* 304.

the household. Women were expected, Penelope-like, to tend the hearth, and to spin and weave: 'domum servavit, lanam fecit', as was said of the famous Claudia.[135] Clytaemestra, by contrast, weaves not to clothe but to kill her husband. Again, she tends not a domestic fire but a huge chain of beacons, involving herself most anomalously with fires in the outside world,[136] the sphere of men. At the end of her recital of her beacon-chain, she compares it to a *lampadedromia*, the best known of which in Athens took place at the Panathenaea.[137] Here again we have a reversal, a woman associated with and, as it were, in charge of a major city rite. Furthermore, Fraenkel remarks that there is a further anomaly, in that at the Panathenaea teams of runners competed against each other, whereas 'a single team, posted from Ida to Argos, is running here and therefore there is no competition, and yet there is mention of a winner as in the Attic Lampadedromia. This paradox must have struck Athenian hearers as something almost grotesque'.[138]

More contentiously perhaps, the anomalous trial at the Buphonia sacrifice might bear comparison with the trial of Orestes.[139] The justification for such a comparison would be that, once the year-end schema was brought into play, then all aspects of it were available for the consideration of the actions on stage. Furthermore, the Buphonia trial and that of Orestes are, by their very newness, characterisable as anomalous, and both institute a new way of solving a 'legal' problem. Both of them make a point of involving not just the people most immediately implicated in the problem but also a wider section of the community: in Orestes's case, the Areopagus, in the

---

[135] *Carm. lat. epig.* 52 (Buecheler); cf. R. Lattimore, *Themes in Greek and Latin Epitaphs* (Urbana, 1962), 271.

[136] S. V. Tracy, 'Darkness from light: the beacon fire in the *Agamemnon*', *CQ* 36 (1986), 257–60 relates the beacons to the (possible) use made of them by Mardonius to signal his capture of Athens (cf. Hdt. 9.3.1); another Persian element in Clytaemestra's account is ἄγγαρος (282), which recalls the *aggareion* system of horse-riding messengers (Hdt. 8.98.2). Persian echoes would further blacken the picture of the queen, as in the case of the Amazons; cf. K. J. Dover, 'The red fabric in the *Agamemnon*', in *Greek and the Greeks* (n. 5), 151–60 (= *Dioniso* 48 (1977), 55–69), esp. 156–60 on the Spartan king Pausanias and Agamemnon.

[137] Cf. Fraenkel ii.166–9 on this rite (with bibliography).

[138] Ibid. 168–9.

[139] The fullest account of the Buphonia is in Porph. *de abst.* 2.28 ff., which is followed here.

Buphonia, 'all' the citizens. The aetiological story told of one Sopatros, a farmer in Attica but not an Athenian, who killed in anger an
ox which ate his sacrificial cakes; he then fled to Crete.[140] Drought
struck Attica, and the oracle did not demand the expiation of the
crime but rather its repetition, and the subsequent consumption of
the animal. In return for the gift of citizenship and the promise that
all would take part in the rite, Sopatros effected the repetition. The
strange trial followed. Like the men who struck the ox in myth and
ritual, Orestes has fled, though like Sopatros he does not flee the trial
completely, but is brought to it by the oracle at Delphi. In this way, in
each case, a problem is resolved without further suffering: the ox
slain by Sopatros is exhumed, skinned, stuffed and yoked to a plough
as it was in life, and reparations are made to the Furies.

There are a number of ways in which the trial of Orestes demonstrates its superiority to the 'comedy of innocence'[141] acted out at the
Buphonia. In the trial at the festival, after the blame had been passed
from group to group involved in the sacrifice, 'they convicted the
knife [that skinned the ox] of the slaughter, because it was voiceless
(οὔσης ἀφώνου)'.[142] We may detect echoes of the voiceless Iphigeneia
here. Furthermore, the repetitive and predictable nature of the rite's
outcome also makes it unsuitable as a model for any practical law-
court, which would have to deal with cases of greater complexity
where resolution could not always depend on an unusual demand
from Delphi, as in the case of Sopatros, or on the convenient fiction
that the 'murder-weapon' was guilty. The passing of the blame from
one group at the Buphonia to another is, finally, reminiscent of
similar attempts by the murderers and their apologists in the trilogy
to pass the blame to, for instance, *dike*. At the same time, however,
ancient convention is not totally abandoned in the new legal system,
in that restitution and the involvement of the wider community
appear in the new courts, both in Orestes's time and in Aeschylus's.

The year-end periods of abnormality, violence and disruption are
brought to a conclusion by the Panathenaea, as the city remakes its

[140] Another version of the story has Diomos 'taking the others, who were present
when the ox ate the cakes, as *sunergoi* and slaughtering it' (Porph. *de abst.* 2.10).

[141] For the phrase, K. Meuli, 'Griechische Opfergebräuche', in *Phyllobolia (Fest.
P. Von der Mühll)* (Basel, 1946), 275–6.

[142] Porph. *de abst.* 2.30.

unity and faces a new start. The question must then be: may not the disruption surrounding the recent reforms to the Athenian legal system be similarly concluded? They too be can seen as marking the end of one period and the start of another, with the violence and disruption that such changes traditionally may, but need not inevitably, involve. Athena and Poseidon, normally together on the Acropolis, are ritually split apart each year, but this is done the better to cement their unity for the coming twelve months. Mythology and ritual regularly depict such dislocations and reunifications in terms of violence and upheaval, which lead to a better state of affairs, though inevitably with winners and losers. The *logos*-based courts provide the best available place for resolutions of such conflicts in the future. The mythical first Areopagus even provides a model for the behaviour of the losers: if the Furies need further persuasion, the defeated jurors do not complain.

There is therefore, a considerable range of mythical reference into which the contemporary events are situated. Parallels are given from mythology, especially Athenian mythology, for the kind of change that has happened, making it comprehensible and even giving it a perspective through changes of a much greater kind on a cosmic scale. Then there are references to Athenian rituals and their myths, which carry the message that Athens has met and coped satisfactorily with crises of this kind before, coped indeed better than other places and peoples. These references either pervade the whole trilogy, as in the cases of the Mysteries or the year-end festivals, or are placed at significant junctures in the narrative, as in the evocations of the Arcteia at the sacrifice of Iphigeneia or of the Anthesteria at the time of Agamemnon's murder.

All of these myths and rituals can be pressed into service to think about the recent changes. They might, but need not, be read as simply supportive of them. The stories themselves have problems in them, such as Zeus's violent treatment of his father, the war in the Athenian foundation myth, or the patriarchal nature of the Amazonian stories. Furthermore, the Delphic succession myth, which provides the non-violent model for the play's changes, appears to have been made up by Aeschylus himself by the suppression of more violent versions, and some of the rituals involve blatant cases of Athenian myth-making: rhetoric is as much part of the manipulation of myth and ritual as it is of legal debate. The imagery of the trilogy creates constant ambiguities, whereby Orestes can be both the snake, chthonic creature of darkness, and the 'light' of the house, but these mythic and ritual references offer more positive ways of looking at the events in the play and in 'reality', which can suggest that what Ephialtes has done is not so very much against Athenian tradition. What our Proteus himself felt about the changes we cannot know, but he has provided a rich variety of means for his contemporaries to come to terms with them.[143]

[143] I am very grateful to Christiane Sourvinou-Inwood for her careful criticism of this article, parts of which also benefited from comments at the Warwick Classical Association conference and seminars in London and Oxford. The views expressed remain the responsibility of the author.

13

The Prometheus Trilogy

M. L. West

The evidence against the Aeschylean authorship of the *Prometheus* is now overwhelming; or so it appears to me, considering the question without preconception and in that hebdomad of life in which, according to Solon, περὶ πάντα καταρτύεται νόος ἀνδρός. Those who still maintain that the play is by Aeschylus may probably be divided into three categories: those who have not read Mark Griffith's recent book on the subject;[1] those who are incapable of unlearning anything they grew up believing, at any rate concerning such an important matter; and those who, while not constitutionally incapable of conversion, nor unimpressed by the evidence, yet have a rooted feeling, which they are unwilling to discount, that the play is like Aeschylus. The first group is easy to prescribe for. The second is incurable. To the third I would say that although instinct may certainly on occasion be worth a hundred arguments, its reliability as a pointer to the truth depends on its sources. When it represents a rational calculation performed by the subconscious from considerations or observations of which the conscious mind has not yet taken stock, so that upon reflection it can be put on an objective basis, well and good. There is no doubt an element of such calculation in the

---

[Editor's note. The author has omitted two drawings which appeared in the original publication, added some translations, and supplied a postscript.].

[1] *The Authenticity of Prometheus Bound* (Cambridge, 1977). See also O. Taplin, *The Stagecraft of Aeschylus* (Oxford, 1977), 460–9.

present case, for of course the *Prometheus* does have some Aeschylean
features. (So did the early plays of Sophocles, according to himself.)
But who can boast a subconscious programmed with a concept of
Aeschylean drama that is not based in part on the *Prometheus* itself?
It is one of the first plays of the transmitted seven that the student
reads; it is one liable to make a striking impression on him, and so to
contribute more than its share to his concept of Aeschylus. He reads
in handbooks about Aeschylus' love of spectacle and interest in
theological problems, he finds these supposed characteristics exemplified nowhere more clearly than in the *Prometheus,* and he accordingly registers these aspects of the play as peculiarly Aeschylean. On
such foundations the developing scholar builds up his concept of
Aeschylus, and it is little wonder if, some decades later, he is unable to
fight the conviction that the *Prometheus* is profoundly Aeschylean
and that Aeschylus is incomplete without the *Prometheus.* But the
time has come now to face the facts; to stop pretending that they are
explained if Aeschylus wrote the play in Sicily, or when he was rather
ill; and to construct a new, more homogeneous picture of the Father
of Tragedy.

The purpose of this article is to reconsider the old but still unresolved problems of the staging of the extant *Prometheus,* to contribute to the reconstruction of the trilogy, and to advance arguments for
dating it to the year 440 or shortly after.

It is generally accepted that the other plays of the trilogy were the
Prom. Lyomenos and *Prom. Pyrphoros,* though opinion is sharply
divided (and has been for over a century) on whether the latter was
the third play or the first. There are good reasons for the belief
that these three plays did form a trilogy. The scholiast on *PV* 511
states that Prometheus 'is released in the following play', and on 522
that he 'is keeping what he has to say for the next play'.[2] We know
enough about the *Lyomenos* to see that it continued the story of
Prometheus in exactly the way foreshadowed in the *Desmotes* and in
exactly the same style, with another chorus of sympathetic but
ineffectual deities and with lengthy catalogues of remote peoples

---

[2] ἐν γὰρ τῷ ἑξῆς δράματι λύεται; τῷ ἑξῆς δράματι φυλάττει τοὺς λόγους. The
suggestion that this could mean 'the next play' in some collected edition is absurd,
particularly in view of the second passage. Ancient critics never refer to other plays in
such a way.

and places, partly in instruction of a passing wanderer from Greece. Heracles' route through the west complemented Io's through the east. Even in the few fragments quoted we observe some of those stylistic features whose frequency in the *Desmotes* sets it apart from the work of Aeschylus,[3] and some close parallels of diction. If ever two plays were composed together, these two were. We are bound to assume that there was a third.[4] Among the plays ascribed to Aeschylus, *Prom. Pyrphoros* is virtually the only candidate,[5] and its title is certainly promising. Although next to nothing is recorded of its contents, we do know that it referred to Prometheus' bondage as being for τρισμυρία ἔτη ('thrice-myriad years'), which links it with *PV* 94 τὸν μυριέτη χρόνον ἀθλεύσω ('I shall endure my myriad-year term').[6] The idea is not found in any other early treatment of the Prometheus myth, and it presupposes an account which embraces both the binding and the release—that is to say, where drama is concerned, a Prometheus trilogy.

Taplin has suggested that the titles of the plays indicate that they did not belong together in a trilogy.[7] The argument runs: epicleses such as *Desmotes, Lyomenos*, were invented by Alexandrian scholars to distinguish between plays of the same name; the author's title would simply have been *Prometheus* in each case; but the author would not have given the same title to different plays within a trilogy. The first premise is unsound. In a number of cases, epicleses are obviously inspired by some striking *visual* feature of a particular scene: *Ajax* μαστιγοφόρος ('goad-bearing'), *Hippolytus* στεφανηφόρος ('garlanded') and καλυπτόμενος ('veiled'), and others. Such names will not

---

[3] Initial anapaest in the trimeter (Griffith (n. 1), 77–8); irregular caesura in anapaests (Griffith (n. 1), 70–1); address with the bare proper namer (Griffith (n. 1), 120–1).

[4] The hypothesis of a dilogy (Bernhardy, Dindorf, Bergk, Focke) cannot be supported by any solid parallel so far as the Dionysia are concerned. It would be possible at the Lenaia, when it was the custom for tragic poets to exhibit two plays, though we do not know that these were ever connected in subject. This option is not available to those who maintain that *Desm.* is by Aeschylus, as tragic performances at the Lenaia only began *c.*440.

[5] Against H. Lloyd-Jones's theory that it was the *Aitnaiai* see the just criticisms of Taplin (n. 1), 464–5.

[6] There is no contradiction, since these are not meant as precise numbers. Cf. 257–8, 512.

[7] 'The title of *Prometheus Desmotes*', *JHS* 95 (1975), 184–6.

have originated with scholars who knew the plays mainly from reading but with people who knew them as spectacles. They must have been current in the book trade long before the Alexandrians set to work. A man buying an *Ajax* needed to be sure which one it was: to be told that it was 'that one where Ajax appeared brandishing a whip' was just what he wanted. Such designations, like all book titles in the classical period, were initially informal and not exclusive. The same play might be called Φρύγες or Ἕκτορος λύτρα.[8] There is no certainty that the plays of our trilogy were recorded in Didaskaliai under 'Prometheus' titles: they might have been designated after their choruses, as so often happened, or just collectively as Προμηθεία τετραλογία, '*Prometheia* (tetralogy)' (cf. *TrGF* i, DID B 5. 8; C 4a. 7; C 24). The greater importance of the virtuoso actor after the fifth century perhaps encouraged the later use of protagonist-titles. But any of our plays might at any time have been referred to as a *Prometheus*, and whoever needed to distinguish between them could at any time attach the suitable epiclesis.

PROMETHEUS PYRPHOROS

The *Pyrphoros* was certainly the first play, not the third. The arguments used by Pohlenz nearly fifty years ago[9] should have been accepted as conclusive.

(i) By the end of *Ly.* Prometheus was free and wearing the crown that commemorated his bondage and was subsequently worn by men in remembrance of it. This already establishes an aition for cult practice, something we would expect to come at the end of the trilogy. Those who place *Pyrph.* last assume that it had to do with the establishment of the Attic Promethia. But this cannot have required more than a few lines at the end of a play, and could very well have been dealt with in *Ly.* It is impossible to see how a whole further play could have been filled.

[8] See in general E. Nachmanson, *Der griechische Buchtitel* (Darmstadt, 1969).

[9] *Die griechische Tragödie*, 1st edn. (Leipzig, 1930), 70 ff.= 2nd edn. (Göttingen, 1954), 77–8. Cf. A. D. Fitton-Brown, 'Prometheia', *JHS* 79 (1959), 52–60, at 53; Griffith (n. 1), 15–16; T. Gargiulo, *Boll. Com.* 27 (1979), 91–100.

(ii) If *Pyrph.* came first, it dealt with Prometheus' theft of fire. The plan of the trilogy was then Crime–Punishment–Reconciliation. This, and not Punishment–Reconciliation–(?), is surely the scheme that would naturally have occurred to the poet.

(iii) The perfect tense in sch. *PV* 94 (= fr. 208a Radt), ἐν γὰρ τῷ Πυρφόρῳ τρεῖς μυριάδας φησὶ δεδέσθαι αὐτό, 'for in the *Pyrphoros* he says that he was (has been) bound for three myriad (years)', used to be taken as an indication that *Pyrph.* came later than *Desm.* But in fr. 199 what was actually a prophecy to Heracles, ἥξεις δὲ Λιγύων εἰς ἀτάρβητον στρατόν κτλ., 'you will come to the fearless host of the Ligyans' etc., is turned by Hyginus into *Aeschylus autem in fábulá quae ínscríbitur Prometheus Lyomenos Herculem ait... iter fécisse per Ligurum fínés* etc. The scholiast may likewise be referring to a passage that was actually in the future tense. Indeed, this duration for the bondage could only be given at or before its beginning, since in fact Prometheus was released much sooner than Zeus anticipated, in the thirteenth human generation. Fifth-century writers were quite used to converting so many generations into so many hundred years.

It has often been argued that the fullness with which anterior events are related in *Desm.* makes it unlikely that another play preceded. But not all of these events need have fallen within the compass of *Pyrph.*; *Desm.* itself shows that the author was much given to repeating himself; and on the other hand Prometheus is not explicitly identified in the opening scene till line 66, not as early as we might expect if he had not been seen before. An audience is not normally required to deduce the identity of a character from a statement of what he has done (7–8), an address as indistinctive as Θέμιδος αἰπυμῆτα παῖ (18), or an assessment of the general situation.

Pyrph., then, was concerned with Prometheus' theft of fire and its transmission to mankind. He carried it in a fennel-stalk,[10] and the play's epiclesis πυρφόρος, like *Ajax* μαστιγοφόρος and *Hippolytus* στεφανηφόρος, doubtless recalled a particular scene where he appeared with this property. There seems to be a reflection of it in *Birds* 1494 ff., where Prometheus appears veiled and furtive, afraid of being seen by Zeus, in a situation where no fires are burning on

---

[10] *PV* 109, after Hes. *Th.* 567, *Op.* 52; also on vases, perhaps after Aesch. *Prom. Pyrkaeus.*

mortal altars (1516–18). His 'I detest all the gods, as you know' in
1547 (~ *PV* 975 'in a word, I hate all the gods') confirms the allusion
to the Prometheus trilogy, which had been parodied by Aristophanes
earlier[11] and by Cratinus before him.[12] It is difficult to account for
the *Birds* scene without the tragic model.[13]

Prometheus appeared with the smouldering fennel, furtively,
λαθὼν Δία τερπικέραυνον, 'eluding the eye of Zeus whose sport is
thunder' (Hes., *locc. citt.* n. 10), but visible to the chorus. Presumably
he did not carry it away again to give to mankind off stage, but gave it
to mankind or to some intermediary in the course of the scene. It is
natural to guess that he gave it to the chorus and that a small fire was
kindled on the altar in the middle of the orchestra; it may then have
been covered over with ashes. Cf. Hyg. *Fab.* 144 (*ignem*) *Prometheus
in ferulá detulit in terras hominibusque mónstravit quomodo cinere
obrutum seruarent.*[14]

Were the chorus then mortal men? Perhaps, but it does say in the
Life of Aeschylus (T 129 Radt, ἐκ τῆς Μουσικῆς Ἱστορίας) that his
Prometheus plays διὰ μόνων οἰκονομοῦνται θεῶν ... τὰ γὰρ δράματα
συμπληροῦσιν οἱ πρεσβύτατοι τῶν θεῶν, καὶ ἔστι τὰ ἀπὸ τῆς σκηνῆς
καὶ τῆς ὀρχήστρας θεῖα πάντα πρόσωπα ('are managed through gods
alone ... for the plays are filled by the most senior gods, and on stage
and orchestra it is all divine characters'). Io at least is an exception; but
a chorus of mortals would be a more flagrant one. I would suggest as a
possibility that the chorus represented the tree-nymphs known as the

[11] Griffith (n. 1), 11–12; add *Ach.* 704 ~ *PV* 2.

[12] See below on *Ly.* Was any play of Aeschylus made so much use of by comedians?

[13] Certain of the things Prometheus says in it might be echoes of the trilogy: 1500
βουλυτὸς ἢ περαιτέρω; 'ox-unyoking time or beyond?' (πέρα and περαιτέρω three
times in *Desm.*, not otherwise in Aeschylus); 1514 ἀπόλωλεν ὁ Ζεύς, 'Zeus is finished'
(Prometheus might have said this to the Titans in *Ly.*, alluding to the disaster that
awaited Zeus if he did not buy Prometheus' secret); 1538 ἥπερ ταμιεύει τὸν κεραυνὸν
τοῦ Διός, 'she who is warden of Zeus' thunderbolt'. Zeus' thunderbolt may have been
important in the trilogy as the foundation of his power, cf. *PV* 922. In *Eum.* 827–8 it is
Athena who alone has access to the building where it is kept. In Pl. *Prot.* 321d it is
from the house that she shares with Hephaestus that Prometheus steals fire, though in
Desm. we only hear of Hephaestus as its owner. Plato, at least, was thinking of the
Periclean Hephaesteum overlooking the agora, shared by Hephaestus and Athena.

[14] The passage goes on to relate the nailing of Prometheus to the Caucasian rock
for 30,000 years, the eagle, and its dispatch by Heracles. Another account, 'Probus' on
Virg. *Ec.* 6. 42 says 'fúrem Iuppiter insequebatur, sed ille, qui non posset subterfugere,
in silicem ferulam adlísit eique ignem commendauit'.

Meliai. Hesiod said that following Prometheus' trick Zeus 'did not give fire to the μελίαι' (*Th.* 563). A scholiast explains the word as meaning men, because they were descended from the Meliai. Others may have understood it to mean the Meliai themselves, as those from whom men take fire, stored up in trees as it is (cf. my note on the passage). Our poet had Hesiod's account very much in mind, and might have had the idea of making the Meliai the intermediaries who received fire from Prometheus and from whom mankind would afterwards obtain it. If so, it becomes a little easier to understand how he came to think of making the Oceanids, nymphs of springs and groves, the chorus of the following play. The hypothesis also allows us to accommodate in *Pyrph.*, if we wish, Aesch. fr. 379 (*fab. inc.*),

> ὑμεῖς δὲ βωμὸν τόνδε καὶ πυρὸς σέλας
> κύκλῳ περίστητ᾽ ἐν λόχῳ τ᾽ ἀπείρονι
> εὔξασθε,

> But take your stand all round this altar and bright fire
> and in unbroken band utter prayer,

which we know from Porphyry who quotes it to have been addressed to a female chorus.[15] Mette inserts it in his fr. 343 = 204a/b Radt, a Prometheus-play in which the chorus rejoices in the novelty of fire and is confident that it will attract Naiads. I agree with Fraenkel and others that this is a satyric chorus, in which case the play will be Aeschylus' *Prometheus Pyrkaeus* of 472.[16] But the scene is at least suggestive as a model for *Pyrph.*

In Hesiod the theft of fire followed its withdrawal by Zeus in response to the trick that Prometheus played on him at Mekone over the division of meat. It was itself followed by the creation of the first woman and her reception by Epimetheus. These matters are entirely ignored in *Desm.*, however, and we must take what we find there as our guide to the context of the theft in *Pyrph.* Prometheus relates (199 ff.) that when the younger gods began to rebel against

[15] The injunction to pray does not exclude the addressees' being divine themselves. Hera prays to Earth, Heaven, and the Titans in *Hymn. Ap.* 332 ff.; the Erinyes pray to their mother Night in *Eum.* 321 and 844 and to the Moirai in 961.

[16] E. Fraenkel, *Proc. Brit. Acad.* 28 (1942), 245 ff.; B. Snell, *Gnomon* 25 (1953), 435–6; H. Lloyd-Jones, appendix to the Loeb *Fragments of Aeschylus*, p. 562; Radt in *TrGF* iii.

the Titans, he, advised by his oracular mother Themis–Gaia,[17] tried to persuade his brothers to resist them by craft, not with force. They would not listen to him, so he changed sides and helped Zeus to victory. Zeus banished Kronos and his allies to Tartarus, and assigned to the new gods their various privileges. For mortals he had no concern: he proposed to wipe them out and create a new race. Only Prometheus resisted, and he saved them from destruction, gave them hope of life in place of certainty of death, and fire from which they would develop many skills.[18]

It is doubtful whether all this could have been encompassed in a tragedy. If it was, the *Pyrphoros* must have moved at a tremendous pace, wholly unlike that of the Brucknerian *Desmotes*. I think it much more likely that it began with Zeus already in power, the Titans already in Tartarus, and mortal men floundering in misery, deprived of the easy life they had enjoyed in the reign of Kronos and unequipped for the realities of the new world. The first part of the play will have been devoted to the representation of this situation by means of choral songs, dialogue between Prometheus and the chorus, and perhaps dialogue of a less friendly sort between Prometheus and some representative of Zeus' regime. If the chorus consisted of the Meliai, their sympathy for mankind is understandable, because they could be considered the mothers of mankind, in accordance with those traditions which had men born from trees.[19]

Two fragments attributed to Aeschylus but not to a specific play might have stood here. One is 312 R.,

αἱ δ' ἐπ' Ἄτλαντος παῖδες ὠνομασμέναι
πατρὸς μέγιστον ἆθλον οὐρανοστεγῆ
κλαίεσκον, ἔνθα νυκτέρων φαντασμάτων
ἔχουσι μορφὰς ἄπτεροι Πελειάδες.

---

[17] In the genuine Aeschylus, *Eum.* 3, Themis is the daughter of Ge and her successor as the incumbent of the Delphic oracle.

[18] Cf. 110. Later, in 442 ff., Prometheus speaks as if mankind has already acquired all its arts, directly taught by him. The poet's conception has clearly evolved between the first passage and the second, and nothing of what is new in the second must be projected back into *Pyrph.* By 714 there are iron-working Chalybes.

It is doubtful what, if any, sense can be given to the statement in 331 that Oceanus shared and dared everything with Prometheus. He cannot have played any part in the theft of fire.

[19] Hesiod may have considered them so. See my notes on *Th.* 187 and *Op.* 145–6.

> While the seven known as Atlas' Daughters
> lamented their father's unequalled labour of the sky-roof
> from where they appear in their nocturnal forms
> as Doves without wings.

The labour imposed on Atlas is twice referred to in sympathetic terms in *Desm.* (347 ff., 425 ff.), and Prometheus may have told the chorus about it in *Pyrph.* The other is 344, translated from the Armenian source as *Iouem a sceleratorum genere semouet et ab iniústo léx*, i.e. Zeus can do by virtue of his position things for which anyone else would be called a criminal. That does not sound like genuine Aeschylus, but it might well represent an exchange between Prometheus and a Jovite:

> How is Zeus not unrighteous, if he acts like this?
> —He is not; the law exempts him from that name.

The theft of fire will have been preceded by a scene in which Prometheus obscurely intimated to the chorus that he intended to do something to alleviate man's lot. They will have questioned him wonderingly in a passage of stichomythia, but he probably did not reveal everything: this the most likely context for fr. 208,

> σιγῶν θ᾽ ὅπου δεῖ καὶ λέγων τὰ καίρια,
>
> keeping silent where need be and saying what is called for,

especially in view of its immediate model, *Cho.* 582, where Orestes has been explaining his bold plan to the chorus. It is also a possible context for fr. 301 (*fab. inc.*),

> ἀπάτης δικαίας οὐκ ἀποστατεῖ θεός.
>
> A god does not disdain deception that is righteous.

That this verse came from the Prometheus trilogy is suggested by the following considerations:

1. It is a justification of some deception by a god, a justification presented presumably by himself. It does not look like a line from a longer speech (as of a *deus ex machina*) but a complete response to a query or reproach in stichomythia; addressed, moreover, to someone of less lofty status. There cannot have been many plays in which these circumstances arose.

2. Aeschylus knows that the gods deceive in the ultimate interest of justice, but the provocative, aphoristic formulation as an *ad hoc* self-justification reminds us more of the sophistic manner of *PV.*
3. The initial anapaest is, as has been noticed, markedly more frequent in the Prometheus-poet than in the genuine Aeschylus.

Prometheus left the stage, and the chorus no doubt sang in a mood of anxious anticipation. Presently he returned with the fennel, the fire was lit on the altar, and after all due formalities had been attended to, the chorus sang again, joyfully, like the satyrs in the *Pyrkaeus* papyrus, and like other tragic choruses who think that everything is turning out all right.

But the crime had been detected. What noisy god now entered to charge Prometheus with it we cannot be sure; perhaps Hermes, who is introduced in *PV* 941 as if we had all seen him before. Hyginus in the passage cited above gives Mercury, not Vulcan, as the one who nailed Prometheus to the rock, and this could be the result of telescoping the proceedings at the close of *Pyrph.* with those of the opening of *Desm.* At any rate we may be sure that a tense scene ensued between a defiant Prometheus and an indignant emissary of Zeus. There may have been an announcement of the further hardships now to be imposed on mankind through Pandora, τοῦ πηλοπλάστου σπέρματος θνητὴ γυνή, 'the mortal woman of clay-moulded seed' (fr. 369). *Trag. adesp.* 352 would fit well here:

> εἱμαρμένον δὲ τῶν κακῶν βουλευμάτων
> κακὰς ἀμοιβάς ἐστι καρποῦσθαι βροτοῖς (v.1. -ούς).
>
> It is fated that for those ill designs
> mortals shall reap an ill return.

This was not a statement of a universal principle, as those who quote it understand: 'fated' implies a particular situation. A god is announcing how mankind is going to be punished.[20]

What is more certain is that the scene culminated in the announcement of Prometheus' punishment. We know that Hephaestus was appointed to carry it out (*PV* 3–4). There is no need to suppose, however, that he was brought onto the stage for this purpose in

[20] I suspect that the gnomological tradition has substituted εἱμαρμένον for πεπρωμένον (cf. *PV* 103, 512, 518–19, 753, 815, *Ly.* fr. 199. 3) and τῶν for σῶν.

Pyrph. Prometheus was probably told 'you will be fastened to a rock with unbreakable shackles forged by Hephaestus; there you will stay ἔτη τρισμυρία' (fr. 208a, cf. above);

> χροιὰν δὲ τὴν σὴν ἥλιος λάμπων φλογί
> αἰγυπτιώσει.
>
> And your complexion the sun's torchlike flame
> will Egyptify.[21]

At the end Kratos and Bia may have been called forward as κωφὰ πρόσωπα to lead him away, for this seems the obvious way of bringing the exodos about. The chorus would follow after him as helpless sympathizers, lamenting his fate and man's and the harshness of Zeus.

It remains to consider where the action was supposed to take place. The divine drama hardly needs a definite locale, but it would be contrary to tragic practice not to specify one. Karl Reinhardt thought that it would have had to be Olympus, if *Pyrph.* was the first play in the trilogy, which he did not believe.[22] That is surely the last place it could be. We want a place on earth associated with Prometheus or with the origin of fire. The Hesiodic Mekone meant little to the Athenians or to anyone else. One possibility is Academia outside Athens, where Prometheus was honoured with Hephaestus and Athena.[23] Its pleasant groves, a favourite resort from the city since Cimon's gardening works, would be appropriate for the Meliai. The strongest candidate, however, must be Lemnos, in view of Cic. *Tusc.* 2. 23 *ueniat Aeschylus... Quo modo fert apud eum Prometheus dolorem quem excipit ob fúrtum Lémnium!* Cicero's testimony is not conclusive, for shortly afterwards he locates Prometheus' bondage in the Caucasus, and even imports the Caucasus into his translation of the Titan's first speech in *Ly.* He has been conditioned to that by the mythographical vulgate,[24]

---

[21] *Trag. adesp.* 161, cf. PV 22–3 σταθευτὸς δ' ἡλίου φοιβῇ φλογί | χροιᾶς ἀμείψεις ἄνθος. The fragment can only be addressed to someone who is going to be kept immobile in the open for a long period.

[22] *Tradition und Geist* (Göttingen, 1960), 210 n.

[23] Rose Unterberger, *Der gefesselte Prometheus des Aischylos* (Stuttgart, 1968), 134. She believes that *Pyrph.* was the third play.

[24] As have Strabo 4. 1. 7 (fr. 199) and the writer of the *Desm.* Hypothesis, who states that the scene of the play is set in Scythia at Mt. Caucasus. It is clear from 422 and 719 that the scene is not the Caucasus. To suppose that Prometheus emerged

and when he writes *fúrtum Lémnium* he may not be thinking of *Pyrph.*, which is not the Aeschylus he wants to quote: he adorns the phrase with a quotation from Accius' *Philoctetes*, where Ulysses, pointing out the landmarks of Lemnos, referred to the shrine of Hephaestus on the mountain where fire first came from heaven[25] and the grove where Prometheus shared it secretly with mortals. This is Cicero's immediate source. Accius may be recasting something from Aeschylus' *Philoctetes* or Euripides', but if so he has transferred it from a different context in the play. The grove he mentions would certainly do very well as the scene of *Pyrph.*, and the statements that Prometheus stole the fire from Hephaestus (*PV* 7, 38) suit Lemnos.

PROMETHEUS DESMOTES

On the left-hand side of the orchestra in the theatre of Dionysus there was at one time an outcrop of limestone which formed a natural eminence of some size, about 5 m across. At some stage in the theatre's development it was removed, but N. G. L. Hammond has made a good case for believing that it was still there in Aeschylus' time and that he sometimes made use of it to represent a hill or mound.[26] Taplin, *Stagecraft* 448–9, is inclined to accept this for the *Septem* and *Supplices*, but thinks that the rock was removed before the *Oresteia*, at the same time as the introduction of a stage set on the far side of the orchestra from the audience. But his argument is merely the negative one that the rock's only use in the *Oresteia* 'would be for the Areopagus in *Eum.*, and it seems implausible that the whole Areopagus should be represented by a small [*sic*] outcrop rather than left entirely to the imagination'. Because the trilogy could have been performed without a rock, it does not follow that the rock had been removed; and in fact, if Hammond is right in supposing

---

from the rock's embrace (1019) in a completely different place, for the sake of absolving Cicero from his error, is the height of absurdity.

[25] Lightning struck a tree: Tz. in Lyc. 227, cf. Hellan. 4 F 71, Diod. 1. 13. 3.

[26] 'The conditions of dramatic production to the death of Aeschylus', *GRBS* 13 (1972), 387–450, at 409 ff.

that it served as Darius' grave-mound in the *Persae*,[27] then it could serve as well for Agamemnon's tomb in the *Choephoroe*,[28] and for the appearance of Clytaemestra's ghost in the *Eumenides*. The introduction of a stage set *c*.460 in no way depended on, or made advisable, the removal of the rock—least of all if, as Taplin thinks (457), the diameter of the orchestra was simultaneously reduced, leaving the rock further out of the performers' way.

In the plays we have from the last third of the fifth century, rocks and hills are scarcely called for,[29] and tombs seem to be small altar-like structures.[30] We may conclude that the outcrop had gone at least by *c*.430, for otherwise we cannot explain the persistent failure to make use of it, which is in such contrast with its almost constant appearance in Aeschylus. Its removal must surely be connected with the comprehensive reconstruction of the theatre undertaken in the Periclean period, which involved an enlargement of the skene area, the re-siting of the orchestra and *eisodoi*, and the re-contouring of the auditorium within new supporting walls.[31]

In *Prometheus Desmotes* and for a large part of *Lyomenos* the focus of attention is a rock, described as high and rugged, constantly called a πάγος (20, 117, 130, 270; so of the hill in *Supp.* 189), πέτρα, or φάραγξ. It was not imposed on the poet by the story, for in the Hesiodic version Prometheus is fastened to a pillar. Hammond (n. 26, 422 ff.) is surely right in assuming that the Titan was bound on the

---

[27] Hammond (n. 26), 423, 428. Cf. especially *Pers.* 659 ἔλθ' ἐπ' ἄκρον κόρυμβον ὄχθου.

[28] 4 τύμβου δ' ἐπ' ὄχθῳ τῷδε. Hammond (n. 26), 436–7.

[29] The main exception is Andromeda's rock. Pirithous was also bound to a rock, but the *Pirithous* may have been composed before 430; at least if it is by Euripides, it belongs to his early work. The rocky peak from which Euadne leaps in *Suppl.* 980–1071 rose up behind the *skene*; it is fully discussed by N. C. Hourmouziades, *Production and Imagination in Euripides* (Athens, 1965), 32–3. Rocky caves in which people live (*Ichneutae, Cyclops, Philoctetes*, etc.) are essentially different; they were certainly represented by adapting the *skene*. On them see W. Jobst, *Die Höhle im griechischen Theater des 5. und 4. Jahrhunderts vor Chr.* (Vienna, 1970), 24 ff.

[30] P. D. Arnott, *Greek Scenic Conventions* (Oxford, 1962), 61–3, 137. In Sophocles' *Polyxena* (fr. 523 + Longin. π. ὕψ. 15. 7) Achilles' ghost apparently rose from his tomb; this may have been an early play.

[31] W. Dörpfeld, *Ath. Mitt.* 49 (1924) 89; A. W. Pickard-Cambridge, *The Theatre of Dionysus at Athens* (Oxford, 1946), 15 ff.; Hammond (n. 26), 410–11. It is now known that the newer temple of Dionysus behind the skene area does not date from this period but from the fourth century: *Deltion* 18 (1963) Χρον. 14–15.

natural rock to the left of the orchestra and not, as is usually
supposed, on an artificial construction in the centre of the skene area.

The play opens with the unusual spectacle of four actors entering
together:[32] Prometheus, held by Kratos and Bia, and Hephaestus
carrying a hammer and a collection of shackles (54, 56). The prisoner
is taken up onto the rock, which, as we can gather from other plays,
is easily ascended from the orchestra.[33] The actual shackling is
simulated, of course, because he has to be able to remove himself at
the end, but it is simulated vividly, with ringing blows of metal
against stone (133).

Hephaestus, Kratos, and Bia descend and depart. Prometheus'
anapaests in 93–100 presumably accompany their exit; if they go by
the east *eisodos*, they are soon out of sight behind the rock.

Presently the Oceanids arrive. How they arrive is one of the two
great problems in the staging of the play. On a literal reading of the
text (114–35 + 271–83), they come flying into view with a multitu-
dinous flapping of wings that suggests a flock of birds. They are
seated in a winged vehicle or vehicles, in which they remain aloft for
some 150 lines. Prometheus then invites them to descend to earth,
and they do so, stepping nimbly (ἐλαφρῷ ποδί) out of whatever they
were sitting in. All kinds of explanations have been offered of the
means by which these manoeuvres were represented: some ludicrous,
some unworkable, some simply feeble. They may be divided as
follows:

(i) Some think that there were no vehicles at all: the chorus danced
in, miming flight, and the rest was left to the imagination.[34] There are
two serious objections. Why are the Oceanids, nymphs of springs,
represented as flying at all? It is not in their nature to fly, and other
gods reach the place on foot without difficulty. The author's only
motive for bringing them by air is to achieve a spectacular effect, and
if they are in fact merely dancing, there is none.[35] And secondly, if
they are not in actual vehicles (aloft or aground) at 271, why all the
fuss about their now getting down out of them? Fictitious vehicles
would have been far better forgotten.

[32] Cf. Taplin (n. 1), 240–1.   [33] Hammond (n. 26), 421.

[34] G. Thomson, *CQ* 23 (1929), 160–1, and *Aeschylus: The Prometheus Bound*
(Cambridge, 1932), 142–4.

[35] Cf. Griffith (n. 1), 144, Taplin (n. 1), 259–60.

(ii) Some think that they came in wheeled vehicles at ground level or on the roof of the skene or some other elevated platform.[36] It is difficult to conceive that any impression of flight could be so achieved, whether with a communal cattle-truck or a squadron of Bath chairs, or that the audience readily accepted the creaking of axles in place of the whirring of wings. What were the means of propulsion? 'Attendants who would be regarded by convention as non-existent' (Sikes–Willson)? Hardly convincing aviation. Hidden ropes and winches? Think how awkwardly they would move forward. As for the skene roof, it is doubtful whether there was one at this period substantial enough for dodgems, and if there was, its boards would add fearfully to the creaking and rumbling. Ancient wheels had no rubber tyres. And how were the vehicles concealed from the view of the spectators in the upper rows before the chorus's entry? The skene roof cannot have been more than about 8 ft high in Euripides' time,[37] whereas the auditorium went up about 85 ft higher. No alternative elevated track is conceivable in the theatre as we know it. That only leaves the ground; and does anyone really believe that the Oceanids were trundled (uphill) up the *eisodoi*, sat there like an invalids' outing for a quarter of an hour, and then dismounted to find places in an orchestra littered with abandoned transport?

(iii) Some think that they really were borne through the air by means of the *mechane*, either in one container[38] or in individual winged chairs of the pattern used by Triptolemos.[39] It will be granted that the last method would be visually satisfactory, if it could be carried out, and that it is really the only one that approaches being so.

The objections raised to both versions of the crane theory are on practical grounds.[40] On all other known occasions when the crane was used in drama, it carried not more than two persons, or one on a

---

[36] e.g. E. E. Sikes and S. J. B. W. Willson, *Prometheus Vinctus of Aeschylus* (London, 1908), p. xlvi; F. Focke, *Hermes* 65 (1930), 282–3; Pickard-Cambridge (n. 31), 39; Unterberger (n. 23), 10; T. B. L. Webster, *Greek Theatre Production* (2nd edn., London, 1970), 12; Arnott (n. 30), 76–7; Hammond (n. 26), 424.

[37] Arnott (n. 30), 43.

[38] A surprisingly popular option: Wilamowitz, *Hermes* 21 (1886), 610 = *Kl. Schr.* i. 161, *Aischylos. Interpretationen* 116, Headlam, Smyth, Mazon, Groeneboom, and others.

[39] E. Fraenkel, *Kleine Beiträge* i. 398 ff.

[40] Sikes and Willson (n. 36), p. xlvi, Pickard-Cambridge (n. 31), 39, Arnott (n. 30), 76, Taplin (n. 1), 254, Hammond (n. 26), 424, etc.

(model) horse or other animal. It must have been designed for tasks of that order, and we cannot believe that the same machine was capable of carrying an entire chorus, weighing with their vehicles a ton or more and occupying not less than 250 cu. ft of space. The Athenians did have building cranes that enabled them to raise stone blocks of up to 12 tons or more to the top of an edifice.[41] But the theatre crane probably had little in common with those. It had not only to lift a man but to move him easily up, down, or sideways as required. It was worked by a single operator,[42] and appears to have functioned in the manner of the κηλώνειον, consisting basically of a counterweighted boom on an altazimuth mounting.[43] It was probably no larger than it needed to be to swing its load up over the skene façade. For a whole chorus a far larger machine would have had to be built, and it is doubtful whether it would have been operable.

A more plausible solution to the problem is to suppose that several cranes were used. Six would certainly suffice for a chorus of twelve,[44] possibly four, if each were made to bear three cars and passengers. We have no evidence for more than one crane being used on other occasions, true; but then we have no other text that calls for a chorus to fly.[45] Staging *Desm.* was by any account a uniquely ambitious and expensive undertaking. There is, moreover, a practical reason why cranes could not proliferate in the period after *c.*435, in which most

[41] See J. J. Coulton, *JHS* 94 (1974) 1–19, and *Greek Architects at Work* (London and New York, 1977), 84, 144.

[42] Ar. *Peace* 174, frr. 160, 192 Kassel–Austin; Strattis fr. 4 K.–A.

[43] See P. Oxy. 2742 fr. 1, Poll. 4. 128, 131; Pickard-Cambridge (n. 31), 127–8; Arnott (n. 30), 72–5. I am not sure whether the τροχός which the operator may ἐὰν ἀνεκάς in Ar. fr. 192 is a winch enabling the actor to be lowered from the boom, or simply a counterweight with which the operator guides the machine.

[44] The argument is not greatly affected if the chorus was of fifteen. Taplin (n. 1), 323 n. 3 suspects that the tragic chorus always numbered fifteen. As he observes, the ancient statements that Sophocles increased it from twelve to fifteen may be based solely on the belief that *Ag.* 1348–71 implies a chorus of twelve. But to me that belief seems justified (cf. Fraenkel's edition, iii. 633–5; Pickard-Cambridge, *The Dramatic Festivals of Athens*, 2nd edn., 235). What we lack is any equally good evidence from the plays that the chorus ever numbered fifteen. Presumably it did attain that size before the end of the fifth century, for it is not likely to have been increased at any later date in view of the chorus's declining significance. But a later writer may have ascribed the change to Sophocles simply because he came next after Aeschylus, for whom twelve was attested.

[45] Not even *Clouds* or *Birds*.

of our plays fall: a large part of the width of the stage was occupied by a permanent roofed building. The *mechane* was confined to a screened but unroofed area at the side.[46] Earlier, from the time of its first use *c.*460, the skene had probably been what its name suggests, a light temporary structure erected anew for each festival and easily removable for a play set in desert regions.

On the other hand there would be difficulties in staging *Desm.* in the way I have suggested if we take it back to the time of Aeschylus, when the width of the stage was not more than about 18 m.[47] A crane carrying two riders would require, I reckon, some 4 m clear working space, given that both ends of the boom had to move in a lateral arc. For three riders one would have to allow more. For the operation to be carried out without severe congestion, we need the enlarged stage of the Periclean theatre, laid out to the same width as the Parthenon stylobate, 100 Attic feet $= 30.89$ m.[48]

Here, then, is an important consideration bearing on the date of the trilogy. The text of *Desm.* indicates, as clearly as we could wish, that the Oceanids were intended to enter flying. The only feasible and effective way of achieving this presupposes a stage which has been widened but not yet built over. The rock beside the orchestra has not yet been removed; the east *eisodos* has to skirt it. It follows that the *Prometheus* and its companion plays could only have been conceived and produced at a certain fairly short transitional period in the development of the Theatre of Dionysus, say between *c.*445 and *c.*435.

Beyond Prometheus' rock, then, I suppose the audience to see a new stage, 100 feet wide, across which run two wooden screens, some 2 m high, on either side of a central gap. Above the screens, which are painted to suggest mountainous scenery, the tops of several cranes inevitably project, possibly camouflaged with branches. As Prometheus exclaims ἆ ἆ ἔα ἔα, and breaks into his unforgettable snatch of song (if it is song),

τίς ἀχώ, τίς ὀδμὰ προσέπτα μ' ἀφεγγής;

[46] On the left, if Poll. 4. 128 may be taken as evidence for this period.

[47] Hammond (n. 26), 414.

[48] I infer this from the post-holes in the breccia base, originally ten in number, which held the support posts of the skene façade: they extend over a distance of 28.5 m.

the Oceanids start to rise into view, sitting barefooted in their winged thrones which sway and hover like a flight of birds just in front of the screens. The astonished spectator surmises that this must be the chorus, and receives confirmation when they begin to sing. But they remain hanging in mid-air throughout the ensuing scene (in which Prometheus' singing voice is tested no more).

At 271 the poet decides that it is time to bring them to earth, and he makes Prometheus persuade them to descend so that they may hear about his future prospects. ἀκούσατε, he says, as if about to reveal all. They are willing; they desire to hear the whole story. Their vehicles sink low enough for them to step down.[49] But instead of the entertainment they have been promised, their father Oceanus suddenly barges forth over the fence on a griffin, and the next 113 lines are devoted to dialogue between him and Prometheus uninterrupted by a word from the chorus. They then sing an ode as if nothing had happened, after which they do hear Prometheus' story—all that he did for men, and the first hints of what is to come. Not surprisingly, the Oceanus scene has been suspected of being an insertion.[50] I think there is no real doubt that it was composed by the same poet as the rest. It has all his trademarks, some of them in abnormal measure. On the other hand it seems safe to say that when he composed 271–83 he was not planning this as the immediate sequel. The chorus would still have had to land if he had been, to free a crane for Oceanus' use, but some different reason would have been provided. As it is, the poet must have had a prior motive for bringing them down when he does. The obvious one is so that they can dance—as they do the moment Oceanus departs. They sing *inter alia* of Atlas, who is introduced (425 ff.) as if we had not already heard about him from Prometheus in the Oceanus scene (347–50). The stasimon as a whole would stand satisfactorily after 283. The silence for which Prometheus apologizes in 436 is his delay in continuing after his promise in 271–6: his intervening dialogue with Oceanus obscures

---

[49] The crane operators perhaps lift the counterweights up onto supports, so as not to be suddenly supporting them themselves, and then unhook them and swing the booms back.

[50] Wilhelm Schmid, *Untersuchungen zum gefesselten Prometheus* (Tübingen, 1929), 5–15.

the connection, just as it disrupts the whole sequence of action. The poet inserted it presumably because he found that his play was turning out too short or that the plot was advancing too rapidly. It is hastily written, dramatically weak and repetitious, inflated by the irrelevant digression on Atlas and Typhoeus (for whose sufferings Prometheus was not responsible), and in the end ludicrous; no wonder the griffin becomes impatient. The chorus are silent throughout not because they have temporarily disappeared[51] but because the poet has entirely neglected to harmonize the scene with its context. Having decided to add it, he has let his mind run exclusively on what Oceanus might say to Prometheus and Prometheus to Oceanus.[52]

Oceanus' griffin (as the scholiast convincingly interprets the 'four-legged bird') is, like his daughters' winged chairs, gratuitous spectacle. Rider and mount were carried by the crane, as were Bellerophon and Pegasus in Euripides' *Bellerophon* and *Stheneboia* (both early plays) and Trygaeus and his giant beetle in Aristophanes' *Peace*. Their combined weight may have approached that of a pair of Oceanids, so that the same counterweight could be used. But the operator and the Oceanids concerned would have had to work very fast at 277–83 to enable Oceanus to appear without an awkward delay—a further embarrassment caused by the insertion.[53]

We may now pass to the closing scene and the problem of what happens to the various people present. I agree with Taplin ((n. 1), 269–70) and most commentators that Hermes stalks off at 1079. The question is what becomes of Prometheus and the chorus. The indications given in the text may be summed up as follows:

[51] Against this theory of Wilamowitz and others see Taplin (n. 1), 256–7. In 281 χθονὶ τῇδε πελῶ they tell us as clearly as could be wished that they are alighting on the ground in full view of everyone.

[52] He does not in fact give the chorus much to say in the later scenes with Io and Hermes.

[53] The manoeuvre could perhaps have been speeded up a little by using Oceanus as the counterweight to a pair of his daughters. A couple of stage-hands would have had to hoist him up on their shoulders when the Oceanids dismounted and then bear him round towards the fence; two others would seize the free end of the boom as soon as it came within reach and haul it down, and Oceanus would be up and away. All this may of course be far from the truth, but it is important to discuss these questions in the most concrete practical terms.

1016–21 (Hermes) Zeus will shatter the rock with thunder and
lightning, and Prometheus will be concealed inside it for a lengthy
period.

1043–52 (Prom.) Let him employ thunder, lightning, furious winds,
shake the earth from its foundations, confound sea and sky, and
throw me into darkest Tartarus.

1060–79 (Hermes) Anyone who stays here will hear terrifying thunderclaps and be in danger of disaster. (Cho.) We shall stay nevertheless.

1080–8 Now there really is an earthquake, thunder, lightning, dust-
laden whirlwinds; sky and sea are confused.

Not all of these phenomena could be simulated in the theatre, but
thunder and lightning could be and no doubt were. The impious
Salmoneus' methods, dragging cauldrons and inflated skins behind
his chariot and hurling torches into the air, are already known to
pseudo-Hesiod and alluded to by Sophocles.[54] There is evidence for
mechanical thunder and lightning at least in the later theatre,[55] and
we may be sure that even if they had never been used before, an
author so given to spectacular effects as the poet of *Desm.* would not
have left them to the imagination at the climax of his play.[56]

Did they just die away after Prometheus' last words, while he and
the chorus remained in full view waiting for someone to start
applauding? That would be a dreadful anticlimax, besides being
'unparalleled in the stage technique of Greek tragedy since it would
be the only exit or entry which is actually left to the imagination'
(Taplin (n. 1), 274). The chorus have been offered a good excuse
for leaving, in keeping with their timorous nature, and they have

[54] [Hes.] fr. 30. 4–10, cf. Apollod. 1. 9. 7; Soph. fr. 10c. 6, and probably his *Salmoneus*.

[55] Sch. Ar. *Nub.* 294, Poll. 4. 130, Tz. *Prol. de com.* p. 36. 79–81 ~ 46. 83–6 Koster; A. E. Haigh, *The Attic Theatre* (3rd edn., Oxford, 1907), 218; Pickard-Cambridge (n. 31), 133; Arnott (n. 30), 89–90.

[56] Scholars are perhaps at present too taken with the idea of effects being left to the imagination in ancient drama. One has only to read the plays of Kālidāsa to appreciate the difference between drama which limits itself to what it is possible to represent visually, as the Greek does, and drama which does not, as the prop-less, scenery-less Sanskrit does not. And we know, for example, that when someone was supposed to be flying in a Greek play, he was really hoisted through the air.

unexpectedly declined the opportunity. The poet must have thought of an alternative means of exit for them, as unconventional as their entrance. As for Prometheus, the whole notion of his being concealed in the rock for a time has no point unless it corresponds to an actual vanishing act at the end of the play and his absence during the interval before *Ly.* But was there a way of vanishing from the rock beside the orchestra? If we are right about its use by Darius and Clytaemestra in Aeschylus, there was. For those royal ghosts were able to rise up out of the earth without having been seen to arrive, and disappear back into it.[57] This suggests that there was some kind of concealed approach to the top of the rock from the *eisodos* behind. Geologically this is plausible. Limestone tends to weather into steps on the scarp side; the stratification in the area would indicate that this was the north-east side of the rock, which agrees most satisfactorily with the evidence that it was easily ascended from the orchestra (west) side. So there might have been a natural staircase on the east face. Alternatively there might have been a fissure on the south side, as the joints in limestone are commonly widened and deepened by chemical solution.[58] If something of the sort existed, all that was necessary was for the chorus to go up onto the rock sometime after 1063 (as the Danaids had done in *Supplices*) and cluster round Prometheus, hiding him from view: he would then make his escape, delivering his last words as he went, and they would rapidly follow him out of sight amid the final thunderclaps.

PROMETHEUS LYOMENOS

Centuries have passed. Prometheus' temporary entombment is forgotten; he resumes his place on the rock-face for the beginning of the third play.[59] His appearance is perhaps somewhat changed. Emphatic

---

[57] Cf. Hammond (n. 26), 423.

[58] I am indebted to Dr David Bell of the Oxford Department of Geology and Mineralogy for instruction in these matters.

[59] Convention allowed characters to walk in at the start of a play and take up a position which for the purposes of the drama they were supposed to have been in for a considerable time. See Taplin (n. 1), 134–6.

380 M. L. West

predictions (above p. 369) have prepared us for a darkening of his skin.[60] Also he should have a wound where the eagle attacks him.

The Titans come tramping up the *eisodos*.

> ἥκομεν ...
> τοὺς σοὺς ἄθλους τούσδε Προμηθεῦ
> δεσμοῦ τε πάθος τόδ' ἐποψόμενοι.

> We are come ...
> to view these ordeals of yours, Prometheus,
> and this bondage you endure.[61]

The anapaests went on with a catalogue of the places they had passed on their way (frr. 191–2, 203). It included Aethiop territory by the Ocean where the sun sets, the Red Sea, the warlike Heniochi of the Caucasus, and the Phasis, which the poet regards as the boundary of Europe and Asia and therefore locates at the Crimea.[62] Roughly speaking, then, the Titans have followed in reverse the route laid down for Io, traversing Africa and Asia before reaching Europe from the east. Where was their starting-point? We must assume that since their release from Tartarus they have been settled in the Isles of the Blest.[63] It looks as if the poet located these off the west coast of Africa, in the Canaries, as did some later writers.[64]

They probably commented on Prometheus' shrivelled and decayed appearance. This is suggested by the echo in Cratinus' *Ploutoi*, fr. 171 K.–A., where the chorus describe themselves as Titans who, now that their bondage is over and the tyrant Zeus overborne by the Demos,[65]

[60] Merely a dramatic device to underline the lapse of time, or did his complexion have to be brought into accord with a statue familiar to the Athenians. A potters' god might have a scorched and sooty face: cf. Hom. *Kaminos* (*Vita Homeri Herodotea* 32) 22–3 with G. M. Richter, *The Craft of Athenian Pottery* (New Haven, 1923), 76–7.

[61] Fr. 190. Cf. *PV* 1 ἥκομεν, 284–5 ἥκω ... πρὸς σὲ Προμηθεῦ, 298–9 καὶ σὺ δὴ πόνων ἐμῶν | ἥκεις ἐπόπτης;

[62] Cf. *PV* 730–5 and 790; J. D. P. Bolton, *Aristeas of Proconnesus* (Oxford, 1962), 56–7. πῆ μὲν is suspect in fr. 191 (τῇ μὲν, ἐπὶ μὲν have been conjectured); perhaps Arrian took ἐπῆμεν from an earlier metron. The Titans must have crossed the river to reach Prometheus on the European side.

[63] H. Weil, p. xi of his edition of the play; Wilamowitz, *Aischylos-Interpretationen* (Berlin, 1914), 151. See Hes. *Op.* 173a–c, Pind. *Ol.* 2. 70 ff. For the genuine Aeschylus (*Eum.* 650–5) Kronos is still in bondage.

[64] Str. 1. 1. 5, 3. 2. 13, Mela 3. 10, Juba 275 F 44, Ptol. 4. 6. 34.

[65] There seems a clear allusion here to Pericles' deposition from the strategia. Lenaia 429 follows as the probable date for the *Ploutoi*. So W. Luppe, *Wissenschaftliche*

δεῦρ᾽ ἐσύθημεν πρὸς ọ.[
αὐτοκασίγνητόν τε παλαιὸν
ζητοῦντε[ς] ϙεἰ σαθρὸν ἤδη.

We have hastened hither to the [
and looking for our ancient brother
albeit now decrepit.

If P. Heidelberg 185 (= fr. 451u) is to be assigned to *Ly.* and to its first scene, the Titans' emotion boiled up into dochmiacs before Prometheus addressed them. But there are serious difficulties in the identification.[66]

Prometheus' speech, known from Cicero's translation (fr. 193), must have been followed by further dialogue before anyone else entered. Trag. adesp. 342,

ἐλαφρὸν παραινεῖν τῷ κακῶς πεπραγότι,

It is easy to offer advice to one sunk in misfortune,

might belong here in view of its similarity to *PV* 263 ff. (Prometheus to the Oceanids),

ἐλαφρόν, ὅστις πημάτων ἔξω πόδα
ἔχει, παραινεῖν νουθετεῖν τε τὸν κακῶς
πράσσοντα.

We have noted before this poet's habit of repeating himself,[67] and also his weakness for initial anapaests.

It is commonly assumed that the next person to make an appearance was Ge, perhaps rising out of the earth to waist level.[68] The

---

Zeitschrift der Martin-Luther-Universität Halle-Wittenberg 16 (1967), Gesellsch. u. Sprachwiss. Reihe, 1. 68, 83. Cratinus also parodied *PV* in his *Seriphioi* (*c.*423?), frr. 222–3 and 343 K.–A. A series of fragments of Varro's *Prometheus Liber* come from a passage in which the bound Titan described his sufferings in terms no doubt largely inspired by Aeschylus (423–7 Astbury); they include (424) *tum ut si subernus cortex aut cacumina | morientum in querqueto arborum áritudine*, (425) *atque <ex artubus> | exsanguibus dolore euírescat colós*, (427) *leuis méns umquam somnurnas imagines | affatur, non umbrantur somno púpulae.*

[66] K. Reinhardt, *Hermes* 85 (1957), 12 ff. and *Eranos-Jahrbuch* 25 (1957), both in his *Tradition und Geist* (182 ff., 221). Reinhardt assigns the fragment to *Pyrph.*, but his reconstruction of it is altogether too hypothetical.

[67] See W. Schmid (n. 50), 9–11 and 69.

[68] This hypothesis apparently inspired the similar epiphany of Erda in *Das Rheingold* (P. Maas, *Kl. Schr.* 650). An Apulian calyx-crater of about the third quarter of the

belief that she had a role in the play is based on the list of characters
preceding the text of *Desm.*, for in most manuscripts it includes Ge
and Heracles in addition to the characters who actually occur in that
play, and Heracles certainly had a part in *Ly.* It is accordingly supposed that a fragment from a *dramatis personae* for *Ly.* has somehow
become conflated with that for *Desm.* This explanation seems never to
have been questioned,[69] yet no convincing reason has been given for
believing that the *dramatis personae* of different plays were in any
circumstances written out side by side. There is at least one possible
alternative explanation that ought to be borne in mind. Whoever
compiled the list presumably did so by running his eye down the
margins of the text he was concerned with and collecting the names
that marked characters entering. He might easily include by mistake
a name that had been written in the margin for a different reason.
There happens to be in *Desm.* a place where both *Γῆ* and *Ἡρακλῆς*
might have been written in the margin in close proximity as glosses:
871–4,

> σπορᾶς γε μὴν ἐκ τῆσδε φύσεται θρασύς,
> τόξοισι κλεινός, ὃς πόνων ἐκ τῶνδ᾽ ἐμέ
> λύσει· τοιόνδε χρησμὸν ἡ παλαιγενής
> μήτηρ ἐμοὶ διῆλθε Τιτανὶς Θέμις.

If this is the source of their appearance in the cast-list, we should
expect them to come between Io and Hermes. In fact Io is out of
sequence (as is Prometheus) in the manuscripts in question, but
Ge and Heracles do appear in the predicted place before Hermes.
The evidence for an appearance of Ge in *Ly.*, then, is at best
doubtful. She is certainly not required to advance the plot, since
Prometheus has already received all the instruction he needs from her
before *Desm.* begins. I am much more inclined to believe that his first
visitor after the Titans—following a choral song by them—was
Heracles.

---

fourth century, decorated with a painting based on *Ly.* (the play as a whole, not any
particular scene), shows a featureless female to the right of the bound Prometheus,
but her identification as Ge seems to be arbitrary. (Berlin 1969.9; T. B. L. Webster and
A. D. Trendall, *Illustrations of Greek Drama* (London, 1971) iii. 1. 27.)

[69] Wilamowitz (n. 63), 128, is evidently none too happy with it, but finds no better
one.

Heracles, like Io, is a wanderer who arrives at Prometheus' rock by chance. He is on his way to Geryones or, according to Posidonius, to the Hesperides (fr. 199). Prometheus will give him directions, as before he gave them to Io. But the scene contained other business of more relevance to Prometheus. The eagle, whose attacks every second day he had described to the chorus (fr. 193, cf. *PV* 1021–5), made its appearance on one of the cranes and was shot down by Heracles in full view of the audience[70]—the only killing in tragedy to take place on stage, though Artemis in Sophocles' Niobe was seen above the house shooting arrows into it. And Hermes' statement in *PV* 1026–9, that Prometheus' suffering would not end

πρὶν ἂν θεῶν τις διάδοχος τῶν σῶν πόνων
φανῇ θελήσῃ τ᾽ εἰς ἀναύγητον μολεῖν
Ἅιδην κνεφαῖά τ᾽ ἀμφὶ Ταρτάρου βάθη,

found fulfilment. The god, according to the only known version of the story, was Chiron, whom Heracles had accidentally wounded in the fray that followed Pholos' drinking party and who chose to give up his immortality to Prometheus and die rather than live in incurable pain.[71] After shooting the eagle, we are told in that version, Heracles παρέσχε τῷ Διὶ Χείρωνα θνῄσκειν ἀθάνατον <ὄντα> ἀντ᾽ αὐτοῦ θέλοντα ('produced Chiron to Zeus as an immortal willing to die in his own place').[72] Heracles was indeed the only possible intermediary between Chiron and the bound Prometheus. According to Stesichorus, Heracles was entertained by Pholos while on his way to Geryones.[73] Our poet, then, or his source for the Chiron story, could represent Heracles as having wounded Chiron earlier on the same journey that brought him to Prometheus. Knowing of the Centaur's desire to die, and learning of Prometheus' need of just such a sacrifice, he could then assure the Titan that this requirement

[70] This is certain in view of fr. 200, where Heracles, 'preparing to aim his bow at the bird', prays that Apollo may guide the arrow straight. Rightly Reinhardt, *Tradition und Geist*, 219.
[71] Apollod. 2. 5. 4. 4–5, 5. 11. 10, from Pherecydes, cf. 3 F 83 with Jacoby.
[72] 2. 5. 11. 10. The Vatican epitome omits ἀθάνατον. In 2. 5. 4. 5 we should read ἀντιδόντος Διὶ Ἡρακλέους Προμηθέα (instead of Διὶ Προμηθέως) τὸν ἀντ᾽ αὐτοῦ (sc. Χείρωνος) γενησόμενον ἀθάνατον.
[73] *PMGF* 181 = S 19 (p. 162 Davies); surely not on his way back, when he had a herd of cattle to manage.

of Zeus' was fulfilled; perhaps also that he, being Zeus' son, knew that his father would accept the arrangement as made by him.[74]

Did Heracles himself release Prometheus from the rock? 'Probus' on Virg. *Ec.* 6. 42, in a version of the myth that is based in outline on the trilogy but departs from it in detail, says that Heracles killed the vulture (*sic*) but was afraid to free Prometheus, *ne offenderet patrem*. Prometheus subsequently warned Jupiter against the union with Thetis, and Jupiter in gratitude released him. Hyginus, *Fab.* 54, puts it the other way round: Prometheus agreed to reveal his secret if Jupiter released him, Jupiter promised, Prometheus spoke, and Thetis was given to Peleus; Hercules was sent to kill the eagle, after which Prometheus was released. Philodemus, π. εὐσεβείας 5860 ff. Obbink, explicitly ascribes to Aeschylus (p. 306 Radt) the proposition that Prometheus was freed ὅ[τι τὸ λ]όγιον ἐμή[νυσε]ν τὸ περὶ Θέ[τιδ]ος κτλ. ('because he disclosed the oracle about Thetis', etc.). But these accounts conflict with the clear programme presupposed by repeated statements in *Desm.*: Prometheus will not reveal the secret about Thetis *until* he has been released and offered compensation (172–7, 770, 989–91); and he will be released by Heracles (771–4, 785, 871–3; cf. 27).[75] It is implied that the release takes place with Zeus' consent (176, 375–6).[76] These data constitute our most reliable evidence for the course of events in *Ly.*, and it is not wise to reject them on the strength of summary statements and renarrations in later sources. In fact, by allowing Heracles to free Prometheus the dramatist can avoid an awkward dilemma, for

[74] H. Weil, *Études sur le drame antique* (Paris, 1897), 78, 80, followed by T. Zieliński, *Tragodumenon libri tres* (Cracow, 1925), 34 ff., pointed out that the Chiron story properly belongs to a version where Prometheus is punished in Hades–Tartarus (Hor. *C.* 2. 13. 37, 18. 35) and does not make much sense in one where he is punished in the upper world. One can envisage Heracles' mediation in the context of the Cerberus Labour: he could as well converse with the bound Prometheus in Hades as with the bound Pirithous in the play of that name. Our tragedian knows something about Prometheus' being consigned to Hades, but makes this a dramatic interlude (in more senses than one); above p. 379.

Chiron's desire to die might have prompted the remark (fr. 706, *fab. inc.*) ὡς οὐ δικαίως θάνατον ἔχθουσιν βροτοί, | ὅπερ μέγιστον ῥῦμα τῶν πολλῶν κακῶν, 'how wrong men are to hate death, the greatest salvation from many ills'.

[75] Heracles releases him also in Apollod. 2. 5. 11. 10 (Pherecydes? but sch. A.R. 4. 1396 = 3 F 17 mentions only shooting the eagle), Hyg. *Fab.* 144, Pediasimus 11.

[76] 771 ἄκοντος Διός (ἄρχοντος Pauw) is not to be taken as counter-evidence. As Weil explained ((n. 74), 91), it means 'if' (or 'seeing that') Zeus is unwilling.

otherwise either Prometheus must abandon his four-hundred-year-old resolve and spill his secret before being released, or Zeus must capitulate to the Titan.

The sequence of events from Heracles' arrival to his departure may have been something like this:

Prometheus hails his destined liberator; Heracles learns the situation (including the danger his father is in), and expresses his concern. The eagle appears and is shot.

Heracles offers to release Prometheus altogether on condition that he reveals the secret to Zeus, but is told that Prometheus cannot become free to live the life of an immortal until another immortal opts for death. He explains that he knows such a one. Prometheus promises to save Zeus. Mounting the rock, Heracles applies his club to the shackles with two or three resounding blows (punctuated by trimeters), and they fall away.[77]

Short choral song of the sort that may be sung while characters remain on stage.

Prometheus gives Heracles directions for the continuation of his travels, and he leaves.[78]

Stasimon.

As has been mentioned, Heracles' destination is given both as Geryones and as the Hesperides. Both may be correct, for although some fifth-century accounts separated the two localities, the older authorities placed the Hesperides' island near Erytheia. It belonged indeed to the same story, the birthplace of Geryones' herdsman Eurytion; golden apples grew there, but there seems originally to have been no question of Heracles' taking them.[79] That developed

---

[77] They must be broken either by strength or by art; if not by Heracles, then by Hephaestus who made them. So Schmid (n. 50), 100.

[78] In this context one might put fr. 315 τῷ πονοῦντι δ' ἐκ θεῶν | ὀφείλεται τέκνωμα τοῦ πόνου κλέος ('to the man who toils the gods owe toil's offspring, glory') and Adesp. 410/410a πολλοῦ σε θνητοῖς ἄξιον τίκτει πατήρ· | καὶ μή τι παυσώμεσθα δρῶντες εὖ βροτούς ('your father begot you to be of great value to mortals; let us not cease doing them good'). (The two verses are not to be separated, for the first would not have been quoted for its own sake; the addressee is surely Heracles, and the speaker another philanthropic god.)

[79] Hes. *Th.* 215 f., 274–94, 333–6, 517–19; Stes. S 7–8 with C. M. Robertson, *CQ* 19 (1969), 215–16. Hesiod evidently knew an eighth-century epic on the subject. He

subsequently as a separate Labour, requiring a separate journey. The Prometheus poet kept Geryones and the Hesperides together. Whether both represented Labours is uncertain, but the discrepancy between the sources in fr. 199 suggests at least that they were both mentioned with some emphasis. The conventional (Stesichorean) Iberian location was retained, for Heracles' route, as Prometheus described it to him, was to take him through the nomad Scyths and Abioi (196, 198),[80] across the Ister (197),[81] and through Ligyan territory (199).[82]

If Heracles leaves Prometheus free, how is the sequel to be imagined? How and why is Zeus warned about Thetis? Even if Prometheus has promised to tell him, a plausible setting for the revelation is needed. Nothing has happened to make Prometheus feel particularly benevolent towards Zeus. He has referred to Heracles, after being delivered by him, as ἐχθροῦ πατρός μοι τοῦτο φίλτατον τέκνον, 'dearest child of a father I hate' (201). He is even less likely now to respond to demands from Hermes than when he was in fetters. But clearly some new character has got to appear. Much the most attractive hypothesis, I think, is that it is Thetis herself, fleeing from Zeus' embraces. This was suggested by A. D. Fitton-Brown ((n. 9), 57), who pointed out that a (Byzantine) commentator on *PV* 167 says of Zeus and Thetis οὗτος γὰρ ἐρασθεὶς αὐτῆς ἐδίωκεν αὐτὴν ἐν τῷ Καυκάσῳ ὄρει ὅπως συγγένηται αὐτῇ, ἐκωλύθη δὲ ὑπὸ Προμηθέως εἰπόντος αὐτῷ ὅτι ὁ μέλλων

represents the serpent who guards the apples as alive and well (336), whereas later authors say Heracles slew it.

[80] It is hard to see why the poet should have changed the Homeric Abioi (*Il.* 13. 6) into Γάβιοι (196. 3), as sch. Hom. l. c. and Stephanus of Byzantium assert. Possibly the originator of this statement mistakenly combined the word, which begins a trimeter, with a stichometric symbol; $\overline{\Gamma}$ (300) would be a surprisingly low figure, but one could also think of $\overline{I}$ (900).

[81] Conceived to flow down from the Rhipaean mountains and divide into the Danube and Po. In sch. A.R. 4. 282–91b (p. 280. 8–10 W.) read καὶ τὸ μὲν {εἰς τὴν καθ' ἡμᾶς θάλασσαν ἐκβάλλειν ῥεῖθρον, τὸ δὲ} εἰς τὴν Ποντικὴν θάλασσαν ἐκπίπτειν, τὸ δὲ εἰς τὸν Ἀδριατικὸν κόλπον. Cf. p. 281. 9–12.

[82] Hyginus says that the Ligyans were encountered on the return journey, and that they tried to rob Heracles of Geryones' cattle. But at least the second part of this is an invention; Strabo quotes the original verses, and they say not a word about the cattle. Heracles may have returned through Africa, or the poet may have said nothing about his return route, having already dealt with all other sectors of the earth in connection with Io and the Titans.

γεννηθῆναι ἐξ αὐτῆς ἔσται κρείττων κατὰ πολὺ τοῦ οἰκείου πατρός, 'for he, struck with desire for her, was chasing her in the Caucasus with a view to having intercourse with her, but he was stopped by Prometheus, who told him that the son due to be born from her would be much more powerful than his father'. (Cf. Nonn. *D.* 33. 355–69.) Fitton-Brown assumed that Prometheus was still bound and had to give up his secret now because once Zeus actually took Thetis, it would have no further value. But that is not a convincing motivation for Prometheus, who can expect to be released anyway if Zeus falls from power. It is more plausible that he should speak out (*a*) to honour a prior undertaking to Heracles and (*b*), when the time comes, to save Thetis. For the dramatic presentation of an amorous pursuit the poet had a model in Aeschylus' *Supplices*. The singing actor who had been Io in *Desm.* would now appear as Thetis, voicing her distress in lyrics much as before. In terms of composition, the Thetis scene may have been prior to the Io scene. After some dialogue between Thetis and Prometheus, Hermes would arrive, imperious as the Egyptian herald in *Supplices*, demanding Thetis for Zeus. Prometheus would now at last play his trump, letting out the old oracle about Thetis' child through a passage of stichomythia.

Exit Hermes to report to Zeus. Stasimon. Final scene in which Prometheus receives compensation (cf. *PV* 176), in the form of honours to be paid to him in future by men, in particular at Athens, where regular torch-races will commemorate his bringing of fire.[83] It is also laid down that in memory of his bondage he will henceforth wear a crown.[84] On the Apulian vase-painting mentioned earlier

---

[83] Cf. Hyg. *Astr.* 2. 15. 2. On the Attic Promethia see L. R. Farnell, *The Cults of the Greek States* (Oxford, 1896–1909) v. 378 ff.; Wilamowitz (n. 63), 142–4; L. Deubner, *Attische Feste* (Berlin, 1932), 211–12; W. Kraus, *RE* xxiii. 654–5.

[84] Ath. 674d = fr. 202. Cf. 'Prob.' on Virg. *Ec.* 6. 42, Hyg. *Astr.* 2. 15. 4. Athenaeus and Hyginus treat this as the aition for festive wreaths in general. Athenaeus has earlier quoted a passage of Menodotus (541 F 1) according to which Prometheus' wreath was of withy, and so perhaps in Aeschylus' *Sphinx* fr. 235. Artistic representations show him with a diadem or a wreath of bay or willow even before his release: L. Eckhart, *RE* xxiii. 707–8, 712, 719–20. Apollod. 2. 5. 11. 10 says (Heracles) τὸν Προμηθέα ἔλυσε, δεσμὸν ἑλόμενος τὸν τῆς ἐλαίας ('freed Prometheus, taking for himself the olive band'), which seems to be confused. Several authors say also that Prometheus put on an iron finger-ring with a piece of the rock set in it ('Prob.', Hyg.; Plin. *HN* 33. 8, 37. 2), but this is not ascribed to 'Aeschylus', and Hyginus implies that his authority for the ring did not mention the crown.

(n. 70) we see this crown being brought to him by Athena, and it is likely enough that it was she who came in this closing scene to announce his reward.

As for Thetis—the other female figure on the vase?—it is decreed that she shall marry Peleus: her son shall be mightier than his father indeed, a glorious hero, but not mightier than Zeus, whose regime is now secure for ever. The Titans will return to the Isles of the Blest, never to be seen on earth again. *Exeunt omnes,* Athena perhaps by air to Olympus, the Titans celebrating the power and wisdom of Zeus in their final anapaests.

So much for the probable action of the play. But there is still a good deal to be said about Heracles' travels and how the poet's idea of them relates to tradition.

As Erytheia was located beyond Ocean from at least the eighth century, Heracles' journey there—and his journey to the Hesperides, when that became an independent story—provided poets and prose writers who wished to compile connected accounts of his adventures with an all-embracing frame in which to set any exploits that lay outside the ordinary Greek orbit. Thus those Pontic Greeks who traced the Scythian peoples back to a union between Heracles and Echidna (Hdt. 4. 8–10) said that he met her on his way back from the land of Geryones, only they made this more plausible by placing Geryones ἔξω τοῦ Πόντου, i.e. somewhere in the north or north-east.[85] We have seen that Stesichorus had told the tale of the Centaurs' drinking-party, at which Heracles accidentally shot Chiron, in his *Geryoneis,* and perhaps other incidental exploits too.[86]

Of particular relevance to *Ly.* is the detailed narrative of Heracles' peregrinations compiled by an Athenian logographer of the mid-fifth century, Pherecydes.[87] In his second book Pherecydes gave the following account of the hero's quest for the golden apples. Certain 'Nymphs of Zeus and Themis'[88] dwelling in a cave by the Eridanus

[85] It seems to be Herodotus who attaches the conventional location by Cadiz.
[86] J. Vürtheim, *Stesichoros' Fragmente und Biographie* (Leiden, 1919), 20, goes much too far in inferring that the poem was 'eine ganze Heraklea' in which 'sämtliche Taten des Herakles werden vor Augen geführt'.
[87] 3 F 16–17, 75–6, 7~Apollod. 2. 5. 11.
[88] Zeus and Themis are the parents of the Horai and Moirai in Hes. *Th.* 901–6.

showed him where and how to catch Nereus, who, after vainly trying to escape by changing into all kinds of forms, told him the way to the Hesperides. He arrived at Tartessus—almost at his journey's end? No: from there he crossed over to Libya, where he killed Antaios, and continued to Memphis, where he killed Busiris, and to Arabia, where he killed Emathion. Then he went up the Nile, through the mountains of Abyssinia, into the furthest wastes of Africa, clearing it of wild beasts. Reaching Ocean in the far south, he embarked in the Sun's golden cup. Surely now he is about to find the Hesperides? No again: he sails east to the Caucasus, and in response to Prometheus' entreaties kills the eagle that plagues him. He also answers Prometheus' need of a god to die in his place by 'providing' Zeus with Chiron, whom he had shot in an earlier escapade (above p. 383). Prometheus rewards him with a new load of advice about the golden apples. He should go to Atlas, who is located in the far north, and get him to fetch the apples for him while he himself supports the sky. Heracles does this. Atlas tries to leave him permanently holding the sky, but Heracles induces him to take it back, using a ruse taught him by the foresighted Prometheus. He then returns to Mycenae with the apples.

It is obvious that this preposterous concatenation of events is the result of a two-stage expansion from a much simpler story. Twice Heracles seems about to reach the Hesperides, and twice they are withdrawn to a more remote location. In the original story, adapted from Stesichorus,[89] the Hesperides' isle is near Tartessus. The first expansion removes it (and the journey in the Sun's cup) to the southern Ocean, enabling the African adventures to be brought in; this corresponds to the version of Panyassis, cf. fr. 12 Bernabé (Busiris), 11 (Hesperides located *qua cedunt medii longe secreta diei*).[90] The second expansion, no doubt due to Pherecydes himself, brings in Prometheus and Atlas, and transfers the Hesperides to the

---

[89] For Nereus see Paradox. Vat. 32 p. 340 Giannini (= S 16a Davies p. 160) παρ' Ὁμήρῳ Πρωτεὺς εἰς πάντα μετεμορφοῦτο, καθὰ Θέτις παρὰ Πινδάρῳ καὶ Νηρεὺς παρὰ Στησιχόρῳ καὶ Μήστρα ('in Homer Proteus changed into all forms, like Thetis in Pindar and Nereus in Stesichorus, and Mestra'). The episode is shown on vases from the early sixth century.

[90] Avien. *Phaen.* 179, 'where the unknown south retreats', never allowing the traveller to find its limits. Not understood by V. Matthews, *Panyassis of Halikarnassos* (Leiden, 1974), 70.

far north, because Atlas is now located under the Pole about which
the stars revolve.[91] Heracles no longer has to cross to the Hesperids'
isle himself or kill the serpent, because Atlas gets the apples for him.

In *Ly.* as in Pherecydes, the traditional eagle-shooting is placed in
the context of the journey to the Hesperides, in despite of geography;
Prometheus gives Heracles directions; and Chiron is found willing to
die in Prometheus' place. It cannot be supposed that these coinci-
dences between two approximately contemporary Athenian publications are fortuitous. I cannot see anything to be said for postulating
yet a third work containing these details as a common source. It is
after all likely that the Prometheus poet, with his encyclopaedic
interest in mythology, had direct knowledge of Pherecydes' work if
it was published first, or, if not, that Pherecydes was present when the
trilogy was performed. In short, one surely drew upon the other.
Which upon which?

I do not think certainty is attainable, but a number of considerations can be adduced in favour of the priority of Pherecydes.

(i) The common features in question reflect the approach of a
mythographer, of someone who strings myths together in a continuous narrative. Heracles' visit to Prometheus is seen as part of the
story of a particular Labour; and Prometheus' exchange of death with
Chiron, with whom he has no other connection, is the invention of a
storyteller whose Heracles narrative encompassed both Pholos' party
and Prometheus' liberation.

(ii) To make Heracles encounter Prometheus on his way to the
Hesperides was more natural for Pherecydes, whose Heracles is
coming from the far south and heading for the far north, than for
the tragedian, who has him heading for the far west and would have
had to invent *ad hoc* an explanation of his presence in Scythia.

(iii) The advice which Heracles received from Prometheus in
Pherecydes concerned the method of getting the apples and tricking
Atlas, and was thus in keeping with Prometheus' essential nature as
the clever, foresighted one. In *Ly.*, so far as we can see, Prometheus
merely functioned as an oracle and had no practical devices to
impart. It is unlikely that the tricking of Atlas appeared, since Atlas

[91] Cf. Critias, *TrGF* 43 F 3. 5 (the two Bears τὸν Ἀτλάντειον τηροῦσι πόλον); Eur.
HF 403 οὐρανοῦ θ᾽ ὑπὸ μέσσαν ... ἕδραν.

is represented as Prometheus' brother by whose fate he is deeply grieved (*PV* 347–50).

Pherecydes' *floruit* is given by Eusebius as 456/5; Jacoby writes 'der ionische Dialekt...weist ihn doch wohl vor den Peloponnesischen Krieg'. I would advance two reasons for thinking that the part of his work that concerns us was composed after the date given by Eusebius. The first is to do with the ruse by which Heracles gets Atlas to take the sky back again: he asks him just to take it for a moment while he arranges a σπεῖρα, a carrying-pad, on his head. As a specimen of Greek trickery this does not strike us as very inspired; only an imbecile would have been taken in by it. I suspect that it is an autoschediasm of Pherecydes', and that the pad was suggested to him by that metope of the temple of Zeus at Olympia, completed in time for the games of 456, which shows Atlas bringing the apples to Heracles, who stands supporting the sky with the help of a large pad or bolster.[92] The sculptor evidently knew the version of the Hesperides story that Pherecydes followed, in so far as it is Atlas who fetches the apples, but he does not know Pherecydes' story of Atlas' attempt to remain free and Heracles' trick, for Atlas is offering him the apples in an eager and helpful manner,[93] and Heracles is already using a pad. The new temple and its sculptures must have been scrutinized with interest by every visitor to the Olympic games in 456, 452, and subsequently. There are few works of art outside Athens that Pherecydes is more likely to have examined.

My second reason is that Pherecydes' account of Heracles' progress towards the Hesperides appears, as we have seen, to be built upon Panyassis'. Panyassis probably died in the 450s.[94] His *Herakleia* may have been completed some time before. But an epic by a Halicarnassian noble which never achieved real popularity would not automatically become widely known across the Aegean within a few years. Who brought it to Athens? Who more likely than the poet's cousin (or nephew) Herodotus, likewise a man of letters, banished by the

[92] Illustrated e.g. in H.-V. Herrmann, *Olympia: Heiligtum und Wettkampfstätte* (Munich, 1972), pl. 57; J. Boardman, *Greek Art* (4th edn., London, 1996), 138 fig. 128.

[93] Similarly on a white-ground lekythos by the Athena Painter, Athens 1132: C. H. E. Haspels, *Attic Black-Figure Lekythoi* (Paris, 1936), pl. 47. 3; Boardman, *Athenian Black Figure Vases* (London, 1974), fig. 252.

[94] See Matthews (n. 90), 12–19, with my qualifications in *CPh* 71 (1976), 172–4.

same tyrant, and known to have been in Athens around 445?[95] If so, Pherecydes' Book 2 is not earlier than the 440s.

THE DATE OF THE TRILOGY

The results of the various stylistic, metrical and dramaturgical studies of *Desm.* assembled by Griffith strongly suggest that it belongs to a stage in the development of Attic tragedy which was not reached for a decade or two after Aeschylus' death. In many respects it has more in common with the techniques of extant Sophocles and Euripides than with those of Aeschylus. It would be hazardous to base a dating on such observations alone, even though a large number of separate criteria point in the same direction. But other considerations lead to a dating fully consistent with them.

A *terminus ante quem* of 430 is given by Cratinus' *Ploutoi*, probably produced at the Lenaia in 429 (n. 65).

The poet was something of a polymath, with an interest in mythology of the synoptic kind as represented by Hesiodic poetry and the logographers, and in geography, ethnography, and the history of culture. He was well versed in contemporary and older literature. A survey of the authors that are or may be used by him will help to define the *terminus post quem*.

(*a*) Hesiod. No earlier poet appears so imbued with the *Theogony* and *Works and Days*. They provide him not just with the Prometheus myth, but with the Titanomachy, the oracular Gaia, the figures of Kratos and Bia, and incidental details such as Memory as mother of the Muses (*PV* 461) and the alleviation of human misery by Hope (250).

(*b*) Aristeas, *Arimaspeia*. See J. D. P. Bolton, *Aristeas of Proconnesus*, 44–64.

(*c*) The *Titanomachy* ascribed to Eumelus. See *JHS* 122 (2002), 113–14.

---

[95] For this visit see Jacoby, *RE* Suppl. ii. 226–9, 233–42, 247. Lygdamis' tyranny belongs to the 450s (Matthews (n. 90). 16–17), and Herodotus was in Halicarnassus for a time after its fall (*Suda*; Jacoby 225).

(*d*) Acusilaus of Argos. This logographer (2 F 34) would seem to be the source for Prometheus' marriage to the Oceanid Hesione (*PV* 559).

(*e*) Aeschylus. He naturally knows Aeschylus' plays, and imitates some of the more obvious features of his style. He is particularly likely to have been influenced by *Prometheus Pyrkaeus*. This satyr-play appears to have inspired several vase-paintings in the period 440–420, and Beazley suggested that it had recently been revived.[96]

(*f*) Pindar. The Typhon passage *PV* 351–72 is certainly dependent on *Pyth*. 1. 15–28 (470 BC); the unusual metaphor ἱπούμενος in 365 may come from *Ol*. 4. 7 (452 BC), if not from some parallel passage in a lost poem. *Pyth*. 4. 291 (462 BC) is our only source apart from *Ly*. for Zeus' release of the Titans collectively. The myth of the prophecy about Thetis comes from *Isth*. 8. 26 ff. (478 BC) or from some epic which Pindar has closely followed.[97]

(*g*) Protagoras. The poet's picture of the evolution of human civilization, with the gift of fire by Prometheus leading to the growth of arts and crafts (*PV* 110, 254, 442 ff.), is most closely paralleled in the myth that Plato puts in the mouth of Protagoras (*Prot*. 320c ff., 321d), which is generally agreed to follow the lines of Protagoras' own work περὶ τῆς ἐν ἀρχῇ καταστάσεως.[98] Accounts of man's progress from a beastlike condition and of his development of technical skills appear in several tragedians and other writers from the second half of the fifth century and nowhere earlier.[99] It is likely that this conception originated in a particular sophist's account— Protagoras'. If we may trust the indications in Plato's dialogue, Protagoras visited Athens for the first time in the 440s (or late 450s) and for the second time in about 433.[100] The second date is too late to account for the *Antigone* chorus. If our premises are

[96] *AJA* 43 (1939), 618–19; 44 (1940), 212. Cf. F. Brommer, *Satyrspiele* (2nd edn., Berlin, 1959), 45–9.

[97] Weil (n. 74), 75; Wilamowitz (n. 63), 133.

[98] See W. K. C. Guthrie, *History of Greek Philosophy* (Cambridge, 1962–81), iii. 63 ff.

[99] Soph. *Ant*. 332 ff., Eur. *Supp*. 201–13, Critias *TrGF* 43 F 19, etc.; Guthrie (n. 98), iii. 79 ff.; E. R. Dodds, *The Ancient Concept of Progress* (Oxford, 1973), 7 ff. The twentieth Homeric Hymn is undated, but probably of the same period.

[100] *Prot*. 310e: Hippocrates was a child the first time, and is still νεώτερος, whereas Socrates was old enough to have become acquainted with him the first time.

correct, then, Protagoras promulgated his Prometheus culture-myth at Athens sometime between 452 and 442.

(*h*) Pherecydes of Athens. See above. This is another source that seems to bring us down to the 440s.

(*i*) Sophocles. Many parallels of expression have been noted between *Desm.* and Sophocles.[101] They are particularly frequent in *Ajax* and *Antigone*, suggesting that the Prometheus trilogy may be near in date to those plays. Of course, for any given instance there may have been many more parallels in lost plays; but that consideration does not alter the significance of the concentration of instances, within the extant Sophoclean plays, in two which are generally regarded as close to each other in date. In no case is it possible to demonstrate that one passage is directly inspired by the other. There are, however, four cases where it seems to me that Sophocles uses a phrase in a more natural and spontaneous way than the Prometheus poet, and none of a contrary kind.

Tr. 1095 ἱπποβάμονα στρατόν ∼ *PV* 804–5 στρατόν … ἱπποβάμονα. In Sophocles of the Centaurs who *walk as* horses, in *PV* of the Arimaspoi who *ride on* horses.

Aj. 227 ὤμοι φοβοῦμαι τὸ προσέρπον ∼ *PV* 127 πᾶν μοι φοβερὸν τὸ προσέρπον.

Aj. 447–8 κεἰ μὴ τόδ᾽ ὄμμα καὶ φρένες διάστροφοι | γνώμης ἀπῇξαν τῆς ἐμῆς ∼ *PV* 673–4 εὐθὺς δὲ μορφὴ καὶ φρένες διάστροφοι | ἦσαν. Less natural as a predicate.

Ant. 492 λυσσῶσαν … οὐδ᾽ ἐπήβολον φρενῶν ∼ *PV* 443–4 νηπίους ὄντας τὸ πρίν | ἔννους ἔθηκα καὶ φρενῶν ἐπηβόλους. An odd sense for the phrase.

One may say that this is merely evidence of Sophocles' superiority as a poet; but I submit that it creates a presumption that, if the Prometheus trilogy is close in date to *Ajax* and *Antigone* and shares phraseology with them for that reason, the priority belongs to Sophocles. *Antigone* is datable to 441 or 440, *Ajax* is usually put not long before it. *Trachiniae* is now thought by many to be earlier still.

---

[101] W. Aly, *Rh. Mus.* 68 (1913), 539 n. 1; Schmid (n. 50), 17–18; Groeneboom on *PV* 644; Griffith (n. 1), 296 n. 13.

A dating of the Prometheus trilogy shortly after *Antigone* would fit perfectly with the inferences previously drawn regarding the poet's use of Protagoras and Pherecydes. It will also be recalled that earlier an entirely separate line of reasoning, from the form of the theatre presupposed by *Desm.*, led to the conclusion that it could hardly have been conceived as it stands except in the transitional period between *c.*445 and *c.*435.

There may have been a particular stimulus to compose a Prometheus trilogy about 440, apart from the interest aroused by Protagoras' theory of civilization. A magnificent new temple of Hephaestus had just been completed above the agora.[102] There must have been a dedication ceremony at which fire was kindled on the altar for the first time—holy fire specially brought from a pure source, another altar, by runners. The occasion called for a torch-race. Such races were a feature of several Athenian festivals, and probably already established in the cult of Hephaestus.[103] At the Promethia the teams lit their torches at Prometheus' altar in the Academia and raced through the Ceramicus to some goal in the city. As Prometheus and Hephaestus are connected in worship in the Academia, and the connection is reflected in our trilogy—Hephaestus was robbed by Prometheus in *Pyrph.*, felt sympathy for him in *Desm.* because of τὸ συγγενὲς ἤ θ᾽ ὁμιλία, and must have been united in honour with him at the end—it is not unlikely that the runners in the Promethia finished at an altar of Hephaestus, or that at the time of the dedication of the new temple a new race was instituted, or an existing one newly regulated, to bring its holy fire from the old altar of Prometheus.[104] Such an occasion might well give the cue for a revival of Aeschylus' thirty-year-old satyr play *Prometheus Pyrkaeus*, as well as for the composition of a tragic trilogy on the Prometheus story which culminated in the establishment of the Promethia and the striking of the balance between Prometheus and Hephaestus.

[102] The Hephaesteum is believed to have been begun c. 449 and to have been completed in the late 440s, but an exact date cannot be given.
[103] See Frazer on Paus. 1. 30. 2; Deubner, *Attische Feste* 212–13.
[104] Some kind of reorganization of the torch-race at the Hephaestia in 421/0 is attested by *IG* i³ 82, but the inscription is not well preserved.

POSTSCRIPT 2004

The foregoing paper was published in 1979. As I noted in the opening paragraph, I was then in the hebdomad of life which Solon (fr. 27. 11) associated with the attainment of intellectual maturity. I am now in the one at whose completion, according to the same authority, death would not be premature. But I have not rewritten the paper from the changed vantage-point of the early twenty-first century. I have merely retouched it in a few places and updated references to ancient sources. I have not taken issue with more recent secondary literature. I would, however, draw attention to the important book by Robert Bees, *Zur Datierung des Prometheus Desmotes* (Stuttgart, 1993). He comes to similar conclusions to mine about the date of the drama, and he makes a persuasive case for the playwright's familiarity with the work of Herodotus, who ought therefore to be added to my list of the authors he knew.

I have built on the present paper in two further essays, which I commend to the reader's notice. In the third chapter of my *Studies in Aeschylus* (Stuttgart, 1990) I have developed additional arguments against Aeschylus' authorship of the Prometheus trilogy and given reasons for ascribing it to his son Euphorion. In a subsequent article entitled '*Iliad* and *Aethiopis* on the stage: Aeschylus and Son' (*CQ* 50 (2000), 338–52) I have argued that Euphorion was also responsible for parts of the Memnon trilogy, namely the *Psychostasia* (or at least its opening and closing scenes) and the *Europa*, and that he may have had something to do with the spurious ending of the *Seven Against Thebes*.

Glossary

aition	cause, explanation
alastōr	avenging spirit
anagnōrisis	recognition
archōn	Athenian official
atē	madness, disaster
aulos	pipe (reed instrument)
daemon, daimon	spirit concerned with the destiny of an individual
dēmos	people
didaskaliai	dramatic records
dikē	justice, lawsuit, trial
eisodos	side-entrance to the stage
ephebe	youth (around the age of 18)
epiclēsis	additional name
Erinys (-yes)	goddess(es) concerned with punishment
ēthos	moral disposition, character
euandria	manliness
habros	delicate, luxurious
hubris	wanton violence or injustice
kommos	ritual lament
kratos	strength, power, rule
krokōtos	saffron-coloured robe
lampadēdromia	torch race
logos	word, speech, reason
mēchanē	crane used in the theatre
metoikos	metic, resident alien
nostos	return home
oikos	household
orchēstra	dancing area of the chorus in the theatre
pannychis	night-festival
peithō	persuasion
peplos	robe
philos	friend, loved one, relation
phthonos	envy

polis	city-state
pompē	procession
scholiast	ancient commentator
scholion	note by scholiast
skēnē	stage building
skolion	drinking song
stasis	civil strife
theomachos	fighter against the gods
timē	honour
xenos	guest, host
Zeugitae	members of the third of the four Athenian property classes

General Index

Accius 52, 370
Agamemnon 7, 20–35, 36, 40, 43–4, 69, 115, 126 n. 73, 128 n. 77, 130 n. 79, 147, 194–5, 211–43, 245–64, 265–301, 302–15, 316–22, 323–58
Agathon 69
Aigina 346 n. 94
Aigyptioi 17, 41, 48–9, 182–7, 194, 196, 208–9
Aitn(ai)ai 50 n. 41, 361 n. 5
Akousilaos 63, 393
alastor 257, 260, 261, 397
Alexander, 'the Great' 104, 121 n. 63
Alkibiades 104
Alkmaionids 106, 251–2
Alkmene 50 n. 41, 69
Amazoneion 335
Amazons 34, 176, 334–6, 342
Amymone 41, 48–9, 58
anachronism 19–20, 193, 199, 201–2
anagnorisis 7, 397
Anthesteria 35, 343–7
anthropology 29, 32, 291–2
Aphrodite 18, 175, 187, 189–95
Apollo 190, 216, 238 n. 75, 283–4, 331–4
Apollodoros (mythographer) 218
Apollonios of Rhodes 40
archery 308–9
archon basileus 247
Areopagos 23–5, 28, 34, 126 n. 73, 248–51, 264, 271–5, 280 n. 39, 285–7, 301, 324–5, 327, 335, 343, 370
Ares 335
Argeiai 64–6
Argo 66–7
Argonauts 336
Argos 19, 23–4, 95, 190–2, 201–2, 246–7, 268–71
Aristarchos 40
Aristeas of Proconnesos 392
Aristophanes 32–3

Assemblywomen 97 n. 10
Birds 37, 363–4
Frogs 110, 170, 229
Lysistrata 22 n. 71, 97 n. 10, 219–20, 221
Peace 377
Wasps 82, 97 n. 10, 274
Aristophanes of Byzantium 61
Aristotle 2, 69, 94, 98 n. 11, 161–2, 171, 235–6, 238, 279 n. 38, 280; see also *Athenaion Politeia*
Arkteia 339–43
Arktinos 54
Artemis 21, 34, 63, 190, 216, 218–26, 259, 339–43
Aspasia 113
Atalanta 69 n. 109
Athamas 64
Athena 34, 119, 266–8, 337, 351–4
Athenaion Politeia 23–4, 249–50, 274
Atlas 367, 376, 377, 389–92
audience address 254, 278
Augustine 292–3
aulos 109, 110, 121, 132, 397
autochthony 13

Bakchai 61–4
barbarians 5–7, 19, 100–2, 111–12, 119, 122, 123 n. 69, 205–6
Bassarides 41, 47–8, 62 n. 80
Beattie, J. 291–2
Beethoven, L. van 33
Bouphonia 354–6
Brauron 21 n. 71, 34, 219–23, 339–43
'bricolage' 326
Bruckner, A. 366
Brynner, Yul 100, 132 n. 83
bulls 340

calculus Minervae (vote of Athena) 283 n. 49
'cancelled entry' 379 n. 59

Index of Greek Words

Index of Passages in Aeschylus

This index refers to passages in the seven extant plays. References to lost plays can be found in the General Index. Titles are given in transliterated form. See p. xv above for alternative versions of the titles.

792: 86
794: 86
795: 91
799: 114
800: 72, 80
816: 82
818: 82
821: 102 n. 20
825: 123
826: 73 n. 7, 86, 114
827–8: 121, 123, 125
829–31: 123 n. 69
832–51: 126 n. 73
832–4: 90, 117
833: 91
834–6: 89
837–8: 117
842: 86
843–4: 80
845–8: 6 n. 16, 80, 89, 91
849–51: 90, 91, 117
851: 118
855–6: 121
856: 77
857: 122
861: 122
866: 122
880–906: 128 n. 77
897: 86
899: 72, 74, 81
903: 72
906: 114
907–1077: 126 n. 73
913: 89
914–17: 121, 123
914: 102 n. 20, 124, 125, 126 n. 73
918–1037: 126
918–21: 230
919: 91
920: 91
923: 102 n. 20
925–7: 80
925: 72, 102 n. 20
926–7: 81
928–30: 89, 114, 128 n. 77
940: 81
955–61: 84
955: 72
956: 81

957: 83
960: 83
966–71: 84, 123
968: 83
971: 83
972: 83
978–85: 73, 84
978: 102 n. 20
979: 102 n. 20
982: 83
986: 81
987–91: 102 n. 20
989: 102 n. 20, 125
993: 73, 81, 90
1000–1: 90
1014–15: 92
1017: 84, 92
1020: 84
1024: 80
1030: 90
1036: 80, 84, 114, 126
1038–77: 126
1049: 103 n. 21
1056–7: 91
1060: 90
1062: 91
1065: 126
1073: 101 n. 17
1077: 126

Prometheus Desmotes
1: 380 n. 61
3–4: 368
7–8: 363, 370
18: 363
20: 371
22–3: 369 n. 21
27: 384
38: 370
54: 372
56: 372
66: 36 n. 110, 363
88: 37
93–100: 372
94: 36, 361, 363
101–5: 232 n. 57
103: 368 n.
108: 232 n. 57
109: 363 n.